Royal Irish Constabulary Officers

ROYAL IRISH CONSTABULARY OFFICERS

A Biographical Dictionary and Genealogical Guide, 1816–1922

Jim Herlihy

With a foreword by W. E. Vaughan

FOUR COURTS PRESS

Set in 11pt on 13pt Ehrhardt by
Mark Heslington Ltd, Scarborough, North Yorkshire for
FOUR COURTS PRESS
7 Malpas Street, Dublin 8, Ireland
www.fourcourtspress.ie
and in North America for
FOUR COURTS PRESS
c/o ISBS, 920 N.E. 58th Avenue, Suite 300, Portland, OR 97213.

First published 2005
Paperback reprint 2016

A catalogue record for this title is available
from the British Library.

ISBN 978-1-84682-626-9

Printed in Ireland
by SPRINT-Print, Dublin.

Foreword

This is Jim Herlihy's fifth book on the Irish constabulary, which makes him the James Paterson of the Irish police. His characteristic tools are the database and the website, not the hammer and chisel, but he shares with the Scots exemplar the qualities of perseverance and piety. Any historian interested in the identity of policemen whose names are found in the Chief Secretary's Office Registered Papers, Convict Reference Files in the National Archives, or the Larcom Papers in the National Library, or newspaper references will be forever in his debt. Names that heretofore could be only sketchily identified can now be given a generous biographical identity.

The officers' names have already appeared in *The Royal Irish Constabulary: a complete alphabetical list of officers and men, 1816–1922* (1999). The entries in this latest volume are substantial biographical items. Henry William Wray's entry, for example, contains the information that he was born in 1804, at Convoy, Co. Donegal, that his wife was a native of Co. Cavan, that his daughter Mary Mabel died 18 March 1855 at Queenstown, aged 15; that he was appointed sub inspector (third class) in 1827, county inspector, 1851; that he died 28 March 1866 at Julia Mount, Wexford; that his will was proven on 7 May 1866, that his widow lived at Sidmonton, Bray, Co. Wicklow, and that his effects were under £800. Where the author has used sources other than the Officers Registers, they are indicated: in Wray's case they include records of the Church of Jesus Christ of Latter Day Saints and the *Cork Examiner*. Jim Herlihy writes in his introduction that the process in supplementing the information contained in the Officers Registers was 'a painstaking task'. This is an understatement.

The entry for Henry William Wray is not exceptionally long. There are many long ones. Benjamin Woods' entry covers nearly a whole page: he joined the Peace Preservation Force in 1815 and rose to the rank of district head constable in the Irish Constabulary, emigrated to Sydney in 1839, 'where he was still seeking employment when in early 1840 the recently appointed chief police magistrate, Willoughby Shortland, offered him the position of chief constable'. In spite of mixed fortunes, Woods is described 'as the most important police officer in Northern New Zealand between 1840 and 1853'. Sir Neville Chamberlain's entry runs to two and a half pages. Not only did Sir Neville have a distinguished official career (he was inspector general, 1900–16) but he invented the game of snooker, which, according to Sir Compton Mackenzie, 'added so much to the gaiety of nations'.

In addition to the 1,700 biographical entries, there are 273 illustrations, which are mainly portraits of constabulary officers, including one of Thomas Hartley Montgomery, a second-class sub inspector, who was hanged for murder at Omagh on 26 August 1873. The biographical list is preceded by a Glossary that will be invaluable to any scholar who uses the Registered Papers or the Convict Reference Files (terms such as justice of the peace, stipendiary magistrate, and resident magistrate are defined; particularly useful, for example, is the definition of constable, sergeant, chief constable and head constable). There are nineteen appendices that give important succession lists (inspectors general, commandants of the depot in the Phoenix Park, private secretaries to the inspectors general, for example). Appendix 1 contains eleven tables that analyse the data from the biographical entries; the first two tables show officers' birthplaces; Dublin accounted for 24 of those born in Ireland (10 per cent); Carlow accounted for only 14; Antrim and Down combined accounted for only 64. A very considerable number were born outside Ireland, amounting to about 15 per cent; England and Scotland accounted for most of these (185 out of 225); the balance, however, was remarkably exotic – with Austria, Belgium, Prussia, France and Spain accounting for eight!

W.E. Vaughan
Trinity College
Dublin

To the memory of

Patrick Joseph Carroll

(1897–1982)

Deputy Commissioner, Garda Síochána

Irish police historian and author

Contents

Abbreviations

AAD	Army Archives, Dublin	Div. Commr.	Divisional Commissioner
ACI	Acting County Inspector	Div. Mag.	Divisional Magistrate
ADC	Aide-de-Camp	DL	Deputy Lieutenant
ALD	Allen Library Dublin	DMP	Dublin Metropolitan Police
Adjt	Adjutant	DSC	Distinguished Service
AIG	Assistant Inspector General		Cross
ADRIC	Auxiliary Division Royal	DSO	Companion of the
	Irish Constabulary		Distinguished Service
A/Con	Acting Constable		Order
A/Sgt.	Acting Sergeant	DSPCA	Dublin Society for the
BA	Bachelor of Arts		Prevention of Cruelty to
BIF	*Burke's Irish Family Records*		Animals
BL	Bachelor-at-Law	E.R.	East Riding
BLG	*Burke's Landed Gentry of*	F.P.	Full pay
	Ireland	FRCSI	Fellow of the Royal College
BP	*Burke's Peerage &*		of Surgeons of Ireland
	Baronetage	GAA	Gaelic Athletic Association
Bt	Baronet	GBE	Knight Grand Cross of the
CarNB	Patrick Carroll's Notebooks		Order of the Bath
CB	Companion of the Order of	GCH	Knight Grand Cross of the
	the Bath		Royal Hanoverian Guelphic
CBE	Companion of the Order of		Order
	the British Empire	GCMG	Knight Grand Cross of the
CC	Chief Constable		Order of St Michael and St
CE	*Cork Examiner*		George
CI	County Inspector	GCVO	Knight Grand Cross of the
C-in-C	Commander-in-Chief		Royal Victorian Order
CM	Chief Magistrate	GM	Garda Museum
CMG	Companion of the Order of	GOC	General Officer
	St Michael and St George		Commanding
CO	Colonial Office series	GS	Garda Síochána
Col.	Colonel	H/Con.	Head Constable
Comdt	Commandant	HMSO	Her Majesty's Stationery
CSI	Companion of the Order of		Office
	the Star of India	HO	Home Office series
CSO LB	Chief Secretary's Office	H.P.	Half pay
	Letter Books	IG	Inspector General
CSORP	Chief Secretary's Office	IRA	Irish Republican Army
	Registered Papers	IRB	Irish Republican
DI	District Inspector		Brotherhood
DIG	Deputy Inspector General	IRP	Irish Revenue Police

JP	Justice of the Peace	PRO K	Public Record Office, Kew
KCB	Knight Commander of the Order of the Bath	PRONI	Public Record Office, Northern Ireland
KCH	Knight Commander of the Royal Hanoverian Guelphic Order	P/Sec.	Private Secretary to the Inspector General
KCMG	Knight Commander of the Order of St Michael and St George	PSNI	Police Service of Northern Ireland
KH	Knight of the Royal Hanoverian Guelphic Order	QC	Queen's Counsel
		RA	Royal Artillery
		RAF	Royal Air Force
KOSB	King's Own Scottish Borderers	RAMC	Royal Army Medical Corps
		RFC	Royal Flying Corps
KPM	King's Police Medal	RIA	Royal Irish Academy
Kt	Knight	RIC	Royal Irish Constabulary
LDS	Church of Jesus Christ of Latter Day Saints	RM	Resident Magistrates
		RMA	Royal Military Academy
		RN	Royal Navy
LG	*London Gazette*	RNVR	Royal Navy Volunteer Reserve
Lt.	Lieutenant		
Lt-Col	Lieutenant-Colonel	RUC	Royal Ulster Constabulary
LLB	Bachelor of Laws	RUI	Royal University of Ireland
LLD	Doctor of Laws	SFTCD	Senior Fellow of Trinity College Dublin
LMP	London Metropolitan Police	Sgt	Sergeant
MA	Master of Arts	SI	Sub Inspector
MBE	Member of the Order of the British Empire	SM	Stipendiary Magistrates
		S.R.	South Riding
MVO	Member of the Royal Victorian Order	SRM	Special Resident Magistrate
		TCD	Trinity College Dublin
NA	National Archives, Dublin	TCI	Temporary County Inspector
N.R.	North Riding		
NLI	National Library of Ireland	VC	Victoria Cross
OP	Official Papers	WO	War Office
PC	Privy Councillor	W.R.	West Riding
PMG	Paymaster General	WWI	World War One
PPF	Peace Preservation Force		

Preface

In writing this book I have reason to feel gratified by the courtesy which has been exhibited towards me in the several repositories I have visited in the course of my research. I wish to acknowledge the assistance of the staffs of the National Archives (formerly the Public Record Office), Kew, Richmond, Surrey; the British Library, Newspaper Library, Colindale Avenue, London; the National Archives, Gregory O'Connor in particular for his assistance with records relating to Resident Magistrates; the National Library, Director Brendan O'Donoghue, Collette O'Daly, Periodicals/Newspaper Librarian for procuring, at my request, microfilm copies of the *Constabulary Gazette* and John Farrell, Exhibits Officer; Lar Joye, Assistant Keeper, the National Museum of Ireland, Collins Barracks, Dublin; the Royal Irish Academy; Jean O'Hara and Mary Kilcline Cody, Alumni Proctor's Office, Trinity College Dublin for verifying the names of RIC officers who graduated from TCD; Professor W.E. Vaughan, TCD; Rev. J. Anthony Gaughan; Brendon Colvert, in-house editor, *IPA Journal*; Pádraig Ó Macháin, School of Celtic Studies, Dublin Institute for Advanced Studies, for his assistance in identifying officers of the Peace Preservation Force; the staff in Mount Jerome Cemetery, Harold's Cross, Glasnevin Cemetery, Deansgrange Cemetery, Dublin and Michael O'Sullivan, St Joseph's Cemetery, Cork; Lelia O'Flaherty for locating and photographing the graves of several RIC officers; Wendy Quirke of the Church of Jesus Christ of Latter Day Saints Family History Centre, Wilton, Cork; the General Registrar's Office, Dublin; the Guards Museum, London; Tim Cadogan, Niamh Cronin and Kieran Wise, Cork County Library; Kieran Burke, Cork City Library; Commandant Victor Laing and the late Commandant Peter Young, Army Archives; Brian Griffin, Bath Spa University College; Sergeant Michael O'Connor, Garda Headquarters, Phoenix Park, Dublin for his assistance in identifying officers by way of their insignia; Inspector Richard Abbott, Police Service of Northern Ireland, and Sergeant Anthony Rae, Lancashire Constabulary for their assistance in identifying the Officers Roll of Honour; the late Reginald A. Hale, police historian, Cheltenham, Gloucestershire for identifying hitherto unknown sources of research; Roger Willoughby, Nottingham for his assistance in verifying RIC officers awarded Visit to Ireland Medals; Paul Turnell, Middlesex, for his expertise in finding newly released sources in the Public Record Office, Kew; military historian and artist F. Glenn Thompson in particular for identifying very early constabulary officers by their uniforms and insignia.

The late curator and founder of the Garda Museum, Sergeant Gregory Allen, was always available to give advice and assistance. In a variety of ways this publication would not have been attempted without his pioneering work in identifying, salvaging, preserving and displaying artifacts in the original Garda Museum at Garda Headquarters, Phoenix Park, Dublin. The most valuable acquisition to the Garda Museum and Archives at the behest of Gregory Allen and the late Sean Sheehan, Assistant Commissioner Garda Síochána, were the indexed and penciled notebooks of the late Patrick Joseph Carroll, (1897–1982), Deputy Commissioner, Garda Síochána, son of an RIC man who had a life-long interest in police history.

In 1997 the Garda Museum was transferred to the Record Tower, Dublin Castle. Gregory Allen's successor as curator, Inspector John Duffy, drew my attention to the significance of P.J. Carroll's notebooks and this book had its beginning. I could indeed scarcely find words adequate to convey my sense of indefatigable assistance I have received at his hands throughout the progress of this work and of the benefits I have at all times derived from his experience and highly-prized advice. Thank you to Sergeant Pat McGee, the current Garda Museum curator and the staff at the Garda Museum, Donal Kivlehan and Pauline Duffy who were always helpful when I practically made the museum a second home. Thanks are also due to the chairman, Chief Superintendent John Kelly, the committee and members of the Garda Síochána Historical Society for their encouragement and providing a forum for renewed interest in Irish police history. Garda Jim Groarke, Anglesea Street Garda Station, Cork, has been exceptional in his upkeep of the website of the Garda Síochána Historical Society and in keeping the history of the RIC very much alive for internet users.

I wish to pay a special thanks to the staff of Four Courts Press for their efficiency and professionalism. For encouragement and advice at the very outset when this book was just a thought, I wish to thank Professor Kevin B. Nowlan, Professor Emeritus, Modern History, University College, Dublin. Deserving a special thanks are the hundreds of RIC officers descendants with whom I have met or with whom I have corresponded. I am indebted to Professor W.E. Vaughan, Trinity College, Dublin for providing a foreword. For whatever errors that may have crept, unconsciously on my part, into the memoirs of those who have afforded me information, I can only express my regret and suggest as an excuse the impossibility, in a work embracing so immense a body of facts, of avoiding occasional inaccuracies.

Glossary

Acting Constable
Introduced in 1859 and re-designated in 1883 by the rank of acting sergeant. The bearer of this rank wore two gold stripes or chevrons in his right sleeve. Rough riders in the mounted troop usually held this rank.

Acting Sergeant
Replaced the rank of acting constable in 1883 and was discontinued in 1918. The bearer of this rank wore two gold stripes or chevrons in his right sleeve.

Adjutant (of the Depot)
The chief assistant of the commandant to whom he afforded every information relative to the Depot and reported any breaches of the rules and regulations of the Force or standing orders of the Depot which came under his notice. All orders to the Depot were issued through the adjutant. He examined all recruits on their joining the Depot and kept a roster book of all duties of officers and men in the Depot. He received on parade on a daily basis all companies of men.

Assistant Inspectors General
In 1836, the Act of 6 and 7 of Wm. IV, cap.13, sec.7, authorized the Lord Lieutenant to appoint the four 'County Inspectors'. In 1839, the Act 2 and 3, Vic., cap.75, secs.10 and 11, reduced the number to two and altered their title to that of 'Provincial Inspectors.' In 1846, the Act 9 and 10 Vic. cap.97, sec. 6, changed the titles to that of 'Assistant Inspectors General.' In 1859, the Act 22 and 23 Vic., cap 22, sec.3, authorized the Lord Lieutenant to appoint one additional Assistant Inspector General. It was the third highest rank in the Constabulary. One was employed in the Constabulary Office, Dublin Castle and the other was commanding the Educational Department at the Phoenix Park Training Depot.

Auxiliary Division RIC
The Auxiliary Division of the Royal Irish Constabulary (ADRIC) was formed in July 1920 and had a headquarters staff comprised of an adjutant, quartermaster, transport officer, quartermaster sergeant and intelligence officer. Outside of its headquarters it was divided into companies each of which was made up of a commander, second in command, platoon commander, section commander, intelligence officer, quartermaster and assistant quartermaster. Companies were made up of 100 'Temporary Cadets' who were ex-army officers.

Cadets
There is no reference in the 1837 Irish Constabulary Code to the cadet system, which was introduced in 1842. The regulations on the subject, issued on 17 November 1842, stipulated that: 'Except in extraordinary cases, no gentleman shall be appointed to the office of sub inspector who shall not have undergone a course of cadet training.' The training requirement coincided with the completion of the Depot in the Phoenix Park. The door was, for all practical purposes, closed to promotion from the ranks. The age limit was 30 years and candidates underwent a preliminary examination of an unspecified standard. During training the cadets received the pay of a constable, but wore the uniform and performed the duties of an officer. Initially, their number was limited to two at a time, but in later years it grew to six. In addition to a constable's pay, a cadet received £50 per year, half of which had to be lodged with the

Depot Paymaster. Cadets were taught to command a body of men and, when competent, were promoted to the rank of third class sub inspector (before 1883; district inspector after 1883) as vacancies occurred and took charge of a constabulary district

Chief Constable
The rank of chief constable was introduced into the baronial constabulary in 1787 under 27, Geo. III, cap.40 to take charge of a district comprised of one or more baronies. A chief constable commanded sixteen sub constables who were appointed by the Grand Jury. Chief constables were appointed to the Peace Preservation Force under 54, Geo. III, cap.131, passed on 25 July 1814; they were subject to a chief magistrate and took command of fifty sub constables and served in an area proclaimed by the Lord Lieutenant to be disturbed.

Chief Magistrate of Police
A chief magistrate of police was appointed with the powers of a justice of the peace under the Peace Preservation Act, 1814 by the Lord Lieutenant of Ireland to take charge of areas proclaimed to be in a state of disturbance. These magistrates were expected to reside in their areas. Each was at the head of a force of constabulary.

Chief of Police
The office of Chief of Police, created on 15 May 1920, replaced that of the inspector general of the RIC. The first to hold the office was Major-General Sir Henry Tudor (1871–1965), who had been the Police Adviser since February 1920. The Deputy Chief of Police and Director of Intelligence, 1920–2 was Brigadier-General Sir Ormonde de l'Epee Winter, CB, CMG, DSO, KBE (1875–1962). For two or three nights Tudor's office was in a small hotel on the north bank of the Liffey; it afterwards moved to Park Lodge on the opposite side of the river. In early October 1920 the Chief of Police moved into Dublin Castle.

Commandant (of the Depot)
The Commandant of the Depot held the rank of county inspector between 1842 and under 22 & 23, Vic., cap.22 passed in 1859, it was directed that one of the Assistant Inspectors General should bear the title Commandant of the Depot. He resided constantly in the Depot and was answerable for the discipline, efficiency and general conduct of the officers and men under his command. He issued orders of the inspector general. He was responsible for the interior economy of the Depot, the instruction in police and detective duties and the drilling of cadets and recruits. He received on parade and inspected the Depot Force on each Tuesday.

Constable
The rank of Constable before 1883 was in effect the same as sergeant as he wore three stripes or chevrons on his right sleeve. From 1883 the rank of Sub Constable was re-designated Constable and the rank of Constable was re-designated Sergeant.

Constabulary Districts
In 1787, by 27 Geo. III, cap.40 (Irish), power was given to the Lord Lieutenant and Privy Council in Ireland to establish Districts, for each of which 16 constables might be appointed by the Grand Jury and one chief constable by the Lord Lieutenant who took charge of a Constabulary District. These were 'barony constables' and were paid out of the county cess. In 1792, by 32 Geo. III, cap.16, (Irish) further power of appointing barony constables was given to Grand Juries.

Constabulary of Ireland
Otherwise referred to as the County Constabulary which was formed in 1822 and continued until 1836. However, 'Constabulary of Ireland' is stamped on cap badges after 1836 to 1867 when the Irish Constabulary was granted the prefix 'Royal'.

County
Territorial divisions created from the late twelfth century onwards as part of the Anglo-Norman colonization. Commanded by a county inspector, with the exceptions of counties Cork, Galway and Tipperary who were commanded by two county inspectors.

County Constabulary
In 1822, by Geo. IV, cap.103, the right of appointing 'barony constables' was transferred from the Grand Juries to the county magistrates and an inspector of such constables was appointed for each Province, called a Provincial Inspector General.

County Inspector
A rank of three classes and who commanded a constabulary division of one of the thirty-two counties of Ireland. Each of the three largest counties had two county inspectors, each in charge of a division called a Riding: Cork East Riding, Cork West Riding; Galway East Riding, Galway West Riding; Tipperary North Riding and Tipperary South Riding. In addition, from 1865, the Town Inspector and Commissioner of Police in Belfast held the constabulary rank and pay of county inspector. Retirement age for county inspectors and upwards was 65 years or having completed 40 years' service. The Surgeon and Veterinary Surgeon and the Barrackmaster at the Phoenix Park Depot also held the rank of county inspector, as did the Commandant of the Depot between 1842 and 1859 when it was upgraded to the rank of assistant inspector general. County Inspectors were seconded as Divisional Commissioners between 1919 and 1921 and at that time the rank of temporary county inspector was introduced to replace those on secondment.

Depot & Reserve
The training depot at Phoenix Park Dublin was purpose built and opened in 1842 and remained the main training depot for the RIC until disbandment in 1922. The Depot was formed for two main objects, namely, the instruction of recruits for the Force generally and the establishment of a reserve force (of which it was to be its headquarters), pursuant to Vic 2 & 3, cap. 75, and it was commanded by one of the superior officers of the Force.

Depots, Sub Depots and Camps
Richmond Barracks Sub Depot was used to train officers from the British colonies in 1907 and 1908. North Dublin Union Depot was used between March 1920 and March 1921. Beggars Bush Barracks RIC Depot was used to house the Auxiliary Division of the RIC between February 1921 and March 1922. The RIC Camp at Gormanston was used for the Convoy Division of the RIC between September 1920 and March 1922 and there was also the RIC Camp in Newtownards, Co. Down, from November 1920 to May 1922.

Deputy Inspectors General
In 1836, the Act of 6 and 7 of Wm. IV, cap.13, sec.5, authorized the Lord Lieutenant to appoint one or two Deputies to the Inspector General. The Act 22 and 23 Vic., cap.22, sec.2, passed in 1859, reduced the number of Deputies to one, to be appointed by the Lord Lieutenant. It was the second highest rank in the Constabulary and he was employed in the Constabulary Office, Dublin Castle.

District Inspector
The rank district inspector was of three classes who commanded a constabulary district. Introduced in 1883, replacing the rank of Sub Inspector. He prosecuted cases in the Petty Session Courts. Retirement age was 60 or 40 years' service.

Divisional Commissioner (1889–98) & (1920–22)
The office of Divisional Commissioner was the re-designation name given in 1889 to Divisional Magistrates, who were introduced in October 1883. They were revised on 11 March

1920 under the Chief of Police Office formed on 15 May 1920 – under Major-General Sir Henry Tudor (1871–1965), who had been the Police Adviser since February 1920. Each Divisional Commissioner appointed between 1920 and 1921 was paid a salary of £1,200 p.a., locomotion allowance and a house allowance of £80. The Senior Divisional Commissioner was paid a further £200 p.a. He was over all the Martial Law area which included counties Clare, Cork, Kerry, Kilkenny, Limerick, Tipperary, Waterford and Wexford. The Divisional Commissioners in Cork, Clonmel and Limerick were subordinate to him. Each Divisional Commissioner was supplied with a Crossley Tourer and an RIC driver. The Treasury allowed a maximum of £250 p.a. for the maintenance of each car..

Divisional Magistrate
The title Divisional Magistrate was the re-designation name given in October 1883 to Special Resident Magistrates, who were originally appointed in August 1882. In 1889 Divisional Magistrates were re-designated Divisional Commissioners and abolished in 1898.

Head Constable
The rank of head constable was the most senior non-commissioned rank; head constables were usually stationed at district headquarter stations.

Head Constable Major
The head constable major was the highest non-commissioned rank in the constabulary and employed at the Phoenix Park Depot. He was the connecting link between the adjutant, head constables, sergeants, acting sergeants and constables. He was the master of the drill exercise and was acquainted with the manner of performing every duty of all ranks in the Depot. He paraded and inspected all guards and other parties previous to the adjutant's inspection and on every occasion was the first man on parade. Each day he read all the orders to the orderly sergeants of companies and, on Saturday, the standing orders of the Depot to the men.

High Constable
By the Statute of Winchester, passed in the reign of Edward I, the hundred, a territorial division comprising of several towns and villages, was bound to answer for all robberies committed therein, unless the robber was taken. This statute also created the office of High Constable, two of these officers being appointed in each hundred, and with a view of better keeping the peace they were directed to inspect all matters relating to arms and armour.

Inspector General
In 1836, the Act of 6 and 7 of Wm. IV, cap.13, sec.5, authorized the Lord Lieutenant to appoint the Inspector General of the Constabulary Force in Ireland. The inspector general was the Constabulary's administrative, executive and operational head.

Instructor of Musketry
He was charged with the full musketry training of all recruits and the further annual training of the Depot and Reserve forces as directed by the inspector general. He carried out monthly inspections of all arms at the Depot.

Irish Constabulary
Established in 1836 with the amalgamation of the four provincial constabularies, it was given the prefix 'Royal' on 6 September 1867 for its success in suppressing the Fenian rising.

Justice of the Peace
A Justice of the Peace was appointed for a County and he could act as a Justice anywhere in the County but he generally attached himself as a matter of convenience and etiquette to the particular Petty Sessions Court near which he resided. Justices of the Peace had three main sets

of duties, viz.: (1) They heard and finally disposed of minor 'offence cases' (e.g., simple drunkenness, common assault, etc.) and also certain 'civil cases' (e.g. small debts) dismissing such cases as they considered not proven and inflicting such punishment or making such order in proven cases as they thought proper and as lay within their power. (2) In the more serious classes of crime and offences (e.g., murder, manslaughter, burglary etc.) they decided whether there was or was not sufficient evidence against the accused to warrant his return for trial at a higher court. If they thought not, they ordered the discharge of the accused (this was called 'refusing informations'); if the contrary, they ordered him to stand trial before the higher court (Quarter Sessions or Assizes), and took precautions that he should do so, either by having him kept in custody in the meantime or getting security ('bail') for his appearance at such higher court. (3) Acting in some instances in or as a court, and in other instances merely as citizens of known integrity, they performed a great number of duties, some connected with the authorization of police to arrest suspected persons, some not directed against any culprit but done merely for the convenience of the public generally or of particular persons, e.g. taking declarations or committing lunatics to asylums. These Justices of the Peace were assisted by paid Magistrates, commonly called Resident Magistrates. On 20 December 1922, the Adaptation of Enactments Act (Act 2 of 1922) became law by which the Justices of the Peace and the Resident Magistrates were deprived of their powers, which were thenceforward exercised by District Justices (Section 6 of the Act) and JPs were replaced by Peace Commissioners.

Paymaster
Appointed under 6 & 7, Wm. IV, cap.36 in 1836 and discontinued in 1851 under 14 &15, Vic, cap.85. Each paymaster was allocated two counties.

Peace Preservation Force
In 1814, by 54, George III, cap.131, the Lord Lieutenant was empowered, with the assent of the Privy Council, to proclaim any county, or barony, to be in a state of disturbance and to appoint therein a chief magistrate, chief constable and not more that 50 sub constables. These were called the Peace Preservation Force as distinguished from the 'barony constables', but, like them, they were paid from local rates. Their employment ceased on the restoration of peace in the particular district for which they were appointed.

Petty Constables
They were instituted in the reign of Edward III (1327–77). They discharged the duties of the ancient tithing-man in addition to assisting the High Constable.

Petty Sessions Court
The petty sessions courts were held on any day of the week and presided over by a resident magistrate and accompanied by one or two justices of the peace.

Police Instructor & Schoolmaster
The role and title of Depot Schoolmaster was introduced in October 1846 with the appointment of Constable John Nixon, RIC 8883 and in 1854 he was replaced with 2nd Class Head Constable John Corbett, RIC 8989. In 1869 the title was changed to Police Instructor and Schoolmaster with the appointment of 1st Class Head Constable John Egan, RIC 4438. His replacement in the same rank in 1877 was John Bodley, RIC 10049 and he was promoted District Inspector in 1884. Henceforth a district inspector was in charge with the title changing to Chief Police Instructor in 1893.

Private Secretary to the Inspector General
Introduced in 1860 and of the seventeen appointed up to 1922, ten were later appointed resident magistrates.

Provincial Inspector General
In 1822, by Geo. IV, cap.103, the right of appointing 'baronial constables' was transferred from
the Grand Juries to the county magistrates and an inspector of such constables was appointed
for each of the four provinces of Munster, Ulster, Leinster and Connaught and such were titled
'Provincial Inspectors General'. They were discontinued in 1836 with the amalgamation of the
provincial constabularies into the Irish Constabulary.

Receiver
The Receiver was the financial manager of the Constabulary and established by Section 40 of
the Constabulary Act, 1836. Arthur Beresford Cane was appointed the Receiver for the
Phoenix Park Depot on 1 February 1843 and died on 13 May 1864 at Marseilles, France, late
of Collinstown House, Clondalkin, Co. Dublin. The Constabulary Office was formed on 1 June
1836. The Receiver's Office was formed in April 1851 following the abolition of the
paymasters. In July 1873 the offices of Inspector General and Receiver were amalgamated and
the duties of the Receiver were transferred to the inspector general.

Reserve Force
In 1839, by 2 & 3, Vic., cap.75, a Reserve Force was established in Dublin which might be sent
to any part of the country as required. It consisted of 2 chief constables or sub inspectors, 4
head constables and not more than 200 sub constables.

Resident Magistrate
The term resident magistrate is used first in the title of the Act of 1853. These resident
magistrates were appointed in 1836 by the Lord Lieutenant to reside in areas he thought fit and
were not to hold offices in the constabulary. These magistrates reported regularly to the chief
secretary on the state of their districts. The inspector-general acquired the right to appoint
from the constabulary, to every third vacancy in the resident magistracy, a right which Curtis
says was exercised up to 1862. Reference to a printed list of 70 resident magistrates in 1871,
however, shows that 10 of them were serving as sub inspectors in 1855, all appointed RMs
between 1858 and 1867. Four of them were appointed after 1862, so that sub inspectors still
continued to be eligible, even if not directly nominated by the inspector-general. At least 9 of
the sub inspectors serving in 1873 can be traced as still serving in 1894 as resident magistrates.
By 1909, 25 of the resident magistrates out of a total of 66 had seen RIC service, whilst by 1918
the figure was 18 out of 58. Writing in 1909, Leatham says: 'Every third vacancy in the list of
resident magistrates is filled by the promotion of a District Inspector'. On 20 December 1922,
the Adaptation of Enactments Act (Act 2 of 1922) became law by which the Justices of the
Peace and the Resident Magistrates were deprived of their powers, which were thenceforward
exercised by District Justices (Section 6 of the Act).

Riding
A division of the three largest counties commanded by a county inspector, namely Cork East
Riding, Cork West Riding, Galway East Riding, Galway West Riding, Tipperary North Riding
and Tipperary South Riding.

Riding Master
Introduced in 1843 with the special appointment of 1st Class Head Constable Richard
Pilkington, RIC 5509 attached to the Reserve at the depot in charge of Cavalry and Drill, from
the 5th Dragoon Guards. He was replaced by Sub Inspector George Roche Cronin, whose
successor in 1866 was Sub-Inspector John Mulcahy, a survivor of the Charge of the Light
Brigade. Further appointments were made from former sergeant-majors in dragoon and hussar
regiments until 1917. Riding masters held the honorary rank of a first class district inspector.

Sergeant

The rank of constable was re-designated sergeant in 1883, the holder of which wore three stripes or chevrons on his right sleeve.

Special Resident Magistrate (1881–3)

When Ireland was seriously disturbed in December 1881, six Special Resident Magistrates were appointed, each of whom was responsible for co-ordinating and directing the activities of the forces of law and order in a group of counties. In a circular to Resident Magistrates dated 22 June 1882, the territorial jurisdiction of the SRM Divisions was established under the charge of a Special Resident Magistrate, to which they were appointed in August 1882: Div. I – HQ at Mullingar for counties Leitrim, Cavan, Longford, Westmeath and Meath; Div. II – HQ at Westport for counties Sligo, Roscommon, and Mayo; Div. III – HQ at Galway for counties Galway and Clare; Div. IV – HQ at Limerick for counties Limerick, Tipperary, and Waterford; Div. V- HQ at Cork for counties Cork and Kerry; Div. VI – HQ at Maryborough for King's County and counties Kildare, Queen's County, Kilkenny and Carlow. The SRMs were reduced from six to four and re-designated Divisional Magistrates in October 1883. Though these officers had the powers of a JP their duties were executive.

Station Party

Small bodies of on average three or five members of the constabulary 'stationed' at almost all villages, at many of the hamlets, and even at places where no clusters of houses existed. These, besides preserving the peace in small circumjacent districts, carried expresses from station to station, escorted prisoners and promulgated government notices and proclamations.

Stipendiary Magistrate

Paid magistrates were first appointed under the Peace Preservation Act, 1814 in an area proclaimed by the Lord Lieutenant to be disturbed. In 1822 the Lord Lieutenant was further empowered to appoint magistrates for any district, who would be constantly resident with the powers of a justice of the peace, on the application of the justices of the county. Such paid magistrates were not connected with the constabulary. These paid magistrates were replaced by Resident Magistrates in 1836.

Storekeeper / Barrackmaster

The role of barrackmaster was introduced in 1841 with the appointment of John Mason Pooley as Depot Paymaster and Barrackmaster, with the rank and pay of a county inspector. The triple regimental duties of adjutant, assistant barrackmaster and storekeeper were performed by Sub Inspector Thomas Fleming from 1842 to 1854.

Sub Constable

The rank of sub constable was first introduced in 1787 with the establishment of the 'barony constables'. From 1822 to 1883 the lowest form of entry into the constabulary was that of a second class sub constable. After one year's service he was elevated to the rank of first class sub constable. From 1883 the rank of sub constable was re-designated constable.

Sub Inspector

In 1828 the rank of sub inspector was introduced as the officer in charge of the constabulary in a county. The Act of 1836 re-designated the rank of sub inspector to that of county inspector. In 1839 the rank of sub inspector was re-introduced and was of three classes and who commanded a constabulary district, replacing the rank of Chief Constable and re-designated District Inspector in 1883. He prosecuted cases in the Petty Session Courts.

Superintending Magistrate
Chief Magistrates appointed under the Peace Preservation Act, 1814 were often referred to as 'superintending magistrates'.

Surgeon
Employed at the Phoenix Park Depot with the rank and pay of a county inspector. Introduced in 1839 and only a total of five appointed up to 1922. He inspected recruits on joining and previously to their being approved of. He was in charge of the Depot Hospital which he attended daily to inspect the convalescents and men who reported themselves sick, whether from the country or the Depot.

Veterinary Surgeon
Employed at the Phoenix Park Depot with the rank and pay of a county inspector. Introduced in 1842 and abolished in 1916, with a total of only four appointed. He was responsible for the proper care and treatment of the horses of the whole establishment and took charge of sick and lame horses, the hospital stables, pharmacy and forge. He inspected all the horses of the Depot on a daily basis.

Introduction

The idea of compiling a biographical dictionary and genealogical guide of all officers who served in the Royal Irish Constabulary and its predecessor forces came about in a variety of ways. To the RIC officers, it was long overdue that some exertion should be made to furnish a public memorial of the services performed, the dangers braved, the honours attained, the disappointments suffered, by those officers who preserved the peace for almost the entire nineteenth century and early twentieth century. For many years I had collected information on individual officers; this led to the publication of *The Royal Irish Constabulary: A Short History & Genealogical Guide*, which generated a vast amount of queries from RIC descendants worldwide, mostly related to tracing relatives in the RIC General Registers of Service.

The reception given to this book led me to assemble *The Royal Irish Constabulary:*

1 Patrick Carroll (1897–1982), Deputy Commissioner, Garda Síochána, police historian and author, photographed as a Garda superintendent and member of the first and only Garda cadet class of 1923.

A Complete Alphabetical List of Officers and Men, 1816–1922 which was alphabetically arranged and which contained the surname, Christian name and unique sequential registered number of each of the 85,028 members of the RIC (except cadet officers). In the case of officers, this book included the names extracted from the Officers Registers (HO 184, vols 45–8 inclusive) which covers the period from 31 January 1817 to 17 September 1921. This represents a total of 1,531 officers; 635 of these do not have registered numbers; they joined the RIC as cadets and are represented in the alphabetical list by their surname, Christian name and 'Cadet' in lieu of the registered number. The names of the remaining 896 are italicized in the alphabetical list, indicating that they had been promoted to the officer class.

The archives of the Chief Secretary's Office, namely the Chief Secretary's Registered Papers (CSORP) and its associated offices for the period 1790–1922 now housed in the National Archives, Dublin, contain reports made to the Chief Secretary by officers of the Peace Preservation Force from 1814 and constabulary officers from 1822. The fact that the PPF were disbanded on completion of their work in areas proclaimed to be disturbed meant that the chances of registers of officers in this force surviving were remote. Also it was apparent to me that the RIC Officers Registers, although dated from 31 January 1817, only contain the names of officers who were serving in 1836 on the formation of the Irish Constabulary as a national police force. They were written retrospectively in 1836 because the Officers Registers did not contain the names of officers who had joined before 1836 and who by then had left the service by way of resignation, dismissal, retirement or death. This theory was reinforced on discovering the penciled notebooks of Patrick Joseph Carroll, Deputy Commissioner, Garda Síochána, which had been donated to the Garda Museum. Patrick Joseph Carroll, the son of a member of the Royal Irish Constabulary joined the Garda Síochána as a member of the first and only cadet class on 1 July 1923 having qualified as a national schoolteacher. He retired on his 65th birthday on 5 November 1962 as a deputy commissioner, a rank he had held for three years. A keen police historian and author of several articles published in the *Garda Review*, he had spent practically every afternoon since 1935 in the former State Paper Office in Dublin Castle taking copious notes and detailed extracts of police sources from the State Papers covering the first half of the nineteenth century. (The premises of the former State Paper Office in the Record Tower at Dublin Castle were vacated in August 1991, and the headquarters of the National Archives moved from the Four Courts to Bishop Street in September 1992.)

The names of constabulary officers contained in P.J. Carroll's notebooks enabled me to identify all of the constabulary officers mentioned in the State Papers who had served in the Peace Preservation Force from 1814 and in the County Constabulary from 1822, but who had left the service by reason of retirement, resignation, death or dismissal. These amounted to a 169 officers; coupled with the officers who were serving in 1836 to 1922, this made a total of 1,700, who are all identified in this book.

THE LIST

In the case of the 1,531 RIC Officers whose names appear in the RIC Officers Registers the following information has been extracted and contained in THE LIST on pages 47 to 330: surname, Christian name(s); RIC Registered Number in the case of officers promoted from the ranks; ADRIC Cadet number in the case of RIC officers who were seconded for service in the Auxiliary Division of the RIC and ADRIC officers who transferred as officers into the RIC; LDS Microfilm and page number of each RIC officer whose name appears in the RIC officers service registers which were microfilmed by the Church of Jesus Christ of Latter Day Saints; birth year or date of birth where known; county or place of birth; previous occupation and duration if known or in the case of previous army service, the rank held and the regiment in which he served; date of appointment as an officer i.e. as a chief constable before 1836, as a 3rd class sub inspector before 1883 and a 3rd class District Inspector after 1883; subsequent promotions and dates to the ranks of county inspector, assistant inspector general, deputy inspector general and inspector general; dates of secondment as special resident magistrates, divisional magistrates and divisional commissioners; posts held at headquarters; date of resignation, dismissal, retirement or death in the service or on superannuation

In the case of the 169 RIC Officers identified in P.J. Carroll's notebooks the following information is contained in THE LIST: surname, Christian name; year of birth; county of birth; date or year of appointment to the PPF or constabulary; period of service in the Peace Preservation Force; place of service as a chief constable in the PPF or constabulary; date of resignation, dismissal, retirement or death.

GENEALOGICAL INFORMATION

The process of supplementing the information contained in the Officers Registers with further genealogical information was a painstaking task. I was facilitated in this process when the Garda Museum & Archives purchased microfilm copies of the Home Office (HO 184) RIC Officers Registers and microfilm copies of the Royal Irish Constabulary Lists which were published bi-annually from 1840 to 1921. The RIC Lists contain the names of serving, superannuated and deceased officers. They also contain the names of officers who received academic qualifications, were awarded campaign medals prior to enlistment and who were seconded for service in the Crimea and the First World War as commissioned officers. I verified and extracted information on their military careers from the Army Lists and their individual War Office files in the National Archives formerly (the Public Record Office), Kew, Richmond, Surrey.

Since RIC officers were prohibited by their regulations from serving in their native county, the index to Griffith's Valuation of Ireland, 1848 to 1864 on CD-Rom was particularly useful in locating officers who were in lodging during this period. Since many of the officers had very unusual surnames, the index was also helpful in

2

2 *Constabulary of Ireland*, watercolour attributed to Edward Hayes, RHA (1797–1864).   3 Early print showing a chief constable of the Irish Constabulary in full dress uniform which was worn for formal duties with a shako cap and crimson sash.   4 Early print showing a chief constable in undress uniform and wearing a cheese-cutter cap which features a black shamrock braid.

3   4

6

7

5

8

9

5 Constabulary of Ireland chief constable in full dress *c.*1836 drawn by Alan Mounce. 6 Constabulary of Ireland's officer's gilt epaulette. 7 Constabulary of Ireland officer's brass shoulder scales, *c.*1840. 8 Constabulary of Ireland officer's epaulette, *c.*1845. The cloth is rifle green; the braid of gold lace and the crescent and tipstaffs are gilt. 9 Constabulary of Ireland officer's shoulder belt plate *c.*1860.

pinpointing the exact location of the birth place of such officers. The 1881 British Census and National Index on CD-Rom was invaluable in identifying the exact origin and birthplaces of RIC officers born in England, Scotland, and Wales, some of which were found attending boarding schools and colleges prior to their joining the RIC.

In cases where RIC officers were appointed as chief magistrates and stipendiary magistrates from 1814 prior to 1836, the dates of appointment are given from the information in P.J. Carroll's notebooks as are the resident magistrates appointed in 1836 to 1850. The careers of former RIC officers appointed as resident magistrates were verified from the RIC Lists from 1840 to 1921 and from the Resident Magistrate Records of Service Books and Letter Books in the National Archives.

Civil registration began in England and Wales on 1 July 1837. The birth, marriage and death indexes, arranged alphabetically by quarter year, are in the Family Records Centre in Islington. Civil registration in Ireland began on 1 January 1864 pertaining to births, marriages and deaths and in the case of non-Catholic marriages from 1845. These indexes are in the General Registrar's Office, Dublin and have been microfilmed by the Church of Jesus Christ of Latter Day Saints, copies of which are available for research at LDS Family History Centers. I have searched and verified the 1,700 RIC Officers against both sets of birth, marriage and death indexes from 1837 in the case of England and Wales and from 1845 in the case of Ireland up to 1922. In all cases where I have found birth, marriage and death entries relating to an officer I have supplemented the RIC officers record with the following information: Registrar's District, Year, Quarter Year, Volume No., Page No. The foregoing information will enable the researcher to apply for and obtain a birth, marriage or death certificate of the officer.

The index to Irish wills and administrations from 1858 is alphabetically arranged in relation to Ireland in the National Archives, Dublin. In England there is a similar index on microfiche, alphabetically arranged in the National Archives (formerly the Public Record Office), Kew, Richmond, Surrey. I have extracted the information from both indexes in relation to RIC Officers who died in Ireland and England and added the relevant information to the individual RIC Officers entry. The CD-Rom Index of Irish Wills, 1484–1858 in the National Archives, published by Eneclann, also contained the names of several RIC Officers, particulars of whom have also been added. Wills of officers before 1858 in England were found on line on the National Archives website.

I searched on microfilm each issue of the *Irish Times* from 1859 and the *Cork Examiner* from 1842 up to 1922 and both newspapers proved invaluable in providing a wealth of genealogical information on RIC officers. Most of the officers retired to areas of south County Dublin, the vast majority of whom are buried in Mount Jerome Cemetery, Harold's Cross. Deansgrange Cemetery also contains many officers' graves, including that of the only cadet officer to be promoted inspector general, namely, Sir Andrew Reed. His epitaph reads: – 'I have no greater joy than to hear that my children walk in truth' (3 John 4). Other epitaphs of officers I have found were of

10

11

10 RIC officer's full dress belt plate, *c*.1868 worn on the black patent leather shoulder belt. 11 RIC officer's waist belt plate, *c*.1880. 12 RIC officer's full dress cocked hat of black beaver with gold pattern shamrocked lace, gold netted wire button and gold spiralled bullions at each tip. The plumes are white swan feathers with rifle green feathers under same. These patterned cocked hats were worn by the inspector general and staff. 13 Plumes for RIC officer's cocked hat. 14 RIC officer's cocked hat complete with plumes.

12

13

14

15   16

15 Rifle Brigade officer's patrol jacket, *c.*1900, of rifle green cloth with black velvet collar, cuffs and black mohair braid.   16 RIC officer's full dress tunic and helmet, *c.*1910. The tunic of black cloth with black velvet collar and cuffs with mohair braid.   17 RIC officer's full dress helmet covered with rifle green cloth with blackened bronze or white metal fittings, *c.*1902–10.   18 RIC officer's silver mountings worn on the black patent leather full dress shoulder belt, *c.*1911–22.   19 RIC officer's full dress black patent leather pouch with silver badge, *c.*1900.

17   19

18

DI William Harding Wilson in St Mary's Church of Ireland Cemetery, Templemore, Co. Tipperary, who was murdered there on 16 August 1920. It reads simply: 'His life to his country, his soul to God.' Sir Richard Willcocks, a veteran of the Peace Preservation Force and inspector general for Munster, is buried in St Laurence's churchyard, Chapelizod, Dublin and his epitaph reads: 'Praises on Tombs are trifles vainly spent; a man's good name is his own monument.' Chartres Brew from Corofin, Co. Clare, former chief constable in the Irish Constabulary and founder of the police in British Columbia, is buried in Barkerville Cemetery, British Columbia where his epitaph reads: – 'A man imperturbable in courage and temper, endowed with a great and varied administrative capacity, a most ready wit, a most pure integrity and a most human heart.' District Inspector William Limerick Martin was stoned to death while attempting to arrest the parish priest in Derrybeg, Gweedore in 1889. A monument in his honour stands in the grounds of St James' Church, Dublin, and a commemorative silver bust of him in uniform is in the PSNI Museum, Belfast. Two memorial windows in the Church of Ireland, Gorey, by the celebrated stained-glass artist Harry Clarke were commissioned by the Order of Freemasons and Dr Marie Lea-Wilson, the widow of DI Percival Samuel Lea-Wilson, who was murdered in Gorey on 15 June 1920.

Numerous RIC Officers were found in *Burke's Peerage and Baronetage*, *Burke's Landed Gentry* and *Burke's Irish Family Records* which confirmed the intermarriage of numerous RIC Officers families. The *Constabulary Gazette* published weekly from 3 April 1897 and 28 January 1922 contains several photographs of RIC officers, references to which have been extracted and entered in THE LIST.

Candidates for the RIC had to be personally known, in the majority of cases, to a RIC sub inspector (re-titled district inspector after 1883), stationed in the district where the candidate was a native of or resided. In such cases, the recommending Sub Inspector (abbreviated SI) or District Inspector (abbreviated DI), followed by the officer's Surname only was entered in the Recommendations column of the candidate's service record. All such recommending officers are identified in this book. By consulting the service recommending RIC officer, the researcher can discover the constabulary district where he was stationed at that time.

THE FIRST OFFICERS

The calibre and choice of the first officers of the Peace Preservation Force drawn from the old Dublin Police was instrumental in its success. John Wills, born in 1788, of Esker Lodge, Lucan, Co. Dublin, a veteran of the Dublin Police, 1797–1812, was one of three (of the first government (the others being Richard Willcocks and Edward Wilson)) appointed magistrates on the recommendation of Lord Cathcart by the Earl of Hardwicke in 1802 sent out without police; special magistrate 1808; in 1813 he was ordered to take charge of the disturbed areas of Cos. Roscommon, Galway, Leitrim,

20

20 RIC buttons, *c*.1900–22. Left column of blackened white metal from top to bottom: late Victorian, Edward VII. Centre Column, of blackened horn: late Victorian top two and George V. Right Column, of blackened white metal: Edward II top two and George V. 21 RIC officer's rank insignia worn on the shoulder strap of the dark green serge undress tunic of 'frock'. The insignia is that of a county inspector, the crown and star of blackened bronze, *c*.1903–22. 22 RIC officer's full dress cocked hat, *c*.1880 of black beaver with black silk shamrock pattern lace and loop over the cockade with black netted button on rifle green feathered plumes. This pattern has been worn by a staff officer, veterinary surgeon.

22

21

Cavan, Wexford and Westmeath; as a chief magistrate 14 December 1815 he took charge of the barony of Clanwilliam, Co. Tipperary; in February 1817 took charge of the proclaimed barony of Castleraghan, Co. Cavan; removed with the Revenue Police in April 1817 to the proclaimed baronies of Offaly, Kilcullen, Connell, Carberry, Clane and Naas in Co. Kildare and Philipstown in King's County; in November 1818 sent to Donegal to organize the Revenue Police; recalled in February 1819 to take charge of the proclaimed parishes of Killyon, Killyconnigan and Clonard in the baronies of Clune and Moypenrath, Co. Meath; on 14 November 1819 he was sent to Co. Roscommon, residing in Rockley Park, Roscommon and remained there until the County Constabulary came into operation on 24 April 1824 when he retired to Esker Lodge, Lucan, Co. Dublin on a pension of £500 per annum.

Richard Willcocks was appointed the first chief magistrate of the Peace Preservation Force on 6 September 1814 by Robert Peel in the barony of Middlethird, Co. Tipperary and based at Cashel. The success of Peel's Peace Preservation Force was due primarily to the extensive work of Richard Willcocks (*Mr Secretary Peel – The life of Sir Robert Peel to 1830* (Cambridge, Mass., 1961) pp. 182–3, 200–1). Willcocks sent a letter of thanks to Robert Peel for granting him leave to visit his family from Cashel to Palmerston at Christmas 1817. He was appointed provincial inspector general for Munster from 6 November 1822. He tendered his resignation on 14 October 1827, 'owing to my late very severe illness and the general debilitated state of my health.' His reply pays high tribute and adds that the Lord Lieutenant 'feels it to be a duty to provide adequately for the retirement of a respectable and deserving public servant,' all meticulously set down in Wellesley's own hand; knighted 1827; a summary in 1827 of the service and the esteem in which Sir Richard Willcocks was held appears in the papers of Sir Edward John Littleton (1791–1863), 1st Baron Hatherton, Chief Secretary to the Lord Lieutenant of Ireland, 1833–4 (Staffordshire Record Office D260/M/01/1086): '1827, Sir Richard Willcocks – In 1803, he obtained and communicated to the Government the first information of (Robert) Emmet's designs, and thereby prevented the insurgents from gaining possession of Dublin. On that occasion he narrowly escaped assassination; eight persons having been stationed in different places for the purpose of attacking him. Immediately afterwards he organized a Yeomanry Corps in the County of Dublin, with the assistance of which he maintained the tranquillity of his own neighbourhood. He apprehended and committed to prison 35 persons concerned in Emmet's insurrection. He was subsequently employed from 1807 to 1827, in active service in different parts of Ireland. He was sent as a Stipendiary Magistrate, from time to time, into the Counties of Kerry, Limerick, Tipperary, Cork, Waterford, Kilkenny, Meath, and Westmeath; by his own exertions unaided by police, he successively tranquillized those counties. This was affected chiefly by obtaining private information, apprehending the principal offenders, bringing them to trial, securing witnesses, and preventing them from being tampered with. He was afterwards appointed Chief Magistrate under the Peace Preservation Act, and

23   24

23 RIC officer sketch.   24 RIC officer sketch.   25 DI 1st class sketch.

25

ultimately Inspector General of Munster, under the Constabulary Act. It is universally allowed that there never was a more efficient Magistrate. The honour of Knighthood was conferred on him on retiring.'

Edward Wilson served in the Dublin Police from 1788 to 1808 as Chief Peace Officer, Workhouse Division. Arrests made by him are mentioned in the *Freeman's Journal* of 25 October 1793, 6 June 1801, 9 August 1803, 2 August 1804, 25 September 1804, 4 October 1804 and 6 April 1805 and he made several arrests of the leaders in Robert Emmet's Rising in 1803. He was appointed a special government magistrate in 1808, by the Duke of Wellington. From 1811 he served as a special magistrate for Dublin Castle in Roscommon, Westmeath, Waterford and Queen's County. Appointed chief magistrate in the PPF in the barony of Kilnamanagh, Co. Tipperary on 3 May 1815. He was pensioned in 1828.

A sister of Thomas D'Arcy, PPF chief magistrate of police, Eliza (1767–1829), married on 16 August 1791 Major Henry Charles Sirr (1764–1841), Town Major, Dublin Castle. PPF Chief Magistrate, Samson Carter's mother, Maria Swan, was the daughter of Major William Swan, JP, Co. Dublin, who assisted Major Sirr in the capture of Lord Edward Fitzgerald. The majority of RIC officers had fathers, sons or brothers in the RIC or either they or their siblings married into RIC families.

Three generations of the Fleming family served as officers in the (Royal) Irish Constabulary. Thomas Fleming, born in 1800, London, England, ran away from home at the age of fifteen and joined the 3rd Battalion of the Rifle Brigade giving his age as seventeen and served as a private, corporal, sergeant and colour sergeant from 14 September 1815 to 16 February 1838. He joined the Irish Constabulary as a sub constable and drill instructor on 6 March 1838 at the Leinster Depot; promoted constable, 1 June 1838, 2nd class head constable, 1 September 1839, 1st class head constable, 1 December 1842, extra head constable, 1 October 1846; 3rd Class SI on 1 June 1848 and the first Adjutant of the Phoenix Park Depot having the triple regimental duties of adjutant, barrackmaster and storekeeper which he performed until 1 May 1854. He was the father of Sub Inspector Thomas Sylvanus Fleming and grandfather of County Inspector, Major Cyril Francis Fleming who was responsible for recruiting the 'Black and Tans' and the Auxiliary Division of the RIC in London.

The Cadet system was introduced in 1842; however, three officers resigned in their commissions in favour of having their sons obtain a commission, namely, William Henry, in favour of his son, William Henry Jnr in 1841; Edward J. Kirwan in favour of his son, Henry Kirwan, in 1842 and John Faithful Fortescue in favour of his son George Edward Fortescue, in 1844.

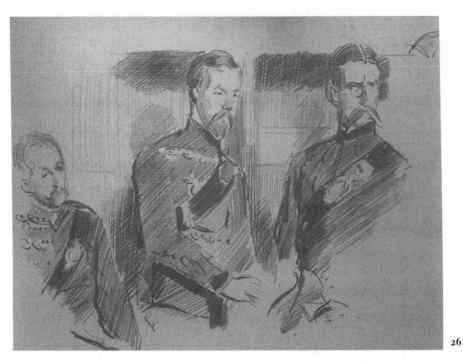

26

26 RIC Officers at the Parnell Commission.   27 Silver snuff box dated 1 March 1828 presented to Sir Richard Willcocks, Inspector General of the Munster Constabulary, by chief constables of the Limerick Constabulary on the occasion of his retirement.   28 Silver candelabra now in the Garda Officers Club – one of a pair presented to the RIC Officers Mess by Robert Fitzwilliam Starkie on the occasion of his appointment as a Resident Magistrate in 1893.

27

28

RIC OFFICERS IN THE UNITED KINGDOM
AND THE COLONIES

The first county chief constable to be appointed in England was Anthony Thomas Lefroy (1802–90) who was chief constable of Gloucestershire from 1839 to 1865; prior to his appointment he was chief constable in Rathdrum, Co. Wicklow. Former RIC officers served as chief constables in England: Sir Leonard Dunning, chief constable of Liverpool, 1902–12 and H.M. Inspector of Constabulary, 1912–30, Sir John William Nott-Bower, chief constable of the City of Leeds, 1878–81, Liverpool, 1881–1902 and commissioner of the City of London, 1902–25, Sir Hugh Stephenson Turnbull, chief constable of Cumberland and Westmoreland, 1920–25 and commissioner of police for the city of London, 1925–50, John Hayes Hatton, chief constable of East Suffolk, 1840–2 and chief constable of Staffordshire, 1842–56, John Hatton, chief constable of Ipswich, 1841–2, chief constable of East Suffolk, 1843–69 and Beccles in 1844, Walter Congreve, chief constable of Staffordshire, 1866–1888, James Brown Wright, chief constable of Newcastle-upon-Tyne, 1899–1925, William Alfred Smith, assistant chief constable of Liverpool, Henry Allbut, chief constable of Bristol, 1894–1906, Philip Theodore Briarly Browne, chief constable of Bootle, Lancashire, 1920–26 and chief constable of Cumberland and Westmoreland, 1926–51, Francis C. Coleridge, chief constable of Devonshire, 1892–1907, Walter Stocks Davies, chief constable of Birkinhead, 1898–1912, Valentine Goold, chief constable of Somerset, 1856–84, Major Michael J.A. Egan, chief constable of Southport, Lancashire, 1920–42 and H.M. Inspector of Constabulary, 1942–50, George Morley, chief constable of Hull, 1910–22 and chief constable of Durham County, 1922–42, Charles Haughton Rafter, chief constable of Birmingham, in 1899–1935, followed by Cecil Charles Hudson, Moriarty, assistant chief constable of Birmingham, 1918–1935 and chief constable, 1935–1941. Scotland also benefited from cadet-trained RIC officers, namely, William Pearce, chief constable of Glasgow City, 1847–8, James Verdier Stevenson, chief constable of Glasgow City, 1902–22, Colin Campbell Robertson-Glasgow, chief constable of Ayrshire in 1911–19 and Lieutenant Hugh Stephenson Turnbull, chief constable of Argyle, 1913–20. Benjamin Woods, a veteran of the Peace Preservation Force, was appointed chief constable of Auckland from 1840 to 1853. In 1845 Irish Constabulary Sub Inspector Thomas Thompson was appointed superintendent in charge of the police in Ceylon and was succeeded by a fellow Irish Constabulary officer, William Macartney, in 1847. The British Columbia Territorial Police Force was organized by ex-Irish Constabulary Sub Inspector Chartres Brew. RIC District Inspector James Samuel Gibbons was seconded on 11 October 1886 on his appointment as Inspector General of the Egyptian Police with the title 'Pasha'. Similarly, RIC District Inspector Pierre B. Pattisson served as captain superintendent of police in Shanghai from 1897 to 1898, and another RIC Officer, Thomas Andrew Howe, served as deputy captain superintendent of police at Hong Kong from 1897 to 1898.

29 RIC Officers Mess dining room, Phoenix Park, Dublin – now the Garda Síochána Officers Club.

IRISH REVENUE POLICE

Between 11 November 1838 and 8 August 1845 five former lieutenants in the Irish Revenue Police transferred as 3rd class sub inspectors in the Irish Constabulary, namely, Thomas F. Fitzsimon, Henry R. Johnstone, Giles William Cullen, Edward Smyth Corry and Robert Gore. When the Irish Revenue Police was disbanded on 1 December 1857 a further twenty-eight lieutenants were appointed 3rd class sub inspectors in the Irish Constabulary, namely, George Keating Auchmuty, Vershoyle Crawford Brommel, John Byrne (2), Daniel McCarthy Downing, William Daniel Foley, Richard Garrett, Edwin Edward Graves, Thomas Hamilton, Thomas Pierrepoint Hewitt, William Stuart Irvine, Thomas LeBan Kennedy, George MacCarthy, Percy MacMahon, Edward J. McDermot, Edward McDermott, Frederick George Patterson, Morgan Joseph Quill, Thomas Rodwell, Augustus Rudge, Samuel Henry Stephens, John Studdert, William St Lawrence Tyrrell, William Henry Vallancey, Henry Frederick Ward, Henry Ware, Henry Archdall Wood and George Hill Wray.

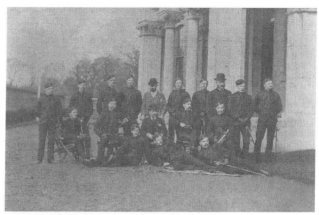

30

31

32

30 Cadet Class 1883 outside the RIC Officers Mess. **31** RIC Headquarters Officers, 1901.
32 Co. Tipperary District Inspectors, in Tipperary Town, 1890.

THE CRIMEA

Four officers were killed while serving with the Commissariat in the Crimea: Thomas C. Anderson, William Peter Coppinger, George Du Bourdieu, John Fitzgerald Studdert; and a further twelve survived: Edward Joseph Banon, Harris Bindon, Chartres Brew, Thomas Peter Carr, Christopher Joseph DeGernon, William Fosberry, Valentine E. Goold, W.H.S. Hemsworth, William Somerset Keogh, Robert James Reamsbottom, Henry Badham Thornhill, John S. Watkins. RIC inspectors general, Col. Robert Bruce, Lieutenant-General Duncan McGregor and Col. Sir John Steward Wood, were veterans of the Crimea. RIC Riding Master John Mulcahy was a survivor of the Charge of the Light Brigade, and Major Thomas Esmonde, later RIC deputy inspector general, won the Victoria Cross, while James Ross, a Crimean veteran, was appointed a sub inspector in 1867.

DUBLIN METROPOLITAN POLICE

The DMP relied on former RIC officers as its commissioners, namely, Major George Baxter Browne, joint commissioner (1837–58), Sir David Harrel, chief commissioner (1883–93), John Joseph Casimir Jones (1893–1901), William Moorehouse Davies, acting commissioner (1914), William Charles Forbes Redmond, second assistant commissioner on 1 January 1920 and Denis Barrett on 23 February 1920.

FIRST WORLD WAR

In the First World War, one county inspector and thirty-three district inspectors were seconded for service, and one former district inspector enlisted as commissioned officers in the British Army. Of these, nine were wounded and the following six were killed: Captain Edward Graham Mylne, Captain Osbourne George de Courcy Baldwin, Captain Valentine Charles Joseph Blake, Lieutenant-Colonel William Alfred Smith, George Edward Saville Young and Captain Robert Peter Villar. A total of 26 rejoined including 6 of the wounded. DI Harry Smyth was killed in Ashbourne, Co. Meath, on 28 April 1916 during the Easter Rising and County Inspector Alexander Gray died of his wounds on 10 May 1916.

WAR OF INDEPENDENCE

In the course of the Irish War of Independence, twenty-five RIC officers were assassinated: two in 1919: John Charles Milling, RM (formed DI) and Michael Hunt; ten in 1920: William Charles Forbes Redmond, Second Assistant Commissioner,

Dublin Metropolitan Police (former DI), Alan Bell, RM (former DI), Percival Samuel Lea-Wilson, Brevet Lieutenant-Colonel Gerard Bryce Ferguson Smyth, DSO, Divisional Commissioner for Munster, William Harding Wilson, Oswald Ross Swanzy, James Joseph Mary Brady, Philip St John Howlett Kelleher, Francis William Crake, Philip John O'Sullivan; twelve in 1921: Thomas James McGrath, Tobias O'Sullivan, William Clarke, Philip Armstrong Holmes Divisional Commissioner (former DI), Francis Worthington Craven DSO, DSC, DSM, Michael Joseph Cahill, Gilbert Norman Potter, Harry Biggs, Cecil Arthur Maurice Blake, Michael Francis McCaughey, Cyril Robert Mason; one in 1922: Michael Keany. A total of six RIC officers were wounded: Albert Augustine Roberts; Philip Valentine McDonagh and Michael Fallon in 1920; William Herbert King and Frederick George Lancaster in 1921 and Hubert Leslie Baynham in 1922.

GARDA SÍOCHÁNA

The Civic Guards (later styled the Garda Síochána) was formed in February 1922 to police the Irish Free State and the following RIC officers were involved in its establishment: Patrick Walsh, Bernard O'Connor, Patrick Riordan, John A. Kearney and Thomas McGetrick. Michael Horgan who had retired from the RIC in 1920 at the age of fifty-seven was appointed a superintendent in the Garda Síochána on 9 April 1924, pioneering the weights and measures section at Garda Headquarters, Dublin, and was pensioned on 1 July 1934 in his 71st year. Patrick Walsh was appointed deputy commissioner in the Garda Síochána on 6 April 1922. In May 1922 when a faction of the Garda Síochána mutinied in Kildare, Commissioner Michael Staines tendered his resignation; Patrick Walsh also resigned in loyalty to the Commissioner, but continued to serve the Provisional Government as a civilian advisor. On the recommendation of Commissioner Eoin O'Duffy, he was re-appointed assistant commissioner, his former office having been filled by Deputy Commissioner Eamon Coogan. He retired from the Garda Síochána in 1936. Bernard O'Connor was appointed as a superintendent on 1 April 1922, chief superintendent in 1923 and retired in 1934.

ROYAL ULSTER CONSTABULARY

The Royal Ulster Constabulary was formed in Northern Ireland on 1 June 1922 and the following 51 officers transferred from the RIC: Thomas James Allen, James Armstrong, William Atteridge, William Ball, Frederick Ambrose Britten, Patrick Cahill, Henry Connor, Edward J. Conran, Charles Frederick Fellowes Davies, John Cunningham Dudgeon, Robert Dunlop, John Patrick Ferris, Thomas Henry Fletcher, Henry Arthur Geelan, John Fitzhugh Gelston, Ernest Oswald Gerity,

Ewing Gilfillan, John Kearney Gorman, George Hall, Ronald Trant Hamilton, Richard Dale Winnett Harrison, Richard Robert Heggart, Thomas Hunter Herriot, George Louis Hildebrand, Donald Charles Blake Jennings, Francis William Lewis, William John Lynn, Jacob Frederick Martin, William John McBride, George Andrew McFarland, John McNally, Samuel McNeill, William Verner Miller, Joseph Roger Moore, William Sneyd Moore, Thomas Dawson Morrison, Ronald Leslie Murray, Henry Lancelot Neligan, Samuel Nevin, John William Nixon, Cornelius O'Beirne, Richard Pike Pim, John Martin Regan, Henry Seymour Robinson, Andrew Scott, John Charles Lionel Silcock, Reginald Rowland Spears, Frederick Rufane St Lawrence Tyrrell, Henry Jordan Walshe, Charles George Wickham and George Williams. Charles George Wickham was the first appointed inspector general of the RUC and served until 1945 when he was succeeded by a fellow former RIC officer Richard Pike Pim until 1961.

PALESTINE GENDARMERIE

In March 1922 the following 10 RIC officers joined the Palestine Gendarmerie (British Section): Cecil Joseph Burke Dignan, Harold Edward Fitzgerald, Gerald Robert Evans Foley, William Farrell Martinson, Michael Joseph McConnell, John McFarland, James Munro, Michael Sylvester O'Rorke, Howard Douglas D.C. Tiley and Robert Lewkenor Worsley. Major General Henry Hugh Tudor took charge as Inspector General of Police and Prisons on 15 June 1922. Gerald Robert Evans Foley was appointed assistant inspector general of the Palestine Police and William Farrell Martinson who had been commandant of the ADRIC Depot at Beggars Bush Barracks Dublin since 7 February 1921 was appointed adjutant to the headquarters staff of the Palestine Police.

PERSONALITIES

Robert O'Hara Burke (1821–61) served in the Irish Constabulary from 1849 to 1852 when he resigned and emigrated to Australia joining the Victoria Police. He was promoted to the rank of superintendent. He commanded the expedition, organized by the Royal Society of Victoria and supported by the government, fitted out to explore the centre of Australia which started from Melbourne on 20 August 1860, reached Cooper's Creek on 11 November 1860, crossed the continent and reached the Gulf of Carpentaria on 10 February 1861 where he died of starvation on 28 June 1861. He was buried with a public funeral at Melbourne on 21 January 1863.

RIC Inspector General, Col. Sir Neville Chamberlain (1856–1944), invented the game of snooker in Ooty, India in 1874, while stationed there as a young subaltern with the Devonshire Regiment. In 1901 he resided at The Hermitage, Cullenswood,

Rathfarnham, Co. Dublin and added a billiards room to the house which would be the home of the poet and patriot, Patrick Pearse (1879–1916). District Inspector Thomas St George MacCarthy (1862–1943) was capped for rugby for Ireland and was one of the seven co-founders of the Gaelic Athletic Association, who attended its inaugural meeting in Thurles, Co. Tipperary in 1884. Joseph Alphonsus Carbery was recognized internationally as a dog-breeder, judge and exhibitor. He owned kennels and bred the 'Of Boyne' Irish setters which won a world-wide reputation, and exported them to all parts of the world; his dogs won thousands of prizes and one hundred and fifty championship certificates and Green stars; he also exhibited and won with pointers, setters, retrievers, spaniels and Kerry Blue setters; for over forty years his judging engagements, mostly as an all-round judge, extended all over Great Britain and Ireland, Sweden, Italy, Norway and Holland. He was a member of more than twenty dog societies and was Vice-President of the old Irish Kennel Club at the date of its abolition and was one of the first to assist the Governing Body of which he had acted on the General Purposes Committee for more than nine years. He was also a senior member of the Irish Redsetter Club of which he acted as Hon. Treasurer for 21 years. He was a regular contributor to the *Irish Field* and to cross-channel

32a Sub Inspector Joseph Cox
Irish Constabulary, Cashel, Co. Tipperary,
1848

32b Sub Inspector Thomas Trant,
Irish Constabulary, Callan, Co.
Kilkenny, 1848

Pen and ink sketches by William Tinsley (1804–1885), at the State Trial of William Smith O'Brien (1803–64), held at Clonmel, Co. Tipperary in October 1848 (reproduced in *Journal of the Royal Society of Antiquities in Ireland* (1953), vol. lxxxiii, part 1). Both officers were awarded the first Constabulary Medals on 1 September 1848, and received a reward of £50 each for their roles in suppressing the Young Ireland Rising at the 'Battle of Farrinrory' at the widow McCormack's Famine Warhouse, Boulagh Common, Co. Tipperary on 29 July 1848.

periodicals dealing with dogs. He judged a number of times at Crofts International Show.

The community of Blaketown, Newfoundland takes its name from its former governor (1887–9), Sir Henry Arthur Blake (1840–1918), who served as a sub inspector in the RIC (1859–1876), resident magistrate (1876–81), special resident magistrate (1881–4), Governor of the Bahamas (1884–7), Jamaica (1889–97), Hong Kong (1897–1903) and Ceylon (1903–7). He was a botanist and Fellow of the Royal Geographic Society who discovered a new species of orchid in Hong Kong which was named in his honour, 'Bauhinia Blakeana'. In 1965 the flower was adopted as the City Flower of Hong Kong and in 1997 was chosen as the emblem for Hong Kong SAR. He is buried in the grounds Myrtle Grove, Youghal, Co. Cork, where Sir Walter Raleigh is reputed to have smoked the first tobacco and planted the first potatoes in Ireland. His granddaughter married the author, Claud Coburn (1904–81), who coined the phrase: 'Never believe anything until it has been officially denied.'

Anthony Thomas Lefroy (1802–90), a former chief constable in the Irish Constabulary in 1839, was the first appointed chief constable of Gloucestershire, which was also the first appointment of a chief constable to the county constabulary in England. His cousin, Thomas Lefroy, married Anna Austen, a niece of the novelist, Jane Austen (1775–1817). The poetess Mrs Felicia Dorothea Hemans (1793–1835) was the sister of Major George Baxter Browne (1790–1879), county inspector, Irish Constabulary and joint commissioner, Dublin Metropolitan Police. Sir Thomas Wyse (1791–1862), first cousin of Irish Constabulary County Inspector, Thomas Wyse (1823–78), married Letitia Bonaparte (1824–71), niece of Napoleon I Bonaparte (1769–1821), Emperor of the French. RIC DI Pierre B. Pattisson (b.1857), married on 20 November 1885 at the parish church, Clontarf, Co. Dublin, Bertha Maude, youngest daughter of Lieutenant-Colonel James Balcombe, of 1, Marino Terrace, Clontarf, Co. Dublin. Her sister, Florence Balcombe (b.1858), an aspiring actress who had been courted by the poet and playwright Oscar Wilde (1854–1900), married on 4 December 1878, at St Ann's Church, Dublin, Bram Stoker (1847–1912), author of *Dracula*, published on 26 May 1897; Bram Stoker, whose maternal grandfather was Thomas Thornley (1795–1850), SI RIC, was born at 15, The Crescent, Clontarf, Co. Dublin and his first book, published in 1879 was *The Duties of Clerks of Petty Sessions in Ireland*; Pattisson's wife, Bertha Maude, was an authoress of several articles in the *Sketch*, the *Illustrated Sporting and Dramatic News*, *Temple Bar* and the *English Illustrated Magazine*. The painter, decorator and author of *The Ragged Trousered Philanthropist*, first published in 1914, the classic English working-class novel, Robert Tressel (1870–1911), claimed in his daughter's birthday book that he was born in Dublin in April 1870, the son of Samuel Croker, resident magistrate and former chief constable Irish Constabulary. Margaret Barrington (1896–1992), daughter of RIC District Inspector Richard Barrington (1865–1949), married firstly, Edmund Curtis (1881–1943), author and historian, and secondly, the novelist, Liam O'Flaherty (1896–1984).

Thomas Hartley Montgomery, a sub inspector in Newtownstewart, Co. Tyrone, befriended a bank cashier named William Glass and in due course used that friendship to gain entry to the bank, murder his friend and steal £1,600 in notes. The murder took place on 29 June 1871, a day when the bank manager was at another bank and most of the local police were on 'fair duty' in a neighbouring village. Montgomery was tried on three occasions, in the first and second trials the jury disagreed but in the third, on 22 July 1873, he was arraigned at Omagh Assizes, found guilty and surprised all by making a matter of fact confession of guilt. Part of the *Belfast Newsletter* helped to convict him as the stolen money was eventually recovered wrapped in that part of the daily newspaper that had been missing from the scene of the crime. He was hanged at Omagh, Co. Tyrone on 26 August 1873, where RIC men had the doubtful distinction of seeing their former sub inspector executed. The episode was heightened in local folklore by a tremendous thunderstorm on the evening of the execution. The hangman was William Marwood.

District Inspector James Ellis French was arrested on 15 July 1884 for his involvement in indecency with a group of Dublin Castle officials. He tried unsuccessfully to plead 'insanity' on 19 August 1884 and 30 October 1884. He was tried for conspiracy on 31 October 1884, 3 November 1884 and 19 December 1884 and found guilty on 20 December 1884 and sentenced to two years' imprisonment with hard labour from the date of arrest.

Obviously, the core of this book is to be found in its huge LIST, which mentions every (Royal) Irish Constabulary officer and Peace Preservation Force officer. This LIST covering, 1,700 officers, expands the officer genealogical content, who are identified by name only in the huge *The Royal Irish Constabulary: A Complete Alphabetic List of 85,028 Officers and Men, 1816–1922* which I published after *The Royal Irish Constabulary: A Short History and Genealogical Guide*. In addition, the other appendices identify every officer and their roles who served at the RIC Headquarters in the Phoenix Park Depot, from 1842 to 1922 and its sub depots. In a separate appendix the constabulary divisions and districts to which RIC officers were allocated are identified. An officers' Roll of Honour is also provided.

THE LIST

A

Abbott, George; RIC 962; LDS 2097/210; born 1812, Kent, England; wife a native of Co. Mayo; his third daughter, Julia C. Abbott, Ivy Cottage, Ballinrobe, Co. Mayo; married on 13/10/1869, John R. Kelly, of Ballykine House, Clonbur at Ballinrobe Church, Co. Mayo (*Cork Examiner* 18/10/1869); 3rd SI 21/5/1857; pensioned 1/4/1875; died 7/1/1894 at The Rectory, Annaghdown, Claregalway, Co. Galway (Galway Registrar's District, 1894, March Quarter, vol. 4, p. 219); buried at Headford, Co. Galway on 10/1/1894; will proved on 24/4/1894 at Tuam by the oath of Davis R. Young, Gent. and Robert J. Dixon, clerk, of Castlebar, Co. Mayo, the executors – effects £385.7s.0d.

Abbott, Samuel Tydd; LDS 2097/080; CarNB; born 1793, Silvermines, Co. Tipperary; fourth son of John Abbott, Esq., baronial head constable, Upper Ormond, Silvermines, Co. Tipperary; PPF; enlisted as a constable, 1/2/1824; wife a native of Co. Longford; 3rd SI 1/2/1833; pensioned 20/12/1866; his eldest daughter, Elizabeth, married Dr Patrick Horne at Ballinasloe, Co. Galway on 25/5/1854 (Ballinasloe Registrar's District, vol. 1, p. 619); died 1/10/1873 at the residence of his son-in-law, Dr Patrick Horne, Ballinasloe, Co. Galway; C.C. Ballinasloe, Co. Galway.

Ackland, Henry; CarNB; born Lagavooreen, Drogheda, Co. Louth; son of John Ackland; captain, 3rd SI 1824; C.C. Roscommon, Co. Roscommon.

Acklom, John Evatt; LDS 2097/112; born 1803, Cornwall, England; ensign, 19/6/1825, lieutenant, 19/9/1826, captain 1/6/1832, 28th Regiment of Foot (North Gloucestershire Regiment); captain half pay, Ionian Militia from June 1835 to November 1838; 3rd SI 18/4/1837; pensioned 8/1/1844.

Adams, William Somerville; RIC 82930; LDS 2099/035; born 29/7/1892, Co. Westmeath; (Mullingar Registrar's District, September Quarter, 1892, vol. 3, p. 218); married on 1/4/1918, wife a native of Sussex; captain, East Lancashire Regiment, 13/3/1915–20/5/1920; ADRIC, 10/8/1920–25/8/1920; 3rd DI 20/9/1921; pensioned 8/5/1922.

Adderley, Albert W.; RIC 47862; LDS 2098/237; born 6/2/1863, Innishannon, Co. Cork; married on 5/9/1901 (Rathdown Registrar's District, September Quarter, vol. 2, p. 806); 3rd DI 10/12/1908; pensioned 30/6/1920.

Alcock, Mason; RIC 23953; LDS 2097/223; born 1836, Roughgrove, near Bandon, Co. Cork; ensign in the South Cork Militia from 12/10/1855 to 12/9/1856; married on 8/3/1888 at Desertserges (Inishowen Registrar's District, March Quarter, 1888, vol. 2, p. 151), Diana, third daughter of John Miller, Buncrana, Co. Donegal; 3rd SI 14/10/1858; pensioned 1/7/1899; died 5/5/1901 at Sandon, Clontarf, Dublin; will proved at the Principal Registry on 19/6/1901 by the oath of Henry James Hungerford and Henry Thomas White, solicitor – effects £6,502; buried in Mount Jerome Cemetery, Dublin.

Aldworth, Richard Fitzjohn; RIC 24628; LDS 2097/228; born 22/10/1836, Youghal, Co. Cork; third son of Rev. John Aldworth (b.28/12/1800, d.12/6/1878), Rector of Youghal, 1836 and of Glanworth, Co. Cork, 1847 who married on 5/5/1826, Anne (d.7/11/1845), eldest daughter of Charles Deane Oliver (1771–15/2/1829), of Spa Hill, Co. Limerick and Rock Mill Lodge, Co. Cork; clerk in Ennis National Bank for two years to April 1859; 3rd SI 23/4/1859; married firstly 7/4/1869, at St Paul's Church, Upper Norwood, Elizabeth MacGregor (d.3/5/1889), second daughter of William Hutton, of Headview House, Lismore, Co. Waterford

(*Cork Examiner* 16/4/1869), and they had one son, Oliver Fitzmaurice (1870–84); married secondly, Maria Louisa Fitzgerald, daughter of Rev. E. Loftus Fitzgerald, of Templemichael, Co. Waterford; pensioned 21/6/1890; died 10/2/1893 at Marino, Youghal, Co. Cork; will proved on 28/9/1893 at the Principal Registry by the oath of Maria Louisa Aldworth, of Marina, Youghal, Co. Cork, the widow, sole executrix – effects £894.0s.10d.

Allbutt, Henry; RIC 50479; LDS 2097/323; born 1858, Warks., England; 3rd DI 15/11/1882; his wife was from Surrey; resigned 17/10/1886 on his appointment as Deputy Chief Constable of Liverpool; Chief Constable of Bristol City, 11/91/894 to 19/9/1906.

Allen, Charles; CarNB; 3rd SI 1823; died February 1826 at Mount Talbot; C.C. Loughrea, Co. Galway; his widow, Elizabeth was residing in Ballinasloe, Co. Galway in 1830.

Allen, Henry Augustine; RIC 27393; LDS 2097/241; born 1842, Co. Clare; 3rd SI 6/6/1862; CI 1/9/1886; pensioned 23/10/1899; his daughter, Mary Stuart married on 11/4/1901 at St Paul's Church, Fremantle, Western Australia, Harry Ingram, youngest son of Rev. John Cecil Rogers, of Nohoval, Co. Cork, by Rev. Edward Saunders.

Allen, Richard; RIC 27829; LDS 2098/034; born 1844, Arklow, Co. Wicklow; 3rd DI 1/5/1887; died 9/11/1894 at Killaloe, Co. Clare (Scariff Registrar's District, 1894, December Quarter, vol. 4, p. 233); administration granted on 14/12/1894 at the Principal Registry to Anna Allen, of 58, Raymond Street, Dublin, the widow – effects £151.10s.0d.

Allen, Thomas James; RIC 56026; LDS 2098/097B; born 25/9/1872, Co. Leitrim; (Mohill Registrar's District, 1872, vol. 13, p. 262); 3rd DI 10/2/1919; awarded the Constabulary Medal, 1922; pensioned 31/5/1922; transferred to the Royal Ulster Constabulary on 1/6/1922.

Alworthy, Charles; LDS 2097/157; 3rd SI 21/4/1847; dismissed as unfit by the Surgeon, 21/4/1847.

Alworthy, Samuel; LDS 2097/023; born 1784, Co. Kilkenny; private and corporal in the Kilkenny Militia from 1810 to 1814 (WO 13/2942–60); PPF Clerk 21/12/1815; PPF constable, 1/2/1817 in Co. Tipperary; his fifth daughter, Susan, married on 11/6/1864, at Dunedin, New Zealand, Joseph Martin, Esq., of South Yarra, Melbourne, Australia (*Cork Examiner* 31/8/1864); 3rd SI 10/3/1818; C.C. Moate, Co. Westmeath and Ballymahon, Co. Longford; pensioned 1/12/1849; died 29/7/1859.

Anderson, John; LDS 2097/086; born 1801, Co. Dublin; clerk from 8/4/1824 to 24/9/1834; wife a native of Dublin City; 3rd SI 24/9/1834; his only son, captain John Anderson, 19th Regiment of Foot (Green Howards), married on 4/6/1863, at St David's Church, Exeter, Devon, England, Harriet, youngest daughter of Charles Brutton, Northernhay (*Cork Examiner* 6/6/1863); CI 17/10/1856; pensioned 15/12/1869; died 13/6/1875 at New Ross, Co. Wexford; (New Ross Registrar's District, 1875, vol. 9, p. 61).

Anderson, Louis; LDS 2097/037; born 10/11/1800, Prospect House, Dunbell, Co. Kilkenny; second son of John Anderson (b.1757) (d.1/4/1839), of Woodville and Prospect House, Dunbell, Co. Kilkenny, who served in the Gowran Yeomanry Cavalry in 1798 and who married on 7/10/1787, Jane (b.1/4/1767; d.16/7/1836), eldest daughter of Abraham Denroche, of Newhouse, Co. Kilkenny; father of Louis John Anderson, SI, RIC; educated at Kilkenny College; married in 1834 Elizabeth Dillon (d.1/5/1883 aged 82 years), eldest daughter of William Despard, JP, of Killaghy Castle, Mullinahone, Co. Tipperary; 3rd SI 28/1/1823; CI 21/1/1840; resided at Ballinahone House, Co. Armagh, Evington, Co. Carlow and Belgrave Square, Dublin; pensioned 1/8/1867; died 11/3/1888 at 46, Belgrave Square, Rathmines, Dublin; buried in Mount Jerome Cemetery, Dublin on 14/3/1888; administration granted on 2/7/1888 at the Principal Registry to Olympia Anderson, of 46, Belgrave Square, Rathmines, Dublin, spinster, the sole executrix – effects £2,158.12s.3d.

Anderson, Louis John; LDS 2097/205; born 8/6/1835, Killaghy Castle, Co. Tipperary; son of Louis Anderson, CI, RIC; educated at the Royal School, Armagh; married on 14/7/1858 (Dundalk Registrar's District, vol. 5, p. 419), Frances Ann (d.22/1/1911), daughter of Edward

George Brunker, MD, of Roden Place, Dundalk, Co. Louth and Minore House, Co. Monaghan, by his wife Frances, youngest daughter of William Smyth, JP of Gurteen, Co. Tipperary; he had three sons and two daughters, one of which, Isabella (1845–80) married Andrew O'Brien Carleton, DI, RIC; 3rd SI 3/10/1854; died 28/2/1867 at Gorey, Co. Wexford (Gorey Registrar's District, vol. 2, p. 788); gratuity to his widow of £113.17s.11d.; buried in Mount Jerome Cemetery, Dublin with his wife Frances Anne Anderson, died 22/1/1911 aged 73 years and their daughter died 23/2/1947 aged 87 years; administration granted at the Principal Registry on 16/4/1867 to Frances Anne Anderson, of Roden Place, Dundalk, Co. Louth, widow of the deceased – effects under £1,000.

33 Louis Anderson.

Anderson, Thomas Charles; RIC 13936; LDS 2097/184; born 1823, Co. Kildare; 3rd SI 31/5/1850; seconded to the Commissariat Department in the Crimea on 6/7/1854 where he died on 11/8/1854.

Andrews, Alexander R.; RIC 51007; LDS 2097/334; born 1860, Co. Kilkenny; 3rd SI 14/11/1883; resigned 28/4/1888 at Rathfriland, Co. Down.

Anketell, John; LDS 2097/155; born 1825, Anketell's Grove, Emyvale, Co. Monaghan; 3rd SI 2/4/1847; pensioned 10/7/1867.

Annesley, Arthur Geoffrey Grove; RIC 53927; LDS 2098/059; born 24/6/1867, Co. Kilkenny, eldest son of Henry Robert Grove Annesley, CI, RIC; (Kilkenny Registrar's District, 1867, vol. 13, p. 527); married on 22/6/1898 (Rathdown Registrar's District, June Quarter, 1898, vol. 2, p. 771), Mary Edith, daughter of the late William J. Roe, Kingstown (Dunlaoghaire), Co. Dublin; 3rd DI 31/1/1890; pensioned 19/4/1922; died 12/1/1954.

Annesley, Henry Robert Grove; RIC 19012; LDS 2097/206; born 22/4/1831, Annesgrove, Castletownroche, Co. Cork; son of Lieutenant-General Arthur Grove Annesley and Elizabeth (d.26/2/1863 at Annesgrove)(*Cork Examiner* 4/3/1863), daughter of John and Lady Charlotte Mahon; his sister, Frances St Lawrence Grove Annesley married on 29/10/1850 (Naas Registrar's District, vol. 8, p. 341), George Montgomery Vaughan, Esq., of Quilly House and Villa, Co. Down at Ballymore Eustace, Co. Kildare (*Cork Examiner* 30/10/1850); his sister, Catherine Grove Annesley married on 20/1/1863 at Castletownroche Church, Co. Cork (Fermoy Registrar's District, vol. 6, p. 6), by the Rev. C.A. Maginn, MA, rector of the parish, Lieutenant, Henry Albert Platt, 69th Regiment of Foot (South Lincolnshire Regiment), youngest son of Samuel Platt, Esq., JP, DL, of 9, Eastern Terrace, Brighton and nephew of the Hon. Sir Thomas Platt, Kt., formerly one of the Judges of Her Majesty's Court of Exchequer (*Cork Examiner* 22/1/1863); employed for five years in the General Post Office Dublin; married 20/11/1862 (Rathdown Registrar's District, vol. 9, p. 519), by special license, at the residence of the bride's father, by the Rev. William Marrable, uncle of the bride, to Kathleen Letitia (d.25/12/1919), only daughter of Benjamin Ivan Tilly (d.1953), of Chantilly, Co. Dublin (*Cork Examiner* 24/11/1862); 3rd SI 16/10/1854; CI 16/10/1877; pensioned 23/12/1891; died 3/11/1908 at Highthorn, Kingstown, Co. Dublin; will proved at the Principal Registry on 4/12/1908 by the oath of Kathleen L.G. Annesley, the widow and Frederick William Westrey, Esq. – effects £7,392.15s.5d.

Archer, Robert H.; CarNB; born, Co. Dublin; C.C. Clashmore, Co. Waterford.

Armstrong, Archibald; LDS 2097/036; born 1779, Co. Sligo; lieutenant and captain, 71st Regiment of Foot (Highland Light Infantry); 3rd SI 28/1/1823; died 11/6/1841.

Armstrong, Bertie MacVicar; RIC 72025; LDS 2098/192B; born 5/6/1884, Lincs., England; captain, H.E.H; married on 31/5/1921 (Drogheda Registrar's District, June Quarter, 1921, vol. 2, p. 425), wife a native of Co. Wicklow; 3rd DI 10/1/1920; pensioned 31/8/1922.

Armstrong, Charles Edward; LDS 2098/101; born 2/4/1872, Dingle, Co. Kerry; (Dingle Registrar's District, 1872, vol. 10, p. 258); married on 9/6/1909 (Rathdown Registrar's District, June Quarter, 1909, vol. 2, p. 779), wife a native of Co. Leitrim; 3rd DI 26/4/1894; King Edward VII Visit to Ireland Medal, 1903; resident magistrate 3rd class 14/6/1919; appointed an additional RM for Co. Westmeath by warrant dated 21/9/1920, principally to enable him to act during the absence of John Peter Byrne, RM, at Athlone (p. 174. RM Records of Service Book, National Archives, Dublin).

Armstrong, Edward Jenkins; RIC 21906; LDS 2097/212; born 1834, Co. Louth; accountant and cashier in the Belfast Bank for five years; 3rd SI 28/10/1857; pensioned 24/7/1878; died 4/1/1881.

Armstrong, James; RIC 51924; LDS 2098/128B; born 1866, Co. Fermanagh; (Enniskillen Registrar's District, 1866, vol. 12, p. 84); married on 6/9/1874 (Belfast Registrar's District, September Quarter, 1894, vol. 1, p. 534), wife a native of Co. Armagh; 3rd DI 8/1/1920; pensioned 31/5/1922; transferred to the Royal Ulster Constabulary on 1/6/1922.

Armstrong, James; LDS 2097/073; born 1796, Co. Tipperary; PPF; enlisted as a sub constable, 1/5/1819; 3rd SI 1/3/1832; wife Mary; died 11/12/1845; C.C. Borrisoleigh, Co. Tipperary.

Armstrong, John; CarNB; born 1786, Drogheda, Co. Louth; wife, Eleanor; PPF; C.C. Drogheda, Co. Louth from 1806; died July 1829; will proved at Drogheda sub-registry by the oath of William Dawson, Peter Street, Drogheda, Co. Louth (NA Reference: IWR/1828/F/13).

Armstrong, Thomas; RIC 787; LDS 2097/080; born 1803, Co. Fermanagh; PPF; enlisted as a sub constable 1/5/1819; wife a native of Co. Fermanagh; baronial chief constable from 7/11/1823 to 1/9/1825; his youngest daughter, Margaret, married on 6/12/1871, Henry Reay, Esq., of Ardee, Co. Louth, at the Parish Church, Dundalk, Co. Louth (Dundalk Registrar's District, vol. 17, p. 743) (*Cork Examiner* 4/12/1871); 3rd SI 1/2/1833; pensioned 1/6/1864; died 10/3/1886 at Ardee, Co. Louth; will proved on 6/5/1886 at Armagh by the oath of George Armstrong, of Dundalk, Co. Louth, National School Teacher, one of the executors – effects £247; C.C. Hackballscross, Co. Louth.

Armstrong, Thomas James; RIC 16324; LDS 2097/299; born 1833, Co. Tipperary; 3rd SI 27/1/1879; his daughter was born in Moylough, Co. Galway on 1/1/1884; died 24/6/1887 at The Cottage, Killaloe, Co. Clare; administration granted on 6/9/1907 at Limerick to Catherine Armstrong, The Cottage, Killaloe, Co. Clare, the widow – effects £622.9s.6d.

Armstrong, William; LDS 2097/145; born 1825, Co. Sligo; 3rd SI 19/6/1844; died (date not entered in register).

Armstrong, William E.: LDS 2097/154; born 1825, France; Imperial and Royal Austrian Cavalry for three years and six months; 3rd SI 2/9/1846; resigned 18/09/1850.

Arnold, Richard Ernest; RIC 78414; LDS 2098/245B; born 12/3/1893, Co. Wexford; (Enniscorthy Registrar's District, June Quarter, 1893, vol. 4, p. 546); captain, Royal Field Artillery; ADRIC; 3rd DI 2/7/1921; pensioned 20/5/1922.

Arthur, Patrick; RIC 2767; LDS 2097/093; born 1817, Co. Clare; 3rd SI 22/1/1836; dismissed 27/4/1837.

Arthur, Thomas; LDS 2097/131, born 1817, Co. Clare; 3rd SI 1/7/1840; broke his arm in April 1851; pensioned 1/7/1863; died 21/11/1893 at Drinagh Cottage, Mountmellick, Queen's County; administration granted on 18/12/1893 at the Principal Registry to William Arthur, of 32, Circus Road, St John's Wood, London, surgeon, the universal legatee – effects £216.13s.4d.

Ashberry, Edward; LDS 2097/078; born 1796, Shinrone, King's County; PPF; enlisted as a sub constable, 1/6/1821; 3rd SI 14/12/1832; his eldest son, William, aged 19 years, died at

34   35

34 William Atteridge in District Inspector's RIC uniform, 1916. 35 William Atteridge in District Inspector's RUC uniform, 1924. 36 William Atteridge in County Inspector's RUC uniform, 1930 with Señor Hermán Montoya (left), from Colombia, South America, and Prince Tunku Yahaya, son of the Sultan of Kedah, Malaya, who were studying police methods at the Royal Ulster Constabulary Depot, Newtownards, Co. Down.

36

Kilmacthomas, Co. Waterford on 9/1/1848; he received an injury in the leg when on patrol at Goresbridge in Co. Kilkenny on 10/5/1834; pensioned 1/9/1849; died 1853.

Atkin, Walter; LDS 2097/115; born 1811, Careystown, Cloyne, Co. Cork; enlisted as a sub constable on 10/9/1829; wife a native of Queen's County; 3rd SI 1/9/1839; died 14/8/1859 at Rathdowney, Queen's County; administration granted at the Principal Registry on 20/3/1860 to Martha Atkin, of 75, Harcourt Street, Dublin, the widow of said deceased – effects under £300.

Atkinson, Charles; LDS 2097/038; born 1798, Tedavnet, Co. Monaghan; 3rd SI 28/1/1823; C.C. Newtownlimavady, Co. Derry, 1831; died 12/4/1836 at Carrickmacross, Co. Monaghan.

Atkinson, Robert Charles; LDS 2097/046; born, Tedavnet Co. Monaghan; Monaghan Militia (WO 13/3160–79); while residing in Rathgar, Co. Dublin he married Eliza Sparrow in 1809 (Marriage Licence Bonds for the Diocese of Dublin); 3rd SI 1/10/1823; on 20/11/1829 his wife died in Strokestown, Co. Roscommon and he applied for two months leave to place some of his seven children with friends; dismissed 1838 having been found guilty by the constabulary court of sending forged barrack rent to the paymaster; was given a gratuity in consideration of the length of his service.

Atteridge, William; RIC 55620, LDS 2098/008B; born 1/8/1873, Co. Limerick; joined the Merchant Navy in 1889 until he enlisted in the RIC as a constable on 16/11/1892; served in Athy, Co. Kildare for five years until his promotion to acting sergeant in 1899 and transferred to Co. Galway E.R.; promoted sergeant in 1900 and Office Inspector of Weights and Measures; married on 22/8/1901 (Gort Registrar's District, September Quarter, 1901, vol. 4, p. 109), Jane Forde, a native of Co. Galway; they had a son who died young and two daughters, Kathleen and Maud; promoted head constable in 1906 and served in Loughrea, Co. Galway; 3rd DI 3/1/1910 and transferred to Tubbercurry, Co. Sligo; transferred to Moate, Co. Westmeath in December 1910; 2nd class DI 24/5/1911; transferred to Belfast in charge of Springfield Road 'B' District in December 1914; 1st class DI 1/5/1920; TCI 16/11/1920 in charge of Co. Clare until the signing of the Treaty and transferred to Belfast; awarded a 3rd class favourable record and £3 for courage and tact in a riot in Belfast on 26/4/1919; pensioned 31/5/1922; transferred to the Royal Ulster Constabulary on 1/6/1922; promoted RUC county Inspector in 1927 in charge of Co. Fermanagh and in January 1929 he was transferred to Co. Antrim; awarded the MBE in 1923; author of *The Royal Ulster Constabulary Guide*, 1935; pensioned on 1/8/1933 on his sixtieth birthday; died 26/7/1957; buried in Breandrum Cemetery, Enniskillen, Co. Fermanagh; (Photo in the Irish *Daily Telegraph*, 21/7/1933).

Attfield, Richard Albert; RIC 82943; LDS 2099/046; born 28/5/1880, Surrey, England; married on 4/6/1915, wife from London; 1st lieutenant, 3rd Battalion (Special Reserve) Prince Albert's (Somerset Light Infantry), 15/7/1915; served with the Machine Gun Corps in Mesopotamia; wounded 14/1/1917; nominated for a commission in the RIC by Lord Balfour of Burleigh and General Sir Nevil Macready; ADRIC, October 1920 to July 1921; 3rd DI 20/9/1921; pensioned 26/5/1922; died in 1962; (WO 339/34723).

Aubrey, Benjamin; RIC 4188; LDS 2097/273; born 1821, Co. Cork; 3rd SI 1/6/1868; died 14/2/1876 at Tubbercurry, Co. Sligo; (Tubbercurry Registrar's District, 1875, vol. 4, p. 374).

Auchmuty, George Keating; LDS 2097/218; born 1836, Co. Westmeath; joined the Irish Revenue Police as a lieutenant on 29/12/1856, serving in Ballyvary, Co. Mayo; 3rd SI 1/2/1857; dismissed 10/10/1869 for 'continued habits of intemperance'.

Aurose, Samuel I.W.; LDS 2097/335; born 1861, Co. Cork, 3rd DI 29/2/1884; resigned 3/11/1894.

Aylmore, George Hart A.; RIC 77810; LDS 2098/235B; born 15/2/1888, Essex, England; (West Ham Registrar's District, 1888, March Quarter, vol. 4a, p. 298); 2nd lieutenant, 1st Essex Regiment; ADRIC; married on 20/7/1921; 3rd DI 2/7/1921; pensioned 8/5/1922.

B

Babbage, Henry Whitmore; RIC 44400; LDS 2097/301; born 1855, Middlesex, London, England; (Marleybone Registrar's District, 1855, June Quarter, vol. 353, p. 353); clerk in the War Office for four years and articled to a firm of brewers for two years; wife from Co. Tipperary; 3rd DI 3/5/1879; CI 27/4/1901; pensioned 4/4/1908 as being permanently unfit for duty by the surgeon of the Force; died 27/4/1911 at Church Street, Cavan, Co. Cavan; will proved at the Principal Registry on 3/6/1911 by the oath of Elmima N. Babbage, the widow – effects £371.18s.1d.; (photo in the *Constabulary Gazette*, vol. XV, no. 5, 23/4/1904).

Bagge, William; CarNB; born Kilgobnet, Co. Waterford; C.C. barony of Kilkenny West; Glasson, near Athlone, 1828 and Kinnegad, Co. Westmeath, 1831.

Bagley, Richard William; LDS 2097/122; born 1817, Co. Westmeath; served two years in the British Legion in Spain as a captain in the artillery; 3rd SI 13/12/1838; pensioned 17/1/1859 in Co. Antrim; died 10/6/1903 at Coolmagee, Portrush, Co. Antrim; buried in Coleraine Cemetery on 13/6/1903.

Bagnell, E.T.; LDS 2097/334; born 1860, Co. Dublin; 3rd DI 26/2/1884; dismissed 1/4/1884.

Bailey, Edward William; RIC 34405; LDS 2097/270; born 1850, Co. Cavan; wife a native of Co. Cavan; 3rd SI 24/6/1868; pensioned 9/12/1893; died 31/12/1918.

Bailey, James Luttrel; LDS 2097/270; born 1804, Queen's County; 3rd SI 14/7/1832; CI 1/6/1859; Commissioner of Police and Town Inspector of Constabulary, Belfast from 1/9/1865 to 1/10/1882; received a favourable record on 31/12/1869 for complete and successful organization of arrangements for the preservation of the police on an occasion of hostile gatherings; pensioned 1/6/1883; died 22/2/1896 at 10, Mountcharles Street, Belfast (Belfast Registrar's District, 1896, March Quarter, vol. 1, p. 283); will with one codicil proved on 29/4/1896 at Belfast by the oath of William Frederick Bailey, of No. 9, Brockvale Avenue, Belfast, MD and James Cunningham, of Waring Street, Belfast, stocks and shares broker, the executors – effects £10,476.16s.0d.; C.C. Gowran, Co. Kilkenny; (photo in the *Constabulary Gazette*, vol. VI, no. 13, 23/12/1899, p. 390).

Bain, Andrew; RIC 52409; LDS 2098/026; born 1862, Melrose, Roxburgh County, Scotland; assistant master in the Mannaward School, Plymouth from April a884 to April 1887; residing at 6, Salisbury Street, Edinburgh, Scotland in 1881 (Census); 3rd DI 1/6/1887; author of *Police Duties and Drill*, 1894; captain, Royal Engineers; Ashanti War Medal, 1895–6; seconded 5/3/1900 while employed in active service in South Africa; resigned 2/5/1903 on his appointment as Commissioner of Police, Nigeria.

Baldwin, Osborne George De Courcy; RIC 65959; LDS 2098/027B; born 4/4/1885, Yorks., England; (York Registrar's District, 1885, June Quarter, vol. 9d, p. 51); son of Rev. W.H. De Courcy Baldwin and Mary Osborne De Courcy Baldwin, of 'Mickledown', Ewell, Surrey; educated at Rockington School, East Yorkshire; lieutenant, 3rd (Reserve) West Yorkshire Regiment; lieutenant, 3rd Battalion West Yorkshire Regiment, from 5/9/1906 to 28/4/1911; qualified to act as an instructor of musketry while a subaltern; captain, 'C' Coy, 8th Battalion Royal Munster Fusiliers from 9/11/1914; his mother, Mary, resided at Ballyhubba, Charleville, Co. Cork from where he enlisted in the RMF; 3rd DI 8/4/1911; King George V Visit to Ireland Medal, 1911; killed 26/1/1916, Pas de Calais, France; buried in Mazingarbe Communal Cemetery Extension, south of Bethune (Grave no. 101); administration granted at the District

Registry of Cork on 13/6/1916 to his mother Mary, of Pennington Cross, Lymington, Hants., widow – effects £129.12s.od.; (WO 339/13385).

Ball, Frederick James; RIC 43063; LDS 2097/294; born 1852, Co. Clare; regimental sergeant major, 4th Dragoon Guards; 3rd DI 16/10/1877; CI 14/2/1899; AIG 1/4/1908; Commandant of the Phoenix Park Depot from 1/4/1908 to 26/10/1909; pensioned 1/7/1912; died 27/3/1918 at Sandon, Castle Avenue, Clontarf, Co. Dublin; will proved at the Principal Registry on 2/5/1918; (photo in the *Constabulary Gazette*, vol. XXVI, no. 13, 11/12/1909).

Ball, Townley Brabazon Balfour; RIC 23834; LDS 2097/306; born 1837, Co. Westmeath; son of Edward Ball, Belfield, Raheny, Dublin and Anna Jane Ball (d.14/9/1880) (*Cork Examiner* 20/9/1880); grandson of George Ball of Ballsgrove, Drogheda, Co. Louth, Captain in the 18th Light Dragoons and ADC to Sir John Moore at the Corunna Campaign, 1808–9; 3rd SI 7/2/1880; pensioned 10/11/1889; died 15/5/1896 at his sister-in-law's residence, 3, Marino Terrace, Clontarf, Dublin (Dublin North Registrar's District, 1896, June Quarter, vol. 2, p. 329); buried in Raheny Cemetery, Dublin; will proved at the Principal Registry on 25/8/1896 on the oath of William Carruthers, of 6 Westmoreland Street, Dublin, solicitor and William J. Gibson, of 7 Castle Avenue, Clontarf, Dublin, M.D. – effects £10,653.13s.2d.

Ball, William; LDS 2097/066; born 1787, Co. Fermanagh; ensign (by purchase) 22nd Regiment of Foot (The Cheshire Regiment), 25/1/1810; lieutenant (by purchase) 11/3/1813, in exchange of receiving the difference in consequence of ill health from a residence of twelve years in India; lieutenant half pay, 9/11/1820; married at Enniskillen, Co. Fermanagh, 12/8/1823; 3rd SI 6/11/1826; pensioned 31/8/1847; died 28/4/1861 at Windlehunt, Lancashire; will proved on 16/1/1862 at the Principal Registry by the oath of Samuel Frith Esq., of Enniskillen, Co. Fermanagh, the sole executor – effects under £7,000; (WO 25/750 fol. 128).

Ball-Lenthall, Henry Benson Wyndham; RIC 64495; LDS 2098/239; born 22/5/1887, Co. Dublin; BA 1908, Trinity College Dublin; changed his Surname from 'Ball' to Ball-Lenthall on 2/4/1916; married on 16/6/1915, E.A. Lenthall, a native of England; 3rd DI 17/1/1909; ACI 11/12/1920; pensioned 31/5/1922; transferred to the Royal Ulster Constabulary on 1/6/1922.

Balmer, Richard; CarNB; born Forkhill, Co. Armagh; captain; dismissed 25/11/1830 for gambling and being frequently in arrears to his men; his wife Mary is buried in St Nicholas Burial Ground, Dundalk, Co. Louth and her inscription reads: 'This stone was erected by Richard Balmer of Forkhill in memory of his wife Mary Balmer who departed this life on the 7th of July 1813, aged 36 and also two of his children who died young'; C.C. Castleconnell, Co. Limerick; Ballinspittal and Innishannon, Co. Cork.

Bane, John Joseph; RIC 53171; LDS 2098/043B; born 31/8/1870, Co. Tipperary; married on 17/9/1897 (Limerick Registrar's District, September Quarter, 1897, vol. 5, p. 224), wife a native of Co. Limerick; 3rd DI 2/3/1913; King George V Coronation Medal, 1911; pensioned 30/9/1920.

Banon, Edward Joseph; LDS 2097/103; born 1816, Irishtown House, Mullingar, Co. Westmeath; son of James Banon (1781–1847) and Mary Bridget (d.1833), second daughter of Count Patrick Awly Magawly de Calry, of Temora, King's County; his cousin, Sir Nicholas Fitzsimon, DL, MP succeeded to the Broughal Castle estates in 1849, and on his death were succeeded to by his brother, Christopher (1810–24/5/1863), of Irishtown and Edward Joseph Banon succeeded to the Broughal Castle estates on 24/5/1863; his brother, Andrew (b.1823) married on 1/6/1864 at St Michan's Church, Dublin, Nannie, daughter of Edward T. Ffrench Beytagh, Esq., barrister-at-law, of 74 Blessington Street, Dublin (*Cork Examiner* 4/6/1864); married on 18/8/1857, at the Catholic church of St Asaph, North Wales, Ellen Mary, eldest daughter of the late John Fitzgerald of Carrick-on-Suir, Co. Tipperary (*Cork Examiner* 26/8/1857); daughters born on 8/3/1862 at Tallyard, Co. Meath (*Cork Examiner* 12/3/1862) and 30/12/1864 (*Cork Examiner* 5/1/1865); 3rd SI 20/10/1836; seconded to the Commissariat Department in the Crimea on 6/7/1854 to 11/2/1855; resident magistrate 5/2/1858; died on

10/9/1873 at Broughal Castle, Parsonstown, King's County; (Parsonstown Registrar's District, 1873, vol. 18, p. 433); will with one codicil proved on 11/11/1873 at the Principal Registry by the oath of Andrew Banon, of 43 Eccles Street, Dublin, Esq., the brother and one of the executors – effects under £450.

Barlow, Michael; CarNB; 3rd SI 1/7/1821; C.C. barony of Kilmain and Ballinrobe, Co. Mayo.

Barnes, Thomas Simpson; LDS 2097/133; born 1821, Co. Armagh; 3rd SI 8/10/1840; died 29/7/1845.

Barnivill, John; RIC 28201; LDS 2098/012; born 1843, Co. Tipperary; married on 11/6/1871 (Galway Registrar's District, vol. 9, p. 132), wife a native of Galway City; 3rd DI 1/2/1886; pensioned 1/6/1904; died 28/4/1907 at 35, Morehampton Terrace, Donnybrook, Dublin; will proved on 12/7/1907 at the Principal Registry by the oath of Mary Barnivill, widow – effects £494.0s.9d.

Barnivill, Richard Thomas; LDS 2098/100; born 1874, Co. Cavan; (Cavan Registrar's District, 1874, vol. 8, p. 117); 3rd DI 1/4/1894; resigned 10/2/1900.

Barrett, Denis; RIC 58485; LDS 2098/076B; born 21/8/1876, Cork City, Co. Cork; (Cork Registrar's District, 1876, vol. 15, p. 185); employed as a station master before joining the RIC as a constable on 15/10/1898; 3rd DI 10/2/1917; resigned 23/2/1920 on his appointment as third Assistant Commissioner of the Dublin Metropolitan Police until his retirement on 31/3/1925.

Barrington, Richard; RIC 52080; LDS 2098/001B; born 5/5/1865, Enniscorthy, Co. Wexford; son of Thomas (d.1886) a saddler and Mary Frayne, a native of Co. Donegal (d.1884), who were married on 21/6/1861 at Kilpatrick Church, Wexford (Wexford Registrar's District, vol. 10, p. 587); he had five sisters and two brothers; Richard was part owner of the saddlery business at Duffrey Street, Enniscorthy; married on 18/6/1895 (Inishowen Registrar's District, June Quarter, 1895, vol. 2, p. 93), Charlotte B. Scott, a native of Co. Sligo; they had three children, Margaret born on 10/5/1896 in Malin, Co. Donegal and she married twice, firstly in 1922 to the historian and writer, Edmund Curtis (1881–1943), and secondly to the novelist, Liam O'Flaherty (1896–1984) and she died in Kinsale, Co. Cork in 1982; the second daughter, Adelaide Charlotte was born in Magheragh, Co. Derry and she came to Canada in 1926 and married Loftus Dudley Ward, her first cousin, son of John Ward, RIC; the third daughter, Henrietta was born in Malin, Co. Donegal in 1900 and died on 29/12/1919; 3rd DI 19/3/1909; pensioned 4/6/1922. Richard came to Canada in 1926 with his daughter Charlotte in 1926 and retired in Victoria, British Columbia, Canada where he died in hospital of heart disease on 24/9/1949. He is buried in Saanich Royal Oak Cemetery, Victoria, British Columbia. Richard was a Protestant most of his life and for some reason turned to Catholicism, a move that separated him from his wife Charlotte. This may be the reason that his wife remained in Ireland and he died in British Columbia.

Barron, Netterville Guy; born 8/12/1867; educated at Haileybury and Royal Military Academy, Woolwich; married on 5/9/1952, Esme Catherine Mary (d.5/11/1952), daughter of Robert Borradaile Lloyd, banker, of Fir Grove, Farnham, Surrey; commissioned in the Royal Artillery, 1887; served in WWI (wounded, despatches); commanded the Heavy Artillery XVII Corps, 1917–19; RIC Divisional Commissioner for Munster, 7/4/1920–31/8/1922; DSO, 1918; CMG, 1919; CBE, 1923; brigadier-general; retired 1920; died 21/4/1945.

Barry, David; RIC 55103; LDS 2098/044B; born 14/2/1870, Cahirciveen, Co. Kerry; (Cahirciveen Registrar's District, 1870, vol. 20, p. 50); married on 9/11/1905 (Kinsale Registrar's District, December Quarter, 1905, vol. 5, p. 195); 3rd DI 2/9/1913; pensioned 20/5/1922.

Barry, David John; LDS 2097/081; PPF; 3rd SI 1/12/1832.

Barry, Dominick; LDS 2097/300; born 1835, Co. Galway; joined the Irish Revenue Police as a lieutenant on 23/8/1852; wife from Queen's County; 3rd SI 1/4/1879; pensioned 1/8/1896; died 20/1/1907 at Richmond Road, Fairview, Dublin; will proved on 7/2/1907 at the Principal Registry by the oath of Kate M. Barry, the widow – effects £596.5s.0d.; his daughter Elizabeth

37

38

37 Osbourne George De Courcy Baldwin.   38 Denis Barrett – Assistant Commissioner, DMP;
portrait in Garda Museum, Dublin Castle.   39 Denis Barrett – Assistant Commissioner, DMP,
1922.   40 Richard Barrington.

39   40

Angela (Lizzie) married on 14/2/1900 at the Church of the Visitation, Clontarf, Dublin, Henry Edward Herrd, Woodford House, Santry, Co. Dublin.

Barry, James; CarNB; captain; anonymous complaint made on 9/8/1824 against him of owning a private horse and feeding him with government forage; C.C. Clonakilty, Co. Cork, 1824.

Barry, Robert; LDS 2097/042; born 1785, Co. Cork; coroner of Co. Tipperary from 19/1/1814 to 30/6/1823; 3rd SI 30/6/1823; died 7/5/1845; widow, Margaret.

Barry, Thomas Robert; LDS 2097/091; born 1810, Co. Tipperary; enlisted as a constable, 1/5/1830; his son Robert Thomas Barry married on 28/9/1875 by special licence Lucy Moreton Cox, Esq., daughter of Stephen Moreton Cox, of New England, New South Wales; 3rd SI 1/12/1835; received an approbation on 31/3/1852 for judicious and successful patrolling, whereby an assassination was prevented and the suspected persons were arrested and brought to justice; received a grant from the Reward Fund on 30/9/1853 for indefatigable exertions in bringing to justice the conspirators in a murder case; received a favourable record and a grant from the Reward Fund on 31/12/1870 for having made effective and successful arrangements which led to the suppression of formidable riots in Cork; CI 22/12/1860; pensioned 10/7/1882; died 4/8/1895 at 45, Morehampton Road, Dublin (Dublin South Registrar's District, 1895, September Quarter, vol. 2, p. 416); will proved on 25/10/1895 at the Principal Registry by the oath of Caroline Weir, of 45, Morehampton Road, Dublin, the widow – effects £519.2s.1d.

Barry, William; LDS 2097/291; born 1825, Co. Galway; wife from Co. Waterford; 3rd SI 1/11/1872; died 27/10/1883 at Derrygonnelly, Co. Fermanagh; administration with the will annexed granted on 12/2/1884 at Armagh to Mary Barry of Ship Street, Tuam, Co. Galway, the widow and a legatee – effects £656.19s.0d

Batt, William Holmes; LDS 2097/070; born 1806; son of Samuel Batt, gent., of Banagher, King's County and Jane Holmes, of Drogheda, Co. Louth, who were married in 1791; married in 1833, in St Michael's Parish, Limerick, Mary Lydia Blundell, daughter of a Limerick jeweller and they had seven children, Samuel (b.1834), John Charles (b.1835), William Holmes (b.1840), Sarah Ellen, born and died in 1847, Thomas (b.1850) and Araminta (b.1852); PPF; 3rd SI 1/7/1831; severely reprimanded on 1/2/1839; died in Dublin in 1852; C.C. New Quay, the Burren and Newmarket-on-Fergus, Co. Clare.

Battersby, James; LDS 2097/031; born 1789, Co. Monaghan; wife a native of Co. Dublin; ensign and lieutenant, 20th Regiment of Foot (East Devonshire Regiment) and 30th Regiment of Foot (Cambridgeshiire Regiment) from May 1810 to March 1817; awarded one medal and four clasps for Orthes and Toulouse; 3rd SI 13/12/1822; severely wounded on 19/10/1823 while suppressing a riot; CI 21/9/1840; died 27/5/1853 in Dundalk, Co. Louth (*Cork Examiner* 6/6/1853).

Bayly, Henry Lambert; LDS 2097/130; born 9/12/1808, Ballyarthur, Co. Wicklow; second son of Rev. Henry Lambert Bayly, of Ballyarthur, Co. Wicklow; 3rd SI 31/1/1840; married on 9/12/1851 at St Peter's Church, Dublin (Dublin South Registrar's District, vol. 5, p. 355), Margaret, the eldest daughter of the late Rev. Thomas Acton, and niece of Colonel Acton, MP and VL for Co. Wicklow, of West Aston, Co. Wicklow (*Cork Examiner* 12/12/1851); Col. Acton's youngest son, Major Charles Acton, 51st Regiment of Foot (King's Own Light Infantry), married on 6/8/1869 at Christchurch, Lancaster Gate, London, Georgina Cecilia, youngest daughter of George Annesley, Esq., of Queen's Gardens, Hyde Park, London (*Cork Examiner* 7/8/1869); resigned 1/5/1849 and appointed Chief Constable of Northamptonshire on 12 May 1849 until July 1875; he was also Chief Constable of Peterborough Liberty from 10 March 1857 to 1 February 1876; died 1886.

Baynham, Hubert Leslie; RIC 69949; LDS 2098/106B; born 8/12/1892, Swansea, Glamorgan, Wales; educated at the Municipal Secondary School, Dynecor Place, Swansea, 1907–12, Technical College, Swansea and St Paul's College, Cheltenham; he matriculated at London University, qualified for the Board of Education Training Certificate and was studying for a science degree at London at the outbreak of WWI; held the Welsh record for the high jump and the 100 yards; joined Royal Garrison Artillery as a gunner, regimental no.105843 on 11/7/1916 and commissioned as a lieutenant on 12/5/1918; married on 23/6/1920 (Cork Registrar's District, June Quarter, 1920, vol. 5, p. 113), wife a native of Co. Cork; 3rd DI 4/1/1920; wounded, Ballybricken House, Callan, Co. Kilkenny 12/3/1921; musketry instructor from 1/6/1921 to 26/5/1922; pensioned 5/5/1922; (WO 330/75870).

Beirne, Patrick; RIC 42499; LDS 2098/171; born 1858, Co. Dublin; married on 8/10/1889 (Rathdown Registrar's District, December Quarter, 1889, vol. 2, p. 807); wife a native of Co. Dublin; 3rd DI 14/4/1900; King Edward VII Visit to Ireland Medal, 1903; pensioned 11/12/1919; died in 1946; buried in Esker Cemetery, Lucan, Co. Dublin.

Bell, Alan; RIC 44799; LDS 2097/304; born 8/8/1857, Banagher, King's County; BA, Dublin University; 3rd DI 10/9/1879; resident magistrate 3rd class 10/11/1898, 2nd class 1/8/1903, 1st class 11/1/1915; was brought to Dublin Castle in November 1919 as a counter intelligence officer for the Directorate of Intelligence at Scotland Yard. He investigated the Ashtown ambush and the assassination of second Assistant Commissioner Redmond, the DMP's senior investigator of political offences. He was shot dead on 26/3/1920 at Merrion, Dublin, late of 19 Belgrave Square, Monkstown, Co. Dublin; buried in Deansgrange Cemetery, Dublin; will proved at the Principal Registry on 3/5/1920; (p. 113, RM Records of Service Book, National Archives, Dublin).

Bell, James; RIC 35559; LDS 2098/104; born 1849, Co. Cavan; 3rd DI 17/11/1893; pensioned 29/9/1909; died 7/12/1919 at Larne, Co. Antrim; (Larne Registrar's District, 1919, December Quarter, vol. 1, p. 418).

Bernard, Frank Cyril; RIC 79228; ADRIC no. 903; LDS 2099/040; born 9/8/1886, Malaga, Spain; attached to Fort Garry Horse as a trooper on 12/2/1915; 2nd lieutenant, 4th Battalion Royal Irish Fusiliers on 12/8/1915; wounded at Guillemont on 4/9/1916; demobilized on 9/2/1919; 3rd DI 20/9/1921; pensioned 27/4/1922; (WO 339/38284).

Bernard, Joshua William Vitringa; RIC 27017; LDS 2097/239; born 1842, Balbriggan, Co. Dublin; son of Rev. Joshua L. Bernard, curate of St Mary's, Donnybrook, Dublin; married on 10/8/1871 (Cookstown Registrar's District, vol. 11, p. 541), at Cookstown, Co. Tyrone, Annie, only surviving daughter of the late Lieutenant-Colonel Charles Irvine, 38th Regiment of Foot (1st Staffordshire Regiment) (*Cork Examiner* 16/8/1871); 3rd SI 1/9/1861; received a favourable record on 30/6/1871 for solving a case of dangerous stabbing in tracing the weapon which inflicted the wound; died 22/9/1886 at Enniskerry, Co. Wicklow, late of Limavady, Co. Derry; administration granted on 5/11/1887 at Derry to Mary Irwin, Great James' Street, Derry, widow, universal legatee – effects £679.3s.6d.

Berne, Connor; RIC 37472; LDS 2098/096; born 1847, Co. Roscommon; married on 13/1/1883 (Ballinrobe Registrar's District, March Quarter, 1883, vol. 4, p. 31), wife a native of Co. Mayo; 3rd DI 1/2/1893; Queen Victoria's Visit to Ireland Medal, 1900; King Edward VII Visit to Ireland Medal, 1903; chief police instructor at the Phoenix Park Depot from 1/2/1893 to 1/2/1902; pensioned 2/3/1912; (photo in the *Constabulary Gazette*, vol. 2, no. 39, p. 1, 24/12/1897 & vol. XXXI, no. 6, 20/4/1912).

Berreen, James Joseph; RIC 54890; LDS 2098/130B; born 1869, Co. Sligo; married on 18/9/1907 (Belfast Registrar's District, September Quarter, 1907, vol. 1, p. 542), wife a native of Co. Sligo; 3rd DI 8/1/1920; pensioned 17/5/1922.

Bews, John; LDS 2097/096; born 1786, Orkney, Scotland; paymaster 73rd Regiment of Foot (Pertshire Regiment) from 1811 to 1836; married Mary Elizabeth Reid on 8/6/1817 at St Pancras, London; 3rd SI 1/10/1836; paymaster 1/10/1836 for Co. Mayo; received the inspector general's approbation on 22/6/1841 and was dismissed; (WO 25/799 fol. 31).

Biggs, Harry; RIC 72325; ADRIC no. 133; LDS 2098/215B; born 20/6/1894, Hants., England; (Farnham Registrar's District, 1894, September Quarter, vol. 2a, p. 99); lieutenant, 3rd Hussars; 3rd DI 12/1/1920; killed 14/5/1921, Coolboreen, Co. Tipperary.

Bigley, William; RIC 17934; LDS 2097/300; born 1835, Drum, Co. Roscommon; wife from Gloucestershire; 3rd SI 25/4/1879; pensioned 1/8/1896; died 19/5/1912 at Parkmount, Portadown, Co. Armagh; will proved on 25/7/1912 at Armagh by the oath of Francis William Hudson Bigley, MD and Richard Wilson Mullock, MD – effects £980.18s.5d.

Bindon, Harris; LDS 2097/153; born 1826, Clooney House, Quin, Co. Clare; 3rd SI 8/4/1846; seconded to the Commissariat Department in the Crimea from 6/8/1854 to 1/10/1856; daughter, Amy Jane Frances, born on 17/2/1868 at Tullamore, King's County (Tullamore Registrar's District, vol. 8, p. 818) (*Cork Examiner* 20/2/1868); pensioned 18/4/1869; died 14/3/1900.

Bindon, John Read; LDS 2097/027; born 1775, Co. Cork; entered the Navy from the Royal Naval Academy on 21/6/1793 as a First Class Volunteer on board the *Captain* 74, Captain Samuel Reeve. He served on shore in August following at the occupation of Toulon, and in December witnessed the destruction of the French shipping at that port; was further employed as a midshipman with the land fore at the reduction of St Fiorenza and Bastia in the island of Corsica in February and May 1794 and on 14/3/1795 and 13 /7/1795 participated in Hotham's partial actions with the French fleet. In 1796 he joined the *Andromache* 32, Captain Charles John Moore Mansfield, one of the in-shore squadron off Cadiz and on 31/1/1797 during a close and destructive engagement of 40 minutes with the Algerian ship of similar force, when an attempt was made by the latter to board the British frigate, he received several sabre and gunshot wounds. On 14/2/1797 he was also present in the action off Cape St Vincent. Proceeding to the West Indies in the early part of 1799, he was there promoted from the *Prince of Wales* 98, bearing the flag of Lord Hugh Seymour, to a Lieutenancy on 31/7/1799 in the *Invincible* 74, Captain William Cayley, while under whose command he served on shore with the army during the operation which led to the conquest of the Dutch colony of Surinam. He was subsequently appointed on 26/6/1800 to the *Cyane* 18, Captain Henry Matson, also stationed in the West Indies; on 26/3/1801 to the *Daphne* 20, Captain Richard Matson, in which vessel he returned to England; on 1/2/1803 to the *Russell* 74, Captain Robert Williams, whom he accompanied to the East Indies; on 13/4/1804 to the *Stately* 64, Captain George Parker, employed in the North Sea and in September 1806 to the command of a signal-station on the west coast of Ireland, which he retained until 20/6/1814. He was placed on the Junior List of Retired Commanders on 23/11/1830 and on the Senior List on 23/12/1843. He married on 31/1/1806, Sarah Eliza Vereker, cousin of Lord Gort and niece of Col. William O'Dell, MP for Co. Limerick and a Lord of the Treasury, by whom he had issue an only daughter; 3rd SI 21/10/1821. The only river police organized at that time was initiated by Warburton, Inspector General of Constabulary for Connaught in November, 1821, when he arranged for six boats as a patrol in the Shannon estuary to prevent the importation of arms from adjoining counties. To take charge of the party he swore in Lieutenant John Read Bindon, RN, as Chief Constable at Kildysart on 21/10/1821. Government did not think the Waterguard Police good value for money, and by May 1823 Warburton had disposed of four of his boats, retaining two as a communication with Co. Limerick, and transferring Bindon to ordinary duty at O'Brien's Bridge; pensioned in 1849; died 3/10/1863 at the Old Leighlin Glebe, Co. Carlow; will and one codicil proved at Kilkenny on 6/11/1863, by the oath of Rev. William Francis Bindon, of Old Leighlin Glebe (Leighlin Bridge), Co. Carlow, aforesaid Clerk A.M. the sole executor – effects under £1,500.

Bingham, Lucan; LDS 2097/177; born 1822, Boyle, Co. Roscommon; daughter born on 7/7/1863 at Kilkenny (*Cork Examiner* 9/7/1863); 3rd SI 9/11/1848; died 13/9/1881 at Annefield House, Maryborough, Queen's County; administration granted at Kilkenny on

41

42

41 Netterville Guy Barron, Divisional Commissioner, RIC.

42 George Garrett Black – 'The Little Inspector'.

28/10/1881 to Helena Binghan, of Annefield House, Maryborough, widow of the said deceased – effects £1,128.4s.10d.

Bird, John Bowyer; RIC 59751; LDS 2098/183; born 21/8/1874, Bucks., England; (Eton Registrar's District, 1874, September Quarter, vol. 3a, p. 442); married Elizabeth Purcell, a native of Co. Cork; 3rd DI 1/12/1901; King Edward VII Visit to Ireland Medal, 1903; Company Officer, Richmond Barracks Sub Depot from 17/9/1907 to 10/4/1908 and 1/7/1908 to 15/10/1908; major, 2nd Battalion Irish Guards; CI 1/8/1920; pensioned 14/5/1922.

Bissett, David William; LDS 2097/103; born 1785, Co. Cork; captain, Royal Pertshire Militia, 16/6/1825; clerk in the Naval dockyards in Cork Harbour and Kinsale from January 1801 to May 1807; Local Inspector, Convict Department from July 1835 to October 1836, 3rd SI 11/10/1836; paymaster 11/10/1836 for Co. Galway; pensioned 31/5/1851 on the abolition of the office of paymaster; cited in the Incumbered Estates Rental for Ballygroman Upper, Co. Cork in April 1854; died 18/5/1852 at Cambridge Terrace, Rathgar, Co. Dublin and formerly of Salisbury Terrace, Dublin; buried in Mount Jerome Cemetery, Dublin; will and one codicil proved at the Principal Registry on 26/6/1858 by the oath of Aaron Moffett, of No. 48, Lower Dominick Street, Dublin, one of the executors – effects under £3,000.

Black, George Garrett; LDS 2097/205; born 1835, Co. Dublin; married on 8/1/1861 (Dublin North Registrar's District, vol. 5, p. 84), Jane Rebecca, daughter of Dr Abraham Cronyn, of Callan, Co. Kilkenny (*Cork Examiner* 14/1/1861); son born on 6/3/1863 at 9, Bessborough Terrace, Dublin (*Cork Examiner* 9/3/1864); daughter, Rebecca Mary, born on 28/7/1866 at Newry, Co. Down (Newry Registrar's District, vol. 11, p. 823); daughter, Ida Jane Isabel (Newry Registrar's District, vol. 11, p. 485) born on 4/7/1869 at Newry, Co. Down (*Cork Examiner* 8/7/1869); 3rd SI 2/10/1854; CI 3/1/1871; pensioned 3/4/1895; died 5/3/1910 at Ellerslie, Hollybrook Road, Clontarf, Co. Dublin; will proved on 9/4/1910 at the Principal Registry by the oath of Maud A. Black, spinster – effects £5,397.13s.6d.; his eldest surviving son William Tyndall Black, Barlum House, Carlow, Lieutenant Wicklow Artillery, Southern Division, Royal Artillery, on 20/4/1897 was married by the Rev James Sheppard, MA, at St Thomas' Church,

Charlton, Kent to Katherine Edith Frances, youngest daughter of Captain Isaac Colqhoun, Chief Constable, Swansea, South Wales; (photo – Garda Museum & Archives, Dublin Castle).

Blackhall, Robert; CarNB; C.C. barony of Lower Ormond; Tullamore, King's County, 1821; discharged 1824.

Blair, William James; RIC 55407; LDS 2098/151B; born 1875, Co. Roscommon; married on 5/10/1915 (Dundalk Registrar's District, December Quarter, 1915, vol. 2, p. 743), wife a native of Co. Louth; 3rd DI 20/9/1920; pensioned 25/04/1922.

Blake, Cecil Arthur Maurice; RIC 73512; ADRIC no. 521; LDS 2098/201B; born 20/2/1885, Hants., England; (Christchurch Registrar's District, 1885, June Quarter, vol. 2b, p. 641); the son of a veterinary surgeon, he served in the Hampshire Yeomanry, the Royal Horse Guards (blues) Regiment, 29/8/1902–28/8/1904 as a rough-rider, sergeant and riding instructor in the Denbighshire Hussars; lieutenant, 9th Reserve Battery, Royal Horse Artillery on 26/1/1915; injured at Ramburelles on 23/1/1916; married in 1906 and divorced in 1919; wife remarried as Irene Young; one son, Peter Willington Blake (b.3/4/1918); relinquished his commission 11/12/1919; 3rd DI 12/1/1920; killed 15/5/1921, Ballyturin House, Gort, Co. Galway: (WO 339/22133).

Blake, Henry Arthur Sir; RIC 24511; LDS 2097/225; born 18/1/1840, Co. Limerick; son of Peter Blake (1809–50), CI, RIC and Jane daughter of John Lane, of Lanes Park; the Blake family were founded by one Robert Blake who accompanied Prince John of England to Ireland in 1185; educated at Dr St John's Academy and Sentry College; was a student of Queen's College Galway and employed as a clerk in the Bank of Ireland for one year and six months before securing a cadetship in the RIC; married firstly in 1862 (Dublin South Registrar's District, vol. 5, p. 268), Mary Jeannie (d.23/10/1871 in New Orleans, Louisiana – *Cork Examiner* 20/11/1871), daughter of Andrew Irwin Esq., of Ballymore, Boyle, Co. Roscommon, and by her had a son Harry Irwin, born on 23/10/1871 in New Orleans, Louisiana (*Cork Examiner* 20/11/1871); daughter born on 22/6/1863 at Headford, Co. Galway (*Cork Examiner* 30/6/1863); daughter Jemima born and died on 27/3/1864 (Tuam Registrar's District, vol. 9, p. 338) at Tuam, Co. Galway and she had a twin sister, Susan (Tuam Registrar's District, vol. 4, p. 467) (*Cork Examiner* 1/4/1864); married secondly on 7/2/1874, Edith, elder daughter and co-heir of Ralph Bernal, later Bernal-Osborne, Esq. (26/3/1808–4/1/1882), MP by his marriage on 20/8/1844 to Catherine Isabella Osborne (d.20/6/1880), of Newton Anner, Co. Tipperary, daughter and heir of Sir Thomas Osborne, Esq. (1757–3/6/1821), 9th Bt., MP; Catherine Isabella's sister, Grace Bernal-Osborne (d.18/11/1926), married a month earlier on 3/1/1874, William Amelius Aubrey Beauclerk (15/4/1840–11/5/1898), 10th Duke of St Albans; Henry Arthur Blake had two sons, Arthur, b.15/1/1877 and Maurice, b.6/6/1878 and a daughter, Olive (1875–12/9/1953), who married on 8/6/1903, Major John Bernard Arbuthnot (1875–1950), MVO, Scots Guards; their son, Commander Bernard K.C. Arbuthnot, DSC, RN (8/11/1909–14/9/1975), married on 15/4/1939, Rosemary Harold Thompson (9/7/1917–29/8/1978), whose daughter, Patricia Evangeline Anne (17/3/1914–89), author and artist, married firstly, on 10/10/1933, Arthur Cecil Byron and married secondly in 1940, Claud Cockburn (1904–81), author and journalist who coined the phrase: 'Never believe anything until it has been officially denied', son of Henry Cockburn; another son, Major Myles Henry Arbuthnot, MBE, Royal Corps of Signals was killed in active service in Italy on 16/10/1943 and is buried in the Bari War Cemetery, Carbonara, Italy; 3rd SI 1/3/1859; received a favourable record on 30/6/1871 having received intelligence that a large flock of geese, having peculiar marks had been stolen on the previous day and found that upon enquiry that a crate of live fowl had been forwarded for London by an early train. He telegraphed and had them stopped resulting in the offender being traced and convicted by a variety of links of evidence and in the face of much difficulty; received a favourable record on 30/6/1871 for gallant exertions in saving life and property at a fire; received a favourable record on 31/12/1871 for solving a barbarous murder; resident magistrate 7/1/1876; special resident magistrate 1/12/1881; Governor of Bahamas, 4/1/1884–7; transferred to Newfoundland as governor, 1887–9 and knighted in 1887 during a controversy over fishing rights in Newfoundland waters. The terms of the 1818 fishing convention which gave American fishermen substantial rights to the waters and to Newfoundland shores for processing were up for discussion. Britain and the United States, however, had planned to meet without Newfoundland's knowledge. Outraged Newfoundland Prime Minister, James Winter demanded to attend and eventually did. During this time Blake acted mostly as a mediator; Governor of Jamaica, 1889–97, Hong Kong, 1897–1903 and Ceylon, 3/12/1903–11/7/1907; Knight of the Justice of St John of Jerusalem; Fellow of the Royal Geographical Society; GCMG. In 1910 he became chairman of the newly-formed Newfoundland Oilfields Limited which explored oil deposits in the Parsons Pond area. The community of Blaketown is named in his honour; died 23/2/1918, at Myrtle Grove, Youghal, Co. Cork; (Youghal Registrar's District, 1918, March Quarter, vol. 4, p. 513); he was buried on 27/2/1918 in the garden of Myrtle Grove, Youghal, Co. Cork beneath four great yew trees, which were planted there by Sir Walter Raleigh (1552–1618), poet and colonist, who was Mayor of Youghal, 1588–9, who is credited with planting the first potato in Ireland in this garden in 1589 and with having smoked the first pipe of tobacco under a tree also in this garden. In 1965 the flower 'Bauhinia blakeana' was adopted as the City Flower of Hong Kong and later chosen as the emblem for Hong Kong SAR in 1997. The tree was first discovered on the shore of Hong Kong Island near Pok Fu Lam around 1880 and described as a new species in 1908 by Dunn. The species is characterized by its purplish red blossoms and its two-lobed heart shaped leaves. It was named after Hong Kong governor Sir Henry Arthur Blake who had a strong interest in botany; (photo in the *Constabulary Gazette*, vol. VI, no. 13, 23/12/1899, p. 390).

Blake, Henry B.; LDS 2097/069; born 1807, Co. Carlow; PPF; 3rd SI 1/6/1831; pensioned 16/11/1849.

Blake, Isidore; LDS 2097/045; born 1791, Tower Hill, Ballyglass, Cong, Co. Mayo; cornet (by purchase) 17th Light Dragoons, 10/5/1810; lieutenant, 13/8/1813; lieutenant half pay, 8th Light Dragoons, 1/9/1823; married in Kaina, East India, 12/8/1813; children: Isidore, born 27/7/1817, Fanny, born 29/11/1819; Maurice, born 26/2/1825, John, born 15/6/1826 and died at Prospect Hill, Galway on 1/2/1849; 3rd SI 13/10/1823; residing at Tubbercurry, Co. Mayo, 1824–8; CI 22/1/1836; died 31/3/1849; (WO 25/750 fol. 328).

Blake, John; LDS 2097/096; born 1783, Rathfarnham, Co. Dublin; 3rd SI 1/10/1836; paymaster 1/10/1836; a defaulter in the sum of £1,616 on 1/2/1845 and dismissed on 13/3/1845.

Blake, John; LDS 2097/166; born 1826, Co. Galway; 3rd SI 13/5/1848, died 24/1/1849.

Blake, John Joseph; LDS 2097/090; born 1811, Co. Galway; married on 17/4/1856 at the Parish Chapel of Kilteevan, Co. Roscommon, Ellen, youngest daughter of the late Charles O'Connor, of Cloontuskert, Co. Roscommon (*Cork Examiner* 23/4/1856); 3rd SI 24/11/1835; pensioned 21/9/1863; died 30/12/1879 at Fermoy, Co. Cork; (Fermoy Registrar's District, 1879, December Quarter, vol. 4, p. 441).

Blake, Maurice A.; LDS 2097/148; born 1825, Co. Galway; 3rd SI 23/1/1844; died 30/4/1848.

Blake, Peter; LDS 2097/066; born 1809, Corbally Castle, Co. Galway; son of Patrick Blake, Corbally Castle, Co. Galway and Mary Morgan, Monksfield, Loughrea, Co. Galway; father of Sir Henry Arthur Blake (1840–1918) SI RIC; married Jane daughter of John Lane, of Lanes Park, near Killenaule, Co. Tipperary; daughter born at Richmond, near Kilkenny on 30/10/1849 (*Cork Examiner* 31/10/1849); his ninth child, a son was born on 8/7/1851 at Lanes Park, Co. Tipperary (*Cork Examiner* 14/7/1851); his eldest daughter, Susan Maria, married on 15/12/1864 (Dublin North Registrar's District, vol. 17, p. 533); in Clontarf, Co. Dublin, Charles Symes, second son of the late Charles Symes Gifford, solicitor, of Annsbrook, Clontarf, Co. Dublin (*Cork Examiner* 19/12/1864); his third son, John Lane Blake, married on 5/3/1866

43 Henry Arthur Blake, 1887, Governor of Newfoundland.   44 Henry Arthur Blake, 1897, Governor of Hong Kong.   45 Orchid 'Bauhinia Blakeana' called after Sir Henry Arthur Blake. 46 Hong Kong flag bearing the 'Bauhinia Blakeana' emblem.   47 Myrtle Grove, Youghal, Co. Cork, burial place of Sir Henry Arthur Blake.

(Dublin North Registrar's District, vol. 2, p. 688) in St Thomas' Church, Dublin, Kate Edith, eldest daughter of John Gibbs, of Seville Place, Dublin (*Cork Examiner* 8/3/1866); 3rd SI 1/8/1827; CI 1/9/1838; died 17/11/1850 in Co. Kilkenny after three days illness (*Cork Examiner* 22/11/1850); transcript of will in 1830 in the Prerogative Court, executrix – Jane Blake, Lismore, Co. Waterford (NA Reference: IWR/1830/F/256).

Blake, Robert; CarNB; CI Magunihy, Co. Kerry; Eyrecourt, Co. Cavan; Westport, Co. Mayo and Roscommon, Co. Roscommon.

Blake, Valentine Charles Joseph; RIC 63671; LDS 2098/226; born 17/12/1885, Co. Mayo; (Castlereagh Registrar's District, March Quarter, 1886, vol. 4, p. 112); son of Valentine and Mary Blake; 3rd DI 5/5/1908; captain, 1st Battalion Irish Guards from 3/11/1914; killed 28/1/1916, Pas de Calais, France; buried at Rouge Croix, M.22A.8.2 Map Sh.36.1/40,000; administration granted at Principal Registry on 20/4/1916 to the Hon. Mary Blake, Maryborough, Queen's County, his mother – effects £207.34s.8d.; (WO 339/37108).

Blakeny, George; LDS 2097/163; born 1811, Co. Roscommon; ensign and lieutenant, 83rd Regiment of Foot from 30/11/1826 to 10/11/1835; his wife was a native of Co. Derry; 3rd SI 15/1/1848; died 22/8/1853 in Carndonagh, Co. Donegal.

Blakeny, Thomas; LDS 2097/087; born 1791, Co. Dublin; enlisted as a sub constable, 5/2/1819; 3rd SI 15/10/1834; pensioned 1/2/1859 in Co. Roscommon; died on 21/6/1863 at Strokestown, Co. Roscommon; letters of administration granted at the Principal Registry on 1/8/1863 to Anthony Kirwan, of No. 27, Rutland Street Lower, Dublin, Gentleman, the first cousin twice removed only next of kin of the deceased.

Blascheck, Robert Alexander; RIC 55391; LDS 2098/092; born 1870, Trieste, Austria; master at Paignton School, Devon for two years; married on 24/4/1895 (Ballinrobe Registrar's District, June Quarter, 1895, vol. 3, p. 25), Miss L.M. Burke, a native of Co. Mayo; 3rd DI 1/9/1892; pensioned 1/10/1902.

Blayney, William; LDS 2098/179; born 5/8/1877, Co. Antrim; (Ballymena Registrar's District, 1877 vol. 6, p. 148); clerk in the Civil Service for 4 years; married on 25/4/1917 (Dublin South Registrar's District, June Quarter, 1917, vol. 2, p. 615), Mary F. Beveridge; 3rd DI 25/6/1901; King Edward VII Visit to Ireland Medal, 1903; musketry instructor from 14/3/1915 to 23/12/1915; Temporary Assistant Commissioner of the Dublin Metropolitan Police, 1914; major, 6th Battalion Royal Dublin Fusiliers from 29/1/1916 to 22/3/1919; musketry instructor from 22/3/1919 to 12/6/1920; TCI 1/8/1920; CI 1/8/1920; pensioned 16/5/1922.

Blennerhassett, William Massy; LDS 2097/141; born 1816, youngest son of Gerald Blennerhassett, of Riddlestown Park, Co. Limerick and Elizabeth Ann Massy (born 1790 and died on 15/3/1872 – *Cork Examiner* 18/3/1872)), daughter of William Massey, Glenville, Ardagh, Co. Limerick; 3rd SI 18/5/1843; married on 9/9/1847 (Rathkeale Registrar's District, vol. 9, p. 599), Margaretta Sophia (dsp.19/4/1872), youngest daughter of Lieutenant-Colonel John Fraunceis Fitzgerald (28/6/1791–25/4/1854), Knight of Glin, of Glin Castle, Co. Limerick and Bridgetta Eyre (1789–1876); pensioned 1/9/1863; resided at Cloughnarald, Rathkeale and later at Shannon Lawn, Glin, Co. Limerick; died 19/11/1903. His brother, Gerald Fitzgerald Blennerhassett, DL, JP was a leading figure in the Colleen Bawn tragedy as the man who arrested Lieutenant Scanlon.

Blood, William; CarNB; born, Fantore, Ennistymon, Co. Clare, son of Richard Blood, of Fantore; ensign 32nd Regiment of Foot (Duke of Cornwall's Light Infantry), 6/11/1811; slightly wounded at Salamanca (*London Gazette* 22/7/1812); lieutenant 15th Regiment of Foot (East Yorkshire Regiment); married on 28/10/1823, Hannah Swete, of Spittle, Abbeymahon, Co. Cork; died 26/8/1826; he had one son, Thomas (b.14/12/1825); C.C. baronies of Ibane and Barryroe, Co. Cork; his brother Thomas Blood (b.1789), enlisted with a recruiting party of the 43rd Regiment of Foot (Monmouthshire Regiment) in Castlebar, Co. Mayo in October, 1810. Joined 2nd Battalion at Colchester, England in February 1811. Joined 2nd Battalion on the frontier of Portugal in July 1811. Appointed corporal in February 1812, sergeant in May 1812 and colour sergeant in August 1813. Ensign to the 6th Regiment of Foot (1st Warwickshire Regiment) on 18/11/1813 and to lieutenant on 8/9/1814. Both appointments were without purchase. Wounded at the Battles of Orthes, 27/2/1814 while serving with the 1st Battalion (*London Gazette*). Received a pension of £70 per annum commencing 28/2/1815. Transferred to the 6th Royal Veteran Battalion in May 1816 and the 8th Royal Veteran Battalion in December 1819. Disbanded in March 1821. Appointed to the Royal 7th Veteran Battalion in December 1821 Replaced on the retired list owing to incapacity to serving from wounds in May 1824; married firstly at St Anne's Church, Dublin Mary Cooke. Married secondly on 7/5/1853, Kitty (d.May 18720, third daughter of Neptune Blood, of Ballykilty, Co. Wicklow; died 26/12/1856.

Bloxham, Mark; LDS 2097/161; born 1795, Dublin; son of Mark Bloxham and Hester Hart, who were married in St Luke's Parish, Dublin on 18/1/1793; Scholar TCD on 5/11/1810, BA, 1815, MA, 1818; 3rd SI 1822; pensioned 30/9/1847; died 13/5/1876 at Tubbercurry, Co. Sligo, late of Sligo, Co. Sligo; administration (and will annexed) granted on 1/7/1876 at the Principal Registry to Alicia Bloxham, of Stephen Street, Sligo, widow and the sole legatee – effects under £400.

Bodkin, Thomas; CarNB; on 18/6/1825 at Lanesborough obtained leave on the death of his mother; C.C. Lanesborough, Co. Longford; Kinlough, Co. Leitrim; Kilcock, Co. Meath; Clonroche, Co. Wexford, 1828; barony of Bantry, Co. Wexford, 1829; Co. Meath 1/5/1830; Corbally, near Athy, Co. Kildare, 1830; Nobber, Co. Meath, 19/9/1830; Dunshaughlin, Co. Meath, 1831; died 20/12/1831, Co. Meath.

Bodley, John; RIC 10044; born 1820; as a 2nd Class Head Constable he was appointed police instructor and schoolmaster at the Phoenix Park Depot on 12/1/1877; 3rd DI 1/1/1884; pensioned 1/11/1889; died 8/7/1907 at 9, St Peter's Road, Cabra, Dublin; buried in Glasnevin Cemetery, Dublin on 10/7/1907; will and two codicils proved on 9/8/1907 at the Principal Registry by the oath of Mary A. Bodley, the widow and John O'Sullivan, solicitor – effects £3,058.7s.8d.

Bodley, William Herbert; RIC 66455; LDS 2098/032B; born 11/9/1887, Co. Dublin; (Dublin North Registrar's District, December Quarter, 1887, vol. 2, p. 576); 3rd DI 9/11/1912; discharged on a gratuity 31/7/1918.

Bolger, James; LDS 2097/119; born 1805, Co. Kilkenny; wife a native of Co. Limerick; 3rd DI 24/5/1838; CI 15/2/1866; pensioned 10/4/1876; died 23/7/1886 at Tullamore, King's County; will proved on 19/8/1887 at the Principal Registry by the oath of Maria Bolger, Tullamore, King's County, one of the executors – effects £440.

Bonis, James; RIC 15787; LDS 2097/317; born 1835, Clongesh, Longford, Co. Longford; 3rd DI 16/1/1882; pensioned 1/8/1896; died 20/2/1918 at Fair Lawn, Moy, Co. Armagh; (Armagh Registrar's District, March Quarter, 1918, vol. 1, p. 88); buried in Kilmore, Rockhill on 22/2/1918.

Bookey, Richard; LDS 2097/141; born 1813, Kilrush, Co. Wexford; wife a native of Co. Wexford; son born on 23/7/1855 at Castlepollard, Co. Westmeath (*Cork Examiner* 8/8/1855); 3rd SI 14/8/1843; dismissed 9/2/1857.

Booth, Joseph Henry; RIC 55209; LDS 2098/092B; born 14/5/1873, Cahirciveen, Co. Kerry; (Cahirciveen Registrar's District, 1873, vol. 10, p. 76); 3rd DI 7/9/1919; awarded medal of the Society for Protection of Life from Fire; pensioned 17/7/1922.

Bourchier, Henry James; RIC 31907; LDS 2097/258; born 14/8/1842, Baggotstown, Rathkeale, Co. Limerick; son of John Bourchier (1811–85), JP, BA, TCD, of Baggotstown, Co. Limerick and Sarah, eldest daughter and co-heir of David Aher, of Castlecomer, Co. Kilkenny who were married on 9/7/1833; educated at St Columba's College, Rathfarnham, Dublin; married on 5/3/1867 (Mitchelstown Registrar's District, vol. 2, p. 1101), Nina Darley (d.1924), eldest daughter of Rev. John Leech, D.D. of Cloocconra, Mitchelstown, Co. Cork; 3rd SI

1/9/1866; received a favourable record on 30/6/1871 for solving a murder; CI 13/11/1891; CI attached to Crime Branch from 14/9/1892 to 1/4/1893; pensioned 15/1/1907; died 2/3/1921 at Baggotstown, Kilmallock, Co. Limerick; (Kilmallock Registrar's District, 1921, March Quarter, vol. 5, p. 199); will proved at the Principal Registry on 21/9/1921; (photo in the *Constabulary Gazette*, vol. XIII, no. 12, 13/6/1903).

Bowles, Cornelius; RIC 57902; LDS 2098/178B; born 30/4/1876, Co. Limerick; married on 27/7/1909, wife a native of Co. Mayo; 3rd DI 16/10/1920; pensioned 9/5/1922.

Boyce, Samuel; RIC 25364; LDS 2097/233; born 1839, Brook-Hall, Coleraine, Co. Derry; clerk in the Coleraine Branch of the Northern Bank for two years and 9 months; wife a native of Co. Wexford; 3rd DI 2/1/1860; received a favourable record on 30/6/1869 for energy and success in defeating a false claim for compensation off the county; accidentally killed on 23/6/1880 when proceeding on duty to Waringstown Station, Co. Down.

Boyle, John; RIC 57246; LDS 2098/229B; born 1875, Co. Donegal; 3rd DI 1/1/1921; pensioned 1/1/1921.

Bracken, James Harton; LDS 2097/082; born 1802, Kilbeggan, Co. Westmeath; father of Patrick James Bracken, SI, RIC; wife a native of Co. Longford; 3rd SI 12/2/1833; presented with an ornamental sabre by the Lord Lieutenant on 1/10/1842; CI 2/7/1851; pensioned 1/8/1872; died 13/3/1885 at 4 Rostrevor Terrace, Clontarf, Co. Dublin, late of Thurles, Co. Tipperary, Kilkenny, Co. Kilkenny and Camac House, Clondalkin, Co. Dublin; administration granted on 9/6/1885 at the Principal Registry to Zillah Elizabeth Harton, of 4 Rostrevor Terrace, Clontarf, Co. Dublin – effects £629.12s.9d.

Bracken, Patrick James; RIC 16057; LDS 2097/194; born 1830, King's County; son of James Harton Bracken, SI, RIC; 3rd SI 13/8/1852; Adjutant, Phoenix Park Depot from 15/10/1875 to 10/3/1885; pensioned 10/3/1885; died 31/3/1916 at 2 South Circular Road, Dublin, formerly of United Services Club, Dublin; (Dublin South Registrar's District, 1916, March Quarter, vol. 2, p. 586); will proved on 18/4/1916 at the Principal Registry by the oath of Joseph McDermott, Solicitor – effects £1,150.16s.0d, resworn £1,131.18s.8d.

Bradshaw, Joseph; RIC 1708; LDS 2097/233; born 1812, Kilcoole, Co. Wicklow; son of Benjamin Bradshaw, former Mayor of Clonmel, Co. Tipperary; 3rd SI 1/1/1860; died on 28/2/1870 at the Adelaide Hospital, Peter Street, Dublin after a tedious illness (*Cork Examiner* 4/3/1870 & 17/3/1870); will proved on 31/3/1870 at the Principal Registry by the oath of Henry Lewis, Arklow, Co. Wicklow and Edward Brock, Grafton Street, Dublin – effects £3000.

Brady, Edward; RIC 56342; LDS 2098/189B; born 7/1/1874, Gort, Co. Galway; (Gort Registrar's District, 1874, vol. 4, p. 367); married on 24/8/1904 (Clonmel Registrar's District, September Quarter, 1904, vol. 4, p. 269), wife a native of Co. Tipperary; 3rd DI 16/10/1920; pensioned 22/4/1922.

Brady, James Joseph Mary; RIC 70381; LDS 2098/110B; born 9/10/1898, Co. Dublin; (Rathdown Registrar's District, 1898, December Quarter, vol. 2, p. 792); lieutenant, Special Reserve Irish Guards; 3rd DI 15/6/1920; killed 30/9/1920, Chafpool, Co. Sligo.

Brady, William Edward; LDS 2097/032; born 1785; sergeant 32nd Regiment of Foot (Duke of Cornwall's Light Infantry), 1804 to 1805; pay sergeant to a company, 1805–6; acting sergeant-major to the left wing of 99th Regiment of Foot (Lanarkshire Regiment) at New Providence, Bahamas, Cuba and Jamaica, 1806–8; paymasters clerk, 1808–10; quarter master sergeant, 1810–12; ensign, 20/2/1812; lieutenant, 4/11/1815; exchanged to 2nd West Indies Regiment, 4/11/1815; lieutenant half pay, 2nd West Indies Regiment at Jamaica, 1/2/1819; severely wounded; married at Barraca, island of Cuba, 29/7/1807 and 10/9/1813 in Isle of Wight; children: Mary Jane Brady, b.23/9/1816, Fanny Brady, b.6/3/1819, Frederick Edward Brady, b.19/3/1821; married secondly, 5/7/1827, Swords, Co. Dublin; daughter, Anna Louisa Brady, b.20/4/1828; 3rd SI 22/12/1822; Chief Constable at Dunshaughlin, Co. Meath, 1823 and Chief Constable, Co. Dublin, residing at Swords, 1823–8. (WO 25/751 fol. 227); his widow, Lucinda

48

49

48 William Blayney. 49 James Harton Bracken, 1857. 50 Col. Henry Brackenbury, RA (1837–1914), Assistant Under-Secretary for Police and Crime. 51 Edward Brady.

51

50

Catherine, younger daughter of Charles S. Forster, solicitor, Dublin, died on 17/5/1887 at Carleton Terrace, Bray, Co. Wicklow; buried in Mount Jerome Cemetery, Dublin on 20/5/1887 (Grave No. C3–5612). W.E. Brady on 16/6/1835 published 'A series of memorials soliciting promotion which have been submitted to the Irish Government by Lieut. W.E. Brady, Chief Constable of Police, during the period of his services in the before-mentioned office, commencing in 1822, to which were added by way of appendix, twenty-four documents from noblemen, general, field and other officers; together with many others from civic and judicial functionaries; bearing the dates from 1805 to 1831, in support of Lieutenant Brady's humble merit and pretensions, both as an officer in the British Army, as well as of his efficiency and usefulness in the Office of Chief Constable, which he now holds in the District of Listowel, Co. Kerry.' (NLI P.1637)

Breally, Victor Sheldrick; LDS 2098/226B; born 30/5/1897, London, England; Royal Navy, Royal Air Force; 3rd DI 12/1/1920; pensioned 14/4/1922.

Brennan, Patrick; LDS 2097/110; born 1805, Co. Kilkenny; 3rd SI 30/1/1837; resigned 23/10/1844 on his appointment as Superintendent of Police, St Lucia; died 6/12/1845, St Lucia.

Brereton, James; RIC 17979; LDS 2097/202; born 1831, Co. Dublin; served an apprenticeship as an attorney and a solicitor but never practised; married on 10/11/1864 (Listowel Registrar's District, vol. 20, p. 278), at Listowel, Co. Kerry, Ursula Caroline Elizabeth, eldest daughter of Richard C. Harnett, Esq., solicitor, Listowel, Co. Kerry (*Cork Examiner* 16/11/1864); son, James William Henry, born on 21/2/1868 at Bantry, Co. Cork (Bantry Registrar's District, vol. 10, p. 33) (*Cork Examiner* 26/2/1868); 3rd SI 25/7/1854; received an approbation on 30/6/1869 for very praiseworthy exertions in extinguishing a fire; dismissed 2/4/1870.

Brett, James Hazlett; RIC 50997; LDS 2097/331; born, 1859, Co. Waterford; BA, Trinity College Dublin, 1882; married on 18/4/1894 (Galway Registrar's District, June Quarter, 1894, vol. 4, p. 106), Mina Constance Martyn, a native of Co. Wexford; 3rd DI 11/9/1883; pensioned 23/6/1920.

Brett, William; LDS 2097/096; born 1789, Co. Dublin; PPF; widower on appointment; 3rd SI 1/10/1836; paymaster 1/10/1836 for Co. Longford and Co. Cavan and for Co. Fermanagh and Co. Tyrone; pensioned 31/5/1851 on the abolition of the office of paymaster; died 11/5/1858 at Enniskillen.

Brett, William Gore; LDS 2097/071; born 1801, King's County; PPF; enlisted as a sub constable, 1/2/1819; constable 1/2/1820; 3rd SI 31/7/1831; wife a native of Kilbrogan, Bandon, Co. Cork; son born on 7/12/1851 at Bandon, Co. Cork (*Cork Examiner* 17/12/1851); received a severe injury in the leg while on duty at Limerick on 10/9/1840; pensioned 21/4/1864; died 10/7/1878.

Brew, Chartres; LDS 2097/152; born 31/12/1815, Richmond House, Corofin, Co. Clare; 3rd SI 3/3/1840, eldest son of Tompkins Brew (1783–1843), Adelphi, Corofin, Co. Clare, stipendiary magistrate and Jane Smith (d.1865); seconded to the Commissariat Department in the Crimea on 6/7/1854 to 26/8/1856, where he was appointed Assistant Commissary-General on 1/2/1856; resigned 16/9/1856. While traveling out to British Columbia, he was a passenger on board the ship *Austria* from Southampton to New York. The ship burned at sea and he was one of the few survivors. As there was not enough room for him in the boat, he and another passenger took turns swimming with one hand on the stern. 58; He served in Cahir, Co. Tipperary and Cork City before serving in the Crimea in 1854–5. He trans-shipped from New York to Aspinwell, traversed the fever-ridden swamps of Panama, and found his way to the Colonies almost on schedule. He was sworn in as Chief Inspector of Police at Fort Langley, the first capital of what became a province, [of British Columbia] on a wet November 19, 1858. He founded the British Columbia Police in 1859, fourteen years before the Royal Canadian Mounted Police was established, and amalgamated with the RCMP in 1950. He became a Gold

Commissioner and County Court Judge. He died at Richfield, Baritoo, British Columbia on 31/5/1870 (*Cork Examiner* 25/7/1870) and he is buried in Barkerville, British Columbia where his epitaph reads: 'A man imperturbable in courage and temper, endowed with a great and varied administrative capacity, a most ready wit, a most pure integrity and a most human heart.'

Brew, Henry Joseph; RIC 25538; LDS 2097/235; born, 1839, Co. Dublin; 3rd SI 15/4/1860; died 28/6/1869 at Lisdoonvarna, Co. Clare, aged 30 years, 'from a disease of the heart, where he was for the benefit of his health', late of Marble Hill, Co. Galway (*Cork Examiner* 7/7/1869); administration granted at the Principal Registry on 6/5/1870 to Frances Alicia Brew, of 2 Palmyra Crescent, Galway, the widow of the deceased – effects under £1,500.

Brew, Richard George; LDS 2097/069; born 20/2/1800, Co. Clare; married on 15/11/1838, Barbara Jane (d.14/12/1871 in Dublin – *Cork Examiner* 15/12/1871), daughter of Christopher Lysaght, Cahirvelly House, Limerick; 3rd SI 1/7/1834; died 25/12/1854 at Skibbereen, Co. Cork.

Brew, Tompkins; CarNB; born 11/03/1783, Applevale, Co. Clare; father of Chartres Brew, SI, RIC; resided at Riverstown, Co. Clare; JP, 1/3/1810; 3rd SI 1/4/1824; married Barbara Jane (d.1865, Dublin), daughter of William Smith of Limerick on 29/9/1818; his daughter, Alice married on 20/9/1855 (Kilrush Registrar's District, vol. 6, p. 396), Andrew Paterson, Esq., C.A., Edinburgh (*Cork Examiner* 24/9/1855); stipendiary magistrate 24/5/1831 for Co. Clare; died at Church Street, Ennis, Co. Clare 25/12/1843; buried at Dromcliffe, Ennis, Co. Clare; C.C. Oranmore, Co. Galway; Corofin, Ennis and Kilrush, Co. Clare.

Britten, Frederick Ambrose; RIC 59038; LDS 2098/160; born 1875, Somerby, Leics., England; (Melton M. Registrar's District, 1875, March Quarter, vol. 7a, p. 2678); son of Thomas C. Britten (b.1833), Nevis, West Indies and Mary A.M., Britten (b.1840), Leicester; under master at St Aubyn's School, Lowestoft for 1 year; BA Keble College, Oxford; married in June 1907 (Loughrea Registrar's District, June Quarter, 1907, vol. 4, p. 157), wife native of Co. Galway; 3rd DI 3/9/1899; King Edward VII Visit to Ireland Medal, 1903; awarded a certificate from the Irish Police and Constabulary Recognition Fund; TCI 20/8/1920; CI 1/10/1920; retired; 31/5/1922; transferred to the Royal Ulster Constabulary on 1/6/1922.

Brommel, Vershoyle Crawford; LDS 2097/216; born 1834, Co. Roscommon; joined the Irish Revenue Police as a lieutenant on 25/1/1855 and served in Plumb Bridge, Co. Tyrone; 3rd SI 1/12/1857; died 1/2/1873 at Wexford, Co. Wexford; (Wexford Registrar's District, 1873, vol. 4, p. 828).

Brooke, Gustavus; CarNB; born Templepatrick, Co. Antrim; died December 1826; his wife's brother, a Mr Bathurst was recommended by Mr G.V. Hart for service as a chief constable; C.C. Longford, Co. Longford.

Brooke, James Thomas; RIC 44152; LDS 2097/298; born 1853, Suffolk, England; (Sanford Registrar's District, 1853, March Quarter, vol. 4a, p. 539); private tutor in Guildford, Norfolk for six years; 3rd SI 7/1/1879; CI 2/10/1899; pensioned 30/4/1910; died suddenly of pneumonia on 20/3/1917 at 74, Constable Road, Ipswich, Suffolk, England; (photo in the *Constabulary Gazette*, vol. V, no. 13, 24/6/1899).

Brown, James William; RIC 38068; LDS 2097/287; born 1848, Co. Limerick; 3rd SI 12/10/1871; King Edward VII Visit to Ireland Medal, 1903; pensioned 7/10/1905 by the surgeon to the Force as being unfit for service; (photo in the *Constabulary Gazette*, vol. XVI, no. 14, 24/12/1904).

Brown, John F.; LDS 2097/022; born 1791, Co. Meath; peace officer from 1/5/1815 to 1/12/1815; PPF Constable 1/12/1815; wife a native of King's County; 3rd SI 31/1/1817; admonished 'for want of energy' on 13/6/1855; pensioned on 1/5/1859 in Co. Donegal; died 3/9/1862 at Carrick-on-Shannon, Co. Leitrim; will proved in the Principal Registry on 11/10/1862 by the oath of Rev. John Wills Brown, of Trentvale, Staffs., England, clerk and one of the executors – effects under £1,500.

Browne, George Baxter; CarNB; born 12/8/1790, Liverpool, Lancs., England; one of six children (three sons and three daughters of George Browne (d.1812 in Canada), Liverpool wine merchant and Felicity Wagner (d.11/1/1827), daughter of the Austrian and Tuscan consul to Liverpool; his father George Browne was a Liverpool merchant who, after some reverses, moved to Brownwylfa, near St Asaph in Flintshire, North Wales; his grandfather was George Browne of Passage West, Co. Cork. His brother was Lieut. General Sir Thomas Henry Browne. His sister, Felicia Dorothea (23/9/1793–15/5/1835), is remembered as the poetess, Mrs Hermans. In 1812 she married an Irish officer, Captain Alfred Hemans, a veteran of the Peninsular Wars and the Low Countries Campaigns and bore him five sons in the first six years of their marriage, but in 1819 he moved to Italy leaving five boys with Felicia, two of which join him in the 1830s. She came to reside in Dublin in 1831, and from her sick bed she dictated her last poem to her brother. She died on 15 May 1835 at the early age of 41 and she is buried in St Anne's Church, Dublin; C.C. Killarney and by 16/8/1828 Browne had been appointed Chief Constable (district officer) and Paymaster in the Leinster Constabulary and allocated to Co. Kilkenny, where Inspector General Sir John Harvey then resided. Within a month or so Chief Constable Beauchamp Colclough Urquhart was removed from the pay clerkship (the equivalent of a county officer) and Browne was appointed in his stead. A further opportunity came in February 1830 when Harvey fell ill and had to take the waters at Cheltenham. With his recovery a few months later, one of his first acts was to commend Browne's conduct of affairs in leaving him a clean slate to begin with. On 25 July 1813 while serving as a young subaltern with the 37th Regiment of Foot (Royal Hampshire Regiment) at the Pass of Roncenvalles he was twice wounded. Captain 37th Regiment of Foot (Royal Hampshire Regiment) from 24/3/1825 to 29 August 1826 when placed on half pay. Awarded one medal with six clasps for Corunna, Albuera, Cuidad Rodrigo, Badajos, Salamanca and Vittoria. Appointment as a stipendiary magistrate came on 25 May 1831 and, six years later, on 1 July 1837 he was appointed joint commissioner of the DMP. He married firstly Harriet Anne (d.5/6/1858 after a few hour's illness) (*Cork Examiner* 8/6/1857), eldest daughter of Martin Whish, Esq., Chairman of the Board of Excise; married secondly the widow of James Patterson, and daughter of Reverend C. Irwin (Belfast Registrar's District, vol. 2, p. 884); CB, 13/6/1857; 12 March 1858, saw the entry into Dublin of the earl of Eglinton, appointed Lord Lieutenant for a second time. It was marred by an outbreak of disorderly ebullience in which the police and the students of Trinity College came into collision. In the upshot Col. Browne was obliged to retire, and thereafter the DMP was guided by a Chief Commissioner with the help of an Assistant Commissioner; died on 12/7/1879 at Clifton Gardens, Folkestone; (Elham Registrar's District, September Quarter, 1879, vol. 2a, p. 458).

Browne, Henry Peter; CarNB; captain; 3rd SI 22/8/1823; died in 1839 at Ilfracombe, North Devon, Devon, England; administration granted in 1839 at the Prerogative Court (NA Reference: Prerogative Grant Book/F/210b); C.C. Taghmon, Co. Wexford; Kells and Summerhill, Co. Meath.

Browne, Jeremiah; RIC 1083; LDS 2097/197; born 1811, Co. Limerick; enlisted as a sub constable on 1/5/1831; wife a native of Scotland; 3rd SI 18/2/1853; retired 10/5/1871; died 2/11/1880 at 2 St Helen's Terrace, Phibsborough, Dublin, late of Phibsborough Avenue, Dublin; administration granted on 14/6/1881 at the Principal Registry to Mary Anne Browne, of 2 St Helen's Terrace and Thomas Browne, Ballingarry, Co. Limerick, farmer and spinster and brother and sister of the deceased – effects under £600.

Browne, John Colclough; LDS 2097/147; born 1821, Co. Wexford; 3rd SI 12/5/1845; died 26/1/1866 at Tullow, Co. Carlow (Carlow Registrar's District, vol. 3, p. 402); administration granted at Kilkenny on 16/3/1866 to Sarsfield Vessy Browne, of Blenheim, Kingstown, Co. Dublin, the brother and one of the next of kin of the deceased – effects under £100.

Browne, John George; LDS 2097/142; born 1810, Upper Canada; captain; wife a native of Co. Carlow; nephew of Major George Baxter Browne, CI, RIC, Commissioner of the Dublin

Metropolitan Police and of the poetess, Mrs Felicia Dorothea Hemans; 3rd SI 8/6/1843; barrackmaster and storekeeper of the Phoenix Park Depot 1/5/1854; died 7/6/1865 at the Phoenix Park Depot (*Cork Examiner* 10/6/1865).

Browne, Martin; LDS 2097/144; born 1823, Co. Roscommon; clerk in the Constabulary Office from 25/11/1840 to 24/3/1844; 3rd SI 30/3/1844; resigned 7/4/1856.

Browne, Patrick; LDS 2097/097; 3rd SI 1/10/1836; paymaster 1/10/1836; held other situations which he surrendered by order of the government; pensioned 10/6/1869.

Browne, Philip Theodore Briarly; RIC 67664; LDS 2098/051B; born 1/9/1890, Glos., England; assistant schoolmaster at St Andrew's, Eastbourne for two and a half years; captain; 3rd SI 11/1/1914; resigned 1/10/1920; Chief Constable of Bootle Borough Police, Lancashire from 7/10/1920 to 17/3/1926 and Chief Constable of Cumberland and Westmorland Constabulary from 4/3/1926 to 1952 when he died in office.

Brownrigg, Henry John (Sir) Kt.; CarNB; born 18/6/1798, eldest son of General Thomas Brownrigg (1767–1826) and Anne, daughter of R. Shearman, esq., of Kilcrain, Co. Kilkenny; 2nd lieutenant Rifle Brigade 6/12/1813; lieutenant 23/12/1819 to 23/4/1826 when he was placed on half pay; his uncle was General Sir Robert B. Brownrigg, Bt., GCB, Colonel 9th Regiment of Foot (Green Howards Regiment); uncle – Lieutenant Henry B. Brownrigg, died in the East Indies; uncle – Lieutenant John B. Brownrigg, 36th Regiment of Foot (Herefordshire Regiment), drowned in the service; brother – Lieutenant Charles C. Brownrigg, 9th Regiment of Foot (East Norfolk Regiment); brother – Lieutenant William M. Brownrigg, 13th Regiment of Foot (1st Somersetshire Regiment); brother – Lieutenant Marcus F. Brownrigg, Royal Navy; first cousin – Lieutenant Colonel Robert B. Brownrigg, killed in Montevideo; his brother, Captain W. Meadows Brownrigg, of Sydney, Australia fifth daughter, Maria Matilda, married on 20/7/1861, at Christchurch, Melbourne, Australia, George Maunsell, Esq., eldest son of Edward Maunsell, of Deerpark, Co. Clare (*Cork Examiner* 28/10/1861); first cousin – Lieutenant-Colonel Robert B. Brownrigg, 52nd Regiment of Foot (Oxfordshire Regiment), died from the effects of the Indian climate; first cousin – Captain J.B. Brownrigg, Royal Navy, died in service in the West Indies; married in 1822, Elizabeth (d.23/1/1880 at Sunnyside House, Folkestone), third daughter of Rev. Thomas Cooke; his second daughter, Bessie Diana died on 22/11/1855 at 7 Pembroke Place, Dublin (*Cork Examiner* 26/11/1855); his second son, Colonel Henry John Brodrick Brownrigg CB, 24/5/1881 and Commissary General to the Forces was born in Co. Cork in 1828 and died on 23/10/1904; 3rd SI 1/10/1826; to the Commission of Peace on 1/11/1832; AIG 1/9/1838; DIG 9/6/1848; CB, 13/6/1857; inspector general 19/10/1858; Knighted by the Earl of Mornington, 1858; author of *Constabulary Manual of Drill* (1859) and *Observations concerning the Constabulary Force in Ireland – Chiefly in reference to certain objections against the present system* (1862); pensioned 8/5/1865; died 25/11/1873 at 12 Talbot Square, Hyde Park, London; (Kensington Registrar's District, December Quarter, 1873, vol. 1a, p. 46); administration granted at the Principal registry on 11/12/1873 to Dame Elizabeth Brownrigg, of 12 Talbot Square, Hyde Park, widow, the relict – effects under £1,500; C.C. Skibbereen and Doneraile, Co. Cork and Tralee, Co. Kerry.

Brownrigg, Herbert George; RIC 54417; LDS 2098/070; born 3/5/1864, Co. Wicklow; (Rathdown Registrar's District, 1864, vol. 7, p. 1,018); on temporary survey staff in Tasmania from 1886 to 1888; married on 6/4/1906 (Dublin South Registrar's District, June Quarter, 1906, vol. 2, p. 567), Letitia Bedella (d.3/9/1967), daughter of Thomas Hope and widow of Dr A. Johnson, of Westport, Co. Mayo; 3rd SI 1/10/1890; King Edward VII Visit to Ireland Medal, 1903; retired 1/10/1920; died 31/10/1953.

Brownrigg, Quin John; RIC 17767; LDS 2097/201; born, 21/1/1832, Co. Kerry; eldest son of Sir Henry John Brownrigg (1798–1873); clerk in the Office of Fines and Penalties for two years and ten months; married 24/4/1861 (Antrim Registrar's District, vol. 1, p. 22), Anne (d.9/10/1905), daughter of William Chaine, Esq., Co. Antrim; by whom he had Herbert George,

52   53

52 Chartres Brew – first inspector general of constabulary, British Columbia, 1858.   53 Herbert
George Brownrigg.   54 Col. Robert Bruce, Inspector General, RIC.

54

b.3/5/1864, John Claud, b.23/8/1878, Mildred Alexander, Eveline Annie, Mary Elizabeth, Edith Jane Dunville, Gertrude Ellen and Kathleen Winifred; 3rd SI 1/4/1854; received a favourable record on 31/12/1870 for prompt and intelligent action on private information received, whereby the perpetrator of an agrarian murder was discovered, arrested and evidence obtained; musketry instructor from 1/4/1876 to 1/10/1876; CI 16/11/1876; retired 1/1/1889; died 2/9/1907 at Ballywillan, Co. Galway, late of Portrush, Co. Antrim; will proved on 15/10/1907 at the Principal Registry to Herbert George Brownrigg, DI, RIC – effects £6,763.7s.2d.

Brownrigg, Thomas Marcus; LDS 2097/139; born 8/6/1823, Co. Limerick; eldest son of Sir Henry John Brownrigg (1798–1873); brother of Quin John Brownrigg, CI, RIC; amateur photographer; member of the Dublin Photographic Society and 'The Linked Ring', a secret society of amateur photographers, in which he was known as 'The Magician'; married on 15/8/1854 (Dublin South Registrar's District, vol. 5, p. 312), Muriel Anna, only surviving daughter of James Duff Watt, Esq., Deputy Commissary-General to the Forces (*Cork Examiner* 18/8/1854); daughter Ida, born on 1/7/1855 at 9, Besborough Terrace, Dublin (*Cork Examiner* 6/7/1855) and she died aged on 5/9/1855, aged two months (*Cork Examiner* 10/9/1855); daughter born on 23/4/1856 at 9, Besborough Terrace, Dublin (*Cork Examiner* 28/4/1856); daughter born on 5/2/1865 at Maryborough, Queen's County (*Cork Examiner* 14/2/1865); daughter, Eleanor Mary, born on 11/8/1872 in Dublin (Dublin South Registrar's District, vol. 12, p. 670) (*Cork Examiner* 13/8/1872); 3rd SI 18/3/1842; Adjutant, Phoenix Park Depot from 30/6/1855 to 30/6/1862; resident magistrate 1/7/1862; AIG, 8/5/1865; pensioned 1/8/1877; died 17/11/1901 at Artington House, Guildford, Surrey, England; (Guildford Registrar's District, December Quarter, 1901, vol. 2a, p. 47); probate of will granted on 16/1/1902 at London to Eleanor Hannah Brownrigg, the widow – effects £6,503.18s.3d.

Bruce, Robert; born 17/2/1825, Downhill, Co. Derry; 2nd son of Sir James Robertson Bruce, 2nd Baronet (4/9/1788–22/4/1836) and Ellen (d.14/7/1864) youngest daughter of Robert Bamford Hesketh, Esq., of Gwyrch Castle, Denbigh County, Wales; educated at the Scottish Naval and Military Academy; 2nd lieutenant Royal Welsh Fusiliers, 31/3/1843, major 21/9/1855; served as a brevet colonel in Canada, Bulgaria, the Crimea and Indian Mutiny campaign; placed on half pay on 2/12/1859; assistant inspector of volunteers in Lancashire 1/3/1865; colonel on 17/5/1867 and placed on half pay on 1/4/1868, retiring as colonel and sold out on 11/12/1872. He married on 1/2/1859, Mary Caroline (d.24/5/1893 at 6, Warwick Square, London SW) daughter of Sir John Montagu Burgoyne, 9th Bt., of Sutton Park, Bedfordshire; he had one daughter, Lilian Amy (d.6/11/1948), who married at St Gabriel's, Warwick Square, London on 3/1/1894, Lieutenant-General, Sir Gerald Francis Ellison (d.27/10/1947), KCB, KCMG, Royal Warwickshire Regiment, second son of Canon Ellison, Rector of Haseley, Oxon.; Chief Constable of Lancashire from 6/2/1868 to 30/12/1876; DIG 1/1/1877; inspector general 12/5/1882; pensioned 21/9/1885; CB (Civil), 14/9/1885; died at 'Bruno', Alexandra Road, Farnborough, Hampshire, 1/9/1899; (Hartley West Registrar's District, September Quarter, 1899, vol. 2c, p. 143); buried in Brompton Cemetery, London (*Times* 2/9/1899); probate granted at London on 11/11/1899 to Henry Denison, retired colonel in H.M. army and Frank Kinder, solicitor – effects £40,326.7s.6d.

Bruce-Norton, John; RIC 81617; ADRIC no. 1216; LDS 2099/031; born 31/3/1895, Madras, India; lieutenant, Royal Flying Corps; 3rd DI 25/6/1921; resigned 23/12/1921.

Buckley, John; RIC 56521; LDS 2099/005; born 1901, Listowel, Co. Kerry; (Listowel Registrar's District, 1901, March Quarter, vol. 5, p. 374); 3rd DI 5/1/1921; awarded the South African Medal serving with the Imperial Yeomanry in 1902; and the medal of the Royal Humane Society; pensioned 30//4/1922.

Bulfin, Thomas; LDS 2097/022; born 1785; PPF; 3rd SI 3/5/1816; pensioned 1/3/1839; died 12/1/1849, Sligo, Co. Sligo.

Bull, Robert George; RIC 33945; LDS 2097/268; born 7/3/1848, Co. Dublin; his son, Edward Joseph, was born on 1/1/1872 at the residence of his father-in-law, Joseph Green, Esq., Barna House, Newport, Co. Tipperary (Nenagh Registrar's District, vol. 3, p. 664) (*Cork Examiner* 4/1/1872); 3rd SI 20/3/1868; resident magistrate 3rd class 8/2/1892, 2nd class 3/1/1896, 1st class 8/2/1909; pensioned 7/3/1913; on 4/6/1917 appointed as temporary resident magistrate during the absence on military service on Henry Toppin, RM; his son, Captain Bull was killed fighting in South Africa in April, 1902.

Buller (Sir) Redvers Henry (1839–1908); PC VC, 1879, KCMG, 1882, KCB, 1885, GCB, 1894, GCMG, 1901, Special Commissioner for Kerry and Clare, 1 August 1886, Under Secretary to the Lord Lieutenant of Ireland, 1886 to 15/10/1887; born 7/12/1839, Downes, Crediton, Devon, England son of James Wentworth Buller, MP, of Crediton, Devonshire and Charlotte, daughter of Lord H.M. Howard. He was the descendant of an old Cornish family, long established in Devonshire, tracing its 'ancestry in the female line to Edward I'; educated at Eton. He entered the army in 1858, and served with the 60th (King's Royal Rifles) in the China campaign of 1860. In 1870 he became captain, and went on the Red River expedition, where he was first associated with Colonel (afterwards Lord) Wolseley. In 1873–4 he accompanied the latter in the Ashanti campaign as head of the Intelligence Department, and was slightly wounded at the battle of Ordabai; he was mentioned in despatches, made a C.B., and raised to the rank of major. In 1874 he inherited the family estates. In the Kaffir War of 1878–9 and the Zulu War of 1879 he was conspicuous as an intrepid and popular leader, and acquired a reputation for courage and dogged determination. In particular his conduct of the retreat at Inhlobane (March 28, 1879) drew attention to these qualities, and on that occasion he earned the VC; he was also created C.M.G. and made lieutenant-colonel and A.D.C. to Queen Victoria. In the Boer War of 1881 he was Sir Evelyn Wood's chief of staff; and thus added to his experience of South African conditions of warfare. In 1882 he was head of the field intelligence department in the Egyptian campaign, and was knighted for his services. Two years later he commanded an infantry brigade in the Sudan under Sir Gerald Graham, and was at the battles of El Teb and Tamai, being promoted major-general for distinguished service. In the Sudan campaign of 1884–5 he was Lord Wolseley's chief of staff, and he was given command of the desert column when Sir Herbert Stewart was wounded. He distinguished himself by his conduct of the retreat from Gubat to Gakdul, and by his victory at Abu Klea (16–17 February), and he was created K.C.B. In 1886 he was sent to Ireland to inquire into the 'moonlighting' outrages, and for a short time he acted as under-secretary for Ireland; but in 1887 he was appointed quartermaster-general at the war office. From 1890 to 1897 he held the office of adjutant-general, attaining the rank of lieutenant-general in 1891. At the war office his 'energy and ability inspired the belief that he was fitted for the highest command, and in 1895, when the duke of Cambridge was about to retire, it was well known that Lord Rosébery's cabinet intended to appoint Sir Redvers as chief of the staff under a scheme of reorganization recommended by Lord Hartington's commission. On the eve of this change, however, the government was defeated, and its successors appointed Lord Wolseley to the command under the old title of commander-in-chief. In 1896 he was made a full general. In 1898 he took command of the troops at Aldershot, and when the Boer War broke out in 1899 he was selected to command the South African Field Force in Natal and landed at Cape Town on 31 October. Owing to the Boer investment of Ladysmith and the consequent gravity of the military situation in Natal, he unexpectedly hurried thither in order to supervise personally the operations, but on the 15 December his first attempt to cross the Tugela at Colenso was repulsed. The government, alarmed at the situation and the pessimistic tone of Buller's messages, sent out Lord Roberts to supersede him in the chief command, Sir Redvers being left in subordinate command of the Natal force. His second attempt to relieve Ladysmith (10–27 January) proved another failure, the result of the operations at Spion Kop (24 January) causing consternation in England. A third attempt (Vaaikrantz, 5–7 February) was unsuccessful, but the Natal army finally accomplished its task in the series of actions which culminated in the victory of Pieter's Hill and the relief of Ladysmith on the 27th of February. Sir Redvers Buller remained in command of the Natal army till October 1900, when he returned to England (being created G.C.M.G.), having in the meanwhile slowly done a great deal of hard work in driving the Boers from the Biggarsberg (5 May), forcing Lang's Nek (12 June), and occupying Lydenburg (6 September). But though these latter operations had done much to re-establish his reputation for dogged determination, and he had never lost the confidence of his own men, his capacity for an important command in delicate and difficult operations was now seriously questioned. The continuance, therefore, in 1901 of his appointment to the important Aldershot command met with a vigorous press criticism, in which the detailed objections taken to his conduct of the operations before Ladysmith (and particularly to a message to Sir George White in which he seriously contemplated and provided for the contingency of surrender) were given new prominence. On the 10 October 1901, at a luncheon in London, Sir Redvers Buller made a speech in answer to these criticisms in terms which were held to be a breach of discipline, and he was placed on half-pay a few days later. For the remaining years of his life he played an active part as a country gentleman, accepting in dignified silence the prolonged attacks on his failures in South Africa; among the public generally, and particularly in his own county, he never lost his popularity. He married in 1882 Lady Audrey Jane Charlotte, daughter of the 4th Marquess Townshend and widow of the Hon. G.T. Howard who survived him with one daughter; died on 2/6/1908.

Burbridge, Richard; CarNB; PPF; PPF Clerk, 6/9/1814; lieutenant, 22nd Regiment of Foot (The Cheshire Regiment); recommended by (later Sir) Richard Willcocks on 12/3/1816: 'The bearer lieutenant Burbridge on the half pay of the 22nd Regiment of Foot is a fit and proper person to fill the office of Chief Clerk in my police establishment in the barony of Middlethird, Co. Tipperary – Approved.'

Burgess, Edward N.; RIC 13766; LDS 2097/183; born 1828, Ballycormack, Co. Carlow; 3rd SI 12/1/1850; dismissed 19/10/1870, having been imprisoned for pecuniary difficulties.

Burke, Dominick Francis; LDS 2097/158; born 1821, Cahernagarry, Kilreekil, Co. Galway, son of Michael Burke; father of Francis Charles Burke, DI, RIC, RM; married Frances 'Fannie' Burke, daughter of Denis Burke, Ballydugan, Loughrea, Co. Galway; 3rd SI 7/5/1847; awarded the Constabulary Medal on 6/9/1867 for defending Tallaght Barracks, Co. Dublin during the Fenian Rising on 30/4/1867; retired 9/11/1870; died 26/3/1904 at 6, Tivoli Terrace, Kingstown, Co. Dublin; buried in Deansgrange Cemetery, Dublin (Upper North Section, Row G2, Grave No. 5) with his wife Fannie (d.30/8/1924), and sons Dominick (d.18/2/1941) and Major Francis Charles Burke (d.13/1/1936), DI, RIC, RM; will with one codicil proved at the Principal Registry on 15/6/1904 by the oath of Fannie Burke, the widow – effects £594.6s.6d.; (photo in the *Constabulary Gazette*, vol. VI, no. 13, 23/12/1899).

Burke, Francis Charles; RIC 58076; LDS 2098/140; born 3/12/1874, 5, Royal Terrace East, Kingstown, Co. Dublin; son of Dominic Francis Burke, SI, RIC, of Cahernagarry, Co. Galway and Frances 'Fannie' Burke, daughter of Denis Burke, Ballydugan, Co. Galway; brother of 2nd Lieutenant John Errol Burke, 2nd Battalion, Connaught Rangers; educated at Belvedere College, Dublin; 3rd DI 1/5/1898; King Edward VII Visit to Ireland Medal, 1903; King George V Visit to Ireland Medal, 1911; captain, Royal Irish Regiment; captain 24/10/1914 and major 18/1/1916, 5th Battalion Connaught Rangers; left Curragh Camp on 4/5/1915 for England on board *Munich*. Arrived at Basingstoke, Hampshire 5/5/1915. Left Liverpool on S.S. *Mauritania* on 8/7/1915. Disembarked 16/7/1915 at Mudros, Greece. Disembarked at Anzac Cove, Gallipoli on 6/8/1915. Received a bullet wound to the head in action on Hill 60, Dardanelles on 21/8/1915 and his brother Lieutenant John Errol Burke was killed gallantly leading a charge at Kaean Kuzu, Gallipoli; severely wounded in the Irish Rebellion, April 1916; temporary adjutant of the Phoenix Park Depot, 1/8/1918 to 27/4/1919; resident magistrate 3rd class 8/8/1919; died 13/1/1936; buried in Deansgrange Cemetery, Dublin (Upper North Section, Row G2,

55   57

55 Dominick Burke, 'The Hero of Tallaght', 1867.   56 Dominick Burke, *Siege of Tallaght*, 1867.
57 Dominick Burke, 1897.

56

Grave No. 5) with his father Dominick Francis Burke, SI, RIC (d.26/3/1904), mother Fannie (d.30/8/1924), and brother Dominick (d.18/2/1941); (p. 177, RM Records of Service Book, National Archives, Dublin); (WO 339/13602).

Burke, John; CarNB; born, Pallasgreen, Co. Limerick; lieutenant 23rd Dragoons; lieutenant 16th Dragoons; captain; half pay 44th Regiment of Foot; author of *Exposure of Frauds and Malversions carried on by the Leinster Constabulary* (London, 1828); C.C. Arthurstown, Co. Wexford; Trim, Co. Meath; Ballincollig, Co. Cork and Pilltown, Co. Kilkenny.

Burke, Mark; RIC 88; LDS 2097/206; born 1802, Co. Mayo; joined as a constable, 1/10/1823; wife a native of Co. Leitrim; 3rd SI 17/10/1854; pensioned 1/11/1865; died 23/5/1892 at Ballisodare, Co. Sligo; administration granted on 15/8/1892 at the Principal Registry to Denis Burke, of 57 Grand Parade, Cork, auctioneer, the nephew – effects £78.9s.5d.

Burke, Mark-O'Malley; LDS 2097/128; born 1814, Co. Mayo; 3rd SI 13/7/1839; dismissed 10/4/1842.

Burke, Myles Blake; LDS 2097/160; born 17/6/1826, Bantry, Co. Cork; eldest son of Chief Constable Stephen Burke (1791–1855); married on 9/8/1849 at 6 Bridge Street, Cork, by the Rev. Thomas Barry, V.G., Anna, only daughter of Denis McCartie, of Derrigh, Newmarket, Co. Cork; 3rd SI 2/11/1847; pensioned on 1/6/1887 and retired to Carlisle House, Monkstown, Co. Dublin; died 21/12/1906 at 34 Eccles Street, Dublin, late of the Shelbourne Hotel, Dublin; funeral from St Joseph's, Berkeley Street on 24/12/1906 to Glasnevin Cemetery, Dublin; will proved on 15/4/1907 at the Principal Registry by the oath of Walter Blake Burke, ex-major – effects £2,061.6s.7d.

Burke, P. J.; CarNB; C.C. Croom, Co. Limerick; Naas, Kilcock and Leixlip, Co. Kildare.

Burke, Robert-O'Hara; RIC 13609; LDS 2097/182; born February 1821, at Dominick Street, Galway; baptized in St Nicholas' Collegiate College Church on 30/7/1822; second eldest son of James Hardiman Burke (d.1854), Mayor of Galway, 1820–22, of St Clerans, Co. Galway and Anne Louisa O'Hara (d.1844), of Raheen, Co. Galway, who were married in 1817; his father served with the 7th Royal Fusiliers and was involved in the capture of the islands of Martinique in 1809 and Guadeloupe in 1810 during the Napoleonic Wars; his brothers both served in the army; his eldest brother John Hardiman Burke was a colonel in the 88th Regiment of Foot (Connaught Rangers) serving in the Mediterranean, Nova Scotia, the West Indies and the Crimea seeing action at the battles of Alma, Balaklava and Inkerman; his younger brother James Thomas served as a lieutenant with the Royal Engineers and was the first British officer to be killed in the Crimea at the battle of Giurgevo on the Danube on 7/7/1854; Robert O'Hara Burke was educated at Woolwich Military Academy which he entered on 12/5/1835, aged 14 years and 3 months and discharged on 9/12/1836; cadet, 1840, 2nd lieutenant, 1/8/1842 and 1st lieutenant, 1/4/1847, Austrian Service, Prince Regent's 7th Hussar Regiment; 3rd SI 6/11/1849; resigned 20/11/1852 and emigrated to Australia in 1853; acting inspector at Carlsruhe, Victoria Police; senior inspector, Beechworth, 1854–8; superintendent of police, Castlemaine district, 1858–60; commanded the expedition organized by the Royal Society of Victoria and supported by the government fitted out to explore the centre of Australia which started from Melbourne on 20/8/1860; reached Cooper's Creek on 11/11/1860; crossed the continent and reached the Gulf of Carpentaria on 10/2/1861 where he died of starvation on 28/6/1861. He was buried with a public funeral at Melbourne on 21/1/1863. A bronze statue was erected in Collins Street, Melbourne in 1864 at a cost of £4,000; biography – *The Shimmering Waste: The Life and Times of Robert O'Hara Burke* by William Henry, Galway 1997.

Burke, Stephen; LDS 2097/036; born 15/12/1791, Co. Galway; son of Myles Burke, whose father Dominick was the third son of Ulick of Ower and Catherine Blake (1760–1853), daughter of Sir Walter Blake, 10th Baronet Menloe, of Menloe Castle; he was the second of three children, his older brother Myles became a medical doctor in Galway and his younger sister Maria married Martin Kirwan of Hillsbrook, Co. Galway; ensign (without purchase) Galway Militia,

24/12/1810 (WO 13/2882–901); lieutenant, 17/2/1812 serving in Limerick; ensign, 2nd Battalion 47th Regiment of Foot (Lancashire Regiment), 11/6/1812 serving in Spain and was present at the Battle of Vittoria on 21/6/1813; lieutenant, 26/5/1814 and served in India; lieutenant half pay, 24/10/1814; married, 5/5/1824 in Galway, Julia (1802–1860), second daughter of Joseph Blake, of Brookhill, Co. Mayo and Catherine Jennings, of Ballyeurin, Co. Galway, the grandchild of Sir Joseph Hoare, Bt., Co. Cork; children: Elizabeth Mary Teresa, born 25/2/1825, Myles Blake, born 17/6/1826, Chief Constable Irish Constabulary, Catherine, born 18/4/1828; his son Joseph Burke, married on 5/2/1856, at the Roman Catholic Church, Castlecomer, Co. Kilkenny, Matilda Henrietta, only daughter of John Andrew Kirwan, Esq., DL and Resident Magistrate, of Hillsbrook, Co. Galway, who died on 2/1/1869 at Castlecomer, Co. Kilkenny (*Cork Examiner* 4/1/1869) and granddaughter of Major and the Lady Matilda Burke (*Cork Examiner* 8/2/1856); his daughter Elizabeth Mary Teresa married on 22/11/1855, John Savage, Esq., Surgeon, of Newry, Co. Down at Warrenpoint Catholic Church, Co. Down (*Cork Examiner* 28/11/1855); severely wounded at the assault of St Sebastian on 31/8/1813 – ball passed through right thigh; awarded one medal and two clasps for Vittoria and St Sebastian; 3rd SI 28/1/1823 when residing at 40 Leinster Road, Rathmines, Dublin; residing in Killarney, Co. Kerry 1823–4 and Bantry, Co. Cork, 1824–8; CI 8/1/1844; pensioned 15/12/1851 and retired to 40, Leinster Road, Rathmines, Co. Dublin where he died on 21/6/1855 (*Cork Examiner* 25/6/1855); buried in Glasnevin Cemetery, Dublin (Plot WA66ALL), with his wife Julia (d.25/10/1860); (WO 25/751 fol. 368).

Burke, William Rickard; LDS 2097/095; born 1812, London, England; enlisted as a sub constable in November 1834; wife a native of Co. Cork; daughter born on 21/3/1855 at Thurles, Co. Tipperary (*Cork Examiner* 23/3/1855); 3rd SI 14/4/1836; CI 11/3/1865; AIG 8/4/1872; pensioned 16/11/1876; died 19/1/1880 in Skibbereen, Co. Cork; Skibbereen Registrar's District, 1880, June Quarter, vol. 5, p. 507); buried in Glasnevin Cemetery. His diary, 1865–1872 was acquired by the National Library of Ireland in 2001.

Butler, Antoine Sloet; resident magistrate, 1853–82; divisional magistrate 1882; captain, 7th Dragoon Guards; awarded Medal for the Kaffir War; CB.

Butler, George Beresford; CarNB; PPF.

Butler, James; LDS 2097/145; born 1801, Co. Tipperary; wife from Co. Tipperary; 3rd SI 22/6/1844; received a grant from the Reward Fund on 31/5/1848 for uniformly zealous and successful exertions in making offenders amenable; pensioned 1/12/1856 in King's County; died 1861.

Butler, Patrick; RIC 53720; LDS 2098/230B; born 1871, Co. Tipperary; wife a native of Co. Kerry; 3rd DI 1/1/1921; pensioned 3/5/1922.

Butler, Xaverius Henry Blake; LDS 2097/198; born 1832, Chester, Ches., England; 3rd SI 13/8/1853; pensioned 1/6/1870; died 6/11/1880.

Bygott, Harold M.; RIC 72102; ADRIC no. 6; LDS 2098/236B; born 2/1/1885, Lancs., England; lieutenant, 2nd Leicester Regiment; 3rd DI 2/7/1921; pensioned 12/4/1922.

Byrne, George; RIC 4623; LDS 2097/278; born 1823, Longford; wife from Co. Derry; 3rd SI 15/7/1869; died 31/5/1875 at Naas, Co. Kildare; (Naas Registrar's District, 1875, vol. 9, p. 611).

Byrne, James; RIC 61813; LDS 2098/213B; born 14/12/1887; Co. Roscommon; (Roscommon Registrar's District, December Quarter, 1887, vol. 3, p. 256): army; 3rd DI 11/2/1920; pensioned 17/7/1922.

Byrne, John; LDS 2097/215; born 1834, Co. Cork; joined the Irish Revenue Police as a lieutenant on 20/1/1854 and served in Carrigart and Kilcar, Co. Donegal; 3rd SI 25/3/1858; CI 15/2/1879; divisional commissioner 15/2/1889; died in 1898; (photo in the *Constabulary Gazette*, vol. VI, no. 13, 23/12/1899, p. 390).

Byrne, John; RIC 24863; LDS 2097/220; born 1832, Co. Dublin; uncle of RIC Inspector General, Brigadier-General, Joseph Aloysius Byrne; joined the Irish Revenue Police as a

58 59

58 Robert O'Hara Burke, explorer. 59 Robert O'Hara Burke, grave in Melbourne, Australia.
60 John Peter Byrne. 61 Brigadier-General Sir Joseph Aloysius Byrne, Inspector General,
RIC.

60 61

lieutenant on 26/1/1853 and served in Co. Donegal; his youngest son, Charles Frederick, aged 13 months died on 18/5/1864 of croup at Gorey, Co. Wexford (Gorey Registrar's District, vol. 12, p. 339) (*Cork Examiner* 21/5/1864); 3rd SI 1/12/1857; CI 14/9/1881; died 9/1/1883 at Cloone Constabulary Barracks, near Mohill, Co. Leitrim; will proved on 5/4/1883 at the Principal Registry by the oath of Thomas Byrne, Church Street, Cork, merchant and brother – effects £3,426.2s.4d.

Byrne, John Peter; RIC 50412; LDS 2097/320; born 1/12/1859, Co. Dublin; MA 1880, LLB 1884, BL, Trinity College Dublin; 3rd SI 9/11/1882; adjutant, Phoenix Park Depot from 9/5/1901 to 1/5/1903; resident magistrate 3rd class 1/5/1903, 2nd class 16/5/1908, 1st class 1/10/1919; died of septicaemia 3/2/1921 at The Moorings, Athlone, Co. Westmeath; will proved at the Principal Registry on 2/6/1921; (photo in the *Constabulary Gazette*, vol. XII, no. 17, 17/1/1903).

Byrne, Joseph Aloysius (Sir); LDS 2098/071B; born 2/10/1874, Pump Street, Derry, Co. Derry, Northern Ireland, son of Dr Joseph Byrne (d.1910), DL, Derry, and Emily Egan; nephew of John Peter Byrne, DI, RIC, RM; married 1908, Marjorie, daughter of Alan Ferguson Joseph, Cairo; two daughters, Eithne (b.1901) and Clodagh (b.1910); educated at St George's College, Weybridge and Maison de Melle, Belgium. Knight of Grace of the Order of St John of Jerusalem; joined the Royal Inniskilling Fusiliers in 1893 and served in the South African War in the Siege of Ladysmith where he was wounded. He was afterwards employed with the Central Judicial (Claims) Commission in Pretoria; with the rank of Assistant Adjutant General he served at the War Office; granted the rank of Brevet Lt. Col. at the War Office on 1/4/1915; Deputy Adjutant General, Irish Command, 27/4/1916, with the rank of Brigadier-General (despatches and CB); Inspector General of the RIC from 1/8/1916 to 11/3/1920 when he was placed on sick leave with full pay for a year. In 1921 he was offered the post of Assistant Commissioner of the London Metropolitan Police on the retirement of Sir Basil Home, KCB but declined same. He was called to the (Lincolns Inn) Bar in 1921; Governor of the Seychelles, 1922–7; Governor of Sierra Leone, 24/9/1927–24/9/1929 & 1930–23/5/1931; Governor and Commander-in-Chief in Kenya, 1931–7; CB, 1917; KBE, 1918; KCMG, 1928; GCMG, 1934. He died on 13/11/1942; (photo in the *Constabulary Gazette*, vol. XXXIX, no. 7, 2/9/1916).

Byrne, William James Joseph; RIC 52878; LDS 2098/041; born 1863, Co. Tipperary; married on 19/4/1894, Mary Widdicombe, a native of England; 3rd DI 1/5/1888; dismissed 25/9/1901 for insubordination.

C

Cahill, C. S.; LDS 2097/110; 3rd SI 30/1/1837.

Cahill, Michael Joseph; LDS 2098/197B; born 16/8/1895, Co. Tipperary; lieutenant, Royal Irish Fusiliers; 3rd DI 10/1/1920; accidentally shot and killed 23/4/1921, Swords, Co. Dublin; late of 6 Queen Street, Clonmel, Co. Tipperary; administration granted on 23/8/1921.

Cahill, Patrick; RIC 56228; LDS 2098/188B; born 1873, Co. Tipperary; (Tipperary Registrar's District, 1873, vol. 3, p. 764); married on 20/9/1905 (Tullamore Registrar's District, September Quarter, 1905, vol. 3, p. 436), wife a native of Co. Limerick; 3rd DI 16/10/1920; pensioned 31/5/1922; transferred to the Royal Ulster Constabulary on 1/6/1922.

Cahill, Thomas; LDS 2097/315; born 1860, Co. Clare; 3rd SI 4/1/1882; King George V Coronation Medal, 1911; died 15/11/1919 at Ballymurphy, Kilfenora, Co. Clare; will proved at the Principal Registry on 6/9/1920.

Calderwood, Douglas Boyd; RIC 73514; ADRIC no. 515; LDS 2098/234B; born 2/5/1893, Yelverton, Devon, England; (Tavistock Registrar's District, 1893, June Quarter, vol. 5b, p. 514); educated at Merchiston Castle School, Officer Training Corps, Edinburgh, Scotland; 2nd lieutenant Royal Field Artillery, 14/9/1914 and proceeded overseas with D Battery 48th Brigade RFA; invalided home (concussed by a shell) at Ypres on 23/9/1915 and on recovery transferred to the Royal Flying Corps as a lieutenant on 1/11/1915. On being gazetted a Flying Officer on 27/7/1916 he was appointed a flying instructor in England where he remained until he went overseas to join No. 7 Squadron, RFC in February 1917.On being invalided home he was gazetted captain on 1/1/1918 and appointed to command No. 4 Training Squadron RAF and demobilized in 1919; joined the ADRIC as a cadet and appointed to command the ADRIC Transport Division; 3rd DI 2/7/1921; pensioned 31/3/1922; (WO 330/20357).

Caldwell, William; LDS 2097/054; born 1798, Co. Fermanagh; port officer in the Customs from February 1820 to July 1824; 3rd SI 10/8/1824; died 19/5/1858.

Callaghan, Robert; RIC 51809; LDS 2098/129B; born 1866, Co. Down; married on 4/9/1894 (Lisnaskea Registrar's District, September Quarter, 1894, vol. 3, p. 157), wife a native of Co. Fermanagh; 3rd DI 8/1/1920; pensioned 22/5/1922.

Cameron, Charles Ewen Allen; RIC 26122; LDS 2097/237; born 1841, Co. Leitrim; son of Russell Bedford Cameron, CI, RIC and father of John Bedford Russell Cameron, DI, RIC: spent five years at sea as a midshipman; 3rd SI 1/10/1860; received an approbation on 31/12/1870 for spirited conduct in securing a furious stallion and saving a boy who had fallen off him; CI 5/5/1884; married Marchioness Conyngham, from Co. Cork; Commissioner of Police and Town Inspector of Constabulary, Belfast from 15/3/1887 to 3/10/1889; AIG 3/10/1889; divisional commissioner 3/10/1889 and attached to Crime Branch at Headquarters; pensioned 27/4/1901; died 30/3/1914 at Mount Plunkett, Roscommon; will proved on 24/6/1914 at the Principal Registry to Sarah A. Cameron, widow effects £7,861.5s.4d.; he bequeathed a mortgage debt charged on the estate of Rev. John Stewart Gumley to the children of his first marriage and the remainder to his wife.

Cameron, John Bedford Russell; RIC 55035; LDS 2098/082; born 1869, Gort, Co. Galway (Gort Registrar's District, 1869, vol. 4, p. 390); son of Charles Ewen Allen Cameron, CI, RIC married on 27/4/1899, wife a native of Co. Kerry; 3rd DI 23/12/1891; resigned 20/7/1899.

Cameron, Russell Bedford; LDS 2097/065; born 1807, Scotland; father of Charles Ewen Allen Cameron, CI, RIC; 3rd SI 1/11/1826; CI 1/3/1839; pensioned 1/6/1850; died 31/10/1863 at Aughamore House, Co. Leitrim; administration granted at the Principal Registry on 20/10/1864 to Helen Cameron, of Aughamore House, Co. Leitrim, widow of the deceased – effects under £200; his son George d'Halberg Cameron, manager of the Provincial Bank, Nenagh, Co. Tipperary died at Henry Street, Nenagh on 2/1/1904.

Cameron, Oswald Alexander; RIC 66465; LDS 2098/035B; born 17/11/1890, Middlesex, London, England; (Hampstead Registrar's District, 1890, December Quarter, vol. 1a, p. 593); army tutor for one year; 3rd DI 13/11/1912; died from tetanus as a result of a motor cycle accident on 17/2/1913 in Sligo; (Sligo Registrar's District, 1913, March Quarter, vol. 2, p. 207).

Campbell, James; LDS 2097/169; born 1804, Co. Antrim; enlisted as a sub constable on 1/5/1825; 3rd SI 1/6/1848; pensioned 28/5/1870; died 29/10/1874 at Belfast, Co. Antrim; will proved on 18/11/1874 at Belfast by the oath of William Campbell, Carryclough, Ballymoney, Co. Antrim and Alexander McCloy, Ballymoney, Co. Antrim (deceased domiciled in Ireland) – effects in the United Kingdom under £3,000.

Campbell, James Douglas; RIC 72014; LDS 2098/191B; born 25/3/1894, Co. Antrim; (Belfast Registrar's District, June Quarter, 1894, vol. 1, p. 237); lieutenant, army; 3rd DI 10/1/1920; retired 24/6/1922.

Campbell, John; CarNB; C.C. barony of Coshmore and Coshbridge, Tallow, Co. Waterford, 1824; died April 1825 as a result of a fall from his horse.

Cannon, Henry Charles; RIC 16550; LDS 2097/195; born 1831, Co. Kildare; son of Thomas Cannon, Esq., Resident Magistrate (d.1853); 3rd SI 17/12/1852; pensioned 10/4/1868; died 6/4/1872 at No. 3, Park Terrace, Stillorgan, Co. Dublin; will proved on 11/6/1872 at the Principal Registry by the oath of Susannah Cannon, 3 Park Terrace, Stillorgan, widow, the sole executrix – effects £5; his daughter Ellen, who was also the granddaughter of Major James Tandy, Millbank, Naas, Co. Kildare, married Charles, the only son of Charles Vawser, Esq., Cambridgeshire and Boxholme Hall, Lincolnshire at Bray, Co. Wicklow on 21/10/1899; buried in Mount Jerome Cemetery, Dublin.

Canny, Jeremiah; LDS 2097/161; born 1818, Co. Clare; 3rd SI 22/9/1847; died 24/8/1853 in Claremorris, Co. Mayo.

Carbery, Joseph Alphonsus; RIC 43849; LDS 2098/159; born 1860, Co. Leitrim; son of Denis Carbery, RIC Sub Constable 15200, who was married on 8/12/1859 in Co. Leitrim; journalist; married on 9/6/1896 (Dublin South Registrar's District, June Quarter, 1895, vol. 2, p. 685), wife a native of Caermarthen, Wales; 3rd DI 2/9/1899; King Edward VII Visit to Ireland Medal, 1903; awarded a certificate from the Irish Police and Constabulary Recognition Fund; pensioned 15/6/1920; on retirement he remained in Beech Grove, Drogheda, Co. Louth being recognized internationally as a dog-breeder, judge and exhibitor. He owned kennels and bred the 'Of Boyne' Irish setters which won a world-wide reputation, and exported them to all parts of the world; his dogs won thousands of prizes and one hundred and fifty championship certificates and Green stars; he also exhibited and won with pointers, setters, retrievers, spaniels and Kerry Blue Setters; for over forty years his judging engagements, mostly as an all-round judge, extended all over Great Britain and Ireland, Sweden, Italy, Norway and Holland. He was a member of more than twenty dog societies and was Vice-President of the old Irish Kennel Club at the date of its abolition and was one of the first to assist the Governing Body of which he had acted on the General Purposes Committee for more than nine years. He was also a senior member of the Irish Redsetter Club of which he acted as Hon. Treasurer for 21 years. He was a regular contributor to the *Irish Field* and to cross-channel periodicals dealing with dogs. He judged a number of times at 'Crofts' International Show drawing large entries. In 1931 he drew an entry of 368 dogs when judging Irish Setters; died 24/12/1940 at Brookfield, Castlepark Road, Dunlaoghaire, Co. Dublin; buried in the New Cemetery, Drogheda, Co. Louth; his eldest son, Rev. J.J. Carbery, SJ,

62

63

62 Joseph Alphonsus Carbery, Head Constable, champion dog breeder.   63 Joseph Alphonsus Carbery.   64 Michael John Carney.   65 Major Samson Carter, Peace Preservation Force, Grave in Mount Jerome Cemetery, Dublin.

64

65

Rathfarnham, Co. Dublin, aged 21 years died at Beech Grove, Drogheda, Co. Louth on 17/1/1818 and was buried in Glasnevin Cemetery, Dublin on 19/1/1918.

Carden, Arnold Philip; RIC 48497; LDS 2097/319; born 9/2/1859, Co. Cavan; fourth son of Andrew Carden (28/9/1815–27/11/1876), of Barnane, Co. Tipperary, DL, JP, High Sheriff, 1873; Captain 60th Rifles and Anne (b.11/11/1824)(d.1869), daughter of Lieutenant-General Sackville Hamilton Berkeley (1780–1863), of Lisbuoy House, Beragh, Co. Tyrone who were married on 4/8/1847; 3rd SI 17/3/1882; CI 1/3/1904; King George V Coronation Medal, 1911; married in 1884 (Armagh Registrar's District, September Quarter, 1884, vol. 1, p. 47), Eva (d.1939), daughter of Robert Hamilton; he had one son, Philip Berkeley Hamilton Carden, Lieutenant, Royal Engineers (b.1904) and died unmarried in the Gold Coast in 1928; he had two daughters one of which, Eva F.A. Carden married on 10/1/1908 at St James' Church, Belfast, Henry Ernest Kearney, Northern Bank, Downpatrick, Co. Down, son of William Kearney, 128, Inverness Terrace, Belfast; pensioned 31/12/1910; died 23/11/1915 at Ardlin, Upper Newtownards Road, Belfast; buried in Dundonald Cemetery, Belfast on 25/11/1915; will proved at the Principal Registry on 17/7/1916 by the oath of Constance E, Carden, the widow – effects £132.4s.0d. (photo in the *Constabulary Gazette*, vol. XIII, no. 9, 23/5/1903).

Carleton, Andrew O'Brien; RIC 26522; LDS 2097/238; born 1842, Co. Kildare; only son of Andrew Carleton, Esq., QC; 3rd SI 24/4/1861; married Isabella Anderson (b.1845) (d.2/6/1880), fourth daughter of Louis John Anderson, DI, RIC; died 1/9/1889 at Lucan, Co. Dublin; will proved on 11/12/1889 at the Principal Registry by the oath of Ellen Carleton, of Ardlanstown, Ballinhassig, Co. Cork – effects £1,248.3s.11d.

Carlisle, David Windrum; RIC 65418; LDS 2098/014B; born 15/10/1866, Berks., England; employed for five years in Belfast for a glass bottling company and for six months in the oil colour business; married on 12/11/1914 (Clifden Registrar's District, December Quarter, 1914, vol. 4, p. 79), Irene Mary, daughter of Henry A. Robinson and Annie M. Robinson, Roundstone, Co. Galway; 3rd DI 9/10/1910; captain, Royal Garrison Artillery from 16/2/1916 to 24/2/1919; pensioned 15/4/1922; died in Dublin on 8/1/1918.

Carney, Michael John; RIC 62529; LDS 2099/009; born 1887, Roscrea, Co. Tipperary; (Roscrea Registrar's District, September Quarter, 1887, vol. 3, p. 498): son of William Carney (1852–1927), RIC 38604; married on 12/12/1916, Edith Kenny, a native of Cahir, Co. Tipperary and daughter of Joseph P. Kenny, Head Constable RIC 35031 and Catherine Isabella Whetstone, daughter of John Whetstone (1816–96), Keeper of the Bridewell, Cahir; as an acting sergeant he joined the Royal Irish Regiment and was sent to France in 1917. The Regiment's first battle was fought on the Messines Ridge front and later moved to the Hindenburg Line front. After the third battle of Ypres he was sent as an instructor to the 3rd Army Musketry School near Amiens and returned home in December 1917 on leave after which he was an instructor to the School of Musketry in Dollymount Strand, Dublin in order to introduce a new system of musketry until March 1918. He returned to France where he found that the French School of Musketry had been overrun by the Germans. With a considerable amount of difficulty he rejoined his Regiment at Le Touquet and was given charge of an ammunition dump near Bayonne until he was discharged and returned to Ireland in July 1919 and rejoined the RIC; 3rd DI 5/1/1921; pensioned 22/4/1922; died in 1975 and is buried in Deansgrange Cemetery, Dublin.

Carpenter, William; LDS 2097/093; 3rd SI 1/2/1836; dismissed 8/12/1838.

Carr, Charles Andrews; RIC 24638; LDS 2097/228; born 1840, Co. Roscommon; 3rd SI 1/6/1859; pensioned 1/7/1899; died 8/2/1917; buried in Esker Cemetery, Lucan, Co. Dublin where he erected a headstone to his daughter: 'Sacred to the memory of Margaret Henrietta Carr, who died at Lucan on 5/4/1893, aged 17 years, second and fondly loved daughter of Charles A. Carr, DI, RIC, forever with the Lord.'

Carr, Frederick; LDS 2097/054; born 1798, Castlebar, Co. Mayo; baronial chief constable 1/10/1821 to 1/4/1824; wife a native of Co. Mayo; 3rd SI 10/8/1824; received an injury at

Tubbernamanagh, near Elphin on 8/9/1836; CI 1/1/1848; pensioned 7/7/1866; died 27/1/1869 at Tullamore, Co. Offaly; (Tullamore Registrar's District, 1869, vol. 2, p. 564); administration granted at Mullingar, Co. Westmeath on 15/3/1869 to Elizabeth Carr, of Tullamore, Co. Offaly, widow of the deceased – effects under £200.

Carr, Thomas Peter; RIC 13610; LDS 2097/182; born 1830; Co. Galway; 3rd SI 23/11/1849; seconded to the Commissariat Department in the Crimea on 27/8/1854 to 26/12/1855; received a favourable record on 31/12/1868 for discipline, coolness and courage during a party riot when several arrests were made; received a favourable record on 30/6/1869 for tact and unwearied exertions in the discovery of an offender who had abstracted a large sum of money from a safe; CI 29/10/1874; Commissioner of Police and Town Inspector of Constabulary, Belfast from 25/9/1885 to 15/3/1887; pensioned 15/3/1887; died 6/11/1908 at Ballyveeny Lodge, Ballycroy, Co. Mayo.

Carr, William; RIC 82080; LDS 2099/024; born 11/4/1896, Co. Limerick; (Limerick Registrar's District, 1896, June Quarter, vol. 5, p. 251); lieutenant, Royal Munster Fusiliers; 3rd SI 25/6/1921; pensioned 13/5/1922.

Carroll, Henry George L.; RIC 38312; LDS 2097/289; born 1850, Co. Dublin; BA 1872, MA 1879, Trinity College Dublin; 3rd SI 18/4/1872; pensioned 20/2/1888.

Carroll, Joseph; CarNB; 3rd SI 1829; died 13/1/1831; C.C. Carlow, Co. Carlow; Kingscourt, Co. Cavan; Nobber, Co. Meath.

Carroll, Joseph J.T.; RIC 64531; LDS 2098/242; born 28/6/1885, Co. Dublin; (Dublin South Registrar's District, September Quarter, 1885, vol. 2, p. 565); BA, Royal University of Ireland; married on 5/1/1922, Miss Ethel Edith Koe; 3rd DI 23/12/1908; captain, 6th Battalion Royal Dublin Fusiliers from 22/11/1914 to 24/9/1918; twice wounded; attached to Crime Special Department from 24/9/1918 to 1/5/1920; on 1/2/1921 he was awarded a 1st class favourable record for good duty in connection with an ambush at Ballyrichard, near Midleton, Co. Cork on 29/12/1920; TCI 24/11/1920; pensioned 8/5/1922.

Carroll, Patrick; LDS 2097/028; born 1785, Co. Limerick; baronial chief constable from 1810 to 1815; constable PPF 15/5/1815; widower on appointment; 3rd SI 1/1/1822; pensioned 15/12/1851; died in 1855.

Carroll, Richard; RIC 24; LDS 2097/182; born 1803, Co. Kildare; enlisted as a sub constable on 13/6/1821; injured his left leg when in the mounted force as a result of falling from a horse in October 1821; married in November 1826; wife a native of King's County; 3rd SI 16/11/1849; pensioned 1/10/1853; died 13/2/1875 at Ardee, Co. Louth; (Ardee Registrar's District, 1875, vol. 7, p. 288).

Carter, Herbert Cyril; RIC 76833; LDS 2098/184B; born 1894, Dewsbury, Lancs., England; (Dewsbury Registrar's District, 1894, June Quarter, vol. 9b, p. 643); 3rd DI 16/10/1920.

Carter, John Colles; RIC 38846; LDS 2097/290; born 1850, Queen's County; 3rd SI 1/10/1872; CI 16/1/1897; King Edward VII Visit to Ireland Medal, 1903; pensioned 15/8/1912; (photo in the *Constabulary Gazette*, vol. XIII, no. 15, 4/7/1903).

Carter, Peter D.; LDS 2097/134; born 1816, Co. Carlow; 3rd SI 22/12/1840; dismissed 12/6/1847.

Carter, Samson; CarNB; PPF; born 1777, Co. Cork; son of Samson Carter, of Brunswick Street, Dublin and Maria Swan, daughter of Major William Swan, JP, Co. Dublin (who assisted in the capture of Lord Edward Fitzgerald); who were married on 31/10/1771 (Hoey's Dublin Mercury); major; chief magistrate 12/2/1820 in the proclaimed barony of Ennishowen and based at Seaview, Carndonagh, Co. Donegal; in Doneraile, Co. Cork in 1822 in the proclaimed baronies of Duhallow, Orrery and Kilmore, Fermoy, Condons and Clongibbon; in Kilmacthomas, Co. Waterford in 1826–7; married on 25 May 1830, by Rev. J.M. Poole at Cashel Cathedral, Co. Tipperary, Elizabeth Mary, third daughter of Richard Creaghe Esq., of Castle Park, Golden, Co. Tipperary, Deputy Lieutenant for Co. Tipperary; stipendiary magistrate 1826 in Co. Tipperary, based in Cashel; appointed a JP in 1828 for King's and Queen's Counties; in Ballybay, Co. Monaghan in 1829; in Borrisokane, Co. Tipperary in November 1829; in Castlebar, Co. Mayo in January 1831; in January 1833 his second son, Samson Carter junior (1804–60), civil engineer and surveyor, married Mary, second daughter of Rev Henry Pasley, Rector of Ballyhane, Co. Mayo in Turlough Church and resided afterwards at Castleview, Co. Kilkenny; an attempt to assassinate Major Carter was reported in the *Limerick Evening Post* and *Clare Sentinel* on 27/5/1831: 'On Tuesday at noon, Major Carter of Thurles, Chief Magistrate of Police, was walking with his lady in his own lawn about 200 yards from the house, a ruffian rushed upon him from behind a thicket, and discharged a musket at him, a ball from which wounded him in the side. Our account states, that the Major is out of danger, and adds that were it not for the presence of mind of Mrs Carter, whose screams brought out the servants and others, both could have fallen under the hands of this lawless ruffian'; resident magistrate 1/10/1836; pensioned 1/12/1839; died 3/2/1854 at Barneen, Rathmines Upper, Co. Dublin; buried in Mount Jerome Cemetery, Dublin on 6/2/1854,(Registry No. 104) (Section C, Grave No. 91, Grant No. 859P), with his sons William Bellingham Carter (d.1/4/1891, aged 59 years) and Samson Carter, Jnr. (d.1/12/1860, aged 56 years).

Carter, Samuel R.; RIC 33105; LDS 2097/263; born 1846, Co. Dublin; 3rd SI 22/7/1867; King Edward VII Visit to Ireland Medal, 1903; pensioned 1/9/1907.

Cary, Annesley; CarNB; PPF; died 18/10/1826; C.C. barony of East Idrone and St Mullins, Co. Carlow.

Cary, Deering; LDS 2097/053; born 1792, King's County; father of Henry George Cary, CI, RIC; ensign, lieutenant and captain, 44th Regiment of Foot (East Essex Regiment), from February 1810 to July 1817; married at Portarlington, 20/7/1818 to Laetitia_____; 3rd SI 10/8/1824; severely wounded while suppressing a riot in Kilrush, Co. Clare in 1827; pensioned 1/12/1840; died 1853; (WO 25/732 fol. 73); (WO 25/3239 fol. 40).

Cary, Edward George; RIC 50166; LDS 2097/321; born 1861, Co. Galway; son of Henry George Cary, CI, RIC; 3rd DI 12/10/1882; King Edward VII Visit to Ireland Medal, 1903; detective director at Belfast, 1/4/1905; CI 29/5/1905; King George V Coronation Medal, 1911; pensioned 16/6/1920.

Cary, Henry George; RIC 16853; LDS 2097/197; born 1835, Co. Mayo; son of Captain Deering Cary, 44th Regiment of Foot (East Essex Regiment), SI, RIC; father of Edward Cary, CI, RIC; married on 4/3/1856, at St George's Church, Dublin (Dublin North Registrar's District, vol. 5, p. 60), Caroline Jane, fourth daughter of the Late Rev. John Low, Rector of Dunshaughlin, Co. Meath (*Cork Examiner* 7/3/1856); son born on 14/12/1856 at Trim, Co. Meath (*Cork Examiner* 17/12/1856); 3rd SI 1/6/1853; received a favourable record on 31/12/1871 for prompt and effective arrangements and personal activity resulting in the recapture of an escaped convict; received a favourable record on 30/6/1872 for activity and intelligence in bringing to justice a notorious and systematic swindler; CI 1/10/1876; pensioned 1/12/1894; died 26/3/1897 at 6, Martello Terrace, Dun Laoghaire, Co. Dublin (Rathdown Registrar's District, 1897, March Quarter, vol. 2, p. 911); will proved on 12/5/1897 at the Principal Registry by the oath of John Low, of Eastwood, Dundrum, Co. Dublin and George Sydney Cary, of Laurel Lodge, Terenure, Co. Dublin – effects £2,785.16s.11d.; buried in Deansgrange Cemetery, Dublin (South Section, Row W, Grave No. 13) on 29/3/1897 with his wife Caroline Jane (d.21/11/1916), his son Arthur D.L. Cary (d.25/3/1926) and daughter-in-law Caroline Eleanor (d.30/11/1946) aged 91, daughter of Rev. Stephen Radcliffe, rector of Lisnadill, Co. Armagh.

Cary, Henry J. Litton; RIC 48965; LDS 2097/311; born 1860, Co. Meath; 3rd SI 8/6/1881; King George V Visit to Ireland Medal, 1911; pensioned 24/11/1917.

Cary, Robert; LDS 2097/114; born 1799, Co. Wexford; baronial chief constable, from 1/3/1837 to 1/7/1837; wife a native of Co. Wexford; 3rd SI 1/7/1837; died on 11/12/1851 at Bruff, Co. Limerick after a very short illness (*Cork Examiner* 15/12/1851).

Casey, John; RIC 58289; LDS 2099/015; born 17/10/1875, Boyle, Co. Sligo; (Boyle Registrar's District, 1875, vol. 19, p. 97); married on 27/4/1908 (Dublin North Registrar's District, June Quarter, 1908, vol. 2, p. 489); 3rd DI 17/9/1921; pensioned 20/4/1922.

Cashman, James M.; LDS 2097/121; born 1814, Co. Cork; 3rd SI 19/10/1838; dismissed 1/4/1841.

Caulfield, John; LDS 2097/161; born 1828, Co. Kildare; son born on 15/12/1853 at Bruff, Co. Limerick, prematurely and only survived only a few hours (*Cork Examiner* 26/12/1853); 3rd SI 27/9/1847; received a favourable record on 31/12/1869 for untiring exertions in protecting voters against formidable mobs and arresting many of the rioters and house wreckers; resigned 27/8/1888; died 4/1/1900 at the residence of his son-in-law, Solomon Darcus, Plasnewydd, Killiney, Co. Dublin, late of Cartref, Greystones, Co. Wicklow; administration granted on 2/4/1900 at the Principal Registry to Charlotte Caulfield, widow, effects £23.10s.1d.

Cave, James Geoffrey; LDS 2098/109; born 20/2/1871, Hendley in Arden, Warks., England; (Leicester Registrar's District, 1871, June Quarter, vol. 7a, p. 221); son of Martin Cave (b.1816) Co. Mayo and Elizabeth Cave (b.1840, Wilmcote, Warwickshire; clerk in an auctioneers office with W.C.B. Cave, Birmingham for 4 years; married on 17/12/1901, wife a native of Co. Galway; 3rd DI 10/11/1894; resigned 31/3/1902.

Cawley, John Wandrum: RIC 82084; ADRIC no. 578; LDS 2099/028; born 3/6/1894, The Nest, New Road, Windsor, Berks., England; (Windsor Registrar's District, 1894, September Quarter, vol. 2c, p. 416); enlisted as a private in the 4th Battalion, Royal Berkshire Regiment on 3/3/1911, Regimental No. 1541; lance corporal, 5/8/1914, acting-corporal, 5/10/1914, lance sergeant, 19/12/1914, sergeant, 2/3/1915, company quartermaster sergeant, 19/8/1916, company sergeant major, 13/9/1916; commissioned as a 2nd Lieutenant, 14/10/1916; acting captain, 30/6/1918; wounded by a bomb on 27/8/1918, Asiago, Italy; awarded the Military Cross and the Military Medal; demobilized, 30/11/1919; 3rd DI 25/6/1921; pensioned 25/4/1922; (WO 374/12952).

Chamberlain, Neville Francis Fitzgerald, Col. (Sir); LDS 2098/222; born 13/1/1856, Upton Park, Upton, Bucks., England; (Upton Registrar's District, 1856, March Quarter, vol. 3a, p. 362); the only son of Lieutenant Colonel Charles Francis Falcon Chamberlain (1826–1870), CB, 26th Regiment of the Bombay Native Indian Army, and Marian Ormsby (who married secondly, 1878, Rev. Jacques Massis, of Clermont, Ferrand, France) daughter of George H. Drury, M.C.S.; his uncle was Field Marshal Sir Neville Bowles Chamberlain, GCIE, CSI (10/1/1820–18/2/1902); he married in St Mark's Church, Bangalore, India on 1/9/1886, Mary Henrietta (1866–26/7/1936), daughter of Major-General Alexander Charles Hay, Bengal Staff Corps. They had one daughter, Nora Mary (Lady Wigram), born in India in 1887 and died 5/1/1956; she married on 5/12/1912, at Christ Church, Down Street, Mayfair, London, Colonel Sir Clive Wigram, PC, GCB, GCVO, CSI, [born on 5/7/1873, Madras (now Chennai) India, son of Herbert Wigram, Madras Civil Service; educated at Winchester College (Fellow 1938) and the Royal Military Academy, Woolwich; a first class cricketer with Marleybone Cricket Club and Europeans (India); joined the Royal Artillery, 1893; ADC to Lord Elgin Viceroy of India, 1894–5; exchanged to 18th Lancers, 1897; served in the Tirah Expedition, North West Frontier, India, 1897–8; ADC to Lord Curzon Viceroy of India, 1899–1904; served in South Africa with Kitchener's Horse Regiment (mentioned in Despatches); Assistant to the Chief of Staff during HRH the Prince of Wales' Visit to India, 1905–6; Brevet Majority, 1906; Brevet Lieutenant-Colonel, 1915; Brevet Colonel, 1919; Military Secretary to Lieutenant-General Sir Horace Smith-Dorrien at Aldershot; Assistant Private Secretary and Equerry to the King, 1910–31; Private Secretary to the King, 1931–5 and Private Secretary and Keeper of HM Privy

66

67

66 Col. Neville Chamberlain, *c*.1899 in South Africa, inventor of Snooker.   67 Fernhill Palace, Ooty, India.   68 John Roberts Jnr, 1885 Billiards Champion.

68

Purse, 1935–6; created 1st Baron Wigram, 25/6/1935; Deputy Constable and Lieutenant-Governor, Windsor Castle and Keeper of His Majesty's Archives, 1936–45; Royal Victorian Chain, 1937; Permanent Lord in Waiting and Extra Equerry to King George VI, 1936–52; Permanent Lord in Waiting and Extra Equerry to the Queen, 1952–60; died in Westminster, London, 3/9/1960]. Lord and Lady Wigram had three children: (George) Neville Clive, the 2nd Baron Wigram; Francis, Captain Grenadier Guards, killed in action, September, 1943 and Mary Amy Anne; Col. Sir Neville Chamberlain was educated abroad and Brentwood School, Essex; joined the army as a Sub Lieutenant on 9/8/1873, serving with the 11th (Devonshire) Regiment and promoted Lieutenant on 9/8/1874; Bengal Staff Corps on 25/7/1876 serving with the Central India Horse, 1876; served on the staff of Sir Frederick Sleigh Roberts (1832–1914), throughout the Afghan War, 1878–80 and present at the capture of Peiwar Peital, action at Mungiar defile, expedition into Khost Valley, battle of Charasiah, operations at and around Kabul in December, 1879; March from Khabul to Khandahar and the battle of Khandahar of 1 September (wounded). Despatches (*London Gazette*, 4/9/1879, 16/1/1880 and 4/5/1880); Medal and four clasps and the Bronze Star; ADC to Sir Frederick Sleigh Roberts, commander-in-Chief, Madras, 28/11/1881–17/8/1885; promoted Captain on 9/8/1885 and Brevet Major on 7/11/1885; Persian Interpreter to the Commander-in-Chief, India, 28/11/1885–31/12/1889; served with the Burmese Expedition, 1886–7 as DAA and QMG (Medal and clasp); Despatches (*London Gazette*, 2/9/1887). Military Secretary to the Kashmir Government and reorganized the Kashmir Army, 1890–7; promoted Major on 9/8/1894, Brevet Lieutenant-Colonel 1/7/1887, Brevet Colonel, 6/1/1894 and Colonel on 6/2/1899; Commanded the Khyber Force, 1899; Private Secretary to Field Marshal Lord Roberts in the South African War, 1899–1900; Operations in the Orange Free State, February to May 1900, including operations at Poardeberg (17th to 26th February); actions at Poplar Grove, Driefontein, Vet River (5 and 6 May) and Zand River; operations in the Transvaal in May and June, 1900, including actions near Johannesburg, Praetoria and Diamond Hill (11 and 12 June); operations in the Transvaal east of Praetoria, July, 1900 (Despatches, *London Gazette* 8/2/1901); Afghan Medal, 1878–80, with four clasps for Peiwar Kotal, Charasia, Kabul and Kandahar; Kabul to Kandahar Star, 1878–80; India General Service Medal, 1854, with one clasp for Burma, 1885–7; Queen's South Africa Medal, 1899–1902, with five clasps for the Cape Colony, Paardeberg, Driefontein, Johannesburg and Diamond Hill; inspector general 1/9/1900; CB (Military), 1900; KCB (Civil), 1903; King Edward VII Visit to Ireland Medal, 1903; KCVO (Civil), 1911; awarded in 1915 the King's Police Medal, 1909; King George V Coronation Medal, 1911; pensioned 31/7/1916; in retirement he resided at Brookville House, Raheny, Dublin and later at The Wilderness, Ascot, Berkshire where he died on 28/5/1944.

The Inventor of Snooker: Col. Sir Neville Chamberlain: In the early days of snooker, it was generally accepted that the game originated in the British Army garrisons of India as a combination of the various billiard games, particularly English billiards, which where then commonly played. Beyond this nobody laid claim to its specific origins until a debate began in the late 1930s. One thing is certain though, the game which Colonel Sir Neville Chamberlain of the Devonshire Regiment claims to have named *snooker* ('snooker' once being a derogatory term for a first-year cadet of the Royal Military Academy of Woolwich in England) in 1875, and which for many years was referred to as *snooker's pool*, bore more relation to the existing billiard games of the time than the modern game of snooker – fewer balls were used, they were positioned on different spots, had different values, and the scoring sequence and rules would be unrecognizable to a follower of today's game of snooker. Who brought about the changes which form the modern game remains a mystery, but they were generally in place by 1900. They probably evolved through a series of individuals in the Army Officers' Mess, or it is even thought the English gentleman at the club in the Ootacamund hills of India added more balls to the game – perhaps this is why Chamberlain waited over 60 years until the late 1930s before making his claim to be

69

70

69 Col. Sir Neville Chamberlain, 1900, Inspector General, RIC. 70 Mary Henrietta Lady Chamberlain and her daughter, Nora Mary. 71 Cullenswood House, Rathfarnham, Co. Dublin.

71

the originator of snooker. Here follows a letter by Compton McKenzie which appeared in the *Billiard Player* publication of April 1939. The details of the letter have become accepted as fact as to the origins of the game of snooker.

The Billiard Player: April 1939: Last year an article in *The Field* put forward the theory that the game of snooker had its origin at the Royal Military Academy (RMA), Woolwich, where officers of the Royal Artillery and the Royal Engineers receive their training as cadets. The theory was plausible, because a first-year cadet at 'The Shop', as the RMA is familiarly known, is called 'snooker,' the soubriquet being time's corruption of the original word for a newly-joined cadet, which was 'Neux.' It must be remembered that the RMA was founded as long ago as 1741. The writer of the article stated that the original rules of snooker were copied out by Lord Kitchener from those at 'The Shop,' brought by him to Ootacamund, India, and there hung up in the Club. This assertion was formally contradicted by General Sir Ian Hamilton in a letter to *The Field* of July 11, 1938. In point of fact Lord Kitchener never visited India until many years after snooker had become a popular game out there. Investigation has established that so far from snooker having originated at 'The Shop', the game was invented at Jubbulpore in the year 1875 by Colonel Sir Neville Chamberlain, who is fortunately still with us and whose memory is perfectly clear on the subject. It befell during the 'Rains' that Sir Neville, who was then a young subaltern in the Devonshire Regiment, anxious to vary the game of Black Pool which was being played every long wet afternoon on the Mess billiard table, suggested putting down another coloured ball, to which others of different values were gradually added.

One day a subaltern of the Field Battery at Jubbulpore was being entertained by the Devons, and in the course of conversation told young Chamberlain about the soubriquet 'snooker' for first year cadets at Woolwich. To quote Sir Neville's own words: 'The term was a new one to me, but I soon had an opportunity of exploiting it when one of our party failed to hole a coloured ball which was close to a corner pocket. I called out to him: "Why, you're a regular snooker!"'

'I had to explain to the company the definition of the word, and, to soothe the feelings of the culprit, I added that we were all, so to speak, snookers at the game, so it would be very appropriate to call the game snooker. The suggestion was adopted with enthusiasm and the game has been called snooker ever since.'

In 1876 Sir Neville Chamberlain left the Devons to join the Central-India Horse, taking with him the new game. A year or two later came the Afghan War, a more serious potting game in which young Chamberlain was himself potted. However, fortunately for himself and the great game which we enjoy so much today, he recovered from his wound, and when at the close of 1881 General Sir Frederick Sleigh Roberts became Commander-in-Chief of the Madras Army, the inventor of snooker served on his personal staff, and was with Roberts when every summer he moved to the hill station at Ootacamund known to all and sundry as 'Ooty'. Here came officers from big garrisons like Bangalore and Secundderabad and planters from Mysore. All of them enjoyed snooker as a speciality of the 'Ooty' Club where the rules of the game were drawn up and posted in the billiards room, but not by Lord Kitchener. During the eighties rumours of the new game in India reached England. One evening Sir Neville Chamberlain when dining in Calcutta with the Maharaja of Cooch Behar was introduced to a well-known professional billiards player whom he had engaged from England for some lessons.

This professional told the Maharaja he had been asked in England to obtain the rules of the new game snooker and the Maharaja introduced Sir Neville Chamberlain to him as the best person to give him the information he wanted because he was the inventor of it. In a letter to *The Field* of March 19, 1938, Sir Neville regretted he did not know the name of the professional but thought he was probably a contemporary of John Roberts and W. Cook. A week or two later Mr F.H. Cumberlege wrote to Sir Neville Chamberlain to say that the professional must have been John Roberts himself who came out to Calcutta in 1885. Mr Cumberlege added that he remembered showing the Maharaja the new game of snooker at Cooch Behar after a shooting party in the spring of 1884. Sir Neville Chamberlain has received from several other distinguished authorities confirmation of his claim to be the inventor of snooker: Major-General William Arthur Watson (25/9/1860–27/6/1944), CB, CMG, CIE, Honorary Colonel of the Central India Horse (his old regiment) wrote: 'I have a clear recollection of you rejoining the regiment in 1884. You brought with you a brand new game, which you called snooker or snookers. There were the black, the pink, the yellow and the green. We all understood it was your own invention. We took to it very keenly.' Major-General Sir John Hanbury Williams (19/10/1859–19/10/1946), GCVO, KCB, KCVO, CMG, CVO (Colonel of the 43rd Oxfordshire and Buckinghamshire Light Infantry) wrote: 'I was always under the impression that you introduced the game of snooker to the 43rd in 1884–85. Certainly the 43rd never played snooker till you came and introduced it to us. Hope you will stick to the honour of its invention.' Field Marshal William Riddell Birdwood, 1st Baron Birdwood (13/9/1865–17/5/1951), GCB, KCB, CB, GCSI, KCSI, GCMG, KCMG, GCVO, CIE, DSO, MA, LLD, Hon. Litt., LLD wrote: 'I remember well you introducing the game of snookers into the 12th Lancers' Mess, when I was a subaltern in the Regiment at Bangalore in '85.' Sir Walter (Roper) Lawrence, 1st Bt. (9/2/1857–25/5/1940), GCVO, GCIE, KCIE, CB, CIE, Under-Secretary to the Punjab Government, 1884–86 and to the Government of India, 1887–9 wrote: 'When we first met in Simla in 1886, when you were with Lord Roberts, the Commander-in-Chief, and afterwards when we served together in Kashmir, I always looked upon you as the inventor of snooker, and I know that this idea was common to many of my friends. Quite recently, last year (1937) I was telling some of my friends in England who were discussing snooker, that I had the honour of knowing very intimately the inventor of the game.' The testimony of these and other highly distinguished officers finally disposes of the theory advanced with some emphasis by the writer in *The Field* that the game of snooker originated at the Royal Military Academy, Woolwich, and it has been a privilege for me to assemble in print such incontrovertible evidence. There is nothing to add except that all the many thousands of snooker players the world over will wish Colonel Sir Neville Chamberlain, who is now in his 84th year, many another year to enjoy the honour of being the inventor of a game, now 63 years old, which has added so much to the gaiety of nations. – Compton McKenzie. (1938).

Chambers, William; LDS 2097/314 born 1859, Co. Armagh; 3rd DI 29/12/1881; resigned 23/11/1896 at Castlebar, Co. Mayo.

Channer, John William; LDS 2097/147; born 1816, Co. Dublin; wife a native of Co. Clare; son born on 10/9/1852 at Adare, Co. Limerick (*Cork Examiner* 13/9/1852); 3rd SI 8/1/1845; died 20/4/1867 at half-past three o'clock, on Saturday, at his residence, William Street, Limerick, aged 50 years (*Cork Examiner* 29/4/1867); (Limerick Registrar's District, 1867, vol. 10, p. 327).

Channer, William; LDS 2097/050; born 1787, Herefs., England; troop sergeant major, 19th and 23rd Lancers from 1/4/1805 to 31/8/1821; enlisted as a constable 11/9/1821; 3rd SI 1/3/1824; on 14/10/1829 he reported of Ballinasloe constabulary barracks, Co. Galway 'through carelessness of the mess woman (who is a sister to one of the men) in neglecting to extinguish a candle between 9pm and 10pm'; residing at 3 Frances Street, Kilrush, Co. Clare in 1846 (Slater's Directory, 1846); pensioned 14/2/1851; died 2/2/1863 at 5 Home Terrace, Haddington Road, Dublin, formerly of 81 Glanmire Road, in the Parish of Shandon, City of Cork; will proved at the Principal Registry on 14/3/1863, by the oaths of Fanny and Elizabeth Channer, both of Home Terrace, aforesaid spinsters and executrixes – effects under £400.

Chatterton, Sinclair Dickson Smith; RIC 44147; LDS 2097/298; born 1853, Mount Olive, Raheny, Co. Dublin; BA, Trinity College, Oxford, 1877; 3rd SI 1/1/1879; CI 1/7/1899; King Edward VII Visit to Ireland Medal, 1903; King George V Coronation Medal, 1911; pensioned 10/12/1913; died 13/3/1914 at Innisfail, Dundalk, Co. Louth; will proved on 30/4/1914 at the Principal Registry to Eleanor A.A. Chatterton, spinster, effects £10,643.11s.4d.; buried on 16/3/1914; (photo in the *Constabulary Gazette*, vol. XVI, no. 14, 24/12/1904).

72   73

72 Col. Sir Neville Chamberlain, *c.*1905.   73 Col. Sir Neville Chamberlain, 1916.   74 Medal awards and decorations, Col. Sir Neville Chamberlain.

74

Cheesman, Charles; RIC 61139; LDS 2098/195; born 1879, Peckham, Surrey, England; son of Ernest Cheesman (b.1843), Peckham Surrey and Anne Cheesman (b.1856), Houghton, Hampshire; married on 9/1/1908, wife a native of Oxford; 3rd DI 5/6/1903; King Edward VII Visit to Ireland Medal, 1903; King George V Visit to Ireland Medal, 1911; attached to Crime Special Branch from 17/8/1917 to 18/6/1918; TCI 20/8/1920; CI 1/10/1920; awarded the King's Police Medal 1921; pensioned 8/5/1922; (photo in the *Constabulary Gazette*, vol. XXX, no. 14, 16/12/1911, p. 231 & vol. XXXIII, no. 23, 16/8/1913).

Church, Edward; RIC 14407; LDS, 2097/185; born 1828, Co. Leitrim; 3rd SI 7/10/1850; discharged on a gratuity 26/1/1865; died in 1865 in Dublin; (Dublin North Registrar's District, 1865, vol. 12, p. 347); buried in Mount Jerome Cemetery, Dublin with his wife, Mary and daughters, Florence Mary (d.17/12/1937, aged 74 years) and Adelaide Frances (d.31/1/1940, aged 79 years).

Clancie, Thomas William; LDS 2097/040; born 1791, Co. Clare; 3rd SI 27/3/1823; CI 1/10/1836; pensioned 11/4/1859 in Queen's County; died 28/11/1868 at Portrane, Queen's County (*Cork Examiner* 12/12/1868); will proved on 15/12/1868 at Kilkenny by the oath of Michael Kelly, of Portsmouth, Hants., England, Surveyor of Taxes, the sole executor – effects under £2,000.

Clark, Arthur Gordon Lyon; RIC 82093; ADRIC no. 975; LDS 2099/037; born 1/3/1886 and baptized at St Michael's Church, Samambagh, India, 9/5/1886 by J.H. Beck, Planter's Chaplain; son of William Lyon Clark (Tea Planter) and Ada Constance Sophia, Semambagh Tea Estate, Syllub, India; educated at the Oratory School, Birmingham, 1898–1904 and Cedar Court, Rockhampton from August 1904 to July 1905; married on 20/8/1913, wife from Somerset; Royal Military College, September 1905 to June 1906; 2nd Lieutenant, King's Own Yorkshire Light Infantry, 29/8/1906–1/6/1909; 2nd Lieutenant South African Field Artillery, 1/9/1915; captain, 4B Reserve Battery, Royal Field Artillery, 1/11/1915; fluent in French and Hindustani; awarded the French Croix de Guerre (*London Gazette* dated 31/8/1916); completed army service on 14/10/1920; 'H' Company ADRIC in Tralee, 1920 to 25/8/1921; 3rd DI 20/9/1921; pensioned 15/4/1922; (WO 339/6572).

Clarke, John; LDS 2097/058; born 1800, Co. Galway; father of Thomas H. Clarke, SI, RIC; 3rd SI 1/1/1825; C.C. Ballymena, Co. Antrim, 1831; pensioned 1/6/1865; (WO 339/6572).

Clarke, Patrick; RIC 54946; LDS 2098/184B; born 14/3/1871, Co. Meath; married on 5/7/1898 (Wexford Registrar's District, September Quarter, 1898, vol. 4, p. 389), wife a native of Co. Wexford; 3rd SI 16/10/1920; pensioned 15/4/1922.

Clarke, Philip; RIC 6970; LDS 2097/272; born 1826, Co. Louth; 3rd SI 16/9/1868; received a favourable record on 30/6/1872 for detection under very peculiar circumstances of persons implicated in dictating, writing and sending two threatening letters; died 9/3/1884 at Carrick-on-Shannon, Co. Leitrim, formerly of Glenties, Co. Donegal; will with one codicil proved on 8/4/1884 at the Principal Registry by the oath of Michael Clarke, Head Constable and Peter McKenna, Constable, Carrick-on-Shannon, Co. Leitrim, the executors – effects £1,354.15s.11d.

Clarke, Richard W.; LDS 2097/121; born 1812, Co. Dublin; PPF; PPF Clerk 1/7/1834; clerk in the Constabulary Office from 1837 to 1/11/1838; wife a native of Co. Galway; 3rd SI 1/11/1838; pensioned 1/7/1856 in Co. Down; died 21/2/1859.

Clarke, Thomas H.; LDS 2097/146; born 1826, Co. Antrim; eldest son of John Clarke, SI, RIC; his health was impaired with a wetting in October 1848; 3rd SI 5/7/1844; died of consumption on 9/6/1852 at Arthurstown, Co. Wexford (*Cork Examiner* 16/6/1852).

Clarke, William; RIC 72020; LDS 2098/159B; born 2/8/1892, Co. Armagh; lieutenant, Royal Irish Rifles; 3rd DI 10/1/1920; killed 20/1/1921 Glenwood, Co. Clare.

Clarke, Wogan; CarNB; died in Castlemartyr, Co. Cork 'on Saturday morning 6/1/1827 after a painful illness, Wogan Clarke Esq. chief constable and paymaster of the police in the east riding of this county (Cork)'; C.C. Castlemartyr, Co. Cork.

Clayton, Edward Myles; RIC 52875; LDS 2098/036; born 1863, Co. Kildare; clerk to Messr's Carnegie and Co., 40 Dame Street, Dublin for four years; married firstly on 1/6/1892 (Dublin South Registrar's District, June Quarter, 1892, vol. 2, p. 539); married secondly on 22/4/1896; 3rd DI 1/5/1888; King Edward VII Visit to Ireland Medal, 1903; CI 6/8/1910; awarded a certificate from the Irish Police and Constabulary Recognition Fund; AIG 15/4/1920; divisional commissioner for Munster No. 2 Division, 11/3/1920–14/4/1920; pensioned 31/8/1922.

Clements, James; LDS 2097/088; born 1785, King's County; enlisted as a constable on 1/4/1822; 3rd SI 18/3/1835; died 5/12/1839 and buried in the Church of Ireland Cemetery, Limerick; he and his wife Elizabeth had three children baptized in Limerick churches, Anne on 17/10/1829, Elizabeth on 2/8/1831 and James on 6/10/1835; his daughter, Matilda married Hugh Persse Joynt of Limerick on 29/6/1840 at St John's Church, Limerick and she died in February 1900 at Sheen Lodge, Limerick.

Clerkin, John; RIC 39595; LDS 2098/157; born 1853, Co. Monaghan; 3rd DI 1/7/1899; King Edward VII Visit to Ireland Medal, 1903; pensioned 17/3/1907.

Clifford, Stephen; RIC 56129; LDS 2098/185B; born 6/2/1874, Killarney, Co. Kerry; (Killarney Registrar's District, 1874, vol. 5, p. 379); married on 2/5/1905 (Cork Registrar's District, June Quarter, 1905, vol. 5, p. 94), wife a native of Co. Cork; 3rd DI 16/10/1920; pensioned 8/5/1922.

Clinch, Bernard; LDS 2097/116; born 1805, Dublin City; 3rd SI 6/9/1837; died 11/3/1842.

Clune, Martin; LDS 2097/106; born 1808, Co. Clare; wife a native of Co. Galway; his only daughter, Louisa Josephine, married on 3/3/1866 (Dunmanway Registrar's District, vol. 5, p. 311), by special License, at the residence of the bride at Dunmanway, Co. Cork, by the Rev. John Walsh, brother of the bridegroom, assisted by the Rev. John Hurley, P.P., Rev. Denis O'Donoghue, P.P., Enniskeane and Rev. James O'Keeffe, Dunmanway, Dr David John Walsh, B.A, Staff Assistant Surgeon, Her Majesty's Indian Army (Bengal), son of David Walsh, Esq., Ballincollig, Co. Cork – after dejeuner the happy pair left for Dublin en route for Calcutta (*Cork Examiner* 8/3/1866); 3rd SI 16/11/1836; pensioned 20/12/1866; died 19/6/1873 at Dublin; (Dublin South Registrar's District, 1873, vol. 7, p. 637).

Coburn, John; LDS 2097/074; born 1803, Co. Leitrim; PPF; enlisted as a sub constable, 17/10/1823; wife a native of Co. Dublin; 3rd SI 13/4/1832; died 1/5/1851.

Coe, John; 3rd SI 1/6/1848 in Sligo; pensioned in 1857; died on 14/5/1857 in Sligo.

Coffey, Edward Patrick; LDS 2097/210; born 1837, Co. Galway; 3rd SI 15/2/1857; dismissed 3/7/1875 by order of the Lord Lieutenant on the recommendation of the inspector general.

Coffey, William; LDS 2097/067; born 1789, King's County; PPF; enlisted as a sub constable, 1/5/1816; married Louisa Lucy Davies, sister of James Davies, CI, RIC and they had three children, Georgina who married Patrick Teaffy, William Thomas, born in Galway City in 1833, who married Jane Anderson in 1864 and died in Liverpool in 1903 and Alfred; 3rd SI 30/11/1828, CI 15/12/1851; died 20/6/1858 in Dublin.

Coghlen, William Francis; LDS 2097/043; born 1794, Co. Mayo; 3rd SI 25/8/1823; pensioned 31/8/1847; died in June 1857.

Colbert, John; RIC 54039; LDS 2098/148B; born 1868, Youghal, Co. Cork; (Youghal Registrar's District, 1868, vol. 4, p. 1065); married on 29/10/1896, wife a native of Co. Tipperary; 3rd DI 20/9/1920; pensioned 17/7/1922.

Colclough, Henry; CarNB; born *c*.1784, Mount Sion, Co. Carlow; son of Henry Colclough (d.1836), High Sheriff,1803 and Anne (m.1783), daughter of Alexander Crawford of Millwood, Co. Fermanagh and brother of McCartney Colclough (1794–1860); lieutenant, 30th Regiment of Foot (Cambridgeshire Regiment); died 28/7/1830; C.C. Glenarm, Co. Antrim; Newtownbellew, Co. Galway

Colclough, McCarty; LDS 2097/051; born 1794, Mount Sion, Co. Carlow, son of Henry Colclough (d.1836), High Sheriff, 1803 and Anne (m.1783), daughter of Alexander Crawford of

Millwood, Co. Fermanagh and brother of Henry Colclough; ensign in the Carlow Militia from 1810 to 1811 (WO 13/2627–46); ensign and lieutenant, 62nd Regiment of Foot (Wiltshire Regiment) from April 1811 to August 1817; married in 1819, Margaret (d.1851), daughter of James Cooke, of Kilkenny; widower on appointment; 3rd SI 1/7/1824; C.C. Enniskillen, Co. Fermanagh, 1831; CI 3/10/1846; died 21/12/1860 at Wexford, Co. Wexford; will and one codicil proved at Waterford by the oath of Beauchamp Colclough, now of Glasgow in Scotland and Edward Hill of Bandon in the County of Cork, inspectors of constabulary, the executors – effects under £9,000.

Cole, Bertram Eric; RIC 72023; LDS 2098/160B; born 11/1/1897, Wilts., England; (Melksham Registrar's District, 1897, vol. 51, p. 108); lieutenant, Wiltshire Regiment; 3rd DI 10/1/1920; permitted to resign on 14/3/1922.

Cole, James Joseph; RIC 62060; LDS 2098/251B; born 1887, Co. Roscommon; (Roscommon Registrar's District, September Quarter, 1887, vol. 3, p. 274); brother of Thomas Edward Cole, DI, RIC; 3rd DI 4/1/1921; pensioned 17/7/1922.

Cole, John Willabey Sneed; LDS 2097/138; born 1815, Co. Dublin; wife a native of Co. Derry; 3rd SI 21/2/1842; received a approbation on 31/12/1848 for eliciting the unqualified approbation of the Mayor and the local authorities of Derry, by his unremitting and humane exertions in rendering assistance to the survivors of the catastrophe on board the steamer 'Londonderry', as well as identifying the dead, securing their money and other property and finally assisting in their interment; pensioned 16/6/1862; died 17/10/1870 at Dublin; (Dublin North Registrar's District, 1870, vol. 17, p. 536).

Cole, Thomas Edward; RIC 57098; LDS 2098/086B; born 24/2/1877, Co. Roscommon; (Roscommon Registrar's District, 1877, vol. 4, p. 184); brother of James Joseph Cole, DI, RIC; married on 8/8/1910 (Dublin North Registrar's District, September Quarter, 1910, vol. 2, p. 497), wife a native of Co. Longford; 3rd DI 1/2/1918; pensioned 17/7/1922.

Colegrave, John Manby; LDS 2097/104; born 1811, Africa; cornet and lieutenant to 8/1/1836; 3rd SI 1/11/1836; CI 21/5/1858; appointed a resident magistrate on 1/3/1860 but the appointed was immediately cancelled at his own request; 'proceeded to England, having obtained three weeks leave of absence' (*Cork Examiner* 19/2/1862); AIG 11/2/1869; died 17/1/1880.

Coleman, James; LDS 2097/178; born 1816, Co. Meath; 3rd SI 1/5/1849; paymaster 1/5/1849 for Co. Armagh and Co. Louth; discharged on a gratuity 31/5/1851 on the abolition of the office of paymaster.

Coleman, John; RIC 28343; LDS 2098/073; born 1845, Co. Kildare; 3rd SI 25/3/1891; died 24/6/1901 at Rossmult Cottage, Ballycahill, Thurles, Co. Tipperary; will proved on 15/7/1901 by the oath of John H. Coleman, railway clerk – effects £492.10s.od.; his wife, Mary Teresa (b.1854), predeceased him at New Line House, Portumna, Co. Galway on 13/4/1895 (Portumna Registrar's District, 1895, June Quarter, vol. 4, p. 259).

Coleman, Peter; LDS 2097/137; born 1809, Louth, Co. Louth; 3rd SI 1/8/1841; paymaster 1/8/1841 for Counties Kerry and Limerick; discharged on pension on the abolition of the office of paymaster on 31/5/1851; died 6/11/1895 at Ashville, Dunleer, Co. Louth (Ardee Registrar's District, 1895, December Quarter, vol. 2, p. 247); buried in Louth Cemetery on 9/11/1895.

Coleridge, Francis Randolph Cyril; RIC 37556; LDS 2097/285; born 1852, Devon, England; (Honiton Registrar's District, 1852, March Quarter, vol. 5b, p. 27); 3rd SI 28/4/1871; musketry instructor from 1/4/1887 to 18/1/1892 when he resigned on his appointment as Chief Constable of the Devonshire County Constabulary to 31/3/1907.

Colgan, Matthew; CarNB; born King's County; lieutenant; his wife Mary complained on 18/2/1829 that he was not paying the agreed sum for her maintenance; C.C. Glenties, Co. Donegal and Cootehill, Co. Cavan, 1830.

Collins, Charles; RIC 52135; LDS 2098/236; born 25/6/1865, Ardee, Co. Louth; (Ardee Registrar's District, 1865, vol. 12, p. 399); school teacher in Co. Louth for one year; married on 8/1/1919 (Granard Registrar's District, March Quarter, 1919, vol. 3, P. 135), Jane E. Brabazon, a native of Co. Longford; 3rd DI 10/5/1905; pensioned 1/8/1920.

Colomb, Wellington; RIC 15375; LDS 2097/189; born 1827, England; 3rd SI 12/12/1849; Adjutant, Phoenix Park Depot from 15/5/1872 to 15/10/1875; CI 15/10/1875; AIG 16/10/1877; pensioned 10/9/1891; died 7/5/1895 at Kirkcudbright, Scotland; administration granted on 5/6/1895 at Kirkcudbright and resealed in Dublin on 11/6/1895 – effects in Ireland £21.16s.4d.

Colthurst, William; CarNB; born 1797; 3rd SI 1824; his father who was rector of Desertmartin, Co. Derry died March 1827; stipendiary magistrate 25/5/1831; C.C. Lurgan and Armagh, Co. Armagh and Tulla, Co. Clare.

Comerford, Francis; RIC 44569; LDS 2098/229; born 9/6/1861, Urlingford, Co. Kilkenny; national schoolteacher for four years; married on 17/8/1892 (Tralee Registrar's District, September Quarter, 1892, vol. 5, p. 302), Mary Browne a native of Tralee, Co. Kerry; 3rd DI 27/4/1908; pensioned 15/6/1920; (photo in the *Constabulary Gazette*, vol. XXV, no. 5, 17/4/1909, p. 618).

Comyns, George Devonport; LDS 2097/095; born 1809, Co. Galway; wife a native of Co. Cork; 3rd SI 23/2/1836; paymaster, 20/10/1856; pensioned 9/8/1852.

Concannon, John; RIC 29750; LDS 2098/035; born 1845, Co. Mayo; 3rd DI 10/8/1887; Detective Director from 3/4/1895; died 16/1/1902 at Delvin Co. Westmeath; (Delvin Registrar's District, 1902, March Quarter, vol. 3, p. 103); buried at Templetuohy, Co. Tipperary on 17/1/1902; (photo in the *Constabulary Gazette*, vol. VI, no. 13, 23/12/1899 & vol. XI, no. 4, 19/4/1902).

Condon, David Daniel; LDS 2097/171; born 1791, Co. Cork; PPF; enlisted as a sub constable in May 1823 and left the Peace Preservation Force in Co. Cork in 1826 when the entire Force was discharged; re-enlisted in the Constabulary as a sub constable on 1/1/1830; his daughter, Sarah Carrick, died on 27/10/1861, at Clashmore, Co. Waterford (*Cork Examiner* 31/10/1861): 3rd SI 1/6/1848; pensioned 1/3/1859 in Co. Tipperary; died 2/4/1870 at Killarney, Co. Kerry; (Killarney Registrar's District, 1870, vol. 10, p. 237).

Congreve, William Walter; LDS 2097/103; born 5/4/1804, Congreve, Aldermaston, Staffordshire, and of Burton Hall, Ches., England; son of Richard Congreve (2/8/1778–22/11/1857) and Mary Ann (d.5/8/1820) daughter of George Birch, of Hamstead Hall, Staffordshire who were married on 8/12/1801; educated at Westminster and B.N.C. Oxford; cornet, lieutenant and captain, 3rd Light Dragoons from May 1825 to October 1836; married 29/4/1830, Anna Selina (d.26/3/1859), second daughter of Rev. Henry Lambart Bayly of Ballyarthur, Co. Wicklow; his son, Captain William Congreve, born 5/3/1831 was Chief Constable of Staffordshire County Constabulary from 2 July 1866 to 1888; 3rd SI 24/10/1836; paymaster 24/10/1836; pensioned 1/1/1852; died 20/11/1864.

Conlin, Bernard; RIC 45368; LDS 2098/167; born 3/9/1861, Arvagh, Co. Cavan; father of John Francis Conlin, DI, RIC and Thomas William Conlin, DI, RIC; married on 28/10/1891 (Cookstown Registrar's District, December Quarter, 1891, vol. 1, p. 671), Minnie Bradley, a native of Belfast; his son Joseph Patrick was a doctor as was a daughter, Claire and director of the Blood Transfusion Service for Northern Ireland; her twin brother Arthur was also a doctor; a son Geoffrey worked in the bank in Tipperary and the second eldest son, Bernard Francis Conlin, a brilliant mathematician at Trinity College Dublin and a 2nd Lieutenant in the 28th Brigade, Royal Field Artillery was killed at the Battle of the Somme on 9/10/1916 and is buried in Hilly Station Cemetery, Mericourt-L'Abbee, Somme, Grave III.A.28; 3rd DI 1/2/1900; King Edward VII Visit to Ireland Medal, 1903; pensioned 15/6/1920; died 14/4/1934 at Glenaboy, 156, Botanic Road, Glasnevin, Dublin; buried in Glasnevin Cemetery on 17/4/1934, Dublin (Grave

75

75 Patrick Clarke.   76 Francis Comerford and family.   77 John Concannon.

76   77

KF 225.5); Bernard Conlin had a brother, Thomas Henry Conlin who perished in the sinking of the RMS *Titanic* on 14/4/1912. He boarded at Queenstown, Co. Cork as a third class passenger, ticket number 21332, having paid the fare of £7.14s.8d. and his destination was North Fairhill Street, Philadelphia. He was returning to America after a brief visit home to Arvagh, Co. Cavan. He had first emigrated from Ireland in the 1880s. Described as a general labourer in the embarkation records, he was travelling back to his sister Rosa in Philadelphia, where another sister, Annie also lived. The *Irish World*, published in New York on May 11, 1912 contained this assessment of him: Thomas Conlin, Jnr., thirty years old, of 2238 North Fairhill Street, this city is counted among the victims of the *Titanic* disaster. He was seen on the ill-fated boat by survivors who knew him and was not among those rescued by the *Carpathia*. He was born in Ireland, came to this country when very young and attended the St Edward's School. He was a member of the parish total abstinence society, the BVM Sodality and the Holy Name Society. He was an agent for a machine company and had gone to Ireland to visit his old home. Those aboard the *Carpathia* who knew Tom Conlin were the Murphy sisters, Kate and Margaret, and it is recounted that Conlin took off his coat and threw it to these girls as they were about to descend in a lifeboat dressed only in their nightclothes. He knew he would not need it. It appears that Tom and the Murphy girls were cousins. One story around Cornmore, Co. Cavan claims that Thomas Conlin was engaged to an American woman named Lena Keyes, who later moved to Dobbs Ferry in New York, where she worked as a housekeeper and died in her nineties.

Conlin, John Francis; RIC 69944; LDS 2098/100B; born 30/10/1895, Co. Derry; son of Bernard Conlin, DI, RIC and brother of Thomas William Conlin, DI, RIC; John Francis Conlin was commissioned as a 2nd lieutenant, Royal Field Artillery, 9/10/1914, lieutenant, 2/5/1916, captain, 18/9/1917, acting major, 15/10/1917, relinquished acting rank of major, 20/10/1917; mentioned in despatches (*London Gazette* dated 30/5/1918); released from army service, 13/1/1919 and retained the rank of captain; awarded the Military Cross (*London Gazette* dated 3/6/1919); 3rd DI 4/1/1920; pensioned 31/8/1922; assistant commissioner Indian Police Service, Port Blair, Adam & Nicobar Islands in 1930; superintendent of District Police, Ajmer-Merwara, Ajmer, India in 1938; (WO 339/25259).

Conlin, Thomas William; RIC 72970; ADRIC no. 425; LDS 2099/039; born 1899, Scarriff, Co. Clare; (Scarriff Registrar's District, 1899, vol. 4, p. 333); son of Bernard Francis Conlin, DI, RIC and brother of John Francis Conlin; lieutenant, Royal Field Artillery; ADRIC, September 1920 to 25 August 1921; married Elizabeth (Betty) Spears at Haddington Road Church on 24/7/1935; 3rd DI 20/9/1921; pensioned 2/5/1922; qualified as a doctor and practised in Leeds until his death on 9/10/1969, having served as a Medical Officer with the Royal Army Medical Corps in India in WW2.

Connaughton, John; RIC 18575; LDS 2097/324; born 1835, Cashel, Co. Longford; wife a native of Co. Donegal; 3rd DI 18/10/1882; pensioned 1/8/1896; died 10/1/1918 at Ballyshannon, Co. Donegal; (Ballyshannon Registrar's District, 1918, vol. 2, p. 3).

Connolly, John; RIC 47789; LDS 2098/091B; born 4/5/1877, Co. Galway; (Tuam Registrar's District, 1877, vol. 14, p. 538); married on 27/12/1906 (Londonderry Registrar's District, March Quarter, 1906, vol. 2, p. 591), wife a native of Co. Derry; 3rd DI 7/9/1919; pensioned 17/4/1922.

Connor, Daniel; RIC 27724; LDS 2097/235; born 1814, Co. Tipperary; 3rd SI 1/5/1860; pensioned 1/7/1878; died 12/4/1890 at Waverly, Blackrock, Co. Cork; will proved on 13/5/1890 at Cork by the oath of John Sheehan, of Ashburton Hill, Cork, Gent., and James Walsh of Clonaniclon, Thurles, Co. Tipperary, farmers, the executors – effects £2,162.

Connor, Henry; RIC 58526; LDS 2098/069B; born 31/4/1879, Co. Meath; (Trim Registrar's District, June Quarter, 1879, vol. 2, p. 1061); married on 31/1/1906 (Dublin South Registrar's District, March Quarter, 1906, vol. 2, p. 580), wife a native of Co. Dublin; 3rd DI 6/2/1916;

awarded the King's Police Medal 1922; pensioned 31/5/1922; transferred to the Royal Ulster Constabulary on 1/6/1922.

Conran, Edward J.; RIC 51607; LDS 2098/214; born 15/9/1863, Co. Cork; married in July 1900, wife a native of Co. Clare; 3rd DI 16/5/1906; pensioned 31/5/1922; transferred to the Royal Ulster Constabulary on 1/6/1922.

Considine, Heffernan Fritz James Joseph John (Sir); LDS 2098/172; born 24/10/1846, Co. Limerick; eldest son of Heffernan Considine (1816–1885), JP and DL of Derk, Pallasgreen, Co. Limerick and Mary, daughter of John MacMahon, JP of Firgrove, Co. Clare; his sister Mary married Lieutenant Colonel William MacCarthy-O'Leary (2/1/1849–27/2/1900), DL, Coomlegane, Millstreet, Co. Cork, an officer of the South Lancashire Regiment, who was killed in action on 27/2/1900 while in command of the 1st Battalion of his regiment leading a sabre attack of Pieter's Hill, Natal, during the South African War; Mary's son was Brigadier Heffernan William Denis MacCarthy-O'Leary (2/8/1885–23/2/1948), DSO, MC; Heffernan F.J.J.J. Considine married on 8/1/1880 (Enniscorthy Registrar's District, 1880, March Quarter, vol. 4, p. 422), Emily Mary (d.11/8/1903), daughter of John Hyacinth Talbot, JP and DL of Castle Talbot and Ballytrent, Co. Wexford, formerly MP for New Ross and Eliza, daughter of Sir John Power, Bt., of Edermine, Enniscorthy, Co. Wexford; six sons and four daughters; two of his sons were killed in action in WWI – Heffernan James Considine, MC, Captain 4th Battalion, Royal Irish Regiment, born 3/10/1883, killed 27/10/1916 and Christopher Daniel, 2nd Lieutenant, 5th Battalion, Royal Dublin Fusiliers born 21/12/1887, killed at Ypres 24/5/1915; educated at Stonyhurst, Lancashire; BA, Lincoln College, Oxford; High Sheriff of Co. Limerick, 1881; temporary resident magistrate 7/2/1882 and 3rd class permanent on 9/11/1883, 2nd class on 19/12/1887 and 1st class on 1/7/1898 and served in Newmarket, Co. Cork, Tralee, Co. Kerry and Kilkenny City; received the thanks of the Lord Lieutenant and the Irish Government on six occasions; DIG 18/4/1900; CB, 1902; MVO 4th class, 1903; created a Knight, 1908; Queen Victoria's Visit to Ireland Medal, 1900; King Edward VII Visit to Ireland Medal, 1903; George V Visit to Ireland Medal, 1911; awarded the King's Police Medal, 1909 in 1910; King George V Coronation Medal, 1911; pensioned 8/11/1911; died 12/2/1912; (Rathdown Registrar's District, 1912, March Quarter, vol. 2, p. 65); administration granted on 26/3/1912 at the Principal Registry to Heffernan James Considine – effects £90,593; (photo – Garda Museum & Archives, Dublin Castle).

Conway, Jeremiah Francis; RIC 53767; LDS 2099/006; born 1870, Listowel, Co. Kerry; (Listowel Registrar's District, 1870, vol. 5, p. 553); married on 24/11/1904 (Tralee Registrar's District, December Quarter, 1904, vol. 5, p. 321), wife from Co. Kerry; received a 1st class favourable record & £5 on 26/4/1921 for good police work in capturing armed raiders at Stradbally, Co. Laois and a 3rd class favourable record on 2/1/1922 for breaking up a Sinn Féin Court; 3rd DI 15/2/1921; pensioned 15/7/1922.

Conway, Thomas John; RIC 12832; LDS 2097/178; born 1824, Co. Mayo; 3rd SI 24/4/1849; resigned on 7/6/1849 in consequence of mental derangement.

Cook, James; LDS 2097/140; born 1813, Co. Tyrone; wife a native of Scotland; 3rd SI 6/2/1843; injured when thrown from his gig in September 1852; pensioned 26/3/1858; died 12/8/1869 at Trim, Co. Meath (Trim Registrar's District, 1869, vol. 12, p. 694).

Cooke, Geoffrey Cotton; LDS 2099/033; born 2/6/1893, London, England; captain, Royal East Kent Regiment; 3rd DI 25/6/1921; pensioned 10/5/1922.

Cooke, Hugh J. D.; RIC 72243; ADRIC no. 79; LDS 2098/239B; born 8/3/1895, British Guiana; captain, Royal Fusiliers; married on 8/6/1921; wife a native of Co. Westmeath; 3rd DI 2/7/1921; pensioned 12/4/1922.

Cooke, John Burke; RIC 15216; LDS 2097/189; born 1826, King's County; 3rd SI 26/11/1851; discharged on a gratuity of £83.0d.0d on 15/4/1866.

78   79

78 Heffernan Fritz James Joseph John Considine, Resident Magistrate. 79 Heffernan F.J.J.J. Considine, RM. 80 Heffernan F.J.J.J. Considine, Assistant Inspector General, RIC. 81 Heffernan F.J.J.J. Considine, Deputy Inspector General, RIC.

80   81

Coote, Robert; CarNB; while stationed at Castletownberehaven he married in June 1824 Rebecca Morris (d.10/11/1837, Bridge Street, Limerick) youngest daughter of Theophilius M. Symms, of Waterfall, Co. Cork; C.C. Castletownberehaven and Timoleague, Co. Cork; Dingle, 1831 and Milltown, Co. Kerry.

Coppinger, William Peter; LDS 2097/146; born 1826, Co. Wexford; son of William Henry Coppinger and Elizabeth O'Byrne; grandson of Peter Coppinger and Elizabeth O'Brien 3rd SI 1/12/1844; seconded to the Commissariat Department in the Crimea on 30/7/1854, where he was killed on 11/8/1855; his headstone inscription reads: 'Sacred to the memory of Sub Inspector of Irish Constabulary and serving with the Commissariat in the Crimea. Died 11th August 1855 Aged 29 Years. This stone was erected to his memory by his brother Officers of the Constabulary.'

Corbally, T. M.; LDS 2097/082; PPF; 3rd SI 1/2/1833; C.C. Kilkenny, Co. Kilkenny.

Corbett, Victor Daniel; RIC 71650; LDS 2098/124B; born 23/5/1895, Co. Sligo; (Sligo Registrar's District, June Quarter, 1895, vol. 2, p. 279); educated at Exeter School Officer Training Corps, 1908–9, Corporal Wellington School, Somerset Officer Training Corps Junior Division, 1911–13; medical student at London Hospital Medical College, 1/11/1913 17/11/1914; 2nd Lieutenant Middlesex Regiment, 11/12/1914, lieutenant, 7/12/1916, temporary captain, 17/5/1717, acting major, 19/9/1919–21/1/1920; wounded 25/5/1918; mentioned in despatches (*London Gazette* dated 25/5/1917); awarded the Military Cross (*London Gazette* dated 26/7/1918); awarded the French Croix de Guerre with Silver Star (*London Gazette* dated 17/1/1919); relinquished his commission on completion of army service on 21/1/1920; 3rd DI 8/7/1920; pensioned 12/5/1922; (WO 339/17766).

Cornwall, Francis H.; RIC 13725; LDS 2097/183; born 1828, Co. Dublin; 3rd SI 21/12/1849; died 15/7/1855 in Co. Kildare.

Corr, John D.; LDS 2097/176; born 1827, Durham, Kilbride, near Roscommon, Co. Roscommon; 3rd SI 1/11/1848; CI 10/3/1873; wife connected in Tipperary, Cork W.R. and Dublin; died 26/2/1880.

Corrigan, James; CarNB; C.C. Moylough, Co. Galway, 1820; died before November, 1825.

Corry, Edward Smyth; LDS 2097/148; born 1819, Newry, Co. Down; son of Trevor Corry; lieutenant, Irish Revenue Police from 9/10/1843 to 9/1/1845; wife a native of Somerset, England; daughter born on 3/1/1851 at the house of Mrs Trevor Corry, Abbey Yard, Newry, Co. Down (*Cork Examiner* 10/1/1851) (*Dublin Evening Post*, Thursday 9/1/1851); his brother Trevor Corry died in London on 9/3/1851 (*Dublin Evening Post*, Thursday 20/3/1851); 3rd SI 14/1/1845; pensioned 16/9/1862; died 25/5/1866.

Corry, Somerset; CarNB; born 1796; 3rd SI 1825; C.C. Ballymoney, Co. Antrim, 1825.

Cosgrove, John; RIC 27463; LDS 2098/011; born 1844, Co. Leitrim; married on 26/10/1881, wife a native of Co. Armagh; 3rd DI 1/2/1886; King Edward VII Visit to Ireland Medal, 1903; pensioned 1/10/1904; died 12/11/1921 at 122, Ellenborough Terrace, Belfast and buried in Granard, Co. Longford.

Cotter, James; RIC 12861; LDS 2097/295; born 1831, Co. Donegal; served in the Crimea as a sub-constable with the Mounted Staff Corps; married on 10/9/1859 (Downpatrick Registrar's District, vol. 4, p. 745), wife a native of Co. Waterford; 3rd SI 1/3/1878; pensioned 1/2/1890; died 3/7/1903 at Rosebank Terrace, Tramore, Co. Waterford; will and one codicil proved on 12/10/1903 at Waterford by the oath of Richard Cotter, retired sergeant Victoria Police – effects £3,650.7s.11d.

Cottingham, Thomas; RIC 32953; LDS 2098/093; born 1848, Loughsheelan, Co. Cavan; married on 30/4/1893, wife a native of Co. Down; 3rd SI 8/8/1892; King Edward VII Visit to Ireland Medal, 1903; pensioned 8/11/1908.

Coughlin, William Francis; CarNB; born 1794; died 1854; C.C. barony of Shelburne, Arthurstown and barony of Shelmalier, Taghmon, Co. Wexford, 1828.

Coulahan, Michael; born Lusmagh, King's County; CarNB; PPF; C.C. Corofin, Co. Clare, 1820.

Courtenay, Henry Drury; RIC 72997; ADRIC no. 452; LDS 2098/240B; born 30/10/1891, Zetland Place, Plymouth, Devon, England; son of John Thomas Courtenay, sergeant, 3rd Devon Regiment and Emily Esther (nee Harman), Erine Side House, Ivy Bridge, South Devon; educated at Pembroke College, Oxford; enlisted as a private (No. 4817) in the Inns of Court Officer Training Corps, Berkhampstead on 12/7/1915 to 14/11/1915; lieutenant, 20th Hussars on 15/11/1915; called upon to resign his commission on 20/5/1917 due to financial trouble; 3rd DI 2/7/1920; dismissed 14/3/1921; (WO 374/15820).

Cowen, Thomas; adjutant, 79th Regiment of Foot; shot himself on 8/1/1823; C.C. Clara, King's County, 1823. (*Connaught Journal*, Thursday, 16 January 1823, vol. 69)

Cox, John; LDS 2097/172; born 1799, Co. Wicklow; enlisted as a sub constable on 29/3/1820; wife a native of Co. Wicklow; received an injury on 10/7/1820 whilst on duty at Loughmore, Co. Limerick from a party who assaulted the police with stones; on 21/8/1820 he was severely wounded while escorting a prisoner by a large party; 3rd SI 1/6/1848; died 14/5/1858.

Cox, Joseph; LDS 2097/079; born 1807, Co. Mayo; son of Francis Cox, surgeon; married on 7/7/1846, at Golden, Co. Tipperary, Grace White (1810–1895), daughter of Joseph White, Esq., of Springmount, Golden, Co. Tipperary; enlisted as a constable, 2/10/1823; 3rd SI 31/1/1833; awarded the Constabulary Medal 1/9/1848 and a reward of £50 for his successful defence of The Warhouse, at Boulagh Common, Co. Tipperary against a considerable amount of rebels on 29/7/1848; CI 2/6/1853; resident magistrate 31/10/1859; died 25/2/1868 as a result of rheumatics of the heart at Athy Street, Carlow; (Carlow Registrar's District, 1868, vol. 3, p. 348); buried in Mount Jerome Cemetery, Dublin on 28/2/1868; (Registry No. 222) (Section B, Sub Division 199, Grant No. 3629P); administration granted on 16/3/1868 at Kilkenny to Grace Cox, of Carlow, the widow – effects under £3,000. His widow, Grace Cox died on 21/3/1895, aged 85 years, at Elm Grove. Kimmage Road, Rathfarnham, Co. Dublin, formerly of 8 Northbrook Road, Leeson Park, Dublin (Dublin South Registrar's District, 1895, March Quarter, vol. 2, p. 577); she is also buried in Mount Jerome, Cemetery, Dublin; probate of her will was granted on 23/1/1896 to Richard Chadwick, of Hoar Abbey, Cashel, Co, Tipperary – effects £3,139.8s.4d. – Resworn £3,054.3s.4d.

Cox, William; LDS 2097/074; born 1786, Co. Antrim; PPF; private, corporal, sergeant and troop sergeant major in the army from 25/2/1804 to 29/8/1821; enlisted as a constable, 1/9/1821; 3rd SI 1/4/1832; C.C. Bawnyarroy, Castlecomer, Co. Kilkenny, 1835; died 17/10/1840 at Ballon, Co. Carlow; an inquest into his death returned a verdict that he 'came by his death by poison administered by himself in a state of temporary derangement'; C.C. Co. Westmeath and Castlecomer, Co. Kilkenny

Cradock, James Verschoyle; LDS 2097/127; born 1809, Co. Dublin; son of Rev. Thomas Russell Cradock, MA, formerly Rector of St Nicholas-Within Parish, Dublin; wife a native of Co. Roscommon; 3rd SI 13/5/1839; pensioned 1/10/1859; died 25/10/1880 at 10, Palmerston Road, Rathmines, Dublin; buried in Mount Jerome Cemetery, Dublin on 27/10/1880; his eldest daughter, Elizabeth died on 5/11/1911 at 10 Palmerston Road, Rathmines, Co. Dublin; will proved on 23/11/1880 at the Principal Registry by the oath of Elizabeth Mary Cradock and Francesca Theodosia Cradock, all of 10 Palmerstown Road, spinsters, the executrixes – effects under £6,000.

Craig, George Fitzgerald William; RIC 56625; LDS 2098/113; born 17/6/1869, Naas, Co. Kildare; (Naas Registrar's District, 1869, vol. 12, p. 847); married firstly, Emily Hayes; married secondly on 12/7/1899 (Dublin South Registrar's District, September Quarter, 1899, vol. 2, p. 620), Isabel Roche, a native of Co. Dublin; 3rd DI 1/4/1895; CI 15/6/1920; his wife died at 42 Landsdowne Road, Dublin on 25/9/1918; wounded at the Cork and County Club, Cork on

17/7/1920 in an attack in which RIC Divisional Commissioner Gerard Bryce Fergus Smyth was killed; awarded the King's Police Medal in 1922; pensioned 31/8/1922; he died in 1956.

Crake, Francis William; RIC 72473; ADRIC no. 205; LDS 2093/146B; born 19/4/1893, St Matthew's Parish, Newcastle-upon-Tyne, Northd., England; (Newcastle-upon-Tyne Registrar's District, 1893, June Quarter, vol. 10, p. 55); resided at 232,Westgate Road, Newcastle-on-Tyne; 1st Northumbrian Field Ambulance, 1909–13; 11th Reserve Regiment of Cavalry, 3/9/1914–1/6/1915; private, No. 16957, 1st Battalion Hampshire Regiment, 2/6/1915–13/3/1917; 2nd Lieutenant Bedfordshire Regiment, 10/8/1917 (*London Gazette* dated 20/12/1917); MC; demobilized 21/2/1920; married Guineveve Marie Sykes at Newcastle on 6/8/19143rd DI 14/8/1920; killed 28/11/1920, Kilmichael, Co. Cork; buried Elswick, Newcastle-on-Tyne, Northd., England; (WO 374/16320).

Crane, Charles Paston; RIC 44598; LDS 2097/302; born 12/8/1857, Holden, Yorks., England, the son of Canon William Crane and brother of Hubert William Crane, SI, RIC; BA, Honours, Exeter College, Oxford, 1878; 3rd SI 18/8/1879; Private Secretary to the Inspector General from 18/6/1895 until his appointment as a resident magistrate 3rd class 4/9/1897, 2nd class 19/1/1903, 1st class 24/9/1914; in 1900 was seconded to serve as adjutant of the 12th Imperial Yeomanry in South Africa, where he was mentioned in despatches and received the medal with clasps for Wittebergen, Transvaal and Cape Colony and was awarded the DSO. After the War he returned to his magisterial duties in Ireland, to be seconded again in 1914, when he saw service with the Lancashire Fusiliers and the Irish Guards. Later he commanded the 24th (Hallamshire) Battalion, the York and Lancaster Regiment and the 43rd (Provisional) Battalion. He was promoted Lieutenant Colonel in 1915 and gained the OBE in 1916. He retired on 1/7/1920 and represented Central Wandsworth on the L.C.C. until 1925, later serving on the Chelsea Borough Council. He married in 1908, Mary Alice Caroline, daughter of Colonel and Lady Mary Skrine, of Warleigh Manor, Somerset and niece of Earl Temple, of Newtown Park, Bath; died at 19 Sloane Gardens, Chelsea, London S.W., 18/1/1939; (Chelsea Registrar's District, March Quarter, 1939, vol. 1a, p. 523); probate granted at Bristol on 4/4/1939 to Mary Alice Caroline Crane, widow – effects £49.15s.2d.; (p. 109, RM Records of Service Book, National Archives, Dublin); autobiography, *Memories of a Resident Magistrate, 1880–1920*, University Press, Edinburgh, 1938; (photo in the *Constabulary Gazette*, vol. 2, no. 39, p. 1, 24/12/1897).

Crane, Hubert William; RIC 45346; LDS 2097/307; born 1856, Holden, Yorks., England; (Ludlow Registrar's District, 1856, March Quarter, vol. 6a, p. 500); son of Canon William Crane and brother of Charles Paston Crane, SI, RIC; BA, Exeter College, Oxford, 1878; 3rd SI 7/9/1880; CI 1/4/1902; King Edward VII Visit to Ireland Medal, 1903; King George V Visit to Ireland Medal, 1911; awarded a certificate from the Irish Police and Constabulary Recognition Fund; awarded in 1919, the King's Police Medal, 1909; pensioned 31/12/1919.

Craven, Francis Worthington; RIC 80043; ADRIC 1305; born, 29/2/1898, Barrow-in-Furness, Cumbria, England; (Bradford, Yorkshire Registrar's District, 1898, December Quarter, vol. 9b, p. 97); lieutenant commander, Royal Navy; DSO, DSC, DSM; 3rd DI 20/12/1920; killed 2/2/1921, Ballinalee, Co. Longford; buried in Dalton-on-Furness on 5/2/1921,

Crawford, James; LDS 2097/029; born 1777, Ayrshire, Scotland; ensign 101st Regiment of Foot (Duke of York's Irish Regiment), 1816; lieutenant half pay, 1816; 3rd SI 1/4/1822; CI 17/1/1831; pensioned 1/8/1849; died 1852; (WO 25/754 f.148A).

Crawford, John Vershoyle; CarNB; born 6/1/1800, sixth son of David Crawford (1759–1825), of Ballyshannon, Co. Donegal; C.C. Newtownforbes, 1824; Moydow, Co. Longford, 1827; Longford, Co. Longford, 1829; retired 12/1/1830; died 10/3/1860.

Crawford, S.; CarNB; PPF; C.C. Dunleer, Co. Louth.

Crawford, Shuldham Pooley; LDS 2097/080; born 1812, Co. Derry; 3rd SI 1/2/1833; CI 14/12/1837; presented with an ornamental sabre by the Lord Lieutenant on 29/10/1842; AIG

1/1/1863; pensioned 11/12/1869; died 26/11/1873 at 37, Raglan Road, Dublin; administration granted on 29/1/1874 at the Principal Registry to Deborah Crawford, of Bellaghy, Castledawson, Co. Derry – effects under £5,000.

Crawley, John; LDS 2097/063; born 1780, Co. Armagh; served as a Coast Officer in the Port Department from 1802 to 1821 during which time he served in the yeomanry cavalry; widower on appointment; 3rd SI 1/10/1825; C.C. Carndonagh, Co. Donegal, 1831; pensioned 1/4/1845; died 1847.

Creagh, Andrew; LDS 2097/037; born 1779, Co. Limerick; brother of Col. Sir Michael Creagh and of Major Creagh of the 86th Regiment of Foot (Royal County Down Regiment)); ensign, lieutenant and captain from July 1797 to November 1816; major, 81st Regiment of Foot (Loyal Lincoln Volunteers Regiment); married Mary Head, in Halifax Nova Scotia, 20/12/1804; his daughter, Elizabeth Mary married John J. Scully, solicitor, at Middle Gardiner Street, Dublin on 17/11/1846; 3rd SI 28/1/1823; pensioned 17/8/1843; died 4/4/1857; (WO 25/744 fol. 17).

Creagh, Andrew M.; LDS 2097/127; born 1814, Doneraile, Co. Cork; 3rd SI 14/6/1839; pensioned 1/3/1848.

Creaghe, Philip Crampton; RIC 38313; LDS 2097/289; born 29/9/1850, Clonmel, Co. Tipperary; third son of Richard Fitzroy Creaghe, Melbrook, Clonmel, and Athassel Abbey, Co. Tipperary; 3rd SI 8/4/1872; married on 27/10/1874 at Holy Trinity, Paddington, London, Isabel Emily Chisholm, youngest daughter of John Seton Chisholm, of Calcutta, India; resident magistrate 3rd class 17/2/1896, 2nd class 8/9/1902, 1st class 7/3/1913; pensioned 29/3/1916; (p. 107, RM Records of Service Book, National Archives, Dublin).

Crean, Hugh M.; RIC 51731; LDS 2098/133B; born 8/5/1868, Ballinrobe, Co. Mayo; (Ballinrobe Registrar's District, 1868, vol. 9, p. 49); married on 20/4/1904, wife a native of Co. Sligo; 3rd DI 8/1/1920; pensioned 15/7/1922.

Crean, John William; LDS 2097/238; born 1841, Queen's County; 3rd SI 9/3/1861; dismissed 2/4/1867.

Crean, Patrick; RIC 1503; LDS 2097/193; born 1809, Co. Tipperary; joined as a sub constable on 1/2/1833; married on 20/12/1838; wife a native of Co. Kildare; 3rd SI 10/6/1852; pensioned 16/4/1870; died 5/10/1875 at Claremorris, Co. Mayo; (Claremorris Registrar's District, 1875, vol. 19, p. 97).

Crofton, Malby (Sir) 2nd Bt.; LDS 2097/059; born 21/12/1797, Longford House, Ballisodare, Co. Sligo; son of Sir James Crofton, 1st Bt. and Marion, daughter of John Lyster, D.D., of Rocksavage, Co. Roscommon, Rector of Clonpriest; married 24/1/1821, Sarah Jane (d.14/4/1867), fourth and youngest daughter of Andrew Parke, major, 8th Regiment of Foot (The King's Regiment), brother of Roger Parke of Dunnally, Co. Sligo, Lieutenant Colonel Sligo Militia (WO 13/220–37); JP, 1821; 3rd SI 1/1/1825; C.C. Lisburn, Co. Antrim, 1831; resident magistrate 1/10/1836; stipendiary magistrate 1/2/1837; retired as a RM in 1853; died 15/12/1872 at 53 Pembroke Road, Dublin, late of Longford House, Sligo, Co. Sligo; he was succeeded by his grandson, Sir Malby Crofton, 3rd Bt. (1857–1926); will proved on 21/1/1873 at the Principal Registry by the oath of Marion Louisa Crofton, spinster, the daughter and one of the executrixes – effects under £10,000.

Crofton, William Edward; LDS 2097/097; born 1793, Co. Cork; wife a native of Co. Tyrone; ensign, lieutenant and captain, 91st Regiment of Foot (the Argyllshire Highlanders) from 19/10/1809 to 29/11/1833; awarded one medal and two clasps for Vittoria and the Pyrenees; 3rd SI 1/1/1836; received a severe wound on the temple from a brick or stone whilst on duty on 28/3/1837 from the effects of which his life was considered to be in danger; pensioned 10/6/1869; died 1/8/1870 at Newtownlimavady, Co. Derry; (Newtownlimavady Registrar's District, 1870, vol. 11, p. 535).

Croghan, James Beatty; RIC 212; LDS 2097/204; born 1804, Rathconnell, Co. Westmeath; married in October 1835; his wife, Mary, a native of Co. Sligo died on 10/5/1864 (Parsonstown

Registrar's District, vol. 8, p. 479), at Ferbane, King's County, aged 58 years (*Cork Examiner* 16/5/1864); 3rd SI 21/8/1854; pensioned 15/11/1868; died 17/10/1885, Dublin; (Dublin South Registrar's District, 1885, December Quarter, vol. 2, p. 476; his daughter Ellen Emily, Barley Lodge, Catford, Kent, England, died on 12/6/1901.

Croghan, John R.; RIC 35439; LDS 2097/128; born 1810, Co. Roscommon; wife a native of Co. Louth; 3rd SI 19/7/1839; pensioned 1/11/1859.

Croghan, William Thomas; LDS 2097/277; born 1851, Co. Kilkenny; clerk in Belfast Bank for two years and six months; married on 20/9/1883, wife from Co. Roscommon; 3rd SI 29/3/1869; CI 1/5/1894; King Edward VII Visit to Ireland Medal, 1903; pensioned 13/8/1910.

Croke, Forbes Le Blount; RIC 81629; ADRIC no. 1248; LDS 2099/023; born 7/5/1890, Hendon, Middlesex, England; (Hendon Registrar's District, 1890, June Quarter, vol. 3a, p. 146); Royal Engineers, 18/3/1915; demobilized 8/1/1920; residing at The Grand Hotel, Englebury, Switzerland in May 1921; 3rd DI 25/6/1921; pensioned 31/3/1922; (WO 339/282).

Croker, John; LDS 2097/113; born 1813, Fedamore, Co. Limerick; 3rd SI 24/5/1837; daughter born on 26/2/1853, at his seat, Avonview, Co. Wicklow (*Cork Examiner* 7/3/1853).

Croker, Samuel; CarNB; born 1790, Woodville, Co. Waterford; son of Samuel Croker, of Dunsfort, Co. Cork (d.2/4/1845, at Glanworth, Co. Cork, aged 78 years) and Elizabeth (d.8/6/1833 at Woodville, Co. Waterford), daughter of Francis Crump, of Annagh, Co. Kerry; 3rd SI 1/5/1823; lieutenant; married on 4/9/1827, Jane Ussher Quin, daughter of Arthur Quin, of Dungarvan at Affane by a Waterford or Lismore licence; Jane Ussher died on 23/1/1887 in Liverpool and is buried in Mount Jerome Cemetery, Dublin with her daughter Annie Elizabeth (baptized at Dungarvan on 7/11/1829), who died on Easter Day 1880 and her son Samuel Croker (baptized at Dungarvan on 30/6/1828), who died on 1/1/1889; administration granted in London and resealed in Dublin on 11/11/1887; resident magistrate on 24/12/1838 in Ennis, Co. Clare; pensioned 1/4/1843; residing at 28, Sanford Road, Ranelagh, Dublin in 1868. A birth certificate registered on 7/5/1870 in the No. 3 South District, Dublin, shows that a son, Robert was born on 18/4/1870 to Samuel Croker 'pensioner' and Mary Croker (formerly Noonan), both resident at 37, Wexford Street, Dublin. The baptismal register at St Kevin's Church, Harrington Street, Dublin, confirms that a Robert Croker was christened on 26/4/1870. The priest, Jacobus Baxter, noted the father, Samuel Croker, was a 'Catholicus'. The sponsors were Maria Hannah Croker and the mother, 'Maria Noon', of 37 Wexford Street. However, the tenant of that house was a Dr Daly. The painter, decorator and author of *The Ragged Trousered Philanthropist*, first published in 1914, the classic English working-class novel, Robert Tressel (1870–1911) claimed in his daughter's birthday book that he was born in Dublin in April 1870, the son of Samuel Croker. Mary Anne Noonan and Samuel Croker had a family of three girls and three boys; C.C. Kilmacthomas (1834) and Dungarvan, Co. Waterford (1826) and Carrickbeg, Co. Tipperary; died *c.*1875/1876.

Cronin, George Roche; RIC 18806; LDS 2097/204; born 1831, Co. Kerry; son, George Francis, born on 5/6/1868 at Boyle, Co. Roscommon (Boyle Registrar's District, vol. 14, p. 101) (*Cork Examiner* 10/6/1868); 3rd SI 21/8/1854; in charge of the Mounted Troop at the Phoenix Park Depot from 1856 to 1866; resident magistrate 3rd class 1/3/1866, 2nd class 18/5/1872, 1st class 23/12/1887; pensioned 5/1/1896; died 24/5/1902 in Cork City; (Cork Registrar's District, 1902, June Quarter, vol. 5, p. 140); (p. 11, RM Records of Service Book, National Archives, Dublin); buried in St Joseph's Cemetery, Cork – Section 6.

Cross, Hugh Lionel; RIC 82715; ADRIC no. 1890; LDS 2099/045; born 1890, Worcs., England; army service, 1914–18; married 14/9/1921, wife from Northumberland; ADRIC, May to September 1921; 3rd DI 24/9/1921; pensioned 9/5/1922.

Crossley, Arthur; CarNB; lieutenant; 3rd SI 1/1/1823; stipendiary magistrate 18/11/1829 in Co. Roscommon; died 9/2/1844, Elphin, Co. Roscommon; administration granted at Elphin Diocese on 14/2/1844 (NA Reference: Crossle/Wood/14/1851); C.C. Fermoy, 1823 (the

Constitution or *Cork Morning Post*, 17/3/1823); C.C. Castletownroche, Mitchelstown and Doneraile, Co. Cork; Sligo, Co. Sligo and Athleague, Co. Roscommon.

Crossley, Francis; LDS 2097/043; born, Doneraile, Co. Cork; married Miss Elizabeth Gardiner of Mallow, Co. Cork, on 24/3/1824 at Newberry Church, Co. Cork by Rev. Lombard; 3rd SI 1823; CI 1/9/1838; resident magistrate 1/9/1839; died 5/9/1839; wife Elizabeth in receipt of a pension of £20 P. a. from 6/9/1839; his daughter, Elizabeth Catherine, married on 15/2/1853 at St Anne's Church, Dublin, Robert C. McGowan, Esq., of Portadown, Co. Armagh (*Cork Examiner* 21/2/1853).

Crossley, William; CarNB; born 1796, Shankill, Co. Antrim; 3rd SI 1825; died in Co. Derry in 1836; administration granted at the Derry Diocese to M.A. Crossley, of Derry (NA Reference: IAR/1836/F/24); his youngest son, Arthur Ratcliffe Crossley, aged 18 years, died on board the *Camillus* on his passage home from New Orleans in October 1850 (*Cork Examiner* 14/10/1850); his eldest son died on 2/10/1864 (Belfast Registrar's District, vol. 16, p. 230), at 7 University Square, Belfast, aged 39 years (*Cork Examiner* 25/10/1864); C.C. barony of Lower Maserene, Crumlin, 1825; Derry, Co. Derry, 1829; Antrim and Maghera, Co. Antrim, 1831.

Crowe, William Mordaunt; RIC 31733; LDS 2097/258; born 1842, Ennis, Co. Clare; third son of John Crowe, Captain 93rd Highlanders and Frances Elizabeth, daughter of the Hon. E. Stather, Legislative Council of Nevis, West Indies who were married on 18/8/1829; 3rd SI 1/7/1866; died 23/8/1869 at 14, Waterloo Road, Dublin, late of Bruff, Co. Limerick; administration granted at the Principal Registry on 21/10/1869 to Thomas Carlisle Crowe, of Ennis, Co. Clare, Captain, Royal Artillery, the brother of the deceased – effects under £300.

Crowley, Jerome D.; RIC 59653; LDS 2098/175B; born 30/11/1875, Co. Cork; awarded the Constabulary Medal; married on 25/9/1912, wife a native of Co. Clare; 3rd DI 16/10/1920; pensioned 2/5/1922.

Crozier, Francis Percy; RIC 72229; ADRIC no. 65; born 1879, only son of Major B.R. Crozier; married 1st, 1904, Ethel (d.1921), only child of Colonel R. Cobb, I.M.S.; two daughters; 2nd, 1921, Grace Catherine, 3rd daughter of Dr Croker Roberts of Lough Byrne, Co. Leitrim. Educated at Wellington College. Served in the South African War (Queen's Medal six clasps, King's medal, two clasps); Ashanti, 1900 (medal); Northern Nigeria 1902–5 (medal two clasps, dispatches); Zululand, 1905–6 (medal and clasp); retired, 1908; Captain Canadian Forces, 1908–12; served in the European War, 1914–19; rejoined (from Canadian R. of O.) 1914; Royal Irish Fusiliers as Captain: Major Royal Irish, 1914; Lt.-Col. Royal Irish Rifles, 1 Jan. 1916; Brigadier-General commanding 119th Infantry Brigade, 20 Nov. 1916, DSO, 1917; CMG, 1918; CB, 1919; Croix de Guerre with palm, dispatches seven times; Commanded 3rd Battalion Welch Regiment, 1919; G.O.C. 40th Division (France), March-April 1919; Hon. Brigadier-General 1919; Queen Victoria's Diamond Jubilee Medal, 1897; King Edward's Coronation Medal, 1902; 1914–15 Star; G.S. medal; Victory medal. Served with Lithuanian Army against Bolshevists 1919–20, and on Polish Front, 1919–20; Special Mission to Latvia and Esthonia, 1920; relinquished commission, 1920; Commandant Auxiliary Division of the Royal Irish Constabulary (which he raised), 4 August 1920–1 February 1921, from which he resigned. Publications: *A Brass Hat in No Man's Land*, 1930; *Impressions and Recollections*, 1930; *Five years Hard*, 1932; *Angels on Horseback*, 1932; *Ireland Forever*, 1932; *The Men I Killed*, 1937; died 31/8/1937 at East Lodge, Walton-on-Thames; (Surrey N.W. Registrar's District, September Quarter, vol. 2a, p. 318); (WO 76/207 fol. 98) (WO 76/208 fol. 117).

Cruess, Joseph Robert; CarNB; of Birr, Co. Offaly; marriage to Anne Cruess; marriage licence granted in 1816 in the Killaloe and Kilfenora Diocese (NA Reference: Killaloe & Kilfenora Court Book); C.C. Dingle, Co. Kerry, 1828; in Gowran, Co. Kilkenny in November, 1829 when reported for debt and witholding pay from constables and he was dismissed.

Cruice, John Francis; LDS 2097/190; born 1824, Co. Galway; 3rd SI 11/2/1852; CI 1/3/1876; pensioned 23/12/1891; died 25/3/1910 at Albert Villa, 51, Rathgar Road, Dublin,

82 William Peter Coppinger grave in the Crimea.   83 Charles Paston Crane, RM. 84 Jerome D. Crowley.   85 Brigadier-General Francis Percy Crozier.

formerly of Limerick and afterwards of Tralee, Co. Kerry; will proved on 3/5/1910 at the Principal Registry by the oath of George D. Clancy, solicitor – effects £3,103.14s.9d.

Cruise, Richard Francis Raleigh; RIC 60575; LDS 2098/191; born 1879, Co. Limerick; (Glin Registrar's District, March Quarter, 1879, vol. 5, p. 285); mathematical master at Crescent College, Limerick and St Brendan's College, Kilkenny, 1897–1900; married on 7/10/1910, wife a native of Co. Clare; 3rd DI 7/7/1902; Company Officer, Richmond Barracks Sub Depot from 17/9/1907 to 10/4/1908 and 1/7/1908 to 15/10/1908; TCI 20/9/1920; CI 1/10/1920; divisional commissioner 11/11/1920; pensioned 12/4/1922; his daughter, Betty, aged five years died in Bantry, Co. Cork on 28/1/1919.

Culhane, Patrick; RIC 38454; LDS 2098/169; born 1853, Kilfergus, Co. Limerick; married on 9/1/1893 (Mullingar Registrar's District, March Quarter, 1893, vol. 3, p. 375), wife a native of Co. Westmeath; 3rd DI 3/5/1900; pensioned 31/12/1914.

Cullen, Francis Nesbitt; RIC 14023; LDS 2097/184; born 1831, Skreeney House, Manorhamilton, Co. Leitrim; the youngest son of Colonel John James Cullen (1793–1842) and brother of Giles William Cullen, SI, RIC; his nephew, Captain Francis James Cullen, 66th Regiment of Foot was killed in action at Kushki Nakhud, near Candahar, Afghanistan on 27/7/1880; masters assistant, navy; married on 31/7/1854 (Dublin North Registrar's District, vol. 5, p. 117), Emily Margaret, eldest daughter of the late Andrew Finucane, Esq., DL, of Ennistymon, Co. Clare, and granddaughter of the late Judge Finucane (*Cork Examiner* 2/8/1854); 3rd SI 1/10/1850; CI 1/4/1875; Commissioner of Police and Town Inspector of Constabulary, Belfast from 1/10/1882 to 20/9/1885; AIG 25/9/1885; divisional commissioner, 25/9/1885; died 2/10/1889 in Armagh, Co. Armagh; buried in Manorhamilton, Co. Leitrim on 5/10/1889; will proved on 21/10/1889 at Armagh by the oath of James Soden Manly Cullen, of Shannon Lodge, Carrick-on-Shannon, Co. Leitrim and George Mitchell, of 9 Upper Pembroke Street, Dublin, executors – effects £3,646.17s.5d.

Cullen, Giles William; LDS 2097/137; born 1816, Skreeney House, Manorhamilton, Co. Leitrim; the second son of Colonel John James Cullen (1793–1842) and brother of Francis Nesbitt Cullen, AIG, RIC; lieutenant, Irish Revenue Police from 20/1/1840 to 7/8/1841; married on 11/9/1851 at Maryborough Church, Queen's County (Mountmellick Registrar's District, vol. 8, p. 243), Henrietta Catherine, youngest daughter of Thomas Cannon, of Portrane, Queen's County (*Cork Examiner* 17/9/1851); 3rd SI 13/08/1851; pensioned 13/2/1866.

Cumming, Charles Gordon; LDS 2098/005; born 1859, Bradninch, Devon, England; BA, Trinity College, Oxford, 1880; lodging at Worcester Street, Broomsgrove, Worcester in 1881 (Census); assistant master; married on 16/10/1885; 3rd DI 1/3/1885; resigned 1/3/1894; at the Lancashire Quarter Sessions in July 1899 ex-DI Cumming pleaded guilty to stealing two mackintoshes at Ulverton. It was stated that the accused who had taken his degree at Trinity College, Oxford, travelled with a distinguished explorer in Africa for ten years, and afterwards held a commission in the RIC, resigning the latter because he got into the hands of money lenders, who made him pay 400 per cent. He returned to Africa but he did not succeed and came back to England where he had further trouble, two paper mills in which his family were interested being destroyed by fire. It was added that his wife's health broke down and that she left him after a quarrel. The accused took to drink and committed the thefts while suffering from the effects. The Bench gave the accused the benefit of the First Offenders Act and discharged him (the *Constabulary Gazette*, vol. V. no. 17, p. 515, 22/7/1899).

Cummins, Bernard; LDS 2097/081; born 1791, Gallen, King's County; enlisted as a sub constable, 1/8/1823; wife a native of King's County; 3rd SI 1/2/1833; pensioned 1/8/1859; died 17/9/1871 at Sligo, Co. Sligo; (Sligo Registrar's District, 1871, vol. 12, p. 395).

Cuppage, Henry; RIC 28373; LDS 2097/243; born 1844, Co. Armagh; employed in a merchant' Office Belfast for ten months and in the Northern Bank, Belfast for two years and eight months; 3rd SI 9/2/1863; dismissed 19/6/1875.

Curling, Arthur; LDS 2097/163; born 1822, Kent, England; son of Thomas Curling, Squire, Kent; sergeant, 4th Light Dragoons from 8/10/1838 to 1/6/1844; captain under His Imperial Highness Ali Morad, Persia from 1/6/1844 to 1/3/1847; wife a native of Cornwall, England; 3rd SI 28/1/1848; Adjutant, Phoenix Park Depot from 15/8/1870 to 15/5/1872; CI 15/5/1872; pensioned 27/1/1888; his wife Cornelia Agnes died at Fermoy, Co. Cork on 25/1/1860; died 27/10/1898 at Devonshire Square, Bandon, Co. Cork; will proved on 30/11/1898 at Cork by the oath of Frances N. Curling, of Devonshire Square, Bandon, Co. Cork – effects £9,698.8s.5d, Resworn £9,505.0s.11d.

Curtis, Edward Robert; RIC 18490; LDS 2097/302; born 1835, Co. Roscommon; son of Robert Curtis, CI, RIC; 3rd SI 2/7/1854; died 27/12/1864 at Kilmallock, Co. Limerick (Kilmallock Registrar's District, 1885, vol. 5, p. 291 & vol. 15, p. 210).

Curtis, Robert; LDS 2097/046; born 1801, King's County; father Robert Edward Curtis, SI, RIC; 3rd SI 13/10/1823; CI 2/10/1838; wife a native of County Louth; author of *The Irish Police Officer – Comprising of Identification and other Tales* (1861), *Rory of the Hills* (London, 1870), *The History of The Royal Irish Constabulary* (London, 1889); pensioned 28/5/1867; died 30/12/1874 at 70, Upper Leeson Street, Dublin; buried in Deansgrange Cemetery, Dublin (South Section, Row W, Grave No. 1); will proved on 28/1/1875 at the Principal Registry by the oath of Eleanor Curtis, Upper Leeson Street, Dublin, widow and one of the executors – effects under £1,500.

Curtis, Robert; CarNB; born, Inane, Co. Tipperary; son of Robert Curtis, Inane, Co. Tipperary and Sarah (niece of John Toler (3/12/1745–27/7/1831), 1st Earl of Lord Norbury, the infamous 'Hanging Judge'), second daughter of Daniel Toler (d.c.1755) and Letitia (d.17/2/1794), daughter of Thomas Otway, of Castle Otway, Co. Tipperary; 3rd SI 1822; died 14/8/1829 at Borris-in-Ossory, Co. Laois; his brother was Daniel Toler Curtis; C.C. Kilbeggan, Co. Westmeath, 1828, Borris-in-Ossory, 1829 while residing in Bagenalstown, Co. Carlow.

Cusack, Francis; RIC 38226; LDS 2098/121; born 1854, Kilkenny West, Co. Westmeath; 3rd DI 3/10/1896; died 5/10/1905 at Rathkeale, Co. Limerick; administration granted on 1/2/1906 at Limerick to James Cusack, Land Steward – effects £277.8s.1d.

D

Dagg, George Amyralde de Montmorency Edwin; RIC 43556; LDS 2097/295; born 1856, Co. Dublin; eldest son of George W.J. Dagg, Quartermaster General's Office, Dublin Castle; sister born on 12/6/1854 at Dublin Castle (*Cork Examiner* 16/6/1854); brother born on 21/1/1858 (*Cork Examiner* 23/1/1856); MA, LLB, Dublin University; married on 15/10/1880 (Dublin South Registrar's District, 1880, December Quarter, vol. 2, p. 583); temporary civilian clerk in the Recruiting Pay Office, Dublin for one year; granted a first class certificate of military qualification on 23/5/1873 at the School of Gunnery, Kingston, Ontario, Canada; 3rd SI 8/4/1879; author of *Devia Hibernia: The Road and Route Guide for Ireland* (Dublin, 1893); died 8/8/1904 at Johnstown, Co. Kilkenny; administration granted on 31/10/1904 at the Principal Registry to Margaret N. Dagg, widow – £1,155.14s.1d. buried in Mount Jerome Cemetery, Dublin on 10/8/1904 with his father George W.J. Dagg, died 28/4/1891, aged 69 years and stepbrother, Thomas Sidney Charles Dagg, MA, LLB, BL, died 29/12/1964, aged 90 years.

Dale, Isaiah; RIC 21315; LDS 2097/327; born 1838, Killeevan, Co. Monaghan; 3rd DI 1/11/1882; pensioned 17/1/1888; died 9/1/1901 at the residence of his son at Osborne House, Colchester; (Colchester Registrar's District, March Quarter, vol. 4a, p. 395).

Dale, John Henry Wellington Loftus; RIC 55390; LDS 2098/091; born 1870, Co. Fermanagh; married on 11/8/1898 (Schull Registrar's District, September Quarter, 1898, vol. 5, p. 293), Georgina May Gilpin, a native of Co. Dublin; 3rd DI 2/7/1893; King Edward VII Visit to Ireland Medal, 1903; pensioned 13/4/1922; (photo in the *Constabulary Gazette*, vol. XVI, no. 19, 19/11/1904 & vol. XXXIII, no. 24, 6/9/1913, p. 380).

86

87

86 George D'Amyralde de Montmorency Edwin Dagg.

87 Richard Dease grave, WW2 fighter pilot.

Dalton, Matthew Aylmer; CarNB; died 1831; C.C. Kilworth and Castletownroche, Co. Cork and Killenaule, Co. Tipperary.

Daly, James Vincent; LDS 2098/044; born 1861, Co. Louth; assistant veterinary surgeon in Dublin for two years; 3rd DI 1/10/1886; Queen Victoria's Visit to Ireland Medal, 1900; King Edward VII Visit to Ireland Medal, 1903; King George V Visit to Ireland Medal, 1911; Veterinary Surgeon to the RIC from 1/10/1886 to 1/12/1916; resided at 29, Liffey Bank, Conyngham, Dublin; (photo in the *Constabulary Gazette*, vol. 2, no. 39, p. 1, 24/12/1897).

Daly, John; RIC 55740; LDS 2098/183B; born 10/4/1872, Co. Cork; married on 25/8/1908 (Kanturk Registrar's District, September Quarter, 1908, vol. 5, p. 153), wife a native of Co. Cork; 3rd DI 16/10/1920; received a first class favourable record for gallantry during an ambush at Killenaule, Co. Tipperary on 24/1/1921; pensioned 20/4/1922; died 5/5/1958.

Daly, John Hickman; LDS 2097/068; born 1793, Co. Clare; private in the Ennis Yeoman Cavalry from 1810 to 1813; enlisted as a sub constable 1/11/1822; wife a native of the Isle of Man; in 1826 at the Galway Election he received a slight injury to his head from a blow of stones; constable 1/4/1831; 3rd SI 1/5/1831; pensioned 1/2/1856 in Co. Antrim; died 6/7/1870.

Dames, John A.; LDS 2097/027; born 1799, Ballyburly, King's County; 3rd SI 14/11/1821; resigned 9/1/1840.

D'Arcy, Edmond Kelly; LDS 2097/118; born 1810, Co. Roscommon; 3rd SI 1/2/1838; pensioned 23/2/1865; died 15/10/1866 at Dunleer, Co. Louth (Ardee Registrar's District, vol. 17, p. 246); administration granted on 20/11/1866 at the Principal Registry to Kate D'Arcy, of Dunleer, the widow of said deceased – effects under £450.

D'Arcy, Nicholas; CarNB; born Ballyforin, Co. Roscommon; 3rd SI 1820; described by Major George Warburton on 2/10/1832 to 'be in wretched state of health.' C.C. Glenamaddy, Co. Galway, 1821; Ballyhaunis, Co. Mayo, 1827 and Ballaghadereen, Co. Roscommon, 1830.

D'Arcy, Thomas; CarNB; born Killucan, Co. Westmeath, one of eight children (3 sons and 5 daughters of James D'Arcy (1700–1758) of Dunmowe, Co. Meath and Elizabeth Judge (d.1773), daughter and co-heiress of Thomas Judge, of Grangebeg, Co. Westmeath; PPF; in 1803 as a half pay captain he was appointed brigade major of yeomanry in Co. Longford; in 1807 he was made a justice of the peace for Westmeath, Longford, Roscommon and Leitrim; in 1812 the government took over completion of the Royal Grand Canal from Coolnahay, Co. Westmeath to near Termonbarry, Co. Roscommon. Contractors had to give up through activities and atrocities against workmen by members of a combination who called themselves 'Carders' and 'Thrashers'. The military were brought in and D'Arcy was much engaged in night patrol and thirty miles of canal was completed in three years. In 1816 he was sent to Innishowen, Co. Donegal following the murder of Mr Norton Butler, at Grouse Hall, six miles from Moville and Carndonagh, Co. Donegal on 3/7/1816 close to his own home by two assassins in the view of a considerable amount of people who were engaged in turf-cutting, none of which rendered him assistance; appointed a PPF chief magistrate 29/7/1817 and made a JP for counties Donegal, Derry and Tyrone, in the two of the latter counties he was frequently involved in government missions. He resided with a force of military at Grouse Hall in the proclaimed barony of Ennishowen East with twenty members of the PPF. He was provided with thirty men from the Board of Excise for the detection of illicit distillation and he was so successful that there was not one case before the Spring and Summer Assizes for prosecution. On the success of this measure was founded the Irish Revenue Police in 1832; at the beginning of 1820 seven more proclaimed baronies were added under the Peace Preservation Act in Co. Galway making a total of thirteen baronies resulting in all of Co. Galway, with the exception of Connemara being proclaimed and he took up residence in St Clerans; he was appointed inspector general for Ulster in November 1823 and though moving to Belfast remained in charge of the PPF in Co. Galway until August 1824 when the County Constabulary took over its role; married firstly, Sarah Anne Tilly, aunt of Robert Murray Tilly (1842–93), CI and Barrackmaster, RIC; married secondly in 1804, Eliza, daughter of Captain Buchanan, of Rockfield, Co. Westmeath. They had two sons and three daughters; eldest, William James, of Rhynne Mount, Co. Longford was called to the Irish Bar on 25/5/1834, d.s.p.1846; moved his family to Holly Hill, Strabane, Co. Tyrone in June 1826; pensioned 1833; died 1833; Thomas D'Arcy's sister, Eliza (1767–1829) married on 16/8/1791, Major Henry Charles Sirr (1764–1841), Town Major, Dublin Castle, 68th Regiment of Foot (Durham Light Infantry) and had two sons, Rev. Joseph D'Arcy Sirr, Rector of Kilcoleman and Henry Charles Sirr.

Davies, Charles Frederick Fellowes; RIC 61869; LDS 2098/213; born 3/12/1884, Co. Dublin; (Dublin South Registrar's District, December Quarter, 1884, vol. 2, p. 593); assistant teacher at St Andrew's College for 6 months; captain and promoted major, 6th Battalion Royal Inniskilling Fusiliers in January 1918; acting lieutenant-colonel of a regimental battalion Connaught Rangers from 25/2/1919 to 23/4/1919; Decorated by the King of Serbia with the Order of the White Eagle & Sword; 3rd DI 18/7/1906; Adjutant, Phoenix Park Depot from 15/6/1920 to 1/10/1920; CI 1/10/1920; Commandant, RIC Camp Gormanstown from 22/11/1920 to 1/3/1922; pensioned 31/5/1922; awarded the OBE; (WO 339/12370); transferred to the Royal Ulster Constabulary on 1/6/1922.

Davies, James; LDS 2097/114; born 1810, Killian, near Balinasloe, Co. Galway; eldest son of Thomas Davies, of Newcastle, Aughrim, Co. Galway and Bidelia Anne Blake, eldest daughter of Michael Blake of Kiltolla and Anne Ffrench. Thomas was the eldest son of James Davies of Newcastle and Catherine Cruise; father of James Taaffe Davies, SI, RIC; married firstly on 21/12/1839 at St John's Cathedral, Sligo, Maria, only daughter of John Taaffe, of Glenesk, near Lough Talt, Co. Sligo; Maria Davies died on 28/2/1864 (Boyle Registrar's District, vol. 4, p. 57) – administration granted to James Davies at Boyle, Co. Roscommon on 13/2/1865; married secondly on 18/8/1868 at Kildallow Church, Edith, aged 21 years, eldest daughter of David White, Esq., JP, Lisanaly House, Kildallow, Co. Cavan and Mountjoy Forrest, Co. Tyrone (*Cork Examiner* 21/8/1868); 3rd SI 10/7/1837; died of typhoid fever 17/6/1869 at Castlebar, Co. Mayo (*Cork Examiner* 26/6/1869); buried in the Church of Ireland Cemetery, Castlebar, Co. Mayo; administration granted on 1/11/1869 at Ballina to Edith Davies of Castlerea, Co. Roscommon, the widow of the deceased – effects under £600.

Davies, James Taaffe; RIC 30257; LDS 2097/252; born September 1844, Co. Sligo; son of James Davies, CI, RIC; married in 1882 Agnes Eveleen Beytagh from Co. Dublin who died at 21 Garville Avenue, Rathgar, Co. Dublin on 29/4/1937; 3rd SI 1/11/1865; pensioned 6/5/1905; died 26/10/1907 at 12, Dromard Terrace, Kingstown, Co. Dublin; he had six children: Mary St Clare, b.12/8/1883, Upper Gardiner Street, Dublin, who married J.J. Hayes in New Jersey, USA and they had a daughter Moira who was an actress; Herbert Joseph, captain Merchant Navy, born 16/3/1885, Kilrush, Co. Clare and died unmarried in Stornoway and is buried there. He was awarded the Lloyd's silver medal for gallantry; Edward James, born in 1887, Shinrone and died on 23/2/1941 in a London clinic following an operation. He was manager of the Hong Kong and Shanghai Bank; Mary Eveleen Rosemary was born in Shinrone in 1888. She married Harry Neville Roberts in Dublin on 28/4/1921 and she died in Dublin in September 1934; Noel John, born in Shinrone in March 1891 and joined 8th Battalion, Royal Dublin Fusiliers, 2nd Lieutenant and was killed in action in France on 27/4/1916; Douglas Joseph, born in New Ross in September 1893 and joined the Royal Dublin Fusiliers, Special Reserve as a lieutenant and was awarded the Military Cross. He was interned by the Japanese in WW2 and later was in the government service in Malaya. He died in NSW Australia on 15/11/1952.

Davies, Walter M.C.; RIC 72016; LDS 2098/193B; born 10/2/1900, Ches., England; RNVR; married on 9/3/1922, wife a native of Cork E.R.; 3rd DI 10/1/1920; pensioned 31/8/1922.

Davies, Walter Stocks; LDS 2097/333; born 1859, Notts., England; (Nottingham Registrar's District, 1859, September Quarter, vol. 7b, p. 251); son of Rev. E. Davies, Rector of Wilford, Notts., and brother of William Moorehouse Davies, DI, RIC; 3rd DI 14/11/1883; married on

27/8/1890 (Bawnboy Registrar's District, September Quarter, 1890, vol. 3, p. 23), wife a native of Co. Cavan; resigned 30/4/1898 on his appointment as Chief Constable of Birkinhead Borough Police on 30 April 1898 to 1912; died 11/4/1913, 5, St George's Crescent, Llandudno, Caernarvon, Wales; (Conway Registrar's District, June Quarter, 1913, vol. 11b, p. 623); administration granted on 29/4/1913 to Adela Gertrude Davies, widow – effects £622.7s.4d.

Davies, William Moorehouse; RIC 44600; LDS 2097/303; born 1858, Notts., England; son of Rev. E. Davies, Rector of Wilford, Nottingham and brother of Walter Stocks Davies, DI, RIC; apprenticed to Mr Thomas Adams & Co. (Shippers) London for three years; married on 28/9/1886 at Kedlock, Mary Brown Millar, elder daughter of Walter Millar, Esq., Kedlock and Cupar Fife, New Brunswick; AIG 17/2/1910; King George V Visit to Ireland Medal, 1911; acting Chief Commissioner, Dublin Metropolitan Police, 5/8/1914 to 14/1/1915; DIG 15/12/1916; pensioned 13/3/1920; (photo in the *Constabulary Gazette*, vol. XXXV, no. 23, 15/8/1914, p. 246).

Davis, Francis; CarNB; born 1788, Moneymore, Louth, Co. Louth; sergeant in the PPF in Co. Louth for three years and six months; 3rd SI 1818; died 1824; wife Susannah Davis applied for a widows pension on 31/12/1824; C.C. Tallanstown, Co. Louth.

Davis, Hugh; RIC 15338; LDS 2097/296; born 1832, Co. Fermanagh; married on 10/2/1864 (Dublin North Registrar's District, vol. 2, p. 639), wife a native of Co. Dublin; 3rd DI 9/8/1878; pensioned 10/4/1894; died 25/5/1924; buried in Borrisokane Cemetery, Co. Tipperary.

Davis, James Henry; LDS 2098/170; born 1876, Banbridge, Co. Down; (Banbridge Registrar's District, 1877, vol. 6, p. 209); 3rd DI 4/11/1900; pensioned 11/12/1913; died 15/9/1916.

Davis, John Hubert; RIC 57881; LDS 2098/124; born 1874, Millford, Co. Donegal; (Millford Registrar's District, 1874, vol. 12, p. 266); 3rd DI 3/11/1896; Queen Victoria's Visit to Ireland Medal, 1900; King Edward VII Visit to Ireland Medal, 1903; King George V Visit to Ireland Medal, 1911; pensioned 21/11/1920.

Davis, William; RIC 16820; LDS 2097/309; born 1834, Co. Cork; wife from Co. Sligo; 3rd SI 14/12/1880; pensioned 1/8/1896.

Dean, Sidney Harry; RIC 82015; ADRIC no. 193; LDS 2099/021; born 14/5/1894, Staffs., England; (Wolverhampton Registrar's District, 1893, June Quarter, vol. 6b, p. 592); lieutenant, Tank Corps; 3rd DI 25/6/1921; pensioned 18/4/1922.

Deane, Henry J.; RIC 49211; LDS 2097/319; born 1858, Ashen Street, Ashen, Essex, England; (Lewisham Registrar's District, 1857, December Quarter, vol. 1d, p. 619); son of William J. Deane (b.1824) Lymington, Hampshire and Sophia A.L. Wynch (b.1829), Calcutta, India; three years in the Suffolk Militia; 3rd SI 24/6/1882; resigned 15/2/1886 from Spiddal, Co. Galway.

Dease, Richard Edmund Anthony; RIC 71649; LDS 2098/127B; born 19/2/1897, Tralee, Co. Kerry; (Tralee Registrar's District, 1897, March Quarter, vol. 5, p. 520); only son of Major Edmund T. Dease (1/10/1861–1/10/1945), RM, DL, JP, Royal Irish Fusiliers, of Rath House, Ballybrittas, Co. Laois and Mabel More O'Ferral; South Irish Horse; lieutenant, Royal Irish Fusiliers; 3rd DI 8/7/1920; pensioned 23/4/1922; joined the Indian Police; in 1923 he married Irene Eleanor, of Hendon, Middlesex, the daughter of a colonel in the Worcestershire regiment; during WW2 he served as a pilot officer in the RAF Volunteer Reserve, service no. 86844 and was killed in action on 24/11/1940; buried in Shrewsbury General Cemetery (Old part, Sec.38, Div.4, Grave H), Shropshire, England.

Decluzeau, John James; LDS 2097/053; born 1792, Co. Dublin; brother of Sinclair Henry Decluzeau, CI, RIC; 3rd SI 1/8/1824; C.C. Strabane, Co. Tyrone, 1831; pensioned 1/3/1848; died 1860.

Decluzeau, Sinclair Henry, LDS 2097/047; born 1793, Co. Dublin; brother of John James Decluzeau, SI, RIC; wife a native of Co. Louth; 3rd SI 10/11/1823; CI 8/4/1844; pensioned 21/4/1859 in Annesley Terrace, Newcastle, Co. Down; died 30/9/1872 at Kilkeel, Co. Clare; (Kilkeel Registrar's District, 1872, vol. 11, p. 368).

DeCourcy, Thomas Hare; LDS 2097/245; born 1843, Co. Limerick; 3rd SI 2/12/1863; dismissed 8/2/1867.

DeGernon, Christopher Joseph; LDS 2097/126; born 1816, Middlesex, England; 3rd SI 2/4/1839; received an approbation on 30/6/1852 for spirited exertions in endeavouring to save life and property at a fire; seconded to the Commissariat Department in the Crimea from 6/7/1854 to 8/12/1855; awarded additional pay on 20/5/1858 while in charge of the Curragh Camp, Co. Kildare; resident magistrate 10/8/1860; died 25/1/1875 at Glenogra, Co. Limerick, formerly of Roseborough House, Co. Tipperary, the Abbey, Rathkeale and Kilmore House, Co. Limerick; will proved on 5/3/1875 at Limerick by the oath of Daniel Charles Riordan, MD, of Bruff, Co. Limerick, the sole executor – effects under £7,000.

Deignan, James; RIC 56369; LDS 2098/067B; born 1873, Boyle, Co. Sligo; (Boyle Registrar's District, 1873, vol. 9, p. 113); married on 5/4/1902, wife a native of Co. Sligo; 3rd DI 26/5/1916; pensioned 12/5/1922; died 20/5/1960.

Deignan, John; RIC 61063; LDS 2098/121B; born 1882, Westport, Co. Mayo; (Westport Registrar's District, March Quarter, 1882, vol. 4, p. 582); 3rd DI 15/6/1920; pensioned 31/8/1922.

Delany, Laurence Joseph; RIC 52618; LDS 2098/118B; born 19/3/1869, Queen's County; married firstly on 2/7/1896 (Limerick Registrar's District, September Quarter, 1896, vol. 5, p. 227); married secondly on 22/2/1900 (Clogheen Registrar's District, March Quarter, 1900, vol. 4, p. 381); 3rd DI 14/5/1920; pensioned 12/5/1922.

Denny, Henry; RIC 18808; LDS 2097/204; born 1836, Tralee, Co. Kerry; married on 1/12/1864 at St Anne's Church Dublin, by the Rev. Richard Hore, Janie, eldest daughter of Joseph Armstrong, Esq., of Bray, Kingscourt, Co. Cavan (*Cork Examiner* 3/12/1864); 3rd SI 1/10/1854; died 9/11/1872 at Ennis, Co. Clare; (Ennis Registrar's District, 1872, vol. 19, p. 137).

Dermody, Joseph; RIC 4150; LDS 2097/267; born 1820, Knocktopher, Co. Kilkenny; wife a native of Queen's County; 3rd SI 1/12/1867; pensioned 1/4/1875; died 19/11/1896.

Despard, George; LDS 2097/142; born 1784, Clonenagh, Queen's County; married in Dublin, 6/1/1826; his youngest daughter, Gertrude Priscilla, married on 6/1/1869, at Lacca Church, Queen's County (Mountmellick Registrar's District, vol. 3, p. 541), Matthew Henry Franks, Esq., of Westfield, Queen's County (*Cork Examiner* 15/1/1869); ensign 53rd Regiment of Foot (The King's Shropshire Light Infantry Regiment), 1815; lieutenant, 1833; 3rd SI 1/12/1823; stipendiary magistrate, 2/4/1835; resident magistrate, 1/10/1836; pensioned 9/1/1844; died 13/6/1860; (WO 25/755 fol. 247).

Dickson, George; LDS 2097/079; born 1802, Loughgall, Co. Armagh; wife a native of Co. Armagh; 3rd SI 1/1/1833; CI 11/7/1853; died 10/3/1865 at Monaghan, Co. Monaghan (Monaghan Registrar's District, vol. 3, p. 253); will and three codicils proved on 20/4/1865 at Armagh by the oaths of Edward Dawson Atkinson, of Tandragee, Co. Armagh, Gentleman, Solicitor and Margaret Kirkpatrick, of Richmond Terrace, Belfast, Co. Antrim, widow, two of the executors – effects under £3,000; a gratuity of £142.10s. 4d. was granted to the guardians and three orphan children on 21/3/1865.

Dickson, H.E.; captain; divisional commissioner for Leinster, 1920; resigned 14/3/1920.

Dickson, William Atkinson; LDS 2097/269; born 1850, Co. Down; married on 15/4/1880, wife from Co. Donegal; 3rd SI 27/4/1868; resigned 16/3/1883.

Dignan, Cecil Joseph Burke; RIC 71646; LDS 2098/141B; born 18/3/1899, Co. Roscommon; (Roscommon Registrar's District, 1899, June Quarter, vol. 3, p. 262); lieutenant, South Irish Horse; 3rd DI 8/7/1920; pensioned 22/3/1922; seconded for service to the Palestine Gendarmerie on 22/3/1922.

Dixon, William H.; LDS 2097/153; born 1825, Dublin City, Co. Dublin; 3rd SI 3/6/1846; dismissed 1/11/1848; C.C. Ballybought, Newry, Co. Down, 1845.

Dobbin, John James; RIC 79317 & 82942; ADRIC no. 973 & 1431; LDS 2099/052; born 1895, Co. Meath; (Navan Registrar's District, December Quarter, 1895, vol. 2, p. 733); army service, 1914–19; 3rd DI 20/9/1921; pensioned 11/5/1922.

Dobbin, William; CarNB; resigned 7/4/1827 from Clonmel, Co. Tipperary; C.C. barony of Lower Ormond, Borrisokane, Co. Tipperary, 1824.

Dobbyn, Alexander MacManus Rowan; RIC 58442; LDS 2098/148; born 1874, Lisburn, Co. Antrim (Lisburn Registrar's District, 1874, vol. 6, p. 697); son of George Henry Walker Dobbyn, CI, RIC; BA 1894, Trinity College Dublin; 3rd DI 20/10/1898; King Edward VII Visit to Ireland Medal, 1903; ACI 29/4/1920; CI 27/7/1920; pensioned 22/4/1922.

Dobbyn, George; LDS 2097/075; born 1804, Newtown, Co. Westmeath; PPF; enlisted as a sub constable, 1/5/1824; recommended by Chief Constable Henry Walker Thompson on 19/3/1832 for service as a chief constable in the constabulary as 'being one of the most zealous men I have ever met and responsible for (in troubled times) the hanging and transporting of more ribbonmen that the rest of the Westmeath police put together'; 3rd SI 6/6/1832; pensioned 1/1/1851; died 30/1/1867 at Abbeylara, Co. Longford (Granard Registrar's District, vol. 3, p. 193); will proved at the Principal Registry on 29/3/1867 by the oath of George Henry Walker Dobbyn, of the Constabulary Barracks, Phoenix Park, Dublin, Sub Inspector of Constabulary, the sole executor – effects under £5,000.

Dobbyn, George Henry Walker; RIC 25774; LDS 2097/236; born 1842, Co. Westmeath, father of DI Alexander MacManus Rowan Dobbyn; 3rd SI 14/6/1860; CI 11/4/1884; pensioned 1/3/1904; died 28/5/1908 at Fahan House, Fahan, Co. Donegal; will proved at the Principal Registry by the oath of Annie Dobbyn, the widow – effects £8,608.8s.1d.

Doherty, James; RIC 3414; LDS 2097/312; born 1837, Co. Donegal; 3rd DI 20/5/1881; pensioned 1/2/1883; died 20/12/1883 at Letterkenny, Co. Donegal; administration granted on 21/11/1883 at Derry to Elizabeth McConologue, of Gortnacorrib, Co. Donegal, wife of Anthony McConologue, the sister – effects £382.

Dolan, Philip; RIC 55229; LDS 2098/099B; born 1/10/1871, Co. Cavan; 3rd DI 10/2/1919; pensioned 3/5/1922.

Dolan, Thomas; RIC 58564; LDS 2098/063B; born 15/9/1876, King's County; (Parsonstown Registrar's District, 1876, vol. 15, p. 585); married on 24/1/1914 (Athlone Registrar's District, March Quarter, 1914, vol. 3, p. 14), wife a native of Co. Galway; 3rd DI 14/3/1915; pensioned 22/5/1922.

Donelan, John; CarNB; C.C. Claremorris, 1827 and Castlebar, Co. Mayo, 1830.

Donelan, Malachy H.; CarNB; stipendiary magistrate; severely wounded in 1823; residing with his brother at 21, Great Charles Street, Mountjoy Square, Dublin in 1828; died 1844; C.C. Ferbane and Edenderry, King's County, 1828.

Donnellan, Peter; RIC 60047; LDS 2098/174B; born 24/5/1879, Mohill, Co. Leitrim; (Mohill Registrar's District, June Quarter, 1879, vol. 3, p. 271); married on 10/6/1908 (Ennis Registrar's District, June Quarter, 1908, vol. 4, p. 114), wife a native of Co. Antrim; 3rd DI 16/10/1920; awarded the Constabulary Medal on 9/9/1921 for gallant and meritorious service during the Kilmeena ambush, Co. Mayo; pensioned 27/4/1922.

Donnelly, Edward James; RIC 54316; LDS 2098/081B; born 8/8/1870, Co. Derry; married on 21/6/1897 (Belfast Registrar's District, June Quarter, 1897, vol. 1, p. 560), wife a native of Co. Antrim; 3rd DI 13/12/1917; pensioned 15/10/1920.

Donoghue, Jeremiah, RIC 65374, 2098/186B; born 11/4/1880, Kenmare, Co. Kerry; (Kenmare Registrar's District, March Quarter, 1880, vol. 5, p. 310) wife a native of Co. Cork; 3rd DI 16/10/1920; pensioned 17/7/1922.

Donoghue, John; LDS 2097/129; born 1816, Co. Cork; enlisted as a sub constable on 5/2/1827; 3rd SI 1/12/1839; CI 1/12/1839; pensioned 1/6/1856 in Co. Wicklow; died 16/4/1857 in Co. Wicklow.

Donovan, John; LDS 2097/158; born 1812, Co. Kerry; 3rd SI 10/5/1847; received grants from the Reward Fund on 31/5/1848 and on 30/9/1849 for uniformly zealous and successful exertions in making offenders amenable; CI 1/1/1870; died 25/9/1881 at Nenagh, Co. Tipperary; will proved on 14/10/1881at Limerick on the oath of Mary Dillon, of Listowel, Co. Kerry, widow, the sole executrix – effects £718.12s.od.

Doolan, Thomas; CarNB; born Borrisokane, Co. Tipperary; married in January 1842, Kate, eldest daughter of Christopher Sharpe, of Dublin at St Andrew's Church, Dublin; author of *Munster – Memoirs of a Chief Constable* (Dublin, 1831); C.C. Kilmallock and Hospital, Co. Limerick.

Doolan, William; CarNB; son of Thomas Doolan, Wingfield, King's County; son-in-law of Dr John Conolly, Clonmel, Co. Tipperary; tendered his resignation from Thurles on 14/7/1830, having through gambling been found frequently in arrears to his men; C.C. Athy, Co. Kildare; Croom, Co. Limerick and Thurles, Co. Tipperary.

Dougan, James Hamilton; RIC 72009; LDS 2098/171B; born 31/10/1895, Co. Derry; (Derry Registrar's District, December Quarter, 1895, vol. 2, p. 167); lieutenant, army; 3rd DI 10/1/1920; pensioned 9/5/1922.

Douglas, Edmund Alexander; CarNB; born, 1797, 3rd SI 1/10/1824; CI 1/1/1835; resident magistrate 1/10/1836; C.C. Claudy, Co. Derry and Ballybay, Co. Monaghan, 1831.

Douglas, James; LDS 2097/290; born 1838, Lancs., England; (Lancaster Registrar's District, 1838, December Quarter, vol. 21, p. 443); sergeant major 17th and 18th Hussars from 17/4/1858 to 30/6/1872; 3rd SI 1/7/1872; RIC Riding Master; died 11/3/1873 in Dublin; (Dublin North Registrar's District, 1873, vol. 2, p. 551).

Dowling, Patrick J.; LDS 2098/005B; born 28/10/1889, Co. Clare; 3rd DI 2/3/1910; on 22/4/1921 he received a 1st class favourable record in leading a counter attack against an ambush at Swanlinbar on 17/12/1920; pensioned 9/5/1922; (photo in the *Constabulary Gazette*, vol. XXXV, no. 1, 13/5/1914).

88 James Hamilton Dougan.   89 Major Laurence Dundas, Peace Preservation Force, c.1864.

Dowling, Thomas R.; RIC 40193; LDS 2098/123; born 12/1/1855, Co. Kerry; married on 5/5/1882 (Athy Registrar's District, 1882, June Quarter, vol. 3, p. 273), wife a native of Co. Tipperary; 3rd DI 2/11/1896; King Edward VII Visit to Ireland Medal, 1903; pensioned 13/3/1915; (photo in the *Constabulary Gazette*, vol. V, no. 4, 22/4/1899).

Downing, Daniel McCarthy; LDS 2097/214; born 1829, Kenmare, Co. Kerry; joined the Irish Revenue Police as a lieutenant on 21/11/1853 and served in Brockagh, Co. Donegal; 3rd SI 1/12/1857; died 15/12/1863 of rheumatic fever at Athenry, Co. Galway (*Cork Examiner*17/12/1863); buried in the family vault in Kenmare, Co. Kerry; administration granted on 12/3/1864 at the Principal Registry to Daniel McCarthy of Prospect House, Skibbereen, Co. Cork, Gentleman, Attorney for the benefit of Eugene Downing, the father only next of kin of the deceased – effects under £100.

Doyle, John; RIC 57246; LDS 2098/229B; born 1900, Co. Donegal; 3rd DI 1/1/1921; application to refuse promotion to the rank of DI was sanctioned on 12/1/1921.

Doyle, Thomas; RIC 1737; LDS 2097/221; born 1812, Co. Kerry; married on 20/12/1838; wife a native of Co. Cork; 3rd SI 17/4/1858; engaged in detective duties in the United States by order of Lord Naas from 28/11/1858 to 25/2/1861 and granted £100 from the Reward Fund for the successful performance of such duty; pensioned 18/11/1870; died 15/3/1876 at New Ross, Co. Wexford; will proved on 1/5/1876 at the Principal Registry by the oath of Margaret Doyle and Johanna (otherwise Anna) Doyle, both of New Ross, spinsters, the daughters and the executrixes – effects under £6,000.

Drew, Cecil Nicholas; RIC 83712; ADRIC no. 532; LDS 2099/053; born 24/4/1891, Hants., England; (Portsea Registrar's District, 1891, June Quarter, vol. 2b, p. 22); enlisted in the motor transport division, 6/1/1915; lieutenant, Royal Air Force, 1/1/1918; 3rd DI 7/1/1921; pensioned 31/8/1922.

Drought, George Meares John; CarNB; second son of John Drought (1751–1814), Whigsborough, Parsonstown, King's County and Meares Isabella Meares, daughter and co-heir of George Meares, of Dublin whom he married on 27/5/1772. He inherited the property of his granduncle Major Fairbrother at Glencarrig, Co. Wicklow and Belmont, King's County and married Jane Acton of West Aston, Co. Wicklow; marriage licence granted in 1805 in the Prerogative Court (NA Reference: M/2464); they had six daughters and three sons, the youngest of which was Captain George Warburton Drought (b.1823)(d.1880), 51st (Yorkshire) Light Infantry, whose wife (his first cousin) Anne Sophia, daughter of Thomas Acton (d.1817) of Westaston, Co. Wicklow, died at Cargine, Co. Roscommon on 3/9/1911 and was buried at Glenealy, Co. Wicklow on 6/9/1911; stipendiary magistrate 14/11/1821 and residing in Reynella, Kilbeggan, Co. Westmeath; resident magistrate 1/10/1836; died 4/3/1844; will proved on 19/3/1844 at the Prerogative Court (NA Reference: Crossle/Drought/n81–2) (T/3283)

Du Bourdieu, George; LDS 2097/152; born 1826, Portsmouth, Hants., England; family from Co. Westmeath; 3rd SI 11/2/1846; received an approbation on 31/3/1850 for gallant exertions when in command of a party of police in saving numerous lives at a fire at the Killarney Auxiliary Workhouse; seconded to the Commissariat Department in the Crimea on 6/7/1854 where he was killed on 3/8/1854.

Dudgeon, John Cunningham; RIC 67627; LDS 2098/049B; born 6/6/1888, Co. Fermanagh; apprenticed for three years to a solicitor; scholar and senior moderator, BA 1911, Trinity College Dublin; 3rd DI 26/5/1914; pensioned 7/6/1922; transferred to the Royal Ulster Constabulary on 8/6/1922.

Dudley, George Vernon; RIC 76115; ADRIC no. 457; LDS 2098/199B; born 31/10/1884, Oxford, Oxon, England; (Headington Registrar's District, 1884, December Quarter, vol. 3a, p. 769); British South African Police Force; Royal North West Mounted Police; enlisted into the Honourable artillery Company (Disembodied Territorial Force) as Gunner 410, 4/8/1914; 2nd Lieutenant, Royal Garrison Artillery, 11/1/1915; lieutenant, 13/2/1915, captain, 18/8/1915; 7

Squadron, Royal Flying Corps, 3/12/1917–7/12/1917; 72 Heavy Artillery Brigade, 24/1/1918–26/1/1918; 1st Heavy Artillery School, 27/12/1918–27/1/1919; acting major, 28/7/1918–20/4/1919; relinquished commission on completion of service on 1/9/1921; Military Cross (*London Gazette* dated 1/1/1918); DSO (*London Gazette* dated 3/6/1919); Mentioned in despatches (*London Gazette* dated 7/7/1919; 3rd DI 12/1/1920; deserted on 5/1/1922 and dismissed on 24/1/1922 by the Chief of Police; (WO 339/22143).

Duff, David; LDS 2097/059; born 1802, Kilglass, Co. Longford; captain, Dublin County Militia (WO 13/2841–60); 3rd SI 1/1/1825; C.C. Dungannon, Co. Tyrone, 1831; resident magistrate 10/8/1836; died on 2/5/1846, aged 43 years at The Hermitage, Kilglass, Co. Longford as a result of a kick in the right side by a horse while he was crossing the lawn. The Hermitage was the residence of his late brother, George Duff, Esq., and David Duff had gone there from Roscommon to arrange the affairs of his brother who had died some five weeks earlier on 22/3/1846, aged 41 years; both brothers are buried in Kilglass Church of Ireland Cemetery (near Abbeyshrule), Co. Longford.

Duff, Samuel; LDS 2097/163; born 1828, Co. Dublin; 3rd SI 17/1/1848; resigned 1853 from Trim, Co. Meath.

Duff, Walter Garden; LDS 2098/037; born 24/11/1863, Auchterless, Aberdeenshire, Scotland; 4th son of Garden William Duff, 9th Bt., of Hatton (b.10/8/1814) and Douglas Isabella Maria, 3rd daughter of Beauchamp Colclough Urquhart (d.19/6/1861), of Meldrum and Blyth, Scotland, who were married on 1/6/1850; pupil at Trinity College, Glenalmond, Monzie, Perthshire, Scotland in 1881 (Census); ranching in America for eighteen months; he married on 5/8/1891, Elizabeth Ann (d.1943), daughter of Major James Leith, VC, born 26/5/1826, Glenkindle, Aberdeenshire and died 13/5/1869, Paddington, London, Scots Greys and 14th Hussars and Isabella Shaw; 3rd DI 1/5/1888; Queen Victoria's Visit to Ireland Medal, 1900; King Edward VII Visit to Ireland Medal, 1903; resident magistrate 3rd class 7/7/1910, 2nd class 24/9/1914; his eldest son Eric Garden Duff, born 1892, died at Navan, Co. Meath in October 1899; his youngest son, Guy Leith Assheton, born 2/10/1893, Captain, Royal Field Artillery, died of wounds received in action on 2/9/1916; (p. 146, RM Records of Service Book, National Archives, Dublin); died 1945.

Duffy, James Joseph L.; RIC 61506; LDS 2098/209; born 14/4/1883, Co. Donegal; (Inishowen Registrar's District, June Quarter, 1883, vol. 2, p. 138); staff clerk with Arthur Guinness & Co., June 1904 to November 1905; captain, 7th (Service) Battalion Royal Munster Fusiliers, 21/12/1914; relinquished his commission and retained the rank of captain, 29/3/1918; 3rd DI 2/1/1906; TCI 1/10/1920; died 28/2/1921 Oughterard, Co. Galway; late of Fiddone House, Tubber, Co. Galway; administration granted at Tuam on 29/7/1921; (WO 339/22483); (photo in the *Constabulary Gazette*, vol. XXI no. 7, 4/5/1907).

Duffy, John; RIC 29288; LDS 2098/054; born 1845, Co. Monaghan; 3rd DI 1/12/1888; pensioned 1/12/1907.

Dumas, Henry; LDS 2097/030; born 1787, Co. Cork; East India Company Service as a cadet, ensign and lieutenant from May 1804 to 1812; 3rd SI 30/10/1822; on 2/5/1831 at the Fair at Castlewellan three fingers on his right hand were disabled from blows of stones; on 19/10/1832 he received a severe injury when returning from the fair at Clough, Co. Down from a bar of iron which was placed on a car, running through his right leg; on 31/8/1834 he was severely injured when returning off duty by the upsetting of the car in which he was travelling; C.C. Downpatrick, Co. Down, 1831; pensioned 13/2/1840.

Duncan, James; CarNB; PPF; served in the 18th Hussars for twenty years before he joined the PPF and then the Constabulary in 1821. In 1830 he was in ill health, had a large family and wished to have his eldest son John Duncan, aged 21 years appointed a chief constable; C.C. Co. Clare; Ballinasloe, Co. Galway and Carrick-on-Shannon, Co. Leitrim.

Duncan, John; LDS 2097/068; born 1809, Edinburgh, Scotland; son of James Duncan; enlisted as a sub constable, 1/7/1825; wife a native of Co. Limerick; daughter born on 20/12/1853 at Summer Hill, Nenagh, Co. Tipperary (*Cork Examiner* 26/12/1853); 3rd SI 10/10/1830; CI 15/12/1851; AIG 30/7/1867; Commandant of the Phoenix Park Depot from 1/8/1867 to 1/10/1882; pensioned 21/2/1882.

Dundas, Laurence; CarNB; born in Ireland in 1787; the son of Laurence Dundas, of Scotland, major, 13th and 26th Light Dragoons (died 1/3/1796 at sea on board HMS *Dictator* off the coast of Madeira on the way to the West Indies) who, whilst serving with the 13th Light Dragoons met and married Ellen Greene in Co. Tipperary on 9/7/1784; major 5th Fusiliers and ADC to the Duke of Wellington; married Charlotte Maria (d.1871), daughter of George Slator, of Swiftbrooke, Co. Dublin in September 1812 in Dublin; he had four sons and two daughters: (twins) Adelaide Maria, Laurence George (b.21/6/1813), Rev. George Charles (b.10/5/1814), Thomas Henry (b.1815, King's County), Sarah Georgina (b.1819) and William John (b.8/7/1820, Dublin); Adelaide Maria married on 7/6/1853 at Monkstown Church, Co. Dublin (Rathdown Registrar's District, vol. 9, p. 622), James White Minchin, captain 63rd Regiment of Foot (West Suffolk Regiment) (*Cork Examiner* 10/6/1853); resided at Clobemon Hall, Ferns, Co. Wexford; his clerk, constable Richard Paige was dismissed on 7/5/1828 for fraud; dismissed in 1828 for making irregular deductions from pay; resided at Hollycourt, Careysfort Avenue, Blackrock, Co. Dublin; died in 1866 (Rathdown Registrar's District, 1866, vol. 12, p. 653); C.C. Wexford, Co. Wexford.

Dunlop, Robert; LDS 2098/097; born 1869, Singapore, Straits Settlements; BA 1891, LLB 1892, Trinity College Dublin; married on 8/8/1894 (Dublin South Registrar's District, September Quarter, 1894, vol. 2, p. 485), L. Evelyn Kildahl, a native of Co. Dublin; 3rd DI 10/12/1893; CI 15/5/1919; senior divisional commissioner 14/2/1921 at Cork; pensioned 31/5/1922; transferred to the Royal Ulster Constabulary on 1/6/1922.

Dunne, Thomas; RIC 7606; LDS 2097/282; born 1826, Dundalk, Co. Louth; wife from Co. Roscommon; 3rd SI 16/11/1870; died 7/2/1890 at Downpatrick, Co. Down; administration granted on 9/4/1890 at Belfast to Letitia Dunne, of Downpatrick, the widow – effects £381.13s.6d.

Dunne, Timothy; RIC 14521; LDS 2097/323; born 1832, Queen's County; wife from Co. Kerry; 3rd DI 18/10/1882; pensioned 1/12/1892.

Dunning, Leonard; RIC 50656; LDS 2097/325; born 17/6/1860, London, England; (St George Hanover Square, Registrar's District, 1860, September Quarter, vol. 1a, p. 216); second son of Simon Dunning (b.11/10/1815) Winkleigh, Devon and died 25/4/1883, 2, Warwick Square, London, England and Elizabeth Mary (b.1834, St Margaret's, Middlesex and died 5/2/1921), daughter of John Border, of Burlington Lodge, Streatham Common, who were married on 19/6/1856; Leonard Dunning married on 19/11/1902, Edith Muriel (d.10/11/1965, aged 86 years), eldest daughter of William Tod, of Drygrange, Allerton, Liverpool; educated at Eton; BA, honours in Jurisprudence, Exeter College, Oxford, 1881; 3rd DI 4/12/1882; resigned 20/10/1895 on his appointment as Assistant Chief Constable of Liverpool City Police on 27 December 1894 and Chief Constable of Liverpool City Police from 1902 to 1912; H.M. Inspector of Constabulary, 1912 to 1930. Knighted in 1917 and created a Baronet 24/6/1930; died 8/2/1941, Beedinglee, Horsham, Sussex, England; probate granted at Liverpool on 24/3/1941 to Dame Edith Muriel Dunning, widow – effects £5,389.9s.4d., resworn, £5,628.16s.10d.; (photo in the *Constabulary Gazette*, vol. XI, no. 5, 26/4/1902, p. 128).

Dunsterville, Edward; LDS 2097/113; born 1810, Co. Cork; father of John William Edward Dunsterville, SI, RIC, RM; wife a native of Co. Fermanagh; 3rd SI 2/6/1837; received a favourable record on 31/12/1868 for prompt proceeding with his party on a long search for the principals of a riotous proceeding, many of which were captured amidst obstruction; pensioned 6/10/1870; died 16/8/1877 at Derry, Co. Derry; administration granted on 22/12/1877 at

90

91

90 Leonard Dunning. 91 Leonard Dunning – Commissioner of the City of London Police.

Derry to John William Edward Dunsterville, of Dungloe, Co. Donegal, SI, RIC, son of the deceased, effects under £7,000.

Dunsterville, John William Edward; RIC 36687; LDS 2097/280; born 13/2/1851, Co. Fermanagh; son of Edward Dunsterville, SI, RIC; 3rd SI 27/6/1870; private secretary to Mr Edward George Jenkinson, KCB, 1888 (1835–1919), Assistant Under-Secretary for Police and Crime on 11/9/1882; resident magistrate 3rd class 15/6/1885, 2nd class 1/1/1893, 1st class 2/8/1907; pensioned 13/2/1916; died 9/2/1918; (p. 14. RM Records of Service Book, National Archives, Dublin).

Dwyer, Charles; RIC 21772; LDS 2097/325; born 1838, Co. Sligo; wife from Chester; 3rd DI 18/10/1882; pensioned 1/6/1898; died 22/4/1917.

Dyas, Joseph; CarNB; captain, 51st Regiment of Foot (2nd Yorkshire West Riding Regiment); stipendiary magistrate 25/5/1831; died 1850; C.C. Kilcullen, 1827; Naas, Co. Kildare, 1828 and Newmarket-on-Fergus, Co. Clare.

Dycer, Edward; born in Dublin City; veterinary surgeon to the Force from 18/11/1842 to 23/5/1855.

E

Eagar, Alexander; LDS 2097/036; born 1786, Clifton Lodge, Killorglin, Co. Kerry; son of Thomas Eagar, of Rathpogue, Co. Kerry and Rosanna (his first cousin), fourth daughter of Alexander Eagar of Ardrinane; ensign in the Kerry Militia from October 1812 to March 1814 (WO 13/2902–22); ensign and lieutenant, 57th Regiment of Foot (West Middlesex Regiment) from March 1814 to April 1816; married in 1817, Margaret, youngest daughter of Eusebius McGillicuddy (granddaughter of the MacGillicuddy of the Reeks), of Tralee, Co. Kerry; he had four sons, Thomas (SI, RIC), Eusebius MacGillicuddy, of Castle Caragh, Francis MacGillicuddy and James MacGillicuddy (SI, RIC) and two daughters, Rosanna Catherine and Margaret (d.1895); 3rd SI 28/1/1823; CI 5/5/1841; pensioned 1/4/1848; died on 7/9/1855 at Clifton Lodge, Killorglin, Co. Kerry in the 69th year of his age (*Cork Examiner* 17/9/1855).

Eagar, James MacGillicuddy; RIC 18807; LDS 2097/203; born 1833, Cloghroe, Co. Cork; fourth son of Alexander Eagar, CI, RIC and a brother of Thomas Eagar, SI, RIC; 3rd SI 21/8/1854; discharged on 1/11/1856 in Co. Derry, having been inflicted with an unsoundness of the mind.

Eagar, Thomas MacGillicuddy; LDS 2097/124; born 1818, Clifton Lodge, Killorglin, Co. Kerry; eldest son of Alexander Eagar, CI, RIC; 3rd SI 16/2/1839; presented with an ornamental sabre by His Excellency, the Lord Lieutenant on 29/10/1842; died 8/7/1847.

Ebhart, William Frederick; LDS 2097/048; born 1795; 3rd SI 1/1/1824; residing at 11 Montgomery Street, Newry, Co. Down, 1830; C.C. Ballinahinch, Co. Antrim, 1831.

Edwards, Joseph; RIC 54120; LDS 2098/144B; born 1868, Co. Dublin; (Rathdown Registrar's District, 1868, vol. 12, p. 904); married on 24/2/1897 (Dublin South Registrar's District, March Quarter, 1897, vol. 2, p. 685), wife a native of Co. Dublin; 3rd DI 20/8/1920; pensioned 12/6/1922.

Egan, Ernest Arthur; RIC 82262; LDS 2099/042; born 11/4/1891, Co. Sligo; (Sligo Registrar's District, June Quarter, 1891, vol. 2, p. 299); sergeant major in the army, 4 years, 327 days; clerk with the Ministry of Labour; 3rd DI 20/9/1921; pensioned 9/5/1922.

Egan, John; RIC 36394; LDS 2098/107; born 30/5/1851, Co. Roscommon; 3rd SI 25/6/1894; King Edward VII Visit to Ireland Medal, 1903; pensioned 1/6/1911.

Egan, John; CarNB; applied for leave on 7/5/1824 from Tuam, Co. Galway due to serious illness; C.C. Co. Cavan.

Egan, Meredith Joseph; RIC 63663; LDS 2098/224; born 19/10/1885, King's County; married on 5/6/1912 (Dublin North Registrar's District, June Quarter, 1912, vol. 2, p. 493), wife a native of Co. Dublin; 3rd DI 23/4/1908; pensioned 7/4/1922.

Egan, Michael J.A.; LDS 2098/232; born 19/4/1884, Co. Limerick; married on 28/9/1909 (Limerick Registrar's District, September Quarter, 1909, vol. 5, p. 261); 3rd DI 11/8/1908; major, Royal Army Service Corps from 15/5/1916 to 11/2/1919; adjutant, North Dublin Union Sub Depot from 18/3/1920 to 31/8/1920; resigned on 31/8/1920 on his appointment as Chief Constable Southport Borough Police Lancashire on 1 September 1920 to 31 August 1942 and appointed H.M. Inspector of Constabulary, 1942 to 1950; awarded CBE in 1935; died whilst holding office on 18/4/1950; (photo in the *Constabulary Gazette*, vol. XXXI, no. 23, 17/8/1912, p. 365).

Egan, Michael Stephen; LDS 2097/23; born 1841, King's County; 3rd SI 1/6/1861; received a favourable record on 31/12/1868 for the arrest of an offender who had fired at the police; received a favourable record on 31/12/1870 for especially distinguishing himself in discharging his duty with alacrity, fortitude and endurance in suppressing formidable riots in Cork; received an approbation on 31/12/1870 for judicious exertions in preventing a collision between military and civilians; barrackmaster of the Phoenix Park Depot 23/6/1880; died 6/3/1890 at 82, Mountjoy Square, Dublin; buried in Glasnevin Cemetery on 8/3/1890; his widow, Christina Kathleen Egan died on 8/7/1916 at Belgrave Lodge, Belgrave Road, Dublin; (photo in the *Constabulary Gazette*, vol. VI, no. 13, 23/12/1899, p. 390).

Egan, William Albert; RIC 66984; LDS 2098/039B; born 4/1/1890, Co. Sligo; (Sligo Registrar's District, March Quarter, 1890, vol. 2, p. 278); married on 3/8/1918, Pauline Gueret, a native of Co. Dublin; 3rd DI 6/1/1913; ACI 1/12/1920; CI 1/1/1921; pensioned 20/5/1922.

Ekins, Thomas Arbuthnott; RIC 81710; LDS 2099/018; born 1/11/1898, Boston, Lincs., England; (Boston Registrar's District, 1898, December Quarter, vol. 7a, p. 427); Royal Air Force and lieutenant, Royal Engineers; married on 5/11/1921, wife from Middlesex; 3rd DI 25/6/1921; pensioned 21/4/1922; appointed assistant superintendent of police, NWFP and was shot by an outlaw near Marden on 7/2/1926; buried at Taikal Payan Cemetery, Peshawar, India; memorial in St John's Church, Peshawar, India – 'In loving memory of Thomas Arbuthnott Ekins, Indian Police, Assistant Superintendent of Police, Peshawar, who was killed on 7 February 1926 by an armed criminal who he was attempting to arrest, he himself being alone and unarmed.'

Ellis, Eyre G.; CarNB; baronial chief constable; stipendiary magistrate 1824; C.C. Dulleek, Co. Meath.

Ellis, Hercules; CarNB; resigned 9/9/1830; his father died in 1829; C.C. Carrickbeg, Carrick-on-Suir, Co. Waterford, 1827.

Elrington, Maurice Collingwood; RIC 16322; LDS 2097/195; born 1832, Templeshambo, Co. Wexford; wife from Co. Antrim; 3rd SI 22/11/1852; resigned 1/3/1871.

Enright, Simon; LDS 2097/120; born 1816, Co. Clare; 3rd SI 4/10/1838; CI 1/3/1867; pensioned 15/5/1872; died 8/10/1873 in Dublin; (Dublin North Registrar's District, 1873, vol. 17, p. 425).

92 | 93

92 William Albert Egan. 93 Major Thomas Esmonde, VC, Deputy Inspector General, RIC.

Esmonde, Thomas VC; born 25/8/1829, Pembrokestown, Co. Waterford; third son of Commander James Esmonde (1791–1842), Royal Navy and Anna Maria (d.25/6/1869 at Landsdowne Road, Dublin – *Cork Examiner* 7/10/1869), daughter of James Murphy of Ringmahon Castle, Co. Cork, and niece of Most Rev. Dr Murphy, Catholic bishop of Cork; married on 24/11/1859, Matilda Marie, daughter of Peter de Pentheny O'Kelly, of Barrettstown, Co. Kildare; he had three daughters and an only son, Thomas Louis (b.14/12/1864), of Ballycourcy, Enniscorthy, Co. Wexford, who married Mary, daughter of George Mansfield, was lost at sea in the sinking of the MV *Leinster* on 10/10/1918 and buried at Glasnevin Cemetery, Dublin on 14/10/1918; one of Thomas Esmonde's daughters married James Comerford and their daughter was Maire Comerford (1893–1982), born in Rathdrum, Co. Wicklow, Cumman na mBan member, political activist and authoress of *The First Dáil* in 1969; awarded the Medal for the Burmese War of 1852 and 1853, the Crimean Medal and the Clasp for Sebastopol and the Turkish Medal. On 18/6/1855 at Sebastopol, Crimea, after being engaged in the attack on the Redan, Captain Esmonde, 18th Regiment of Foot (Royal Irish Regiment), repeatedly assisted, at great personal risk, in rescuing wounded men from exposed situations. Also on 20/6/1855, while in command of a covering party he rushed to a spot where a fireball from the enemy had just lodged, and extinguished it before it could betray the position of his men, thus saving the party from a murderous fire of shell and grape which was immediately opened where the fireball had fallen and for his valour he was awarded the Victoria Cross; (*London Gazette* 25/9/1857); he was the great-uncle of Lieutenant Commander, Eugene K. Esmonde, VC, DSO (1909–42) (*London Gazette* 3/3/42); AIG 24/11/1859; DIG 8/5/1865; discharged on a gratuity 30/7/1867; died 14/1/1873 Bruges, Belgium and his widow resided at Macmine, Co. Wexford.

Evans, Arthur Charles; RIC 16055; LDS 2097/193; born 1832, Co. Wicklow; 3rd SI 3/8/1852; on 14/15/1855 he was reduced six steps in the officers seniority list for appropriating a forage allowance to his own use and control; again reduced six steps for negligence and irregularity in the discharge of his duties and suspended on 25/8/1855; dismissed 25/9/1855.

Evans, Nicholas; LDS 2097/152; born 1825, Templeroan, Doneraile, Co. Cork; 3rd SI 8/4/1846; pensioned 15/4/1876; died 17/6/1882 at Drumcree Cottage, Drumcree, Co. Westmeath; will proved on 23/8/1882 at Mullingar by the oath of William Evans, Gilliardstown, Co. Westmeath, one of the executors – effects £1,514.7s.2d.

Ewart, Frederick W.; RIC 50456; LDS 2097/322; born 1859, Co. Antrim; spent one and a half years in an office in the linen trade; BA, Wadham College, Oxford; married on 14/6/1883 (Belfast Registrar's District, June Quarter, 1883, vol. 1, p. 321), wife a native of Co. Antrim; 3rd SI 15/3/1882; resigned 15/9/1898.

F

Fallon, George Forbes; LDS 2097/162; born 1819, Cashel, Co. Longford; son of Nathaniel Fallon, SI, RIC; 3rd SI 29/11/1847; pensioned 16/10/1875; died 5/2/1884 at Letterkenny, Co. Donegal (Letterkenny Registrar's District, 1884, March Quarter, vol. 2, p. 132).

Fallon, Michael; RIC 52934; LDS 2098/117B; born 7/4/1868, Co. Sligo; wife a native of Co. Westmeath; 3rd SI 14/5/1920; wounded Cloghane/Dingle Road, Co. Kerry 13/7/1920; pensioned 18/4/1922.

Fallon, Nathaniel; LDS 2097/050; born 1784, Co. Longford; father of George Forbes Fallon, SI, RIC; baronial chief constable from May 1811 to May 1824; lieutenant, Wagon Corps, February 1804 to April 1809; widower on appointment; 3rd SI 8/5/1824; pensioned 16/10/1851; died in February 1859.

Fallon, Owen; RIC 26544; LDS 2098/023; born 1840, Co. Mayo; 3rd DI 15/2/1887; pensioned 30/6/1902; died 21/4/1917, at Wood House, Ardara, Co. Donegal; will proved at Londonderry on 18/7/1917 by the oath of H. Falvey, MD and the Reverend Hugh McDwyer, R.C.C. – effects £1,286.18s.3d.

Falloon, Garnett J.; LDS 2097/143; born 1816, Co. Down; wife a native of Hants., England; daughter born on 23/9/1854 at Delvin Cottage, Castletowndelvin, Co. Westmeath (*Cork Examiner* 27/9/1854); 3rd SI 10/1/1844; received an approbation on 30/9/1849 for unremitting exertions in the arrest and conviction of a murderer; pensioned 1/4/1875; died 28/3/1886.

Falvey, Patrick M.; RIC 8903; LDS 2098/010B; born 16/3/1863, Faha, Co. Kerry; married on 24/6/1897 (Kenmare Registrar's District, June Quarter, 1897, vol. 5, p. 141), wife a native of Co. Kerry; 3rd DI 4/1/1910; awarded a 3rd class favourable record and £3 for duty performed during the Sinn Fein Rebellion on 27/7/1916; pensioned 3/9/1920.

Fanning, Rowland Francis Nichol (Sir); LDS 2097/154; born 1827, Co. Dublin, son of John Fanning, Esq., of 6 Duke Street, Drogheda, Co. Louth; married Marry Anne, born, in Kilkenny City (d.1901), daughter of Thomas Stanton, Clonmel, Co. Tipperary; he was one of the first four RIC officers to undergo training on 31/8/1861 at the School of Musketry, Fleetwood, North Lancs., England (*Cork Examiner* 26/8/1861); 3rd SI 3/10/1846; CI 1/1/1870; AIG 16/11/1876; DIG 14/9/1882; pensioned 11/11/1886; Knighted 1886 by order of the Queen by the Lord Lieutenant, in recognition of his long and meritorious service; retired to Dalmore, Bray, Co. Wicklow; died 20/1/1919; (Rathdown Registrar's District, 1919, vol. 2, p. 981); will and two codicils proved on 17/5/1919 at the Principal Registry.

Faraday, John Alexander Mallory; RIC 82012; ADRIC no. 788; LDS 2099/026; born 28/5/1899, San Francisco, United States; captain, Irish Guards; 3rd DI 20/9/1920; pensioned 30/3/1922.

Farrell, James John; veterinary surgeon to the Force from 23/5/1855 to 1/5/1870.

Farrell, Michael; CarNB; born 1778; stipendiary magistrate, 1813; son, Michael (1812–57).

Faussett, Robert; LDS 2097/141; born 1812, Co. Fermanagh; son of Charles Faussett and father of William Willoughby Bernard Faussett, CI, RIC; Scholar Trinity College Dublin on 5/7/1830; BA, 1835; lieutenant, Fermanagh Yeomanry; lieutenant, Fermanagh Militia (WO 13/2861–81); wife a native of Co. Sligo; 3rd SI 2/5/1843; CI 26/9/1868; died 2/1/1877 at Armagh, Co. Armagh; administration granted on 13/2/1877 at Armagh to Rev. Charles Faussett, of Suirview, Newtown, Waterford, Co. Waterford, in Holy Orders, the son of the deceased; effects under £6,000.

Faussett, William Willoughby Bernard; RIC 38048; LDS 2097/286; born 1853, Co. Monaghan; son of Robert Faussett, CI, RIC; married on 29/9/1881, wife from Co. Antrim; 3rd SI 22/9/1871; CI 28/6/1896; King Edward VII Visit to Ireland Medal, 1903; pensioned 11/9/1912; died 8/12/1918 at Dochas, Cowper Road, Dublin; administration granted on 21/4/1919 at the Principal Registry.

Feely, Frank Michael; LDS 2098/007; born 1865, Co. Cork; (Cork Registrar's District, 1865, vol. 10, p. 112); son of Patrick M. Feely, SI, RIC; classical master at Wesley College, Dublin; married in April 1906; 3rd DI 1/10/1885; King Edward VII Visit to Ireland Medal, 1903; died at 3am on 11/1/1908 from septicaemia from injuries received on 30/12/1907; plaque erected in St Mary's Church of Ireland, Killarney reads: 'To the glory of God and in Loving Memory of Frank Michael Feely, Esq., District Inspector, Royal Irish Constabulary, who died 11th January 1908 at Stapleton Place, Dundalk, Co. Louth; Erected by his sorrowing mother, Annie Elizabeth Feely.' Buried in St Patrick's Cemetery, Dundalk, Co. Louth; will proved on 7/3/1908 at Armagh by the oath of Ellen Muriel Feely, the widow – effects £519.13s.7d.

Feely, Patrick M.; LDS 2097/119; born 1800, Co. Roscommon; father of Frank Michael Feely, SI, RIC; wife a native of Co. Roscommon; 3rd SI 8/6/1838; pensioned 17/7/1863; died 16/12/1888 at Castlerea, Co. Roscommon.

Fegan, Peter; RIC 39954; LDS 2098/178; born 1853, Co. Wicklow; 3rd DI 5/1/1901; Queen Victoria's Visit to Ireland Medal, 1900, when he held the rank of head constable; pensioned 1/6/1907.

Fernyhough, Robert; CarNB; died 1828; on 29/12/1825 he reported that a man named Carroll wanted for murder on 'Saturday last' went to the home of Carroll's sister-in-law about a mile from Eyrecourt and found him 'concealed between two beds and three women lying over him'; C.C. (Parsonstown) Birr, King's County, 1825.

Ferrall, Fergus; LDS 2097/045; born 1798, Co. Sligo; widower on appointment; 3rd SI 13/10/1823; pensioned 1/2/1853; resided at Gibraltar House, Co. Dublin; died 25/3/1876; his youngest daughter Anna Maria Victoria, aged 23 years, died at 16, Mount Michael, Glasnevin Road, Dublin on 10/5/1866; his last surviving daughter, Alicia Maria died at 19 Upper Rutland Street, Dublin on 12/10/1877; his son James Thomas Ferrall, aged 58 years died on 13/2/1900 at 16, Middle North Court Avenue, Church Road, Dublin.

Ferrar, William H.; CarNB; police magistrate for the town of Belfast in 1823; died in July 1827 in Belfast, Co. Antrim: will dated 12/9/1825 proved at the Prerogative Court on 22/11/1827 (NA Reference: T/13192); his son Michael answered his correspondence.

Ferris, John Patrick; RIC 57337; LDS 2098/147B; born 1874, Co. Galway; married on 22/8/1903 (Dublin North Registrar's District, September Quarter, 1903, vol. 2, p. 513), wife a native of Co. Kerry; 3rd DI 20/9/1921; pensioned 31/5/1922; transferred to the Royal Ulster Constabulary on 1/6/1922.

Featherstonehaugh, Alfred Hardinge; RIC 80228; ADRIC no. 1278; LDS 2099/048; born 7/4/1901, Ardmanagh House, Glenbrook, Co. Cork; educated at St Bee's College and Trinity College Dublin; served in WWI with the Royal Air Force as a cadet pilot, 1918–19; Chief Game Warden, Federation of Malaya, 1919–21; 3rd DI 20/9/1921; pensioned 20/4/1922; served with the Colonial Service 1928–52; served with F.M.S. Volunteer Force, and Royal Pioneer Corps; Prisoner of the Japanese, 1942–5; married firstly 12/9/1921 (Rathdown Registrar's District, September Quarter, 1921, vol. 2, p. 844), Edna Maude, eldest daughter of William John Smalldridge, 6, Longford Terrace, Monkstown, Co. Dublin; married secondly 7/12/1933, Phyllis Audrey Maud, only daughter and heiress of Henry Aubrey Cox, East Lodge, Glenbrook, Passage West, Co. Cork

Findlay, Francis; RIC 72937; ADRIC no. 352; LDS 2098/220B; born 13/5/1889, Alderwood House, Kinnishead, near Glasgow, Scotland; son of Francis Findlay, Commission Agent and Jane Allison (Nisbet) who were married at Kinnishead on 6/10/1882; baptized on 25/6/1889 by W.S. McAlpine, Minister of Free West Church, Pollokshaur; educated at Shawlands Academy and Glasgow High School; Corporal, No. 107219, 2nd Canadian Mounted Rifles, Machine Gun Section, Victoria, British Columbia, 8/1/1915; 1st Canadian Mounted Rifles Brigade; 2nd lieutenant, Lanarkshire Yeomanry (Territorial Force), 19/12/1916 (*London Gazette* dated 21/3/1917); 4th Battalion, Royal Scots (Territorial Force)(Queen's Edinburgh Rifles), 30/6/1917; lieutenant, 19/6/1918; awarded the Military Cross (*London Gazette* dated 26/7/1918); lieutenant, 9th Battalion Royal Scots (61st Division) resigned his commission and retained the rank of lieutenant (*London Gazette* dated 4/1/1921); 3rd DI 12/1/1920; pensioned 22/4/1922; residing at 190, 21st Street, West Vancouver, British Columbia, Canada in 1938; (WO 374/24256).

Firman, Thomas Pierson; CarNB; born Firmount, Nenagh, Co. Tipperary; son of John Firman; will dated 4/6/1830 was proved on 5/1/1835 by Penelope Chetwynd, who had three sons and came from a Yorkshire family; transcript of administration granted in the Prerogative Court in 1835 granted to Mary Firman, Parsonstown (NA Reference: IAR/1835/F/10) (IWR/1835/F/39); C.C. Eyrecourt, Co. Cavan and Ballinasloe and Clifden, Co. Galway.

Fitzgerald, Daniel O'L'; LDS 2097/188; born 1828, Co. Cork; 3rd SI 6/2/1851; his appointment was not confirmed and he was dismissed 6/2/1851 when he failed the entrance examination at the Constabulary Office.

Fitzgerald, Gerald; CarNB; stipendiary magistrate 20/8/1829 in Co. Tipperary; died 1853 in Ballinasloe, Co. Galway; probate granted on 2/7/1853 in the Prerogative Court (NA Reference: T/17009).

Fitzgerald, Harold Edward; RIC 72003; LDS 2098/157B; born 7/9/1896, Lismore, Co. Waterford; (Lismore Registrar's District, 1896, September Quarter, vol. 4, p. 580); lieutenant, Cheshire Regiment; 3rd DI 10/1/1920; pensioned 12/3/1922; joined the Palestine Gendarmerie as platoon commander on 13/3/1922.

Fitzgerald, John; RIC 45159; LDS 2098/211; born 24/6/1859, Co. Mayo; married in February 1887 (Tralee Registrar's District, March Quarter, 1887, vol. 5, p. 499), wife a native of Co. Kerry; 3rd DI 20/10/1905; pensioned 9/2/1920.

Fitzgerald, Michael E.; RIC 13261; LDS 2097/281; born 1829, Co. Limerick; wife from Co. Dublin; 3rd SI 20/9/1870; received a favourable record on 30/6/1871 for the arrest of an offender on the night of an outrage, in pursuit over an almost inaccessible mountain in utter darkness, the culprit following his arrest forced the injured party to accept a sum of money to compromise the case and was discovered; received a favourable record on 30/6/1871 whereby a systematic robbery had been committed by a postmistress, by opening and retaining American letters and cheques and obtaining the moneys by forgery – by writing privately to the American parties, a clue was obtained which led to the conviction of the offender and the recovery of a considerable sum of money; received a favourable record on 31/12/1871 for perseverance and tact in arresting the offender of a brutal agrarian assault a long way from his station; pensioned 1/8/1878; died 15/2/1893 at Kilmallock, Co. Limerick (Kilmallock Registrar's District, 1893, March Quarter, vol. 5, p. 313)

Fitzgerald, Nugent; RIC 19182; LDS 2097/207; born 1835, Co. Westmeath; 3rd SI 11/5/1856; discharged 31/3/1867, having accidentally wounded himself and lost a leg whilst shooting; granted a gratuity of £8.13s.4d. on 27/11/1857.

Fitzgerald, Thomas Dillon; LDS 2097/121; born 1820, Co. Dublin; clerk in the Constabulary Office from 9/11/1838 to 23/12/1838; wife a native of Co. Tipperary; son born on 11/1/1854 at Caherconlish, Co. Limerick (*Cork Examiner* 18/1/1854); daughter born on 28/5/1855 at

Waterford, Co. Waterford (*Cork Examiner* 8/6/1855); 3rd SI 9/11/1838; resident magistrate 1/3/1860.

Fitzgerald, Thomas George; RIC 17230; LDS 2097/198; born 1834, Co. Tipperary; 3rd SI 15/8/1853; died 27/11/1873 at Tullamore, King's County; administration granted on 18/3/1874 at the Principal Registry to Emily Matilda Fitzgerald, of Tullamore, King's County, the widow of said deceased – effects under £600.

Fitzgibbon, Gerald; LDS 2097/032; born 1788, Co. Tipperary; volunteer, 2nd and 1st lieutenant, 23rd Fusiliers from January 1813 to June 1817, serving two years in Waterloo; married, 1819; 3rd SI 20/12/1822; C.C. Baldoyle, Co. Dublin, 1831; pensioned 30/4/1841; died 1844 in Tralee, Co. Kerry; administration with will annexed granted in 1847 (NA Reference: Char1/14/p51); (WO 25/758 fol. 106).

Fitzgibbon, Gibbon; LDS 2097/148; born 1803, Ballysheedy East, Limerick, Co. Limerick; assistant clerk of security, Excise Department, May 1826 to May 1829 when the office was transferred to London and he was awarded a gratuity of £262.10s.0d. by the Treasury; 3rd SI 13/3/1845; paymaster 13/3/1845 for County Carlow and Queen's County; discharged 31/5/1851 on the abolition of the office of paymaster.

Fitzgibbon, William; LDS 2097/090; born 1810, Co. Limerick; 3rd SI 1/11/1835; died 15/3/1844.

Fitzhenry, Nicholas; CarNB; born, Co. Wexford; C.C. Miltown-Malbay, Co. Clare and Elphin, Co. Roscommon.

Fitzmaurice, George; LDS 2097/055; born 1802, Co. Waterford; 3rd SI 1/9/1824; CI 1/4/1836; JP, 1830; resident magistrate 30/11/1847; pensioned as a RM on 1/6/1869; died 1/11/1870 at Derry, Co. Derry; (Londonderry Registrar's Office, 1870, vol. 17, p. 151).

Fitzpatrick, Edmund; RIC 52396; LDS 2098/132B; born 1870, Co. Leitrim; married on 16/12/1897 (Listowel Registrar's District, December Quarter, 1897, vol. 5, p. 524), wife a native of Co. Kerry; 3rd DI 8/1/1920; pensioned 22/4/1922.

Fitzpatrick, Matthew; LDS 2097/035; born 1792, Clonenagh, Queen's County; ensign 37th Regiment of Foot (Royal Hampshire Regiment), 1813; lieutenant, 1818; 3rd SI 28/1/1823; died 1843; (WO 25/758 fol. 106).

Fitzsimon, Thomas; RIC 14410; LDS 2097/296; born 1831, Queen's County; Jane, his wife died on 6/2/1857, at Oulart, Co. Wexford (*Cork Examiner* 13/2/1857); 3rd SI 18/7/1878; died 14/2/1892 at Kilkeel, Co. Clare, late of Monaghan, Co. Monaghan; (Kilkeel Registrar's District, 1892, March Quarter, vol. 1, p. 578); administration granted on 7/3/1892 at the Principal Registry to Patrick Fitzsimon, of Ballymaners, Stradbally, Queen's County, farmer, the brother – effects £3,034.9s.2d.

Fitzsimon, Thomas F.; LDS 2097/122; born 9/3/1798, Glencullen House, Co. Dublin; third son of Thomas Fitzsimon (1760–1800) and Margaret, daughter and co-heiress (with her sisters, Mrs Esmonde and Mrs Nangle), of Bartholomew Callan, of Osbertstown House, Co. Kildare; his father died of a fever caught when visiting his brother-in-law, Dr Esmonde, who was a political prisoner in Wicklow Jail; joined the Irish Revenue Police as a lieutenant; married Jane Kenny; his only daughter, Anne Margaret, married Richard C. Clifford, lieutenant in the 10th Regiment of Foot (Royal Lincolnshire Regiment) on 18/2/1851 at Oulart, Co. Wexford (*Cork Examiner* 19/2/1851); 3rd SI 11/11/1838; pensioned 10/5/1859 in Co. Galway; died 24/10/1859.

Fitzsimons, James; RIC 35586; LDS 2098/106; born 1851, Co. Donegal; 3rd DI 25/6/1894; King Edward VII Visit to Ireland Medal, 1903; pensioned 3/2/1903; died 4/6/1919 at Shankill, Co. Dublin, late of Somerton, Wexford; buried in Mount Jerome Cemetery, Dublin on 6/6/1919; (photo in the *Constabulary Gazette*, vol. XIII, no. 5, 18/4/1903).

Flanagan, Thomas; RIC 53949; LDS 2098/094B; born 6/1/1872, Co. Sligo; (Sligo Registrar's District, 1872, vol. 2, p. 368); 3rd DI 7/9/1919; pensioned 21/10/1920.

Fleming, Cyril Francis; RIC 57882; LDS 2098/127; born 1875, Fermoy, Co. Cork; (Fermoy Registrar's District, 1875, vol. 9, p. 743); major, Irish Guards Special Reserve on 5/3/1816; married on 24/3/1900 (Dublin North Registrar's District, March Quarter, 1900, vol. 2, p. 457), at St Mary's Church, Donnybrook, Dublin, Helen Gertrude (Nellie), second daughter of F.P. Phelps, Exeter and granddaughter of W.W. Phelps, Archdeacon and Canon of Carlisle; divorced 1921 and remarried in 1926; 3rd DI 21/12/1896; King Edward VII Visit to Ireland Medal, 1903; King George V Visit to Ireland Medal, 1911; Adjutant, Phoenix Park Depot from 16/10/1912 to 16/5/1915; CI 15/6/1920; pensioned 31/3/1922; (photo in the *Constabulary Gazette*, vol. V, no. 12, 17/6/1899, p. 337). He retired to Weston, Trefusis, Flushing, Falmouth, Cornwall where he was appointed deputy lieutenant for the County of Cornwall in 1938 (*The Times*, 7/2/1938); Vice-Chairman, Cornwall Territorial Army Association (*The Times*, 3/1/1941).

Fleming, Thomas; LDS 2097/167; born 1800, London, England; he ran away from home at 15 and joined the 3rd Battalion of the Rifle Brigade giving his age as 17 and served as a private, corporal, sergeant and colour sergeant from 14/9/1815 to 16/2/1838; he joined the Irish Constabulary as a sub constable and drill instructor on 6/3/1838 at the Leinster Depot; promoted constable, 1/6/1838, 2nd class head constable, 1/9/1839, 1st class head constable, 1/12/1842, extra head constable, 1/10/1846; 3rd Class SI on 1/6/1848 and the first Adjutant of the Phoenix Park Depot; in 1850 he was residing at 1 Besborough Terrace, North Circular Road; on 11/7/1851 he received an injury as a result of a fall at the Depot Stores; he was pensioned in Co. Kildare in 1859 and died in Kildare on 25/7/1860. He is buried in Mount Jerome Cemetery, Dublin (Plot C138–1608) with his daughter, Emily, born 27/1/1840 and died on 18/6/1852 at 4 Besborough Terrace, North Circular Road, Dublin (*Cork Examiner* 28/6/1852) and Mary (d.31/7/1861) his eldest daughter. He was the father of Sub Inspector Thomas Sylvanus Fleming and grandfather of County Inspector Cyril Francis Fleming who was responsible for recruiting the 'Black and Tans' and the Auxiliary Division in London.

Fleming, Thomas Sylvanus; RIC 26754; LDS 2097/239; born 1842, King's County; married on 5/9/1865 (Callan Registrar's District, vol. 4, p. 759), wife from, Co. Kilkenny; son, George Alfred, born on 4/2/1868 at Clogheen, Co. Tipperary (Clogheen Registrar's District6, vol. 4, p. 742) (*Cork Examiner* 8/2/1868); son born on 29/1/1871 at Clogheen, Co. Tipperary (*Cork Examiner* 2/2/1871); 3rd SI 1/8/1861; on 18/1/1867 he was reduced in rank and transferred for impugning the character of a magistrate; CI 18/3/1886; Queen Victoria's Visit to Ireland Medal, 1900; died 28/11/1901 at St Anne's Hill, Blarney, Co. Cork, late of Annagh, Clontarf, Co. Dublin; buried in Mount Jerome Cemetery, Dublin on 30/11/1901 (grave No. C138–11275); will proved on 18/2/1902 by the oath of Cyril Francis Fleming, DI, RIC – effects £1,055.2s.0d.

Fletcher, Robert B.; LDS 2097/097; born 1800, Co. Dublin; PPF; PPF Clerk 1/1/1833 to 30/9/1836; 3rd SI 1/10/1836; died 9/4/1849 at Cahirciveen, Co. Kerry.

Fletcher, Thomas Henry; RIC 54971; LDS 2098/083B; born 19/1/1873, Nenagh, Co. Tipperary; (Nenagh Registrar's District, 1873, vol. 3, p. 637); 3rd DI 12/5/1917; pensioned 31/5/1922; transferred to the Royal Ulster Constabulary on 1/6/1922.

Fleury, Alfred E.; RIC 34403; LDS 2097/270; born 1846, Leeson Street Upper, Dublin, Co. Dublin; youngest son of Rev. C.M. Fleury, D.D. of Dublin; 3rd SI 24/7/1868; pensioned 31/8/1896; died 27/1/1910 at Glenwood, Kilworth, Co. Cork; administration granted on 28/4/1910 at the Principal Registry to Anna M. Fleury, the widow – £439.6s.9d.

Flinter, Ephraim Stewart; LDS 2097/026; born 1793, Queen's County; ensign, 97th Regiment of Foot (Royal West Kent Regiment), 8/1/1807; lieutenant, 95th Regiment of Foot (Rifle Regiment), 1812; lieutenant half-pay 1/12/1818; married at Templetuohy Church, Co. Tipperary, 21/11/1816; 3rd SI 1/5/1821; residing at Rossmore 4, Kildare in 1828; CI 1/7/1831; received an injury in the chest when attending a political meeting at Belfast on 21/6/1841; died 1/7/1854 at Ballymena, Co. Antrim, 'in his 60th year as a result of disease of the heart' (*Cork Examiner* 12/7/1854); administration with will annexed granted on 19/8/1854 at Down &

94   95

94 Cyril Francis Fleming.   95 Thomas Fleming, grave in Mount Jerome Cemetery, Dublin.
96 Thomas Sylvanus Fleming.   97 Gerald Robert Edward Foley.

96   97

Connor Diocese (NA Reference: Down and Connor Will & Grant Book/8348); (WO 25/758 fol. 139).

Flower, Robert Glover Cook; RIC 48492; LDS 2097/318; born 1861, Norfolk, England; (Erpingham Registrar's District, 1860, June Quarter, vol. 4b, p. 56); residing at Upton Street, Barton, Gloucester in 1881 (Census); married on 11/8/1885 (Rathdown Registrar's District, September Quarter, 1885, vol. 2, p. 717), wife a native of Co. Wicklow; 3rd SI 17/3/1882; CI 13/1/1903; King George V Coronation Medal, 1911; AIG 30/12/1916; pensioned 15/4/1920; (photo in the *Constabulary Gazette*, vol. V, no. 6, 6/5/1899).

Foley, Gerald Robert Edward; RIC 65911; LDS 2098/024B; born 1/4/1886, Rathkeale, Co. Limerick; (Rathkeale Registrar's District, June Quarter, 1886, vol. 5, p. 521); scholar and gold medallist, BA 1909, Trinity College Dublin; 3rd DI 23/6/1911; captain and major, 5th Battalion, Royal Irish Regiment, from 27/1/1916 to 13/2/1919; awarded the OBE (military) mentioned in despatches; TCI 1/12/1920; pensioned 28/2/1922; appointed superintendent and promoted to Assistant Inspector-General Palestine Police.

Foley, James; RIC 52713; LDS 2098/131B; born 1868, Co. Leitrim; (Carrick-on-Shannon Registrar's District, 1868, vol. 13, p. 79); married on 20/9/1904 (Cork Registrar's District, September Quarter, 1904, vol. 5, p. 113), wife a native of Co. Cork; 3rd DI 8/1/1920; pensioned 20/4/1922.

Foley, John Matthew Galwey; RIC 37562; LDS 2097/285; born 1850, Co. Waterford; father of Thomas Galwey Foley, DI, RIC; married firstly on 25/6/1877 (Dublin North Registrar's District, vol. 7, p. 477); married secondly on 10/11/1904 (Kilkenny Registrar's District, December Quarter, 1904, vol. 3, p. 359), Mary Louise Taylor; 3rd SI 1/5/1871; musketry instructor from 17/1/1892 to 3/4/1895; CI 3/4/1895; residing at Bindon Street, Ennis Co. Clare in 1901, as a widower with two sons, P.N. Barron Foley, aged 12 years and Frederick James Foley, aged 10 years (Census 1901); CI attached to Crime Special Branch 1/5/1901 to 1/11/1902; (photo in the *Constabulary Gazette*, vol. XIX, no. 9, 19/5/1906).

Foley, Thomas Galwey; RIC 59750; LDS 2098/185; born 31/7/1880, Gorey, Co. Wexford; (Gorey Registrar's District, September Quarter, 1880, vol. 2, p. 804); son of John Mathew Galwey Foley, CI, RIC; 3rd DI 17/1/1902; pensioned 22/4/1922.

Foley, William Daniel; LDS 2097/217; born 1831, Co. Cork; joined the Irish Revenue Police as a lieutenant on 15/2/1856 and served in Newbliss, Co. Monaghan; daughter born on 10/5/1861 at Ballinacargy, Co. Westmeath and who survived only for a few minutes (*Cork Examiner* 15/5/1861); his only son, William, aged 13 years, died on 19/4/1872 at Newcastle West, Co. Limerick (*Cork Examiner* 22/4/1872; 3rd SI 1/12/1857; dismissed 16/12/1873.

Foott, Callaghan; RIC 1296; LDS 2097/174; born 1812, Co. Cork; enlisted as a sub constable on 12/3/1832; 3rd SI 1/6/1848; discharged on a pension as a 1st Head Constable of £60.0s.0d. per annum.

Foott, Wade; LDS 2097/039; born 1801, Clonakilty, Co. Cork; son of George Foott, of Springfort House, Mallow, Co. Cork; 3rd SI 10/2/1823; he was severely injured on 23/4/1847 whilst conveying a prisoner to gaol in Thurles by a kick he received in the abdomen; CI 1/1/1841; pensioned 17/11/1862; died 14/5/1866 at Tudor Hall, Monkstown, Co. Dublin (Rathdown Registrar's District, vol. 7, p. 792); administration granted (and will attached) at the Principal Registry on 6/7/1866 to Elizabeth Anne Foott, of Tudor Hall, widow and residuary legatee – effects under £3,000.

Forbes, William Francis; born 15/2/1836, London, Middlesex, England; second son of George John, Viscount Forbes (1785–1836) and brother of George Arthur Hastings Forbes, the seventh Earl of Granard, of Castle Forbes, Newtownforbes, Co. Longford; Leitrim Militia (WO 13/2980–98); captain, Grenadier Guards, from December 1852 to June 1859; honorary colonel 8th Battalion on 15/4/1871, the Prince Consort's Rifle Brigade; JP, DL; Crimean and Turkish Medals with clasp for Sebastopol; wounded at Sebastopol; married 29/10/1863 (Wexford

Registrar's District, vol. 10, p. 10), Phyllis Gabriella (d.20/2/1904), second daughter John Rowe, of Ballycross, Co. Wexford; 3rd class resident magistrate 19/8/1865, 2nd class 18/9/1872, 1st class 6/10/1882; special resident magistrate 1/3/1882 to 1/10/1883 and 1885–89; died 3/2/1899 at Sumville, Curragh Camp, Co. Kildare; will proved at the Principal Registry on 16/3/1899 by the oath of Lady Angela Fitzwygram, of Leigh Park, Hants., and Frances E.N. Paget, of Oxenhoath, Tonbridge, Kent, widow, and Francis R.M. Crozier, of Carrickbrennan, Monkstown, Co. Dublin, solicitor – effects £4,133.14s.11d. (p. 18, RM Records of Service Book, National Archives, Dublin).

Forde, John; LDS 2097/064; born 1801, Co. Louth; 3rd SI 27/1/1826; pensioned 5/8/1846.

Forsayeth, Samuel; CarNB; born, Co. Cork; C.C. Tipperary Town and Clanwilliam, Co. Tipperary.

Fortescue, George Edward; LDS 2097/144; born 27/8/1824, Shebbear, Hatherleigh, Devon, England, son of John Mills Fortescue, SI, RIC; 3rd SI 17/4/1844, appointed in the name of his father, who resigned with that view; CI 18/8/1869; died 29/4/1871 at Monaghan, Co. Monaghan (*Cork Examiner* 5/5/1871); administration granted on 24/7/1871 at the Principal Registry to Sarah Carter, of the Vicarage Bettwys, Abergyle, Denbighshire, Scotland, first cousin once removed of the deceased, effects under £2,000.

Fortescue, John Faithful; LDS 2097/127; born 17/12/1815, Quebec, Canada; son of John Mills Fortescue, SI, RIC; 3rd SI 22/6/1839; received an approbation on 31/3/1852 for indefatigable and successful exertions in bringing to justice the perpetrators of a murder committed up to four years previously; pensioned 1/10/1859; died 10/7/1861 at Ennistymon, Co. Clare (*Cork Examiner* 18/7/1861); administration granted at the Principal Registry to John Mills Fortescue, Dundrum, Co. Dublin on 21/8/1861, the father and only next of kin of the deceased – effects under £800.

Fortescue, John Mills; LDS 2097/068; born 1790, Shebbear, Hatherleigh, Devon, England; married at Stonehenge, Devon, 11/9/1813; children: James, b.16/6/1814, John Faithful, b.17/12/1815 (SI, RIC) Thomas, b.12/2/1815, Henry, b.10/7/1819, George Edward, b.27/8/1824 (SI, RIC); Irish Revenue Police; ensign, 2nd North Devon Militia, 19/1/1807; lieutenant, 1813; ensign 103rd Regiment of Foot (Westmoreland), 19/8/1813; lieutenant, 1817; lieutenant half pay, 1/7/1817, 103rd Regiment of Foot; captain 55th Regiment of Foot (Westmoreland Regiment); Chief Constable of Police, Devon, 1828; 3rd SI 1/1/1829; on 30/6/1829 writing from Devon and applied for an extension of leave as his child was dying; received an injury to his right knee on 17/12/1832 when on duty at the Sligo Election; resigned 16/4/1844 in favour of the appointment of his son George Edward Fortesque; (WO 25/758 fol. 188).

Fosbery, William; LDS 2097/149; born, 1818, Ashgrove, Pallaskenry, Co. Limerick; second son of William Fosbery (1781–1851) and Elizabeth Goff, Carrigfoy, Co. Kerry; married Jane Scott; 3rd SI 2/8/1845; seconded to the Commissariat Department in the Crimea from 2/8/1854 to 10/8/1855; pensioned 21/4/1868; died 2/1/1889 at The Mall, Cahir, Co. Tipperary; will proved on 4/3/1889 at Waterford by the oath of Jane Fosbery, The Mall, Cahir, Co. Tipperary, the widow – effects £3,782.2s.10d.

Foster, John; RIC 52783; LDS 2098/031B; born 16/12/1868, Co. Leitrim; married on 6/10/1896 (Clogheen Registrar's District, December Quarter, 1896, vol. 4, p. 209), wife a native of Co. Tipperary; his son, Ernest John Foster attended The King's Hospital School, Oxmanstown, Dublin from 1914 to 1916; 3rd DI 22/1/1912; ACI 1/12/1920; TCI 1/1/1921; pensioned 15/6/1922.

Fox, Alexander Kingstone; LDS 2097/051A; born 1802, 22, Charlemont Street, Dublin, Co. Dublin; second son of John Fox (b.1774) of Dublin and Sarah, eldest daughter of Alexander Kingstone, of Mosstown; his wife, Paterson was a native of Co. Derry; 3rd SI 1/7/1824; C.C. Muff, Co. Donegal; CI 12/4/1845; died 5/12/1864 at Londonderry (*Cork Examiner*

10/12/1864) (Londonderry Registrar's District, vol. 17, p. 126); administration granted on 28/1/1865 at Londonderry to Catherine Fox, of Londonderry, widow of the deceased – effects under £3,000.

Fox, Andrew; RIC 55596; LDS 2098/134B; born 1871, Co. Tyrone; (Gortin Registrar's District, 1871, vol. 12, p. 915); major, Royal Irish Rifles; 3rd DI 8/1/1920; pensioned 20/5/1922.

Fox, Willoughby George; LDS 2097/150; born 1826, Co. Tyrone; 3rd SI 19/9/1845; resigned 6/2/1857 on his appointment as Chief Constable of Derbyshire County Constabulary from 1857 to 1873.

Foy, Godfrey Ellis; RIC 58070; LDS 2098/130; born 1872, Shankill, Belfast, Co. Antrim; (Belfast Registrar's District, 1872, vol. 1, p. 392); married on 16/5/1917 (Callan Registrar's District, June Quarter, 1917, vol. 4, p. 237), Miss K. Dunbar, a native of Co. Donegal; 3rd DI 24/6/1897; pensioned 9/5/1922; (photo in the *Constabulary Gazette*, vol. 2, no. 39, p. 1, 24/12/1897 & vol. XIX, no. 9, 19/5/1906).

Franks, David Brudenell; LDS 2097/098; born 1813, Carrig Park, Co. Cork; third son of William Franks of Carrig, JP, who married in 1792, Catherine, eldest daughter of William Hume of Humewood, Co. Wicklow; 3rd SI 1/10/1836; paymaster 1/10/1836 for Co. Tipperary; resident magistrate, 11/4/1849; died 7/11/1886 at Coole Lodge, Co. Galway; will with one codicil proved on 3/12/1886 at the Principal Registry by the oath of Louisa Margaret Franks, of Ballinamantine, Gort, Co. Galway, spinster and Charles Gregory, of West Court, Callan, Co. Kilkenny, Esq., the executors – effects £4,663.10s.5d.

Frazer, Charles Henry; RIC 37117; LDS 2097/282; born 1851, Co. Fermanagh; youngest son of William Fraser, Esq., Richmond Place, Dublin; 3rd SI 4/1/1871; pensioned 11/6/1887; died 19/8/1889 at the residence of is brother, Dr H.F. Frazer, Lavender Hill, London, S.W.

Frazer, William; LDS 2097/168; born 1804, Co. Galway; enlisted as a sub constable on 1/11/1824; wife a native of Co. Mayo; his fourth daughter, Charlotte Rebecca, died on 18/11/1863 (*Cork Examiner* 10/12/1863); 3rd SI 1/6/1848; pensioned 15/6/1856 in Co. Mayo.

French, James Ellis; RIC 29244; LDS 2097/247; born 1842, Co. Cork; 3rd SI 28/1/1864; received a favourable record on 31/12/1868 for the highly satisfactory state of the force in his district as tested on a headquarter inspection; received a favourable record on 30/6/1869 for prompt and successful measures for the capture of burglars; received a favourable record on 31/12/1869 for promptitude and determination in the arrest of two offenders out of a large riotous mob; received a favourable record on 31/12/1869 for persevering, ingenuity and zeal (finally attended by success) in the detection and conviction of burglars and recovery of a large amount of property; received a favourable record and a grant from the Reward Fund on 30/6/1870 for ingenious and effective measures adopted by him and admirably carried out by his men for the detection of a case of embezzlement to a serious amount and recovery of the money stolen; received a favourable record on 30/6/1871 for persevering and successful efforts to bring to punishment the keepers of a brothel who were found guilty of having carried on the infamous and detestable practice of decoying very young children for the purpose of prostitution – the constabulary had many difficulties to overcome in obtaining evidence and the importance of this conviction to the community could scarcely be over-rated; received a favourable record and a grant from the Reward Fund on 31/12/1871 in tracing a coiner who was prosecuted and sentenced to seven years penal servitude, without any clue and brought about solely by his plans and the most protracted and patient watching of the offender; detective director from 18/6/1872 to 14/9/1882; residing at 20, Besborough Terrace, North Circular Road, Dublin; CI 14/9/1882; dismissed 30/4/1884; James Ellis French was arrested on 15/7/1884 for his involvement with a homosexual group of Dublin Castle officials. He tried unsuccessfully to plead insanity on 19/8/1884 and 30/10/1884. Tried for conspiracy on 31/10/1884, 3/11/1884 & 19/12/1884 and found guilty on 20/12/1884 and sentenced to two years imprisonment with hard labour from the date of arrest.

French, Robert; LDS 2097/105; 3rd SI 1/11/1836.

Frenzel, Harry; RIC 76811; LDS 2098/182B; 3rd DI 16/10/1920.

Frith, James Moore; RIC 16680; LDS 2097/196; born 1826, Co. Wicklow, son of Rev. John Smith; clerk in the office of the Inspector General of the Irish Constabulary; married Harriet Fannie (died 1886), widow of Captain Jackson, and daughter of Richard Jubb, Cliffe, Yorkshire; 3rd SI 12/2/1853; barrackmaster of the Phoenix Park Depot 8/6/1865; pensioned 16/6/1880; died 28/2/1907 (Descendant of John Frith, The Martyr, b.1503 and was burned at the stake, at Smithfield, as the first Protestant martyr, 4 July 1553).

Frizell, William Hume; RIC 46827; LDS 2097/311; born 1859, Co. Wicklow; married on 24/1/1883 (Borrisokane Registrar's District, March Quarter, 1883, vol. 3, p. 321), wife a native of Co. Dublin; 3rd SI 10/5/1881; pensioned 1/6/1898; died 11/7/1901 at Lawnakilla, Co. Fermanagh; will proved on 29/10/1907 at the Principal Registry by the oath of John A. Frith – effects £1,233.18s.3d.

Fry, Alfred; LDS 2097/293; born 1840, Sheffield, Yorks., England; (Sheffield Registrar's District, 1840, March Quarter, vol. 22, p. 625); troop sergeant major, 5th Dragoon Guards in which he served for 17 years and 6 months; wife a native of Co. Roscommon; 3rd SI 1/10/1875; RIC Riding Master 1/10/1875 until his death on 28/7/1876 in Cork; (Cork Registrar's District, 1876, vol. 15, p. 113).

Fuge, Thomas Hugh Hare; RIC 72007; LDS 2098/161B; born 9/11/1896, Kinsalebeg, Co. Waterford; lieutenant, army; married on 1/6/1921 (Dublin South Registrar's District, June Quarter, 1921, vol. 2, p. 528), wife a native of Co. Dublin; 3rd DI 10/1/1920; pensioned 26/4/1922.

Fulton, Richard Robert; RIC 15584; LDS 2097/191; born 1823, Brussels, Belgium; eldest son of Col. James Forrest Fulton, KH (died on 4/12/1854 at Downpatrick, Co. Down); his brother, Captain Henry Seymour Moore Fulton, 69th Regiment of Foot (South Lincolnshire Regiment); died at Bangor, Co. Down on 4/3/1853, aged 31 years; another brother was Sir Forrest Fulton, KC; daughter, Mary Ormsby born on 27/6/1865 at Castleconnell, Co. Limerick (Limerick Registrar's District, vol. 15, p. 406) (*Cork Examiner* 30/6/1865); his daughter married Lieutenant Colonel Ruttledge; lieutenant, 44th Regiment of Foot (East Essex Regiment); 3rd SI 11/2/1852; Adjutant, Phoenix Park Depot and placed on the temporary rank of second class sub inspector from 1/5/1854 to 30/6/1855; pensioned at Parsonstown, Co. Offaly on 1/7/1886; died 7/4/1906 at Oxmanstown Mall, Birr, Co. Offaly where he had resided since 1876; he was buried in Birr, Co. Offaly.

98   99

98 Matthew Galwey Foley.   99 Godfrey Ellis Foy.   100 James Moore Frith – Barrackmaster, RIC.

100

G

Gaffney, Michael; RIC 64855; LDS 2098/212B; born 1/11/1889, Co. Cavan; lieutenant, Royal Dublin Fusiliers; 3rd DI 12/1/1920; pensioned 11/5/1922.

Galbraith, William; LDS 2097/023; born 1775, Kilthomas, Co. Galway; lieutenant and captain, Royal Irish Artillery from 1/11/1793 to 30/9/1801; lieutenant and captain, Galway Militia from 8/11/1806 to 31/12/1816 (WO 13/2882–901); 3rd SI 1/11/1819; CI 1/1/1832; paymaster 1/10/1836; pensioned 31/5/1851 on the abolition of the office of paymaster; died on 11/8/1851 at Skerries, Co. Dublin (*Cork Examiner* 18/8/1851).

Gallagher, Andrew; RIC 27335; LDS 2097/257; born 1819, Co. Donegal; 3rd SI 16/4/1866; pensioned 16/10/1879; died 22/2/1900 at Newcastle, Co. Down; administration granted on 28/3/1900 at Belfast to Edward Gallagher, merchant and William Gallagher, merchant – £2,462.6s.11d.

Gallagher, Joseph; RIC 55713; LDS 2098/179B; born 1/3/1873, Tubbercurry, Co. Sligo; (Tubbercurry Registrar's District, 1873, vol. 4, p. 604); 3rd DI 16/10/1920; married on 4/2/1900 (Sligo Registrar's District, March Quarter, 1900, vol. 2, p. 311), wife a native of Co. Sligo; pensioned 24/8/1922.

Gallaher, James; RIC 71652; LDS 2097/159; born 1810, Co. Cork; 3rd SI 1/9/1847; paymaster 1/9/1847 for Counties Sligo and Leitrim, Wicklow and Wexford; pensioned 31/5/1851 on the abolition of the office of paymaster.

Gallogly, George Henry; LDS 2098/125B; born 25/1/1895, Edenderry, King's County; (Edenderry Registrar's District, March Quarter, 1895, vol. 4, p. 346); captain, Royal Irish Fusiliers; 3rd DI 8/7/1920; pensioned 23/5/1922.

Gallwey, John; CarNB; born 1783, at 19 Main Street, Killarney, Co. Kerry; second son of Thomas Gallwey (1751–1817), JP, Grand Juror of Killarney, Co. Kerry and Maria (14/3/1758–20/4/1796), daughter of John Mahony of Dunloe Castle, Co. Kerry, by Honora, daughter of William Haly, of Ballyhaly, Co. Cork and Maria his wife, daughter of O'Grady, of Kilballyowen, Co. Limerick; married firstly, 19/6/1819 Bridget 'Biddy the Beautiful' (1795–1/3/1836), eldest daughter of Neptune Blood (1757–4/12/1832), Inspector-General of Excise, of Applevale, Ballintea, Co. Clare and Ellen Blake; Neptune was one of the well-known Clare family who claim descent from the Colonel Thomas Blood (1618–1680) who attempted to steal the Crown Jewels on 9/5/1671; married secondly 30/7/1840, Harriet (d.24/5/1871), daughter of John Cassidy, Monasterevan, Co. Kildare and Killyon, King's County, distiller and landowner; his youngest daughter, Lucy married on 8/1/1857, at the Church of St Andrew, Westland Row, Dublin, Michael McNamara, eldest son of John McNamara, Esq., of Dublin (*Cork Examiner* 9/1/1857); his brother Christopher Gallwey, born 1779 and died on 30/8/1861 at Tramore, Co. Waterford (*Cork Examiner* 3/9/1861), of Killarney, was land agent to Lord Kenmare; captain and major, 16th Regiment of Foot (Bedfordshire Regiment); DIG 1/7/1839; while stationed at Ballincollig, Co. Cork on 26/11/1829 he 'painfully' pleaded for the retention and transfer of sub constable Michael Gallwey, stationed at Passage West since 1822 when appointed by Richard Willcocks and who has been reported for a first offence of drunkenness. Provincial Inspector-General William Miller on 1/12/1829 left the matter open to the lord lieutenant, who ordered dismissal as he had 'made a rule never to look over the offence of drunkenness'; his second son, Neptune Blood Gallwey (1824–84), CI, RIC; his eldest son

General Sir Thomas Lionel John Gallwey (20/7/1821–12/4/1906), KCMG (1889), Colonel Commandant Royal Engineers was born at Farmhill, Killarney, Co. Kerry and educated at the Royal Military Academy, Woolwich, served in West Indies, Canada, Gibraltar and Bermuda and was Governor-in-Chief of Bermuda, 1882–88; Major John Gallwey's grandson Lieutenant Colonel Sir Henry Galway (25/9/1859–17/6/1949) (formerly Gallwey), CMG (1899), KCMG (1910), DSO (1896) was educated at Cheltenham and Sandhurst; joined 30th Regiment in 1878; ADC and Private Secretary to Commander-in-Chief and Governor of Bermuda, 1882–89; Deputy Commissioner and Vice-Consul, Oil Rivers Protectorate, 1891; Acting Consul-General, 1896–98; Acting High-Commissioner Southern Nigeria, 1900; Governor of St Helena, 1902–1911; Governor of the Gambia, 1911–14; Governor of South Australia, 1914–1920; Major John Gallwey died of typhus fever on 30/12/1844 at Barton Lodge, Rathfarnham, Co. Dublin (*Kerry Evening Post*, 8/1/1845); C.C. Ballincollig, Co. Cork.

Gallwey, Neptune Blood; LDS 2097/136; born 1824, Ballincollig, Co. Cork; second son of Major John Gallwey, DIG, RIC; married firstly in 1850 in Sligo, Co. Sligo (Sligo Registrar's District, vol. 10, p. 198), Alice Lawson (d.1856) and they had one daughter, Aphea; married secondly, on 10/11/1857, at St Peter's Church, Castlecomer, Co. Kilkenny (Kilkenny Registrar's District, vol. 6, p. 336) and (Dublin South Registrar's District, vol. 5, p. 358); Harriet Jane, eldest daughter of William Grattan, Esq., Co. Cork, late of the 88th Regiment or Connaught Rangers (*Cork Examiner* 13/11/1857); they had ten children including twins born on 4/8/1862 at the RIC Depot, Phoenix Park, Dublin (*Cork Examiner* 8/8/1862); son Edward, born on 15/1/1864 (Dublin North Registrar's District, vol. 2, p. 492) at the RIC Depot (*Cork Examiner* 20/1/1864); 3rd SI 13/5/1841; residing at the Limerick Road, Killaloe, Co. Clare in 1846 (Slater's Directory, 1846); adjutant, Phoenix Park Depot from 1/7/1862 to 24/1/1869; CI 24/1/1869; dismissed 28/11/1878; died at 5, Lower Dominick Street, Dublin on 11/3/1884; (photo: owned by Anthony McCan).

Gambell, Alexander; LDS 2097/270; born 29/5/1849, Co. Longford; 3rd SI 10/6/1868; CI 8/11/1893; AIG 1/4/1902; Commandant of the Phoenix Park Depot from 1/4/1902 to 16/2/1905; King Edward VII Visit to Ireland Medal, 1903; pensioned 17/2/1910; died on 27/6/1927 and buried in Deansgrange Cemetery, Dublin (South West Section, Row Y, Grave No. 74) with his wife Mary Dorothea Gambell (d.2/7/1943) and her sister Sarah A. Faris, of Corr, Co. Cavan (d.24/1/1946).

Gamble, Robert W.; RIC 18517; LDS 2097/298; born 1838, Knockbride, Co. Cavan; married on 11/11/1870, wife a native of Co. Mayo; 3rd SI 1/1/1879; pensioned 15/7/1897.

Gamble, Thomas Edward Galt; RIC 54996; LDS 2098/077; born 1867, Co. Fermanagh; Royal Dublin Society Librarian from February 1885 to April 1891; married on 12/3/1892 (Dublin North Registrar's District, March Quarter, 1892, vol. 2, p. 459), wife a native of Co. Dublin; 3rd DI 10/9/1891; King Edward VII Visit to Ireland Medal, 1903; CI 9/12/1914; pensioned 7/10/1920; (photo in the *Constabulary Gazette*, vol. 1, no. 15, 10/7/1897).

Gannon, Francis; LDS 2097/174; born 1800, Coolbanagher, Queen's County; brother of Richard Gannon, CI, RIC; enlisted as a sub constable on 25/3/1831; wife a native of Co. Waterford; 3rd SI 1/6/1848; pensioned 16/9/1868; died 3/1/1884 at Waterford (Waterford Registrar's District, 1883, March Quarter, vol. 4, p. 611); his widow, Elizabeth Gannon died at Clonaslee, Queen's County on 20/2/1901.

Gannon, Richard; LDS 2097/086; born 1798, Coolbanagher, Queen's County; brother of Francis Gannon, SI, RIC; PPF; enlisted as a sub constable, 15/9/1819; when serving in the Peace Preservation Force in March 1821 he received an injury at the fair in Cashel from a blow of a stone to the head; married on 20/5/1854 (Dublin South Registrar's District, vol. 5, p. 295), Eliza, eldest daughter of Thomas Lane, Esq., of Coolnabanch, Clonaslee, Queen's County (*Cork Examiner* 29/5/1854); 3rd SI 26/9/1834; CI 20/5/1858; pensioned 17/11/1862; died 4/5/1866, Ennis, Co. Clare (Ennis Registrar's District, 1866, vol. 9, p. 141).

101

101 Neptune Blood Gallwey, *c.*1865.   102 Alexander Gambell.   103 John Fitzhugh Gelston.

102   103

Gardiner, Frederick William; RIC 36896; LDS 2097/282; born 1848, Aghalurcher, Co. Fermanagh; 3rd SI 8/10/1877; died 30/11/1885 at The Hermitage, Dungarvan, Co. Waterford, late of Strabane, Co. Tyrone; administration granted on 19/1/1886 at the Principal Registry to Catherine Hamilton Gardiner, of Providence, Queen's County, the widow – effects £805.15s.0d.

Gardiner, John Charles; RIC 32616; LDS 2097/261; born 23/4/1844, Kilbride, Co. Mayo; 3rd SI 1/4/1868; temporary resident magistrate 27/1/1881; permanent 3rd class RM, 6/6/1881, 2nd class 18/10/1882, 1st class 1/1/1892; pensioned 23/4/1909.

Gardiner, Joshua; RIC 17417; LDS 2097/317; born 1835, Co. Cavan; married on 16/10/1885 (Dublin North Registrar's District, December Quarter, 1885, vol. 2, p. 451); 3rd SI 9/1/1882; pensioned 1/4/1895; died 20/1/1898 at Tritonville Road, Sandymount, Dublin.

Gardiner, Nicholas Roche; RIC 53463; LDS 2098/050; born 1867, Co. Louth; wife a native of Co. Dublin; 3rd DI 2/9/1889; resigned 18/5/1900 on his appointment as Chief Constable of Police of Walsall, Staffs., England on 18/5/1900.

Gardiner, Robert Nicholson; LDS 2097/118; born 1814, Kilmacallan, Co. Sligo; daughters born on 8/12/1852 and 29/11/1855) at Bray, Co. Wicklow (*Cork Examiner* 10/12/1852 & 5/12/1855); 3rd SI 4/11/1837; awarded the Constabulary Medal 30/4/1867; pensioned 1/4/1875; died 19/6/1888 at 'The Lodge', Castlewood Avenue, Rathmines, Dublin.

Gardiner, William; LDS 2097/045; born 1794, Kilmacallan, Co. Mayo; lieutenant and captain in the yeomanry from November 1810 to October 1823; 3rd SI 13/10/1823; pensioned 1/11/1847.

Garraway, Edward Henry; LDS 2097/177; born 1825, Co. Wexford; 3rd SI 10/11/1848; residing at Main Street, Stradbally, Queen's County in 1850; died 8/9/1864 at the General Hospital, Belfast, of 55 Victoria Place, Belfast (Belfast Registrar's District, vol. 11, p. 145); administration granted at Belfast on 30/9/1864 to Jane Garraway, of 55 Victoria Place, Belfast, widow of the deceased – effects under £200; his son Captain Charles W. Garraway, The Royal Irish (Adjutant, Northern Bengal Mounted Rifles) married at St Stephen's Church, Hampstead on 14/8/1895, Etta, only daughter of Lieutenant-Colonel Russell-Royse, Indian Army.

Garrett, Richard; LDS 2097/220; born 28/9/1829, Killoran, Co. Sligo; joined the Irish Revenue Police as a lieutenant on 7/12/1852 and served in Aclare, Co. Sligo; 3rd SI 25/3/1858; CI 11/4/1881; pensioned 1/5/1894; son born at Ballinasloe, Co. Galway on 13/9/1871..

Gavan, Henry; LDS 2097/124; born 1800, Dublin City; 3rd SI 15/1/1839; Superintendent of Police, Ceylon, 30/9/1844 to 1/12/1845; re-appointed 2nd class SI on 1/2/1845; died 5/7/1846; his only daughter, Henrietta Letitia Sophia, married on 28/2/1872, at the Parish Church, Carlow, Co. Carlow, Harri Shackleton, of Kilkea (*Cork Examiner* 4/3/1872).

Geelan, Henry Arthur; RIC 72021; LDS 2098/169B; born 1/3/1900, Co. Armagh; (Armagh Registrar's District, 1900, March Quarter, vol. 1, p. 28); cadet, Royal Air Force; 3rd DI 10/1/1920; pensioned 31/5/1922; transferred to the Royal Ulster Constabulary on 1/6/1922

Geelan, John; RIC 53526; LDS 2098/114B; born 21/3/1868, Co. Leitrim; (Mohill Registrar's District, 1868, vol. 8, p. 310); married on 27/12/1887, wife a native of Co. Leitrim; 3rd DI 14/5/1920; pensioned 31/5/1922.

Gelston, John Fitzhugh; LDS 2098/064; born 1864, Kingscourt, Co. Cavan; son of Rev. Hugh Gelston, MA, Rector of Kingscourt, Co. Cavan; married on 22/4/1895 (Athlone Registrar's District, June Quarter, 1895, vol. 3, p. 1), Edith E. Gray, a native of Co. Westmeath; 3rd DI 21/6/1890; CI 13/11/1912; awarded the King's Police Medal, 1909 in 1917; Commissioner of Police and Town Inspector of Constabulary, Belfast from 11/3/1920 to 31/5/1922; pensioned 31/5/1922; transferred to the Royal Ulster Constabulary on 1/6/1922; his mother, Mrs E.J. Gelston died at Mount Ovid House, Ravenhill Road, Belfast on 4/12/1905, aged 82 years and was buried at Kingscourt, Co. Cavan.

Gerity, Ernest Oswald; RIC 52685; 2098/029B; born 16/1/1867, Cannington, Somerset, England; son of Patrick Gerity (b.1832) and Maria Josephine Gerity (b.1837); residing at East

Street, Ilminster, Somerset in 1881 (Census); married on 7/1/1899 (Galway Registrar's District, March Quarter, 1899, vol. 4, p. 157), wife a native of Co. Cork; 3rd DI 27/6/1911; TCI 7/1/1921; awarded the King's Police Medal, 1921; pensioned 31/5/1922; transferred to the Royal Ulster Constabulary on 1/6/1922.

Gibbons, James; CarNB; father of James Robert Gibbons, CI, RIC; 3rd SI 1825; Kells, Co. Kilkenny in 1828; killed with fourteen constables on 14/12/1831, Carrickshock, Co. Kilkenny; C.C. Pilltown, Co. Kilkenny.

Gibbons, James Robert; LDS 2097/138; born 1822, Co. Westmeath; son of Chief Constable James Gibbons and father of James Samuel Gibbons, CI, RIC; wife a native of Co. Longford; clerk in the Dublin Metropolitan Police Office from 1/5/1839 to 1/3/1842; 3rd SI 1/3/1842; CI 11/2/1869; died 5/2/1886 at Hartland's, Kilkenny, Co. Kilkenny; administration granted on 5/3/1886 at Kilkenny to Anne Bennet Gibbons and Grace Jemima Gibbons, spinsters, of Hartlands, the children and residuary legatees – effects £3,409.5s.4d.

Gibbons, James Samuel; RIC 34684; LDS 2097/271; born 1850, Co. Cavan; son of James Robert Gibbons, CI, RIC; CB; BA, MA, Trinity College Dublin; 3rd SI 19/9/1869; seconded on 11/10/1886 on his appointment as Inspector General of the Egyptian Police with the title 'Pasha'; was awarded the order of the Medidjeh, conferred upon him by His Highness the Khedive of Egypt with the Royal License to accept and wear it and 'Khedive's Bronze Star'; rejoined the RIC on 11/10/1886; CI 31/1/1891; county inspector attached to Crime Department, 31/1/1891 to 1/4/1893; died 28/3/1905 at Oughterard, Co. Galway; (Oughterard Registrar's District, 1905, March Quarter, vol. 4, p. 263).

Gibbons, Lewis William; LDS 2097/159; born 1820, Co. Galway; 3rd SI 2/8/1847; discharged with a gratuity 8/2/1860.

Gibson, John; CarNB; PPF; 3rd SI 3/5/1815; died 1818.

Gibson, Thomas Dunlap; LDS 2097/276; born 5/2/1845, Co. Derry; 3rd SI 20/4/1869; temporary resident magistrate 18/5/1881; permanent RM 3rd class, 2/11/1881, 2nd class, 11/9/1885, 1st class 16/1/1895; pensioned 14/2/1910; (photo in the *Constabulary Gazette*, vol. VI, no. 13, 23/12/1899, p. 390).

Gibsone, Hugh Cecil; RIC 82018; LDS 2099/027; born 30/3/1894, London, England; (Bethnal Green Registrar's District, 1894, September Quarter, vol. 1c, p. 179); captain, Queen's Regiment; married on 6/4/1922 (Cork Registrar's District, June Quarter, 1922, vol. 5, p. 109), M.F. Knox, a native of Co. Cork; 3rd DI 25/6/1921; pensioned 3/5/1922.

Gilchrist, Andrew; RIC 60239; LDS 2098/143B; born 1883, Co. Tyrone; married on 2/7/1912 (Lurgan Registrar's District, September Quarter, 1912, vol. 1, p. 975), wife a native of Co. Armagh; 3rd DI 7/8/1920; pensioned 24/6/1922.

Gilfillan, Ewing; RIC 65125; LDS 2098/007B; born 1/9/1887, Co. Derry; (Derry Registrar's District, September Quarter, 1887, vol. 2 p. 158); married on 17/4/1918 (Dublin South Registrar's District, June Quarter, 1918, vol. 5, p. 583), Sybil A. Palmer, a native of Co. Down; 3rd DI 2/8/1910; pensioned 31/5/1922; transferred to the Royal Ulster Constabulary on 1/6/1922; awarded the MBE in 1923.

Gillis, Charles Henry; RIC 52552; LDS 2098/053B; born 28/10/1867, Co. Carlow; (Carlow Registrar's District, 1867, vol. 18, p. 429); married on 20/8/1898 (Clifden Registrar's District, September Quarter, 1898, vol. 4, p. 61), wife a native of Co. Galway; 3rd DI 30/6/1914; pensioned 1/12/1920.

Gillman, Benjamin Hill; LDS 2097/123, born 1803, Co. Cork; baronial chief constable from March 1831 to January 1839; 3rd SI 3/1/1839; pensioned 1/2/1857; died 1/5/1857 at Chapel Row, Killaloe, Co. Clare.

Gillman, Henry Charles; LDS 2097/275; born 15/3/1849, Kilbrogan, Bandon, Co. Cork; third son of Rev. Henry Gillman, Bandon, Co. Cork (d.18/2/1858 and buried in Kilbrogan Churchyard, Bandon) and Lydia (d.22/12/1856), daughter of George Dunscombe, Esq., of

104

104 James Samuel Gibbons memorial, Carrickshock, Co. Kilkenny. 105 Andrew Gilchrist. 106 Ewing Gilfillan.

105   106

Mount Desert, Cork, who were married on 6/5/1845; he was the grandson of Colonel Henry Gilman; 3rd SI 30/1/1869; pensioned 19/3/1909; died 25/10/1913 at 55, Lindsay Road, Glasnevin, Dublin; will proved on 22/11/1913 at the Principal Registry to Kate Nolan – effects £157.4s.5d.

Gillmor, Gowan; RIC 35525; LDS 2097/278; born 1850, Sligo, Co. Sligo; 3rd SI 22/6/1867; resigned and discharged from the Force on 5/5/1881; daughter born at Clonsingle, Co. Tipperary, the residence of his father-in-law on 1/4/1872 (*Cork Examiner* 4/4/1872).

Gillooly, Michael; RIC 53105; LDS 2098/066B; born 15/8/1869, Co. Sligo; married on 18/8/1910 (Dublin North Registrar's District, September Quarter, 1910, vol. 2, p. 471), wife a native of Co. Roscommon; 3rd DI 12/1/1915; pensioned 20/7/1922.

Gilpin, William; RIC 687; LDS 2097/189; born 1809, Carrigallen, Co. Leitrim; enlisted as a sub constable on 1/12/1830; 1st Head Constable attached to the Reserve on 1/12/1842; 3rd SI 16/11/1851; died 15/5/1886.

Giveen, Fielding; LDS 2097/056; born 1797, Coolderry South, Kildollagh, Co. Derry; 3rd SI 1/10/1824; presented with an ornamental sabre by the Lord Lieutenant on 1/8/1843; CI 9/6/1848; pensioned 15/4/1868; died 5/6/1875 at 4 Clifton Place, Monkstown, Co. Dublin; administration granted on 12/7/1875 at the Principal Registry to Elizabeth Lee, Winton Lodge, Monkstown, Co. Dublin, spinster, the niece of the deceased – effects under £9,000.

Gleeson, James; LDS 2099/011; born 1887, Co. Cork; married on 22/8/1908 (Cork Registrar's District, September Quarter, 1908, vol. 5, p. 89), wife from Co. Waterford; 3rd DI 14/6/1921; pensioned 20/7/1922.

Gleeson, Thomas; LDS 2097/099; 3rd SI 1/10/1836 – record incomplete.

Gloag, John William; veterinary surgeon to the Force from 1/5/1870 to 1/10/1886; holder of the Crimean Medal, with clasps for Alma, Balaklava, Inkerman and Sebastopol; the Turkish Medal; the Order of Knights of the Legion of Honour, the Fifth Class Order of the Medidjeh.

Glynn, George; LDS 2097/060; 3rd SI 10/2/1825 – record incomplete.

Glynn, Michael George; RIC 66985; LDS 2098/040B; born 18/2/1887, Co. Dublin; (Dublin North Registrar's District, March Quarter, 1887, vol. 2, p. 570); 3rd DI 2/4/1913; resigned 19/7/1920.

Godfrey, Mason; RIC 82945; LDS 2099/050; born 11/5/1895, War., England; army service, 1911–20; ADRIC, 1920–1921; 3rd SI 20/9/1921; pensioned 30/4/1922.

Going, Richard; CarNB; born Kilnara, Newport, Co. Tipperary; second son of Richard Going of Bird Hill, Co. Tipperary, JP and Anne, daughter of Henry White, New Ross, Co. Wexford and they had four sons and four daughters; member of the Irish Bar; PPF; major, Tipperary Militia (WO 13/3243–63); his daughter, Georgina Villiers married William Gabbett, Esq., of Strand House, Co. Kerry and she died on 31/8/1854 at Strand House, the sister of Lieutenant-Colonel Going, 1st Royal Regiment (*Cork Examiner* 4/9/1854); his eldest daughter, Angelina Sarah, aged 19 years, died of consumption at Mallow, Co. Cork on 6/2/1823 (the *Constitution* or *Cork Morning Post*, Friday 21/2/1823); chief magistrate for Co. Limerick on 18/4/1820; removed from his command on 5/10/1821; resident magistrate; killed by four armed men on 14/10/1821, Curraheen Cross, near Cappa, Co. Tipperary – one mile from Rathkeale, Co. Limerick; funeral from Rathkeale, Co. Limerick to Newport, Co. Tipperary; left a widow, Joanna, two sons and four daughters; Patrick Neville and James Fitzgibbon were tried at the Limerick Assizes on 12/3/1823, convicted and hanged at Limerick County Gaol on 6/3/1823 (the *Constitution* or *Cork Morning Post*, Monday 17/3/1823); his older brother, Rev. John Going, Rector of Mealiffe, Co. Tipperary, married Frances Anne, eldest daughter of Rev. Walter Shirley, brother of the 4th, 5th and 6th Earl Ferrers; Rev. John Going was murdered at Mealiffe Glebe, Cashel on 23/10/1829, aged 62 years.

Golden, John; RIC 55203; LDS 2098/096B; born 15/8/1871, Killala, Co. Mayo (Killala Registrar's District, 1871, vol. 9, p. 409); awarded the King's Police Medal in 1912; awarded the medal of the Royal Humane Society; married on 22/1/1902; DI 7/9/1919; pensioned 24/8/1922.

Goodwin, Thomas; CarNB; C.C. Ballinasloe, Co. Galway, 1825, Kilconnell, Co. Galway, 1825.

Goold, Valentine E.; LDS 2097/185; born 1814, Yorks., England; ensign in the Queen of Spain's Services for nine months in 1835; 3rd SI 12/4/1844; seconded to the Commissariat Department in the Crimea from 2/8/1854 to 6/7/1855; resigned 22/7/1856 and was appointed Chief Constable of Somerset Police on 1 July 1856 to 30 June 1884.

Gordon, Patrick; RIC 56624; LDS 2098/110; born 6/4/1870, Co. Roscommon; son of John Gordon, Sheepwalk, Co. Roscommon; clerk of the Petty Sessions, Frenchpark, Co. Roscommon; married on 30/1/1901 (Enniskillen Registrar's District, March Quarter, 1901, vol. 2, p. 96), Winifred Una Cassidy, a native of The Graan, Enniskillen, Co. Fermanagh; 3rd DI 29/12/1894; pensioned 23/6/1911; died 14/11/1912 at 4 Rosemount Cottage, New Ross, Co. Wexford; administration granted on 22/2/1913 at the Principal Registry to Winifred Una Gordon, the widow – effects £57.12s.6d.; Winifred Gordon went to Paris and joined the American Ambulance Service and returned to Dublin in 1916, nursed the wounded of the 1916 Rising as a nurse in the Royal City of Dublin Hospital in Baggot Street. She joined Cumann na mBan and sheltered Austin Stack (1879–1929), Deputy Chief of Staff of the IRA (1919–1922) during the War of Independence, whom she married in 1925 and he died at the Mater Hospital, Dublin on 27/4/1929.

Gordon, S.R.; CarNB; born, Belfast, Co. Antrim; died at Crumlin, Co. Antrim on 26/10/1828; C.C. Ballycastle, Co. Antrim.

Gordon, Samuel Thomas; LDS 2098/013B; born 4/5/1849, Co. Dublin; resident surgeon, Richmond Hospital; resided at 11, Hume Street, Dublin; 3rd SI 19/4/1880; surgeon, Turco-Serbian War. Awarded the Turco-Serbian War Medal, 1876 and the Zulu War Medal, 1879; Queen Victoria's Visit to Ireland Medal, 1900; King Edward VII Visit to Ireland Medal, 1903; King George V Visit to Ireland Medal, 1911; surgeon to the Force on 19/4/1880 and pensioned on 21/7/1914.

Gore, Robert; LDS 2097/150; born 1821, Co. Cavan; son of Very Rev., the Hon. George Gore, Dean of Killala, Co. Mayo; lieutenant, Irish Revenue Police from 21/3/1845 to 9/8/1845 3rd SI 8/8/1845; pensioned 18/4/1872; died 13/6/1899 at 35, Upper Mount Street, Dublin, late of Raveagh, Eskragh, Co. Tyrone; will proved on 13/7/1899 at the Principal Registry by the oath of Elizabeth Gore, of Raveagh, Eskragh, Co. Tyrone and William T. Stewart, of 6 Leinster Road, Dublin – effects £1,564.12s.7d.

Gore-Hickman, Thomas O'Brien; RIC 69943; LDS 2098/102B; born 12/7/1892, Tyredagh Castle, Kilrush, Co. Clare; clerk on enlistment; son of Francis William Hickman (1857–1917) of Tyredagh Castle and Kilmore House, Knock, Ennis, Co. Clare and Elizabeth Brown (d.23/4/1953), daughter of Pierce O'Brien, JP, of Durra, Co. Clare, who were married on 16/10/1878; brother of Lieutenant Poole Henry Hickman, 7th Battalion, Royal Dublin Fusiliers; educated at Tipperary Grammar School; Gunner, No. 48700, Royal Garrison Artillery, 1/11/1914; private, No. 18864, 7th (Service) Battalion, Royal Dublin Fusiliers, 7/2/1915; wounded to the face by gunshot at Wytacbaete Ridge, 7/6/1915; second lieutenant, 14/9/1915; lieutenant, 1/7/1917; transferred to the Royal Dublin Fusiliers, 256/3/1918; relinquished his commission and retained his rank of lieutenant, 19/4/1921 (*London Gazette*, dated 19/4/1921); 3rd DI 4/1/1920; pensioned 22/4/1922; married on 6/6/1923, May, daughter of Charles Butler, of Cleethorpes, Lincolnshire; Staff Major, Military District No. 13, Canada, 1940–7; admitted to the Canadian Bar, 1941; Q.C. (Canada) 1955; retired as a magistrate on 30/6/1961; died on 27/12/1982 at Lethbridge, Alberta, Canada; (WO 339/44283).

Gorman, John Kearney; RIC 70141; LDS 2098/108B; born 15/11/1891, Co. Tipperary; major, Royal Artillery; married on 20/4/1922, Annette Mary Josephine O'Brien, a native of Co.

107 Samuel Thomas Gordon, Surgeon.   108 John Kearney Gorman, the last Depot Adjutant, 1922.   109 David B. Graham.   110 Alexander Gray.

Cork; 3rd DI 4/1/1920; Adjutant, Phoenix Park Depot from 16/11/1920 to 14/5/1922; transferred to the Royal Ulster Constabulary on 1/6/1922.

Goslett, Joseph; CarNB; born 1779; appointed PPF Chief Clerk, 14/11/1821 under Major Thomas Philip Vokes in Limerick City until 1831.

Gosselin, Nicholas (Sir); son of Captain Nicholas Gosselin and Selina, daughter of Rev. George Crawford, St Anne's Rectory, Newtownforbes, Co. Longford and Mary West; married Katherine Haslett; major, 4th Battalion Royal Irish Fusiliers; resident magistrate, July 1883; he was given a roving commission in May 1883 to co-ordinate the activities of the RIC political branch in Britain to investigate Fenian organizations; pensioned 1896.

Grace, C.; CarNB; PPF; transferred from Portumna, Co. Galway to Strokestown, Co. Roscommon at the request of Major Matthew Singleton in 1831 for not attending to duties which resulted in infections to horses; C.C. Portumna, Co. Galway and Strokestown, Co. Roscommon.

Graham, David B.; LDS 2097/099; born 1788, Ballynakill, Co. Galway; private and volunteer in the yeomanry cavalry from 1798 to 1808; barony collector for the barony of Shelburne, Co. Wexford, 1828 to 1833; 3rd SI 1/10/1836; paymaster 1/10/1836; discharged on a pension on 31/5/1851 on the abolition of the office of paymaster; died 1861.

Graham, Francis Johnstone; LDS 2097/170; born 1809, Co. Kildare; enlisted as a sub constable on 17/2/1827; wife a native of Co. Kildare; 3rd SI 1/6/1848; received the approbation of the Lord Lieutenant on 31/3/1850 for zeal and activity in detecting two separate attempts to fasten crime on innocent parties; died 28/7/1863.

Grant, Alexander; LDS 2097/065; born 1802, Kilmurry House, Kilworth, Co. Cork; 3rd SI 1/10/1826; died 27/5/1848 at Clonakilty, Co. Cork.

Grant, John; LDS 2097/111; born 1805, Templemichael, Co. Longford; enlisted as a sub constable in October 1823; wife a native of Co. Sligo; 3rd SI 1/11/1838; discharged on medical grounds, 24/3/1858; died 9/5/1861.

Graves, Arthur James; RIC 46286; LDS 2097/310; born 20/7/1858, Cahir, Co. Tipperary (*Cork Examiner* 24/7/1858); son of George Sandes Graves, SI, RIC; married on 24/4/1913, W.L. Alcock from England; 3rd SI 23/2/1881; King George V Coronation Medal, 1911; pensioned 1/11/1914.

Graves, Edwin Edward; LDS 2097/213; born 1828, Co. Limerick; joined the Irish Revenue Police as a lieutenant on 21/11/1849 and served in Plumb Bridge, Co. Tyrone and Swinford, Co. Mayo and residing at Chapel Street, Swinford, Co. Mayo in 1850; 3rd SI 1/12/1857; dismissed 5/10/1875.

Graves, George Sandes; LDS 2097/126; born 1815, Co. Cork; father of Arthur James Graves; married on 14/3/1854 (Dublin North Registrar's District, vol. 5, p. 66); daughter born on 7/3/1856 at Cahir, Co. Tipperary (*Cork Examiner* 12/3/1856); 3rd SI 1/5/1839; CI 10/7/1869; pensioned 16/3/1876; died 10/2/1895 at 63, Morehampton Road, Dublin; administration granted on 26/3/1895 at the Principal Registry to Arthur James Graves, of Kells, Co. Meath, DI RIC, the son – effects £99.6s.11d.

Graves, J.R.; LDS 2097/112; 3rd SI 1/4/1837.

Gray, Alexander; LDS 2097/328; born 1858, Co. Tyrone; BA, Queens University of Ireland; married on 17/12/1894 (Antrim Registrar's District, December Quarter, 1894, vol. 1, p. 45), Helen Stewart Gumley, a native of Co. Antrim; 3rd DI 4/1/1883; Queen Victoria's Visit to Ireland Medal, 1900; King Edward VII Visit to Ireland Medal, 1903; CI 27/10/1906; King George V Coronation Medal, 1911; wounded 28/4/1916, Ashbourne, Co. Meath; died of wounds 10/5/1916; buried in Esker Cemetery, Lucan, Co. Dublin with his wife, Madge who predeceased him; his headstone inscription reads: 'In loving memory of Madge, the beautiful sweet loving wife of A. Gray, DI, RIC who fell asleep 30/4/1901, aged 26 years, "sweet promptness unto kindest deeds were in her very look, we read her face as one who reads a true and holy book," also the above named Alexander Gray CI RIC, aged 57 years, who died on May

10th, 1916 from wounds received in the Ashbourne fight'; will proved at the Principal Registry on 29/6/1917 by Reverend J Merrin, clerk – effects £774.10s.9d.

Greally, John; RIC 64550; LDS 2098/224B; born 29/10/1888, Claremorris, Co. Mayo; (Claremorris Registrar's District, March Quarter, 1889, vol. 4, p. 153); Indian Army Reserve; 3rd DI 1/12/1920; pensioned 9/5/1922.

Greene, George Garrow; RIC 34572; LDS 2097/271; born 1848, Co. Cork; 3rd SI 28/8/1868; pensioned 16/10/1889; author of *In the Royal Irish Constabulary*, Dublin 1905.

Greene, John; LDS 2097/062; born 1796, Co. Waterford; ensign, 90th Regiment of Foot (Perthshire Volunteers), March to December 1812 and ensign and lieutenant, 85th Regiment of Foot (King's Light Infantry), January 1813 to June 1823; 3rd SI 1/10/1825; died 4/9/1840 in Carlow; (WO 25/760 fol. 21).

Greene, John A.; LDS 2097/120; born 1806, Co. Kilkenny; ensign and lieutenant from 1825 to 1836; 3rd SI 21/9/1838; resigned 2/9/1847.

Greene, Joseph; CarNB; lieutenant; JP, 14/8/1806; 3rd SI 1822; CI 1837; stipendiary magistrate, 25/3/1831; resident magistrate, 1/10/1836; died 28/2/1858 at Newtown House, Kilkenny; had a son a clergyman residing in Co. Antrim; C.C. Athy, Co. Kildare; will proved at Kilkenny on 28/5/1858 by the oath of John Newport Greene of the same place, the sole executor – effects under £4,000.

Greene, Pierce E.; LDS 2097/108; born 1815, Co. Waterford; 3rd SI 17/11/1836; died 8/11/1847.

Greene, Reginald; LDS 2097/092; born 1814, Castlecomer, Co. Kilkenny; 3rd SI 1/1/1836; serving in August 1857, record incomplete.

Greene, William John; RIC 33516; LDS 2097/265; born 1848, Co. Wicklow; 3rd SI 7/11/1867; CI 1/5/1892; King Edward VII Visit to Ireland Medal, 1903; pensioned 1/12/1908; died 5/5/1913 at Ivy Bank, Monkstown, Co. Cork; will proved on 7/7/1913 at the Principal Registry to Elizabeth A.D. Greene, the widow – effects £5,687.4s.7d.

Greer, Hugh Conrad; RIC 58071; LDS 2098/132; born 19/8/1873, Clonmel, Co. Tipperary; (Clonmel Registrar's District, 1873, vol. 19, p. 673); son of Thomas Augustus Greer, DI, RIC; he married on 29/4/1908, Inez (d.20/10/1921), daughter of Fairfield Magrane, of Buenos Aires, Argentina; 3rd DI 2/9/1897; King Edward VII Visit to Ireland Medal, 1903; ACI 28/3/1920; CI 15/6/1920; pensioned 17/7/1922; died 30/11/1961; (photo in the *Constabulary Gazette*, vol. 2 no. 39, p. 1, 24/12/1897).

Greer, Thomas Augustus; LDS 2097/226; born 6/7/1838, Glos., England; second son of John Robert Greer (11/9/1800–27/3/1873), of Monkstown Lodge, 6, Richmond Hill, Monkstown, Co. Dublin and Sarah Dinah (d.2/5/1891), daughter of John Strangman, of Summerland, Co. Waterford, who were married on 10/9/1829; father of Hugh Conrad Greer, DI, RIC; clerk in the National Bank for four years up to March 1858; married on 10/10/1867 in Wales, Selina Margaret (d.1921), third daughter of Thomas Hughes, DL, JP, of Ystrad Hall, Denbighshire; his sister, Elizabeth Amelia, married on 27/7/1864, at Monkstown Church, Dublin (Rathdown Registrar's District, vol. 12, p. 796), Anthony Mann Hawkes, Esq., of Horne Castle, Lincs., England (*Cork Examiner* 30/7/1864); 3rd SI 23/3/1859; pensioned 10/6/1879; retired to The Grove, St Lawrence, Jersey; died 24/4/1926 at Brunswick Terrace, Weymouth, Dorsetshire; (Weymouth Registrar's District, June Quarter, 1926, vol. 5a, p. 312); probate granted at London on 2/6/1926 to Frederick Augustus Greer, retired brigadier-general and Hugh Conrad Greer, retired DI, RIC – effects £515.6s.10d.

Gregory, Vere Richard Trench; RIC 56631; LDS 2098/112; born 16/10/1871, West Court, Callan, Co. Kilkenny; son of Henry Charles Gregory, of West Court, Callan, Co. Kilkenny and his first wife, Charlotte Anne (d.5/6/1879) (Callan Registrar's District, vol. 3, p. 189); youngest daughter of Rev. Charles Butler Stevenson, Rector of Callan, and formerly 1st Dragoon Guards (veteran of Waterloo), whom he married on 18/7/1861; half-brother of William Richard

Fetherstonhaugh Gregory, DI RIC; his uncle Lieutenant William Gregory Irish Revenue Police (b.1919) was drowned while sunbathing in Lough Ree, near Athlone in 1849; Vere Richard Trench Gregory married on 26/9/1900, Anne, 2nd daughter of William Faris, of Lurgan and widow of Francis Berry Fetherstonhaugh, of Carrick, Co. Westmeath; BA, LLB 1894, Trinity College Dublin; 3rd DI 21/1/1895; King Edward VII Visit to Ireland Medal, 1903; CI 15/6/1920; pensioned 31/8/1922; author of *The House of Gregory*, Dublin, 1943; (photo in the *Constabulary Gazette*, vol. XIII, no. 22, 22/8/1903, vol. XIV, no. 1, 26/9/1903 & vol. XXXII, no. 14, 14/12/1912).

Gregory, William Richard Featherstonehaugh; RIC 71405; LDS 2098/123B; born 12/7/1892, West Court, Callan, Co. Kilkenny; (Callan Registrar's District, September Quarter, vol. 4, p. 447); son of Henry Charles (10/8/1827–22/7/1918), of West Court, Callan, Co. Kilkenny and his second wife, Alicia Fanny (d.16/9/1929), 2nd daughter of Arthur Gambell, of Washbrook, Co. Westmeath, whom he married on 8/12/1884; half-brother of Vere Richard Trench Gregory, DI RIC; commander, Royal Navy; 3rd DI 13/6/1920; pensioned 5/4/1922; married in 1925, Frances Helen (d.13/3/1969), widow of Frederick Skief, of Baltimore, Maryland USA, and daughter of Elmer Liggett, of Detroit Michigan, USA.

Grene, William David; LDS 2097/247; born 1843, Glos., England; (Chorlton Registrar's District, 1843, September Quarter, vol. 20, p. 285); eldest son of George Greene, Powerstown, Clonmel, Co. Tipperary; married on 12/3/1868 at Thomastown Church, Thomastown, Co. Kilkenny (Thomastown Registrar's District, vol. 4, p. 1027), Alice, the youngest daughter of William Clifford, Millvale, Thomastown, Co. Kilkenny (*Cork Examiner* 13/3/1868); son George (Thomastown Registrar's District, vol. 14, p. 869) born on 3/8/1869 at Thomastown, Co. Kilkenny (*Cork Examiner* 6/8/1869); son, William Robert Clifford (Thomastown Registrar's District, vol. 9, p. 997), born on 21/4/1871 at Thomastown, Co. Kilkenny (*Cork Examiner* 26/4/1871); 3rd SI 29/1/1864; pensioned 11/3/1895; died 15/2/1911; (photo in the *Constabulary Gazette*, vol. VI, no. 13, 23/12/1899, p. 390).

Griffin, James; LDS 2097/168; born 1790, Queen's County; private, corporal and sergeant in the army for thirteen years and ten months, including two years allowed for service in Waterloo; wife a native of Sussex, England; enlisted as a constable on 1/5/1821; 3rd SI 1/6/1848; pensioned 10/5/1856 in Co. Cavan.

Griffin, John Loftus; LDS 2097/058; born 1797, Co. Dublin; married Anne Thompson; 3rd SI 1/1/1825; C.C. Hillsboro, Co. Down,1831; died 16/3/1847; his son Thomas John Augustus Griffin, born 27/71832, Banbridge, Co. Down, joined the Irish Constabulary (RIC 15467) on 24/11/1851 as a former clerk on the recommendation of General Sir Duncan McGregor, Inspector General Irish Constabulary; he was allocated to the Reserve on 1/3/1852 and promoted 1st class sub constable on 1/4/1852, resigned on 18/11/1857 and emigrated to Australia. He served in the police in Victoria and New South Wales, eventually being sent to Rockhampton to take charge of the police at the time of the Canoona Gold Rush in 1857. After Queensland was separated from New South Wales he became clerk of the petty sessions in Rockhampton and Chief Constable at Rockhampton in 1858; he was appointed Gold Commissioner on the Clermont field on 18/10/1863 and in 1867 Gold Commissioner at Rockhampton. In late October 1867 while accompanying police troopers Patrick William Cahill, from Co. Tipperary and John Francis Power, from Co. Waterford, on the Peak Downs Gold Escort, Griffin stole a sum of money (£500) from the escort. Griffin was suave but impecunious from gambling. The escort from the Joint Stock Bank, from Rockhampton to Clermont was performed on the instructions of Griffin in his capacity as gold commissioner. He later realized that when the money was found to be missing he would be suspected so he decided to steal all the money and make it look as though bushrangers had taken it. On the morning on 5 November 1867 the escort party arrived at the Mackenzie River crossing. Camp was pitched there and the three retired for some hours to Bedford's Hotel nearby. Sometime between 2 and 3 a.m. on 6

111   112

111 George Garrow Greene, author.   112 John Loftus Griffin (1832–68), Chief Constable, Rockhampton, New South Wales, hanged for murder, 1868, son of Thomas Griffin (1797–1847), Chief Constable, Irish Constabulary.

November 1867 a number of shots were heard to come from the area of Mackenzie River Crossing. Later next morning the caretaker of Bedford's Hotel, John Peterson found the troopers' bodies at the camp shot through the head and the £4,000 were missing. Griffin had returned earlier that morning to Rockhampton and when news broke concerning the deaths of the two troopers he volunteered to return and assist with the investigation. Griffin came under suspicion when it was learned that money he had paid to some Chinese gold diggers had been part of the money stolen from the escort. The *Queensland Police Gazette* of Wednesday 1 January 1868 (p. 5) reported that 'Griffin was arrested by Sub Inspector Elliott and Detective Kilfeder on suspicion of committing the murder and robbery. Two hundred and fifty three of the stolen notes were recovered and traced to Griffin's possession. Griffin was convicted on 18/3/1868 and sentenced to death for the murder of both troopers after a trial that lasted eight days. Griffin continued to protest his innocence to the hangman's scaffold in Rockhampton Gaol although it was established that he had confessed to one of the prisoners and to Alfred Grant, one of the gaolers. On the morning of 1 June 1868, Griffin was hanged at Rockhampton Gaol.'

Griffin, Robert; RIC 788; LDS 2097/212; born 1811, Dingle, Co. Kerry; 3rd SI 28/11/1857; pensioned 10/9/1869; died 10/4/1884.

Gun, John; LDS 2097/062; CarNB; born, 1790, Rattoo, Ballyduff, Co. Kerry; son of William Gun, Esq. (b.1765); ensign 11/1/1810; lieutenant, 15/10/1812; half pay list 15th Regiment of

Foot 13/11/1817; 3rd SI 19/9/1825; received a severe injury to a knee when quelling a riot at Clonmel, Co. Tipperary on 25/12/1833; received a severe blow to the head on 16/1/1835 from a blow of a stone while protecting the court house at Kinsale from an attack made on it by a mob; residing at William Street, Newtown, Waterford in 1850; his second son, William Gun died in May 1852 in Sierra Leone 'the deceased young gentleman held a high situation in the Customs department' (*Cork Examiner* 20/9/1852); pensioned 1/5/1854; died in 1854 in Canada; C.C. Trim, Co. Meath; Arthurstown, Co. Wexford and Clonmel, Co. Tipperary.

Gun, William Townsend; LDS 2097/164; born 1823, Rattoo, Ballyduff, Co. Kerry; son of Townsend Gun; married twice, his second marriage took place on 26/6/1875 (Enniskillen Registrar's District, vol. 7, p. 58), his second wife was a native of Co. Kerry; 3rd SI 9/2/1848; received a favourable record on 31/12/1870 for especially distinguishing himself in discharging his duty with alacrity, fortitude and endurance in suppressing formidable riots in Cork; CI 1/8/1872; pensioned 24/11/1871; died 23/6/1883 at Wicklow, Co. Wicklow; buried in Lucan Cemetery, Dublin on 8/6/1883; will proved on 31/7/1883 at the Principal Registry by the oath of Isabella Gun, widow, one of the executors – effects £963.16s.0d.; (copy of probate deposited in the National Archives, Dublin – T.679).

Guthrie, Edward; RIC 215; LDS 2097/186; born 1799, Inishmacsaint, Co. Fermanagh; enlisted as a constable on 1/7/1824; wife a native of Co. Fermanagh; 3rd SI 1/5/1851; pensioned 10/2/1858; died 3/10/1875 at Derry, Co. Derry; (Londonderry Registrar's District, 1875, vol. 17, p. 135).

Gwynne, Victor Stuart; RIC 72053; LDS 2098/168B; born 27/03/1897, Co. Antrim; lieutenant, army; 3rd DI 10/1/1920; pensioned 13/4/1922.

H

Hadnett, Richard; LDS 2097/088; born 1807, Co. Tipperary; enlisted as a sub constable, 16/5/1827; his wife, Margaret, youngest daughter of John Mathew, Esq., of Thurles, Co. Tipperary; 3rd SI 1/2/1835; received an injury at the Fair of Thurles on 3/12/1833 from a blow of a stone which fractured his right jaw; was severely beaten on 30/8/1834 while endeavouring to suppress a riot in the City of Cork; at the close of the Cork Assizes in March 1861, Judge Keogh spoke in most complimentary terms of the manner in which Sub Inspector Hadnett had kept the court during the trial case of Johnson against the Cork and Passage Railway (*Cork Examiner* 29/3/1861); died 3/2/1864 at Fisher Street, Kinsale, Co. Cork (*Cork Examiner* 4/2/1864) (Kinsale Registrar's District, vol. 5, p. 288); administration granted on 2/5/1864 at Cork to Margaret Hadnett, of Patrick Street, Cork, the widow of the deceased – effects under £235; his widow, Margaret, died at 4 Anna Villa, North Circular Road, Dublin on 11/1/1883 and was buried in Glasnevin Cemetery, Dublin on 14/1/1883.

Hall, George; RIC 57776; LDS 2098/074B; born 8/5/1876, Co. Monaghan; (Monaghan Registrar's District, 1876, vol. 3, p. 305); married on 10/8/1910 (Cootehill Registrar's District, September Quarter, 1910, vol. 3, p. 101), wife a native of Co. Monaghan; 3rd DI 12/8/1916; pensioned 31/5/1922; transferred to the Royal Ulster Constabulary on 1/6/1922.

Hallaran, Richard Bunbury; RIC 53467; LDS 2098/055; born 1863, Co. Cork; Moderator and Scholar 1885, Trinity College Dublin; 3rd DI 1/1/1889; resigned 20/9/1890.

Haly, Francis Bernard; LDS 2097/038; born 1795, Cork City; 3rd SI 28/1/1823; C.C. Swords, Co. Dublin, 1831; married in February 1825, Anne Alice Duckett, Tramore, Co. Waterford; he was transferred to Ballinspittle, Co. Cork in March 1826; resident magistrate 1840; pensioned 1/4/1843; died in Paris on 25/6/1863; during his long residence in France, he retained undiminished his ardent love for Ireland and interest in her condition and he was himself the type of a true Irish gentleman, honourable, charitable, hospitable and cordial and his death, like his life was that of a pious and devoted Catholic (*Cork Examiner* 30/6/1863); formerly of Maryborough, Queen's County and late of No. 38 Bis in the Rue des Ecuries d'Artois in the City of Paris, France; will proven at the Principal Registry on 29/7/1863 and grant to Anne Alicia Haly, of No. 7, Rue de la Croix in the City of Paris, the widow and Universal Legatee – effects under £800; his eldest daughter, Elizabeth died at Rome on 9/2/1900.

Hamilton, Frederick Lindsay; RIC 76117; ADRIC no. 91; LDS 2098/214B; born 3/10/1891, Surrey, England; (Kingston Registrar's District, 1891, December Quarter, vol. 24, p.); married on 8/4/1919, Mary Lindley a native of Nottingham; commanded 7th Battalion, King's Own Scottish Borderers; 3rd DI 12/1/1920; on 2/2/1921 he was appointed Assistant Commissioner of the Gold Coast Police; however, this appointment was rescinded and he was discharged on 11/5/1921.

Hamilton, Henry; CarNB; captain; 3rd SI and paymaster for Co. Wexford, 1/11828; acting inspector general of Leinster in Dublin on 13/1/1832; (the *Morning Register*, Dublin, vol. ix, Tuesday January 28, 1833).

Hamilton, John; CarNB; lieutenant; went on leave on 7/11/1828 and returned on 24/11/1828. The pay of the Ardfert station party was not issued though received by him. The constables horses, the arms and appointments at Lixnaw station were seized for rent due by him; dismissed 16/12/1828; C.C. barony of Clanmaurice, 1825; Listowel and Lixnaw, Co. Kerry, 1827.

Hamilton, Ronald Trant; RIC 71648; LDS 2098/140B; born 3/2/1898, Co. Dublin; (Dublin South Registrar's District, 1898, March Quarter, vol. 2, p. 598); captain, Royal Irish Regiment; married on 4/2/1921 (Belfast Registrar's District, March Quarter, 1921, vol. 1, p. 592), Kathleen McElroy, a native of Co. Antrim; 3rd DI 8/7/1920; awarded the Constabulary Medal 15/10/1921; pensioned 31/5/1922; transferred to the Royal Ulster Constabulary on 1/6/1922.

Hamilton, Sackville Berkley; RIC 33942; LDS 2097/267; born 1847, Co. Cork; wife from Co. Dublin; 3rd SI 20/3/1868; CI 1/5/1894; King Edward VII Visit to Ireland Medal, 1903; AIG 16/2/1905; Commandant of the Phoenix Park Depot from 16/2/1905 to 22/10/1906; pensioned 1/4/1908; died 4/5/1913 at 15, Regent Terrace, Penzance, Cornwall, England; will proved on 26/6/1913 at the Principal Registry to Eva M.E. Hamilton, the widow – effects £162.17s.1d.; (photo in the *Constabulary Gazette*, vol. XVI, no. 12, 18/2/1905).

Hamilton, Thomas; LDS 2097/213; born 1832, Co. Donegal; joined the Irish Revenue Police as a lieutenant on 3/10/1851 and served in Sligo, Co. Sligo; son born on 9/9/1865 at Tuckey Street, Cork (*Cork Examiner* 11/9/1865); 3rd SI 1/12/1857; he was one of the first four RIC officers to undergo training on 31/8/1861 at the School of Musketry, Fleetwood, North Lancs., England (*Cork Examiner* 26/8/1861); 3rd class resident magistrate 10/10/1867, 2nd class, 18/6/1873, 1st class 1/10/1882; presented with the Medal of the Royal Humane Society on 17/6/1890 for gallant conduct in saving life in Donegal Bay; seconded for service in the Crime Department, Chief Secretary's Office from 1/7/1881 to 7/7/1882; died 18/7/1896 at Salt Hill, Mountcharles, Co. Donegal (Donegal Registrar's District, 1896, September Quarter, vol. 2, p. 27); will proved at Londonderry on 7/7/1897 by the oath of Mary Hamilton, of Beaumount, Belfast, widow and sole executrix – effects – £5,682.16s.9d.; (p. 23, RM Records of Service Book, National Archives, Dublin).

Hamilton, William; RIC 23072; LDS 2097/324; born 1839, Co. Monaghan; wife from Co. Dublin; 3rd DI 18/10/1882; pensioned 1/7/1898; died 6/4/1910 at No. 7, Ellesmere Avenue, North Circular Road, Dublin.

Hamilton, William; CarNB; 3rd SI 1825; described by Major Thomas D'Arcy on 29/11/1825: 'Lieut. Hamilton appears to be an active intelligent officer and promises to be most diligent and zealous, yet temperate in the discharge of his official duties'; death reported on 8/5/1828 by Major D'Arcy from Enniskillen; C.C. Downpatrick, Co. Down, 1826; Muff, Co. Donegal, 1828.

Hampshire, Harold George; RIC 82009; LDS 2099/019; born 27/3/1893, London, England; captain, Machine Gun Corps; wife from Edinburgh, Scotland; 3rd DI 25/6/1921; pensioned 4/5/1922.

Hanna, Joseph; CarNB; PPF; PPF Clerk 12/3/1816; recommended by (later Sir) Richard Willcocks, Palmerston on 19/3/1816 'who served as a lieutenant in my corps of yeomanry from its establishment in the year 1803 until I surrendered my command in 1809.' Clerk in the PPF from 1813 to 1817 at Dundalk, Co. Louth; joined the PPF in Askeaton, Co. Limerick and still serving there in 1832.

Hanna, Samuel; RIC 55384; LDS 2098/086; born 1867, Lisburn, Co. Antrim; Barrister-at-Law; married on 30/8/1893 (Dublin South Registrar's District, September Quarter, 1893, vol. 2, p. 535), wife a native of Derry; 3rd DI 1/9/1892; King Edward VII Visit to Ireland Medal, 1903; CI 5/1/1917; pensioned 1/10/1920; (photo in the *Constabulary Gazette*, vol. X, no. 21, 15/2/1902).

Hannyngton, Thomas C.; LDS 2097/090; born 1815, Co. Tyrone; served for five years in the Ordnance Department under Col. Colby; 3rd SI 1/11/1835; reported for intemperance and warned for removal from County Antrim on 1/8/1840; resigned 10/6/1842.

Hanrahan, Timothy; LDS 2099/010; born 1887, Mitchelstown, Co. Cork; (Mitchelstown Registrar's District, March Quarter, 1887, vol. 4, p. 710); married on 21/10/1906, wife from Co. Monaghan; 3rd DI 13/6/1921; pensioned 31/8/1922.

Harcourt, John; RIC 25254; LDS 2097/231; born 1839, Co. Tipperary; 3rd SI 2/11/1859; pensioned 21/10/1891; died 4/9/1911 at 28, Crabton Close Road, Boscombe, Bournemouth, Hants., England; (Christchurch Registrar's District, September Quarter, 1911, vol. 2a, p. 882); will proved on 25/10/1911 at Winchester, Hants., England and resealed at Dublin on 24/11/1911 – effects in Ireland £1,119.3s.10d.; probate granted to Henrietta Harcourt, spinster – effects in England £8,567.3s.11d., resworn £9,070.12s.1d.

Hardy, William Johnston McKnight; RIC 54178; LDS 2098/061; born 27/3/1865, Co. Derry; tutor of classics and English at Coleraine for one year and Santry, Dublin; married on 22/10/1890 (Dublin South Registrar's District, December Quarter, 1890, vol. 2, p. 553), wife a native of Co. Wicklow; Barrister-at-Law, LLB 1887, Trinity College Dublin; auditor of the TCD Historical Society; 3rd DI 7/3/1890; resident magistrate 3rd class 28/10/1911, 2nd class 16/8/1915; (p. 152, RM Records of Service Book, National Archives, Dublin); (photo in the *Constabulary Gazette*, vol. IX, no. 26, 21/9/1902).

Hare, Gustavus Julius Charles; RIC 30478; LDS 2097/254; born 1841, Bonn, Prussia; 3rd SI 22/9/1865; dismissed 3/9/1868.

Harnett, Falkiner Minchin; LDS 2097/202; born 1831, Co. Limerick; son born on 1/5/1869 at Gorey, Co. Wexford (*Cork Examiner* 6/5/1869); his brother, Captain William Minchin Harnett, 97th Regiment of Foot (Queen's Own Germans Regiment); died on 27/12/1871 at Gorey, Co. Wexford (*Cork Examiner* 2/1/1872); 3rd SI 25/7/1854; died 7/2/1880.

Harper, Andrew Monds; RIC 35094; LDS 2097/275; born 16/8/1850, Co. Sligo; married on 2/6/1883, wife from Worcestershire; 3rd SI 30/1/1869; Private Secretary to the Inspector General from 3/8/1882 until his appointment as a temporary resident magistrate on 17/11/1885; permanent 3rd class RM 5/1/1888, 2nd class 21/3/1893, 1st class 28/10/1905; pensioned 16/8/1915; temporarily reappointed on 30/6/1916 to do duty at Navan, Co. Meath; died 19/6/1917 at Kilfeira, Waterford, Co. Waterford; probate granted at London on 11/8/1917 to Brenda K. Harper, the widow and Ernest E. Bird, resealed at Dublin – effects £2,178.0s.7d.

Harpur, William; LDS 2097/059; born 1788, Co. Cavan; volunteer, private, lieutenant and adjutant in the yeomanry from 1802 to 1811; 3rd SI 22/1/1825; C.C. Lucan, Co. Dublin 1831; died 1842.

Harrel, Alfred Gisborne Wharton; RIC 51176; LDS 2098/009; born 17/2/1865, Clogher, Co. Tyrone; (Clogher Registrar's District, 1865, vol. 3, p. 133); son of Sir David Harrell (1841–1939), DI, RIC, RM and brother of William Vesey Harrel (1866–1956), DI, RIC; BA 1885, Trinity College Dublin; BL; 3rd DI 1/1/1885; resident magistrate 3rd class 27/8/1900, 2nd class 4/11/1907, 1st class 2/6/1916; pensioned 1/12/1920; (p. 120, RM Records of Service Book, National Archives, Dublin).

Harrel, David Alfred (Sir); RIC 24639; LDS 2097/229; born 25/03/1841, Ardglass, Co. Down, son of David Harrel, Mount Pleasant, Co. Down and Jane Wharton (d.1903), of Belfast; married on 11/6/1863 (Newtownards Registrar's District, vol. 9, p. 20), Juliana (b.Co. Armagh), daughter of Rev. Richard Nugent Horner, Rector of Killeeshill, Co. Tyrone; educated at the Royal Naval School, Gosport; 3rd SI 1/8/1859; received a favourable record on 31/12/1868 for the arrest of a violent offender with courage, energy and promptitude; received a favourable record on 31/12/1869 for the capture of a rioter at a faction fight, arrested by the officer whom he assaulted; resident magistrate 31/6/1880–9/1/1883; Chief Commissioner of the Dublin Metropolitan Police from 9/1/1883 to 28/1/1893; Under-Secretary for Ireland, 1893–1902; Member of the Congested Districts Board; Chairman Committee on Production (Arbitration Tribunal under Munitions of War Acts); Arbitrator for the Board of Trade in trade disputes; Independent Chairman of Durham Coal Trade Conciliation Board and of various Railway Conciliation Boards; Chairman, Royal Commission on Railway Conciliation Scheme, 1911; Chairman, Irish inland Fisheries Commission, 1914; Member, Motor Acts Commission Coastguards Commission; Chairman Royal Irish Constabulary and Dublin Metropolitan Police

Commission; KCB, 1895; KCVO, 1900; ISO, 1902; GBE, 1918; GCB, 1920; died 5/12/1939; his eldest daughter, Maude, married J. Home-Ross, F.R.C.P., Ed., only son of Major Hamilton Ross (late I.M.S.), Ballynascreena House, Co. Antrim on 2/11/1899, at St George's Church, Hanover Square, London; (photo in the *Constabulary Gazette*, vol. VI, no. 13, 23/12/1899, p. 390).

Harrel, Joseph Betts; LDS 2098/155B; born 20/8/1898, India; lieutenant, Royal Dublin Fusiliers; 3rd DI 10/1/1920; pensioned 27/4/1922.

Harrel, William Vesey; RIC 51684; LDS 2098/013; born 1866, Clogher, Co. Tyrone; son of Sir David Harrell (1841–1939), DI, RIC, RM; educated at the Royal School, Armagh and Trinity College, Dublin; 3rd DI 24/5/1886; private secretary to the Inspector-General on 9/9/1897; pensioned 29/9/1898 and appointed Inspector of Prisons in Ireland on 29/9/1898; Assistant Commissioner of the Dublin Metropolitan Police on 4/1/1902 until August 1914 when he was retired following the Howth Gun Running on 26/7/1914. The DMP acting under Mr Harrel's orders, attempted unsuccessfully to seize from the Volunteers guns landed at Howth, Co. Dublin. Mr Harrel called the assistance of the military. While the troops were returning to barracks a riot broke out at Bachelor's Walk, Dublin – they fired on them killing a number of them and Mr Harrel was immediately suspended; he served in the European War as a Temporary Commander in the Royal Navy; MVO, 4th Class, 1903; CB, 1912; CBE, 1919; died 6/5/1956 at his home at Clifton Terrace, Monkstown, Co. Dublin; (Obituary – *Irish Times* 7/5/1856).

Harrington, John Henry; RIC 54702; LDS 2098/052B; born 15/4/1874, Co. Fermanagh; married on 30/10/1901 (Balrothery Registrar's District, December Quarter, 1901, vol. 2, p. 395), wife a native of Co. Dublin; 3rd DI 1/12/1914; pensioned 12/5/1922.

Harrison, Richard Dale Winnett; RIC 61870; LDS 2098/215; born 9/5/1883, Rathkeale, Co. Limerick; (Rathkeale Registrar's District, June Quarter, 1883, vol. 5, p. 549); son of Richard J. Harrison, SI, RIC; master in Hughes' Academy, Londonderry for one year and nine months; married in January 1908 (Limavady Registrar's District, March Quarter, 1908, vol. 1, p. 719), Miss C. Miller, daughter of Rev. Miller, a native of Co. Derry; 3rd DI 15/11/1906; TCI 1/10/1920; staff officer to the Special Ulster Constabulary, 4/11/1920; pensioned 31/5/1922; transferred to the Royal Ulster Constabulary on 1/6/1922.

Harrison, Richard J.; RIC 29248; LDS 2097/327; born 1846, Co. Tipperary; father of Richard Dale Winnett, Harrison, CI, RIC; 3rd SI 1/3/1882; pensioned 1/6/1906; buried in Ballyglass Cemetery, Mullingar, Co. Westmeath.

Harvey, Crosbie Maurice; RIC 21226; LDS 2097/209; born 1836, Co. Dublin; Donegal Militia Artillery for one year and three months (WO 13/2772–75); 3rd SI 1/1/1857; in 1862 he applied from Co. Clare to join the Victoria Police supported by nine testimonials (Reference VPRS 937, Unit 199, Bundle 5 – Public Record Office, Victoria, Australia); discharged 25/5/1871, having been found medically unfit by the medical board.

Harvey, John, Col. (Sir); CarNB; born 23/4/1778, England, the son of a Church of England clergyman; PPF; provincial inspector general of Leinster from March 1828–36, residing at 9 Ely Place, Dublin; pensioned 1836; chief magistrate; ensign 80th Regiment of Foot (South Staffordshire Regiment) 18/9/1794; in Holland under the Duke of York, 1796–95; lieutenant and served at the Cape of Good Hope and was present at the surrender of the Dutch Fleet, 1796; on the Egyptian Campaign, 1801; ADC and military secretary to Major General Dowdesdell in India 1803–6; Deputy Adjutant General in Upper Canada 1812–13; assistant adjutant general, 1813–17; in 1813 as a lieutenant colonel he was posted with Major-General John Vincent at Burlington Heights. Following the British defeat at Fort George, Harvey suggested that Vincent's men catch the American's unprepared in a night attack on their camp in Stoney Creek at the farms of James and William Gage. On June 13 at 2 a.m., Major-General Vincent and Lieutenant-Colonel Harvey took 704 men of the 8th (King's) and 49th Regiments from Burlington Heights and marched them in an attack on the 3,500 American soldiers. Twenty three British soldiers were killed, 136 wounded and 55 went missing. However, by morning the British had taken

113   114

113 Alfred Gisborne Wharton Harrel.   114 William Vesey Harrel, Assistant Commissioner, DMP.   115 Sir John Harvey, the hero of the Battle of Stoney Creek, Canada, 1813. 116 Monument to Col. Sir John Harvey, Stoney Creek, Canada, unveiled 6 June 1913.

115   116

several canons and 125 prisoners, including 7 officers, General John Chandler and General William Winder. The rest of the American army was in retreat to Niagra. Most consider the Battle of Stoney Creek to be the battle that turned the War of 1812 to the benefit of Canada and Britain. For his courageous strategy and skill, Harvey received the Star of the Bath and the Star of the Guelph and was knighted Sir John Harvey in 1824. Burlington Heights Park was renamed Harvey Park in his honour on 11 June 1894; Sir John Harvey succeeded Col. Thomas Powell in 1828 as Inspector General for Leinster. He resided at No. 9 Ely Place, Dublin in 1828, 3 Merrion Square North and Clontarf Castle in 1831; Lieutenant Governor of Prince Edward Island, 30/8/1836; Governor of New Brunswick, 1/4/1837; he was recalled from New Brunswick because of his handling of the Maine boundary dispute and was appointed Governor of Newfoundland 20/7/1841. The political situation in Newfoundland was troubled and volatile. Harvey was in part responsible for the revised constitution introduced in 1842, which amalgamated the two houses of the legislature, and he deliberately implemented a policy of conciliation and fairness. He ensured Roman Catholics received government patronage and were represented on the council and persuaded Bishop Fleming to withdraw from politics. At the same time he managed to maintain the support of conservatives, helping the Chamber of Commerce in its efforts to obtain better postal and steamship services, reforming the police force and actively promoting the development of agriculture. In short, Harvey gave the colony a political respite between the storms of the 1830s and the bitter divisions surrounding the campaign for responsible government that was just beginning as he left. Lieutenant governor of Nova Scotia 26/6/1846 to his death; colonel 59th Regiment of Foot (2nd Nottinghamshire Regiment) from 3/12/1844 to his death; LG 9/11/1846; Knighted at King's Lodge, Windsor on 15/12/1824; KCH 19/3/1837; KCB 19/7/1838; died at Halifax, Nova Scotia on 22/3/1852. He married the Hon. Elizabeth, daughter of the 1st Viscount Lake of Delhi (extinct). His eldest son, Sir George Frederick, KCSI (Cr. 24/5/1867), b.1809 and married in 1835 and entered the Indian Civil Service in 1827; his youngest son, Lieutenant Edward Warwick Harvey, 35th Regiment of Foot (Royal Sussex Regiment) died of consumption on 15/2/1846 on board the Royal Mail Steamer *Thames* on his passage from Bermuda to Jamaica; commissioner and political agent at Agra and Delhi during the mutiny 1857–8; retired on annuity in 1863 and died at 122, Sloane Street, London on 4/11/1884.

Harvey, Rodulphus; RIC 24178; LDS 2097/223; born 1/12/1833, Co. Tipperary; served as a junior clerk in the Royal Irish Constabulary Office for 2 years and 7 months; 3rd SI 17/11/1858; Private Secretary to the Inspector General from 1/1/1860 to 1/1/1864; received a favourable record on 31/12/1868 for prompt and judicious action in a case of homicide, whereby failure of justice was averted; received a favourable record on 31/12/1869 for prompt and decisive action with the part under his command in suppressing a riotous mob; detective director from 14/12/1869 until his appointment as a resident magistrate 3rd class 16/6/1872, 2nd class 18/7/1881, 1st class 3/7/1889; pensioned 1/12/1893.

Hatchell, George Melville; surgeon to the Force from 16/3/1848 to 1/7/1857; resided at 13 Hume Street, Dublin; son born on 31/5/1852 at the Phoenix Park Training Depot, Dublin (*Cork Examiner* 9/6/1852); his wife died on 13/6/1854 at the Phoenix Park Training Depot, Dublin (*Cork Examiner* 16/6/1854).

Hatton, John; LDS 2097/123; born 1817, Co. Wicklow; 3rd SI 13/12/1838; resigned 1/12/1843; appointed the first Chief Constable of Ipswich Constabulary on 1/4/1841 to 15/7/1842; Chief Constable of East Suffolk Constabulary on 24/1/1843 to February 1869, and jointly Chief Constable of Beccles from 1844 to August 1857.

Hatton, John Hayes; LDS 2097/032; born 1794, Co. Wicklow; lieutenant in the yeomanry from 1814 to 1822; 3rd SI 13/12/1822; in 1828 his horse fell on him when returning with him off duty which caused the rupture of a blood vessel and his life was for some time despaired of; C.C. Griffinstown, C. Wicklow; appointed the first Chief Constable of East Suffolk County

Constabulary Force on spent long stretches in Mount Juliet, Co. Kilkenny and Portarlington, Queen's County 1/4/1840 to 1/11/1842; on 6/12/1842 he was appointed Chief Constable of Staffordshire until 1856.

Hawkins, Valentine; RIC 55125; LDS 2098/149B; born 1871, Ballinrobe, Co. Galway; married on 13/2/1901 (Ballinrobe Registrar's District, March Quarter, 1901, vol. 4, p. 25), wife a native of Co. Derry; 3rd DI 20/9/1920; pensioned 16/5/1922.

Hawkshaw, Hugh; LDS 2097/035; born 1796, Co. Donegal; son of Rev. Richard Hawkshaw, Rector of Fahan, Co. Derry; entered the Navy on 24/12/1810 as a First Class Volunteer on board the *Fortune* 36, Captain Henry Vansittart, on the Home Station, where he assisted at the capture on 11/10/1811, of Le Vice-Admiral Martin, a notorious privateer, of 18 guns and 140 men, and where he afterwards followed the same captain into the *Clarence* 74. While next attached, between September 1813 and February 1817 to the *Pactolus* 38 and *Severn* 50, both commanded by Captain Hon. Frederick William Aylmer, we find him accompanying the Duke of Cambridge to Cuxhaven and his late Majesty to Scheldt, serving for some time also on the North American station and (besides attending an eminently successful expedition sent in the summer of 1815 to the Gironde in support of the French king) enacting a part in the memorable battle of Algiers on 27/8/1816. He was subsequently for nearly twelve months employed on the African and West India stations in the *Semiramis* 42, Captains Sir James Lucas Yeo and Joseph Harrison; after which he successively joined the *Severn* 50, *Newcastle* 60 and *Leander* 50, commanded on the Home and Bermuda stations by Captains William McCulloch, Arthur Fanshawe and Edward Chetham. He was promoted on 12/7/1819 to a Lieutenancy in the *Newcastle*, bearing the flag of Rear-Admiral Edward Griffith. Commander-in-Chief at Halifax until that ship was paid off in 1822; he married Catherine Eliza, daughter of Robert Miller, Esq., of Blackheath, Kent; daughter born on 5/3/1855 at Athy, Co. Kildare (*Cork Examiner* 9/3/1855); awarded one medal and one clasp for Algiers; 3rd SI 28/1/1823; CI 12/12/1843; pensioned 1/3/1859 in Co. Kildare; died 14/6/1870 at 5, Sydenham Place, Dundrum, Co. Dublin; buried in Deansgrange Cemetery, Dublin (South Section, Row E, Grave No. 32) with Robert Miller Hawkshaw (d.26/2/1869, aged 15 years); will proved on 4/8/1870 at the Principal Registry by the oath of Catherine Elizabeth Hawkshaw, of 5, Sydenham Place, Dundrum, the sole executrix – effects under £9,000; his granddaughter, third daughter of Captain W.S. Hawkshaw, RN, Chilliwick, British Columbia, married on 8/9/1915 at St Thomas' Church, Chilliwick, William Henry Adams Parker, eldest son of John A. Parker, JP, of 20, Newgrove Avenue, Sandymount, Dublin.

Hay, Samuel; LDS 2097/095; born 9/1/1807, Aberdeen, Scotland, brother of the 17th Earl of Errol; ensign, lieutenant and captain from 1/10/1825 to 1/8/1834; married 2/4/1832, Louise, b.18/2/1811, granddaughter of 2nd Earl of Radnor; 3rd SI 1/7/1836.

Hayden, Charles; LDS 2097/089; born 1799, Co. Waterford; wife a native of Dublin City; 3rd SI 1/4/1835; pensioned 14/10/1861.

Hayes, Archibald Edward Ormston; RIC 24612; LDS 2097/226; born 1836, Co. Cork; third son of Francis Hayes, MD, Bandon, Co. Cork; Lieutenant, West Cork Artillery for four years to January, 1859; 3rd SI 24/3/1859; pensioned 1/5/1892; died 7/1/1918 at 100, Lower Baggot Street, Dublin; administration granted on 15/2/1918 at the Principal Registry; (photo in the *Constabulary Gazette*, vol. VI, no. 13, 23/12/1899, p. 390).

Hayes, Denis; RIC 732; LDS 2097/191; born 1807, Co. Limerick; enlisted as a sub constable on 1/2/1830; 3rd SI 11/2/1852; pensioned 11/4/1864; died 4/6/1869 (Newcastle Registrar's District, vol. 10, p. 384) aged 62 years of bronchitis, at his residence, The Square, Drumcollogher, Co. Limerick (*Cork Examiner* 12/6/1869); buried in the family vault in Cloncrew, Co. Limerick on 6/6/1869; will proved at the Principal Registry on 2/6/1870 by the oaths of David Hannigan and Patrick Hannigan of Gardenfield, Co. Limerick two of the executors (By Decree 'Hannigan –v- O'Brien' 10/5/1870) – effects under £200.

Hayes, Thomas; RIC 30259; LDS 2097/253; born 1845, Co. Cork; son of Richard Hayes, Bayview, Carrigaline, Co. Cork; 3rd SI 9/7/1865; CI 28/1/1888; King Edward VII Visit to Ireland Medal, 1903; pensioned 1/12/1905, died 15/10/1915 at Ardmachree, Crosshaven, Co. Cork; will proved on 24/11/1915 at Cork by the oath of Francis G. Hayes – effects £3,655.14s.6d.

Hazlett, James; LDS 2097/180, born 1831, Co. Monaghan; son of John Hazlett, SI, RIC; son born on 2/4/1855 at Castletownberehaven, Co. Cork (*Cork Examiner* 11/4/1855), daughter born on 22/3/1856 (*Cork Examiner* 2/4/1856); son born on 13/3/1863 at Dungarvan, Co. Waterford (*Cork Examiner* 16/3/1863); daughter Emma Eliza born on 1/11/1864 at Ballynamult, Dungarvan, Co. Waterford (Dungarvan Registrar's District, vol. 19, p. 699) (*Cork Examiner* 4/11/1864); 3rd SI 25/8/1849; dismissed 7/12/1870.

Hazlett, John; LDS 2097/061; born 1787, Queen's County; father of James Hazlett, SI, RIC; ensign and lieutenant in the army for 19 years and 6 months; wife a native of Co. Clare; 3rd SI 25/8/1825; at the Monaghan Election in 1826 he received a dangerous wound in the head from stones thrown at him; in November 1837 he was also wounded at Castletownbere, Co. Cork from stones thrown by a mob; C.C. Swanlinbar, Co. Cavan, 1831; pensioned 1846; died 1848.

Hazlewood, George; CarNB; PPF; PPF Clerk 25/3/1817.

Healy, James; RIC 55967; LDS 2097/174; born 1810, Co. Kerry; enlisted as a sub constable on 1/2/1832; awarded a chevron in 1842; married on 17/8/1856 at Ballinderry House, the residence of William Egan, Esq., Kate, the third daughter of the late Matthew McDonogh, of Ballinasloe, Co. Galway (*Cork Examiner* 22/8/1856); 3rd SI 1/6/1848; died 19/10/1863 in Borrisokane, Co. Tipperary; a gratuity of £78.16s.9d. was granted to his widow.

Healy, James; LDS 2098/231B; born 28/1/1868, Swinford, Co. Sligo; (Swinford Registrar's District, 1868, vol. 14, p. 500); 3rd DI 1/1/1921; pensioned 22/4/1922.

Heard, Alexander Edward Stawell; RIC 28306; LDS 2097/243; born 1/7/1839, Co. Kilkenny; clerk in the Provincial Bank, Ennis from 1/3/1858 to 1/9/1859 and in the Census Office, Dublin from 10/6/1861 to 1/12/1862; married on 14/2/1865 at Bruff Church, Co. Limerick (Kilmallock Registrar's District, vol. 5, p. 497), Dora, eldest daughter of Samuel Bennett, M.D., of Adelaide House, Bruff, Co. Limerick (*Cork Examiner* 15/2/1865); son born on 15/12/1865 at Bruff, Co. Limerick (*Cork Examiner* 21/12/1865); 3rd SI 1/1/1863; received a favourable record on 30/6/1871 for judgement and cool determination in suppressing a formidable riot; CI 6/2/1886; divisional commissioner 1/2/1893 to 31/1/1898; received the inspector general's approbation of the excellent services rendered when in charge of six district inspectors and 200 men protecting the Sheriff at the 'Bodyke' evictions; resident magistrate 1/2/1898; pensioned 1/7/1904; his daughter Dorothea Alexandra Heard, aged one year and nine months died at 2, Castle Terrace, Clontarf, Co. Dublin on 2/4/1882; (p. 112, RM Records of Service Book, National Archives, Dublin); (photo in the *Constabulary Gazette*, vol. VI, no. 13, 23/12/1899, p. 390).

Heard, Alexander Wilson Hutchinson; LDS 2097/117; born 1808, Kinsale, Co. Cork; fourth son of Edward Heard, of Compass Hill, Kinsale, Co. Cork and married 1stly in 1832, Esther Elizabeth Phoebe, second daughter of Eustace Stawell (d.7/4/1836) of Coolmaine Castle, Co. Cork and Amy Maria (d.16/9/1864, aged 91 years), daughter of Rev. Richard Griffith, Rector of Kilbrittain, Co. Cork, Chaplain, 3rd Dragoon Guards (*Cork Examiner* 21/9/1864); father of George Bennett Heard, DI, RIC and Wilson Hutchinson Heard, DI, RIC; married secondly, Bessie, daughter of Rev. P. Bolton; 3rd SI 17/10/1837; CI 1/12/1865; received a favourable record on 30/6/1871 for judgement and cool determination in suppressing a formidable riot; pensioned 1/10/1882; died 22/1/1885 at Lizville, Dundrum, Co. Dublin; will proved on 18/4/1885 at the Principal Registry by the oath of Elizabeth Heard, of 81, Upper Leeson Street, Dublin, one of the executors – effects £789.7s.9d.

117 Thomas Hayes.   118 William Reynell Hutchinson Heard.   119 Richard Robert Heggart.
120 Vincent James Hetreed.

Heard, George Bennett; RIC 55064; LDS 2098/083; born 18/3/1870, Kilmallock, Co. Limerick; (Kilmallock Registrar's District, 1870, vol. 10 p. 443); son of Alexander William Hutchinson Heard, DI, RIC and brother of William Hutchinson Reynell Heard, DI, RIC; married Cecilia Louisa Black on 7/11/1893; 3rd DI 18/1/1892; King Edward VII Visit to Ireland Medal, 1903; CI 23/5/1916; awarded a certificate from the Irish Police and Constabulary Recognition Fund; Commandant of the Phoenix Park Depot from 20/4/1920 to 17/5/1922; pensioned 17/5/1922; died 20/12/1961 at Ballinter, Navan, Co. Meath; probate granted on 15/2/1962 at the Principal Registry to William S. Leatham, retired bank manager – effects £1,142.

Heard, Wilson Hutchinson Reynell; RIC 51876; LDS 2098/019; born 1862, Co. Clare; son of Alexander Wilson Hutchinson Heard, DI, RIC and George Bennett Heard, DI, RIC; 3rd DI 10/2/1891; King Edward VII Visit to Ireland Medal, 1903; musketry instructor from 4/1/1907 to 13/3/1909; CI 13/3/1909; King George V Visit to Ireland Medal, 1911; pensioned 1/8/1920.

Hearnden, Arthur Charles; RIC 60576; LDS 2098/193; born 1877, London, Middlesex, England; (Lambeth Registrar's District, 1877, September Quarter, vol. 1d, p. 43); youngest son of William T. Hearnden (b.1836), Ashford, Kent and Valentia, Co. Kerry; residing at 102 Asbury Road, Camberwell, Surrey in 1881 (Census); tutor for 6 months; Gold Medalist, BA 1900, Trinity College Dublin; 3rd DI 1/10/1902; King Edward VII Visit to Ireland Medal, 1903; pensioned on 20/9/1918; died 5/3/1919 at Forster Green Hospital, Belfast; buried in the City Cemetery, Belfast; (photo in the *Constabulary Gazette*, vol. XIV, no. 16, 9/1/1904 & vol. XXIX, no. 16, 1/7/1911, p. 264).

Heath, Francis John; LDS 2097/126; born 1813, Co. Cork; son of Francis John Heath, Monkstown, Co. Cork, Barrackmaster and Ann Farmer, George's Street, Cork who were married at Glanmire, Co. Cork on 24/11/1811; enlisted as a sub constable on 17/8/1829; wife a native of Wales; son born on 21/7/1852 at Carrick-on-Suir, Co. Tipperary (*Cork Examiner* 28/7/1852); 3rd SI 1/5/1839; CI 16/3/1867; pensioned 1/3/1880; died 26/8/1892 at Glengara, Glenageary, Co. Wicklow; will proved on 22/9/1892 at the Principal Registry by the oath of Frances Fredaswitha Heath, of Glengara, Glenageary, Co. Wicklow, spinster, the sole executrix – effects £706.11s.10d.; buried in Deansgrange Cemetery, Dublin (South Section, Row Y, Grave No. 68) on 29/8/1892; his wife, Susan died on 1/1/1883, aged 56 years at the same address and was buried in Deansgrange Cemetery, Dublin on 4/1/1883.

Heatley, John J.; RIC 43019; LDS 2098/155; born 1856, Ballynahinch, Co. Armagh; married on 7/5/1885 (Belfast Registrar's District, June Quarter, 1885, vol. 1, p. 439), wife a native of Co. Antrim; daughter born at Bruff, Co. Limerick on 8/5/1901; 3rd DI 29/4/1899; pensioned 31/10/1917.

Heggart, John Thomas; RIC 53340; LDS 2098/012B; born 17/9/1870, Castleconnell, Co. Limerick; (Limerick Registrar's District, 1870, vol. 15 p. 475); brother of Richard Robert Heggart, DI, RIC; married on 16/9/1896 (Dublin South Registrar's District, September Quarter, 1896, vol. 2, p. 420), wife a native of Co. Clare; 3rd DI 5/1/1910; pensioned 14/4/1922; (photo in the *Constabulary Gazette*, vol. XXVI, no. 13, 11/12/1909, p. 182).

Heggart, Richard Robert; RIC 54660; LDS 2098/228; born 2/9/1872, Castleconnell, Co. Limerick; (Limerick Registrar's District, 1872, vol. 15, p. 434); brother of John Thomas Heggart, DI, RIC; married on 10/4/1899 (Oughterard Registrar's District, June Quarter, 1899, vol. 4, p. 169), wife a native of Co. Galway; 3rd DI 17/4/1908; TCI 1/11/1920 which he refused on 10/11/1920; awarded the Constabulary Medal 27/7/1916; awarded the King's Police Medal 1922; pensioned 31/5/1922; transferred to the Royal Ulster Constabulary on 1/6/1922.

Hemsworth, William Henry Smith; LDS 2097/177; born 1827, King's County; captain, Kilkenny Militia (WO 13/2942–60); 3rd SI 1/5/1849; seconded to the Commissariat Department from 25/8/1854 to 22/9/1855; discharged by the order of His Excellency, the Lord Lieutenant on 25/2/1866; his youngest daughter, Sophia Helen Edith Higginbotham died on

4/3/1918 at 8 St John's Terrace, Clontarf, Co. Dublin and she was buried in the family vault at Clontarf on 8/3/1918.

Hemsworth, William Henry; LDS 2097/064; born 1799, Co. Louth; ensign, lieutenant and paymaster in the Louth Militia from 1812 to July 1822 (WO 13/3079–100); wife a native of Dublin; 3rd SI 1/3/1826; CI 1/6/1850; pensioned 10/6/1869; died 11/5/1871 at 163, Newcomen Terrace, Dublin; will proved on 29/9/1871 at the Principal Registry by the oath of Henry Edward Hemsworth, of 163 Newcomen Terrace, the son and one of the executors – effects under £3,000.

Henderson, Edward; CarNB; born 1756; baronial chief constable; stipendiary magistrate 1800; lieutenant 23rd Regiment of Foot (Royal Welsh Fusiliers), 1805; 3rd SI 1822; pensioned 1826; C.C. Carbury, Co. Kildare and Sligo, Co. Sligo; (WO 25/761 fol. 29).

Henderson, Harold Edmund; RIC 55001; LDS 2098/078; born 1868, Leeds, Yorks., England; son of William G. Henderson (b.1820), Harbridge, Hampshire and Jane M. Henderson (b.1838, Scotland; residing at Mount Morland Grammar School, Leeds, Yorkshire in 1881 (Census); married in April 1905 (Loughrea Registrar's District, June Quarter, 1905, vol. 4, p. 177), Miss Lopdell, a native of Co. Galway; 3rd DI 12/9/1891; King Edward VII Visit to Ireland Medal, 1903; pensioned 25/4/1922.

Henderson, John; CarNB; born, Rathmines, Co. Dublin; lieutenant, 8th Regiment of Foot, 1800; lieutenant, 12th Regiment of Foot (East Suffolk Regiment), 1821; lieutenant half pay, 41st Regiment of Foot (Royal Invalids Regiment), 1825; 3rd SI 1/12/1822; pensioned 1/10/1834; C.C. Navan, Co. Meath; (WO 25/761 fol. 269).

Henderson, William; LDS 2097/030; born 1779, Scotland; PPF; 1/4/1822; ensign (by purchase) 27th Regiment of Foot (Inniskilling Regiment), 5/9/1805; lieutenant, 7/10/1806; captain, 14/9/1815; captain half pay, 1816, 5th Regiment of Foot (Northumberland Regiment); awarded one medal and seven clasps for Salamanca, Niville, Vittoria, Nive, Pyrenees, Orthes and Toulouse; 3rd SI 10/8/1822; married at Castleblayney, Co. Monaghan, 5/1/1825; pensioned 1/2/1859 in Co. Roscommon; died 13/2/1867 at Hollybrook, King's County (Parsonstown Registrar's District, vol. 3, p. 587); will proved at Mullingar, Co. Westmeath on 10/8/1867 by the oath of Elizabeth Mary Susan Carleton (Wife of George Carleton, Major R.A.) of Hollybrook (Ballycumber, Moate, King's County, the executrix – effects under £600. (WO 25/ 751 fol. 298).

Henry, William; LDS 2097/134; born 1823, Co. Monaghan, son of William Henry, SI, RIC; 3rd SI 1/1/1841; pensioned 1/8/1847; died 24/10/1888 at 1 Mespil Road, Dublin; his only son William Frederick Radcliffe Henry, Captain, Royal Irish Fusiliers, died on 14/4/1895, aged 31 years, at 132 Leinster Road, Dublin (Dublin South Registrar's District, 1895, June Quarter, vol. 2, p. 511); will proved on 8/1/1889 at the Principal Registry by the oath of Catherine Eliza Henry, of 1, Mespil Road, Dublin, the widow and sole executrix – effects £3,552.6s.7d.

Henry, William; LDS 2097/051; born 1780, Mountcashel, Co. Waterford; father of William Henry, RIC; lieutenant in the Prince of Wales' Own Donegal Militia from 1/1/1799 to 23/4/1816 (WO 13/2751–71); 3rd SI 1/7/1824; CI 1/7/1824; resigned 31/3/1841 in favour of the appointment of his son William Henry.

Herriot, Thomas Hunter; RIC 72010; LDS 2098/154B; born 23/1/1894, Lanarkshire, Scotland; captain and pilot, Royal Air Force; 3rd DI 10/1/1920; pensioned 31/5/1922; transferred to the Royal Ulster Constabulary on 1/6/1922.

Hetreed, Vincent James; RIC 58444; LDS 2098/154; born 1/11/1874, Kent, England; (Sheppey Registrar's District, 1874, vol. 2a, p. 793); brother of William Charles Patrick Hetreed, DI, RIC; clerk in the Land Commission for 1 year and 6 months; married on 15/9/1915, Violet C. McKeon, a native of Co. Leitrim; 3rd DI 17/3/1899; CI 27/7/1920; pensioned 18/5/1922.

Hetreed, William Charles Patrick; RIC 53464; LDS 2098/051; born 1864, Kent, England; (Sheppey Registrar's District, 1864, June Quarter, vol. 2a, p. 672); brother of Vincent James Hetreed, DI, RIC; tutor at St Brendan's College, Killarney, Co. Kerry and Clongowes Wood

College for two years and ten months; married firstly on 26/4/1892 (Mullingar Registrar's District, June Quarter, 1892, vol. 3, p. 203), wife a native of King's County; married secondly on 12/10/1897 (Dublin North Registrar's District, December Quarter, 1897, vol. 2, p. 513), wife a native of Co. Limerick; 3rd DI 1/1/1889; King Edward VII Visit to Ireland Medal, 1903; his daughter married Lieutenant Skinner at Tramore, Co. Waterford on 10/5/1917; chief police instructor at the Phoenix Park Depot from 1/1/1902 to 1/4/1905; CI 13/8/1910; pensioned 18/11/1917; (photo in the *Constabulary Gazette*, vol. XII, no. 18, 24/1/1903).

Hewgill, Francis; RIC 36839; LDS 2097/281; born 1848, Warks., England; (Warwick Registrar's District, 1848, September Quarter, vol. 16, p. 550); apprentice to general brokers in Liverpool for four and a half years; married on 4/7/1872, Ellen, third daughter of Alexander Patton, Esq., of Finglas, Co. Dublin (Dublin North Registrar's District, vol. 12, p. 453) (*Cork Examiner* 9/7/1872); 3rd SI 26/8/1870; died 13/6/1876; (photo in the *Constabulary Gazette*, vol. VI, no. 13, 23/12/1899, p. 390).

Hewitt, James Malcolm; LDS 2098/020; born 1862, Co. Armagh; eldest son of Thomas Pierrepoint Hewitt, SI, RIC; lieutenant, Carlow Militia (WO 13/2627–46); married on 21/1/1893 (Dublin South Registrar's District, March Quarter, 1893, vol. 2, p. 607), Georgina Charlotte Mahon of Bellville, Co. Galway; his aunt married Mr Joseph Stewart, the celebrated New York Banker; Armagh Militia (WO 13/2603–24); 3rd DI 1/9/1886; died 17/12/1897 at Buncrana, Co. Donegal (Innishowen Registrar's District, 1897, December Quarter, vol. 2, p. 77).

Hewitt, Thomas Pierrepoint; 2097/218; born 1836, Co. Roscommon; son of Henry Hewitt, who died at Kingstown on 10/4/1877, brother of Edward Story Hewitt, who died at Edenderry, King's County on 10/8/1866 and the father of James Malcolm Hewitt, SI, RIC, was born in Co. Armagh in 1862, and who died at Buncrana, Co. Donegal on 17/12/1897 (Innishowen Registrar's District, 1897, December Quarter, vol. 2, p. 77); joined the Irish Revenue Police as a lieutenant on 8/9/1856; 3rd SI 1/12/1857; pensioned 1/3/1875; died 30/5/1883; there is a memorial tablet to him and his family at Castropetre Church, Edenderry, King's County on the left wall just beside the pulpit. Castropetre is derived from the Castle or Camp of Peter Bermingham, a descendant of Sir John de Bermingham who founded the abbey in the area in 1325.

Hickey, John Creagh; RIC 28829; LDS 2098/017; born 1844, Cork; wife a native of Co. Kerry; 3rd DI 15/7/1886; King Edward VII Visit to Ireland Medal, 1903; pensioned 31/3/1905; died 28/3/1913 at St John's, Stillorgan, Co. Dublin; buried in Glasnevin Cemetery, Dublin; (photo in the *Constabulary Gazette*, vol. V, no. 8, 20/5/1899).

Hicks, Richard; RIC 51795; LDS 2098/056B; born 21/1/1868, Westport, Co. Sligo; married on 1/7/1893 (Westport Registrar's District, September Quarter, 1893, vol. 4, p. 197), wife a native of Co. Wexford; 3rd DI 12/1/1914; on 9/1/1917 was awarded a 1st class favourable record for being employed on crime special duty in Cahirciveen District; pensioned 1/1/1921.

Hickson, Edward Fitzgerald; LDS 2097/264; born 18/2/1848, Co. Cork; married in October 1884 (Dublin North Registrar's District, December Quarter, 1884, vol. 2, p. 479), wife a native of Co. Dublin; 3rd SI 15/9/1867; received a favourable record on 30/6/1870 for the discovery and conviction of the writer of several threatening letters (a woman), who was sentenced to five years penal servitude; barrister-at-law; temporary resident magistrate 7/9/1888; permanent RM 3rd class 26/10/1889, 2nd class 19/8/1894, 1st class 1/5/1908; pensioned 26/10/1911; (p. 87, RM Records of Service Book, National Archives, Dublin).

Higginson, John McConnell; LDS 2097/181; born 21/11/1826, Belfast, Co. Antrim; son of Henry Theophilius Higginson (17/3/1798–20/6/1869), of Lisburn, Co. Antrim and Carnalea House, Co. Down, High Sheriff of Carrickfergus, Co. Antrim, MA, TCD, Captain Commandant of the Derryaghy Yeomanry, Registrar of the United Diocese of Down and Connor and Charlotte, only surviving daughter and heiress of John McConnell, of Killyleagh, Co. Down, by his wife Elizabeth, only daughter of Andrew Bogle, MD, of Strabane, Co. Tyrone, a claimant to the dormant earldom of Monteith; Registrar of the Probate Court of Belfast; married on 20/11/1850, Susan Arabella Gertrude (Longford Registrar's District, vol. 7, p. 457), born in Co. Longford (d.14/4/18910), only daughter of Captain Robert Conry, 90th Regiment of Foot (Perthshire Volunteers Regiment), of Clonahee, Co. Roscommon; 3rd SI 15/8/1849; resigned 1/1/1852 in consequence of delicate health; died on14/4/1891 at Carnalea House, Crawfordsburn, Co. Down; will proved on 17/7/1891 at Belfast by Charles W.S. Higginson, of Royal Avenue, Belfast, solicitor, one of the surviving executors – effects £6,932.3s.0d., resworn £5,993.10s.6d.

Higman, Bernard Drake; RIC 73518; ADRIC no. 543; LDS 2099/032; born 6/12/1894, Oak Villa, St Austell, Cornwall, England; son of Henry Wheeler Higman, Oak Lodge, St Austell, Cornwall, solicitor and Emily Martha Pearce; employed as a solicitor's clerk; private No. 3387, Inns of Court Officer Training Corps, 26/4/1915; 2nd lieutenant, 3/25th Battalion, London Regiment, 15/12/1915; lieutenant, 1st Balloon Squadron, Royal Air Force, 18/3/1919; relinquished his commission, 15/4/1919; 3rd DI 25/6/1921; pensioned 9/5/1922; (WO 374/33298).

Hildebrand, George Louis; RIC 59413; LDS 2098/173; born 1874, Co. Sligo; (Sligo Registrar's District, 1874, vol. 2, p. 365); master in Larne Grammar School for one year and six months; married on 19/2/1903 (Dublin South Registrar's District, March Quarter, 1903, vol. 2, p. 581), Lydia Anne Hamilton, a native of Co. Antrim; 3rd DI 18/5/1900; Queen Victoria's Visit to Ireland Medal, 1900; King Edward VII Visit to Ireland Medal, 1903; CI 15/6/1920; pensioned 31/5/1922; transferred to the Royal Ulster Constabulary on 1/6/1922; died in Bangor, Co. Down in 1947.

Hill, Edward; LDS 2097/186; born 1814, Co. Dublin; 3rd SI 1/7/1835; paymaster 1/7/1835; on 1/7/1843 was cautioned by the government as to his conduct; on 1/6/1845 drank a political

121 George Louis Hildebrand (fourth from left, standing) and family.

toast at a dinner and was warned to prepare for his removal from County Armagh; received a grant from the Reward Fund on 31/3/1854 for indefatigable exertions in the suppression of crime and in particular in the conviction of James McArdle for ribbonism; CI 1/10/1860; pensioned 10/3/1873; died 12/8/1884 at Ashbury, Bray, Co. Wicklow; will with one codicil proved at the Principal Registry on 23/9/1884 by the oath of Elizabeth Hill, of Ashbury, Bray, Co. Wicklow, widow and Beauchamp Henry Colclough, of St Joseph's Crescent, Glasnevin, Co. Dublin, Esq., two of the executors – effects £9,772.14s.1d.

Hill, Edward Eustace; LDS 2097/098; captain, 77th Regiment of Foot (East Middlesex Regiment); 3rd SI 1/10/1836; paymaster 1/12/1839; resident magistrate 20/12/1838; residing at Feraghfad, Ballymacormick, Co. Longford in 1850; retired as a RM on 14/8/1860.

Hill, George I.; RIC 13362; LDS 2097/191; born Co. Monaghan; 3rd SI 11/2/1852; received a grant from the Reward Fund on 30/6/1854 for giving important evidence in a Ribbon Case and generally zealous exertions in furthering the ends of justice; died in 1853 in Co. Tyrone.

Hill, George Stewart; LDS 2097/077; born 1811, Co. Antrim; wife a native of Co. Armagh; 3rd SI 1/12/1832; pensioned 1/4/1854; died 11/6/1860 at Warrenpoint, Co. Down; will proved at Belfast on 1211/1860 by Lucy Hill, his widow – effects under £1,500.

Hill, Godfrey; LDS 2097/061; born 1802, Co. Derry; 3rd SI 5/8/1825; in November 1832 he received a slight fracture in the skull in quelling a riot at Glenties, Co. Donegal; C.C. Glenties, Co. Donegal, 1831; dismissed 2/1/1845.

Hill, Hugh Blacker; LDS 2097/084; born 1809, New Ross, Co. Wexford; wife a native of North Wales; birth of a daughter still-born on 19/9/1863 at Devonshire Square, Bandon, Co. Cork (*Cork Examiner* 21/9/1863); wife, Maria Matilda, died of dropsy on 26/9/1863, aged 42 years at Devonshire Square, Bandon, Co. Cork (*Cork Examiner* 28/9/1863); 3rd SI 21/6/1833; CI 11/4/1859; pensioned 1/11/1870; died 20/9/1884; his third son, Matthew Thomas Hill, married on 28/9/1885 at St Nicholas' Church, Cork, Jennie Tresiliam, fourth daughter of Hezebrah O'Callaghan, Cork.

Hill, Hugh O'Halloran; RIC 45250; LDS 2097/307; born 1857, Co. Wexford; 3rd SI 5/4/1880; CI 1/12/1901; King George V Coronation Medal, 1911; his sister, Miss Helen Henrietta Hill died at The Residency, Omagh, Co. Tyrone on 31/5/1904 and was buried in Omagh; Commissioner of Police and Town Inspector of Constabulary, Belfast from 1/4/1906 to 1/6/1909; awarded a certificate from the Irish Police and Constabulary Recognition Fund; pensioned 31/12/1919; died 18/12/1926; buried in Deansgrange Cemetery, Dublin (South West Section, Row X, Grave No. 88) with his brother Matthew T. Hill (d.24/7/1931) and Jane T. Hill (d.12/2/1942).

Hill, James Ponsonby; LDS 2097/092; born 1816, Co. Derry; married Alice Walsh Pratt (died at 3 St John's Terrace, Blackrock, Co. Dublin on 15/6/1901, aged 87 years), daughter of Rev. W.O'B. Pratt, Vicar of Donagh, Glaslough, Co. Antrim; daughters born on 16/7/1850 and 18/6/1853 at Ballickmoyler, Queen's County (*Cork Examiner* 24/7/1850 & 24/6/1853); 3rd SI 1/1/1836; received an approbation on 30/9/1854 for praiseworthy exertions when in command of a party at a fire; CI 1/1/1863; pensioned 1/10/1876; died 5/11/1880 at Jonesboro House, Flurry Bridge, Co. Armagh; will proved with one codicil on 3/8/1881 at Armagh by the oath of John Hill, of Bellaghy Castle, Derry, one of the executors – effects under £245.

Hill, John; CarNB; born 1803; 3rd SI 1825; C.C. Newtownhamilton, Co. Armagh, 1826.

Hill, Richard; CarNB; born 1781; C.C. Newry, Co. Down; Newbliss and Clones, Co. Monaghan.

Hill, Richard Middleton; RIC 48498; LDS 2097/318; born 1858, Beaumaris, Anglesey, England; (Bangor Registrar's District, 1858, March Quarter, vol. 11b, p. 465); teaching at Felstead Grammar School, Felstead, Essex in 1881 (Census); BA, New College, Oxford, 1880; 3rd SI 17/4/1882; Adjutant, Phoenix Park Depot from 1/9/1893 to 28/12/1896; resigned 20/12/1896 on his appointment as Chief Constable of Cornwall County Constabulary on 20 December 1896 to 16 October 1909.

Hill, Thomas M Hamilton Jones; RIC 21224; LDS 2097/209; born 1834, Bellaghy, Co. Derry; third son of John Hill, Esq., JP, Castle, Bellaghy, Co. Derry; married on 26/1/1861 at St Peter's Church, Dublin, Frances Kate Hamilton (Dublin South Registrar's District, vol. 5, p. 305), daughter of Thomas Bryan, Esq., Prospect Hill, Co. Cork (*Cork Examiner* 28/1/1861); 3rd SI 1/12/1856; discharged on medical grounds 1/4/1863.

Hillas, Robert; LDS 2097/115; born, Templeboy, Co. Sligo; 3rd SI 1/9/1837; died 10/2/1880.

Hillas, Robert B.; RIC 8252; LDS 2097/168; born 1800, Doonecoy, Templeboy, Co. Sligo; enlisted as a sub constable on 15/4/1825; 3rd SI 1/6/1848; pensioned 25/3/1858.

Hilliard, George; RIC 61208; LDS 2099/008; born 1901, Irvinestown, Co. Tyrone; (Irvinestown Registrar's District, 1901, June Quarter, vol. 2, p. 134); 3rd DI 15/2/1921; pensioned 18/5/1922.

Hillier, George Edward; born 10/12/1820, Devizes, Wilts., England; son of Col. George Hillier, of Devizes; joined the army in 1838; served with the 5th Lancers; lieutenant-colonel; ADC to the Governors General of India, Lords Auckland, Ellenborough and Hardinge, 1840–7, and in that capacity at the Gevalior campaign, 1843, the Sutlej campaign, 1845–6, he was awarded the Bronze Star for Maharajpore and Medal for Mudki; married firstly in 1848, Catherine Elizabeth, daughter of William Hawkins, of the Cape of Good Hope; married secondly, Olivia Maria, widow of James Barry, of Ballyclough, Co. Cork and daughter of Francis and Anna Maria Drew (d.22/5/1861 in Dublin) of Mocollop Castle, Lismore, Co. Waterford; Francis Drew's brother, Dr Henry Drew died on 9/8/1866 at Wynberg, Cape of Good Hope (*Cork Examiner* 2/10/1866); Olivia Maria Hilier died on 26/11/1884 and is buried in Mount Jerome Cemetery, Dublin; her will with one codicil was proved on 19/2/1885 at the Principal Registry with effects of £7,153.3s.6d.; he retired from the army in 1864; AIG 1/1/1860; Commandant of the Phoenix Park Depot from 1/1/1860 to 1/8/1867; DIG 30/7/1867; inspector general 19/9/1876; author of *Constabulary Manual* (1880); resigned 11/5/1882; died 11/3/1895, aged 74 years, at Mocollup Castle, Lismore, Co. Waterford (Lismore Registrar's District, 1895, March Quarter, vol. 4, p. 506); (*Irish Times* 13/3/1895). (WO 25/768 fol. 608).

Hoare, Bernard; RIC 60181; LDS 2098/249B; born 1879, Tuam, Co. Galway; (Tuam Registrar's District, March Quarter, 1879, vol. 4, p. 596); awarded the Constabulary Medal on 28/5/1920; 3rd DI 3/7/1921; pensioned 22/4/1922.

Hobart, Patrick; LDS 2097/070; born 1802, Cappoquin, Co. Waterford; PPF; enlisted as a sub constable on 1/12/1820; constable 1/9/1826; 3rd SI 1/7/1831; CI 1/1/1852; C.C. Marble Hill, Loughrea, 1835; married on 27/11/861 at Ballingarry Church, Co. Tipperary, Mary Matilda, daughter of Ralph Smith, Esq., of Ballymona House, Co. Tipperary (*Cork Examiner* 29/11/1861); pensioned 20/9/1870; died 29/1/1880 at 1 Pembroke Road, Dublin; will proved on 25/3/1880 at the Principal Registry by the oath of Robert Warren, Killiney, Co. Dublin and Owen Armstrong, of Clifton Terrace, Monkstown, Co. Dublin – effects under £12,000.

Hobbins, Thomas; RIC 35005; LDS 2098/137; born 1850, Co. Tipperary; 3rd DI 2/7/1910; pensioned 7/2/1910.

Hobbs, George; CarNB; C.C. Ennistymon, Co. Clare, 1824; Gorey, Co. Wexford; Co. Westmeath, 1828; Dunshaughlin, Co. Meath, 1829; temporarily employed in Corbally, Queen's County, 1830; Mountmellick, Queen's County, 1831; his eldest son George (son of the late George Hobbs, sub inspector of constabulary) aged 24 years died on 29/4/1851 of consumption (*Cork Examiner* 2/5/1851).

Hodge, Isaac Lang; RIC 61145; LDS 2098/197; born 1879, Plymouth, Devon, England; (Wigton Registrar's District, 1880, September Quarter, vol. 10b, p. 514); son of John M. Hodge (b.1848), Plymouth, Devon and Janny Lang Hodge (b.1850) Exeter, Devon; residing at 38 Tavistock Place, Charles The Martyr, Plymouth, Devon in 1881 (Census); schoolmaster for two years; BA University College, Dunelm.; married on 29/8/1907, Mabel Huddleston, a native of London; 3rd DI 8/8/1904; King Edward VII Visit to Ireland Medal, 1903 as a head constable; pensioned 13/4/1922.

Hogben, Henry Arthur; LDS 2098/058; born 1869, Co. Tyrone; son of Thomas D. Hogben, SI, RIC and brother of Thomas James Hogben, SI, RIC; 3rd DI 3/10/1889; dismissed 25/10/1892 for drunkenness.

Hogben, Thomas D.; RIC 3619; LDS 2097/226; born 1821, Co. Cork; married 12/2/2852; father of Henry Arthur Hogben, SI, RIC and Thomas James Hogben, SI, RIC; 3rd SI 22/3/1859; pensioned 6/1/1883; died 12/4/1898 at Bonvil House, Cupar, Fifeshire, Scotland; his son Edgar Hogben, MD, died on 4/9/1899 at Stratnighe, Fifeshire, Scotland; administration granted on 8/9/1898 at Cupar, Fifeshire, Scotland and resealed on 11/10/1896 at Dublin – effects in Ireland £168.7s.9d.

Hogben, Thomas James; RIC 39177; LDS 2097/292; born 1854, Co. Donegal; son of Thomas D. Hogben, SI, RIC and brother of Henry Arthur Hogben, SI, RIC; 3rd SI 6/4/1879; pensioned 1/9/1886; died 22/10/1893.

Hogge, Michael; RIC 53813; LDS 2098/116B; born 24/6/1867, Co. Sligo; (Sligo Registrar's District, 1867, vol. 7, p. 346); married on 22/5/1913 (Boyle Registrar's District, June Quarter, 1913, vol. 4, p. 45), wife a native of Co. Roscommon; 3rd DI 14/5/1920; pensioned 17/7/1922.

Hojel, James; LDS 2097/224; born 1837, Co. Wicklow; 3rd SI 20/1/1859; CI 1/10/1882; died 12/11/1891 at Bandon, Co. Cork; (Bandon Registrar's District, 1891, December Quarter, vol. 5, p. 2); his widow, Alice, aged 81 years, died at Cooteville, Maryborough (Portlaoise), Co. Laois and was buried in Bandon, Co. Cork on 11/7/1916 .

Holland, Edward; LDS 2097/244; born 1843, Pembrokeshire, Wales; son, Frederick John Tredigar Penrose, born on 21/12/1871 in Sixmilebridge, Co. Clare (Ennis Registrar's District, 1872, vol. 4, p. 319) (*Cork Examiner* 28/12/1871); married secondly in September 1884 (Fermoy Registrar's District, September Quarter, 1884, vol. 2, p. 27); 3rd SI 17/9/1867; pensioned 1/1/1888.

Holmes, Benjamin Hayes; LDS 2097/098; lieutenant, 36th Regiment of Foot (Herefordshire Regiment), 13/8/1812; lieutenant half pay, 25/3/1817; awarded one medal and two clasps for Salamanca and the Pyrenees; 3rd SI 1/12/1839; paymaster 1/12/1839; resident magistrate 16/8/1841; removed on reduction of resident magistrates on 15/1/1842; re-appointed resident magistrate on 22/1/1844; residing at Underhill, Fanlobbus, Co. Cork in 1850; (WO 25/762 fol. 170).

Holmes, Francis George; RIC 17508; LDS 2097/200; born 1834, Malta; 3rd SI 1/10/1853; resigned 19/2/1855 from Co. Antrim.

Holmes, George; RIC 31300; LDS 2097/255; born 1847, Co. Armagh; son of Gordon Holmes, CI, RIC; father of Philip Armstrong Holmes, Divisional Commissioner, RIC; 3rd SI 1/3/1865; CI 10/9/1891; pensioned 1/7/1898; died 23/2/1917 at 73 Sandymount Avenue, Dublin; buried in Mount Jerome Cemetery, Dublin; will proved on 25/6/1917 at the Principal Registry by the oath of Harriette C. Holmes – effects £1,689.5s.8d.

Holmes, Gordon; LDS 2097/133; born 1804, Co. Longford; father of George Holmes, SI, RIC; wife a native of Co. Roscommon; enlisted as a sub constable in January 1831; 3rd SI 26/11/1840; received a grant from the Reward Fund on 30/9/1853 for indefatigable exertions in the capture of persons concerned in an important case the murder of Mr Bateson; received a favourable record on 31/1/1868 for surprising when on patrol an armed party engaged in illegal drilling and arresting several of the principals; CI 1/7/1868; pensioned 1/8/1875.

Holmes, John Robert; RIC 25087; LDS 2097/230; born 1841, Co. Armagh; classical teacher in Drogheda for two years; 3rd SI 18/9/1859; died 4/5/1868 at Glenties, Co. Donegal (Glenties Registrar's District, 1868, vol. 7, p. 70).

122   123

122 Joseph Edward Leo Holmes.   123 Philip Armstrong Holmes, Divisional Commissioner, RIC.   124 Philip Armstrong Holmes grave in Mount Jerome Cemetery, Dublin.   125 Michael Horgan.

124   125

Holmes, Joseph Edward Leo; RIC 50985; LDS 2097/329; born 1858, Marleybone, London, Middlesex, England; (Marleybone Registrar's District, 1858, March Quarter, vol. 1a, p. 370); son of Jesse Holmes (b.1828) Ireland and Ann E. Holmes (b.1832), Bloomsbury, London, Middlesex; residing at 3 Alma Square, Marleybone, London in 1881 (Census); married on 11/6/1884 (Rathdown Registrar's District, June Quarter, 1884, vol. 2, p. 784), wife from Co. Dublin; 3rd DI 22/2/1883; King Edward VII Visit to Ireland Medal, 1903; CI 23/1/1908; King George V Coronation Medal, 1911; awarded a certificate from the Irish Police and Constabulary Recognition Fund; CI attached to Crime Special Department from 9/11/1911 to 18/7/1920; pensioned 18/7/1920.

Holmes, Michael; RIC 43374; LDS 2098/147; born 1859, Co. Tipperary; married on 8/12/1885 (Ballinasloe Registrar's District, December Quarter, 1885, vol. 4, p. 7), wife a native of Yorkshire; 3rd DI 19/10/1898; pensioned 7/6/1919.

Holmes, Philip Armstrong; RIC 58074; LDS 2098/144; born 1876, Co. Cork; (Castletown Registrar's District, 1876, vol. 15, p. 57); son of George Holmes, CI, RIC and grandson of Gordon Holmes, CI, RIC; 3rd DI 1/7/1898; major, 5th Battalion, Royal Irish Regiment from 22/1/1916 to 7/5/1919; CI 15/6/1920; divisional commissioner 30/8/1920, Munster No. 2 Division; wounded 28/1/1921, Toureengarriv, Co. Cork and died 29/1/1921; buried in Mount Jerome Cemetery, Dublin; will proved at the Principal Registry on 3/3/1921.

Holmes, Stanley Brereton; RIC 82934; LDS 2099/044; born 1898, Kells, Co. Meath; (Kells Registrar's District, 1898, March Quarter, vol. 2, p. 767); army service, 1915–20; ADRIC, 1/9/1920–1/6/1921; 3rd DI 20/9/1921; pensioned 12/5/1922.

Holmes, Stephen (Sir); KH (1833); veteran of the Peninsular War; holder of the Waterloo Medal; ensign, 2/11/1806, 6th Garrison Battalion; lieutenant, 21/7/1808; lieutenant 24th Regiment of Foot (2nd Warwickshire Regiment); captain, 4/2/1814, 78th Regiment of Foot (Highland or Shire Buffs); captain, 3/2/1820, 90th Regiment of Foot (Pertshire Volunteers Light Infantry Regiment); major half-pay, 24/12/1825 unattached; knighted 1833; lieutenant colonel, 28/6/1838; DIG, 15/3/1838 to 1/7/1838; retired from army in 1840; (Will of Stephen Holmes, Lieut. Colonel in the Army and DIG of the Constabulary of Rathmines, Dublin – PRO, Kew, Catalogue Reference: PROB 11/1922 / Dept: Records of the Prerogative Court of Canterbury and related Probate Jurisdictions: Will Registers / Name of Register: Arden Quire Numbers: 51–100 / Date: 5 February 1840 / Image Reference: 425/366).

Horgan, Matthew; RIC 59172; LDS 2098/167B; born 1881, Co. Cork; (Cork Registrar's District, June Quarter, 1881, vol. 5, p. 191); son of Cornelius Horgan (1826–1902), RIC 14204 and brother of Michael Horgan, DI, RIC and Denis Horgan (1861–1933), RIC Head Constable 44496 and Petty Sessions Clerk, Nenagh, Co. Tipperary (1904–22 and District Court Clerk, Nenagh (1922–33); a third brother, Cornelius Horgan was a teacher in Glasgow, Scotland; married on 15/11/921 (Trim Registrar's District, December Quarter, 1921, vol. 2, p. 846), Mary Elizabeth Tier, a native of Trim, Co. Meath; 3rd DI 1/101920; pensioned 20/7/1922. Weights & Measures Inspector, Cambridge, England in 1933.

Horgan, Michael; RIC 47760; LDS 2098/238; born 19/9/1863, Hospital, Co. Limerick; son of Cornelius Horgan (1826–1902), RIC 14204 and brother of Mathew Horgan, DI, RIC and Denis Horgan (1861–1933), RIC Head Constable 44496 and Petty Sessions Clerk, Nenagh, Co. Tipperary (1904–22) and District Court Clerk, Nenagh (1922–33); a third brother, Cornelius Horgan was a teacher in Glasgow, Scotland; he was a former teacher; married on 31/7/1900 (Lismore Registrar's District, September Quarter, 1900, vol. 4, p. 279), at Mount Melleray; 3rd DI 11/11/1908; pensioned 20/9/1920; was appointed a superintendent in the Garda Siochána on 9/4/1924, pioneering the weights and measures section at Garda Headquarters, Dublin and pensioned on 1/7/1934 in his 71st year; died 29/1/1949.

Horigan, James; RIC 34165; LDS 2098/102; born 1849, Fohinagh, Co. Galway; married on 3/11/1897 (Ballinrobe Registrar's District, December Quarter, 1897, vol. 4, p. 13), wife a native of Co. Mayo; 3rd DI 1/9/1893; pensioned 2/6/1909.

Horne, Alfred Edward; RIC 30256; LDS 2097/251; born 14/3/1843, Co. Meath; assistant master at Clonmel Model School from 26/8/1861 to 8/4/1865; 3rd SI 1/6/1865; received a favourable record on 31/12/1869 for persevering and successful pursuit of a serious offender in the mountains; son Alfred Edmund Charles (Clonmel Registrar's District, vol. 4, p. 777) born on 26/2/1870 at the residence of his father-in-law in Clonmel, Co. Tipperary (*Cork Examiner* 4/3/1870); married secondly on 11/11/1874 at St Stephen's Church, Dublin, Martha Caroline, youngest daughter of Rev. Joseph Morton, incumbent of Bumlin, Diocese of Elphin (Dublin South Registrar's District, vol. 17, p. 591); temporary resident magistrate 11/12/1882; permanent RM 3rd class 9/11/1883, 1st class 3/7/1889; appointed to the Commission of Peace for Co. Dublin for the purpose of an inquiry under the Explosives Act in Dublin under warrant dated 4/12/1893; pensioned 1/5/1908; died 1/6/1916 at Palmerstown, Co. Dublin; will probated at the Principal Registry on 7/7/1916 by the oath of Ernest Dunkels, BL – effects £5,228.12s.6d., resworn £4,944.8s.10d.; (p. 29, RM Records of Service Book, National Archives, Dublin).

Howard, Thomas; LDS 2097/076; born 1789, King's County; lieutenant in the King's County Militia from September 1805 to 26/10/1811 (WO 13/2961–79); ensign and lieutenant in the army from 25/10/1807 to 1/12/1811; 3rd SI 15/8/1832; died 17/8/1840.

Howe, Thomas Andrew; RIC 50671; LDS 2097/325; born 1857, Co. Fermanagh; tutor, Trinity College Dublin; wife from Co. Fermanagh; 3rd DI 6/12/1882; Deputy Captain Superintendent of Police at Hong Kong 9/9/1897 to 20/9/1898; King Edward VII Visit to Ireland Medal, 1903; CI 19/7/1906; King George V Coronation Medal, 1911; pensioned 31/10/1919; (photo in the *Constabulary Gazette*, vol. XIV, no. 22, 20/2/1904 & vol. XVI, no. 14, 24/12/1904).

Huddy, Gideon Ouseley; RIC 20052; LDS 2097/305; born 1838, Corofin, Co. Clare; father of Richard Henry Brabazon Huddy, DI, RIC; wife from Dublin City; 3rd SI 14/1/1869; pensioned 31/12/1896; died 5/5/1899 at Dunmanway, Co. Cork; administration granted on 21/7/1899 at Cork to Adelaide Huddy, of Dunmanway, Co. Cork, spinster, the universal legatee – effects £248.14s.10d.

Huddy, Richard Henry Brabazon; RIC 51685; LDS 2098/016; born 1867, Co. Limerick; son of Gideon Ouseley Huddy, SI, RIC; 3rd DI 24/5/1886; died 16/1/1898 at Ballylinan, Queen's County; administration granted on 6/6/1898 at the Principal Registry to Gideon Ouseley Huddy, DI, RIC, father of the deceased, of Dunmanway, Co. Cork – effects £620.12s.8d.

Hudson, Gilbert Samuel; LDS 2098/198B; born 11/4/1895, Co. Dublin; (Dublin South Registrar's District, June Quarter, 1895, vol. 2, p. 594); army; married on 8/9/1920; 3rd DI 7/12/1920; pensioned 9/6/1922.

Huggins, David George; RIC 26954; LDS 2098/018; born 1843, Kilmoon, Co. Clare; brother of Joshua Alexander Huggins, SI, RIC; married on 19/9/1895 (Cahirciveen Registrar's District, September Quarter, vol. 3, p. 25), Lavinia Graves, a native of Co. Kerry; 3rd DI 15/7/1886; King Edward VII Visit to Ireland Medal, 1903; pensioned 31/3/1905; died 27/2/1927; buried in Mount Jerome Cemetery with his wife, Lavinia C.K. Huggins (d.26/10/1941).

Huggins, Joshua Alexander; RIC 21727; LDS 2097/313; born 1838, Kilmoon, Co. Clare; brother of David George Huggins, SI, RIC; married on 12/10/1893 (Dundalk Registrar's District, December Quarter, 1893, vol. 2, p. 671), wife from Co. Louth; 3rd SI 20/10/1881; pensioned 1/6/1898; died 8/2/1904 at Ardcarn, Co. Roscommon; will proved on 2/5/1904 at Tuam; will proved on 20/7/1904 by the oath of Anne Elizabeth Huggins, widow – effects £1,686.3s.0d.

Hughes, John; LDS 2098/062; born 1867, Co. Tipperary; son of Mr Thomas W. Hughes, of Dalkey, Co. Dublin; BA 1878, Trinity College Dublin; 3rd DI 7/3/1890; Queen Victoria's Visit to Ireland Medal, 1900; King George V Visit to Ireland Medal, 1911; pensioned 1/1/1921.

Hume, Joseph Samuel Hoare; RIC 24627; LDS 2097/227; born 16/5/1835, West Canada; cashier at the establishment of Messrs. McBirney, Colles & Co. Dublin from November 1853 to June 1856; 3rd SI 21/4/1859; pensioned 1/5/1898; died 27/1/1919 at Prospect House, Bushy Park Road, Terenure, Co. Dublin; will proved at the Principal Registry on 14/5/1919.

Hunt, Edward; LDS 2097/089; born 1809, Cork; 3rd SI 1/4/1835; dismissed 28/10/1848.

Hunt, Michael; RIC 55727; LDS 2098/022B; born 3/9/1873, Co. Sligo; son of John Hunt; married on 16/5/1900 (Athy Registrar's District, June Quarter, vol. 3, p. 215), wife a native of Monasterevan, Co. Kildare; 3rd DI 1/1/1911; awarded a 1st class favourable record in connection with a Sinn Féin Meeting on 9/9/1919; killed 23/6/1919, Main Street, Thurles, Co. Tipperary; late of Railway House, Thurles, Co. Tipperary; buried in Monasteraden Catholic Cemetery, Co. Sligo on 26/6/1919; administration granted at the Principal Registry on 2/8/1919.

Hunt, Michael John; RIC 70010; LDS 2098/109B; born 16/61898, Athy, Co. Kildare; (Athy Registrar's District, 1898, June Quarter, vol. 3, p. 305); captain, Royal Irish Regiment; married Nina Moore Swinden, a native of Lancashire; 3rd DI 4/1/1920; pensioned 19/5/1922.

Hunt, William; CarNB; 3rd SI 1819; father-in-law of Chief Constable John Wright (d.1853); in September 1824 he was severely wounded in the left leg in quelling a riot at Tubberbracken fair, when the whole police party was attacked by an immense mob of the peasantry. Also received a blow of a stone in the chest from which he suffered from debility and frequent spasms; pensioned 1/4/1825; retired to Kilrush, Co. Clare where on 27/5/1825 he lost his right eye; on 10/4/1827 he was residing in Caermarthen, Wales; died 1830; C.C. Athenry, Co. Galway, 1820.

Hurley, Michael; RIC 17987; LDS 2097/315; born 1835, Co. Cork; married on 9/6/1883, wife from Co. Cork W.R.; 3rd SI 18/6/1881; Private Secretary to the Inspector General from 24/11/1885 until 11/8/1893; CI and barrackmaster of the Phoenix Park Depot 11/8/1893; pensioned 1/9/1900 and from his home in 4, Rathdown Terrace, North Circular Road, Dublin administered the RIC branch of St Joseph's Young Priests Society until his death on 27/6/1911 at 4 Rathdown Terrace, North Circular Road, Dublin; will proved on 27/9/1911 at the Principal Registry by the oath of Mary Jane Hurley – effects £1,344.14s.6d.; (photo in the *Constabulary Gazette*, vol. 2, no. 39, p. 1, 24/12/1897).

Hurst, George; RIC 51165; LDS 2098/001; born 1865, Co. Kildare; married on 27/3/1889 (Parsonstown Registrar's District, March Quarter, 1889, vol. 3, p. 487), wife a native of Co. Dublin; 3rd DI 12/7/1884; King Edward VII Visit to Ireland Medal, 1903; CI 20/12/1908; King George V Coronation Medal, 1911; pensioned 8/12/1916; his brother, Gerard Hurst, RIC, died in Athlone, Co. Roscommon on 7/10/1887; (photo in the *Constabulary Gazette*, vol. XIII, no. 24, 5/9/1903).

Hurst, Gerard; RIC 2408; LDS 2097/254; born 1817, Enniskillen, Co. Fermanagh; wife from Co. Cork; 3rd SI 1/6/1865; pensioned 1/10/1882; died 23/4/1888 at Newtownstewart, Co. Tyrone.

Hussey, William Hawthorne; RIC 40018; LDS 2098/141; born 1856, Kiltullagh, Co. Roscommon; married on 21/10/1886; (Belfast Registrar's District, December Quarter, 1886,vol. 1, p. 371); 3rd DI 1/7/1898; King Edward VII Visit to Ireland Medal, 1903; pensioned 31/10/1917; died 12/4/1919 at Parkmount, Portadown, Co. Armagh; buried in the City Cemetery, Belfast; (photo in the *Constabulary Gazette*, vol. VI, no. 14, 30/12/1899).

Hutchinson, John; RIC 30255; LDS 2097/252; born 1847, Co. Kilkenny; 3rd SI 1/6/1865.

Hyde, John Oldfield; RIC 45353; LDS 2097/308; born 1/11/1854, Co. Roscommon; son of Rev. Arthur Hyde, Frenchpark, Co. Roscommon; scholar, Trinity College Dublin; 3rd SI 1/11/1880; died 11/2/1896 at 5, Stillorgan Park, Dublin, late of the Cottage, Kenmare, Co.

126

126 Michael Hunt. 127 George Hurst. 128 John Oldfield Hyde, brother of Dr Douglas Hyde, President of Ireland, 1938–45. 129 John Oldfield Hyde.

127

128

129

Kerry; buried in Deansgrange Cemetery, Dublin (South Section, Row Z, Graves 21–22) on 12/2/1896 with his grandmother Anne (d.20/3/1894, aged 92 years), widow of the Venerable J. Oldfield, Archdeacon of Elphin, his aunt Christine Wilson (d.5/4/1918) widow of Rev. P. Wilson, his aunt Sara Oldfield (d.20/7/1923) and his aunt Emily Oldfield (d.3/7/1921); administration granted on 16/3/1876 at the Principal Registry to Douglas Hyde, of Ratra House, Frenchpark, Co. Roscommon, Esq., LLB, the brother – effects – £228.1s.7d.

Hylton, Edgar Walter; RIC 79876; ADRIC no. 1167; LDS 2099/022; born 22/2/1900, Middlesex, England; (Chelsea Registrar's District, 1900, March Quarter, vol. 1a, p. 435); lieutenant, Durham Light Infantry; 3rd DI 25/6/1921; pensioned 29/3/1922; joined the Palestine Police on 30/3/1922.

I

Ibbotson, Leslie Henry Parker; RIC 78038; ADRIC no. 803; LDS 2098/237B; born 24/10/1892, Bourdon, Altrincham, Ches., England; (Altrincham Registrar's District, 1892, December Quarter, vol. 8a, p. 184); son of Walter Ibbotson, Donnybrook, South Downs Drive, Ashley Heath, Altrincham, Cheshire; private, No. 5103, Public Schools Battalion Royal Fusiliers, 5/9/1914; lieutenant, 2nd Leicester Regiment, 5/9/1915; 19th Battalion, Manchester Regiment, 1916; 3rd DI 2/7/1921; pensioned 15/3/1922; joined the Palestine Police on 29/3/1922; (WO 339/38081).

Ievers, John Henry; RIC 34756; LDS 2097/272; born 1847, Co. Galway; son of Robert John Ievers (1800–1872), of Castle Ievers, Co. Limerick, wine merchant and Elizabeth (m.1845) 3rd daughter of Major M.P. Browne, of Woodstock, Co. Mayo; 3rd SI 2/10/1868; his sister, Frances, married on 17/6/1858, at Knockavilla Church, Co. Cork, William Browning Gardner, Esq., solicitor, of Cork City (*Cork Examiner* 19/6/1858); discharged with a gratuity on 31/12/1877 due to ill-health; emigrated to Australia and applied to join the police in Melbourne, Victoria (Public Record Office, Melbourne – Reference: VPRS 937, Unit 493, Bundle 3); died unmarried in Australia in 1879.

Ireland, DeCourcey Plunkett; LDS 2097/145; born 1823, Co. Galway; married on 28/12/1871, at St Peter's Church, Dublin, when residing at Abbeyville, Clonmel, Co. Tipperary, Ada, second daughter of the late Robert Hall, Esq., of Merton Hall, Borrisokane, Co. Tipperary (*Cork Examiner* 1/1/1872); 3rd SI 11/6/1844; CI 18/5/1869; received a favourable record on 30/6/1871 for solving a murder; received a favourable record on 31/12/1871 for solving a barbarous murder; died 3/1/1891 at Seaview Cottage, Dalkey, Co. Dublin, late of Merton Hall, Borrisokane, Co. Tipperary; will proved by the oath of Ada Ireland, of Merton Hall, Borrisokane, Co. Tipperary, the sole executrix – effects £1,081.6s.9d.

Ireland, Frederick; RIC 29189; LDS 2097/246; born 1845, Co. Dublin; father of Frederick Crawford Vincent Ireland, CI, RIC; 3rd SI 14/1/1864; received an approbation in 1868 for exertions at a fire and mounting the roof of burning premises which contained spirits, wines, oils and tallow; resigned 18/12/1868.

Ireland, Frederick Crawford Vincent; RIC 53460; LDS 2098/046; born 1869, Co. Dublin; (Rathdown Registrar's District, 1869, vol. 17, p. 885); son of Frederick Ireland, SI, RIC; educated at Portarlington School, Armagh Royal School and Dublin High School; married on 29/9/1894 (Rathdown Registrar's District, September Quarter, 1893, vol. 2, p. 735), Edith A. Whitton, a native of Co. Dublin; 3rd DI 1/6/1889; King Edward VII Visit to Ireland Medal, 1903; CI 3/7/1912; awarded a certificate from the Irish Police and Constabulary Recognition Fund; pensioned 1/10/1920; died 10/12/1930 at 19, Mespil Road, Dublin; (Dublin South Registrar's District, 1930, December Quarter, vol. 2, p. 357); will proved at the Principal Registry on 23/3/1931 by the oath of Alexander Frederick Boyle and Rupert Henry Giltrap, solicitors – effects £2,173.2s.4d.

Ireland, James; LDS 2097/135; born 1804, Low Park, Co. Roscommon; wife a native of King's County; enlisted as a sub constable in April 1825; 3rd SI 17/11/1841; resigned 16/6/1868.

Ireland, James Stanley; CarNB; born 1780, Low Park, Co. Roscommon; son of Richard Ireland and grandson of Rev. William Ireland who died near the abbey of Cong, Co. Mayo in 1787 and Magdalene, daughter of John Irwin, Esq., of Lysballaly, Co. Sligo, by Magdalene, his wife, daughter of John Kelly, Esq., of Castle Kelly; ensign without purchase, 87th Regiment of Foot (The Prince of Wales' Irish Regiment), 10/1/1810, lieutenant without purchase, 22/9/1812; acting deputy assistant commissary general in the Peninsular War; one of six brothers who served in the army, two were killed before the Castle of Burgos, one at the Battle of Fuentes de Horor, and another in India. The remaining brother survived as a half-pay officer; married on 19/1/1815 in Athlone, Matilda Davies, sister of Thomas Davies, of Newcastle, Aughrim, Co. Galway and aunt of James Davies, CI, RIC; father of Richard Davies Ireland (1816–17) BA, TCD, 1837, BL, 1838, Solicitor-General, Victoria, Australia; 3rd SI 1/1/1823; C.C. Roscommon in 1825; CI 1/3/1824; resident magistrate 1/5/1830; pensioned 15/8/1842; died on 7/3/1856 at Chateau Hunaudieres, near Le Mans, France, aged 75 years, late of the 87th Regiment and many years resident magistrate for the county of Galway (*Cork Examiner* 19/3/1856); (WO25/763/Fol.211); C.C. Ballinamore, Co. Leitrim and Ahascragh, Co. Galway.

Irvine, William Stewart; LDS 2097/216; born 1834, Co. Tyrone, the son of John Irvine, Rector of Kilmoon, Diocese of Meath and he joined the Revenue Police on 14/11/1854 as a lieutenant and served in Malin, Co. Donegal; daughter born on 1/11/1862 at Rathfriland, Co. Down (*Cork Examiner* 6/11/1862); married secondly on 15/11/1893 (Enniskillen Registrar's District, December Quarter, vol. 2, p. 65); 3rd SI 1/12/1857; received a favourable record on 30/6/1869 for effectively aided by his party succeeded upon a slight clue in a detection of the crime of infanticide; CI 27/2/1879; pensioned 21/4/1891; died 22/12/1896 at Douglas, Isle of Man.

Irwin, Charles Dillon; RIC 13272; LDS 2097/181; born 1827, Fernhill, Co. Roscommon; fourth son of John Irwin, Esq., of Fernhill, Co. Roscommon; married on 20/4/1853 at the Metropolitan Church, Marlborough Street, Dublin, Julia, youngest daughter of George Cornelius Smyth, Esq., Solicitor, of Dublin (*Cork Examiner* 4/5/1853); 3rd SI 15/8/1849; dismissed 28/6/1869.

Irwin, John; RIC 42537; LDS 2098/202; born 1/3/1859, Co. Clare; married in September 1890, Molly, eldest daughter of John O'Sullivan, Bandon, Co. Cork; his wife died at Roundstone, Connemara, Co. Galway on 5/10/1910, aged 41 years and was buried in Bandon, Co. Cork; 3rd DI 10/1/1904; died 7/11/1914 at Cahirciveen Barracks, Co. Kerry.

Irwin, John; LDS 2097/051A; born 1799, Co. Leitrim; 3rd SI 1/7/1824; C.C. Carrickmacross, Co. Monaghan 1831; pensioned 1/9/1848.

Irwin, John King; RIC 21859; LDS 2097/211; born 1834, Co. Armagh; 3rd SI 12/9/1857; died 17/5/1868 at Raphoe, Co. Donegal (Strabane Registrar's District, vol. 7, p. 252) (*Cork Examiner* 23/5/1868); administration granted at Londonderry on 6/6/1868 to Isabella Mary Irwin, of Raphoe, the widow of the deceased – effects under £800.

Irwin, John Thomas; LDS 2098/002, born 1859, Queen's County; 3rd DI 12/7/1884; died 28/4/1886 at Shillelagh (Shillelagh Registrar's District, 1886, June Quarter, vol. 22, p. 804).

Irwin, Joseph Burke; RIC 25537; LDS 2097/234; born 19/1/1838; Co. Roscommon; 3rd assistant clerk, Head Police Office, Dublin on 26/6/1856; junior clerk, Receiver's Office, Dublin Metropolitan Police, 28/10/1856 to 16/2/1860; 3rd SI 3/4/1860; married on 22/5/1866 (Dublin South Registrar's District, vol. 7, p. 702), Alicia, second daughter of the late Andrew Graves, Esq., Derrynaseera, Queen's County, at the Church of St Andrew, Westland Row, Dublin (*Cork Examiner* 24/5/1866); received two favourable records on 31/12/1870 for zealous and persevering efforts in the discovery and capture of an offender under circumstances of difficulty and taking judicious steps for the discovery of a robbery of money by soldiers; temporary resident magistrate 28/7/1882; permanent RM 3rd class 28/10/1882, 2nd class 3/7/1889, 1st class 1/1/1892; pensioned 19/1/1903.

Irwin, Thomas; RIC 5405; LDS 2097/269; born 1823, Co. Tyrone; wife a native of Co. Limerick; his daughter, Barbara Hannah aged 18 years, died on 9/9/1869 after a long illness (C. 14/9/1869); 3rd SI 14/3/1868; pensioned 1/5/1888; died 3/6/1895 at Town View, Tinahely,

Co. Wicklow (Shillelagh Registrar's District, 1895, September Quarter, vol. 2, p. 674); his wife Annie died at Tinahely, Co. Wicklow on 7/1/1891; administration granted on 10/10/1895 at the Principal Registry to Anna M. Irwin, of Tinahely, Co. Wicklow, the widow – effects £223.

Irwin, William; RIC 41428; LDS 2098/072; born 1857, Hants., England; 3rd DI 25/3/1891; King Edward VII Visit to Ireland Medal, 1903; King George V Coronation Medal, 1911; CI 11/12/1913; pensioned 1/9/1918; died 17/9/1918 at Downpatrick, Co. Down; (Downpatrick District, 1918, vol. 1, p. 563).

Irwin, William S.; LDS 2098/008; born 1862, Co. Westmeath; senior classical master, Carrig School, Kingstown, Co. Dublin; BA 1883, Trinity College Dublin; married M.G. Robinson, a native of Co. Mayo; 3rd DI 1/10/1885; son born in Maryborough, Queen's County on 30/1/1908; pensioned 15/6/1920.

J

Jackson, Benjamin; LDS 2097/057; born 1802, Co. Clare; enlisted as a constable 1/10/1822; 3rd SI 1/11/1824; wife a native of Co. Kerry; his daughter Alice married on 13/2/1862 at the Roman Catholic Chapel of St Nicholas, by the Lord Bishop of Galway, Joseph Butler, Assistant Surgeon, Tipperary Artillery, only son of John Butler, Esq., of Winterfield House, Co. Galway, and late captain, 62nd Regiment of Foot (Wiltshire Regiment) (*Cork Examiner* 18/2/1862); his daughter 'Bessey' Elizabeth Anne, married on 19/5/1863 in Galway (Galway Registrar's District, vol. 6, p. 49), John Gill, Esq., Surveyor of Income Tax (*Cork Examiner* 23/5/1863); his eldest son, Burton Jackson, married on 3/2/1864 (Listowel Registrar's District, vol. 5, p. 499 & vol. 5, p. 516), at Ballyduff, Co. Kerry, by the Most Rev. Dr Moriarty, Ellie Gertrude, daughter of Kerry Supple, Esq., of Ballyhorgan House, Co. Kerry (*Cork Examiner* 12/2/1864); at Listowel, Co. Kerry on 26/11/1829 he was granted leave for a surgical operation on his jaw; CI 1/4/1849; pensioned 1/6/1865; died 19/8/1872 at Palmyra Crescent, Galway, Co. Galway; administration granted on 5/12/1872 at the Principal Registry to Anne Jackson, Palmyra Crescent, Galway – effects under £6,000; his second son, Benjamin R. Jackson, aged 22 years died on 6/7/1873 at Montpelier Terrace, Galway.

Jackson, Francis; RIC 64280; LDS 2098/231; born 29/8/1883, The Manse, Ballycastle, Co. Antrim; (Ballycastle Registrar's District, September Quarter, 1883, vol. 1, p. 69); 3rd DI 15/9/1908; captain, 6th (Service Battalion) Royal Irish Fusiliers on 28/10/1914 to 31/3/1919; assumed duty at the War Office, 2/6/1916 and General Staff Officer (Grade III) in the Directorate of Military Intelligence at the War Office, 23/2/1918–28/2/1919; mentioned in a communiqué to the Press, 13/3/1918; wounded in the head and right hand at Suvla Bay, Gallipoli, 9/8/1915; pensioned 31/5/1921 on grounds of ill health; attached to the Nautical Training School, Heswall, Cheshire in 1922; (WO 339/11955).

Jacques, William; RIC 7517; LDS 2097/279; born 1828, Fiddown, Co. Kilkenny; 3rd SI 1/4/1870; detective director from 22/1/1881 to 20/4/1883; pensioned 10/11/1889; died 23/9/1899 at Hilberry, Ballydollaghan, Co. Down; administration granted on 19/2/1900 at Belfast to Frances Jacques, the universal legatee – £1,496.13s.2d.

Janns, Frederick William; 2097/128; born 1814, Devon, England; 3rd SI 1/7/1839; CI 1/8/1867; died 28/10/1874.

Jenkins, Edward; LDS 2097/039; born 1790, Glamorgan, Wales; ensign, November 1814 to October 1821, 77th Regiment of Foot (East Middlesex Regiment); clerk, January 1808 to March 1814; acting purser, May 1813 to March 1814; held the Commission of Peace for the Counties of Louth, Armagh and Down for 9 years and 4 months; his eldest daughter, Frances married on 11/6/1855 in Dublin (Dublin South Registrar's District, vol. 5, p. 312), Christopher Brennan, Esq., of Mountmellick, Queen's County (*Cork Examiner* 15/6/1855); 3rd SI 10/2/1823; CI 1/10/1825; stipendiary magistrate 7/4/1844; died 1849; C.C. Dundalk, Co. Louth.

Jennings, Charles; LDS 2097/122; born 1803, Warks., England; enlisted as a constable on 11/5/1823; 3rd SI 11/12/1838; died 11/12/1841.

Jennings, Daniel Corley; LDS 2097/107; born 1816, Newry, Co. Down; father of Ignatius Ronayne Bray Jennings, DI, RIC; married Johanna Bray from Tipperary N.R.; 3rd SI 17/11/1836; CI 1/4/1865; pensioned 1/10/1882; died 15/11/1896 at 18 Morehampton Road, Dublin (Dublin South Registrar's District, 1896, December Quarter, vol. 2, p. 426); will proved on 12/12/1896 at the Principal Registry by the oath of Johanna M. Jennings, of 18 Morehampton Road, Dublin, widow – effects £1,309.19s.8d.; buried in Glasnevin Cemetery, Dublin on 18/11/1896.

Jennings, Donald Charles Blake; RIC 68402; LDS 2098/057B; born 21/11/1892, Co. Westmeath; (Mullingar Registrar's District, December Quarter, 1892, vol. 3, p. 206); son of Ignatius Ronayne Bray Jennings; 3rd DI 15/12/1915; pensioned 31/5/1922; transferred to the Royal Ulster Constabulary on 1/6/1922; awarded the MBE in 1923.

Jennings, Ignatius Ronayne Bray; RIC 35879; LDS 2097/279; born 1850, Co. Galway; son of Daniel Corley Jennings, CI, RIC and Johanna Bray; father of Donald Charles Blake Jennings; married in April 1884 (Thomastown Registrar's District, June Quarter, 1884, vol. 4, p. 377), Henrietta Elizabeth, daughter of James Blake and Cornelia Ronayne, of Co. Kilkenny; 3rd SI 17/9/1869; CI 1/11/1894; pensioned 1/8/1910; spent his retiring years in the Public Record Office, Four Courts, Dublin researching the wills of Co. Waterford families. His wills extracts are of great significance as many of the wills were destroyed in the attack on the Four Courts in 1922 during the Civil War. He also served on the committee of St Joseph's Young Priest's Society from 3/3/1912 until his death on 20/6/1928 at 60 Eccles Street, Dublin; (Dublin North Registrar's District, 1928, June Quarter, vol. 2, p. 238); will proved at the Principal Registry on 5/11/1928 by the oaths of Henrietta Jennings, widow and Donald Charles Blake Jennings, DI, Royal Ulster Constabulary – effects £157.10s.2d.; (photo in the *Constabulary Gazette*, vol. 1, no. 27, 2/10/1897).

Jephson, Charles Denham Hayden Jeremy; RIC 44601; LDS 2097/302; born 1857, Essex, England, the son of John Monteney Jephson (1819–1865), BA, FSA, Vicar of Childerditch, Essexand Ellen, daughter of Isaac Jeremy, of Stanfield Hall, MA, Barrister-at-Law, of Norfolk, Recorder of Norwich; 3rd SI 18/4/1879; married on 2/9/1885 (Rathdown Registrar's District, September Quarter, 1885, vol. 2, p. 739), Queenie Emily Georgina, daughter of George Meyler, of Dundrum house, Co. Dublin; they had four daughters; resident magistrate 3/3/1899; died 1951.

Johnson, Harry Hill; RIC 72267; ADRIC no. 96; LDS 2098/241B; born 1/9/1889, Leics., England; mining engineer; captain, 13th Hussars; married on 25/9/1920 in England; 3rd DI 2/7/1921; pensioned 5/5/1922; (WO 339/21727); (photo – Garda Museum & Archives, Dublin Castle).

Johnson, John F.; LDS 2097/181; born 1828, Co. Monaghan; 3rd SI 8/9/1849; died 1/8/1853 in Co. Donegal.

Johnston, John Frederick; LDS 2097/048; born 1789, Co. Derry; married in London, 5/8/1817; son, Frederick, b.12/8/1818; cornet, 6th Inniskilling Dragoons, 4/4/1810; lieutenant (by purchase), 18/2/1813; lieutenant, 19th Light Dragoons, 21/8/1817; captain (by exchange paying the difference), 17th Lancers, 24/6/1824; captain unattached (by purchase), 8/4/1826; widower on appointment; 3rd SI 26/1/1824; CI 1/2/1836; died 11/12/1853 in Killybegs, Co. Donegal; (WO 25/763 fol. 138); C.C. Monaghan, Co. Monaghan, 1831 and Newtownmountkennedy, Co. Wicklow.

Johnston, Thomas; LDS 2097/105; 3rd SI 1/11/1836; dismissed 15/9/1838.

Johnston, William; CarNB; lieutenant; C.C. Newtownmountkennedy, Co. Wicklow

Johnstone, Henry Robert; LDS 2097/124; born 1818, Co. Westmeath; lieutenant, Irish Revenue Police from December 1828 until May 1830; 3rd SI 16/2/1839; dismissed 9/8/1843, but was afterwards permitted to substitute resignation for dismissal on 31/8/1843; emigrated to Australia and from Forest Creek, Victoria applied to join the Victoria Police in 1853 (Reference VPRS 937, Unit 5, Bundle 2 – Public Record Office of Victoria, Australia).

Johnstone, John; LDS 2097/151; born, 1826, Co. Down; 3rd SI 8/11/1845; dismissed 19/8/1847.

130

130 Edward George Jenkinson (1835–1919), Assistant Under-Secretary for Police and Crime.
131 Ignatius Ronayne Bray Jennings.   132 Charles Denham Hayden Jeremy Jephson.

131   132

Jones, Henry; LDS 2097/083; born 1788, North Wales; 3rd SI 18/2/1833; pensioned 16/12/1843.

Jones, Henry Hawtrey; LDS 2097/291; born 19/4/1851, Co. Kilkenny; married on 13/11/1879 (Carrickmacross Registrar's District, vol. 2, p. 425); 3rd SI 31/10/1872; received a severe blow to the head from a stick when trying to preserve the peace on 26/6/1879; CI 26/12/1897; died 10/9/1903 at Carlow.

Jones, Hume Riversdale; RIC 54998; LDS 2098/076; born 21/6/1866, Co. Clare; educated at The Abbey School, Tipperary; son of the Venerable Richard Bathoe Jones (8/9/1830–15/10/1916), of Roscrea, Co. Tipperary, Archdeacon of Killaloe 1889, Canon of St Patrick's 1884, educated at Trinity College Dublin and Angel, 5th daughter of Rev. Hume Babington, Rector of Moviddy, Co. Cork; married on 9/9/1903 (Tubbercurry Registrar's District, September Quarter, 1903, vol. 4, p. 161), Elizabeth Anne, daughter of Charles Phibbs, of Doobeg, Ballymote, Co. Sligo; Scholar, Moderator; Barrister-at-Law, 1898; LLB, Dublin University; 3rd DI 3/6/1891; King Edward VII Visit to Ireland Medal, 1903; King George V Visit to Ireland Medal, 1911; Crime Special Department from 1/10/1908 to 1/10/1914; resident magistrate 3rd class 18/9/1914, 2nd class 30/4/1919; appointed as RM for Co. Dublin on 4/5/1920 for special duty at Dublin Castle; retired as a RM in 1936; died 5/2/1949; author of *Irish Constable's Guide*, 7th edition (Dublin, 1918); (p. 160, RM Records of Service Book, National Archives, Dublin); (photo in the *Constabulary Gazette*, vol. XVI, no. 14, 24/12/1904 & vol. XXXII, no. 24, 22/3/1913, p. 198).

Jones, John Gore; CarNB; born 1792, Co. Sligo; stipendiary magistrate 25/5/1831 in Co. Roscommon and Eyrecourt, Co. Cavan; his youngest son, Lieutenant Thomas Sheridan Gore Jones, 79th Cameron Highlanders was killed in action on 18/11/1863 on the Peshawur frontier while gallantly performing his duty (*Cork Examiner* 15/1/1864); resident magistrate 1/10/1836; died 6/1/1879 at Templemore, Co. Tipperary; will proved on 11/6/1879 at Limerick by the oath of William Gore Jones, of 116, Sloane Street, Middlesex, rear-admiral, Royal Navy, one of the executors – effects under £2,000.

Jones, John Joseph Casimir; RIC 21698; LDS 2097/211; born 4/3/1839, Co. Cork; daughter born on 9/11/1862 at 24, Northumberland Avenue, Kingstown, Co. Dublin (*Cork Examiner*

133   134

133 Henry Hawtrey Jones.   134 John Joseph Casimir Jones, Commissioner, DMP.

11/11/1862; married secondly on 8/2/1872 at the Catholic Church, Ballybrack, Co. Dublin (Rathdown Registrar's District, vol. 2, p. 948), Teresa Mary, daughter of Robert McMahon, Esq., Prospect House, Limerick (*Cork Examiner* 13/2/1872); 3rd SI 1/8/1857; musketry instructor from 1/10/1876 to 29/11/1878; CI 29/11/1878; resigned 28/1/1893 on his appointment as Chief Commissioner of the Dublin Metropolitan Police until 17/1/1901; (photo in the *Constabulary Gazette*, vol. 1, no. 8, 22/5/1897 & vol. VI, no. 13, 23/12/1899, p. 390).

Jones, Sylvanus; CarNB; lieutenant; 3rd SI 1/8/1823; CI 1/11/1824; stipendiary magistrate 25/5/1831; died in 1847; C.C. Westport, Co. Mayo; Castleblakeney, Co. Galway.

Jones, William; RIC 37550; LDS 2097/284; born 8/4/1847, Co. Tipperary; married on 21/8/1879 (Lurgan Registrar's District, vol. 1, p. 811), wife from Australia; 3rd SI 26/4/1871; received an unfavourable record on 19/6/1879 for being drunk at the Mess dinner; resident magistrate 3rd class 4/8/1892, 2nd class 25/12/1897; died 21/12/1909 at Grosvenor Place, Carlow, Co. Carlow; administration granted at the Principal Registry on 9/2/1910 to Mary Jones, the widow – effects £96.12s.6d.; (p. 96, RM Records of Service Book, National Archives, Dublin).

Jones, William Henry; LDS 2097/038; born 1800, Co. Dublin; 3rd SI 1/2/1823; died 9/4/1845; widow Mary.

Joy, Percival Holt; RIC 48106; LDS 2097/314; born 1858, Leeds, Yorks., England; (Hanslet Registrar's District, 1858, September Quarter, vol. 9b, p. 198); residing with his brother, Douglas G. Joy at South Field, Hessle In Sculcoates, Yorkshire in 1881 (Census); MA, Trinity College, Oxford, 1880; 3rd SI 30/12/1881; King Edward VII Visit to Ireland Medal, 1903; pensioned 16/3/1906 due to being unfit by the surgeon to the Force; died 7/12/1914.

Joyce, James; RIC 955; LDS 2097/072; born 1810, Knocktopher, Co. Kilkenny; 3rd SI 1/11/1831; discharged with a gratuity, 1/5/1839.

Joyce, John; CarNB; born 1781; PPF; 3rd SI 1824; C.C. Portumna, Co. Galway and Enniskillen, Co. Fermanagh.

Joyce, William Henry; RIC 34877; LDS 2097/272; born 17/9/1849, Co. Tyrone; 3rd SI 7/11/1868; received a favourable record on 30/6/1871 for where two hostile factions met in considerable numbers and fought with sticks and stones and severe injuries were inflicted on both sides. Both parties endeavoured to conceal the facts for a long time, but by skill and perseverance evidence was at length procured and several persons convicted; temporary resident magistrate 20/1/1888; permanent RM 3rd class 3/7/1889, 2nd class 3/7/1891; briefed by the Irish Attorney General to coordinate intelligence operations at Dublin Castle in May 1888; seconded to London during the Special Commission in October 1888; pensioned 1/11/1901; (p. 84, RM Records of Service Book, National Archives, Dublin).

Judge, Arthur George; LDS 2097/026; born 1797, King's County; wife a native of King's County; his niece Elizabeth Judge, second daughter of head constable Thomas Judge, married at Watergrasshill, Co. Cork on 11/12/185, Samuel Phillips, Esq., Inland Revenue Officer (*Cork Examiner* 17/12/1851); 3rd SI 12/6/1821; severely wounded in King's County in 1827; pensioned 1/7/1851; died 1/2/1869 at Russellstown House, Athy, Co. Kildare; administration granted to George Judge, of Russellstown House, son of the deceased and a principal legatee – effects under £1,000.

K

Kaufman, Cecil Maurice; RIC 72957; ADRIC no. 380; LDS 2099/047; born 31/10/1896, Norfolk, England; (Aylsham Registrar's District, 1896, December Quarter, vol. 4b, p. 43); married on 25/11/1916, wife Phyllis V. Cogwell from Middlesex; army service, 1914–1920, August 1920 to August 1921; 3rd DI 20/9/1921; pensioned 24/8/1922.

Kavanagh, Patrick; RIC 17222; LDS 2097/299; born 1835, Queen's County; wife from Co. Kildare; 3rd SI 1/4/1879; pensioned 15/2/1883; died 24/2/1896 in Co. Wicklow (Rathdown Registrar's District, 1896, March Quarter, vol. 701, p. 62).

Keany, Michael; RIC 56343; LDS 2098/146B; born 24/9/1867, Curracloona, Manorhamilton, Co. Leitrim; son of James Keany and Catherine Mary McHugh; married on 1/4/1902 at Wexford, Co. Wexford (Wexford Registrar's District, June Quarter, 1902, vol. 4, p. 447), Margaret F. Mulcahy, daughter of Edmund Mulcahy, a native of Co. Tipperary; 3rd DI 25/8/1920; killed 11/2/1922, Clonakilty, Co. Cork as he went there with his young son Edward to collect his furniture and belongings having been transferred on promotion to Tuckey Street Barracks, Cork City; late of Queen's Hotel, Warrens Place, Cork; buried in St Finbarr's Cemetery, Cork on 14/2/1922 (Section D, Row 6, Plot 50); administration granted at Cork on 24/10/1922; his wife Margaret, born 1871, Mitchelstown, Co. Cork died on 23/9/1923 at 10, Campers Avenue, Letchworth, Herts., and is buried with him as is his son, Edward who died of his wounds in the attack on the father; another son, Captain John Keany, 121236, Royal Irish Fusiliers (b.14/4/1915) in the RIC Barracks, Clonakilty, Co. Cork) emigrated to England where he studied in St Joseph's College, London (1925–9), Guernsey, Channel Islands (1929–31), Berlin, Germany and Paris, France (1932–7), Exeter University (1937–9). In 1939 he passed the exam for the British Consular service and on 25/2/1940 was granted an emergency commission in the British Army, serving as a signals officer, 1st Battalion, Royal Irish Fusiliers. Served in Italian East Africa from August 1941 to August 1944 as political officer in Eritrea and personal assistant to the governor. On 2/9/1844 as an Italian-speaking officer was posted to SOE (No. 1 Special Force from the 78th Division Rear), Salerno, Italy. On 20/9/1844 was designated second in command to Major Max Salvadori (1908–92), MC, DSO, Mission CHARLTON for liaison with the Italian partisans in Cinaglio. On 4/5/1945 he dropped with Mission CHARLTON behind enemy lines in Italy and was taken prisoner-of-war and executed by the SS on 8/3/1945; he is buried in Milan War Cemetery, Milan, Italy (Grave IV.B15); (photo in the *Constabulary Gazette*, vol. V, no. 22, 26/8/1899, p. 657).

Kearney, John A.; RIC 55958; LDS 2098/073B; born 16/2/1871, Co. Westmeath, the son of RIC constable Thomas Kearney who had joined the RIC on 8/5/1862; married on 24/6/1902 (Limerick Registrar's District, June Quarter, 1902, vol. 5, p. 258); he was the head constable in charge of Tralee Barracks when Roger Casement was arrested at Banna Strand, Co. Kerry on 21/4/1916; married on 24/6/1902, wife a native of Co. Limerick; 3rd DI 19/8/1916; member of the organising committee of the Civic Guards which met on 9/2/1922; disbanded from the RIC on 5/4/1922 and appointed superintendent in the Civic Guards (later styled the Garda Síochána) on 6/4/1922, assisting the Provisional Government by serving as chairman of the organization Committee and later resigned due to intimidation; died 1946, Barnet, England; (Barnet Registrar's District, March Quarter, 1946, vol. 3a, p. 1381).

135

136

135 Michael Keany grave in St Finbarr's Cemetery, Cork.   136 John Kearney.   137 Philip St John Howlett Kelleher.   138 Archibald Kirkland.

137

138

Keating, John; RIC 4121; LDS 2097/264; born 1821, Co. Wexford; 3rd SI 1/8/1867; 3rd DI 1/10/1882; died 23/3/1908.

Keaveny, Thomas; RIC 39849; LDS 2098/149; born 1854, Co. Roscommon; married on 30/1/1884 (Dublin South Registrar's District, March Quarter, 1884, vol. 2, p. 708), wife a native of Co. Mayo; 3rd DI 12/11/1898; King Edward VII Visit to Ireland Medal, 1903; pensioned 1/1/1915; (photo in the *Constabulary Gazette*, vol. XI, no. 23, 6/9/1902).

Keck, Samuel; RIC 2097/081; born 1805, Fethard, Co. Tipperary; enlisted as a constable, 1/4/1824; 3rd SI 1/2/1833; died 27/12/1846.

Keeffe, Daniel; RIC 46553; LDS 2098/006B; born 23/2/1862, Co. Kerry; married on 8/12/1894, wife a native of Co. Galway; 3rd DI 2/7/1910; pensioned 15/6/1920.

Kiely, John; CarNB; PPF; 3rd SI 6/9/1814; C.C. Cashel, Co. Tipperary; Rathkeale, Co. Limerick; Doneraile, Co. Cork, 1825; Mallow, Cloyne, 1830 and Carrigaline, Co. Cork; Nenagh and on special duty in Thurles, Co. Tipperary, December 1829; Kilkenny, 1832.

Kelleher, Philip St John Howlett; RIC 71645; LDS 2098/142B; born 1/7/1897, South Square, Macroom, Co. Cork, the son of Dr Jeremiah Kelleher and Mary Kate (nee Howlett); educated at Castleknock College, Dublin, 1910–15; candidate for entrance to Trinity College, Dublin; lieutenant, 4th Battalion Leinster Regiment, attached to the Royal Irish Rifles, 12/8/1915; awarded the Military Cross; gunshot wound in the left leg at Messines, 7/6/1917; embarked at Southampton, 4/5/1918; disembarked at Alexandria 9/7/1918; posted to the 2nd Battalion, Leinster Regiment, 19/9/1918 at Calais, France; relinquished his commission on 1/4/1920 and retained the rank of lieutenant (*London Gazette* dated 30/6/1920); 3rd DI 8/7/1920; killed 31/10/1920, at the Greville Arms (Kiernan's) Hotel, Granard, Co. Longford; buried in Millstreet New Cemetery, Co. Cork on 4/11/1920; administration granted at the Principal Registry on 25/11/1920; (WO 339/38294).

Kelly, Burrowes; LDS 2097/179; born 1809, Queen's County; 3rd SI 1/5/1849; paymaster 1/5/1849 for Co. Tipperary; pensioned 31/5/1851 on the abolition of the office of paymaster.

Kelly, Henry George; LDS 2097/125; born 1808, Hants., England; enlisted as a sub constable on 1/11/1829; clerk in the Constabulary Office from June 1836 to 6/3/1837; wife a native of Co. Wicklow; 3rd SI 6/3/1839; pensioned 1/4/1847; son born at Clonroad Cottage, Co. Clare on 22/1/1857; pensioned in 1857; died 25/9/1896.

Kelly, John; captain; baronial chief constable; secretary to the PPF in Galmoy, Co. Kilkenny, 1821–22; death reported in the *Freeman's Journal* on 9/7/1824: 'On Saturday last, at Johnstown, Co. Kilkenny, Captain Kelly, Chief of Constabulary Police of the barony'. His widow, Harriet applied for compensation on 18/9/1827 saying that her late husband arrested the murderers of John Marum, Knockashinna, barony of Galmoy, Co. Kilkenny on 16 March 1824.

Kelly, John; LDS 2097/091; born 1804, Sussex, England; wife a native of Queen's County; PPF; clerk in the office of the inspector general of Leinster from 1/7/1824 to 31/10/1835; 3rd SI 1/11/1835; pensioned 1/6/1853; died 4/7/1882.

Kelly, John Sankey; LDS 2097/028; born 1779, Co. Roscommon; ensign and lieutenant, Roscommon Militia, 12/4/1797 (WO 13/3199–219); ensign 54th Regiment of Foot (West Norfolk Regiment), 1/1/1800; lieutenant, 1/7/1801; lieutenant half pay 4th Regiment of Foot (King's Own Regiment), 1/7/1802; wounded in Egypt, 1803; lieutenant and captain, Roscommon Militia, August 1803 to April 1816 (WO 13/3199–219); married in Cloverhill, Castlerea, Co. Roscommon, 22/12/1804; children: George, born 26/2/1816, Thomas Charles, born 4/3/1807, John Sankey, born 24/2/1810, Norry P., born 11/8/1812, W.F., born 4/4/1815; Margaret Hazel, born 13/3/1818, twins Mary and Catherine, born 8/12/1819, Frances, 7/8/1821, Eliza, born 19/7/1823, Harriet, born 10/1/1826; 3rd SI 1/12/1821; ruptured 14/12/1845 while arresting 'Molly Maguires'; pensioned 16/1/1851; (WO 25/764 fol. 25).

Kelly, Michael; RIC 33683; LDS 2098/095; born 1848, Co. Galway; 3rd DI 12/11/1892; King Edward VII Visit to Ireland Medal, 1903; pensioned 11/10/1908.

Kelly, Michael B.; LDS 2097/077; born 1803, Co. Galway; wife a native of Co. Galway; 3rd SI 31/10/1832; CI 16/3/1858; pensioned 16/3/1867; died 18/11/1880.

Kelly, O'Neill Ferguson; RIC 55380; LDS 2097/304; born 1858, Co. Armagh; married on 3/8/1880 (Cork Registrar's District, vol. 5, p. 53), wife a native of Co. Cork; 3rd SI 1/11/1879; King Edward VII Visit to Ireland Medal, 1903; barrackmaster of the Phoenix Park Depot 7/2/1910; King George V Coronation Medal, 1911; pensioned 1/10/1919.

Kelly, William; LDS 2097/052; born 1804, Kent, England; wife a native of Co. Dublin; 3rd SI 4/7/1824; pensioned 16/10/1871; died 2/1/1881; (p. 29, Reply to Father Fitzgerald's Pamphlet entitled his 'personal recollections of the insurrection at Ballingarry in July, 1848, with remarks on Irish Constabulary and hints to all officials, by Thomas Trant, Esq., retired First Class Inspector of the Irish Constabulary' – printed by McGlashan & Gill, 50 Upper Sackville Street, Dublin, 1862).

Kelly, William Bingham; LDS 2097/250; born 1844, Co. Dublin; married on 14/10/1875 (Dublin South Registrar's District, vol. 17, p. 895), wife from Co. Monaghan; 3rd SI 1/10/1864; pensioned 29/12/1894; died 8/10/1903 Park Avenue, at Omagh, Co. Tyrone; buried in Cappagh Cemetery; administration granted on 8/10/1903 at Derry to Isabella C. Kelly, the widow – effects £783.0s.9d.

Kemshall, Joseph Edgar; RIC 72905; ADRIC no. 351; LDS 2098/217B; born 1/12/1894, Derbyshire, England; (Chesterfield Registrar's District, 1894, December Quarter, vol. 7a, p. 717); enlisted, private No. 1319 (Robin Hood) Battalion, Sherwood Foresters (Territorial Force), 102/1911, corporal, 4/2/1914, sergeant 28/2/1915; 2nd lieutenant, Nottinghamshire and Derbyshire Regiment, 18/11/1915; seconded to the Machine Gun Corps, 19/11/1915; temporary lieutenant, 1/6/1917; lieutenant, 1/7/1917; No. 214 Squadron, Royal Air Force, 14/9/1918; demobilized, 13/3/1919; relinquished commission on completion of service and retained the rank of lieutenant, 30/9/1921 (*London Gazette* dated 19/12/1921); 3rd DI 12/1/1920; pensioned 20/4/1922; (WO 374/39136).

Kennedy, Thomas LeBan; LDS 2097/219; born 1834, King's County; joined the Irish Revenue Police as a lieutenant on 23/11/1853 and served in Carrowkeel, Co. Donegal; 3rd SI 26/3/1858; received a favourable record on 30/6/1869 for prompt and judicious measures leading to the capture of sheep-stealers, by Head Constable Thomas Welby, 4572 in England and their subsequent conviction; pensioned 15/2/1883.

Kennett, Charles Leighton; LDS 2097/024; born 1794, Kent, England; ensign, 21/9/1815 to 1820; captain in the Kent Militia from 5/3/1813 to 1/9/1815; 3rd SI 1/3/1820; pensioned 1/6/1845; died 1860; C.C. Cavan, Co. Cavan.

Keogh, William Somerset; LDS 2097/199; born 1830, France; 3rd SI 1/9/1853; seconded to the Commissariat Department in the Crimea, from 2/8/1854 to 17/11/1854; resigned 8/11/1867; died 14/7/1889 at 9, Lower Mount Street, Dublin, 'the last surviving son of the late George Rous Keogh, Esq., of Kilbride, Co. Carlow.

Keohane, Patrick; RIC 55784; LDS 2098/090B; born 2/7/1872, Co. Cork; married on 27/2/1900 (Limerick Registrar's District, March Quarter, 1900, vol. 5, p. 284), wife a native of Co. Limerick; 3rd DI 7/9/1919; pensioned 26/4/1922.

Kerin, Charles Maxwell; LDS 2097/115; born 1812, Co. Clare; father of Edward Joseph Kerin, SI, RIC; his first wife was a native of Co. Galway and she died of fever on 18/11/1853 at Dungarvan, Co. Waterford (*Cork Examiner* 21/11/1853); his sister who was single died on 19/2/1863 at his residence in Tullamore, Co. Offaly (*Cork Examiner* 24/2/1863); remarried and his son was born on 20/8/1867 at Dundalk, Co. Louth (*Cork Examiner* 26/8/1867); 3rd SI 1/8/1837; CI 1/8/1865; pensioned 11/4/1881; died 1/5/1888 at 16 Belvedere Place, Dublin; buried in Glasnevin Cemetery, Dublin on 3/5/1888; will proved on 12/6/1888 at the Principal Registry by the oath of Jane Kerin, widow, one of the executrixes – effects – £1,518.19s.11d.

Kerin, Edward Joseph; RIC 37291; LDS 2097/283; born 1851, Co. Waterford; son of Charles Maxwell Kerin, CI, RIC; married on 30/8/1873 at The Cathedral, Marlborough Street, Dublin (Dublin North Registrar's District, vol. 17, p. 554), Susan Winnifred, second daughter of Mr Patrick Kelly, Esq.; 3rd SI 4/3/1871; pensioned 1/7/1899. (Diary of Sub Inspector E.J. Kerin, 1880–82 in the possession of E.L. Malcolm, Institute of Irish Studies, University of Liverpool.)

Kerin, James; surgeon to the Force from 7/11/1839 until his death on 16/3/1848; resided at 11 Holles Street, Dublin.

Kidd, Andrew; RIC 3967; LDS 2097/248; born 1820, Co. Armagh; wife from Co. Cork; 3rd SI 1/5/1864; pensioned 1/10/1882; died 6/8/1892 at Cambridge Terrace, Belfast; administration granted on 14/9/1892 at Belfast to Joseph Bigger, of 43 Dame Street, Dublin, solicitor, the attorney of the sister – effects £184.

Kieser, John Frederick; LDS 2097/331; born, 1859, Blackheath, Kent, England; (Greenwich Registrar's District, 1859, June Quarter, vol. 1d, p. 571); under graduate at Dr Whewell's Buildings, Trinity and Sydney Street, Trinity College, Cambridge in 1881 (Census); married on 1/7/1885 (Longford Registrar's District, June Quarter, 1885, vol. 3, p. 183), wife from Co. Longford; 3rd DI 8/9/1883; pensioned 13/12/1897.

King, Peter; RIC 15936; LDS 2097/303; born 1833, Co. Galway; 3rd SI 23/8/1879; received a scalp wound as a result of a ceiling falling on him in Carrick Station on 24/3/1888; pensioned 21/8/1888; died 11/1/1913 at Belfast; (Belfast Registrar's District, 1913, March Quarter, vol. 1, p. 383).

King, Richard; LDS 2097/047; lieutenant; 3rd SI 1/11/1823; C.C. barony of Scarawalsh, Co. Wexford.

King, William Herbert; RIC 62656; LDS 2098/218; born 4/8/1882, India; BA, Trinity College, Oxford; captain, Army Service Corps Captain from 18/12/1915 to 13/4/1919; married on 20/10/1909 (Killarney Registrar's District, December Quarter, 1909, vol. 5, p. 161), wife a native of Co. Galway; 3rd DI 8/6/1907; TCI 16/12/1920; wounded Mallow Railway Station, Co. Cork 31/1/1921; pensioned 25/5/1922.

King, William L.; RIC 79005; ADRIC no. 834; LDS 2099/007; born 12/9/1884, Co. Derry; (Derry Registrar's District, December Quarter, 1884, vol. 2, p. 191); seconded for service with ADRIC on 7/2/1921; 3rd DI 2/7/1921; pensioned 15/7/1922.

Kingston, Samuel Richard; RIC 42719; LDS 2098/151; born 1858, Cork; married on 14/10/1892, wife a native of Co. Donegal; 3rd DI 2/2/1899; pensioned 2/5/1918; (photo in the *Constabulary Gazette*, vol. XVI, no. 1, 24/9/1904 & vol. XVI, no. 12, 10/12/1904).

Kirke, James; RIC 59508; LDS 2098/250B; born 1879, Bailieborough, Co. Cavan; (Bailieborough Registrar's District, December Quarter, 1879, vol. 2, p. 377); 3rd DI 15/2/1921; pensioned 23/8/1922.

Kirkland, Archibald; RIC 686; LDS 2097/184; born 1809, Co. Cavan; enlisted as a sub constable on 4/1/1830; 1st Head Constable attached to the Reserve on 1/12/1842; Head Constable Major from 1/6/1848 to 1/5/1850; 3rd SI 1/5/1850; pensioned 16/4/1872; he married Caroline Turner from Co. Armagh and died 1/8/1898 at Ballyhamage, Doagh, Co. Antrim; buried in Donegore Cemetery, Co. Antrim.

Kirwan, Edward J.; LDS 2097/024; born 1780, Co. Galway; father of Henry Kirwan, SI, RIC; ensign, 16/7/1800 to 24/8/1802; ensign, lieutenant and captain, Galway Militia from 23/9/1807 to 31/3/1816 (WO 13/2882–901); 3rd SI 1/3/1820; wounded in an attack on the police on protection duty at an election in Monaghan on 24/6/1826; resigned 25/8/1842 in favour of the appointment of his son, Henry Kirwan; C.C. Monaghan, Co. Monaghan.

Kirwan, Henry Persse; LDS 2097/132; born 1818, Triston Lodge, Killererin, Co. Galway; son of Edward J. Kirwan, SI, RIC: ensign and cornet in the Galway Militia (WO 13/2882–901); 3rd SI 26/8/1842; CI 1/10/1867; pensioned 15/10/1875; his adopted daughter, Sarah Annette

Foster (d.1913) married on 19/12/1879 at Monkstown Parish Church, Dublin, the lawyer and politician, Sir Edward Carson (1854–1935).

Kirwan, Martin; LDS 2097/035; born 1781, Co. Galway; ensign and lieutenant in the South Mayo Militia from 1809 to 1814 (WO 13/3121–40); 3rd SI 28/1/1823; pensioned 1/5/1843; died in 1855.

Kittson, Francis; LDS 2097/094; born 1812, Listowel, Co. Kerry; wife a native of Co. Tipperary; enlisted as a sub constable, 30/5/1823; son born on 25/9/1854 at Clonmel, Co. Tipperary, 'which survived only a few hours' (*Cork Examiner* 4/10/1854); 3rd SI 1/2/1836; pensioned 15/3/1875; died 3/4/1883 at Waterloo Road, Dublin; will proved on 24/7/1883 at the Principal Registry by the oath of Mary Kittson, 4 Waterloo Road, Dublin, widow, the sole executrix – effects £454; buried in Mount Jerome Cemetery, Dublin on 7/4/1883.

Kittson, John B.; CarNB; born Listowel, Co. Kerry; C.C. Curryglass, Co. Cork; Nenagh, Co. Tipperary.

Knox, George William Patrick; RIC 51683; LDS 2098/014; born 1866, Oughterard, Co. Galway; (Oughterard Registrar's District, 1866, vol. 4, p. 519); married on 6/7/1881, wife a native of Canada; 3rd DI 24/5/1886; pensioned 15/10/1920.

Knox, Henry Bernard; RIC 35269; LDS 2097/276; born 1847, Co. Down; married on 14/4/1877 (Dublin South Registrar's District, vol. 7, p. 551); 3rd SI 20/4/1869; dismissed 17/3/1886.

Knox, John; RIC 2969; LDS 2097/229; born 1820, Co. Mayo; 3rd SI 1/8/1859; pensioned 1/10/1882; died 29/10/1901 at Quay House, New Ross, Co. Wexford.

Kydd, James Samuel; RIC 56816; LDS 2099/002; born 8/8/1876, Fermoy, Co. Cork; (Fermoy Registrar's District, 1876, vol. 14, p. 709); son of constable James Kydd, RIC 34304 and Frances (a native of co. Kilkenny); married on 17/10/1903 (Cork Registrar's District, December Quarter, 1903, vol. 5, p. 41), Jeannie Agnes Rothwell (3/7/1880–23/5/1951) wife a native of Newcastle, Co. Tipperary; he had three sons, Herbert Edward (b.20/8/1908); James Rothwell (b.21/11/1910); Charles John French (b.15/7/1915) and three daughters, Mabel Frances (b.20/5/1905); Ruby Lillian (b.19/10/1907) and Alys Dorothy (b.22/12/1913); 3rd DI 1/4/1921; pensioned 27/5/1922; died 27/3/1957 in Upminster, Essex, England; buried in St Laurence Churchyard, Upminster, Essex; (photo – Dr Brian W. Beeley, Tonbridge Wells, Kent, England).

Kyffin, Alexander Lindsay; CarNB; son of Captain J. Willington Kyffin, Mountmellick, Queen's County; on 4/5/1824 he reported from Goresbridge to Major Thomas Powell that he had been on half pay when he joined and had been appointed on full pay with the 47th Regiment of Foot (Lancashire Regiment) and wished to go to London to get back on half pay so that he could retain his post as chief constable. His request was granted; transferred to Wexford on 1/5/1830; pensioned 15/9/1834; C.C. Borris and Mountmellick, Queen's County.

L

Lambert, Burton Persse; CarNB; C.C. Listowel, Co. Kerry; Borrisokane, Co. Tipperary.

Lancaster, Frederick George; RIC 76109; ADRIC no. 22; LDS 2098/202B; born 16/3/1890, Surrey, England; (Epsom Registrar's District, 1890, June Quarter, vol. 2a, p. 18); ex-member of the Grimsby Borough Police and captain, West Yorkshire Regiment; 3rd DI 12/1/1920; wounded Ballymalis, Co. Kerry 17/5/1921; pensioned 25/8/1922.

Langhorne, William Henry; LDS 2098/028; born 1866, Tonbridge, Kent, England; (Keighley Registrar's District, 1865, March Quarter, vol. 9a, p. 187); son of John Langhorne (b.1837) Giggleswick, Yorks., England and Frances Annisley Langhorne (b.1844), Dublin; residing at Vines Crow Lane Grammar School, Rochester, Kent in 1881 (Census); tutor at Newport, Salop for one year; married on 23/1/1895 (Cork Registrar's District, March Quarter, 1895, vol. 5, p. 73), Mary Gertrude Rice Wade of Kildysart, Co. Clare; 3rd DI 1/6/1887; King Edward VII Visit to Ireland Medal, 1903; CI 1/5/1910; pensioned 1/12/1920.

Lanyon, Louis Mortimer; RIC 38128; LDS 2097/288; born 1846, Belfast, Co. Antrim; married on 20/5/1879, wife from Kent; 3rd SI 1/12/1871; pensioned 1/7/1899; died 3/11/1900 at 34 Norton Road, Hove, formerly of West End, Mallow, Co. Cork; (Steyning Registrar's District, December Quarter, 1900, vol. 2b, p. 164); his will dated 26/9/1889 was proved by the oath of Mr Henry Cecil Phillips, of Castletownroche, Co. Cork; effects £16,014 gross and £15,685.14s.1d. net was bequeathed to his widow Mrs Laura Lanyon; resworn in London in March 1902, £17,592.4s.2d.; (photo in the *Constabulary Gazette*, vol. VI, no. 13, 23/12/1899, p. 390).

Laurenson, William John; LDS 2097/031; born 1789, Kenmare, Co. Kerry; PPF Chief Constable from April 1820 to November 1822; 3rd SI 25/11/1822; pensioned 30/6/1839.

Lavelle, William; LDS 2097/173; born 1810, Derryaghy, Co. Antrim; enlisted as a sub constable on 1/8/1830; 1st Head Constable attached to the Reserve on 1/12/1842; 3rd SI 1/6/1848; pensioned 10/10/1862; died 9/1/1867 at Carrick-on-Suir, Co. Tipperary (Carrick-on-Suir Registrar's District, 1867, vol. 4, p. 487).

Law, William Black; RIC 38983; LDS 2097/292; born 1848, Co. Dublin; wife a native of Co. Cork; 3rd SI 27/12/1872; CI 1/2/1898; King Edward VII Visit to Ireland Medal, 1903; pensioned 13/11/1912.

Lawless, George Edmund Francis; RIC 55383; LDS 2098/084; born 1871, Co. Kilkenny; son of William Edmund Lawless, DI, RIC; 3rd DI 22/5/1893; married Isabella Henrietta Butler, of Dublin on 28/6/1893 (Rathdown Registrar's District, June Quarter, 1893, vol. 2, p. 787); resigned 23/1/1899.

Lawless, Philip; LDS 2097/111; born Dublin City, Co. Dublin; 3rd SI 30/1/1837.

Lawless, William Edmund; RIC 28374; LDS 2097/243; born 1843; Co. Tipperary; son of Rev. G. Lawless, Chaplain to the Forces and father of George Edmund Francis Lawless, DI, RIC; 3rd SI 10/2/1863; died 21/1/1898 at 146 Leinster Road, Rathmines, Dublin; administration granted on 2/3/1898 at the Principal Registry to Josephine F.T. Lawless, of 24, Sandycove Avenue, West, Kingstown, Co. Dublin, widow, the universal legatee – £1,674.1s.11d.; buried in Mount Jerome Cemetery, Dublin on 22/1/1898 (Grave No. B83–353–10273).

Lawlor, John Elliott Cairnes; LDS 2097/266; born 1848, Co. Derry; son of John Hilliard Lawlor, Ballylinan, King's County; 3rd SI 13/12/1867; died 10/9/1899 at Guy's Hospital,

London, late of Edenderry, King's County; (St Olave's Registrar's District, September Quarter, 1899, vol. 1d, p. 137); will proved on 9/11/1899 at the Principal Registry by the oath of M.H.J. Lawlor, of the Provincial Bank of Ireland, Galway, Co. Galway and Arthur C. Lawlor, of 19, Corrig Avenue, Kingstown, Co. Dublin – effects £1,564.12s.7d.

Lawson, Charles Humble; LDS 2097/155; born 1827, Co. Cork; son of Samuel Humble Lawson, CI, RIC; 3rd SI 1/4/1847; pensioned 6/11/1862; died on 16/12/1868 at Finisklin, Co. Sligo (Sligo Registrar's District, vol. 17, p. 203); administration granted on 9/3/1869 at the Principal registry to Annabella Sophia Lawson, of Finisklin, Co. Sligo, the widow of the said deceased – effects under £200.

Lawson, Samuel Humble; LDS 2097/034; born 1791, Co. Kilkenny; father of Charles Humble Lawson, SI, RIC; ensign, 6/3/1807; lieutenant, 1/4/1808; captain, 95th Rifle Corps, 15/1/1815; half-pay 30/1/1833; awarded one medal and six clasps for Badajoz and forlorn hope,

139

140

139 James Samuel Kydd, Trim, Co. Meath, 1922. 140 Charles Western Leatham. 141 William Stanley Balfour Leatham. 142 William Stanley Balfour Leatham.

141

142

Salamanca, Pyrenees, Niville, Orthes and Toulouse; wife a native of Co. Cork; his daughter, Alice (d.1856) married in 1850 in Sligo, Neptune Blood Gallwey (1824–84), CI, RIC (Sligo Registrar's District, vol. 10, p. 198); 3rd SI 25/1/1823; CI 1/9/1838; pensioned 1/6/1859 in Co. Sligo; died 4/3/1874 at Albert Street, Sligo, Co. Sligo; will proved on 23/5/1874 at the Principal Registry by the oath of Edward Weekes Lawson, of Derby, Esq., one of the executors – effects under £450; Edward Weekes Lawson was the son of Samuel Humble Lawson, CI, RIC and the brother of Charles Humble Lawson, SI, RIC; he was born in 1833 and died in Southport, Lancashire on 12/3/1915, having married Isabella Alexandria Stewart (b.1835) in Belfast, Co. Antrim on 5/5/1857 (Belfast Registrar's District, vol. 2, p. 880); he was appointed superintendent of the County Constabulary in Derbyshire in 1858 and retired in 1889 as Deputy Chief Constable of Derbyshire.

Lea, Stephen Henry; RIC 55387; LDS 2098/085; born 1859, Warks., England; BA, Keble College, Oxford; 3rd DI 12/1/1893; pensioned 16/4/1922.

Leahy, John Anthony Francis; LDS 2098/047B; born 10/7/1869, Co. Antrim; married on 7/4/1915 (Dublin South Registrar's District, June Quarter, 1915, vol. 2, p. 735), Isabel Pender, a native of Co. Antrim; 3rd DI 7/8/1914; pensioned 14/10/1919.

Leatham, Charles Western; RIC 31544; LDS 2097/256; born, 1846, Co. Tyrone, father of William Stanley Balfour Leatham, DI RIC, RM; married firstly on 10/6/1872 (Rathdown Registrar's District, vol. 7, p. 836); married secondly on 27/1/1894 (Belfast Registrar's District, March Quarter, 1894, vol. 1, p. 365), Marion, daughter of Rev. George Shaw, of Belfast; 3rd SI 15/4/1866; CI 21/4/1891; Commissioner of Police and Town Inspector of Constabulary, Belfast from 1/12/1901 to 1/4/1906; King Edward VII Visit to Ireland Medal, 1903; pensioned 1/4/1906; author of *Questions in the Petty Sessions (Ireland) Act, 1861* (Dublin, 1895), *Sketches and Stories of the Royal Irish Constabulary* (Dublin, 1919); (photo in the *Constabulary Gazette*, vol. 1, no. 30, 23/10/1897).

Leatham, William Stanley Balfour; RIC 58446; LDS 2098/152; born 1879, Co. Antrim; (Belfast Registrar's District, March Quarter, 1879, vol. 1, p. 531); son of Charles Western Leatham, CI, RIC; 3rd DI 14/2/1899; King Edward VII Visit to Ireland Medal, 1903; King George V Visit to Ireland Medal, 1911; musketry instructor from 13/3/1912 to 14/3/1915; major, 6th Battalion Royal Irish Rifles from 1/2/1916 to 22/2/1919; GSO Intelligence Branch, Northern Irish District; severely wounded during the Irish Rebellion, 1916; resident magistrate 3rd class 19/3/1920; died 6/11/1933 at Hopefield Cottage Hospital, Portrush, Co. Antrim leaving his effects to his widow Cecilia Gibson Leatham; (p. 182, RM Records of Service Book, National Archives, Dublin).

Lea-Wilson, Percival Samuel; RIC 65448; LDS 2098/018B; born 22/4/1887, Kensington, Kent, England; (Kensington Registrar's District, June Quarter, 1887, vol. 1a, p. 169); great-grandson of Samuel Wilson, Lord Mayor of London in 1838; educated at Winchester College, 1900 and later at new College, Oxford where he was awarded a BA in 1919. Married Marie E. Ryan, daughter of a Catholic solicitor in Charleville, Co. Cork on 27/1/1914 (Kilmallock Registrar's District, March Quarter, 1914, vol. 5, p. 287); 3rd DI 27/1/1911; lieutenant and captain, 5th Battalion Royal Irish Regiment as a musketry instructor from 25/1/1916 to 17/7/1917 and served in Dublin during the Easter Rising; after the Rising he was in charge of 250 prisoners who had surrendered and were taken under strong military guard to the gardens in front of the Rotunda Hospital, Dublin. Some of the prisoners were concerned by the alleged stripping and ill-treatment Lea-Wilson had given some of their number and in particular to two of their leaders, Tom Clarke and Ned Daly. Two of the prisoners present at the Rotunda were Michael Collins and Liam Tobin, who was later to become Collin's chief intelligence officer and who vowed to have revenge for their ill-treatment; Lea-Wilson rejoined the RIC on 17/7/1917 and was posted to Gorey, Co. Wexford; at 9.45am on 15/6/1920 he was shot and killed near the bridge at Gorey, Co. Wexford; buried on 19/6/1920 with his father in Putney Vale Cemetery,

143

144

143 Percival Samuel Lea-Wilson. 144 Percival Samuel Lea-Wilson, Captain, Royal Irish Regiment, 1916. 145 Stained glass memorial window, Church of Ireland, Gorey, Co. Wexford by Harry Clarke dedicated to Percival Samuel Lea-Wilson, commissioned by his wife.

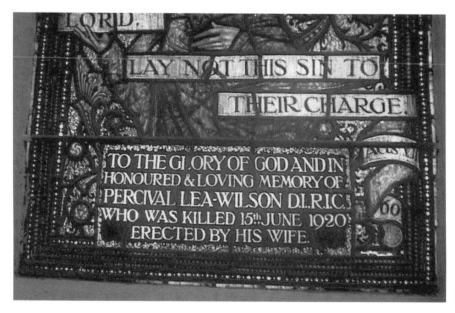

145

Stag Lane, London, England; (photo in the *Constabulary Gazette*, vol. XXIX, no. 12, 3/6/1911, p. 202); his widow commissioned the celebrated stained glass artist memorial window in his honour in the Church of Ireland, Gorey and a second window was commissioned by the Order of Freemasons. She pursued her medical studies and became a leading paediatrician. During a student holiday in Edinburgh in 1921 she purchased a painting. The plaque on the frame read 'Gherardo Della Notte', the popular name given to the famous seventeenth century Dutch artist, Gerard von Honthorst (who specialized on night scenes). Dr Marie Lea-Wilson returned to Ireland and brought the painting with her and placed it in her hall in Fitzwilliam Square, Dublin. Distraught over the killing of her husband, she sought spiritual direction from the Jesuit Father Finlay in Dublin. In gratitude for his help, in the early 1930s she donated the painting to the Jesuit Fathers of the house of St Ignatius at Lower Leeson Street, Dublin. It remained hung in the dining room with the Jesuits for almost sixty years and in 1990, the father superior, Noel Barber, SJ, asked Sergio Benedetti, the chief restorer of the National Gallery of Ireland, to restore the painting. Benedetti, an expert on Italian seventeenth century art, recognized the painting as 'The Taking of Christ' by the Italian artist Michelangelo Merisi, better known as Caravaggio (1571–1610). The painting now hangs in the National Gallery of Ireland on permanent loan from the Jesuit community.

Le Clerc, Eugene; surgeon to the Force on 1/7/1857 to 19/4/1880; resided at Booterstown Avenue, Dublin; died 8/9/1884.

Ledger, Edward; LDS 2097/130; born 1811, Kilbreedy, Bruree, Co. Limerick; wife from Cork E.R.; 3rd SI 30/12/1839; received an approbation on 31/3/1850 for gallant exertions when in command of a party of police in saving numerous lives at a fire at the Killarney Auxiliary Workhouse; died 23/10/1852 in Co. Cork W.R.; his second son, William Sharpe Ledger, died on 3/3/1864 (Dublin North Registrar's District, vol. 2, p. 541), aged 23 years in Dublin (*Cork Examiner* 7/3/1864); his widow, Mary, died on 13/11/1865, aged 50 years (Cork Registrar's District, vol. 20, p. 107), at Grattan's Hill, Cork (*Cork Examiner* 14/11/1865).

Lee, James; CarNB; PPF; 12/3/1816.

Lees, Thomas Orde Hastings; RIC 35091; LDS 2097/274; born 22/2/1846, Ballymacward, Co. Galway, the son of Rev. John and Lady Louisa Lees (daughter of 11th Earl of Huntington); married Grace, daughter of Joshua Wigley Bateman of Guilsborough, Northamptonshire (secretary to the Duchy of Cornwall); educated at the Royal Naval School; Newcross; Royal Academy, Gosport; MA 1869, Barrister-at-Law 1879, Trinity College Dublin; 3rd DI 30/1/1869; received a favourable record on 31/12/1870 for the spirited arrest of a riotous man who had struck a sub constable and his capture after a fierce struggle; received a favourable record on 31/12/1871 for tracing the offenders of a brutal assault who had fled to England resulting in their capture; resigned 10/11/1875 and appointed Chief Constable of Northamptonshire County Constabulary on 25/11/1875 (together with Peterborough Liberty from 2/2/1876) until 1881; called to the Bar (Mid Temple, 1881) returned to English Midland Circuit as a Barrister 1881–1890; unsuccessfully contested parliamentary seat of Northampton 1886; appointed the first Chief Constable Isle of Wight 1890 to 1/3/1899; (received Jubilee Medal from Queen Victoria herself for handling police arrangements for 1896–97 Jubilee at Osborn House). Personal friend of Captain Charles Boycott (of 'Boycott' fame, who came to Northampton in 1886 on the hustings for Lees); author of *The Constable's Pocket Book*, and other technical works; editor of *Snowden's Police Officer's Guide*; died 30/9/1924, at Buckmore, Petersfield, Hampshire, late of 3, Temple Gardens, Middlesex; (Petersfield Registrar's District, December Quarter, 1924, vol. 2c, p. 166); administration granted at London on 31/12/1924 to Grace Lees, widow – effects £701.0s.7d.

Lefroy, Anthony Thomas; LDS 2097/049; born 1802, Alnwick, Northumberland, England; eldest son of Anthony Lefroy (19/10/1777–7/9/1857), Captain 65th Regiment of Foot (2nd Yorkshire North Riding Regiment) for many years Barrackmaster of York and Elizabeth

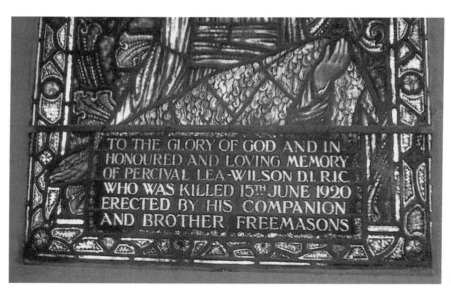

146

146 Stained glass memorial window, Church of Ireland, Gorey, Co. Wexford by Harry Clark dedicated to Percival Samuel Lea-Wilson, commissioned by the Order of Freemasons.
147 RIC Crest in stained glass window.

147

(m.5/11/1798), daughter of William Wilkin, of Appleby, Westmoreland; 3rd SI 1/2/1824; on 16/7/1828 he reported Dennis Hilliard, constable reg. no. 1984, Redcross, Co. Wicklow as having been fined 10 shillings. Lefroy had ordered Hilliard and two men to Rathdrum on 12/7/1828 and at 11pm that night to march his men home at 11.10pm. At 12.35am on Sunday morning he found them drinking in a pub. Hilliard was fined before for drunkenness and in this case he was reduced to the rank of sub constable; A.T. Lefroy resigned on 1/12/1839; he emigrated to England where he was appointed the first County Chief Constable in England and also the first Chief Constable of the Gloucestershire Constabulary, on 1 December 1839, until his retirement on 1 July 1865. He married Amelia Jane Elliott on 12 May 1851 at Cheltenham, daughter of Lettsome Elliott, Bombay CS and he died on 23 March 1890 at Cheltenham. His uncle was the Rt. Hon. Thomas Langlois Lefroy, PC, LLD of Carriglass, Co. Longford (1776–1869), Barrister-at-Law 1797, Bencher of the Kings Inns, 1819, MP for Dublin University, 1832–1842, a Baron of the Exchequer, 1842–1852, Chief Justice of the Court of the Queen's Bench, 1852–1866, who married Elizabeth Cottingham (d.9/11/1900) daughter of James Cottingham and sister of Jane Cottingham (d.30/1/1899), both buried in Deansgrange Cemetery (South Section, RowM1, Grave31). He was residing at 2, Segrave Place, Cheltenham, Gloucestershire in 1881 (Census). His cousin, Thomas Lefroy married Anna Austen, a niece of the novelist, Jane Austen (16/11/1775–18/7/1817). He brought with him to England 13 constables one of who was Charles Reilly who became Deputy Chief Constable of the Gloucestershire Constabulary on 7/1/1840; A.T. Lefroy died 23/3/1890.

Lennon, John Sherlock; LDS 2097/171; born 1802, Drumraney, Co. Westmeath; enlisted as a sub constable on 1/3/1828; awarded a chevron in June 1843; wife a native of Co. Longford; 3rd SI 1/6/1848; died 21/3/1867 in Athlone, Co. Westmeath, the verdict of the Coroner's Jury being suicide; (Athlone Registrar's District, 1867, vol. 18, p. 3).

Lennon, William; RIC 30154; LDS 2097/251; born 1845, Co. Wicklow; son of John Sherlock Lennon, SI, RIC and father of William Sherlock Lennon, DI, RIC; married on 29/4/1879 (Dublin South Registrar's District, June Quarter, 1879, vol. 2, p. 659); 3rd SI 1/4/1865; died by suicide 15/1/1897 at Castle Street, Lisburn, Co. Antrim (Lisburn Registrar's District, 1897, March Quarter, vol. 1, p. 649); administration with the will granted on 22/3/1897 at the Principal Registry to Annie Lennon, of Castle Street, Lisburn, Co. Antrim, widow, the universal legatee – effects £2,402.16s.6d.

Lennon, William Sherlock; RIC 60527; LDS 2098/189; born 5/2/1880, Eyre Square, Co. Galway; (Galway Registrar's District, March Quarter, 1880, vol. 4, p. 283): son of William Lennon, SI, RIC and Annie Sherlock; educated at the Galway school; tutor; matriculated to TCD on 20/6/1898; BA Degree, 1905 and LLB, 1908, Trinity College Dublin; recommended for a Commission in the Army by the Inspector General of the RIC with a reference supplied by L.L. Nicol, Brigadier-General, commanding 30th Infantry Brigade; captain, 6th Battalion Royal Dublin Fusiliers, 19/11/1914 and temporary major on 18/1/1916; Governor of Kilmainham Gaol, Dublin, March to July 1916 and residing at 23, Marlborough Road, Dublin; attached to the Egyptian Army from 18/2/1917 to 16/10/1919; he received a gunshot wound to the right forearm in action at Suvla Bay, Gallipoli on 15/8/1915; 3rd DI 25/5/1902; King Edward VII Visit to Ireland Medal, 1903; pensioned 1/8/1920; seconded for service with the Sudan Government from 2/9/1920 as Assistant District Commissioner; died 1/4/1923 of appendicitis on board the hospital ship *Lady baker* on the River Nile near Kosti, White Nile Province, Sudan, Egypt; administration granted at the Principal Registry, London on 19/1/1924 to his mother, Annie Lennon, 22 Norham Road, Oxford as no executor appointed in his will – effects £1,885.0s.3d.; administration granted to his mother on 7/5/1924 in the High Court, Dublin – effects in Ireland £255.6s.3d.; (PRO reference PMG4875); (WO 339/13484); (Obituary in the *Irish Times*, 16/4/1923).

148

149

148 Anthony Thomas Lefroy, the first appointed Chief Constable in England in 1839.
149 George Henry Samuel Lester. 150 George Henry Luxton. 151 William Lynn.

150

151

Leo, William; LDS 2097/262; born 1848; Co. Kilkenny; 3rd SI 24/6/1867; died 11/11/1874 at Carrick-on-Shannon, Co. Leitrim.

Leonard, Peter; RIC 38810; LDS 2098/174; born 1853, Co. Sligo; brother of Thomas Leonard, DI, RIC; married on 10/11/1894 (Dublin North Registrar's District, December Quarter, 1894, vol. 2, p. 552), wife a native of Co. Roscommon; 3rd DI 24/6/1900; awarded medal and clasp of the Royal Humane Society and silver medal of the Royal Society for the Protection of Life from Fire; pensioned 16/8/1913; died 31/10/1930 in Loughrea, Co. Galway; (Loughrea Registrar's District, 1930, vol. 4, p. 175); administration granted at the Principal Registry on 2/12/1930 to Mary R. Leonard, widow – effects £240.9s.10d.

Leonard, Thomas; RIC 31739; LDS 2098/103; born 1847, Co. Sligo; brother of Peter Leonard, DI, RIC; married on 25/11/1897 (Dublin North Registrar's District, December Quarter, 1897, vol. 2, p. 526), Mary Kerins, a native of Co. Mayo; 3rd DI 17/11/1893; pensioned 1/5/1908 at Dingle, Co. Kerry; died 10/9/1917 at Fernleigh, Beltra, Co. Mayo; will proved on 2/11/1917 at Ballina, Co. Mayo by the oath of Sarah M. Leonard, spinster – effects £490.2s.2d.; buried in Dromard, Co. Sligo on 12/9/1917 at Farnleigh, Beltra, Co. Mayo.

Lester, George Henry Samuel; RIC 71606; LDS 2098/165B; born 13/05/1898, Rathdrum, Co. Wicklow; (Rathdrum Registrar's District, 1898, June Quarter, vol. 3, p. 305); Royal Air Force; married on 30/3/1921, wife a native of Co. Cork; 3rd DI 10/1/1920; pensioned 25/5/1922.

Lewis, Francis William; RIC 71610; LDS 2098/194B; born 11/5/1893, Co. Carlow; (Carlow Registrar's District, June Quarter, 1893, vol. 3, p. 355); son of head constable John Lewis RIC 7187 (b.1826), Co. Wicklow, who was present at the siege of the widow McCormack's house at Ballingarry, Co. Tipperary in 1848, who died at 4 Albert Lane, Sligo on 15/3/1910 and was buried in Glasnevin Cemetery, Dublin; brother-in-law of Michael O'Rorke, DI, RIC; lieutenant, Royal Field Artillery; 3rd DI 10/1/1920; pensioned 31/5/1922; transferred to the Royal Ulster Constabulary on 1/6/1922.

Lewis, John; LDS 2097/094, born 1795, Co. Tipperary; baronial chief constable from March 1813 to March 1823; enlisted as a sub constable, 20/8/1823; 3rd SI 1/2/1836; pensioned 1/10/1858 in Co. Kildare; died 1/10/1869 at Parsonstown, Co. Offaly (Parsonstown Registrar's District, 1869, vol. 18, p. 429).

Lewis, William; RIC 43816; LDS 2098/227; born 23/4/1860, Co. Mayo; married on 22/12/1891 (Castletown Registrar's District, December Quarter, 1891, vol. 3, p. 322), wife a native of Co. Kilkenny; 3rd DI 4/9/1908; pensioned 15/6/1920.

Lewis, William; LDS 2097/044; born 1792, Co. Waterford; lieutenant in the yeomanry from 1/5/1807 to 30/9/1823; 3rd SI 2/10/1823; CI 1/10/1836; died 29/12/1847.

Lilly, Charles James; RIC 44149; LDS 2097/297; born 1857, Leics., England; (Shordlow Registrar's District, 1857, June Quarter, vol. 7b, p. 347); married 14/12/1887 (Dublin North Registrar's District, December Quarter, 1887, vol. 2, p. 442), wife a native of Co. Tipperary; 3rd SI 1/7/1879; King Edward VII Visit to Ireland Medal, 1903; pensioned 15/3/1919; (photo in the *Constabulary Gazette*, vol. XXXI, no. 14, 15/6/1912).

Lindsay, Owen Henry; LDS 2097/210; BA, Trinity College Dublin; married on 14/12/1878; 3rd SI 1/2/1857; CI 8/4/1878; pensioned 1/11/1886.

Little, William; LDS 2097/076; born 1802, Kiltennell, Co. Carlow; wife a native of Co. Wexford; enlisted as a sub constable, 1/11/1824; 3rd SI 1/10/1832; died 28/7/1859.

Littledale, Herbert Francis; RIC 82023; LDS 2099/020; born 28/4/1882, Co. Westmeath; (Athlone Registrar's District, June Quarter, 1882, vol. 3, p. 3); wife from Berkshire; captain, Royal Artillery; awarded the Military Cross; awarded an unfavourable record for neglect of duty at the Galway Races on 3/8/1921; 3rd DI 25/6/1921; pensioned 18/4/1922.

Loch, George Granville Gower; RIC 57880; LDS 2098/120; born 1875, Co. Galway; employed in the Public Record Office as copyist for 3 months; married on 18/4/1907, Miss R.S.

Parker, a native of England; 3rd DI 3/10/1896; died 15/10/1919; (photo in the *Constabulary Gazette*, vol. XXXIII, no. 23, 30/8/1913, p. 363).

Loch, James; RIC 27732; LDS 2097/241; born 1844, Co. Dublin; son of John Loch, CI, RIC; married on 4/2/1872; 3rd SI 16/6/1862; CI 1/11/1886; died 1/12/1903 at Portland, Downpatrick, Co. Down; administration with will granted on 12/1/1904 at the Principal Registry to Angel Constance Loch, widow – effects £771.4s.0d.; (photo in the *Constabulary Gazette*, vol. 1, no. 12, 19/6/1897).

Loch, John; LDS 2097/094; born, 1812, Berwickshire, New Brunswick, Canada; father of James Loch, CI, RIC; wife a native of Co. Armagh; 3rd SI 16/2/1836; CI 6/12/1864; died 2/1/1873 at Cathedral Square, Waterford, Co. Waterford; will proved on 27/3/1873 at Waterford by the oath of Henrietta Elizbeth Loch, widow and the sole executrix – effects under £600.

Lodge, John; LDS 2097/160; born 1798, Monadrishane, Kilworth, Co. Cork; enlisted as a sub constable on 1/11/1831; 3rd SI 16/9/1847; pensioned 1/7/1864; died 19/4/1889 in Dublin; (Dublin South Registrar's District, 1889, June Quarter, vol. 2, p. 493).

Logan, William; CarNB; born 1791; stipendiary magistrate; pensioned 1839; died 1843.

Long, Robert; RIC 48845; LDS 2098/037B; born 21/1/1865, Clogher, Co. Tyrone; (Clogher Registrar's District, 1865, vol. 3, p. 133); 3rd DI 16/8/1912; Company Officer, North Dublin Union Sub Depot from 18/3/1920 to 25/3/1921; chief police instructor at the Phoenix Park Depot from 25/3/1921 to 30/7/1922; pensioned 31/7/1922.

Lopdell, Francis Blake; RIC 31446; LDS 2097/255; born 22/12/1846, Castle Lodge, Co. Galway; the youngest son of Mr John Lopdell, BL, of Raheen Park, Athenry, Co. Galway; married on 24/4/1877 (Dublin South Registrar's District, vol. 7, p. 539); 3rd SI 15/4/1866; received an approbation on 30/6/1870 for spirited exertions in preventing the spread of fire and saving property; received an approbation on 31/12/1870 for spirited and perilous exertions in extinguishing a fire; CI 1/10/1888; King Edward VII Visit to Ireland Medal, 1903; pensioned 1/2/1907; died 10/11/1911 at Burncleuth, Ailsbury Road, Dublin; buried in Athenry, Co. Galway on 13/11/1911; will proved on 11/8/1911 at Tuam by the oath of Christopher Thomas Lopdell and William Keating Blake – effects £4,012.4s.10d.

Lowndes, Hugh Massy; RIC 55386; LDS 2098/088; born 1/11/1867, Norfolk, England; married on 24/2/1903 (Rathdown Registrar's District, March Quarter, 1903, vol. 2, p. 813), Miss Norris, a native of Co. Wicklow; 3rd DI 1/12/1892; Queen Victoria's Visit to Ireland Medal, 1900; CI 23/11/1917; pensioned 16/5/1922.

Lowndes, John; RIC 21073; LDS 2097/304; born, 1834, Oldcastle, Co. Meath; wife from Co. Meath; 3rd SI 19/12/1879; pensioned 1/11/1896; died 15/12/1920 at 79, Whitworth Road, Drumcondra, Co. Dublin; will proved at the Principal Registry on 5/2/1921.

Lowndes, Thomas Francis; RIC 52408; LDS 2098/029; born 3/9/1867, Swords, Co. Dublin; (Dublin North Registrar's District, 1867, vol. 12, p. 582); married on 3/9/1903 (Rathdown Registrar's District, September Quarter, 1903, vol. 2, p. 827), wife a native of Germany; 3rd DI 1/9/1887; King Edward VII Visit to Ireland Medal, 1903; pensioned 31/8/1922; died 12/12/1936 in England; buried in the RIC Plot, Mount Jerome Cemetery, Dublin.

Lowrie, Alexander; LDS 2097/067; born 1780, Banffshire, New Brunswick, Canada; private, Prince of Wales' Aberdeen Fencibles from 1/3/1795 to 1/4/1803; corporal and sergeant, 93rd (Sutherland) Highlanders from 1/4/1803 to 31/8/1821; enlisted as a constable in November 1821; married Elizabeth Burgess on 9/4/1814 in the Settlement of Good Hope, South Africa; constable 1/11/1821; 3rd SI 15/1/1828; C.C. barony of Owney and Arra, Co. Tipperary, 1828, Tully, Ballinasloe, Co. Galway, 1835; pensioned 1/6/1843; died 1860.

Lumsden, John; CarNB; born Houseland, Templetown, Co. Wexford; brother of Chief Constable William Lumsden; died 1830; C.C. Innishowen, Co. Donegal; C.C. Orrery & Kilmore,

1823 (the *Constitution* or *Cork Morning Post*, 17/3/1823); C.C. Mitchelstown and Kildorrery, Co. Cork.

Lumsden, William; LDS 2097/022; born 1788, Houseland, Templetown, Co. Wexford; brother of Chief Constable John Lumsden; PPF; 3rd SI 1/9/1817; at the burning of the barracks at Churchtown, Co. Cork on 31/1/1822, he received several severe wounds to the head and had his left arm broken; pensioned 1/12/1839; died 12/1/1849.

Luxton, George Henry; RIC 72496; ADRIC no. 228; LDS 2098/232B; born 29/3/1895, Islington, London, England; (Islington Registrar's District, 1895, June Quarter, vol. 1b, p. 500); captain, 13th Norfolks Regiment; 3rd SI 2/7/1921; pensioned 31/3/1922; joined the Palestine Police on 30/3/1922; (photo - *The Irish Constabularies, 1822–1922: A Century of Policing in Ireland*, by Donal J. O'Sullivan, Brandon Press, Dingle, Co. Kerry, 1999).

Lynar, Richard A.F.; LDS 2097/149; born 1823, Co. Dublin; 3rd SI 17/4/1845; resigned 8/6/1849 in King's County.

Lynar, William W. (Sir); stipendiary magistrate, Birr, King's County; residing at Marlborough Street, Dublin in 1835; died 1845; widow Isabella; his son, William Lynar, Esq., died on 6/6/1872 at 28 Upper George's Street, Dublin (*Cork Examiner* 10/6/1872).

Lynch, Henry Butler; RIC 25256; LDS 2097/231; born 1837, Co. Galway; married on 15/4/1864 (Dublin South Registrar's District, vol. 7, p. 469) at St Peter's Church, Dublin, Louisa Catherine, daughter of the late John White, solicitor, of North Great George's Street, Dublin (*Cork Examiner* 20/4/1864); daughter, Aphrasia Agusta, born on 10/9/1868 at Belmont, Boyle, Co. Roscommon (Boyle Registrar's District, vol. 19, p. 85) (*Cork Examiner* 15/9/1868); son born on 18/11/1870 at Belmont, Boyle, Co. Roscommon (*Cork Examiner* 23/11/1870); 3rd SI 1/11/1859; pensioned 1/12/1899; died on 15/2/1905 at the residence of his nephew-in-law Rev. Canon White Bell, Doone Glebe, Cappamore, Co. Limerick; buried in St Munchin's Cemetery, Limerick City.

Lynch, John; LDS 2097/061; born 1796, Co. Mayo; wife a native of Co. Clare; 3rd SI 25/8/1825; CI 1/11/849; pensioned 5/2/1853; died 15/4/1861 at Clogher House, Co. Mayo (*Cork Examiner* 29/4/1861).

Lynch, John R.; LDS 2097/109; born 1807, Co. Limerick; wife a native of Dublin City; 3rd SI 7/11/1836; died 12/7/1856 in Co. Tyrone; buried in St Mary's Cemetery, Cloughcor, Strabane, Co. Tyrone.

Lynch, Martin Joseph; RIC 14810; LDS 2097/187; born 1825, Lavally, Co. Galway; son of Thomas Lynch, Esq. (1805–1872), of Lavally, Co. Galway; 3rd SI 12/5/1851; died 18/9/1854 at Mullingar, Co. Westmeath 'after a protracted illness in the 29th year of his age' (*Cork Examiner* 25/9/1854).

Lynch, Patrick; RIC 19332; LDS 2097/208; born 1835, Co. Galway; 3rd SI 1/6/1856; resigned 1/11/1858.

Lynn, William John; RIC 59162; LDS 2098/119B; born 1879, Co. Antrim; (Antrim Registrar's District, December Quarter, 1879, vol. 1, p. 15); 3rd DI 15/6/1920; pensioned 31/5/1922; transferred to the Royal Ulster Constabulary on 1/6/1922.

Lyon, Claude William; RIC 54177; LDS 2098/066; born 1865, Oborne, Dorset, England; residing at Haileybury, Great Amwell, Hertfordshire in 1881 (Census); tutor at Windlesbane House, Brighton, Sandringham House, Southport and Drawbridge House, Waterloo from 1883 to 1887; married on 5/8/1896 (Dublin South Registrar's District, September Quarter, 1896, vol. 2, p. 527); 3rd DI 10/8/1890; Queen Victoria's Visit to Ireland Medal, 1900; King Edward VII Visit to Ireland Medal, 1903; pensioned 30/9/1912.

M

Macafee, David Lindsay; RIC 25365; LDS 2097/233; born 1841, Co. Antrim; 3rd SI 13/1/1860; resigned 20/1/1865.

Macartney, William Isaac; LDS 2097/116; born 1816, Co. Down; 3rd SI 20/9/1837; on 1/12/1847 appointed Superintendent of the Ceylon Police, replacing Sub Inspector Thomas Thompson, Irish Constabulary; his wife gave birth to a daughter on 15/9/1853 at Frankfort Lodge, Merrion Avenue, Dublin: 'the lady of William Macartney, Esq., Chief Superintendent of Police, Ceylon' (*Cork Examiner* 26/9/1853); he had 17 children, one of whom was a planter in Waloya Delta, Ceylon and married the daughter of George Wall, a well-known planter and mercantile man. George Wall's son, Frank wrote the marvelous exhaustive natural history book *The Snakes of Ceylon*; the youngest son, Sir Edward Macartney was Agent General for the Queensland Australia Government in England in 1929; William Isaac Macartney died in Hollywood, near Belfast in 1868 (Belfast Registrar's District, vol. 11, p. 243); his wife died on 17/4/1882 when on a visit to her eldest son in Ceylon and is buried in the Holy Trinity Church, Nuwara Eliya, high up in the Ceylon hill country.

Macauley, Henry Renny; LDS 2097/203; born 1834, Co. Dublin; 3rd SI 21/8/1854; died suddenly on 27/9/1858 at Galway.

MacCarthy, George Thomas; LDS 2097/217; born 21/5/1832, Spa Hill, Tralee, Co. Kerry; father of Thomas St George MacCarthy, DI, RIC; joined the Irish Revenue Police as a lieutenant on 24/11/1855 and served in Rathmullen, Co. Donegal; 3rd SI 1/12/1857; married Margaret Doherty from Rathmullen, Co. Donegal; temporary resident magistrate 22/4/1870; permanent RM 3rd class 3/1/1871, 2nd class 21/4/1880, 1st class 1/1/1893; served as a RM in Trim, Co. Meath 23/4/1870, Tipperary, Co. Tipperary 1/12/1873, Clifden, Co. Galway, 10/8/1881, Kells, Co. Meath 1/8/1882 and Killeshandra, Co. Cavan 15/3/1890; injured at the Tipperary Election and received £400 for injuries sustained on 29/12/1875; pensioned as a RM 21/5/1897; died at 33, Rutland Square, Dublin on 29 November 1902, in a hotel owned by a Susan Vaughan from Ennistymon, Co. Clare. His will (T.11921/National Archives) was probated in the High Court, Dublin on 12 January 1903 and he left an estate of £1,629.2s.10d. to his widow Margaret who was then residing at Walkers Row, Fermoy, Co. Cork; (p. 40, RM Records of Service Book, National Archives, Dublin).

MacCarthy, Thomas St George; RIC 50837; LDS 2097/328; born 9/6/1862 (*Cork Examiner* 14/6/1862) and baptized 11/6/1862, Bansha, Co. Tipperary; son of George Thomas MacCarthy (1832–1902), CI, RIC. He was educated at Tipperary Grammar School, the Erasmus Smith foundation situated in Tipperary Town. This school had a rugby team and it was here that his rugby career began. He moved to Dublin in 1879 where he came to know Michael Cusack, who since 1877 was running a cramming school – Cusack's Academy – which prepared young men for entry examinations for Trinity College, the medical and law schools, the army, constabulary and navy. In 1879 MacCarthy played for Cusack's Academy rugby team, and it was Cusack who coached him for his RIC cadetship examination in 1882, in which MacCarthy took first place. In 1881 he joined Trinity College rugby club and in January 1882 MacCarthy played rugby for Ireland against Wales, and later that year won a Leinster Senior Cup medal with Dublin University Rugby Club. He was the first of nine former Tipperary Grammar School pupils to win 'caps' for Ireland between 1882 and the closure of the school in 1923.

152   153

152 Thomas St George MacCarthy, GAA co-founder.   153 Thomas St George MacCarthy in retirement (standing).   154 Thomas St George MacCarthy grave in Deansgrange Cemetery, Dublin.

154

The friendship between Thomas St George MacCarthy and Michael Cusack explains MacCarthy's presence in Hayes Hotel, Thurles, Co. Tipperary on 1/11/1884 at the inaugural meeting of the Gaelic Athletic Association. He was stationed in Templemore, Co. Tipperary and attended the meeting with the well-to-do builder, Joseph Kevin Bracken (born Ardvullen House, Kilmallock, Co. Limerick and died in1904), member of the Irish Republican Brotherhood, father of politician and publisher, Viscount Brendan Bracken (15/2/1901–8/8/1958), Winston Churchill's closest friend and Minister of Information, 1941–45. Members of the RIC were banned from GAA sports in 1888. He had joined the RIC as a cadet on 21/11/1882; 3rd Class DI on 3/1/1883, 2nd Class on 16/3/1887 and 1st Class DI on 1/8/1896. He was allocated to Templemore, Co. Tipperary on 1/6/1883 and Derrygonnelly, Co. Tipperary on 1/3/1885; Limavaddy on 15/11/1887; Dundalk, Co. Louth on 1/12/1894; Robertstown, Co. Kildare on 15/12/1903; Newpallas, Co. Limerick on 1/4/1905; Newport, Co. Mayo on 25/7/1909; and Ballymahon, Co. Longford on 15/9/1911. In September 1894 he was presented with a complimentary illuminated address accompanied by a purse of sovereigns from the magistrates, clergy and inhabitants generally of the county of Londonderry on the occasion of his transfer to Dundalk; expressive of regret at his removal from amongst them, bearing testimony to the ability, tact and firmness with which he invariably discharged his duties while stationed at Limavady and as a token of their esteem and regard. Resolutions were also passed by the presiding magistrates at Limavady and Claudy Petty Sessions on 4 and 7 December 1894 respectively, expressing regret at his leaving. He was one of seven persons who founded the Gaelic Athletic Association because he was concerned about young persons who were drunk and if they participated in games they were less likely to indulge themselves in liquor. He was awarded the King Edward VII Visit to Ireland Medal, 1903. He was pensioned on 23/1/1912. He played rugby for Trinity College Dublin and was capped for Ireland against Wales in 1882. His sister Kathleen died at an early age and is buried in Bansha Cemetery. He married Mary Lucy Lynch in Dublin's Pro-Cathedral on 18/11/1887 (her father was born in Galway and practiced as a solicitor in Great Charles Street, off the North Circular Road, Dublin). He had a son who practiced law at Edmonton, Canada and a daughter, Kathleen who after acting in the Abbey Theatre immigrated to Melbourne, Australia. He died at Linden Convalescent Home, Blackrock, Co. Dublin on 12/3/1943; buried in Deansgrange Cemetery on 15/3/1943 (Registry No. 55580) (Grave No. 53, Section L3); (photo – Police Service of Northern Ireland Museum, Belfast).

MacDermot, Edward Joseph; LDS 2097/266; born 22/3/1846, Fairhill, Clonbur, Co. Galway; son of Henry MacDermot, SI, RIC and brother of Henry Roderick MacDermot, CI, RIC; married on 6/5/1873 (Castlereagh Registrar's District, vol. 14, p. 69); 3rd SI 23/12/1867; resident magistrate 3rd class 29/10/1892, 2nd class 11/2/1898, 1st class 25/5/1910; pensioned 22/3/1911; (p. 97, RM Records of Service Book, National Archives, Dublin); died 30/9/1941; buried in Deansgrange Cemetery, Dublin (Lower North Section, Row B, Grave No. 9) with Arabella MacDermot, of Coolavin, Sligo (d.29/11/1922), Fannie MacDermot, 5 Park Road, Monkstown, Co. Dublin and Wilfred MacDermot, 5 Park Road, Dunlaoghaire, Co. Dublin (d.16/7/1957).

MacDermot, Henry; LDS 2097/108; born 1809, Coolavin, Co. Sligo; father of Edward Joseph MacDermot, SI, RIC and Henry Roderick MacDermot, CI, RIC; married Mary (b.Kenmare, Co. Kerry and died at Williamstown on 25/6/1878) niece of Daniel O'Connell, 'The Liberator'; 3rd SI 17/11/1836; pensioned 25/3/1870; his youngest daughter, Katie married on 4/10/1880, as Swinford, Co. Mayo, Daniel J. Lyne, MD, JP, Castletownberehaven, Co. Cork (*Cork Examiner* 11/10/1880).

MacDermot, Henry Roderick; LDS 2097/276; born 1850, Fairhill, Clonbur, Co. Galway; son of Henry MacDermot, SI, RIC and brother of Edward Joseph MacDermot, SI, RIC, RM; married on 6/1/1883, wife from Co. Roscommon; 3rd SI 24/2/1869; CI 1/5/1894; pensioned 5/7/1909; died 12/9/1915 in Dublin; (Dublin North Registrar's District, 1915, September

Quarter, vol. 2, p. 309); buried in Deansgrange Cemetery, Dublin (Lower North Section, Row B, Graves 9–11) with his wife Mary (d.25/6/1878) his daughters Kathleen, Mary (d.24/4/1897, aged 12 years) and Patrick MacDermot (d.23/8/1986), Rory (d.21/2/1942), Josephine MacDermot (d.26/11/1971), Florence Frankfort (d.290/5/1959); Florence Margaret Mary (Rita) died at Laytown, Co. Meath on 22/7/1904 and was buried in Deansgrange Cemetery on 25/7/1904.

MacDermott, Anthony Joseph; RIC 28371; LDS 2097/244; born 25/12/1839, Co. Galway; 3rd SI 11/2/1863; temporary resident magistrate 16/8/1881; permanent RM 3rd class 28/10/1882, 2nd class 1/8/1886, 1st class 19/7/1896; pensioned 25/12/1904; (p. 41, RM Records of Service Book, National Archives, Dublin).

MacDougall, William B.; CarNB; born Dublin City, Co. Dublin; 3rd SI 1/6/1825; pensioned 1827; C.C. Tallow, Co. Waterford.

MacInerney, Edward O'Connor; LDS 2097/252; born 1841, Co. Galway; son of John MacInerney, Esq., of Bleakmount House, Gort, Co. Galway; 3rd SI 9/5/1865; resigned 22/1/1868.

Mackintosh, John; RIC 72489; ADRIC no. 221; LDS 2098/242B; born 28/10/1888, Inverness, Scotland; Inverness Constabulary, May 1907 to September 1912; Kilmarnock Constabulary from September 1912 to July 1915; married Isabella Bain on 12/10/1913; lieutenant, 3rd Camerons; 3rd DI 2/7/1921; pensioned 17/7/1922.

MacLeod, John; CarNB; born 1791; father of John Sheridan Johnston MacLeod, SI, RIC, RM; captain; CI 1/8/1824; stipendiary magistrate 2/2/1836; resident magistrate, 1/10/1836; wife Caroline; killed at Garradice, near Ballinamore, Co. Leitrim 29/1/1845. He was the means of bringing to justice several of the lawless gang called 'The Molly Maguires' in the Leitrim District and for this it is supposed he was murdered (Annual Register, 1845, p. 236); buried in Rossorry Cemetery, Enniskillen, Co. Fermanagh on 31/1/1845; C.C. Omagh, Co. Tyrone; Cavan, Co. Cavan, 1831.

MacLeod, John Sheridan Johnston; LDS 2097/135; born 31/12/1821, Co. Sligo; son of John MacLeod, RM; captain; wife a native of Co. Cork; 3rd SI 4/5/1841; resident magistrate 3rd class 11/6/1861, 2nd class 28/6/1866, 1st class 10/6/1881; pensioned 31/12/1891; died 25/11/1899 at 6 Royal Marine Road, Dun Laoghaire, Co. Dublin; (Rathdown Registrar's District, 1899, December Quarter, vol. 2, p. 270); administration granted at the Principal Registry on 22/12/1899 to Mary C. Chambers, The Red House, Camberley, Surrey, married woman, the daughter – effects £194.1s.1d.; (p. 42, RM Records of Service Book, National Archives, Dublin).

MacMahon, Percy; LDS 2097/219; born 1831, Co. Clare; joined the Irish Revenue Police as a lieutenant on 6/10/1850 and served in Shrade, Co. Donegal; 3rd SI 25/3/1858; died 23/4/1861.

MacNamara, James F.; RIC 48090; LDS 2097/314; born 1858, Co. Louth; worked in the Admiralty for two years and ten months; 3rd SI 9/11/1881; died 22/5/1898 at Downpatrick, Co. Down; (photo in the *Constabulary Gazette*, vol. V, no. 14, 1/7/1899).

Madden, Robert Alfred; LDS 2098/181; born 1877, Co. Limerick; assistant master at Kingstown Grammar School; 3rd DI 26/9/1901; temporary adjutant of the Phoenix Park Depot from 1/11/1916 to 1/8/1918; TCI 20/8/1920; CI 1/10/1920; pensioned 16/6/1922.

Madders, Ambrose Samuel; RIC 32846; LDS 2097/261; born 1843, Co. Meath; son of William Madders, SI, RIC; married on 14/3/1877 (Claremorris Registrar's District, vol. 4, p. 559); 3rd SI 15/4/1867; pensioned 16/2/1901; died 2/11/1903 at 1, Rathmines Park, Dublin; buried in Mount Jerome Cemetery, Dublin on 4/11/1903; will proved on 8/12/1903 at the Principal Registry by the oath of Dr F.H. Taaffe and Charles Madders – effects £4,096.4s.5d.

Madders, William; RIC 815; LDS 2097/227; born 1813, Co. Waterford; father of Ambrose Samuel Madders, II, RIC; wife a native of Co. Monaghan; 3rd SI 22/4/1859; pensioned 1/7/1878; died 8/10/1888 at 25, Cambridge Road, Rathmines, Dublin; buried in Mount Jerome Cemetery, Dublin with his wife Mary (d.19/4/1896 aged 78 years) and his fourth son Henry J.

155 156

155 General Sir Duncan MacGregor.   156 Medal awards – General Sir Duncan MacGregor.
157 John Sherlock MacLeod, RM.

157

Madders (d.21/2/1902), Fleet Surgeon, Royal Navy; administration granted on 15/11/1888 at the Principal Registry by Mary Madders, of 25, Cambridge Road, Rathmines, widow – effects £197.6s.4d.

Maffett, Oswald Bayly; RIC 51006; LDS 2097/334; born 1859, Dublin City, Co. Dublin; son of William H. Maffett, Barrister-at-Law, of St Helen's, Finglas, Dublin; married on 24/2/1891 (Sligo Registrar's District, March Quarter, 1891, vol. 2, p. 321), wife a native of Co. Sligo; 3rd DI 14/11/1883; pensioned 11/4/1900; died 1/12/1914 at 19, Adelaide Street, Kingstown, Co. Dublin; will proved in the Principal Registry on 31/8/1915 by the oath of Elizabeth A.E. Maffett, the widow – effects £895.7s.0d.

Magan, Percy; CarNB; born 1796, Co. Roscommon; 3rd SI 1823; at the parish church, Clonallon on 20/9/1865 his son, Percy Magan, of Marlfield House, Co. Wexford was married by the Venerable, the Archdeacon of Dromore, uncle and the Rev. Lewis Richards, brother of the bride, Annie Catherine, only daughter of the Rev. Edward Richards, rector of Clonallon and Chancellor of Dromore (*Cork Examiner* 30/9/1865) and a son was born on 13/11/1867 at Marlfield House (*Cork Examiner* 18/11/1867); C.C. Marlfield, Gorey, Co. Wexford, Rathdown, Co. Wicklow, Sandyford, Co. Dublin.

Magan, Richard; CarNB; born 1794, Togherstown, Co. Westmeath; stipendiary magistrate 15/2/1832; C.C. Woodford, Co. Galway and Belfast, Co. Antrim, 1831; Clonmany, Carndonagh, Co. Donegal, 1832.

Magee, David; RIC 36094; LDS 2098/056; born 1846, Co. Cavan; wife a native of Co. Down; 3rd DI 20/4/1899; pensioned 20/3/1908 and retired to Northern Ireland; awarded Medal of the Dublin Society for the Prevention of Cruelty to Animals.

Magner, Edward Joseph; RIC 71647; LDS 2098/137B; born 25/8/1895, Co. Cork; captain, 3rd Battalion, Leinster Regiment and Royal Air Force; 3rd DI 8/7/1920; dismissed 13/5/1922.

Magrath, Henry; RIC 8.5; LDS 2097/208; born 1801, Co. Roscommon; married in March 1823, wife a native of Co. Roscommon; 3rd SI 1/7/1856; pensioned 3/1/1868; died 3/3/1878 at Delvin, Co. Westmeath; (Delvin Registrar's District, 1878, March Quarter, vol. 3, p. 148); (WO 339/44042).

Maguire, Berrill Henry; LDS 2097/162; born 1821, Co. Meath; ensign, 77th Regiment of Foot (East Middlesex Regiment) from 25/10/1843 to 5/8/1845; wife a native of Co. Kerry; daughter born on 14/8/1861 at St John's Place, Kilkenny (*Cork Examiner* 19/8/1861); his daughter, Margaret, aged five years and ten months died on 2/6/1865 (Kilkenny Registrar's District, vol. 18, p. 355) and his son John Thomas, aged nine years and ten months died on 5/6/1865 (Kilkenny Registrar's District, vol. 18, p. 355), at St John's Place, Kilkenny (*Cork Examiner* 10/6/1865); 3rd SI 29/11/1847; CI 8/4/1872; pensioned 1/9/1886; died 15/9/1894 at 5, Corrig Avenue, Kingstown, Co. Dublin (Rathdrum Registrar's District, 1894, September Quarter, vol. 2, p. 603); buried in Glasnevin Cemetery, Dublin on 18/9/1894; will proved on 15/10/1894 at the Principal Registry, by the oath of Sara Maria Maguire, of 5, Corrig Avenue, Kingstown, Co. Dublin, the sole executrix – effects £3,152.10s.0d. (Will T.15281 / National Archives).

Maguire, Francis Joseph; RIC 57481; LDS 2098/093B; born 1/1/1874, Longsight, Lancs., England; (Chorlton Registrar's District, 1874, March Quarter, vol. 8c, p. 677); son of Roger Maguire (b.1845) Ireland and Annie Maguire (b.1846), Old Swan, Lancashire; married on 21/7/1910 (Belfast Registrar's District, September Quarter, 1910, vol. 1, p. 536), wife a native of Belfast; 3rd DI 7/9/1919; pensioned 17/6/1922.

Maguire, Joseph Cartmail; RIC 29188; LDS 2097/246; born 1843, Co. Sligo; temporary clerk in the Census Office for three months; 3rd SI 1/6/1864; dismissed 15/5/1869.

Mahon, Edmund; CarNB; born 1793, Co. Galway; ensign 70th Regiment of Foot (Surrey Regiment), 12/3/1812; lieutenant, 15/6/1815; lieutenant half pay, 4/11/1817; married in Galway City, 16/8/1824; children: Monimia Mahon, born 22/9/1826 and Thomas Mahon, born

9/4/1828; resided in Galway City, Glenmore, near Ballymahon, Co. Longford and Newmarket-on-Fergus, Co. Clare, 1823–8; pensioned 1/4/1834; died 1864, Co. Galway (Ballinasloe Registrar's District, 1864, vol. 14, p. 5); C.C. Newmarket-on-Fergus, Co. Clare; (WO 25/767 fol. 100).

Mahony, Daniel; CarNB; born Killarney, Co. Kerry; 3rd SI 1/11/1826; resigned at Bantry, Co. Cork, 1/1/1830; C.C. Erris, Co. Mayo; Bantry, Co. Cork.

Mahony, Darby; CarNB; born Cahir, Co. Tipperary; C.C. Clashmore and Dungarvan, Co. Waterford (Transcript of will proved at the Prerogative Court in 1834, James O'Connell, Lakeview – executor; NA Reference: IWR/1834/F/664); (Will of Darby Mahony, Chief Constable of Police of Cork – PRO, Kew, Catalogue Reference: PROB 11/2049 / Dept: Records of the Prerogative Court of Canterbury and related Probate Jurisdictions: Will Registers / Volume number: 2 Quire Numbers: 51–100 / Date: 28 January 1847/ Image Reference: 52/45).

Mahony, Owen; RIC 35287; LDS 2098/125; born 1849, Co. Mayo; married on 2/6/1891 (Belfast Registrar's District, June Quarter, 1891, vol. 1, p. 433), wife a native of Co. Louth; 3rd DI 4/11/1896; King Edward VII Visit to Ireland Medal, 1903; pensioned 5/9/1910; (photo in the *Constabulary Gazette*, vol. XIV, no. 3, 10/10/1903).

Mallon, Hugh; LDS 2098/017B; born 11/4/1887, Newry, Co. Down; (Newry Registrar's District, June Quarter, 1887, vol. 1, p. 789); 3rd DI 23/12/1910; died 8/2/1913 at The Sligo Fever Hospital, Sligo, late of Coloorey, Co. Sligo; administration granted on 24/4/1913 at the Principal Registry to Hugh Mallon, farmer – effects £481.16s.6d.

Malone, John; LDS 2097/073; born 1789, Cappagh, Co. Tyrone; PPF; enlisted as a sub constable, 1/5/1815; private, corporal and sergeant in the South Mayo Militia from August 1805 to August 1815 (WO 13/3121–40); wife a native of Co. Westmeath; on 25/12/1821 his skull was fractured by a blow of a stone at Archerstown, Co. Tipperary while escorting a prisoner; on 1/3/1823 he occasioned a pitchfork wound in the hip from one of a party that had set fire to a dwelling house on the lands at Cullohill, Co. Tipperary; 3rd SI 1/3/1832; pensioned 19/9/1859; died 7/6/1875; C.C. Taghmon, Co. Wexford; Borrisokane, Co. Tipperary.

Mansfield, Robert; LDS 2097/050; born 1798, Killygordon, Co. Donegal; midshipman from 1/1/1804 to 1/6/1809; ensign in the Prince of Wales' Own Donegal Militia from 12/1/1814 to 18/6/1816 (WO 13/2751–71); 3rd SI 1/4/1824; C.C. Lurgan, Co. Armagh,1831; pensioned 15/9/1845; died 1854.

Mara, Timothy; RIC 56077; LDS 2098/079B; born 11/12/1873, Mountmellick, Queen's County; (Mountmellick Registrar's District, 1873, vol. 18, p. 553); married on 12/10/1905 (Dublin North Registrar's District, December Quarter, 1905, vol. 2, p. 485), wife a native of Co. Dublin; 3rd DI 13/10/1917; pensioned 17/5/1922.

Markham, Patrick; RIC 68804; LDS 2098/039; born 1844, Co. Clare; 3rd DI 10/2/1888; pensioned 23/6/1901; died 12/2/1904 at 34 Eccles Street, Dublin; will proved on 15/3/1904 by the oath of Michael Humphreys and William O'Connor, merchants – effects £1,086.18s.0d.

Marks, John Alexander; RIC 43531; LDS 2098/186; born 9/3/1858, Bermuda; married on 5/4/1889 (Belfast Registrar's District, June Quarter, 1889, vol. 1, p. 317), wife a native of Co. Down; 3rd DI 4/1/1902; Queen Victoria's Visit to Ireland Medal, 1900 as a head constable; King Edward VII Visit to Ireland Medal, 1903; pensioned 31/5/1919.

Marrinan, Patrick Aloysius; RIC 56970; LDS 2098/036B; born 17/3/1877, Drogheda, Co. Louth; (Drogheda Registrar's District, 1877, vol. 2, p. 546); son of sergeant Patrick Marrinan, RIC 16873 and brother of sergeant James F. Marrinan, RIC 58261; married on 14/9/1910 (Ballymoney Registrar's District, September Quarter, 1910, vol. 1, p. 183), Sarah Boyle, a native of Co. Antrim; they had six children, three sons and three daughters: RIC heavyweight champion boxer; founder member of the Irish Amateur Boxing Association, 1911; 3rd DI 26/3/1912; committee member of the First All Ireland RIC Representative Body, 1919: CI 15/6/1920; divisional commissioner 25/9/1920, Leinster Division; pensioned 24/8/1922, awarded the CBE

158   **159**

158 Patrick Aloysius Marrinan, co-founder of   **159** Patrick Aloysius Marrinan.
the Irish Amateur Boxing Association.

in 1922; called to the Bar in Dublin and Northern Ireland, 1925; died in Belfast, 8/11/1940; (photo in the *Constabulary Gazette*, vol. XVII, no. 10, 27/5/1905 and the Royal Irish Constabulary Magazine, vol. 1, no. 4, pp. 119–120).

Marshall, Thomas; CarNB; C.C. Newport-Pratt, Co. Mayo.

Marshall, Thomas Michael; RIC 56346; LDS 2098/046B; born 20/10/1875, Longford, Co. Longford; (Granard Registrar's District, 1875, vol. 18, p. 190); married on 1/2/1912 (Limerick Registrar's District, March Quarter, 1912, vol. 5, p. 303), wife a native of Co. Limerick; 3rd DI 16/8/1913; pensioned 17/6/1922.

Martin, Cecil Percy; RIC 68406; LDS 2098/058B; born 9/5/1892, Co. Dublin; (Dublin South Registrar's District, June Quarter, 1892, vol. 2, p. 577); married on 1/3/1917 (Tullamore Registrar's District, March Quarter, 1917, vol. 3, p. 479), Kathleen Humphreys, a native of King's County; 3rd DI 13/2/1915; lieutenant, Royal Irish Regiment from 13/1/1916 to 3/4/1920; pensioned 17/7/1922.

Martin, Jacob Frederick; RIC 60752; LDS 2099/001; born 1902, Glenamaddy, Co. Galway; (Glenamaddy Registrar's District, 1900, June Quarter, vol. 4, p. 252); married on 22/8/1917 (Lisnaskea Registrar's District, September Quarter, 1917, vol. 3, p. 137), wife a native of Co. Fermanagh; 3rd DI 4/1/1921; pensioned 31/5/1922; transferred to the Royal Ulster Constabulary on 1/6/1922.

Martin, Samuel Deacon; LDS 2097/023; PPF; born 1787, Co. Cavan; private, corporal and sergeant in the Cavan Militia (WO 13/2647–66); joined the army in 1803, serving in 26th Regiment of Foot (Scotch Rifles) and 91st Regiment of Foot (The Argyllshire Highlanders) and left the Cameronians on 12/1/1815; PPF Constable 16/4/1815; in the spring of 1817 he received an injury to both legs by a fall from his horse while on duty; 3rd SI 16/10/1818; C.C. Rathcoole, Co. Dublin; died 30/7/1840.

Martin, William Limerick; LDS 2097/268; born 1845, Co. Clare; wife a native of Co. Galway; 3rd SI 1/4/1868; killed 3/2/1889, Derrybeg, Gweedore, Co. Donegal; administration granted on 26/2/1889 at Derry to Henrietta Martin, Ballyshannon, Co. Donegal, the widow – effects £240.3s.3d.; monument erected to him in the grounds of St James Church, Dublin; (silver commemorative bust – Police Service of Northern Ireland Museum, Belfast and memorial in the grounds of St James Churchyard, James Street, Dublin).

Martinson, William Farrell; RIC 72405; ADRIC no. 173; LDS 2098/247B; born 1892, Shanghai, China; served in the British Army; 3rd DI 2/7/1921; seconded for service with ADRIC as Commandant, Beggars Bush ADRIC Depot from 2/7/1921 to 15/3/1922; awarded King's Police Medal, 1909 for distinguished service in 1921, the citation of which read: 'DI Martinson has served as Adjutant of the Auxiliary Division, RIC, for the past eight months and has shown untiring energy and devotion to duty'; pensioned 15/3/1922; joined the Palestine Police as Adjutant.

160 Cecil Percy Martin.   161 William Limerick Martin, silver bust in PSNI Museum.
162 William Limerick Martin, memorial in St James Cemetery, Dublin.

Marum, Edmund; CarNB; son of John Marum, Galmoy, Co. Kilkenny who was murdered on 16 March 1824; C.C. Ballybay, Co. Monaghan; Dromore and Hillsborough, Co. Down, 1826; resigned 1827; emigrated to the United States in 1849 and died of a fever on arrival there. The will of his uncle, Edmund Marum is in the National Archives, Dublin (Transcript of will proved in the Prerogative Court in 1837 – E. Staunton, executor. NA Reference: IWR/1837/F/275).

Mason, Cyril Robert; RIC 72174; ADRIC no. 47; LDS 2098/238B; born 25/10/1895, Ches., England; (Hinckley Registrar's District, 1895, December Quarter, vol. 7a, p. 43); lieutenant, 3rd Ox. Bucks; 3rd DI 7/2/1921; accidentally killed 16/6/1921, Wexford, Co. Wexford; late of Saxonhurst, Old Chester Road, Rock Fermoy, Birkinhead, Chester; administration granted at the Principal Registry on 20/12/1921.

Mason, Oliver Anselim Tibeaudo; LDS 2097/207; born 1832, Co. Dublin; son or Rev. John Henderson Mason and Rector of St Werburgh's and Chancellor of St Patrick's Cathedral, Dublin; daughter born on 29/9/1870 at South View, Bagenalstown, Co. Carlow (*Cork Examiner* 6/10/1870); 3rd SI 11/5/1856; received a favourable record on 31/12/1871 for solving a threatening letter case from a meagre clue resulting in the conviction of the offender who was sentenced to five years penal servitude; pensioned 11/9/1891; died 9/7/1911 at 54, Marlborough Road, Donnybrook, Dublin; his eldest daughter, Olive, married at St Mary's, Donnybrook on 23/12/1901, William Lawson, son of Richard Laferre, Esq., Londonderry, by Rev. M.B.A. Byrn.

Mathew, William Horgan; LDS 2097/069; born 1804, Queen's County; enlisted as a sub constable 15/2/1822; constable 4/7/1825; wife a native of Co. Armagh; 3rd SI 20/5/1831; the inspector general expressed his dissatisfaction of his discreditable manner while in attendance at a constabulary court at Dublin Castle on 28/3/1854; was attacked and dangerously assaulted by constable John Holden from the effects of which he lost the sight of an eye on 5/12/1859; he was awarded £100 from the Reward Fund in consequence of his eye injury; pensioned 28/6/1871; died 17/6/1889.

Mathew, Meredith; CarNB; PPF; son born on 21/5/1855 at Roche's Point, Co. Cork to Mrs Bradley Sole, eldest daughter of the late Mathew Meredith, Sub Inspector of Constabulary (*Cork Examiner* 23/5/1855); C.C. Bandon, Co. Cork.

Matthews, William Charles; RIC 73029; ADRIC no. 482; LDS 2098/218B; born 1893, Glos., England; 1st Battalion Manchester Regiment; 3rd DI 12/1/1920; resigned 18/5/1921.

Maude (Sir) George Ashley; born 11/11/1817; second son of Rev. John Charles Maude (16/9/1792–21/6/1860), Rector of Enniskillen, Co. Fermanagh and Mary, eldest surviving daughter of Cely Trivilian, of Midenley, Somerset, who were married on 10/9/1813; nephew of Captain Sir James Ashley Maude, Royal Navy; 2nd lieutenant, Royal Artillery, 19/12/1833; captain 27/3/1837; adjutant 1/4/1846; son born on 31/7/1852 at 6 Harcourt Street, Dublin (*Cork Examiner* 6/8/1852); lieutenant-colonel and retired as colonel in 1858; commanded a Royal Horse Artillery Troop in Lord Lucan's Cavalry Division in the Crimean War (severely wounded at the Battle of Balaclava and invalided home); lieutenant-colonel commanding the Royal Horse Artillery at Woolwich; ADC to his Royal Highness, the Duke of Cambridge, 1856; military attaché with mission to Coronation of Czar of Russia, 1856; DIG 19/10/1858; resigned 7/8/1860; Crown Equerry and Secretary to the Master of the Horse to Her Majesty, Queen Victoria from 1859; CB (Civil), 1855; CB (Mil.), 1885; KCB (Civil) 1887; Knight of the Medidjeh; married 5/4/1845, Catherine Katinka (5/1/1812–1/6/1882), daughter of Charles George Beauclerk, of St Leonard's Lodge, Horsham, Sussex; died 31/5/1894.

Maunsell, John; RIC 58403; LDS 2098/098B; born 14/1/1879, Tulla, Co. Clare; (Tulla Registrar's District, March Quarter, 1879, vol. 4, p. 617); the son of John Maunsell (1840–1927), of Ballyshannon and Mary (d.16/6/1899), daughter of John Johnston, Co. Fermanagh; his grandfather, John Maunsell (d.8/4/1880) joined the RIC in 1836, serving in the Inspector General's Office and organized the RIC Lists from 1840; married 22/8/1905 (Omagh Registrar's District, September Quarter, 1905, vol. 2, p. 261), Sarah Walker (d.14/12/1960), daughter of

163

164

163 Robert John Maunsell.   164 George Maxwell.

John Sproule, of Ballybogey, Co. Antrim; 3rd DI 2/10/1919; pensioned 10/5/1922; died 3/3/1972, Bangor, Co. Down and buried in Clandebove Cemetery, Bangor.

Maunsell, Robert Joseph; RIC 54419; LDS 2098/071; born 1870, Co. Dublin, the son of John Maunsell (d.1897) and grandson of John Maunsell (1802–79) who founded the Royal Irish Constabulary List & Directory in 1841; 3rd DI 31/1/1892; Queen Victoria's Visit to Ireland Medal, 1900; King Edward VII Visit to Ireland Medal, 1903; CI 25/2/1913; pensioned 1/12/1920; (photo in the *Constabulary Gazette*, vol. 1, no. 21, 21/8/1897 & vol. 2, no. 36, 4/12/1897, p. 1).

Maunsell-Eyre, Richard Henry; RIC 72013; LDS 2098/156B; born 19/9/1868, Bandon, Co. Cork; captain, 4th (Reserve) Battalion, Royal Munster Fusiliers; 3rd DI 10/1/1920; pensioned 24/8/1922; (WO 339/29974).

Maxwell, Charles Leonard Dobbyn; RIC 54418; LDS 2098/069; born 1866, Co. Fermanagh; son of Thomas Dobbyn Maxwell; employed in the Ulster Bank for three and a half years; 3rd DI 23/8/1890; resigned compulsorily on 4/5/1899; (photo in the *Constabulary Gazette*, vol. 2 no. 39, p. 1, 24/12/1897).

Maxwell, George; LDS 2098/168; born 24/12/1874, Co. Kilkenny; (Castlederg Registrar's District, 1874, vol. 7, p. 21); married on 5/5/1909 (Delvin Registrar's District, June Quarter, 1909, vol. 3, p. 129), wife a native of Co. Westmeath; 3rd DI 16/2/1900; King Edward VII Visit to Ireland Medal, 1903; TCI 16/12/1920; CI 1/4/1921; pensioned 8/5/1922; died 12/6/1937.

Maxwell, George; RIC 59039; LDS 2097/247; born 1843, Co. Tyrone; clerk in the Ulster Bank, Belfast and Donegal; married on 15/4/1876, wife from Co. Donegal; 3rd SI 15/1/1864; pensioned 17/1/1895; died 28/3/1919 at Laurel Mount, Highfield West, Cork; (Cork Registrar's District, 1919, June Quarter, vol. 5, p. 117); will proved at Cork on 6/5/1919; buried in St Finbarr's Cemetery, Cork on 31/3/1919.

Maxwell, Thomas Dobbyn; RIC 13803; LDS 2097/183; born 1832, Co. Armagh; father of Charles Leonard Dobbyn Maxwell, DI, RIC; 3rd SI 25/3/1850; married in 1865 (Armagh Registrar's District, 1865, vol. 1, p. 50); died 13/3/1871 at Glasdrummond, Co. Fermanagh (Lisnaskea Registrar's District, 1871, vol. 3, p. 176); will proved on 12/7/1871 at the Principal Registry by the oath of Elizabeth Wilhelmina Maxwell, of Belturbet, Co. Cavan – effects £200.

May, Walter M.C.; RIC 76104; ADRIC no. 164; LDS 2098/204B; born 20/3/1888, Lancs., England; (West Derby Registrar's District, March Quarter, 1888, vol. 8b, p. 652); captain, army; married on 23/12/1914, Ada Calderwood, a native of Hampshire; 3rd DI 12/1/1920; dismissed 6/4/1921 by the Chief of Police for absenting himself from his station.

Mayne, Charles Edward Bolton; RIC 24613; LDS 2097/225; born 13/1/1840, Dublin City, Co. Dublin; 3rd SI 21/3/1859; married Charlotte Emily Henrietta Sweetman and their daughter was the novelist, Ethel Colburn Mayne; son Edward Colborn (Kinsale Registrar's District, vol. 10, p. 465) born on 5/1/1869 at Kinsale, Co. Cork (*Cork Examiner* 13/1/1869); son Charles Sydney Bolton Mayne (Kinsale Registrar's District, vol. 15, p. 409) born on 2/8/1870 at Kinsale, Co. Cork (*Cork Examiner* 6/8/1870) and died aged 27 days at Kinsale on 29/8/1870 (*Cork Examiner* 31/8/1870); temporary resident magistrate 24/7/1882; permanent RM 3rd class 28/10/1882, 2nd class 3/7/1889, 1st class 10/3/1902; pensioned 13/1/1905; (p. 46, RM Records of Service Book, National Archives, Dublin).

McArdle, Daniel; RIC 5621; LDS 2097/265; born 1822, Co. Monaghan; 3rd SI 1/11/1867; pensioned 1/10/1882; died 27/11/1891 at Bundoran, Co. Donegal; administration granted on 30/5/1892 at Derry to Patrick McArdle, Bundoran, Co. Donegal, Gent., the brother – effects £1,148.10s.10d.

McArdle, William Henry; RIC 23096; LDS 2097/312; born 1836, Canada; wife from Co. Wicklow; 3rd SI 1/7/1881; pensioned 1/1/1900; died 10/5/1912 at Ashfield House, Glandore Avenue, Antrim Road, Belfast; buried on 13/5/1912; will proved on 24/6/1912 at Belfast by the oath of Susan McArdle, the widow – effects £791.16s.4d.

McBride, William John; RIC 53152; LDS 2098/115B; born 13/7/1867, Co. Tyrone; (Cookstown Registrar's District, 1867, vol. 11, p. 511); married on 10/4/1901 (Downpatrick Registrar's District, June Quarter, 1901, vol. 1, p. 642), wife a native of Co. Galway; 3rd DI 14/5/1920; Temporary Police Instructor, RIC Camp, Newtownards, Co. Down from 8/11/1920 to 31/5/1922; pensioned 31/5/1922; transferred to the Royal Ulster Constabulary on 1/6/1922.

McCaffrey, James; RIC 29565; LDS 2098/057; born 1844, Co. Fermanagh; wife a native of Co. Fermanagh; 3rd DI 10/10/1889; King Edward VII Visit to Ireland Medal, 1903; pensioned 31/7/1905; died 16/2/1913 at Benview, Swanlinbar, Co. Cavan; will proved on 4/9/1913 at the Principal Registry to Annie McGovern, widow and Robert Mecredy, solicitor – effects £1,013.7s.4d.

McCarthy, Samuel Trant; RIC 19014; LDS 2097/206; born 1833, Co. Cork; 3rd SI 18/10/1854; received a favourable record on 31/12/1870 for the prompt arrest of a murderer and conviction on circumstantial evidence; died 20/1/1871 aged 37 years, at Portlaw, Co. Waterford (*Cork Examiner* 23/1/1871); will proved on 20/2/1871 at Waterford by the oath of Thomas Barry, George's Quay, Waterford, solicitor – effects under £800.

McCartney, James; CarNB; baronial chief constable; C.C. Drogheda, Co. Louth.

McCaughey, Michael Francis; RIC 67290; LDS 2098/211B; born 19/12/1892, Lisburn, Co. Down; (Lisburn Registrar's District, June Quarter, 1892, vol. 1, p. 625); 2nd lieutenant, Irish Guards and transferred to the Indian Army Reserve; 3rd DI 12/1/1920; killed 1/6/1921, Castlemaine, Co. Kerry; (WO 374/43642).

McCauley, William John; RIC 35984; LDS 2098/074; born 1849, Co. Antrim; 3rd DI 25/3/1891; King Edward VII Visit to Ireland Medal, 1903; pensioned 13/9/1909; died 26/1/1918 at Kenbally, Brisbane, Co. Antrim; administration granted on 20/3/1918 at the Principal Registry.

McClelland, Adam; RIC 5212; LDS 2097/288; born 1822, Co. Armagh; father of Thomas Lucas McClelland, DI RIC and Alfred Valentine McClelland, DI, RIC; as a constable he was seconded to the Commissariat Department in the Crimea; wife from Co. Carlow; 3rd SI 1/11/1871; pensioned 19/11/1883; died 24/10/1908; buried in Deansgrange Cemetery, Dublin (South Section, Row M1, Grave No. 35) with his wife Annie (b.1834) (d.24/10/1896 – Dublin

North Registrar's District, 1896, December Quarter, vol. 2, p. 388), son Alfred Valentine (d.6/8/1934, aged 68 years) and daughters Alice (d.8/8/1927, aged 64 years) and Emily (d.27/10/1932, aged 75 years); (photo in the *Constabulary Gazette*, vol. VI, no. 13, 23/12/1899, p. 390).

McClelland, Alfred Valentine; RIC 51682; LDS 2098/015; born 1866, Co. Wicklow; (Rathdown Registrar's District, 1866, vol. 2, p. 1005); son of Adam McClelland, SI, RIC and brother of Thomas Lucas McClelland, SI, RIC; 3rd DI 25/5/1886; barrackmaster of the Phoenix Park Depot 1/10/1919; pensioned 31/8/1922; died 6/8/1834; buried in Deansgrange Cemetery, Dublin (South Section, Row M1, Grave No. 35) with his parents and sisters Alice (d.8/8/1927, aged 64 years) and Emily (d.27/10/1932, aged 75 years).

McClelland, Thomas Lucas; RIC 43062; LDS 2097/294; born 1858, Co. Wicklow; son of Adam McClelland, SI, RIC and brother of Alfred Valentine McClelland, DI, RIC; married on 19/12/1882, wife from Co. Kilkenny; (Callan Registrar's District, 1882, December Quarter, vol. 4, p. 177); 3rd SI 3/11/1877; King George V Coronation Medal, 1911; died 15/7/1916 at 9, Fitzwilliam Terrace, Rathmines, Dublin, late of Boyle, Co. Roscommon; buried in Deansgrange Cemetery, Dublin (South West Section, Row T1, Grave No. 86; will proved on 19/10/1916 at the Principal Registry by the oath of Alfred Valentine McClelland, DI, RIC and Alfred E. Mayston – effects £2,320.7s.4d.

McClintock, George Fitzgerald Hill; LDS 2097/165; born 1826, Sussex, England; Londonderry Regiment; 3rd SI 11/5/1848; received an approbation on 31/12/1855 for zealous exertions in making amenable the perpetrators of the murder of John Gannon; pensioned 31/5/1885; died 27/10/1885 at Rathdrum, Co. Wicklow; will proved on 27/11/1885 at the Principal Registry by the oath of Clementina McClintock, of Charleville Road, Rathgar, Co. Dublin, widow, the sole executrix – effects £1,166.2s.1d.

McClintock, Samuel; LDS 2097/041; of Newtown, Co. Louth and Seskinore House, Omagh, Co. Tyrone; lieutenant, 18th Regiment Foot, Royal Irish Regiment; married firstly, Jane (d.1837), daughter of Lieutenant Colonel Lane; married secondly Dorothea, fourth daughter of John Knox, of Moyne Abbey and they had two sons, Col. George Perry (6/11/1839–26/12/1887) 4th Battalion, Royal Inniskilling Fusiliers and Samuel John (d.1856); 3rd SI 30/6/1823; High Sheriff of Co. Louth, 1843; died 13/12/1852; C.C. Rathkenny House, Navan, Co. Meath, 1835 and Co. Kilkenny.

McConnell, John James; RIC 63141; LDS 2098/180B; born 13/12/1886, Co. Monaghan; (Cootehill Registrar's District, December Quarter, 1886, vol. 3, p. 124); married on 25/1/1916 (Newry Registrar's District, March Quarter, 1916, vol. 1, p. 953), wife a native of Co. Louth; 3rd DI 16/10/1920; pensioned 17/7/1922 at Rathdrum, Co. Wicklow; (WS 509, Bureau of Military History, 1915–1921).

McConnell, Michael Joseph; RIC 67810; LDS 2098/210B; born 1/6/1892, Co. Cork; (Cork Registrar's District, September Quarter, 1892, vol. 5, p. 101); captain, Leinster Regiment; 3rd DI 12/1/1920; Convoy Officer from 8/12/1920 to 25/3/1922 at Gormanstown RIC Camp; pensioned 25/3/1922; transferred to the Palestine Gendarmerie on 26/3/1922.

McCormack, Henry; LDS 2097/172; born 1802, Co. Wicklow; enlisted as a sub constable on 3/11/1823; wife a native of the city of Dublin; 3rd SI 1/6/1848; pensioned 17/11/1862; died 14/5/1868.

McCormick, Francis Edward; LDS 2098/060B; born 6/1/1891, Newtownards, Co. Down; (Newtownards Registrar's District, March Quarter, 1891, vol. 1, p. 794); BA, LLB; 3rd DI 13/4/1915; died 9/7/1917 of tuberculosis at Belper, Dunsany, Dunshaughlin, Co. Meath; will proved at the Principal Registry on 4/9/1917 by the oath of Frederick J. Dempsey – effects £58.13s.3d.

McCormick, John; RIC 10092; LDS 2097/277; born, 1828, Co. Roscommon; 3rd SI 18/4/1869; pensioned 1/7/1879; died 5/1/1885 at Bay View Avenue, North Strand, Dublin;

buried in Glasnevin Cemetery, Dublin on 7/1/1885; administration granted on 13/2/1885 at the Principal Registry to Jane Helen McCormick, 38 Bayview Avenue, North Strand, Dublin – effects £494.1s.0d.

McCoy, John; RIC 43072; LDS 2098/212; born 18/9/1858, Co. Armagh; married on 14/6/1911 (Dublin South Registrar's District, June Quarter, 1911, 2, p. 699), J.V. Bourke, a native of Co. Westmeath; 3rd DI 1/9/1906; pensioned 6/9/1919; his son was born on 21/3/1913 at The Laurels, Newmarket, Co. Cork; (photo in the *Constabulary Gazette*, vol. XIX, no. 25, 8/9/1906).

McCullagh, George; LDS 2097/156; born 1821, Dublin City; clerk in the Dublin Metropolitan Police Office for seven years ending on 11/5/1839; clerk in the Constabulary Office from 11/5/1839 to 11/1/1847; his infant child, William Stratford Manners died on 11/11/1853 at Cashel, Co. Tipperary (*Cork Examiner* 16/11/1853); son born on 9/1/1861 at Arthurstown, Co. Wexford (*Cork Examiner* 14/1/1861); daughter born on 17/11/1863 at Arthurstown, Co. Wexford (*Cork Examiner* 23/11/1863); 3rd SI 20/1/1847; received an approbation on 30/9/1848 for prompt and judicious conduct in the pursuit and arrest of two persons charged with treasonable offences; received a grant from the Reward Fund on 30/9/1854 for prompt and intrepid conduct in the pursuit and capture of armed offenders; pensioned 17/11/1868; emigrated to New South Wales in 1870 for the benefit of his health, where he made an unsuccessful attempt to join the police in Melbourne, Victoria as an officer in citing thirty testimonials in his favour; he was offered a position in the detective police but declined same; died 1/11/1886.

McDermot, Edward J.; RIC 33676; LDS 2097/218; born 1837, Co. Galway; joined the Irish Revenue Police as a lieutenant on 10/6/1857 and served in Creeslough, Co. Donegal; 3rd DI 1/12/1857; resigned 26/11/1858.

McDermot, Hugh John; RIC 29459; LDS 2097/248; born 1845, Kenmare, Co. Kerry; 3rd SI 1/6/1864; received a favourable record on 30/6/1871 for the arrest of an offender of a serious assault and who was about to abscond; pensioned 16/8/1881; died 20/10/1913 at a private nursing home in Dublin.

McDermott, Edmond J.; LDS 2097/221; born 1834, Co. Derry; joined the Irish Revenue Police as a lieutenant on 1/12/1853; 3rd SI 25/3/1858; received a favourable record on 31/12/1870 for promptitude in proceeding to the scene of an agrarian outrage, whereby evidence was obtained which would otherwise have been lost and the guilty punished; pensioned 1/9/1878; died 27/10/1885 Dublin; (Dublin South Registrar's District, 1885, December Quarter, vol. 2, p. 425); (photo in the *Constabulary Gazette*, vol. VI, no. 13, 23/12/1899, p. 390).

McDonagh, Patrick William; RIC 55587; LDS 2098/055B; born 16/4/1872, Co. Derry; 3rd DI 29/9/1914; pensioned 17/10/1920.

McDonagh, Philip Valentine; RIC 52670; LDS 2098/230; born 10/9/1867, Newport, Co. Mayo; (Newport Registrar's District, 1867, vol. 19, p. 427); son of Philip McDonagh (b.1833, Co. Fermanagh), RIC 22497 and Ellen Doherty; married firstly on 2/10/1898 (Kilrush Registrar's District, December Quarter, 1898, vol. 4), Mrs Norah Savage, a native of Co. Clare; married secondly on 19/9/1911 (Cork Registrar's District, September Quarter, 1911, vol. 5, p. 112), wife a native of Co. Limerick; 3rd DI 5/5/1908; wounded, The Quay, Derry 15/5/1920; TCI 9/11/1920; pensioned 23/5/1922; died 16/4/1956; buried in Deansgrange Cemetery (Upper North Section, Row K2, Grave No. 19); with his wife, Mary (d.10/11/1956), his daughter, Doreen (d.3/6/1924) and his son, H.M. Bruce (d.19/5/1981).

McDonald, Augustus LeClerc; LDS 2097/308; born 1857, Athy, Co. Kildare; son of Canon MacDonald, of Athy, Co. Kildare and brother of Charles Montagu McDonald, SI, RIC; clerk in a merchant's office in Belfast for five years; married on 20/6/1883, wife from Co. Mayo; 3rd SI 6/10/1880; King George V Coronation Medal, 1911; pensioned 26/4/1920; (photo in the *Constabulary Gazette*, vol. XIV, no. 20, 2/2/1904).

165

165 Philip Valentine McDonagh.   166 John McGavern.   167 Charles Henry McGowan.

166

167

McDonald, Charles Montagu; LDS 2097/321; born 1860, Athy, Co. Kildare; youngest son of Canon MacDonald, of Athy, Co. Kildare and brother of Augustus LeClerc McDonald, SI, RIC; clerk at the Broadway Courts in Belfast; married on 12/8/1884, wife from Co. Kildare; 3rd SI 6/10/1882; died 19/2/1912 at 175, Rathgar Road, Dublin, late of Bagenalstown, Co. Carlow; will proved on 16/4/1912 to Kate C. McDonald, widow – effects £1,023.8s.5d.

McDonald, Hugh; CarNB; C.C. Co. Clare; Loughrea, Co. Galway.

McDonnell, James Andrew; RIC 65912; LDS 2098/025B; born 16/11/1888, Downpatrick, Co. Down; (Downpatrick Registrar's District, December Quarter, 1888, vol. 1, p. 471); 3rd DI 26/6/1911; King George V Visit to Ireland Medal, 1911; captain, 17th (Reserve) Battalion Royal Irish Rifles, from 11/4/1916 to 9/8/1919; wounded; TCI 1/4/1921; pensioned 13/7/1922.

McDonnell, Randle Frederick; LDS 2097/049; born 1802, Co. Mayo; 3rd SI 20/2/1824; CI 1/2/1838; pensioned 6/1/1844; died 1849.

McDonogh, Nicholas; LDS 2097/040; born 1783, Co. Galway; PPF; PPF Clerk from 15/5/1821 to 13/5/1823 for Counties Carlow, Kildare, Wicklow and Dublin; 3rd SI 13/5/1823; while serving as chief constable at Athy, Co. Kildare on 23 March 1824 he was convicted of the manslaughter on 26 November 1823 of two brothers William and Joseph McDarby, Clontierce, Queen's County and was sentenced to nine months imprisonment of which he served only four months and resumed his post as chief constable; pensioned 12/6/1842; died 16/11/1864 at Lowville, Co. Galway; will proved at the Principal Registry on 21/1/1865 by the oath of James William MacDonogh, of Lowville, near Ahascragh, Co. Galway, Esquire, the sole executor – effects under £3,000 – resworn on 14/9/1877 under £6,000.

McDonough, James; CarNB; 3rd SI 1/12/1828; C.C. Thurles, Co. Tipperary.

McEntee, Patrick; RIC 47381; LDS 2098/002B; born 27/11/1862, Co. Monaghan; married on 9/9/1896 (Dublin North Registrar's District, September Quarter, 1896, vol. 2, p. 508), wife a native of Co. Sligo; 3rd DI 18/1/1909; pensioned 9/7/1920.

McFarland, George Andrew; RIC 72008; LDS 2098/162B; born 28/7/1893, Co. Sligo; (Sligo Registrar's District, September Quarter, 1893, vol. 2, p. 270); army; 3rd DI 12/1/1920; pensioned 31/5/1922; transferred to the Royal Ulster Constabulary on 1/6/1922.

McFarland, John; RIC 72332; ADRIC no. 140; LDS 2098/200B; born 28/2/1891, Co. Leitrim; captain, army; 3rd DI 10/1/1920; pensioned 29/3/1922; joined the Palestine Gendarmerie on 30/3/1922.

McGarry, James Edward; RIC 52387; LDS 2098/050B; born 15/6/1866, Garrison, Co. Fermanagh; (Clones Registrar's District, 1866, vol. 13, p. 160); married on 14/6/1899 (Dublin North Registrar's District, June Quarter, 1899, vol. 2, p. 508), wife a native of Co. Tipperary; 3rd DI 12/11/1913; pensioned 12/5/1922; died 10/2/1952.

McGavern, John; RIC 9997; LDS 2097/278; born 1829, Co. Cavan; wife a native of Co. Monaghan; 3rd SI 4/6/1869; pensioned 16/12/1888; died 3/2/1911 at Ardganagh, Ballsbridge, Dublin; will proved on 16/3/1911 at the Principal Registry by the oath of William J. Seddall, solicitor – effects £303.14s.11d.

McGee, Michael; RIC 22739; LDS 2097/316; born 1839, Co. Tipperary; 3rd SI 16/1/1882; pensioned 1/11/1899.

McGetrick, Thomas; RIC 54165; LDS 2098/030B; born 29/3/1867, Tubbercurry, Co. Sligo; (Tubbercurry Registrar's District, 1867, vol. 19, p. 533); married on 4/8/1908 (Birr Registrar's District, September Quarter, 1908, vol. 3, p. 284), wife a native of King's County; 3rd DI 30/10/1911; pensioned 14/4/1922 and assisted the Provisional Government when transferred to the Civic Guards (later styled the Garda Síochána), serving as chairman of sub committee on conditions of service.

McGinley, William J.; RIC 44323; LDS 2098/192; born 1858, Co. Westmeath; married on 13/11/1888, wife a native of Co. Kilkenny; 3rd DI 25/7/1902; King Edward VII Visit to Ireland

Medal, 1903; pensioned 31/5/1919; (photo in the *Constabulary Gazette*, vol. X, no. 16, 11/1/1902).

McGlin, John; RIC 57819; LDS 2098/223B; born 13/3/1876, Co. Longford; (Longford Registrar's District, 1876, vol. 18, p. 213); 3rd DI 12/1/1920; pensioned 11/4/1922.

McGovern, Bernard; RIC 41494; LDS 2098/188; born 1857, Co. Leitrim; married in April 1883 (Limerick Registrar's District, June Quarter, 1883, vol. 5, p. 265), wife a native of Co. Limerick; 3rd DI 15/5/1902; pensioned 31/5/1919; (photo in the *Constabulary Gazette*, vol. V, no. 19, 1/2/1902).

McGovern, Peter; RIC 55337; LDS 2098/173B; born 23/6/1873, Co. Cavan; married on 2/9/1903 (Larne Registrar's District, September Quarter, 1903, vol. 1, p. 867), wife a native of Co. Antrim; 3rd DI 16/10/1920; pensioned 17/5/1922.

McGowan, Charles Henry; RIC 52858; LDS 2098/075B; born 29/10/1869, Tubberscanavan, Collooney, Co. Sligo; assistant teacher; married on 22/11/1900, wife a native of Co. Limerick; 3rd DI 4/1/1917; pensioned 1/12/1920; died 8/6/1938, Edrington, Birmingham, Warks., England; (Birmingham Registrar's District, June Quarter, 1938, vol. 6a, p. 65); buried in Edrington Abbey Cemetery, Birmingham.

McGrath, Marcus A.; LDS 2097/071; born 1801, Co. Dublin; enlisted as constable in November 1825; 3rd SI 1/8/1831; pensioned 1/10/1855; died 15/7/1872 at Dublin; (Dublin North Registrar's District, 1872, vol. 12, p. 368).

McGrath, Thomas James; LDS 2098/219B; born 30/8/1890, Rathkeale, Co. Limerick; (Rathkeale Registrar's District, September Quarter, 1890, vol. 5, p. 444); lieutenant, West Yorkshire Regiment; 3rd DI 12/1/1920; killed 7/1/1921, Ballinalee, Co. Longford; administration granted at the Principal Registry on 25/8/1921.

McGregor, Duncan (General) Sir; born 16/3/1787; Lieutenant-General James Shaw Kennedy was the first Inspector General following the re-organization of the Constabulary on 1/6/1836 and he was assisted by Major George Warburton, a former Provincial Inspector General for Connaught as his senior deputy. Following Shaw Kennedy's resignation on 15/3/1838 the post was offered to Colonel (afterwards General Sir Duncan) McGregor who was then serving in Canada. Because of the distance and time in receiving his acceptance of the post it became necessary to appoint Major Warburton as Inspector General 'pro tempore' so that some important administrative matters could be dealt with by the Inspector General in person. He relinquished the post on the arrival of Duncan, the candidate favoured by the Government, and this explains his short tenure of office as Inspector General. On 1 July 1838 McGregor was sworn in as Inspector General of the Constabulary of Ireland. He was residing at Drumcondra Castle, Dublin.

A descendant of the McGregor's of Glengyle in Scotland whose family seat bordered Loch Katrine in the Trossacks, north of Aberfoyle, Col. Duncan McGregor's great grandfather had been 'Rob Roy' McGregor, famous for his exploits as a cattle rustler. His grandfather had been badly wounded in 1745 fighting for Prince Charlie at the Battle of Prestonpans. Sir Duncan's own military record is worth quoting as it appears in the Regimental records. He enlisted in the Army as an Ensign on 12/7/1800, aged 13 years; lieutenant in the 72nd Highlanders on 31/8/1801, to the 55th Regiment of Foot (Westmoreland Regiment) on 13/8/1802, captain 78th Regiment of Foot (Fraser's Highlanders Regiment) on 17/4/1804, major on 25/11/1813; lieutenant-colonel on 26/5/1825, colonel on 28/6/1838 and placed on half pay on 27/7/1838 and inspector general on 1/7/1838, lieutenant-general on 12/12/1857, retired as inspector general of the Irish Constabulary on 19/10/1858 and general on 28/10/1864.

He served in Sicily and Italy in the Mediterranean in 1806 and was severely wounded in the shoulder by a musket shot in the Battle of Maida. Thereafter he served in Egypt in 1807; in Holland and in the Peninsular Campaign, 1813–14. He returned to Scotland and was retained on half pay without active service until recalled to leave as a major with the 31st Regiment of Foot

(Huntingtonshire Regiment) for India in February 1825 on the ill fated East India Company's ship *Kent* – a fine ship of 1,350 tons under Captain Henry Cobb. Disaster was to follow: the *Kent* took fire on 1/3/1825 when in the Bay of Biscay and it was necessary to flood the underdeck with sea water in an attempt to extinguish the fire. On board, in addition to the crew of 148, were 20 private passengers, 20 soldiers and 344 soldiers accompanied by 66 children including Mrs McGregor and her infant son.

Efforts to extinguish the fire were unsuccessful and passengers were preparing for a watery grave in the stormy sea when a lookout spotted an approaching ship, the 200 tons *Cambria* with Captain Cook and a group of Cornish miners on board. Despite the dreadful storm and the difficulty in handling the small row boats most of the passengers of the *Kent* were rescued. Having burned for about ten hours the fire reached the ship's magazine and a violent explosion destroyed the *Kent*.

The overladen *Cambria* arrived in Falmouth Harbour on 5 March 1825 and on the following Sunday all the survivors crowded into the local church to thank God for their safe return. In a subsequent report to the Royal Humane Society testimony was given to the efforts of those involved in the rescue and in maintaining discipline on the stricken ship. The Society's silver medals were awarded to Colonel Fearon, Major McGregor and Captain Cobb.

An interesting aside to the *Kent* disaster is the report properly authenticated while the fire was raging and with no hope of rescue Duncan McGregor wrote the following lines to his father. 'The ship *Kent*, *Indiaman*, is on fire. Elizabeth, Joanna and I commit our spirits into the hands of the blessed Redeemer. His grace enables us to be quite composed in the awful prospect of entering Eternity.' He placed the note in a bottle which was left in the cabin and blown into the sea by the explosion which destroyed the *Kent*. It was subsequently picked up on 30 September 1826 on the shore at Barbados and returned to Duncan McGregor.

The life story of Duncan McGregor would not be complete without some reference to Colonel McGregor as Inspector General and for this I quote from Curtis' *History of the RIC* in which he refers to the opinion of Mr and Mrs S.C. Hall, two eminent writers of the day. 'The present inspector-general – is Colonel McGregor, an officer of great experience, derived from sources in various parts of the world. It is admitted on all hands, that no man is better calculated to occupy so important a position; and he has succeeded – a task by no means easy – in governing the force without incurring the charge of recognizing any party. Indeed, the great efficiency of the Force arises from the fact that its chief officers have removed all suspicion of its being biased by undue motives, and to the respect and esteem in which the inspector-general is universally held. He is emphatically popular amongst all classes. In every instance where we consulted the officers or the men upon this point, we received but one answer, given with a feeling akin to personal affection.'

KCB 28/12/1848 for his services in Ireland. Author of a narrative of the loss of the *Kent*, By a Passenger, 1825, 7th ed. 1860. McGregor resided at Belvedere House, Drumcondra, Dublin in 1874, now St Patrick's Training College for teachers. His first son John (1825–92) was a canoeist and philanthropist; among his books was *Our Brothers and Cousins* (1859), an account of his tour in the U.S.A. and Canada. He gave the profits of his books and lectures – some £10,000 – to philanthropic institutions. His second son, Col. Henry Grey McGregor, born 1838, 17th Regiment of Foot (Leicestershire Regiment) was married on 6/8/1863 at St Stephen's Church, by the Right Lord Bishop of Cork, assisted by Rev. P.E. Singer, rector of Stackallen, brother-in-law of the bride, to Rosetta, youngest daughter of the Right Hon. Joseph Napier, ex-Lord Chancellor of Ireland (*Cork Examiner* 8/8/1863). Col. Henry Grey McGregor retired from the army in 1895. Sir Duncan's third son, Sir Evin McGregor, born 1842, became Permanent Secretary of the Admiralty in 1884. His fourth son, Douglas Alexander McGregor enlisted in the army as an ensign in 1853, was promoted lieutenant in 1854 and was killed while serving with the 97th Regiment of Foot (Queen's Own Germans Regiment) on 8/9/1855 in the final storming of the Great Redan, Sebastopol, Crimea (*Cork Examiner* 19/9/1855). Sir Duncan died on 8 June

1881 at 2 Van Brugh Park, Blackheath, Kent and he is buried in Mount Jerome Cemetery, Dublin. (Photograph of painting dated 1837 in *RUC Gazette Supplement P*roceedings dated December, 1995).

McGuire, Ephraim Albert; RIC 44568; LDS 2097/301; born 18/6/1858, Staughton's Row, Tralee, Co. Kerry; son of John McGuire, SI, RIC and brother of John Alexander McGuire, CI, RIC; 3rd SI 23/7/1879; died 21/8/1882 at Tralee, Co. Kerry; administration granted on 17/11/1882 at Cork to John McGuire, father of the deceased – effects £70.9s.0d.

McGuire, John; LDS 2097/166; born 1809, Co. Clare; enlisted as a sub constable in May 1827; wife a native of Co. Tipperary; received a slight injury while defending the police barrack at Templetuohy, Co. Tipperary on 16/11/1828; father of Ephraim Albert McGuire, SI, RIC, born on 18/6/1858 at his residence, Staughton's Row, Tralee, Co. Kerry (*Cork Examiner* 22/6/1858) and John Alexander McGuire, CI, RIC; his fifth son, Francis Henry, aged 10 years died on 10/7/1864 (Tralee Registrar's District, vol. 15, p. 394) in Tralee, Co. Kerry, after forty eight hours illness of scarlatina (*Cork Examiner* 11/7/1864); 3rd SI 30/5/1848; received an approbation on 31/3/1856 for spirited exertions in an arrest and prosecution to conviction in a murder case; pensioned 15/4/1875; died 17/6/1888 at 4 Staughton's Row, Tralee, Co. Kerry; will proved on 24/7/1888 at Cork by the oath of John Alexander McGuire, of Clones, Co. Monaghan, DI, RIC, sole executor – effects £280; his youngest daughter, Alice Susan, died at Staughton's Row, Tralee on 28/6/1873.

McGuire, John Alexander; RIC 39178; LDS 2097/293; born 1853, Co. Cork; son of John McGuire, SI, RIC and brother of Ephraim Albert McGuire, SI, RIC; 3rd SI 7/4/1873; CI 1/7/1898; King George V Coronation Medal, 1911; pensioned 25/2/1913; daughter born on 22/8/1901 at Cartown House, Carrick-on-Shannon, Co. Leitrim; (photo in the *Constabulary Gazette*, vol. XVI, no. 12, 10/12/1904 & vol. XIII, no. 8, 16/5/1903).

McGuire, Owen; RIC 5686; LDS 2097/289; born 1825, Co. Monaghan; wife a native of Co. Dublin; 3rd SI 18/6/1872; died 20/1/1883 at Kilmallock, Co. Limerick (Kilmallock Registrar's District, 1866, March Quarter, vol. 5, p. 271).

McHugh, John; LDS 2098/223; born 16/7/1886; Co. Leitrim; (Bawnboy Registrar's District, September Quarter, 1886, vol. 3, p. 30); son of Patrick McHugh, DI, RIC; second division clerk in the Land Commission for 1 year and 9 months; married on 10/1/1899 (Manorhamilton Registrar's District, June Quarter, 1899, vol. 2, p. 189), wife a native of Co. Kerry; 3rd DI 14/4/1908; resigned 15/2/1910.

McHugh, Patrick; RIC 38552; LDS 2098/117; born 1854, Co. Leitrim; father of John McHugh, DI, RIC; 3rd DI 1/8/1896; King Edward VII Visit to Ireland Medal, 1903; King George V Coronation Medal, 1911; pensioned 1/1/1915; (photo in the *Constabulary Gazette*, vol. V, no. 19, 5/8/1899).

McKean, Richard; RIC 16742; LDS 2097/297; born 1834, Co. Galway; 3rd DI 1/9/1878; died 21/5/1893 at 14, Sandy Street, Newry, Co. Down; will proved on 12/8/1893 at the Principal Registry by the oath of John Mullins, of Ramelton, Co. Donegal, solicitor, the sole executor – effects £743.1s.0d.

McKee, Herbert Malcolm; RIC 69950; LDS 2098/107B; born 6/8/1892, Co. Antrim; (Belfast Registrar's District, September Quarter, 1892, vol. 1, p. 265); lieutenant, Royal Army Services Corps; 3rd DI 14/5/1920; pensioned 4/6/1922.

McKelvey, Alexander; RIC 20259; LDS 2097/249; born 1844, Co. Monaghan; son of Charles McKelvey, SI, RIC; clerk in the Ulster Bank, Downpatrick, Co. Down from 26/3/1863 to 11/6/1864; 3rd SI 1/9/1864; dismissed 6/9/1880.

McKelvey, Charles; LDS 2097/131; born 1800, Co. Fermanagh; father of Alexander McKelvey, SI, RIC; enlisted as a sub constable on 6/2/1820; 3rd SI 1/4/1840; pensioned 7/11/1869; died 26/9/1871 at Belfast, Co. Antrim; (Belfast Registrar's District, vol. 11, p. 238).

McKenna, Stephen Joseph; LDS 2097/212; born 1838, Co. Dublin; 3rd SI 3/11/1857; resigned 3/4/1860 on being gazetted to an ensigncy in the 28th Regiment of Foot (North Gloucestershire Regiment).

McKinstry, Alexander; born Co. Antrim; LDS 2097/114; major; 3rd SI 31/7/1837.

McKinstry, Lee; LDS 2097/125; born 1815, Co. Armagh; 3rd SI 11/3/1839; pensioned 12/10/1860; died 29/10/1872 at Roslin, Sandymount, Co. Dublin, late of Oriel Lodge, Belturbet, Co. Cavan; buried in Mount Jerome Cemetery, Dublin; administration granted on 23/12/1872 at the Principal Registry to Mary Jane McKinstry, Oriel Lodge, Belturbet, Co. Cavan – effects under £6,000.

McKnight, Matthew; CarNB; born 1798, Derrybrusk, Co. Fermanagh; 3rd SI 10/8/1824.

McLean, Anthony; RIC 55200; LDS 2098/065B; born 20/4/1871, Co. Mayo; married on 9/10/1910 (Listowel Registrar's District, December Quarter, 1910, vol. 5, p. 241), wife a native of Co. Kerry; 3rd DI 7/1/1915; pensioned 15/5/1922.

McLoughlin, Roger; RIC 3238; LDS 2097/255; born 1818, Co. Galway; wife a native of Co. Roscommon; 3rd SI 1/12/1865; died 5/10/1880 at Carrick-on-Suir, Co. Tipperary; (Carrick-on-Suir Registrar's District, 1880, December Quarter, vol. 4, p. 351).

McMahon, James; LDS 2098/161; born 1854, Co. Monaghan; married on 6/4/1882 (Claremorris Registrar's District, June Quarter, 1882, vol. 4, p. 69), wife a native of Co. Mayo; 3rd DI 11/9/1899; pensioned 11/1/1917.

McMahon, Patrick; RIC 40356; LDS 2098/128; born 6/7/1855, Co. Monaghan; married on 6/7/1897 (Tulla Registrar's District, September Quarter, 1897, vol. 4, p. 171), Helena Hogan, a native of Co. Clare; 3rd DI 16/12/1896; King Edward VII Visit to Ireland Medal, 1903; pensioned 6/7/1915; died 3/3/1927 in Dublin; (Dublin South Registrar's District, 1927, March Quarter, vol. 2, p. 478).

McMahon, Thomas; RIC 53844; LDS 2098/085B; born 1871, Co. Monaghan; (Monaghan Registrar's District, 1871, vol. 8, p. 339); 3rd DI 1/1/1918; pensioned 13/4/1922.

McMahon, Timothy; LDS 2097/093; born 1810, Co. Clare; 3rd SI 23/1/1836; CI 21/4/1859; pensioned 10/4/1873; died 4/3/1890 at Tulla, Co. Clare (Tulla Registrar's District, 1890, June Quarter, vol. 4, p. 329).

McMahon-O'Byrne, Dermot; RIC 73572; ADRIC no. 634; LDS 2099/034; born 26/9/1889, Co. Dublin; married on 22/12/1918, wife from Co. Monaghan; lieutenant, Royal Army Services Corps and Royal Field Artillery, 12/9/1914–24/6/1919; ADRIC, 27/9/1920–26/8/1921; 3rd DI 25/6/1921; pensioned 21/4/1922.

McMonagle, William Thomas; RIC 72006; LDS 2098/172B; born 15/6/1898, Muff, Co. Donegal; (Derry Registrar's District, 1898, September Quarter, vol. 2, p. 156); educated at the Model School, Derry, Co. Derry; apprentice druggist; acting corporal, No. 34544 Royal Army Medical Corps, 4/9/1914; 2nd lieutenant, 5th Battalion, Rifle Brigade, 5/10/1917; 3rd DI 10/1/1920; pensioned 19/4/1922. He married Violet E. Wafer and emigrated from Ireland to Canada in 1927; (WO 374/45148).

McMullan, James; LDS 2097/169; born 1806, Co. Antrim; enlisted as a sub constable on 1/1/1825; wife a native of Co. Down; 3rd SI 1/6/1848; died 2/5/1861 at Cookstown, Co. Tyrone; letters of administration granted to Margaret McMullan, Cookstown, Co. Tyrone, widow of the deceased, on 4/6/1861 at Armagh – effects under £800.

McNally, John; RIC 55279; LDS 2098/217; born 1/4/1871, Tuam, Co. Galway; (Tuam Registrar's District, 1871, vol. 9, p. 643); married on 13/4/1899, Ballinasloe Registrar's District, June Quarter, 1899, vol. 4, p. 9), wife a native of Yorkshire; 3rd DI 12/1/1906; TCI 8/11/1920; pensioned 31/5/1922; transferred to the Royal Ulster Constabulary on 1/6/1922; (photo in the *Constabulary Gazette*, vol. XXIX, no. 12, 3/6/1911, p. 196).

McNamara, Richard; LDS 2097/131; born 1786, Co. Clare; captain, 2nd Royal Lancers and 20th Dragoons from 1810 to 1817; 3rd SI 1/7/1840; paymaster 1/7/1840; died 7/5/1848.

McNamara, Thomas; RIC 20395; LDS 2097/317; born 1838, Co. Limerick; 3rd SI 9/1/1882; pensioned 16/12/1896; died 2/7/1911 at Millbank Cottage, Mountrath, Queen's County.

McNeale, James Wolfe; CarNB; born, Co. Louth; son of J. Wolfe MacNeale, Carlingford, Co. Louth; 3rd SI 30/12/1824; on 12/1/1826 applied for a week's leave to attended examinations at Trinity College Dublin commencing 20/1/1826 and was refused permission by Under Secretary William Gregory who stated 'Quite impossible to grant leave for such a purpose'; wounded in an attack on the police on protection duty at an election in Monaghan on 24/6/1826 and died of his wounds in January 1827; C.C. Emyvale, Co. Monaghan.

McNeale, John D.; RIC 13121; LDS 2097/179; born 1822, Co. Louth; 3rd SI 13/6/1849; resigned 1/2/1853 'in consequence of pecuniary difficulties.'

McNeill, Samuel; RIC 61715; LDS 2098/187B; born 20/11/1885, Omagh, Co. Tyrone; (Omagh Registrar's District, March Quarter, 1886, vol. 2, p. 267); 3rd DI 16/10/1920; pensioned 31/5/1922; transferred to the Royal Ulster Constabulary on 1/6/1922.

McNess, Jacob; LDS 2097/167; born 1803, Cork City; enlisted as a constable on 11/9/1831; his wife was a native of Boulogne, France; 3rd SI 1/6/1848; received injuries as a result of a fall from his horse on 24/3/1851; received an approbation on 31/12/1855 for zealous exertions in making amenable the perpetrators of the murder of John Gannon; pensioned 8/11/1869; died 25/1/1875 at Belturbet, Co. Cavan; (Cavan Registrar's District, 1875, vol. 3, p. 81); will proved on 4/3/1875 at Cavan by the oath of Rev. Patrick O'Reilly, of Staghall, Belturbet, Co. Cavan, PP, VF, of Drumlane, one of the executors – effects under £600.

McNess, James; RIC 288; LDS 2097/199; born 1806, Dublin City, Co. Dublin; 3rd SI 16/8/1853; died 16/12/1869.

McSweeny, Edward; LDS 2097/106; born 1807, Knocknane, Co. Kerry; 3rd SI 8/11/1836; died suddenly on 23/11/1845.

Meade, Edward Southwell; RIC 17918; LDS 2097/201; born 1832, Kinsale, Co. Cork; 3rd SI 1/6/1854; resigned 1/12/1857 in Co. Antrim.

Meagher, Martin; RIC 7127; LDS 2097/273; born 1826, Co. Kerry; served in the Crimea; 3rd SI 1/1/1869; died 19/5/1871 at Carlow, Co. Carlow; (Carlow Registrar's District, 1871, vol. 3, p. 345).

Mearing, George Edwin; RIC 79209; ADRIC no. 931; LDS 2099/041; born 1894, Reading, Glos., England; (Reading Registrar's District, 1894, vol. 2c, p. 329); army service, 1910–20; 30/9/1920–27/8/1921; married 30/12/1919, wife a native of Padworth, Berks., England; 3rd DI 20/9/1921; pensioned 1/5/1922.

Medlicott, Edward Richard; RIC 16163; LDS 2097/194; born 1832, Dunmurry, Co. Kildare; son of Edward James Medlicott, of Dunmurry, Co. Kildare (b.1790) (d.11/1/1868 – Rathdown Registrar's District, vol. 2, p. 807) and Anne (b.1805)(d.22/8/1866 – Rathdown Registrar's District, vol. 12, p. 654), daughter of Solomon Speer, of Granitefield, Co. Dublin, by his wife, Anne, daughter of Richard Donovan of Ballymore, Co. Wexford; 3rd SI 11/9/1852; he was one of the first four RIC officers to undergo training on 31/8/1861 at the School of Musketry, Fleetwood, North Lancs., England (*Cork Examiner* 26/8/1861); musketry instructor from 1/2/1869 until his death; died unmarried on 25/11/1872 at the Maison de Sante, Charlemont Street, Dublin, late of 37 Parkgate Street, Dublin; administration granted on 4/2/1873 at the Principal Registry to James Edward Medlicott (1827–1913), a brother of the deceased – effects £1,500.

Meehan, Patrick; RIC 29667; LDS 2098/010; born 1846, Co. Down; wife a native of Co. Mayo; 3rd DI 1/9/1885; pensioned 15/11/1906.

Mercer, George Dowers; RIC 29660; LDS 2097/249; born 2/8/1842, Kent, England; father of George Hugh Mercer, DI, RIC, RM; Indian Navy from 1/3/1858 to the abolition of the service on 30/4/1863; married on 18/9/1865, wife from Gloucester; 3rd SI 1/9/1864; temporary resident magistrate 24/7/1882; permanent RM 3rd class 28/10/1882, 2nd class

1/1/1892, 1st class 8/9/1902; pensioned 2/8/1907; (p. 49, RM Records of Service Book, National Archives, Dublin).

Mercer, George Hugh; RIC 55385; LDS 2098/087; born 25/9/1871, Baltinglass, Co. Wicklow; (Baltinglass Registrar's District, 1871, vol. 17, p. 453); son of George Dowers Mercer, SI, RIC, RM; married in January 1904 (Dublin South Registrar's District, March Quarter, 1904, vol. 2, p. 607), Miss Smith, a native of Co. Leitrim and daughter of a resident magistrate; 3rd DI 1/2/1893; King Edward VII Visit to Ireland Medal, 1903; King George V Visit to Ireland Medal, 1911; awarded a certificate from the Irish Police and Constabulary Recognition Fund; Private Secretary to the Inspector General from 27/1/1911 until his appointment as a resident magistrate 3rd class 22/3/1918, 2nd class 7/7/1919; (p. 165, RM Records of Service Book, National Archives, Dublin).

Meredith, Charles George; RIC 51005; LDS 2097/333; born 1862, Co. Louth; BA 1884, Trinity College Dublin; married on 5/6/1912, Miss E.M. Brady, a native of Co. Dublin; 3rd DI 30/10/1883; King Edward VII Visit to Ireland Medal, 1903; died 15/12/1916 at Adare, Co. Limerick; will proved on 12/2/1917 at the Principal Registry by the oath of Agnes L. Meredith, the widow – effects £1,410.0s.4d.

Meredith, William; LDS 2097/072; born 1806, Clonenagh, Queen's County; enlisted as a sub constable 1/10/1825; constable 1/12/1827; wife a native of Co. Tipperary; sons born in Dunfanaghy, Co. Donegal on 30/12/1849 (*Cork Examiner* 31/12/1849) and on 4/10/1861, in Ballaghadereen, Co. Mayo (*Cork Examiner* 7/10/1861); his third son, George died on 17/2/1863, at Ballaghadereen, Co. Mayo (*Cork Examiner* 21/2/1863); 3rd SI 1/9/1831; pensioned 11/04/1864; died 14/2/1872 at Dublin; (Dublin North Registrar's District, 1872, vol. 2, p. 551).

Mildenhall, Samuel Eldon; RIC 10636; LDS 2097/286; born 1828, Bowling Green, Kinsale, Co. Cork; son of Edmund Mildenhall, hotel keeper; married Margaret Rainsbury, from Tipperary S.R. at St Iberies Church in the Union of St Patrick's, Co. Wexford on 20/11/1859 (Wexford Registrar's District, vol. 10, p. 556); his daughter, Elizabeth was born on 3/8/1865 at Arthurstown, New Ross, Co. Wexford (New Ross Registrar's District, vol. 14, p. 818); 3rd SI 15/6/1871; died 19/5/1873 at Frankford, King's County; administration granted on 18/9/1873 at the Principal Registry to Margaret Mildenhall, Frankford, Parsonstown, King's County, widow of the deceased – effects under £300; his daughter, Marion, aged 19 years died on 7/2/1886 at Frankford, King's County (Parsonstown Registrar's District, 1886, March Quarter, vol. 3, p. 465); his son Edmund Mildenhall, RIC Sergeant 43633 died on 16/12/1894, aged 34 years (Dublin South Registrar's District, 1894, December Quarter, vol. 2, p. 511) and is buried in the RIC Plot in Mount Jerome Cemetery, Dublin; (photo: Carol Hale, North Vancouver, British Columbia, Canada).

Millar, William J.; RIC 50982; LDS 2097/329; born 1860, Co. Derry; MA, LLB, Royal University of Ireland; 3rd DI 22/2/1883; CI 15/1/1907; King George V Coronation Medal, 1911; pensioned 15/6/1920; (photo in the *Constabulary Gazette*, vol. XI, no. 22, 23/8/1902).

Miller, Arthur; CarNB; PPF; PPF Clerk 3/5/1816; major, 6th Regiment of Foot (1st Warwickshire Regiment); residing in Taghmon, Co. Wexford in 1826; his widow, Mrs Jane Miller died at 8 South Frederick Street, Dublin on 26/4/1846, aged 93 years.

Miller, James; CarNB; PPF; 3rd SI 14/12/1815; peace officer with the Dublin Police in the Head Police Office until his departure to the PPF in 1816; C.C. barony of Clanwilliam, Co. Tipperary.

Miller, William; CarNB; PPF; born 20/6/1785, Old Cumnock, Ayrshire, Scotland, the son of Rev. Thomas Miller and Janet Stewart. He entered the Army as a cadet in the Royal Artillery at the age of 16 years, 3 months and 10 days. He rose to become a Lieutenant Colonel in November 1851. He served in Sicily and Calabria from May 1806 to December 1807 and in the Netherlands and France from June to September 1815. On being appointed to an unattached Majority he was

168   169

168 Charles George Meredith.   **169** Samuel Eldon Mildenhall.

nominated Aide de Camp to Sir Colquhoun Grant, then Major General on the Staff in Ireland, until being Deputy Inspector General of Constabulary. He was Inspector General for Munster from 16/10/1827 to 1/6/1836, succeeding Sir Richard Willcocks with headquarters in Clonmel, Co. Tipperary and at Fermoy House, Fermoy, Co. Cork from December, 1828. He married at St Anne's Church, Dublin on 13 April 1814 (Marriage Licence granted in 1814 in the Dublin & Glendalough Diocese, NA Reference: M/2464) Frances Levinge, youngest daughter of Sir Charles Levinge (17/4/1751–10/1/796), 5th Bt., of High Park, Mullingar, Co. Westmeath and Elizabeth Frances (17/4/1751–19/5/1828), only daughter of Nicholas Reyney, of Reynella, Co. Westmeath, who were married on 26/6/1779. Frances Levinge Miller died on 9/1/1862 at 6 New Brighton Terrace, Monkstown, Co. Dublin (*Cork Examiner* 13/1/1862). They had the following children: Janette Frances D'Arcy, b.1/1/1815 at Westmeath; Louisa Margaret, b.19/12/1816 at Dublin; William Moore, b.8/11/1818 at Dublin; Charles Stuart, b.7/7/1820 at Dublin; Harriet Alicia, born at Westmeath on 1/4/1824; Selia Anne, born 27/4/1829 at Fermoy, Co. Cork. He was nicknamed 'Indispensable Miller' and he was also a Knight of the Guelphs — a Hanoverian Order instituted in 1815 to Commemorate the raising of Hanover to a Kingdom; however, this later became a foreign order on the accession of Queen Victoria. Col. Miller lived at 'Silverton' in Rathfarnham, Dublin. His son, Counsellor Miller was appointed a stipendiary magistrate in October, 1846 (*Cork Examiner* 7/10/1846); his brother-in-law was William Gregory, Under Secretary of State for Ireland, October 1822–1830; deputy inspector general Irish Constabulary, 1 June 1836, then residing at 4 Fitzwilliam Place, Dublin; pensioned 9/6/1848; Col. Miller died on 19 March 1852; buried in Mount Jerome Cemetery, Dublin (Registry No. 174) on 23/3/1852 (Section C, Grave No. 103, Grant No. 1395P); Chief Magistrate; C.C. Corrofin, Co. Clare. His obituary in the *Gentleman's Magazine* reads: 'At Silverton, Co. Dublin, age 66 years, Deputy Inspector General of the Constabulary of Ireland. Col. Miller was a brother of Dr Miller of Exeter'. (Will of William Miller of Silverton,

Rathfarnham, Dublin – PRO, Kew, Catalogue Reference: PROB 11/2155 / Dept: Records of the Prerogative Court of Canterbury and related Probate Jurisdictions: Will Registers / Volume number: 11 Quire Numbers: 501–550 / Date: 7 June 1852 / Image Reference: 38/28).

Miller, William T.; CarNB; arrested and jailed in Limerick for debt in May 1830; dismissed 25/11/1830 for gambling and being frequently in arrears to the men under his command; C.C. Listowel, Co. Kerry, 1828, Kilfinane, Co. Limerick, 1829.

Miller, William Verner; RIC 72012; LDS 2098/195B; born 27/5/1895, Co. Kilkenny; educated at Bishop Foy High School, Waterford and Trinity College Dublin, 1907–14; 2nd lieutenant, 8th Battalion, 14th Cheshire Regiment, 27/5/1915; wounded in the wrist in June 1915 while serving in Cork; wounded through the lung and liver in Mesopotamia, 11/4/1917; 3rd DI 10/1/1920; acting captain, 29/1/1917; relinquished commission, 19/7/1920 and granted the rank of captain, 19/7/1920 (*London Gazette* dated 19/7/1920); pensioned 31/5/1922; (WO 339/29531); transferred to the Royal Ulster Constabulary on 1/6/1922.

Milling, John Charles; RIC 56627; LDS 2098/115; born 27/3/1873, Glasson, near Athlone, Co. Westmeath; (Athlone Registrar's District, 1873, vol. 8, p. 20); son of Oliver Milling (1844–1906), CI, RIC; attended Ranelagh Endowed School, Athlone; 3rd DI 3/4/1895; married on 23/2/1897 (Dublin South Registrar's District, March Quarter, 1897, vol. 6, p. 658), Elizabeth 'Lilla' Malcolmson, daughter of Robert Malcolmson, solicitor, of Bennykerry Lodge, Carlow. Her sister, Isabel, married Charles Arthur Walsh, CI, RIC; author of *The R.I.C. ABC or Police Duties in relation to Acts of Parliament in Ireland* (Belfast, 1908); resident magistrate 3rd class 31/12/1914; killed 30/3/1919, Westport, Co. Mayo, late of Newport Road, Westport, Co. Mayo; buried in the Church of Ireland Cemetery, Westport, Co. Mayo; administration granted at Ballina on 29/4/1919; (p. 162, RM Records of Service Book, National Archives, Dublin).

Milling, John Thomas; RIC 28156; LDS 2097/242; born 1842, Ardee, Co. Louth; worked in the National Bank, Tralee for three years and the National Bank, Dublin for eight months; 3rd SI 1/11/1862; CI 1/5/1888; died 13/8/1893 at Bindon Street, Ennis, Co. Clare; administration granted on 27/9/1893 at the Principal Registry to Emily Milling, of Ennis, Co. Clare, the widow – effects £2,010.14s.3d.; buried in Mount Jerome Cemetery, Dublin on 16/8/1893 (Grave C114–5251).

Milling, Oliver; LDS 2097/170; born 1810, Ardee, Co. Louth; enlisted as a sub constable on 15/2/1828; wife a native of Co. Cavan; 3rd SI 1/6/1848; awarded the Constabulary Medal on 6/9/1867; CI 3/1/1873; pensioned 1/4/1877; died 5/6/1887 at 3 Glenageary Hill, Kingstown, Co. Dublin; will proved on 20/6/1887 at the Principal Registry by the oath of Harriett Milling, spinster, one of the executors – effects £2,181.

Milling, Oliver; RIC 30260; LDS 2097/253; born 1844, Ardee, Co. Louth; son of Oliver Milling (1810–1887), CI, RIC; 3rd SI 9/7/1865; CI 1/6/1887; King Edward VII Visit to Ireland Medal, 1903; married on 5/3/1867 (Dublin South Registrar's District, vol. 2, p. 839), in Dublin, Lizzie, daughter of John Milling, Esq., of Glenview House, Co. Meath (*Cork Examiner* 111/3/1867); he had four sons and three daughters; one of his sons practised as a dentist in Westland Row, Dublin having obtained a doctorate in dentistry in the United States; one of his daughters, Emma, died of a brain haemorrhage in 1897 and another son, Henry Desmond was killed in a rail accident in 1903 near Ballymoe, Co. Galway. Both children were interred in the Church of Ireland Cemetery in Westport, Co. Mayo; pensioned 29/5/1905; died at Margate, Kent 14/9/1906; buried at Margate on 17/9/1906; his granddaughter, Olive Eleanor Milling, daughter of Henry Milling, DDS, married at St Margaret's, Westminster on 6/12/1915, Captain C.A. McCalden, RAMC, eldest son of David and Mrs McCalden, of Lisnaskea, Co. Fermanagh.

Mills, James Cunningham; RIC 24987; LDS 2097/230; born 1840, Co. Dublin; son, Samuel, born on 8/12/1871 at Shannon Square, Clonakilty, Co. Cork (Clonakilty Registrar's District, vol. 9, p. 997) (*Cork Examiner* 11/12/1871); 3rd SI 19/9/1859; his daughter Josephine married in

1910, George Jordan Ball (b.3/9/1865)(d.4/1/1941), third son of Richard Ball (1812–90), of Moorsides, Clonalvy, Co. Meath; died 28/3/1921.

Mills, Joseph; RIC 8611; LDS 2097/288; born 1829, Co. Wicklow; 3rd SI 12/10/1871; pensioned 1/11/1880; his sister, Mary died at 106 Leinster Road, Rathmines, Dublin on 8/1/1893; died 9/10/1894 at 11 Grand Canal Terrace, Broadstone, Dublin; (Dublin South Registrar's District, 1921, June Quarter, vol. 2, p. 441); late of 25, Morehampton Road, Donnybrook, Dublin; will proved at the Principal Registry on 18/5/1921.

Minchin, William; LDS 2097/099; born 1793, Eversham, Co. Dublin; second son of Captain Falkiner Minchin (1757–1825), 27th Regiment of Foot (Inniskilling Regiment) and Maria, daughter of William Gabbett, of Caherline, Co. Limerick, who were married in 1786; father of William Burnett Minchin, SI, RIC; 3rd SI 1/10/1836; paymaster 1/10/1836; resigned 31/7/1841, having been reported for not surrendering his accounts; died 1843.

Minchin, William Burnett; RIC 25424; LDS 2097/234; born 29/7/1838, Eversham, Co. Dublin; second son of William Minchin (1793–1843), SI, RIC, of Annagh, Nenagh, Co. Tipperary and Georgina Minchin (d.1884), of Holywell House, Hants., who were married in 1829; 3rd SI 10/2/1860; pensioned 25/1/1880; died 3/7/1907.

Moffatt, Aaron; LDS 2097/100; born 1797, Ballymahon, Co. Longford; 3rd SI 1/10/1836; paymaster 1/10/1836 for counties Meath and Westmeath; discharged on pension on 31/5/1851, on the abolition of the office of paymaster; appointed a senior clerk in the Receiver's Office on 1/4/1851 and pensioned from the Receiver's Office on 1/12/1861; resided in retirement at Phillistown House, Co. Meath; his widow remarried William Allman, Esq., of Bandon, Co. Cork and their daughter, Emma, married on 9/11/1865, at St Mary's Church, Dublin, by the Rev. Benjamin Gibson, AM, W.B. Robertson, Esq., Wood Lodge, Monkstown, Co. Dublin and Curraghmore Castle, Co. Cork (*Cork Examiner* 11/11/1865).

Molloy, Louis Drake; RIC 31122; LDS 2097/254; born 1845, Castlepollard, Co. Westmeath; 3rd SI 1/1/1866; died 3/6/1876; administration granted on 7/7/1876 at the Principal Registry to Henry Beauchamp 4, of Castlepollard, Co. Westmeath, the father of the deceased – effects under £600.

Molloy, Michael John; RIC 54694; LDS 2098/038B; born 2/12/1871, Waterford, Co. Waterford; (Waterford Registrar's District, 1871, vol. 19, p. 938); married on 23/1/1901 (Nenagh Registrar's District, March Quarter, 1901, vol. 3, p. 405), wife a native of Co. Tipperary; 3rd DI 10/1/1912; awarded the Constabulary Medal 6/11/1917 'for conspicuous devotion to duty in handling with skill, courage and determination the men under his command at a serious riot' at Listowel, Co. Kerry on 10/10/1917; pensioned 13/4/1922.

Molony, George Arthur; RIC 13122; LDS 2097/180; born 1/3/1829, Co. Galway; 3rd SI 15/6/1849; resident magistrate 3rd class 1/10/1863, 2nd class 17/11/1868, 1st class 25/10/1885; pensioned 1/3/1894; died 11/11/1896 at Omagh, Co. Tyrone (Omagh Registrar's District, 1896, December Quarter, vol. 2, p. 171); will probated on 13/4/1897 by the oaths of William Molony, St James's Gate, Dublin, Esq., and Lewis Buchanan, of Edenfel, Omagh, Co. Tyrone, Colonel Enniskillen Fusiliers – effects – £3,02.17s.9d.; (p. 52, RM Records of Service Book, National Archives, Dublin).

Molony, Harry Brereton; RIC 57879; LDS 2098/118; born 1872, Kiltanon House, Tulla, Co. Clare; master at St Stephen's Green for three years, the Royal School, Armagh and also as a private tutor; BA 1894, Trinity College Dublin; married on 22/4/1914 (Dublin South Registrar's District, June Quarter, 1914, vol. 2, p. 619), Miss Whitney, a native of Dublin City; 3rd DI 1/10/1896; King Edward VII Visit to Ireland Medal, 1903; CI 14/1/1920; resigned 31/3/1920.

Molony, Walter; CarNB; son of Walter Weldon Molony and Mary, daughter of Dr Spelisy; his grandfather was James Molony (b.1717) of Kiltanon, near Tulla, Co. Clare, who married on 8/8/1751, Mary, daughter of Arthur Weldon, of Raheenderry, Queen's County; 3rd SI

1/10/1822; wife, nee Kelly and her five children residing in Claregalway in 1831; severely wounded while suppressing a riot in Galway in 1826; stipendiary magistrate 25/5/1831; retired as a SM in 1848 in Belfast; his son George Molony, Esq., married on 29/4/1852, at Omagh, Co. Tyrone, Susan Anabella, daughter of George Wade, CI, RIC (*Cork Examiner* 7/5/1852); C.C. Drumsna, Co. Leitrim; Gort, Co. Galway.

Molony, Walter Weldon; LDS 2097/129; born 1819, 3 Mountjoy Square South, Dublin, Co. Dublin; father of William Walter Francis Molony, SI, RIC; clerk in the Constabulary Office from 1/11/1838 to 20/11/1839; 3rd SI 21/11/1839; died 19/3/1847; his sister, Eliza Helen married John Croker Esq., of North Great George's Street, Dublin at Castlecomer, Co. Kilkenny on 8/3/1836.

Molony, William Walter Francis; RIC 35902; LDS 2097/279; born 1848, Co. Cavan; son of Walter Weldon Molony (1819–47), SI, RIC; medical student; 3rd SI 30/9/1869; captain, Royal Irish Fusiliers; married his cousin, Mary (Mai) Molony, of Co. Dublin on 9/8/1873; pensioned 16/1/1882.

Monahan, John; LDS 2097/149; born 1800, Co. Tyrone; enlisted as a constable on 1/8/1824; though on the Constabulary strength of Co. Cavan, he never served in that county in that he was employed in Sir Frederick Stovin's office from 1/12/1836 to 1/9/1837; employed in the post office; 3rd SI 16/9/1845; pensioned 25/11/1868; died 3/12/1889.

Monson, Thomas; RIC 36037; LDS 2098/067; born 1850, Boyle, Co. Roscommon; married secondly on 12/8/1895 (Manorhamilton Registrar's District, September Quarter, 1895, vol. 2, p. 1895), Sarah Anne Acheson, a native of Friarstown, Dromahair, Co. Leitrim; 3rd DI 20/1/1890; King Edward VII Visit to Ireland Medal, 1903; pensioned 1/1/1911; his first wife died at The Laurels, Newmarket, Co. Cork on 9/8/1892 and is buried in the Church of Ireland Cemetery, Newmarket, Co. Cork.

Montford, Edward Handcock; LDS 2097/044; born 28/3/1800, Killashee, Co. Longford; son of William Bradish Montfort (1774–1831), of Middleton, Co. Longford, lieutenant 60th Regiment of Foot (Royal American Regiment) and captain, Killashee Infantry and Abigail Handcock (d.16/2/1837) of Portarlington who were married on 8/12/1798; 3rd SI 1/10/1823; while stationed at Mohill, Co. Leitrim on 22/1/1827, he applied for leave from Carrick-on-Shannon on 14/2/1827 to get married to Miss Adelaide Maria West, daughter of John Beatty West, MP for Dublin. In that event, Major George Warburton recommended his transfer. The Lord Lieutenant, Wellesley writes, 'with respect to the removal of the bridegroom, it appears to be a rather harsh measure unless absolutely necessary'; residing at Goose Lodge, Dromahair, Co. Leitrim in 1831; dismissed 11/1/1837 and died *c.*1840; his son William Bradish Montfort (1830–1905) travelled in the USA before settling at Sandringham, Melbourne, Australia, where as a superintendent of police he successfully led the posse that captured the infamous outlaw, Ned Kelly.

Montgomery, John; LDS 2097/151; born 1806, Kinawley, Co. Cavan; father of Thomas Hartley Montgomery, SI, RIC; enlisted as a sub constable on 1/4/1829; 3rd SI 9/12/1845; died 6/8/1870 at Shinrone, King's County; will proved on 14/9/1870 at the Principal Registry by the oath of Thomas Hartley Montgomery, SI, RIC, Newtownards, Co. Down, one of the executors – effects under £800.

Montgomery, Thomas Hartley; RIC 31641; LDS 2097/256; born 1842, Co. Cavan; son of John Montgomery, SI, RIC; worked as an assistant Bank clerk in a Belfast Bank for 7 years and 9 months. He joined the RIC as a Cadet on 4/4/1868, 3rd Class SI on 20/5/1866, 2nd Class SI on 2/4/1870. He was allocated to Co. Down on 1/8/1866. As a sub-Inspector in Newtownstewart, Co. Tyrone he befriended a bank cashier named William Glass and in due course used that friendship to gain entry to the bank, murder his friend and steal £1,600 in notes. The murder took place on 29/6/1871, a day when the bank manager was at another bank and most of the local police were on 'fair duty' in a neighbouring village. Montgomery was tried on three occasions, in

170

170 John Charles Milling.   171 Thomas Hartley Montgomery hanged for the murder of bank clerk William Glass in 1873.   172 William Glass, bank clerk.

171

172

the first and second trials the jury disagreed but in the third, on 22/7/1873 he was arraigned at Omagh Assizes, found guilty, and surprised all by making a matter of fact confession of guilt. Part of the *Belfast Newsletter* helped to convict him as the stolen money was eventually recovered wrapped in that part of the daily newspaper and that had been missing from the scene of the crime. He was hanged at Omagh, Co. Tyrone on 26 August 1873, where RIC men had the doubtful distinction of seeing their former Inspector executed. The episode was heightened in local folklore by a tremendous thunderstorm on the evening of the execution. The hangman was William Marwood.

Mooney, Andrew Martin; RIC 58675; LDS 2098/061B; born 11/11/1879, Co. Monaghan; married on 19/4/1915 (Dublin North Registrar's District, June Quarter, 1915, vol. 2, p. 548), Catherine Buckley, native of Co. Dublin; 3rd DI 15/2/1915; attached to Crime Branch at headquarters from 15/7/1920 to 1/10/1920; Chief Police Instructor from 1/10/1920 to 11/2/1921; pensioned 17/7/1922; died 4/9/1859 Baggot Street Hospital, Dublin; buried at St Mochanog Church, Kilmaconogue, Co. Wicklow.

Moor, Ralph Denham Rayment (Sir); RIC 50672; LDS 2097/326; born 31/7/1860, The Lodge, Furneux Pelham, Buntingford, Sussex, Hertfordshire, England; (Bishop Stortford Registrar's District, 1860, September Quarter, vol. 3a, p. 190); son of William Henry Moor (*c.*1830–*c.*1863) surgeon, and Sarah Pears; spent two and a half years in the tea trade; 3rd DI 6/12/1882; resigned 9/2/1891 after involvement in a divorce case and undertook to raise a constabulary force of Hausa and Gold Coasters to serve in the Oil Rivers protectorate; having impressed the consul-general, Sir Claude MacDonald, by his military efficiency, Moor was transferred to political duties and appointed Deputy Commissioner and Vice-Consul in the Oil Rivers (Niger Coast) Protectorate, 1892; on 1/2/1896 he succeeded MacDonald as Acting Commissioner and Consul-General of what was now called Niger Coast Protectorate, 1896 to 1900. Moor recorded his intention of extending British influence to the interior by peaceful expeditions and collaboration with African rulers, but first saw it necessary to enforce their acknowledgement of British supremacy. Already in 1894, as MacDonald's deputy, Moor had enforced the deposition and exile of the Itsekiri chief Nana Olomu; he now resolved to take strong measures against the Edo kingdom of Benin, and encouraged his deputy, James R. Phillips, in his ill-fated mission of January 1897. Returning from leave, Moor joined the expeditionary force of Admiral H.H. Rawson which within a month avenged the deaths of Phillip's party, looted the art works of Benin city, and established British control. He retired from the post of High Commissioner of Southern Nigeria in October, 1900. Created a KCMG in May, 1897; On 1/10/1903 he retired on grounds of ill health. He had hoped for more than the minor committee appointments offered by the Colonial Office, but he became a director of Alfred Lewis Jones' African Steam Ship Company and worked for the British Cotton Growing Association. In 1898 he had married Mrs. Adrienne Burns, nee Shapman (b.*c.*1871), an attractive divorcee. They had one child, but does not seem to have found happiness and he was found dead as a result of poisoning on 14/9/1909 at his residence at The Homestead, Church Road, Barnes, Surrey, having previously resided at Thurloe Square, London; (Richmond Registrar's District, September Quarter, 1909, vol. 2a, p. 243); administration granted at London on 25/10/1909 to Dame Adrienne Moor, widow – effects £2,671.1s.1d.).

Moore, Henry John; LDS 2098/131; born 16/4/1872, Co. Longford; BA 1894 & 1895, LLB 1905, Trinity College Dublin; married on 10/8/1901, wife a native of Co. Kerry; 3rd DI 17/10/1897; committee member of the First All Ireland RIC Representative Body, 1919; ACI 14/1/1920; CI 15/6/1920; divisional commissioner 11/11/1920 at Clonmel; pensioned 17/7/1922; (photo in the *Constabulary Gazette*, vol. 2, no. 39, p. 1, 24/12/1897 & vol. XXXI, no. 14, 15/6/1912).

Moore, Joseph Roger; LDS 2098/136B; born 25/3/1895, Co. Dublin; captain, Royal Irish Rifles; married on 2/11/1920 (Ballymena Registrar's District, December Quarter, 1920, vol. 1,

173   174

173 Andrew Martin Mooney. 174 Henry John Moore. 175 John Moran, captain, Leinster Regiment. 176 Henry Brown Morell.

175   176

p. 105), Miss Patrick, a native of Co. Antrim; 3rd DI 8/7/1920; pensioned 31/5/1922; transferred to the Royal Ulster Constabulary on 1/6/1922.

Moore, Thomas; RIC 48614; LDS 2098/003B; born 2/3/1863, Co. Antrim; married on 19/7/1890, wife a native of Scotland; 3rd DI 16/9/1909; pensioned 2/9/1920.

Moore, William Sneyd; RIC 53466; LDS 2098/053; born 1864, Co. Cavan; tutor in Co. Antrim for two years; married on 11/10/1894, Miss M. Archdall, a native of Co. Fermanagh; 3rd DI 4/2/1898; King Edward VII Visit to Ireland Medal, 1903; pensioned 31/5/1922; transferred to the Royal Ulster Constabulary on 1/6/1922.

Moran, John; LDS 2098/190B; born 21/10/1892, Athy, Co. Kildare; (Athy Registrar's District, December Quarter, 1892, vol. 3, p. 268); captain, Leinster Regiment; 3rd DI 10/1/1920; pensioned 8/5/1922.

Morant, George Archiebald; RIC 59036; LDS 2098/166; born 1875, India; scholar; BA Pemberton College, Cambridge; married on 12/3/1913, Miss Chearnley, a native of Co. Waterford; 3rd DI 10/1/1900; King Edward VII Visit to Ireland Medal, 1903; Chief Police Instructor at the Phoenix Park Depot from 29/3/1915 to 31/10/1915; Adjutant, Phoenix Park Depot from 9/12/1915 to 1/11/1916; Chief Police Instructor from 1/11/1916 to 14/4/1919; CI 14/4/1919; Private Secretary to the Inspector General from 18/12/1920 until 8/3/1921; acted as second in command of the Phoenix Park Depot from 8/3/1921 to 26/7/1922; pensioned 25/7/1922; (photo in the *Constabulary Gazette*, vol. XXV, no. 14, 19/6/1909, p. 212 & vol. XXXIII, no. 21, 2/8/1913).

Morell, Henry Browne; RIC 49212; LDS 2097/319; born 1858, Co. Tyrone; BA 1884, Trinity College Dublin; married on 22/9/1914 (Dublin North Registrar's District, September Quarter, 1914, vol. 2, p. 439), Miss C. Mooney, a native of Co. Cork; 3rd SI 24/6/1882; King Edward VII Visit to Ireland Medal, 1903; CI 16/2/1905; King George V Coronation Medal, 1911; pensioned 31/12/1919.

Moreton, Thomas; LDS 2097/070; born 1811, Co. Roscommon; enlisted as a sub constable, 1/2/1829; constable, 1/4/1830; 3rd SI 1/7/1831; dismissed 6/9/1847; C.C. Wolf's Hill, Athy, Co. Kildare, 1835.

Morgan, Allen; LDS 2097/146; born 1812, Co. Carlow; 3rd SI 15/7/1844; pensioned 29/6/1868; his brother, J. Morgan, who was in charge of the Powder Magazine, Melbourne, in 1862, recommended an ex-RIC man, John Uzell, RIC 24390, for service in the Victoria Police as Uzell had served under Allen Morgan in Co. Cork.

Morgan, Edward; CarNB; 3rd SI 14/5/1822; the day before he was appointed he was injured in a fall from a horse having been attacked by a mob, four of which were convicted; he was married and had nine children and residing in accommodation in Limerick Prison; received a fracture to the head in a riot in July, 1825 and received assistance in performing his duties by his eldest son John; pensioned 1/2/1829 at £60p.a. having been compelled by 'Rockites' to abandon his property in Co. Limerick; residing at Broad Street, Limerick, c/o Patrick Lynch; on 10/9/1829 reported that he was moving to Co. Kerry and he wished that his three sons who were serving in Slieveardagh, Co. Limerick would be transferred to Co. Kerry; C.C. Killenaule, Co. Tipperary.

Morgan, John; LDS 2097/064; born 1788, Co. Limerick; recommended for service by Major Drought; JP, 8/8/1805; 3rd SI 1/4/1826; C.C. Coolaney, 1826; on 14/11/1826 residing at 59, Lower Gardiner Street, Dublin when he was suspended from duty, reapplied and was reinstated; C.C. Corofin, Co. Clare on 24/7/1831 when his wife died at Riverston, Corofin; died 17/1/1849.

Morgan, Patrick; LDS 2097/086; born 1809, Co. Limerick; enlisted as a sub constable, 15/5/1827; wife a native of Co. Tipperary; 3rd SI 26/9/1834; on 26/6/1843 he was presented with an ornamental sabre by the Lord Lieutenant; received a grant from the Reward Fund on 31/5/1848 for continued success in breaking up gangs of offenders; CI 1/11/1859; pensioned 1/7/1868; died 29/10/1874 at Dublin; (Dublin South Registrar's District, 1874, vol. 17, p. 561).

Moriarty, Cecil Charles Hudson; RIC 60574; LDS 2098/187; born 28/1/1877, Co. Kerry, second son of Rev. Thomas Alexander Moriarty, MA, Rector of Millstreet, Co. Cork; tutor for 6 years; 3rd DI 16/4/1902; married in May, 1906 Muriel Una, daughter of George Tilson Shaen Carter, JP, of Belmullet, Co. Mayo and they had three daughters. He read law at Trinity College, Dublin gaining a BA (Hons.)1899 and LLB 1902 and won a first senior moratorship with a large gold medal. He also played hockey and was capped at rugby in 1899 when Ireland won the Triple Crown. He had been a teacher for six years when he was appointed a 3rd Class DI on 16/4/1902, 2nd Class on 1/3/1906. District inspector in the Detective Department, Constabulary Office, Dublin Castle from 1/2/1914 until he resigned on 6/7/1918 on his appointment as Assistant Chief Constable of Birmingham City Police on 7 July 1918 and Chief Constable of Birmingham City Police from September 1935 to September 1941. He was the author of *Police Law*, 1929; *Police Procedures and Administration*, 1930 in several editions with the view of assisting police officers in the United Kingdom in attaining a working knowledge of the law. Sir Charles Haughton Rafter, KBE, Chief Constable of Birmingham City, said at the Chief Constables Association Meeting on 30 May 1918, 'I do not know of any other book published for the English police forces which gives full and adequate instruction on this subject.' He also wrote: *Questions and Answers on Police Duties*, 1935; *Further Questions and Answers on Police Duties*, 1938; *Emergency Police Law*, 1940 (with J. Whiteside); *Questions and Answers on Police Duties, Third Series*, 1946 (Omnibus Edition, 1954). OBE, 1925; CBE, 1938; Commander of the Order of St John of Jerusalem, 1936; King's Police Medal, 1939; King's Jubilee Medal, 1935; King's Coronation Medal, 1937; died 7/4/1958 Tenbury Wells, Worcestershire; (photo: p. 91, *Policing Birmingham: An Account of 150 Years of Police in Birmingham*, by John W. Reilly, Birminghan, 1989).

Moriarty, Henry Gore; RIC 51164; LDS 2098/003; born 1864, King's County; (Parsonstown Registrar's District, 1864, vol. 8, p. 693); eldest son of Thomas Moriarty, SI, RIC and brother of William Crawford Gore Moriarty, DI, RIC, RM; 3rd DI 12/7/1884; died 22/8/1890 at Steven's Hospital, Dublin, late of Ballymoney, Co. Antrim; buried in Roscommon on 26/8/1890; administration granted on 5/9/1890 at the Principal Registry to Thomas Moriarty of Limerick, DI, RIC, JP, the father – effects – £276.2s.1d.

Moriarty, Thomas; RIC 25255; LDS 2097/232; born 1841, Abbeystown House, Roscommon, Co. Roscommon; son of lieutenant Moriarty, 86th Regiment of Foot (Royal County Down Regiment); father of Henry George Moriarty, SI, RIC and William Crawford Gore Moriarty, DI, RIC, RM; 3rd SI 3/11/1859; ACI 1/7/1883; CI 22/1/1884; Commissioner of Police and Town Inspector of Constabulary, Belfast from 28/9/1896 to 1/12/1901; pensioned 1/12/1901; died 19/5/1915 at Ardnamona, Fortwilliam Park, Belfast; (Belfast Registrar's District, 1915, June Quarter, vol. 1, p. 145); will proved on 28/7/1915 at the Principal Registry by the oath of Ellen F. Hodson Moriarty, the widow and Boughey W.D. Montgomery – effects £2,951.11s.2d.; his eldest daughter Clare married on 12/1/1897 at the Church of St Francis Xavier, Gardiner Street, Dublin, Martin Edward White, third son of Helenus White, Esq., of Mount Sion, Co. Limerick and 71, George Street, Limerick; (photo in the *Constabulary Gazette*, vol. 1, no. 2, 10/4/1897).

Moriarty, William Crawford Gore; RIC 53926; LDS 2098/060; born 5/4/1868, King's County; (Parsonstown Registrar's District, 1868, vol. 8, no. 710); son of Thomas Moriarty, SI, RIC and brother of Henry Gore Moriarty, DI, RIC; 3rd DI 16/10/1889; King Edward VII Visit to Ireland Medal, 1903; Private Secretary to the Inspector General from 5/10/1908 until his appointment as a resident magistrate 3rd class 25/1/1911, 2nd class 11/1/1915; (p. 149, RM Records of Service Book, National Archives, Dublin).

Morley, George; RIC 58445; LDS 2098/146; born 17/11/1873, Bradford, Yorks., England; (Bradford Yorkshire Registrar's District, 1873, December Quarter, vol. 9b, p. 199); son of William James Morley of Heaton, Bradford and Annie, daughter of Richard Brook; lieutenant, Harwich Militia Division, Royal Engineers, 1897–8; tutor at Oxford for 2 years, BA, BCL, Worcester

177   178

177 Charles Cecil Hudson Moriarty. 178 Charles Cecil Hudson Moriarty, Chief Constable
Birmingham Constabulary, 1935–41. 179 Thomas Moriarty. 180 William Crawford Gore
Moriarty.

179   180

College, Oxford, 1893; married on 18/12/1900, Agnes, daughter of Joseph Tetley Milnes, of Hillside House, Bradford and Bishop's Lydeard; 3rd DI 18/10/1898; King Edward VII Visit to Ireland Medal, 1903; resigned 29/9/1910 on his appointment as Chief Constable of Kingston-upon-Hull on 29 September 1910 to 1 October 1922. Released 1914 to command 12th Battalion, East Yorkshire Regiment; Chief Constable of Durham County Constabulary from 1 October 1922 to 19 October 1942, and died at The Slough Emergency Hospital, Slough while holding office, late of 110, Kendall Drive, Slough, Buckinghamshire; (Marleybone Registrar's District, December Quarter, 1942, vol. 1a, p. 433); administration granted on 24/8/1943 to Ellen Agnes Morley, widow – effects £924.17s.11d.

Morrison, Robert Douglas; RIC 48107; LDS 2097/315; born 1858, Co. Derry; married on 16/8/1888 (Rathdown Registrar's District, September Quarter, 1888, vol. 2, p. 713), wife from Co. Down; 3rd SI 30/12/1881; CI 1/11/1902; King Edward VII Visit to Ireland Medal, 1903; King George V Coronation Medal, 1911; pensioned 15/6/1920.

Morrison, Thomas Dawson; RIC 71722; LDS 2098/138B; born 14/9/1893, Co. Down; staff captain, Royal Munster Fusiliers; 3rd DI 8/7/1920; Temporary Adjutant, RIC Camp Gormanstown from 14/9/1920 to 21/11/1920 and permanent Adjutant from 22/11/1920 to 15/3/1922; pensioned 31/5/1922; transferred to the Royal Ulster Constabulary on 1/6/1922; OBE, MC, BL; promoted to the rank of Deputy Inspector General in the Royal Ulster Constabulary.

Morton, Arthur Pratt Winter; RIC 28372; LDS 2097/244; born 1845, France; youngest son of Pierse Morton, Esq., of Kilnacrott House, Co. Cavan; 3rd SI 12/7/1863; died 31/8/1871 at Kilrush, Co. Clare (*Cork Examiner* 7/9/1871); (Kilrush Registrar's District, 1872, vol. 4, p. 292).

Moynihan, John; LDS 2099/013; born 1884, Killarney, Co. Kerry; (Killarney Registrar's District, June Quarter, 1884, vol. 5, p. 310); married on 15/10/1914 (New Ross Registrar's District, December Quarter, 1914, vol. 4, p. 347), wife a native of Co. Wexford; 3rd DI 16/6/1921; pensioned 20/4/1922.

Mulcahy, John; RIC 22742; LDS 2097/259; born 1828, Clonmel, Co. Tipperary; 3rd SI 15/6/1866; RIC Riding Master; joined the 13th Light Dragoons (Army No. 1230) in 1845–6 and was promoted to Troop Sergeant Major on 26/10/1854. He joined the RIC as a sub-constable in January 1858 having served with the 13th Light Dragoon Guards in the 'Charge of the Light Brigade' on 25 October 1854. He was awarded the Crimean Medal and four clasps for the battles of Alma, Balaklava, Inkerman and Sebastopol, and the Turkish Medal. He was also awarded the Distinguished Conduct Medal. His wife was a native of County Tipperary. His eldest son, John Joseph, aged six years died on 3/4/1864 of water on the brain (Dublin North Registrar's District, vol. 7, p. 463), at the Phoenix Park Depot (*Cork Examiner* 6/4/1864). He was promoted to 2nd class Head Constable on 1/1/1858 and 1st class on 1/8/1858. He was promoted 3rd class Sub Inspector and the RIC's first Riding Master on 15/6/1866 (*Cork Examiner* 21/6/1866); founder of the Riding School at the Phoenix Park Depot; 2nd class SI on 25/3/1870. He received one unfavourable record for having been found drunk on 18/10/1870. He died on 10 June 1872 at the Phoenix Park Depot, Dublin and he was buried in Glasnevin Cemetery, Dublin (Grave No. XE 134 Garden).

Mulhall, Charles Joseph M. McDermott; RIC 55516; LDS 2098/081; born 1866, Boyle, Co. Roscommon; (Boyle Registrar's District, 1866, vol. 4, p. 113); 3rd DI 13/11/1891; died 13/4/1900 at Ardee, Co. Louth; (Dublin South Registrar's District, 1900, June Quarter, vol. 2, p. 267); (photo in the *Constabulary Gazette*, vol. 2 no. 39, p. 1, 24/12/1897 & vol. VII, no. 8, 19/5/1900).

Mulherin, James; RIC 55420; LDS 2099/056; born 1870, Ballina, Co. Mayo; (Ballina Registrar's District, 1870, vol. 14, p. 22); 3rd DI 17/9/1921; pensioned 9/5/1922; he was the last District Inspector to join the RIC; his brother William Mulherin, RIC sergeant 61051 was shot dead at the Catholic Church, Bandon, Co. Cork on 25/7/1920.

181

181 Thomas Dawson Morrison, MC.   182 John Mulcahy, lance sergeant, 13th Lancers and survivor of 'The Charge of the Light Brigade' at Balaclava, Crimea, October, 1854 (*sixth from right*).   183 John Mulcahy – Balaclava, Crimea, October, 1854 (*eleventh from the left*).

182

183

Mullarkey, John; RIC 1316; LDS 2097/201; born 1811, Co. Sligo; wife a native of Co. Kerry; 3rd SI 1/5/1854; died 7/8/1875, late of Ballincollig, Co. Cork; administration granted on 8/1/1876 at Cork to Mary Anne Mullarkey, Ballincollig, Co. Cork, widow of the deceased – effects under £600.

Mullen, James Denis; LDS 2097/157; born 1828, Co. Dublin; 3rd SI 21/2/1847; died 7/7/1866 (Dublin South Registrar's District, vol. 12, p. 486).

Mulliner, Ernest W.; RIC 50983; LDS 2097/329; born 1857, Leamington, Warks., England; residing at 9, Binswood Avenue, Leamington Priors, Warwick in 1881 (Census); master; BA, Clare College, Cambridge; married on 1/10/1919, wife from Warwick; 3rd DI 22/2/1883; musketry instructor at the Phoenix Park Depot from 15/12/1901 to 1/10/1904; Queen Victoria's Visit to Ireland Medal, 1900; King Edward VII Visit to Ireland Medal, 1903; CI 1/2/1907; King George V Coronation Medal, 1911; pensioned 31/12/1919; (photo in the *Constabulary Gazette*, vol. 2, no. 36, 4/12/1897, p. 1 & vol. XIV, no. 7, 7/11/1903, p. 182).

Mulock, George Charles; RIC 32720; LDS 2097/262; born 1846, Kilnagarna, King's County; married on 31/3/1874 (Dublin South Registrar's District, vol. 2, p. 679); 3rd SI 20/4/1867; received a favourable record on 30/6/1871 for strenuous exertions in extinguishing a fire; pensioned 21/5/1890; died 14/3/1903 at Kilnagarna, Athlone, Co. Westmeath; administration granted on 26/9/1903 at the Principal Registry to Henrietta C. Mulock, widow – effects £37.17s.11d.

Munro, Horace Frederick Moncreif; RIC 65126; LDS 2098/088B; born 7/2/1884, Midlothian, Scotland; MA, Edinburgh College; 3rd DI 3/1/1910; lieutenant from 10/11/1914 and was promoted captain on 19/1/1915, Royal Army Service Corps to 5/5/1919; TCI 2/11/1920; pensioned 13/7/1922.

Munro, James; RIC 72018; LDS 2098/164B; born 1/7/1894, Scotland; lieutenant, King's Own Scottish Borderers; 3rd DI 10/1/1920; pensioned 24/3/1922; joined the Palestine Gendarmerie on 25/3/1922.

Murnane, David; RIC 41425; LDS 2098/180; born 1858, Co. Limerick; father of James Peter **Murnane, DI**; RIC; married on 8/3/1886, wife a native of Co. Limerick; 3rd DI 23/7/1901; pensioned 31/5/1919; died 20/8/1939; buried in Cahirconlish Cemetery, Co. Limerick with his son Michael (d.10/10/1890); (photo in the *Constabulary Gazette*, vol. XVI, no. 12, 10/12/1904 & vol. XXIX, no. 23, 19/8/1911, p. 376).

Murnane, James Peter; RIC 66457; LDS 2098/034B; born 27/6/1890, Co. Dublin; (Dublin North Registrar's District, September Quarter, 1890, vol. 2, p. 423); son of David Murnane, DI, RIC; taught languages in the Christian Schools, Charleville, Co. Cork for five months; married on 26/2/1920 (Kells Registrar's District, March Quarter, 1920, vol. 2, p. 780), Lilly McCarroll, a native of London; 3rd DI 23/3/1912; pensioned 20/5/1922.

Murphy, Arthur; CarNB; born Navan, Co. Meath; 3rd SI 7/11/1822; on 6/4/1825 he wrote that he was removed from the service for no other cause than 'being advanced in years'.

Murphy, Charles Ouseley; RIC 58443; LDS 2098/150; born 1874, Co. Dublin; eldest son of John Ouseley Murphy, Esq., of St Laurence, Chapelizod, Co. Dublin; married on 10/11/1904 (Dungannon Registrar's District, December Quarter, 1904, vol. 1, p. 757) at St John's Church, Caledon, Marguerite Mont Cargueil, eldest daughter of Mr and Mrs Charles R. Hearn, Annaghroe House, Caledon and of Templenoe, Ballyshannon, Co. Donegal; 3rd DI 24/1/1899; pensioned 12/5/1922; (photo in the *Constabulary Gazette*, vol. X, no. 3, 12/10/1901).

Murphy, D.J.; CarNB; PPF; PPF Clerk 14/12/1815.

Murphy, Harvey Cassidy; RIC 19013; LDS 2097/205; born 1832, Co. Dublin; sons born on 20/1/1867 at Rathkeale, Co. Limerick (*Cork Examiner* 24/1/1867) and on 25/4/1868 (*Cork Examiner* 30/4/1868); son, Henry Lewis Ernest, born on 14/5/1872 at Newport, Co. Mayo

184

185

184 Ernest Mulliner.   185 David Murnane.

186 James Peter Murnane.   187 Thomas Murray.

186

187

(Newport Registrar's District, vol. 14p. 43) (*Cork Examiner* 18/5/1872); 3rd SI 15/10/1854; received a favourable record on 31/12/1869 for untiring exertions in protecting voters against formidable mobs and arresting many of the rioters and house wreckers; CI 1/4/1877; died 10/4/1884 at Castlerea, Co. Roscommon, late of Maryville, Galway; will proved on 27/5/1885 at Tuam by the oath of Ellen Louisa Murphy, of 1 The Mall, Clontarf, Co. Dublin – effects £757.6s.3d.

Murphy, James; RIC 25203; LDS 2098/022; born 1840, Co. Fermanagh; 3rd DI 1/8/1886; pensioned 1/10/1904; died 11/8/1918 (Rathdown Registrar's District, September Quarter, 1918, vol. 2, p. 619).

Murphy, Jeremiah Stack; RIC 16947; LDS 2097/197; born 1833, Templeville, Co. Cork; son of Jeremiah Stack Murphy; married on 31/10/1870 at Kensington and afterwards at St Stephen's Church, Bayswater, Lucy Elizabeth, youngest daughter of Major General Ludlow, late Royal Engineers (*Cork Examiner* 4/11/1870); 3rd SI 1/6/1853; CI 14/5/1876; died 15/2/1883 at Boulogne-Sur-Mer, France; will proved on 22/3/1883 at the Principal Registry by the oath of Elizabeth Stack Murphy, Colville Terrace, London, widow, one of the executors – effects £1,650.2s.9d.

Murphy, John; CarNB; born 1796; 3rd SI 1822; C.C. Balbriggan, Co. Dublin.

Murphy, Patrick; RIC 50516; LDS 2098/221; born 18/8/1864, Co. Clare; wife a native of Co. Mayo; 3rd DI 12/7/1907; pensioned 31/3/1921.

Murphy, Thomas; RIC 32408; LDS 2097/260; born 1843, Co. Wexford; 3rd SI 15/3/1867; received a favourable record on 30/6/1871 for firmness and judgement when in command of a party of police in quelling a riotous mob; dismissed 10/10/1884 for drunkenness and insubordination (*The Times*, 11/7/1885).

Murray, Daniel; LDS 2097/160; born 1821, Co. Wicklow; brother of Thomas Murray, SI, RIC; 3rd SI 15/9/1847; died 6/2/1864 at 20, Upper Merrion Street, Dublin; will proved on 17/3/1864 at the Principal Registry by the oath of Cherry Murray, of Rose Hall, Templeogue, County Dublin, the widow and sole executrix – effects under £1,500.

Murray, Pulteney; LDS 2097/138; born 1812, Pertshire, Scotland; captain, 36th Regiment of Foot from 1825 to 1836; wife a native of Co. Tyrone; 3rd SI 11/4/1842; pensioned 13/8/1872; died 1874 in Galway, Co. Galway; (Galway Registrar's District, 1874, vol. 19, p. 155).

Murray, Ronald Leslie; RIC 69946; LDS 2098/101B; born 5/7/1894, Co. Mayo; lieutenant, Royal Garrison Artillery; 3rd DI 4/1/1920; pensioned 31/5/1922; transferred to the Royal Ulster Constabulary on 1/6/1922.

Murray, Thomas; LDS 2097/107; born 1813, Co. Wicklow; brother of Daniel Murray, SI, RIC; 3rd SI 16/11/1836; dismissed 14/5/1844; nephew of Most Rev. Dr Murray, archbishop of Dublin; died 21/2/1883 at Cooladangan House, Arklow, Co. Wicklow; will proved at the Principal Registry by the oath of Belinda Murray, widow, one of the executors – effects £321.13s.9d.; buried in the New Cemetery, Arklow, Co. Wicklow; (photo of portrait – Michael Murray, TCD).

Mylne, Edward Graham; RIC 61505; LDS 2098/208; born 19/1/1883, Bombay, India; son of Louis George and Amy Frederica Mylne: 3rd DI 22/12/1905; son of Right Rev. Bishop Louis George Mylne and Amy Frederica Mylne, Redcliffe, Battenhall, Worcestershire; educated at Marlborough College and scholarship to Keble College, Oxford; married Annie Frederica Moultrie on 12/6/1914 at Rouen, France; captain, 1st Battalion Irish Guards; died of wounds, 6/12/1915 at the British Red Cross Hospital, Rouen, France; buried in the Cemetery of St Sever, Rouen (grave no.2252) on 13/6/1915; probate granted at the Principal registry on 26/8/1915 to his parents – effects £1,215.1s.1d.; (WO 339/2429).

N

Nangle, Bartholomew; CarNB; PPF; captain; 3rd SI 1/1/1823; chief magistrate 1/1/1823; resident magistrate 1/10/1836; was in charge of a party of police on 3/12/1823 returning to Leamlara, Co. Cork from Glanmire Petty Sessions, one of which was drowned, namely, Constable James Young (the *Constitution* or *Cork Morning Post*, Monday, 8/12/1823); C.C. Rathcormac, Trantstown and Midleton, Co. Cork.

Napier, William Ramsay; RIC 15837; LDS 2097/192; born 1829, Co. Down; 3rd SI 10/5/1852; died 1/11/1895 at 24 Oriental Place, Brighton, Sussex, England; administration granted on 13/1/1896 at the Principal Registry to Rosa Ziemann (wife of H.P. Ziemann) of Lingham House, Gordon Road, Margate, Kent, England, the sister – effects £2,416.18s.2d.

Nash, William; LDS 2097/029; 3rd SI 18/1/1822; resident magistrate 1840.

Naughton, Thomas; RIC 63174; LDS 2098/176B; born 20/7/1882, Co. Mayo; (Claremorris Registrar's District, September Quarter, 1882, vol. 4, p. 166); 3rd DI 16/10/1920; on 15/3/1921 awarded a 1st class favourable record for good police duty in a disturbed area under dangerous conditions; on 30/3/1921 awarded a 3rd class favourable record for the capture of an armed rebel at Thurles, Co. Tipperary; awarded the King's Police Medal, 1921; pensioned 13/7/1922.

Navin, Charles; RIC 55089; LDS 2099/055; born 15/12/1872, Co. Kilkenny; married on 25/6/1912 (Ennis Registrar's District, September Quarter, 1912, vol. 4, p. 103), wife a native of Co. Waterford; 3rd SI 8/1/1921; pensioned 13/04/1922.

Neale, Melville Thomson; RIC 38067; LDS 2097/287; born 1848, Berks., England; ensign, 80th Regiment of Foot (South Staffordshire Regiment) for three years; married a Miss Parkinson on 1/2/1872; 3rd SI 11/10/1871; dismissed 26/10/1875.

Neligan, Henry Lancelot; RIC 66456; LDS 2098/033B; born 8/5/1888, Croydon, Surrey, England; (Croydon Registrar's District, 1888, June Quarter, vol. 2a, p. 265); 3rd DI 7/3/1912; pensioned 31/5/1922; transferred to the Royal Ulster Constabulary on 1/6/1922.

Nesbitt, Francis H.; LDS 2097/060; born 1791, Co. Tyrone; lieutenant in the Prince of Wales' Own Donegal Militia from September 1811 to April 1817 (WO 13/2751–71); 3rd SI 1/8/1825; C.C. Mountcharles, Co. Donegal, 1831; died 17/5/1846 at his residence on Strand Road, Derry, Co. Derry.

Nevin, Samuel; RIC 55428; LDS 2099/014; born 12/5/1872, Ballymena, Co. Antrim; (Ballymena Registrar's District, 1872, vol. 6, p. 166); wife from Co. Armagh; 3rd DI 15/6/1921; pensioned 31/5/1922; transferred to the Royal Ulster Constabulary on 1/6/1922.

Newberry, Basil Richard Chaperre; RIC 72917; LDS 2099/029; born 4/4/1899, Devon, England; (St Thomas Registrar's District, 1899, June Quarter, vol. 5b, p. 33); lieutenant, Devonshire Regiment; 3rd DI 25/6/1921; pensioned 15/5/1922.

Newell, Adam Cooke; RIC 36850; LDS 2097/281; born 26/2/1847, Co. Tipperary; 3rd SI 1/9/1870; resident magistrate 3rd class 8/2/1892, 2nd class 19/7/1896, 1st class 23/4/1909; died 13/4/1910 at Kilgarve, Co. Roscommon; (Dublin South Registrar's District, June Quarter, vol. 2, p. 571); buried in Creagh Cemetery, Ballinasloe, Co. Galway; his widow, Catherine Mary Newell (d.26/7/1922, aged 67 years) and daughters Kathleen Newell (d.14/6/1966) and Gwendoline Alexandria Newell (d.4/4/1977) are buried in Deansgrange Cemetery, Dublin (South Section, Row U1, Grave No. 39); administration granted at Tuam, Co. Galway on

25/7/1910 to Hutchinson Davidson, solicitor and John Mills, Assistant Medical Superintendent – effects £2,640.18s.6d.; (p. 91, RM Records of Service Book, National Archives, Dublin).

Newland, Charles Francis Waters; RIC 51171; LDS 2098/006; born 1864, Gowran, Co. Kilkenny; youngest son of George Edward Newland, AIG, RIC; married at St Patrick's Church, Dublin on 9/6/1887 (Dublin South Registrar's District, June Quarter, 1887, vol. 2, p. 537), Jennie C., eldest daughter of Rev. Canon Jellett Bell, LLD, Rector of St Patrick's Church, Dublin; 3rd DI 10/3/1885; pensioned 24/7/1902; died 3/5/1907 at Old Toll House, Maresfield, Sussex, England; administration granted at Lewes on 28/5/1907 to Jane Carmichael Newland, widow – effects £1,260.1s.0d.

Newland, George Edward; RIC 16679; LDS 2097/196; born 1834, Kilmakillogue, Co. Wexford; father of Charles Francis Waters Newland, DI, RIC; 3rd SI 5/2/1853; musketry instructor at the Phoenix Park Depot from 1/3/1873 to 1/4/1876; CI 1/14/1876; AIG 1/10/1882; Commandant of the Phoenix Park Depot from 1/10/1882 to 1/10/1888; pensioned 1/10/1888; died 18/6/1898 at 3, Burlington Road, Dublin.

Newman, Neville P.; CarNB; born Trim, Co. Meath; C.C. Ballymahon, Co. Longford.

Neylon, Thomas; RIC 56484; LDS 2098/020B; born 9/3/1874, Ennis, Co. Clare; (Ennis Registrar's District, 1874, vol. 4, p. 279); married on 21/2/1911 (Ballyvaughan Registrar's District, March Quarter, 1911, vol. 4, p. 27), wife a native of Co. Clare; 3rd DI 9/10/1910; King Edward VII Visit to Ireland Medal, 1903 as a head constable; King George V Visit to Ireland Medal, 1911; awarded a certificate from the Irish Police and Constabulary Recognition Fund; on 5/2/1920 he was specially promoted to the rank of 1st class District Inspector in recognition of good police services; King's Police Medal 1919; attached to Crime Department at headquarters from 1/10/1919 to 15/6/1920; CI 15/6/1920; pensioned 10/8/1922; at the Co. Mayo Assizes

188

189

188 Edward Graham Mylne.   189 Thomas Neylon.

held in Westport in July 1914, before Mr Justice Madden, appealing the decision of the County Court Judge dismissing his claim for £10,000 compensation for serious injuries received in a riot, DI Neylon was awarded £500 compensation and allowed 24 guineas costs to be levied against the Union and Town of Westport.

Neynoe, Edward Saurin; RIC 16056; LDS 2097/193; born 1833, Co. Dublin; 3rd SI 3/8/1852; died 11/12/1869 at Sligo, Co. Sligo (Sligo Registrar's District, 1869, vol. 218, p. 36).

Nicholson, Joseph; CarNB; born Rathdowney, Queen's County; PPF; captain and in 1798 appointed ADC to General Ralph Dundas and on his staff being broken up in 1803 went to live in the Wicklow mountains where he formed a corps of yeomanry and restored peace in an area known as the Seven Churches; barrackmaster of Wicklow Barracks; appointed a PPF chief magistrate in May 1821 for the baronies of Ossory and Galmoy; in April 1822 given the baronies of Iverk, Kells, Knocktopher and part of Shillelalogher; in May 1823 appointed a stipendiary magistrate in Johnstown, Co. Kilkenny and gave up another situation under the government thinking his situation was permanent; the magistrates of Co. Kilkenny petitioned the Lord Lieutenant that the county was so quiet that a stipendiary magistrate was not required; the Lord Lieutenant agreed and Major Joseph Nicholson was removed in 1825; writing from Castlekevin, Co. Wicklow in 1826 he states that in 1824 was in occupation of a house at Whiteswall in the barony of Galmoy; his nephew, Archibald Nicholson, writing in 1828 stated that Joseph Nicholson died of 'inflammation of the lungs' shortly after his services were dispensed with in 1826; his fourth daughter, Josephine Adelaide Myra Joyce, married on 6/1/1864 at the Union Chapel, Abbey Street, Dublin, William Browne, eldest son of James Browne, Esq. (*Cork Examiner* 9/1/1864).

Nixon, Henry S.; CarNB; born 1794; C.C. Rathfriland, Co. Down; Lifford, Co. Donegal, 1831.

Nixon, John William; RIC 58987; LDS 2098/080B; born 1/6/1877, Co. Cavan; (Cavan Registrar's District, 1877, vol. 30, p. 128); married on 5/6/1920 (Lisnaskea Registrar's District, June Quarter, 1920, vol. 3, p. 181), Nellie Dunbar Moore; 3rd DI 11/8/1917; pensioned 31/5/1922; transferred to the Royal Ulster Constabulary on 1/6/1922.

Noblett, George Harris; RIC 69948; LDS 2098/104B; born 18/5/1898; Co. Dublin; captain, Royal Dublin Fusiliers; married on 24/8/1920 (Castlereagh Registrar's District, September Quarter, 1920, vol. 4, p. 65), Dorothea Georgina Ford, a native of Co. Roscommon; 3rd DI 4/1/1920; pensioned 14/7/1922.

Nolan, John; RIC 34690; LDS 2097/167; born 1796, Co. Dublin; private, 96th Regiment of Foot (The Queen's Own Germans Regiment), from 1/2/1814 to 10/12/1818; Dublin Police, from 1/1/1819 to 1/2/1820; enlisted as a sub constable on 1/2/1820; 3rd SI 1/6/1848; died 22/1/1850.

Norrington, Leonard Charles; RIC 72946; ADRIC CADET no. 355; LDS 2098/216B; born 5/4/1890, Middlesex, England; (London Central Registrar's District, 1890, June Quarter, vol. 1C, p. 22); captain, Royal Irish Fusiliers; 3rd DI 12/1/1920; pensioned 20/5/1922.

Norris, Thomas Duke; RIC 57952; LDS 2098/126; born 1871, Tullamore, King's County; son of William Jones Norris, Tullamore, King's County; married on 27/4/1898, Miss Murphy, of Palmerstown, Co. Dublin; 3rd DI 5/11/1896; King Edward VII Visit to Ireland Medal, 1903; awarded a certificate from the Irish Police and Constabulary Recognition Fund; died 10/8/1919 at Castletown Castle, Dundalk, Co. Louth; administration granted at the Principal Registry on 26/1/1920.

Nott-Bower, John William (Sir); LDS 2097/292; born 20/3/1849; born 17, Micklegate, Yorks., England; (Yorkshire Registrar's District, 1849, March Quarter, vol. 23, p. 704); eldest son of John Bower, esq., D.C.L., barrister and leader of the bar in the ecclesiastical court in the province of York (d.1877) and Charlotte Nott (d.1893), one of fourteen children and youngest daughter of General Sir William Nott, GCB (1782–1845), commander of the army which marched from Kandahar to Kabul in 1842, during the First Anglo-Afghan War; in 1858 the family moved to

190   191

190 John William Nixon.   191 John William Nott-Bower.   192 John William Nott-Bower, Commissioner of Police, City of London.   193 Cornelius O'Beirne.

192   193

Wales, where his father bought some slate quarries; married in 1889, Florence Harrison (d.1893), eldest daughter of Reginald Harrison, Esq., FRCS; from 1862 he was educated at Cheltenham College and from there he entered the Royal Military College, Sandhurst in 1865, where he won the sword of honour and assumed the prefix of Nott by deed-poll in 1911; joined the 5th West York Militia; ensign 33rd and 8th King's Regiments; he left the army at the end of 1872, when he managed to get a much sought-after cadetship in the RIC through the Liberal politician W.E. Forster, a friend of his father, who gave him a letter of introduction to Lord Hartington, chief secretary for Ireland; 3rd SI 18/1/1873; resigned 30/6/1878; Chief Constable of Leeds, 1878–81, where he handled the case of the notorious burglar Charles Peace, tried in Leeds for murder and hanged in 1879; Chief Constable of Liverpool, 1881–1902; Commissioner of Police of the City of London, 1902–25; awarded the King's Police Medal; created Knight, 1911, created CVO, 1911; created KCVO, 1918; Knight of Grace of St John of Jerusalem; Commander of the Order of the Redeemer (Greece); Knight Commander of Order of Military Merit (Spain); Officer of Order of the Crown of Italy; Chevalier of the Legion of Honour (France); married firstly on 1/6/1889, Florence (d.1920), daughter of Reginald Harrison, a Liverpool surgeon. Two of their five sons were killed in the First World War; of the others one, Sir John Nott Bower (1892–1972), followed his father into the police and served as commissioner of the London Metropolitan Police from 1953 to 1958; married secondly on 24/8/1920, Dorothea, Georgina Ford; died 4/2/1939 at The Stuart Hotel, Richmond Hill, Surrey, England; (Surrey N.E. Registrar's District, march Quarter, 1939, vol. 2a, p. 182); buried on 7/2/1939 at Bognor Regis, Sussex; probate granted at London on 23/3/1939 to William Guy Nott-Bower, CBE, civil servant and John Reginald Hornby Nott-Bower, CVO, deputy assistant commissioner of police – effects £10,082.4s.10d.; (photo in the Constabulary Gazette, vol. XI, no. 5, 26/4/1902).

Nowlan, James Christopher; RIC 15050; LDS 2097/188; born 1829, Co. Carlow; 3rd SI 3/7/1851; died 2/5/1852 in Co. Donegal.

Nowlan, William; LDS 2097/173; born 1802, Co. Cork; enlisted as a sub constable on 1/4/1823; 3rd SI 1/6/1848; pensioned 25/1/1864; died 4/6/1867 (Dublin North Registrar's District, vol. 2, p. 464).

Nunan, Andrew; RIC 3780; LDS 2097/265; born 1819, Co. Kerry; married on 7/8/1852, wife a native of Co. Tipperary; 3rd SI 10/5/1867; received a favourable record on 31/12/1870 for spirited conduct in resisting the aggression of a violent mob; pensioned 1/10/1882; died 31/12/1893.

O

Oates, Thomas J.; RIC 55710; LDS 2098/072B; born 9/2/1872, Co. Roscommon; 3rd DI 8/10/1916; pensioned 9/5/1922; breach of promise case taken by a Catherine Molony of Dublin before Justice Kenny on 4/6/1918 resulting in an out of court settlement; (*Constabulary Gazette*, vol. XL, 8/6/1918, p. 760).

O'Beirne, Cornelius; RIC 65420; LDS 2098/016B; born 21/4/1886, Co. Longford; (Longford Registrar's District, September Quarter, 1886, vol. 3, p. 203); married on 30/10/1912, wife a native of Co. Longford; 3rd DI 9/10/1910; captain, 3rd Battalion Royal Irish Regiment from 6/1/1916 to 12/8/1918; TCI 1/12/1920; pensioned 31/5/1922; transferred to the Royal Ulster Constabulary on 1/6/1922; awarded the OBE; appointed district inspector in Belfast, 12/6/1922; assistant commissioner in Belfast, 21/4/1926; promoted county inspector in Co. Fermanagh, 14/3/1929; pensioned from the RUC, 30/9/1942; (photo in the *Constabulary Gazette*, vol. XXX, no. 14, 16/12/1911).

O'Brien, George E.; CarNB; C.C. Clogher, Co. Tyrone.

O'Brien, John; LDS 2097/100; born 1796; 3rd SI 1/10/1836; paymaster 1/10/1836; father of John Mark O'Brien, SI, RIC; resident magistrate, 22/9/1838; re-appointed paymaster on 22/1/1844; re-appointed resident magistrate 31/10/1846; died on 20/9/1857 in Tulla, Co. Clare (*Cork Examiner* 25/9/1857).

O'Brien, John; LDS 2098/114; born 14/2/1872, Co. Cork; 3rd DI 16/3/1895; died 12/4/1915 at L'Abri, Maryborough, Queen's County; (Mountmellick Registrar's District, 1915, June Quarter, vol. 3, p. 363); administration granted on 1/6/1915 at the Principal Registry to Mary O'Brien, the widow – effects £195.11s.8d.; (photo: Garda Museum & Archives, Dublin Castle).

O'Brien, John Mark; RIC 26310; LDS 2097/237; born 1842, Co. Tipperary; son of John O'Brien, SI, RIC, RM; married on 2/2/1869, by the Rev. David Canon Horgan (uncle of the bride), Mary, only daughter of the late S. Gillman, of Abbeyville, Co. Cork (Cork Registrar's District, vol. 5, p. 193) (*Cork Examiner* 3/2/1869); 3rd SI 1/12/1860; received an approbation on 31/12/1868 for exertions in extinguishing a fire at the Cork Steamship Company's Docks; died 1/10/1899 at 36 Eccles Street, Dublin; buried in Glasnevin Cemetery on 3/10/1899.

O'Brien, Robert Joseph; LDS 2097/100; born 1784, Brook Lodge, Co. Waterford; 3rd SI 1/10/1836; paymaster 1/10/1836 for Co. Cork; discharged on a pension on 31/5/1851 on the abolition of the office of paymaster; appointed a senior clerk in the Receiver's Office on 1/4/1851; died 27/2/1863 at 12, Lower Mount Street, Dublin; will proved at the Principal Registry on 16/4/1863 by the oaths of Mary O'Brien, his widow, of Lower Mount Street and Francis Augustus Codd of Corrig Avenue, Kingstown in the County of Dublin, two of the executors – effects under £1,500.

O'Brien, Thomas; RIC 41218; LDS 2098/143; born 1856, Co. Westmeath; married on 4/9/1894 (Dublin North Registrar's District, September Quarter, 1894, vol. 2, p. 45); 3rd SI 1/7/1898; pensioned 31/10/1917; died 1946; (photo in the *Constabulary Gazette*, vol. XIII, no. 23, 29/8/1903); (photo as a sub constable in 1880: Garda Museum & Archives, Dublin Castle).

O'Brien, William Carroll; LDS 2097/084; born 1805, Co. Clare; 3rd SI 15/4/1834; dismissed 28/3/1841.

O'Bryen, Murtagh; LDS 2097/137; born 1814, Co. Clare; wife a native of Co. Galway; daughter born on 29/2/1852 at Ardee, Co. Louth (*Cork Examiner* 10/3/1852); 3rd SI

194   195

194 John O'Brien. 195 Thomas O'Brien. 196 William Arthur O'Connell – Assistant Inspector General, RIC. 197 William Arthur O'Connell.

196   197

198

199

198 Bernard O'Connor.   199 Bernard O'Connor – Chief Superintendent, Garda Siochana.
200 Michael Sylvester O'Rorke.   201 Tobias O'Sullivan.

200

201

23/8/1841; pensioned 1/9/1881; died 1/4/1882 at Glencolumbkill, Co. Clare, formerly of Portlaw, Co. Waterford; will proved at the Principal Registry by the oath of Turlough O'Bryen, of Glencolumbkill, Co. Clare, sole executor – effects £562.0s.11d.

O'Callaghan, Henry Davis; RIC 27018; LDS 2097/240; born 1839, Co. Cork; 3rd SI 14/10/1861; pensioned 1/6/1882.

O'Callaghan, James; LDS 2097/156; born 1780, Co. Armagh; 3rd SI 20/12/1846; paymaster 20/12/1846 for Counties Armagh, Louth and Monaghan; dismissed 4/4/1849.

O'Callaghan, John B.; RIC 56697; LDS 2098/082B; born 14/2/1875, Co. Cork; (Cork Registrar's District, 1875, vol. 20, p. 114); 3rd DI 12/4/1917; pensioned 22/4/1922.

O'Connell, Edward; RIC 17632; LDS 2097/200; born 1833, Co. Roscommon; 3rd SI 11/2/1854; dismissed 31/12/1858.

O'Connell, Timothy; LDS 2097/087; born 1805, Co. Kerry; enlisted as a sub constable, 5/7/1825; 3rd SI 18/10/1834; pensioned 1/1/1850; died 7/2/1884 at Limerick (Limerick Registrar's District, 1884, March Quarter, vol. 5, p. 331).

O'Connell, William Arthur; LDS 2097/305; born 15/12/1856, Co. Clare; Barrister-at Law, 1888; 3rd SI 1/3/1880; Adjutant, Phoenix Park Depot from 1/7/1899 to 9/5/1901; Queen Victoria's Visit to Ireland Medal, 1900; King Edward VII Visit to Ireland Medal, 1903; CI 9/5/1901; CI attached to Crime Special Department from 1/11/1902 to 22/5/1907; AIG 19/4/1911; Commandant of the Phoenix Park Depot from 19/4/1911 to 9/11/1911; King George V Visit to Ireland Medal, 1911; DIG 9/11/1911; awarded in 1914 the King's Police Medal, 1909; pensioned 15/12/1916.

O'Connor, Bernard; RIC 53574; LDS 2098/064B; born 28/3/1869, Ballinameen, Co. Roscommon; son of Bernard O'Connor and Elizabeth Duignan; married on 21/8/1901, Delia McNally, of Clonbur, Co. Galway (Oughterard Registrar's District, September Quarter, 1901, vol. 4, p. 147) and they had three daughters; 3rd DI 5/12/1915. In February 1922, his name having been favourably mentioned by Michael Collins, he was asked to join the Civic Guards (later styled the Garda Síochána) and was appointed as a superintendent on 1/4/1922 based at Howth, Co. Dublin. In 1923 he was promoted chief superintendent at Bray, Co. Wicklow in charge of Counties Dublin and Wicklow and in 1924 was transferred to Mullingar, Co. Westmeath with responsibility for Counties Longford and Westmeath; on his retirement in 1934, the following tribute was paid to him in the *Garda Review*: '[He] was deservedly popular with all ranks. He was efficient, courteous and always ready to assist even the most junior member in matters concerning the public weal or private concern.' The legal profession also paid their tributes to him and said that 'under his control Westmeath was a model to the 26 counties'; died 8/12/1937 at the Mater Hospital, Dublin; buried in Deansgrange Cemetery, Dublin; obituary in the *Westmeath Examiner* reads: 'Deceased when in this country was highly respected and esteemed by a large circle of friends and as a police officer was noted for courtesy, efficiency and kindness.' (photo: Garda Museum & Archives, Dublin Castle).

O'Connor, Edward; LDS 2098/052; born 1864, March, Cambs., England; attending Oundle School, Oundle, Northants., England in 1881 (Census); BA, Oxford University, 1884; 3rd DI 30/1/1889; pensioned 15/10/1905.

O'Connor, James Fitzgerald G.; LDS 2097/046; born 1794, Co. Kerry; married on 31/8/1853 at Castlebar Church, Co. Mayo (Castlebar Registrar's District, vol. 3, p. 337); Lavinia (formerly O'Malley), relict of John Bingham Semple, Esq., of Turlough, Co. Mayo; 3rd SI 18/10/1823; CI 8/11/1838; pensioned 1/8/1865; died 20/11/1880 at 54, Waterloo Road, Dublin; will proved on 29/1/1881 at the Principal Registry by the oath of Lavinia O'Connor, widow, of 54 Waterloo Road, Dublin and Richard Fitzgerald, of River View, Tarbet, Co. Limerick, MD, the executors – effects under £4,000.

O'Connor, William; RIC 41912; LDS 2098/201; born 24/5/1857, Co. Kerry; 3rd DI 4/1/1904; pensioned 1/10/1917.

O'Connor, William F.; RIC 4567; LDS 2097/244; born 1825; Co. Sligo; 3rd SI 10/6/1863; pensioned 1/10/1882; died 26/7/1885 at Nenagh, Co. Tipperary (Nenagh Registrar's District, 1885, September Quarter, vol. 3, p. 332).

Odell, Charles G.; LDS 2097/143; born 1807, Co. Limerick; enlisted as a sub constable on 1/10/1827; married on 20/6/1830 Mary Codd, alias Manifold at Arklow, Co. Wicklow; son born on 28/3/1852 at Nenagh, Co. Tipperary (*Cork Examiner* 5/4/1852); 3rd SI 16/3/1844; received a grant from the Reward Fund on 31/5/1848 for uniformly zealous and successful exertions in making offenders amenable; pensioned 15/7/1867; died 21/5/1880.

Odlum, Richard Edward; LDS 2098/200; born 1854, Dublin City, Co. Dublin; major and riding master with the 7th and 14th Hussars in which he served for 22 years; married in October 1886, wife a native of Co. Dublin; 3rd DI 9/1/1903; King George V Visit to Ireland Medal, 1911; RIC Riding Master from 1903 to 1917; pensioned 7/12/1917; (Sketch in the *Constabulary Gazette*, vol. XV, no. 15, 2/7/1904).

O'Donel, James; LDS 2097/273; born 1818, Co. Donegal; wife from Co. Westmeath; 3rd SI 20/12/1866; pensioned 1/3/1878; died 27/7/1888 at Lisdoonvarna, Co. Clare; will proved on 10/9/1888 at Ballina by the oath of William O'Donel and Francis O'Donel, both of Castlebar, Co. Mayo, executors – effects £581.

O'Donoghue, Daniel Toler; CarNB; born 1776; joined the army in 1795; lieutenant-colonel; PPF; major 1st Garrison Battalion, 4/6/1813; half pay list 4/6/1814; chief magistrate 30/1/1817; stipendiary magistrate 1/1/1823; resident magistrate 1/12/1825; pensioned 1/10/1839.

O'Farrell, John Hubert; RIC 29060; LDS 2097/246; born 1842, Boyle, Co. Roscommon; 3rd SI 16/12/1863; received a favourable record on 31/12/1869 for efficient exertions in procuring evidence against perpetrators of an atrocious case of firing at the person; received a favourable record on 31/12/1869 for discovery by means of tracks of a man who had fired a shot at a person and discovery of concealed arms; died 2/1/1871 at Kells, Co. Meath; administration granted on 21/2/1871 at the Principal Registry to Harward O'Farrell, of Boyle, Co. Roscommon, father of the deceased – effects £328.

O'Halloran, Matthew Thomas; LDS 2097/101; born 1805, Co. Clare; ensign, 82nd Regiment of Foot (South Lancashire Regiment), 1816; employed in the Commissioner's Office in the Office of Examinations of Assessed Accounts, 1813 to 1819 and supervisor in the same department, 1819 to 1825; 3rd SI 1/10/1836; paymaster 1/10/1836 for counties Kilkenny and Waterford; discharged 31/5/1851; died 1862.

O'Hara, Charles Henry; RIC 56623; LDS 2098/108; born 11/5/1871, Clonmel, Co. Tipperary; brother of Patrick Joseph O'Hara, DI, RIC, RM; teacher of modern languages at Kilkenny College for five months; married on 8/4/1907 (Limerick Registrar's District, June Quarter, 1907, vol. 5, p. 237); 3rd SI 1/11/1894; King Edward VII Visit to Ireland Medal, 1903; chief police instructor at the Phoenix Park Depot from 28/3/1910 to 29/3/1915; King George V Visit to Ireland Medal, 1911; CI 22/4/1920; divisional magistrate 22/4/1920; pensioned 19/7/1922; died 1955.

O'Hara, Patrick Joseph; RIC 55990; LDS 2098/098; born 17/3/1868, Clonmel, Co. Tipperary; (Clonmel Registrar's District, 1868, vol. 9, p. 703); brother of Charles Henry O'Hara, CI, RIC; teacher at Rathmines School, Dublin for six months; married on 1/11/1910 (Manorhamilton Registrar's District, December Quarter, 1910, vol. 2, p. 217), wife a native of Co. Antrim; 3rd DI 1/2/1894; resident magistrate 3rd class 25/3/1919; (p. 170, RM Records of Service Book, National Archives, Dublin).

O'Hara, William James; RIC 47707; LDS 2097/312; born 23/6/1857, Coleraine, Co. Derry, son of James O'Hara; educated at Uppingham School; matriculated, 1876; BA, Trinity College, Cambridge, 1880; wife from Co. Kilkenny; 3rd SI 10/10/1881; resident magistrate 3rd class

7/7/1902, 2nd class 1/12/1907, 1st class 30/4/1919; pensioned 15/1/1921; (p. 122, RM Records of Service Book, National Archives, Dublin).

O'Loghlen, Bryan; LDS 2097/155; born 1791, Dysert, Co. Clare; 3rd SI 8/10/1846; paymaster 8/10/1846 for counties Kilkenny and Waterford; discharged 31/5/1859 on the abolition of the office of paymaster.

O'Loghlin, Colman Bryan; RIC 19331; LDS 2097/208; born 1832, Co. Dublin; son of Bryan O'Loghlin of Rockview, Ruane, Co. Clare and nephew of Sir Michael O'Loghlen, Master of the Rolls; 3rd SI 23/7/1856; pensioned 15/8/1885; died 18/4/1908 at Rockview, Ruane, Co. Clare; will proved on 14/12/1908 to Maria O'Loghlen, spinster – effects £469.13s.11d.

O'Malley, Augustus; LDS 2097/129; born 1810, Co. Limerick; 3rd SI 5/12/1839; pensioned on 18/1/1859 in Co. Meath; died 4/11/1859.

O'Meara, M.; LDS 2097/101; 3rd SI 1/10/1836; paymaster 1/10/1836; pensioned 7/11/1839.

O'Neill, Daniel; CarNB; born 1771; 3rd SI 1825; C.C. Lurgan, Co. Armagh; Kilkeel, Co. Down, 1831.

O'Neill, Francis; RIC 39490; LDS 2098/145; born 1854, Queen's County; married on 26/10/1898 (Clones Registrar's District, December Quarter, 1908, vol. 3, p. 98), wife a native of King's County; 3rd DI 1/7/1898; pensioned 15/5/1914; died 22/1/1919; (Rathdown Registrar's District, 1914, March Quarter, vol. 1, p. 518).

O'Reilly, Edward; RIC 26022; LDS 2097/236; born 1840, Co. Kilkenny; spent four years in a merchant office in Dublin (Messrs. Hunt & McCaffrey, No. 4, Merchant's Quay); married on 25/7/1876 (Granard Registrar's District, vol. 3, p. 217), wife a native of Co. Kerry; son born on 4/9/1861, at Eastwood, Glin, Co. Limerick (*Cork Examiner* 10/9/1861); 3rd SI 11/9/1860; pensioned 10/8/1890; died 18/11/1900 at 2, Farrington Square, London, late of Carrickmacross, Co. Monaghan and of Taghmon, Co. Wexford; will proved on 22/12/1900 at the Principal Registry by the oath of Helen O'Reilly, widow – effects £964.2s.0d.

O'Reilly, Mathew George; LDS 2097/165; born 1829, Co. Dublin; 3rd SI 29/4/1848; died 17/6/1868 at Kinsale, Co. Cork (Kinsale Registrar's District, 1869, vol. 12, p. 694).

Ormsby, Charles; LDS 2097/063; born 1797, Tubbervaddy, Co. Roscommon; 3rd SI 20/4/1826; dismissed 14/1/1849.

Ormsby, Robert; LDS 2097/057; born 1797, Castletown, Easky, Co. Sligo; 3rd SI 16/11/1824; chief constable in Ballyhaise, Co. Cavan when he and Major Peter Warburton and a party of police were attacked in December 1826; C.C. Brooksborough, Co. Fermanagh, 1831; died 6/3/1849 in Leeson Street, Dublin; (Certified copy of administration granted in respect of Robert Ormsby, Brooksborough, Co. Fermanagh, formerly of Donail, Co. Sligo at the Prerogative Court in 1849, NA Reference: T/125).

O'Rorke, Michael; RIC 43866; LDS 2098/134; born 1859; Co. Leitrim; married on 22/9/1887, wife a native of Co. Dublin; 3rd DI 16/7/1897; his son, Lewis John O'Rorke, 90 South Circular Road, Dublin died as a result of an accident in Mercer's Hospital, Dublin on 13/1/1914; buried in Glasnevin Cemetery on 17/1/1914; he died on 5/11/1915 at Edenderry, King's County; (Dublin South Registrar's District, 1915, December Quarter, vol. 2, p. 557); administration granted on 21/2/1916 at the Principal Registry to Margaret O'Rorke, the widow – effects £112.3s.2d.

O'Rorke, Michael Sylvester; RIC 69947; LDS 2098/105B; born 28/10/1895, Co. Dublin; (Dublin North Registrar's District, December Quarter, 1895, vol. 2, p. 381); son of Michael O'Rorke, DI, RIC; educated Blackrock School, Dublin; lieutenant, Royal Observer Corps, 1916; transferred to Royal Flying Corps, 1917 as a pilot and promoted captain; 3rd DI 4/1/1920; pensioned 30/3/1922; married in Haifa, Palestine in 1925, Muriel Edith Mawdesley, a native of Oundle, Northants., England; joined the Palestine Police as an assistant superintendent and promoted deputy superintendent, acting district superintendent in Haifa and on 1/4/1932 was personal assistant to the Inspector General of the Palestine Police until 1936 when he was promoted superintendent in charge of the traffic police. In 1938 he was responsible for setting up the Jewish Wing of the Palestine Police. Captain of the Palestine Rugby Team, 1923/25. Master of the Sarafand Foxhounds, 1936/39. In 1940 he was seconded the GHQ Middle East Cairo as Lieutenant Colonel (temp) and responsible for Public Safety and setting up civil police forces in Cyreneca, Abbysinia, Eritrea, Italian, Somaliland and Tripolitania; OBE Military (1942), CBE Civil (1952), CSt.J (1955); transferred to Supreme Headquarters Allied Expeditionary Force in April 1945 as Public Safety Adviser to General Eisenhower; Inspector General of Public Safety in Hamburg in April 1945; Inspector General for Public Safety in the British Zone, Berlin, Germany in 1947; Commissioner of Police, Kenya, 1950/54; Chairman Kenya Film Board of Censors and Commandant of St John's Ambulance (Kenya). Retired in 1962 and moved to Menorca, Spain. In September 1980 he moved to Hampshire, (England); (photo in the *Constabulary Gazette*, vol. 1, no. 16, 17/7/1897); died 3/5/1981 and buried in Glasnevin Cemetery, Dublin.

Osborne, Daniel Toler (Sir); CarNB; born 10/12/1783, Newtown-Anner, Co. Tipperary; son of Sir Henry Osborne, 11th Bt., of Beechwood, Nenagh, Co. Tipperary and Harriet, daughter and coheir of Daniel Toler and niece of John Toler (3/12/1745–27/7/1831), 1st Earl of Norbury ('The Hanging Judge'); married in January 1805, Lady Harriette La Poer Trench (died on 17/11/1855 at Pinner, Middlesex, England, aged 72 years)(*Cork Examiner* 23/11/1855), daughter of William, 1st Earl of Clancarty; they had five sons and five daughters; he succeeded the title as 12th Bt., on the decease of his father, Sir Henry on 27/10/1837; lieutenant-colonel; PPF; 3rd SI 1/7/1822; stipendiary magistrate 1/3/1826; pensioned 1/7/1841; died 25/3/1853 at Kensington Villa, Rathmines, Co. Dublin; buried in Mount Jerome Cemetery, Dublin on 27/3/1853 (Registry No. 235) (Section C, Grave No. 138, Grant No. 107P); C.C. Killucan, Co. Westmeath.

O'Shea, William Edward; RIC 28554; LDS 2097/245; born 1845, Co. Tipperary; 3rd SI 17/7/1863; died 7/2/1876 at Carrick-on-Shannon, Co. Leitrim; administration granted on 8/3/1876 at the Principal Registry to Thaddeus O'Shea, of George Street, Limerick, father of the deceased – effects under £1,500.

O'Shee, John Marcus Poer; RIC 56630; LDS 2098/111; born 17/10/1869, Co. Dublin; second son of Nicholas Richard Poer O'Shee (1821–1902), of Gardenmorris, Co. Waterford, JP and DL, Co. Waterford and Lady Gwendeline Anson (d.15/3/1912), youngest daughter of Thomas William, 1st Earl of Lichfield; he married on 22/9/1900, Myrtle Constance, third daughter of Col. Ynyr Henry Burges of Parkanaur; he had two daughters, Mildred born in 1901 and Gwendoline Constance on 19/4/1903; 3rd DI 17/1/1895; Queen Victoria's Visit to Ireland Medal, 1900; King Edward VII Visit to Ireland Medal, 1903; Adjutant, Phoenix Park Depot from 8/5/1903 to 1/4/1907; Assistant Commandant and Adjutant, Richmond Barracks Sub Depot from 17/9/1907 to 10/4/1908; CI 1/5/1920; Commandant, RIC Camp Gormanston from 11/9/1920 to 22/11/1920; pensioned 5/4/1922.

O'Sullivan, Patrick Augustus; RIC 72017; LDS 2098/153B; born 11/9/1898, Belfast, Co. Antrim; (Belfast Registrar's District, 1898, December Quarter, vol. 1, p. 241); lieutenant, Bedfordshire Regiment; married on 18/9/1920, wife a native of Co. Dublin; 3rd SI 10/1/1920; pensioned 17/4/1922.

O'Sullivan, Philip John; RIC 72019; LDS 2098/166B; born 6/8/1897, Dennis Square, Kinsale, Co. Cork; (Kinsale Registrar's District, 1897, vol. 5, p. 288); the only son of Florence O'Sullivan (b.1868), journalist and co-founder of the *Southern Star* newspaper and Margaret Barry, daughter of Dominick Barry, DI, RIC who were married in 1895; at the outbreak of WW1 he joined the Royal Navy Volunteer Reserve, was commissioned as a lieutenant and given command of a mine-layer. For his role at the Battle of Durazzo he was decorated by the King of Italy and also received the Military Cross for other distinguished conduct; at the end of the War he qualified and practised as a solicitor; 3rd DI 10/1/1920; attached to the Crime Special

Department at Headquarters on 1/10/1920; killed 17/12/1920, Henry Street, Dublin while walking with his fiancée, Alice Moore; late of Denis Quay, Kinsale, Co. Cork; will proved at Cork on 21/1/1921.

O'Sullivan, Tobias; RIC 59193; LDS 2098/222B; born 1877, Oughterard, Co. Galway; (Oughterard Registrar's District, 1877, vol. 14, p. 411); 3rd DI 26/9/1920; killed 20/1/1921, Listowel, Co. Kerry; administration granted at the Principal Registry on 29/7/1921.

Otter, Edwin F.; RIC 50984; LDS 2097/329; born 1860, Co. Westmeath; 3rd DI 22/2/1883; pensioned 1/3/1906; died 18/7/11 at Ennis, Co. Clare; buried at Drumcliffe Cemetery, Co. Sligo; (photo in the *Constabulary Gazette*, vol. 1, no. 23, 4/9/1897).

Oulton, Courtenay C.; RIC 50993; LDS 2097/332; born 1859, Pomeroy, Co. Tyrone; son of Rev. Richard Oulton; BA 1881, Trinity College Dublin; 3rd DI 11/9/1883; CI 4/4/1908; King George V Coronation Medal, 1911; pensioned 15/6/1920.

Owen, Henry Lindsay; RIC 21222; LDS 2097/210; born 1833, Co. Wexford; 3rd SI 1/12/1857; CI 8/4/1878; pensioned 1/11/1886; died 18/11/1886 at Farnham House, Finglas, Co. Dublin, formerly of Newtown and Landsdowne, Co. Waterford; will proved on 9/12/1886 at the Principal Registry by the oath of Adeline Mary Grenville Owen, of 4, Upper Pembroke Street, Dublin, the widow and sole executrix – effects £3,362.11s.0d.

P

Page, William Robert; RIC 51021; LDS 2097/333; born 1859, Middlesex, England; (St George Hanover Square Registrar's District, 1859, March Quarter, vol. 1a, p. 207); son of Charles G. Page (b.1822) Pimlico, London, Middlesex, and Emma Page (b.1824) Suffolk; residing at 51, Wirtemburg Street, Clapham, Surrey in 1881 (Census); 3rd DI 14/11/1883; died 30/6/1884 at Woodford, Co. Galway.

Pain, Brigadier-General Sir George William Hackett; born 5/2/1855; son of George Pain; married in 1898, Sadie, daughter of Sidney Merton, Sydney, New South Wales; entered the army in 1875; captain, 1886; served in the Sudan, 1888 (medal with clasp, Khedive's Star); Nile Frontier Force, 1889 (3rd class Medidjeh); capture of Tokar, 1891 (3rd class Osmanish, clasp to star); Dungola Expeditionary Force, 1896 (despatches, brevet of Lieutenant-Colonel, British medal, Khedive's medal and two clasps); Nile Field Force; Acting A.G. to Egyptian Army to end of campaign; Brevet Colonel, 1901; South African War, 1901–02 (CB, medal and 3 clasps, King's medal and two clasps); Colonel, 1907; command of No. 7 District Southern Command, 1908–11; retired, 1912; raised and commanded 108th Infantry Brigade, Ulster Division, 1914 (Bronze Star, 1915, General Service and Victory medals); commanded 15th Reserve Infantry Brigade in Belfast, 1915; Northern District Irish Command during the Irish Rebellion, 1916 to November 1919; CB (1900), KBE (1919); divisional commissioner for Leinster, 11/3/1920 until the Truce, 1921 (despatches, KBE); MP (C.U.) South Londonderry from 1922; died 14/2/1924.

Park, John; RIC 10869; LDS 2097/280; born 1830, Co. Antrim; 3rd SI 26/5/1870; pensioned 25/6/1873; died 1874 at Ballymena, Co. Antrim; (Ballymena Registrar's District, 1874, vol. 16, p. 80).

Parker, Thomas; LDS 2097/140; born 1816, Co. Tipperary; 3rd SI 1/07/1842; dismissed 15/11/1844.

Parkinson, Garrett Wellesley; LDS 2097/175; born 9/10/1822, Kilrush, Co. Clare; mate and master in the Merchant Navy for nine years; 3rd SI 5/8/1848; resident magistrate 16/2/1865; retired as a resident magistrate on 9/10/1882.

Patrick, George Richard William; RIC 58075; LDS 2098/138; born 1873, Tipperary, Co. Tipperary; (Tipperary Registrar's District, 1873, vol. 8, p. 744); married on 8/6/1911 (Cork Registrar's District, June Quarter, 1911, vol. 5, p. 54), wife a native of Co. Cork; 3rd DI 25/3/1898; King Edward VII Visit to Ireland Medal, 1903; ACI 20/8/1920; CI 1/10/1920; pensioned 10/5/1922.

Patterson, Frederick George; LDS 2097/214; born 1832, Co. Dublin; joined the Irish Revenue Police as a lieutenant on 12/11/1852 and served in Drumkeerin, Co. Leitrim; 3rd SI 1/12/1857; resigned 31/1/1869.

Pattisson, Pierre B.; RIC 45468; LDS 2097/308; born 1857, Essex, England; captain, 5th Battalion, Natal Native Contingent; tutor; awarded the Zulu War Medal with Clasp for 1879; 3rd SI 11/11/1880; married on 20/11/1885 at the parish church, Clontarf, Co. Dublin, Bertha Maude, youngest daughter of Lieutenant-Colonel James Balcombe, of 1 Marino Terrace, Clontarf, Co. Dublin, Secretary of the Clontarf Commissioners, formerly of the 57th Regiment of Foot (West Middlesex Regiment) and Royal South Down Militia (WO 13/2797–814); her sister, Florence Balcombe (b.1858), an aspiring actress who had been courted by Oscar Wilde, married on 4/12/1878, at St Ann's Church, Dublin, Bram Stoker (8/11/1847–20/4/1912),

202 Edwin F. Otter. 203 George William Hackett Pain, Divisional Commissioner, RIC.
204 Pierre B. Pattisson. 205 Pryce Peacock – Surgeon.

author of *Dracula*, published on 26/5/1897; Bram Stoker was born at 15 The Crescent, Clontarf, Co. Dublin and his first book, published in 1879, was *The Duties of Clerks of Petty Sessions in Ireland*; Pattisson's wife, Bertha Maude, was an authoress of several articles in the *Sketch*, *The Illustrated Sporting and Dramatic News*, *Temple Bar* and *The English Illustrated Magazine*; his second son, Arthur Jacob, died at Clonmel, Co. Tipperary, aged one year on 29/6/1896; captain superintendent of police at Shanghai from December 1897 to December 1900; pensioned 6/10/1908; (photo in the *Constabulary Gazette*, vol. 1, no. 31, 30/10/1897).

Patton, David; LDS 2097/057; born 1795, Co. Antrim; assessor of taxes from 18/8/1817 to 1/3/1824; 3rd SI 16/11/1824; C.C. Portadown, Co. Armagh, 1831; pensioned 22/1/1869; died 10/1/1878 at Cavan, Co. Cavan; will proved on 14/2/1878 at the Principal Registry by the oath of James Kerr, of Carlow, Co. Carlow, a captain in the Cavan Militia, one of the executors – effects under £3,000.

Pawle, Reginald Brooks; RIC 79039; ADRIC CADET no. 647; LDS 2098/233B; born 7/6/1894, Essex, England; (Reigate Registrar's District, 1894, September Quarter, vol. 2a, p. 161); son of Ernest Dosselor Pawle, Newport House, Great Baddow, Chelmsford, Essex; educated at Marlborough College; stockbroker; private, 10th (Service) Battalion Royal Fusiliers; reg. no.1079; sergeant, 9/9/1914; lance sergeant, 24/1/1915; 2nd lieutenant, 1st Battalion Hertfordshire Regiment, 8/6/1915; lieutenant, 1/6/1916; wounded by gunshot in the right side, 6/3/1918 and by gunshot wound to the chest, 23/8/1918; disembodied 24/1/1919; ceased to hold a commission in the Territorial army for failing to attend parades (*London Gazette* dated 22/2/1922); 3rd DI 2/7/1921; resigned 4/5/1921; (WO 374/52784).

Paye, Thomas; LDS 2097/104; 3rd SI 1/11/1836.

Peacock, Arthur Wellington; RIC 72859; ADRIC CADET no. 322; LDS 2098/206B; born 9/2/1884, Berks., England; (Camberwell Registrar's District, 1884, March Quarter, vol. 1d, p. 857); captain, Cheshire Regiment; married on 13/4/1918, Edith Hughes, a native of Hampshire; 3rd DI 12/1/1920; pensioned 13/4/1922; (WO 374/54498).

Peacock, Pryce; RIC 21225; LDS 2097/209; born 1832, Co. Limerick; 3rd SI 2/12/1856; died 14/6/1867 at George Street, Limerick; (Limerick Registrar's District, 1867, vol. 10, p. 336); administration granted at Limerick on 7/10/1867 to The Venerable and Reverend Pryce Peacock, of George Street, Limerick, the father and only next of kin of the deceased – effects under £100.

Peacock, Pryce; LDS 2098/054B; born 26/8/1866, Kilrush, Co. Clare; (Kilrush Registrar's District, 1866, vol. 14, p. 376); resided at Castleknock, Co. Dublin; registered on 20/12/1893; L., L.M., R.C.P., 1893; 3rd DI 8/1/1914; Surgeon to the Force; pensioned 12/7/1922; Co-founder of the Irish Automobile Club on 22 January 1901, at the Metropole Hotel, Sackville Street (O'Connell Street), Dublin; (photo & full dress uniform – Garda Museum & Archives, Dublin Castle).

Pearce, William Henry; LDS 2097/029; born 1793, Sussex, England; sergeant, 91st Regiment of Foot (The Argyllshire Highlanders) from August 1807 to August 1814; drill sergeant-major, 18th Hussars from February 1815 to August 1821, with two years service for Waterloo; 3rd SI 1/5/1822; C.C. Kells, Co. Meath, 1832; CI 1/3/1839; resigned 1/5/1847 on his appointment as Chief Constable of the Glasgow Police, Scotland until 10/4/1848.

Pearson, Edward Humble; RIC 45345; LDS 2097/307; born 1859, Co. Galway; married on 28/4/1892 (Kilkeel Registrar's District, June Quarter, 1892, vol. 1, p. 651), wife from Co. Westmeath; 3rd SI 8/6/1880; CI 2/12/1901; King Edward VII Visit to Ireland Medal, 1903; CI attached to Crime Department from 14/8/1907 to 9/11/1911; King George V Visit to Ireland Medal, 1911; AIG 9/11/1911; Commandant of the Phoenix Park Depot from 9/11/1911 to 29/4/1920; pensioned 8/6/1920.

Pelly, John; RIC 25539; LDS 2097/235; born 1838, Co. Galway, fifth son of Cornelius Pelly (d.1863), of Kill, Co. Galway and Mary, daughter of Michael Kelly of Kelly's Grove, Co. Galway;

3rd SI 15/4/1860; died 30/6/1879 at Bray, Co. Wicklow; administration granted on 21/8/1879 at the Principal Registry to Cornelius Pelly, 64 Harcourt Street, Dublin, brother of the deceased – effects under £600.

Pendleton, Samuel Q. Welsted; CarNB; born Belfast, Co. Antrim; army; PPF; chief magistrate 12/3/1816; resigned 1/5/1820; not appointed to the County Constabulary; C.C. Galway; died before 1836.

Pennington, Edwin Grundy; RIC 24629; LDS 2097/227; born 16/5/1835, Suffolk, England; 3rd SI 20/4/1859; musketry instructor at the Phoenix Park Depot from 29/11/1878 to 1/10/1882; CI 1/10/1882; AIG 1/10/1888; Commandant of the Phoenix Park Depot from 1/10/1888 until his death on 27/6/1896 at the RIC Depot, Phoenix Park, Dublin (Dublin North Registrar's District, 1896, September Quarter, vol. 2, p. 291); will proved on 7/8/1896 at the Principal Registry by the oath of Etty de Vere Pennington, RIC Depot, widow – effects £487.1s.2d.; buried in Deansgrange Cemetery, Dublin on 30/6/1896; (South Section, Row W, Grave No. 12) – the inscription on a plinth of a large marble white cross reads: 'In Loving Memory of Edwin Grundy Pennington, Assistant Inspector General and Commandant, R.I. Constabulary, who fell asleep June 27th, 1896 – "I know that my redeemer liveth"'.

Pepper, John Willington; LDS 2097/192; born 1832, Charleville, Co. Cork; second son of Theobald Pepper, Lissinisky, Co. Tipperary, SI, RIC; 3rd SI 3/4/1852; pensioned 1/2/1883; died 17/2/1911 at Belvedere, Meath Road, Bray, Co. Wicklow; buried in Deansgrange Cemetery, Dublin (South Section, Row Q2, Grave No. 76) with his wife Deborah Pepper (d.4/11/1930), only son Captain John Gerald Willington Pepper (d.19/1/1957) late of the Royal Artillery and Ellen M.C. Pepper (d.21/11/1897); administration granted on 8/6/1911 at the Principal Registry to John Gerald Willington Pepper and George R. Pepper – effects £22,583.2s.6d., Resworn £23,256.17s.6d.

Pepper, Theobald; LDS 2097/027; born 1793, Norwood, Lissinisky, Co. Tipperary; father of John Willington Pepper, SI, RIC; ensign 2nd Battalion, 87th Regiment of Foot (Royal Irish Regiment), 1/11/1808; lieutenant, 1/6/1811; lieutenant 3rd Dragoon Guards, 1812; lieutenant half pay, 1/7/1814; married in January, 1823, Margaret, eldest daughter of John Willington, of Castle Willington, Co. Tipperary (*Connaught Journal*, 3/2/1823); children: Jane, born November 1823, Thomas, born December 1825, Ellen, born January 1828; a third son, Hampden Frederick, aged 17 years, died on 14/9/1852 of disease of the heart, at Lissinisky, Co. Tipperary (*Cork Examiner* 20/9/1852); 3rd SI 21/6/1821; pensioned 1/7/1848; died 15/10/1865 at No. 30, Crosthwaite Park, Kingstown, Co. Dublin, formerly of Lissinisky, Co. Tipperary; will with one codicil proved on 8/11/1865 at the Principal Registry by the oath of Margaret Pepper, of Crosthwaite Park, widow of the deceased and one of the executors – effects under £7,000; (WO 25/771 fol. 40).

Percy, Francis; LDS 2097/025; born 1798, King's County; brother of William Percy, SI, RIC; ensign and lieutenant, 51st Regiment of Foot (King's Own Light Infantry Regiment) from 22/7/1813 to 24/12/1818; wife a native of Dublin City; 3rd SI 18/4/1820; CI 24/6/1834; AIG 1/1/1857; pensioned 1/1/1860; died 9/3/1882 at 14, Merrion Square, Dublin; will proved on 31/3/1882 at the Principal Registry by the oath of Rebecca Hamilton, of 14, Merrion Square, widow, the sole executrix – effects £1,667.17s.6d.

Percy, William; CarNB; born, 1793, 11 Russell Street, Dublin, Co. Dublin; brother of Francis Percy, CI, RIC; ensign, 60th Regiment of Foot (Royal American Regiment), 6/11/1809; cornet, 14th Light Dragoons, 5/7/1810; lieutenant, 6/6/1811; lieutenant 74th Regiment of Foot (Highlanders Regiment), 23/1/1812; lieutenant half pay, 36th Regiment of Foot (Herefordshire Regiment), 11/5/1815; 3rd SI 30/10/1822; C.C. barony of Iffa and Offa West, Cahir, Co. Tipperary in 1825; married 9/9/1823 at Knockmourne Church, Co. Cork by Rev. George Gumbleton to Mary Anne, daughter of Robert Warren Gumbleton Esq., of Fort William Park, Co. Waterford and Castleview, Co. Cork; sons: Robert Gumbleton Percy (b.16/2/1826) and

Major John William Percy (b.26/8/1827) (d.15/11/1899), 9th Regiment of Foot (Royal Norfolk Regiment) who is buried in Deansgrange Cemetery, Dublin (South Section, Row O1, Grave No. 26) with his wife Maria Gertrude (20/3/1835–12/12/1903); his brother-in-law, Richard Gumbleton, married on 2/9/1823, at Bath, Somerset, England, Anne Rachel, eldest daughter of the late H. Fowke, Esq., of Tewkesbury (the *Constitution* or *Cork Morning Post*, Wednesday, 3/9/1823); resigned in 1831 following an investigation by provincial inspector general William Miller into the manner in which he paid his men. Miller found 'mistakes of the most reprehensible irregularity largely due to carelessness'; (WO 35/771 fol. 39).

Persse, Dominick; CarNB; born 1782, Killoshulan, Fertagh, Co. Kilkenny; youngest son of Rev. William Persse (d.1813) Rector of Tynagh and Frances Browne, of Woodstock, Co. Mayo; lieutenant, 1808, 71st Regiment of Foot (Highland Regiment); served in the Peninsular War and retired in 1812; married on 11/11/1813, Catharine Henderson (b.1794) (d.24/1/1867 – Millford Registrar's District, vol. 2, p. 194), of Hollymount, Ramelton, Co. Donegal; his youngest son, John G. Persse, Esq., solicitor, of Castleblayney, Co. Monaghan, married on 23/6/1869 at Grangegorman Church, Jane Maria Annette, eldest daughter of Peyton Sheals, of Fortview House, Co. Roscommon, niece to the late and cousin to the present, Sir Hew Crawford-Pollok (d.1885), of Pollok Castle, Renfrewshire, Scotland (*Cork Examiner* 26/6/1869); 3rd SI 1822, Ramelton, Co. Donegal; pensioned 23/10/1835; died on 24/1/1867; C.C. King's County, 1825; Ramelton, Co. Donegal, 1831.

Phillips, James H.; LDS 2097/132; born 1818, Co. Monaghan; 3rd SI 7/7/1840; discharged 1/6/1853, being of unsound mind.

Phillips, John Dunville; RIC 38845; LDS 2097/291; born 1847, Co. Galway; wife from Co. Tipperary S.R.; 3rd SI 2/10/1872; died 31/3/1884 at 7, Newenham Street, Limerick; buried in Clonmel, Co. Tipperary on 2/4/1884; will proved with one codicil on 11/6/1884 at the Principal Registry by the oath of Francis Geraghty, of 1 Clyde Terrace, St John's Terrace, Sandymount, Co. Dublin, accountant to the Irish Land Commission, one of the executors – effects £839.11s.7d.

Phillips, Richard; RIC 21389; LDS 2097/316; born 1839, Co. Monaghan; wife from Co. Sligo; 3rd SI 16/1/1882; pensioned 17/3/1899; in retirement he resided at Rokeby, Terenure, Dublin; he is buried in Mount Jerome Cemetery, Dublin and his headstone inscription reads 'Erected by his sorrowing widow in fond and loving memory of Richard Phillips, DI, RIC, who departed this life on the 3rd March 1911. Here also lie the remains of Frances Anne Phillips, widow of the above named Richard Phillips, who died on 31st day of December 1913, aged 75 years'; will proved on 27/3/1911 at the Principal Registry by the oath of Frances Anne Phillips, the widow – effects £6,290.6s.4d.

Pilkington, Henry Brudenell; LDS 2097/078; born 1809, Geashill, King's County; City of Dublin Police from 1827 to 1829; enlisted as a constable, 1/8/1829; wife a native of Dublin City; 3rd SI 1/1/1836; CI 17/11/1862; pensioned 25/3/1872; died 24/8/1880.

Pim, Richard Pike; RIC 81125; LDS 2099/025; born 20/6/1900, Lisburn, Co. Antrim; (Lisburn Registrar's District, 1900, September Quarter, vol. 1, p. 624); KBE, VRD, DL; sub lieutenant, R.N.V.R; 3rd SI 25/6/1921; pensioned 31/8/1922; transferred to the Royal Ulster Constabulary on 1/9/1922; Inspector General of the Royal Ulster Constabulary from August 1945 to January 1961.

Pinchin, Blennerhassett; RIC 15049; LDS 2097/187; born 1827, Co. Kerry, son of George Pinchin (4/9/1790–4/2/1870), SI, RIC, of Limerick City and Margaret Fitzmaurice; master and assistant master in the Navy, from 1842 to 1845; 3rd SI 16/6/1851; son born on 14/1/1856, at Ballyjamesduff, Co. Cavan (*Cork Examiner* 21/1/1856); died 3/11/1858 at Newtownhamilton, Co. Armagh; a gratuity of £54.8s.8d. was granted to his family on 3/12/1858; administration granted on 9/5/1859 at the Principal Registry to his wife Frances (nee Nowlan) Pinchin, 14 Lennox Street, Dublin.

Pinchin, George; LDS 2097/084; born 4/9/1790, Limerick City, Co. Limerick; father of Blennerhassett Pinchin (1827–1858), SI, RIC: married in 1809, Margaret Fitzmaurice, of Duagh, Co. Kerry; served as a judge of a manor court in 1827; Kerry Yeomanry, 1810; Deputy Clerk of the Peace, from 6/4/1824 to 10/1/1825; Comptroller of Customs at Miramichi, New Brunswick, from 9/5/1828 to 15/2/1834; 3rd SI 15/2/1834; pensioned 10/5/1856; his wife Margaret died on 28/10/1851 at Skibbereen, Co. Cork after a long illness (*Cork Examiner* 3/11/1851); she was a niece of Thomas Fitzmaurice, Lord Baron Ventry and a sister of Lieutenant-Colonel John Fitzmaurice, KH; his eldest daughter, Amelia, married at Skibbereen, Co. Cork, on 8/1/1856 (Skibbereen Registrar's District, vol. 10, p. 110), William Lowth, Esq., of Castle Eyre, Co. Cork (*Cork Examiner* 11/1/1856); his second daughter, Georgina Maria, married at Skibbereen, Co. Cork on 17/3/1853 (Skibbereen Registrar's District, vol. 10, p. 101), William Everitt, Solicitor, of Skibbereen (*Cork Examiner* 25/3/1853); died 5/12/1870 at Ardralla, near Skibbereen, Co. Cork; administration granted on 19/7/1870 at the Principal Registry to Wallis Pinchin, of 10, Beaufort Terrace, Birkenhead, Ches., England, medical doctor, son (by decree Pinchin -v-Pinchin, 21/6/1870) – effects under £500.

Plant, George; RIC 52414; LDS 2098/032; born 1862, Ballymahon, Co. Longford; youngest son of John Plant, Tuome, Ballymahon, Co. Longford; 3rd DI 1/6/1887; died 30/1/1890 at the Adelaide Hospital, Dublin; buried in Kilcammock family burial ground on 3/2/1890.

Plummer, Brudenell; LDS 2097/117; born 1804, Mount Plummer, Monegay, Newcastle, Co. Limerick; second son of Brudenell Plummer, of Mount Plummer, Co. Limerick, JP, High Sheriff, 1808 and Frances Fitzgerald (d.13/5/1849 at Mount Plummer, Co. Limerick), daughter of Thomas Fitzgerald, Knight of Glin, of Glin Castle, Co. Limerick, by his wife, Mary, daughter of John Bateman, of Oak Park, Co. Kerry who were married on 6/1/1755; married Martha, daughter of Rev. Edwin Thomas, of Ballynacourty, Co. Kerry and they had four daughters, Frances FitzGerard, Mary Geraldine, Martha Edwin and Jane Louisa; his youngest daughter, Jane Louisa (d.19/3/1918) married Alexander Boyle (b.8/8/1845)(d.27/3/1920), of Bridge Hill, JP, BA TCD, Barrister-at-Law, King's Inn, Dublin, 1870, Major Londonderry Artillery, eldest son of Edward Boyle (1784–1861), solicitor and law agent to the Marquess of Waterford and Mary Anne Parke, of Stewartstown, Co. Tyrone; 3rd SI 1/11/1837; died 28/12/1869 at The Bungalow, Caw, Londonderry (*Cork Examiner* 3/1/1870); administration granted at Londonderry on 19/1/1870 to Martha Plummer, of The Bungalow, Caw, Londonderry, widow of the deceased – effects under £450.

Plunkett, Christopher; CarNB; born 1793, Co. Westmeath; 3rd SI 1/10/1821; CI 1/9/1824; stipendiary magistrate 1/2/1833; resident magistrate 1/10/1836; pensioned as a RM on 1/11/1850; residing at 5, Kildare Street, Dublin in October 1850 and retired to Brompton, London; C.C. Coleraine, Co. Derry, 1831.

Plunkett, Michael Richard; LDS 2097/034; born 1792, Co. Roscommon; ensign, 2nd Garrison Battalion and 39th Regiment of Foot (Dorsetshire Regiment) from 11/8/1808 to 24/1/1814; 3rd SI 23/1/1823; CI 1/10/1836; stipendiary magistrate 20/10/1846; pensioned a RM on 5/8/1857; residing at 115, Lower Gardiner Street, Dublin in 1850.

Plunkett, R.J.; LDS 2097/142; born 1824, Co. Galway; 3rd SI 24/8/1843; dismissed on 26/10/1852 and his record of dismissal was altered to resignation on 16/6/1855 with the sanction of the Lord Lieutenant on 16/6/1855.

Plunkett, Thomas Oliver Westenra; born 8/4/1838, Co. Louth; second son of Thomas Oliver Plunkett (5/8/1809–26/6/1849), 12th Baron Louth, of Louth Castle, Co. Louth and Anna Maria (d.18/1/1878), youngest daughter of Philip Roche, of Donore, Co. Kildare, by Anna Maria, youngest daughter of 13th Baron of Dunsany; married on 24/7/1862, at St James, Piccadilly, London, by the Rev. Stanley Leathes, MA, Clara Anne (d.27/7/1867), only daughter of John Kirby, Esq., of Sheffield, Yorkshire; married secondly on 20/6/1874, Caroline Alicia Victoria, only daughter of Col. Henry Musters, JP, DL, of Brianstown, Co. Longford; resident magistrate, 14/6/1866; special resident magistrate 1882; captain, 1st Regiment of Foot (1st Royals Regiment); Crimean Medal clasp for Sebastopol and Turkish Medals and also Medal and two clasps for China; died 6/12/1889; buried in Louth on 10/12/1889.

Ponsonby, Richard; LDS 2097/034; born 1796, Crotta House, Kilflynn, Listowel, Co. Kerry; lieutenant in the Kerry Militia from April 1810 to August 1814 (WO 13/2902–22); ensign from September 1814 to August 1816; major; 3rd SI 28/1/1823; died 1/10/1842; his widow Honoria Ponsonby, who was extensively connected among the county families of Kerry died on 16/11/1864 (Tralee Registrar's District, vol. 5, p. 531) aged 76 years, at the residence of her son-in-law, Stephen Sandes, Kilflynn, Co. Kerry (*Cork Examiner* 19/11/1864).

Pooley, John Mason; LDS 2097/136; born 1809, Cornwall, England; paymaster in the Peace Preservation Force from 4/4/1831 to 25/3/1834; clerk in the Tithe Loan Fund Office from March 1834 to July 1835; assistant secretary, Poor Enquiry Commission from July 1835 to June 1836; clerk in the Ordnance Secretary's Office from July 1836 to September 1837; 3rd SI 1/8/1841; paymaster and barrackmaster of the Phoenix Park Depot 1/8/1841 and residing at Shotscourt, 8 Serpentine Avenue, Ballsbridge, Dublin; dismissed 8/11/1850.

Porter, Thomas; LDS 2097/065; born 1786, Milford Haven, Pemb., England; married firstly at St Bride's Church, London, 10/11/1818; wife a native of Co. Westmeath; married secondly Elizabeth, daughter of the late R. Adams, Esq., of Mullingar, Co. Westmeath, on 19/4/1851 at Abbeylara Church, Abbeylara, Co. Longford (Granard Registrar's District, vol. 6, p. 141) (*Cork Examiner* 23/4/1851); son born on 5/1/1856, in Longford, Co. Longford (*Cork Examiner* 16/1/1856); ensign, 66th Regiment of Foot (Berkshire Regiment), 1/6/1813; ensign, Regiment of 28 Foot, 1814; ensign, 35th Regiment of Foot (Royal Sussex Regiment), 1818; ensign, 1st West India Regiment, 1825; lieutenant, 77th Regiment of Foot (East Middlesex Regiment), 1/10/1825; lieutenant half pay, 1/9/1826; awarded one medal and two clasps for Orthes and Toulouse; 3rd SI 1/11/1826; CI 23/11/1850; pensioned 1/6/1865; died 4/4/1866 at Dundalk, Co. Louth; will proved on 28/5/1866 at the Principal Registry by the oath of Elizabeth Porter of Dundalk, Co. Louth, widow and sole executrix – effects under £3,000; (WO 25/771 fol. 144); C.C. Ballymore, 1833.

Potter, Bernard; RIC 3525; LDS 2097/222; born 1815, Co. Roscommon; married on 23/2/1873 at the Cathedral, Cork, Kate, youngest daughter of Denis Reedy, Esq., Skibbereen, Co. Cork; 3rd SI 6/9/1858; pensioned 1/10/1882; died 12/5/1887 at Verdon Row, Cork; administration granted on 18/7/1887 at Cork to Catherine Clancy, of Moylough, Co. Galway, widow, the sister – effects £4,519.13s.7d.

Potter, Gilbert Norman; RIC 59414; LDS 2098/177; born 10/7/1878, Dromahair, Co. Leitrim; married on 9/4/1913 (Dublin South Registrar's District, June Quarter, 1913, vol. 2, p. 565), Lilias Marie Harding, a native of Co. Clare; 3rd DI 27/4/1901; Queen Victoria's Visit to Ireland Medal, 1900 as a cadet; King Edward VII Visit to Ireland Medal, 1903 as a head constable; King George V Visit to Ireland Medal, 1911; kidnapped by the IRA on 22 April 1921 and his wife received a letter saying he had been tried, convicted, sentenced to death and executed on 27 April 1921, at Clogheen, Co. Tipperary; late of Apsley House, Cahir, Co. Tipperary; he left a widow and four children, the eldest 7 and the youngest 4; buried in the Church of Ireland Cemetery, Cahir, Co. Tipperary; administration granted at the Principal Registry on 28/7/1921 – effects were a Ford motor car valued £50, an insurance policy for £300, arrears of pay of £25 and personal belongings valued £50.

Powell, Thomas (Sir); KH (1836); CarNB; born in Wales; adjutant, 11/2/1808 and lieutenant, 14/4/1808 24th Regiment of Foot (Warwickshire Regiment); major, Glengarry Fencibles (British Highland Regiment), 11/5/1815; half-pay major, Rifle Brigade, 11/5/1815; chief magistrate; provincial inspector general 6/11/1822 for Leinster; residing in Corcagh House, Co. Dublin, 1825; resigned, March 1828; captain, 57th Regiment of Foot (West Middlesex

206   207

206 Edward Humble Pearson. 207 Richard Pike Pim, Inspector General Royal Ulster Constabulary, 1945–61. 208 Ivon Henry Price. 209 Lieutenant-Colonel Ivon Henry Price, DSO.

208   209

Regiment), 27/10/1829; major, 2nd (The Queen's Royal) or Light Dragoons; lieutenant colonel, 40th Regiment of Foot (2nd Somersetshire Regiment), 19/2/1836.

Power, Pierce Charles; LDS 2097/238; born 1860, Co. Westmeath; married on 1/5/1903, wife a native of Co. Waterford; son born on 15/9/1861, at Moate, Co. Westmeath (*Cork Examiner* 16/9/1861); 3rd SI 4/1/1883; musketry instructor at the Phoenix Park Depot from 21/12/1896 to 15/12/1901; Queen Victoria's Visit to Ireland Medal, 1900; King Edward VII Visit to Ireland Medal, 1903; CI 28/9/1906; King George V Coronation Medal, 1911; pensioned 1/8/1920; his daughter was born on 17/9/1907 at Spawell House, Wexford, Co. Wexford; (photo in the *Constabulary Gazette*, vol. 2, no. 36, 4/12/1897, p. 1, vol. 2, no. 39, p. 1, 24/12/1897 & vol. XV, no. 23, 27/8/1904).

Power, Pierce Courtenay; RIC 2958; LDS 2097/224; born 1817, Co. Waterford; married on 22/7/1854, wife a native of Co. Sligo; 3rd SI 1/12/1858; died 2/11/1877 at Galway, Co. Galway; administration granted on 26/11/1877 at Tuam to Jane Power, of Galway, widow of the deceased, effects under £600; his only daughter, Lillie, married on 9/12/1886 at Kensington Cathedral, William J. Morton, 124 Marleybone Road, London W.

Power, Redmond; LDS 2097/108; born 1812, Co. Waterford; wife Helen was a native of South Wales and she died at Bantry, Co. Cork on 25/11/1852 (*Cork Examiner* 29/11/1852); 3rd SI 17/11/1836; daughters born at Bantry, Co. Cork on 10/9/1846 and 3/10/1852 and sons born at Bantry on 8/4/1848 and 16/8/1850; pensioned 1/6/1853; died 2/11/1877 at Youghal, Co. Cork; administration granted on 13/12/1878 at Cork to Kate Maria Power, of Youghal, Co. Cork – effects under £100.

Power, William; LDS 2097/106; born 1798, Co. Cork; 3rd SI 8/11/1836; died 11/4/1844.

Prescott-Decie, Brigadier-General Cyril; born 4/8/1865, Bockleton Court, Herefs., England; divisional commissioner 2/4/1920–14/2/1921, Munster No. 1 Division and stationed

210 Edward Jonathan Priestley, Deputy Inspector General, Irish Constabulary, portrait in PSNI Museum, Belfast.   211 Edward Jonathan Priestley – grave in Mount Jerome Cemetery, Dublin.

at Cork City; senior divisional commissioner, 14/2/1921, but resigned his position; brigadier-general Royal Artillery; died in 1953.

Preston, Elystan George Crompton; RIC 58077; LDS 2098/142; born 1873, Lisnaskea, Co. Fermanagh; (Lisnaskea Registrar's District, 1873, vol. 8, p. 244); tutor, 1890 to 1895 and Private Secretary to Col. North, 1895–6; King Edward VII Visit to Ireland Medal, 1903; member of the 4th class Royal Victorian Order, 1903; married firstly on 18/9/1898 (Rathdown Registrar's District, September Quarter, 1898, vol. 2, p. 783), Edith Leatham, Kent, England, dissolved by divorce on 15/7/1921; married secondly on 15/10/1921, Miss M.G. Armit at Longford; 3rd DI 1/7/1898; pensioned 25/7/1922; (photo in the *Constabulary Gazette*, vol. XIII, no. 8, 16/5/1903).

Price, Ivon Henry; RIC 54997; LDS 2098/079; born 1866, Co. Dublin, the son of an engineer; (Celbridge Registrar's District, 1866, vol. 7, p. 507); married on 24/5/1892 (Rathdown Registrar's District, June Quarter, 1892, vol. 2, p. 737), Margaret, daughter of G.L. Kinahan, DL, Wickham, Dundrum, Co. Dublin; son born at Danescourt, Athboy, Co. Meath on 19/5/1901; his son, Lieut. Ernest Dickinson Price, Royal Irish Regiment was born 20/3/1894 at Cappagh House, Co. Tipperary and educated at Mourne Grange, Kilkeel, Co. Down and St Columba's College, Rathfarnham, Co. Dublin; matriculated to Dublin University and served with the Dublin University Officer Training Corps in the Senior Division and left on 5/8/1914; while residing at Tyrone House, Nenagh, Co. Tipperary, he applied for a commission on 10/8/1914 with a preference in a reserve unit of light infantry; appointed to a temporary commission in 2nd Royal Irish Rifles but showed a preference for 2nd Royal Irish Regiment and on the recommendation of his O/C, who added that Price had 'carried out a bombing offensive against the enemy in a most thorough manner some two months ago'; appointed a permanent commission on 4/3/1916; died of wounds at La Targette on 19/3/1916 and buried in Cemetery N.W. of Mont St Eloy (F.9.a. reference map 1/40000 France sheet 51c 1st edition; WO339/37448); 3rd DI 22/10/1891; King Edward VII Visit to Ireland Medal, 1903; Crime Special Department from 16/4/1903 to 1/10/1908; BA 1887, LLD 1890, Trinity College Dublin; DSO; lieutenant-colonel, army & Chief Intelligence Officer at Headquarters of the Irish Command during the Great War; rejoined the RIC on 1/2/1919; CI 12/5/1915; AIG 1/10/1920; pensioned 8/6/1922; died 10/11/1931 at Wellington, Osborne Road, Farnborough, Hampshire; (Hartley West Registrar's District, December Quarter, 1931, vol. 2c, p. 209); administration granted to Ivon Kinahan Price, captain, H.M. army – effects £282.12s.11d.; (photo in the Constabulary Gazette, vol. 1, no. 24, 11/9/1897 & vol. XII, no. 3, 1/10/1902).

Price, Robert; RIC 46852; LDS 2098/220; born 12/2/1861; Co. Leitrim; married on 14/9/1896 (Rathdown Registrar's District, September Quarter, 1896, vol. 2, p. 749), wife a native of Co. Mayo; 3rd DI 26/8/1907; pensioned 15/6/1920.

Priestley, Edward Jonathan; born 4/9/1782, Spring Hall, Yorks., England; third son Thomas Priestley, Esq., Spring Hall, Yorkshire; married firstly in Madras, East India on 27/3/1802; children: John, born 3/2/1803, Hannah Isabella, born 25/12/1805, James, born 1/12/1807; married secondly Mary Anne (1/9/1796–15/7/1870); children: Edward Ramsden (1817–1868), Augusta Lucy (27/5/1837–23/1/1911); joined the 33rd Regiment of Foot (The Duke of Wellington's Regiment) as an ensign and was en route to India in 1809 when he was captured in the Bay of Bengal and taken to Mauritius. He was exchanged at the Cape of Good Hope but was again captured in the Mozambique Channel and remained a prisoner until rescued by a flank company of his own 33rd; adjutant of 33rd Regiment of Foot (The Duke of Wellington's Regiment) and ensign and adjutant, 12th Regiment of Foot (East Suffolk Regiment) 30/12/1813; on half pay 15th Regiment of Foot (The Duke of York's Own Regiment) 4/11/1818; resided in Illingworth near Halifax, Nova Scotia between 1823 and 1828; major, 25th Regiment of Foot (The York Regiment); received the Order of Knighthood of Hanover for his military service and a commission in the Irish Constabulary; AIG 11/6/1836; resident magistrate, 11/6/1842; DIG

9/1/1845; in 1850 resided at 5, Earlsfort Terrace, Adelaide Road, Dublin; pensioned 1/1/1857; died 4/12/1857; buried in Mount Jerome Cemetery, Dublin with his second wife, Mary Anne (d.22/7/1870 – *Cork Examiner* 25/7/1870) his youngest daughter Augusta Lucy, his son 'Edward Ramsden Priestley, Col. and Lieut. Col. 12th Royal Highlanders (The Black Watch, born 21/12/1817, died at Stirling on his landing with his regiment from India on 25/3/1868, aged 50 years' and 'Edith beloved child of E.R. Priestley, 42nd Highlanders and his wife Emma, granddaughter of Major E.J. Priestley, born 12/10/1853, died 1/11/1855'. Another daughter, Anne Philadelphia, aged 13 years died after a long painful illness at his residence on 17/5/1846 (*Cork Examiner*, 22/5/1846); (WO 25/771 fol. 198A).

Purcell, John; RIC 18486; LDS 2097/324; born 1835, King's County; wife from Co. Tipperary S.R.; 3rd DI 18/10/1882; on 18/12/1882 injured as a result of being thrown from his horse while on duty; pensioned 10/2/1891.

Purcell, John Quaid; LDS 2098/043; born 1869, Clonmel, Co. Tipperary; (Clonmel Registrar's District, 1869, vol. 19, p. 685); married on 25/9/1895 (Bawnboy Registrar's District, December Quarter, 1895, vol. 3, p. 37), Eleanor Louisa Moroney, a native of Miltown Malbay, Co. Clare; 3rd DI 10/5/1888; resigned 25/2/1896.

Purcell, William Francis; RIC 23536; LDS 2097/232; born 1838, Co. Tipperary; clerk in a merchant's office, Clonmel for five years; married on 19/3/1859; 3rd SI 13/12/1859; received a favourable record on 31/12/1869 for the prompt arrest of a highway robber, a powerful and desperate character; temporary resident magistrate 24/7/1882; permanent RM 3rd class 28/10/1882; 2nd class 24/10/1889; died 24/8/1893 at Strokestown, Co. Roscommon, late of Ballinagarde, Co. Roscommon; will proved on 30/10/1893 at Tuam, Co. Galway by the oath of Robert Purcell, of Charleville, Co. Cork, bank manager, one of the executors – effects £4,116.7s.8d.; (p. 62, RM Records of Service Book, National Archives, Dublin).

Purdon, Bartholomew Richard; RIC 37551; LDS 2097/284; born 14/5/1850, Rathcore, Co. Meath; 3rd SI 24/4/1871; resident magistrate 3rd class 30/4/1894, 2nd class 18/4/1900, 1st class 6/9/1911; pensioned 14/5/1915; temporarily appointed as a RM to fill a vacancy at Queenstown, Co. Cork caused my a Mr Walter Ernest Everard Callan, RM taking up duty at the Irish Convention from 2/8/1917 to 1/5/1918; (p. 101, RM Records of Service Book, National Archives, Dublin).

Q

Queenan, Michael; RIC 55840; LDS 2099/057; born 27/12/1873, Cuppanaugh, Co. Sligo; (Dromore West Registrar's District, 1872, vol. 19, p. 244); 3rd DI 17/9/1921; pensioned 12/5/1922.

Quill, Gerard Maurice; RIC 26353; LDS 2097/237; born 1841, Co. Kerry; 3rd SI 1/12/1860; dismissed 8/1/1879.

Quill, Morgan Joseph; LDS 2097/215; born 1834, Co. Kerry; joined the Irish Revenue Police as a lieutenant on 10/1/1854 and served in Carn, Co. Donegal; 3rd SI 1/12/1857; resigned 1/6/1860.

Quinn, John; RIC 34350; LDS 2098/068, born 1849, Co. Tipperary; married on 15/2/1892 (Swinford Registrar's District, March Quarter, 1892, vol. 4, p. 314), wife a native of Co. Cork; 3rd DI 1/5/1890; pensioned 1/7/1899; died 30/7/1907 at Cork; (Cork Registrar's District, 1907, September Quarter, vol. 109, p. 56).

R

Rafter, Charles Haughton (Sir); LDS 2097/322; born 1856, Co. Antrim, son of William Pearse Rafter, Belfast; worked as a book-keeper in Co. Antrim; married firstly in 1885 (Rathdown Registrar's District, March Quarter, 1885, vol. 2, p. 813), Olivia Lucy (d.1914), daughter of Arthur Nugent, JP, of Crannagh, Co. Galway; married secondly, 1916, Katharine Veronica, daughter of Dennis Griffin; two sons and one daughter. Educated at Royal Belfast Academical Institutions, Queen's University, Belfast and London University; joined the RIC as a Cadet on 5/9/1882; 3rd DI 16/10/1882 and he resigned on 16/7/1899 to take the post of Chief Constable for Birmingham; author of *RIC Drill Book* (Dublin, 1900); awarded the King's Police Medal, 1909, CBE 1920, KBE 1927, Commander (Brother) of the Order of St John of Jerusalem, 1909. He resided at Elmley Lodge, Harborne, Birmingham and died whilst holding office on 23 August 1935 while on holiday in Co. Galway (his wife's native county); (photo: p. 41, *Policing Birmingham: An Account of 150 Years of Police in Birmingham*, by John W. Reilly, Birminghan, 1989).

212 Charles Haughton Rafter – Chief Constable, Birmingham City Constabulary, 1899–1935.
213 William Charles Forbes Redmond, Second Assistant Commissioner, DMP, grave in Mount Jerome Cemetery, Dublin.

Rainsford, Ross Carthy; RIC 50475; LDS 2097/322; born 1858, Dundalk, Co. Louth; son of Joseph Godman Rainsford, DD (b.1833) (d.21/7/1908) and Maria Susan Carthy (1833–1915), daughter of Ross Carthy, Carlingford, Co. Louth; sister born on 4/1/1856 at the residence of his grandfather, Ross Carthy, Carlingford, Co. Louth (*Cork Examiner* 11/1/1856); tutor; BA 1881, Trinity College Dublin; married on 3/4/1902 (Baltinglass Registrar's District, June Quarter, 1902, vol. 2, p. 389), wife a native of Co. Cavan; 3rd DI 16/11/1882; CI 16/5/1906; King George V Coronation Medal, 1911; pensioned 15/6/1920.

Raleigh, James Walter; RIC 30567; LDS 2097/253; born 1847, Co. Clare; 3rd SI 22/9/1865; died 29/1/1889 at Dunshaughlin, Co. Meath; his only daughter, Mary Thomasina (Mina) died on 6/4/1897 at the residence of her stepfather, J.S. Harbison, Solicitor, Cookstown, Co. Tyrone.

Raleigh, John James; RIC 26523; LDS 2097/238; born 1842, Co. Clare; 3rd SI 3/4/1861; killed 22/8/1863 in a drowning accident, Lahinch, Co. Clare.

Rankin, Edward; CarNB; died 1/8/1831, Kinlough, Co. Leitrim; C.C. Macroom, Co. Cork.

Raymond, Thomas Lill; LDS 2097/048; born 1785; served in the Dublin Police; 3rd SI 1/1/1824; C.C. Virginia, Co. Cavan, 1831; pensioned 5/3/1839.

Reade, Robert Carew; LDS 2097/162; born 1827, Co. Galway; second son of Edward B. Reade, of Tenny Park, Queen's County; 3rd SI 23/11/1847; died on 24/12/1867 (Trim Registrar's District, vol. 17, p. 727), aged 39 years, at Trim, Co. Meath (*Cork Examiner* 31/12/1867).

Reamsbottom, Robert James; RIC 15657; LDS 2097/192; born 1830, Lemanaghan, King's County; 3rd SI 10/5/1852; seconded to the Commissariat Department in the Crimea on 27/8/1854 to 18/1/1855; received a favourable record on 31/12/1870 for efficient and successful exertions for the capture of William Slattery charged with the murder of his wife; CI 16/3/1876; pensioned 22/1/1884; died 12/10/1888 at Moorock Lodge, Ballycumber, King's County; administration granted on 13/11/1888 at Mullingar to William M. Reamsbottom, of Fulwood Park, Preston, Lancashire and Alfred B. Reamsbottom, of Moorock Lodge, Ballycumber, King's County, the sons – effects £835.11s.4d.

Reardon, Michael; LDS 2097/173; born 1805, King's County; enlisted as a sub constable on 1/4/1832; wife a native of King's County; 3rd SI 1/6/1848; died 26/6/1852 in Co. Meath.

Redington, John; RIC 37337; LDS 2098/135; born 1843, Co. Mayo; 3rd DI 9/9/1897; pensioned 1/5/1908; died 20/8/1908 at the Mater Misericordiae Hospital, Dublin, late of Granard, Co. Longford; will proved on 14/10/1908 by the oath of Margaret McGowan – effects £395.16s.4d.

Redmond, Henry Edward; RIC 14068; LDS 2097/185; born 1824, Caen, Normandy, France; lieutenant, 2nd Regiment of Foot (Queen's Royal Regiment) and 54th Regiment of Foot (West Norfolk Regiment) from 20/5/1842 to 31/12/1847; received the special thanks of the Governor and Council and of the Commander-in-Chief in India for his services at the storming of the Forts Monohar and Monsintosh in the Maharatta War; wife a native of Dublin; son born Christopher Fitzsimon Redmond on 25/4/1862 at Tuam, Co. Galway (*Cork Examiner* 29/4/1862), died on 15/8/1863 (*Cork Examiner* 18/8/1863); 3rd SI 10/7/1851; resident magistrate 3rd class 13/9/1860, 2nd class 12/6/1869, 1st class 16/4/1880; pensioned 31/12/1891; (p. 63, RM Records of Service Book, National Archives, Dublin).

Redmond, William Charles Forbes; RIC 57951; LDS 2098/122; born 1872, Armagh; (Armagh Registrar's District, 1872, vol. 6, p. 64); married on 23/10/1902 (Dublin North Registrar's District, December Quarter, 1902, vol. 2, p. 431), wife a native of Co. Dublin; 3rd DI 1/11/1896; King Edward VII Visit to Ireland Medal, 1903; resigned 1/1/1920 on his appointment as second assistant commissioner of the Dublin Metropolitan police; killed 21/1/1920, Harcourt Street, Dublin; buried in Mount Jerome Cemetery, Dublin (Grave No. C39–15725); (photo in the *Constabulary Gazette*, vol. XV, no. 23, 27/8/1904).

GREAT CÆSAR.

214

215

214 Oil painting of Sir A. Reed, KCB which hung in the Officers' Mess at the RIC Depot, paid for by subscription by his fellow officers to the amount of £115. The artist is Walter Osborne (1859–1903), RHA (*Constabulary Gazette,* 15 December, 1900). **215** Andrew Reed, 'Great Caesar'. **216** Andrew Reed, 1899. **217** Andrew Reed, 1900.

216

217

Reed, Andrew (Sir); RIC 25088; LDS 2097/230; MA, LLB, CVO, LLD; born 26/9/1837, Co. Galway, the only son and third of four children (the others of whom died in childhood or adolescence) of John Reed, land agent and his wife Mary, daughter of John Adamson of Moate, Co. Westmeath. His mother died in 1840 when he was three and his father remarried. He attended dame school and Erasmus's School in Galway and at sixteen he was earning his living as a tutor. In 1856 he won a science scholarship, which enabled him to enter Queen's College, Galway from which he obtained an LLB (Gold Medallist). The year in which he took his degree the Earl of Carlisle happened to visit Galway and having inspected the Queen's College, he told the president that he was anxious to give some appointment in the public service to a Galway student of promise. The president said that they had a brilliant young man named Reed, but that he was preparing for the Indian Civil Service, and he feared he would not change his mind. However, the president strongly urged young Reed to accept the Lord Lieutenant's offer of a nomination for a cadetship in the Constabulary. The examination for an Indian Civil Service candidate presented no difficulty and young Reed became a Sub Inspector in no time; 3rd SI 1/10/1859; on 1/11/1868 promoted county inspector and he was invited by Sir John Stewart Wood, the inspector general of the RIC, to become his private secretary. He filled this position for eleven years until 21/7/1879, first under Wood, and then from 1876, under his successor, Lieutenant-Colonel George Edward Hillier. During these years he found time to study law, and in 1873 he was called to the Irish Bar (King's Inn Law Prizeman). At Wood's request, he substantially revised *The Policeman's Manual*, first issued in 1866, and reissued in 1883, 1887, 1891 and 1898. In 1875 he wrote a guide to The Peace Preservation (Ireland) Acts 1856–75, The Liquor Licensing Laws of Ireland in 1889 and produced his own *The Irish Constable's Guide* in 1888 which was to become the Irish policeman's bible; AIG 14/9/1882; filled the office of Divisional Commissioner, Western Division, 14/9/1882–21/9/1885; inspector general 21/9/1885. He married in 1867 (Dublin South Registrar's District, vol. 12, p. 542), Mary Elizabeth (d.1913), only daughter of Mr Hamilton Lyster, of Croghan, Co. Tipperary; her brother, Lieutenant Henry Hamilton Lyster (1830–1922), Bengal Native Infantry was awarded the Victoria Cross for gallantry on 23/5/1858 during the Indian Mutiny. Andrew Reed's only son, Captain Hamilton Lyster Reed (1869–1931), 7th Battery, Royal Artillery, was awarded the Victoria Cross for gallantry at the Battle of Collenso, South Africa on 15/12/1899; for services in connection with the suppression of riots in Belfast, 1886, received the thanks of the Government in the House of Commons; KCB, 1897; CVO, 1900; pensioned 1900; in retirement he was a member of the Royal Dublin Society and the Synod of the Church of Ireland; Governor of the Royal Hibernian School, King's Hospital, Erasmus' School and Vice-President of the Royal Veterinary College; died 7/11/1914 at 5, Dartmouth Road, Leeson Park, Rathmines, Dublin, late of 23, Fitzwilliam Square, Dublin; buried 10/11/1914 in Deansgrange Cemetery, Dublin (South Section, Row M, Grave No. 28) with his wife Elizabeth Mary (d.3/6/1913, aged 69 years), his daughter Mary Reed (d.12/1/1871, aged 4 months) and his eldest daughter Harriet Emily Reed (d.2/4/1952); Epitaph: 'I have no greater joy than to hear that my children walk in truth' (3rd Epistle, John, 4th verse); will proved on 24/11/1914 by Harriet Emily Reed, Olane C. Reed and Mary D. Reed, spinsters – effects £7,665.19s.3d. (Diary of Inspector General Sir Andrew Reed in the possession of his grandson in Tonbridge, Kent).

Reed, James; LDS 2097/053; born 1793, Co. Mayo; father of James Alexander Reed, SI, RIC; supervisor of assessed taxes from 6/12/1815 to 1/8/1824; wife a native of Co. Cork; 3rd SI 1/8/1824; CI 1/5/1847; pensioned 17/10/1856 in King's County; died 25/5/1876 at Dublin; (Dublin South Registrar's District, 1876, vol. 7, p. 649).

Reed, James Alexander; RIC 25536; LDS 2097/234; born 1841, Co. Roscommon; son of James Reed, SI, RIC; 3rd SI 28/3/1860; dismissed 6/3/1862 for having withdrawn himself from his duties without leave; his second daughter, Charlotte died on 17/9/1901 at 194, Rathgar Road, Dublin.

218   219

218 Sir Andrew Reed, grave in Deansgrange Cemetery, Dublin.   219 Hamilton Lyster Reed, VC, son of Sir Andrew Reed.

Reeves, Norman William; RIC 82017; ADRIC CADET no. 15; LDS 2099/017; born 3/7/1896, Hampstead, London, England; (Lewisham Registrar's District, 1896, September Quarter, vol. 1d, p. 1,200); captain, Leicester Regiment for seven and a half years; 3rd DI 25/6/1921; pensioned 27/4/1922.

Reeves, Thomas; RIC 29868; LDS 2097/250; born 1844, Co. Antrim; married on 7/2/1878 (Ballinasloe Registrar's District, March Quarter, 1878, vol. 4, p. 25), wife from Co. Galway; 3rd SI 1/1/1865; received a favourable record on 31/12/1869 for prompt and successful pursuit of an abductor and recovery of a young girl unharmed; received an approbation on 31/12/1870 for spirited conduct in the arrest of leaders of a riotous party; CI 1/4/1887; pensioned 1/5/1888; died 5/3/1919 at Blarney, Newlands Avenue, Southampton, Hants.; (Southampton Registrar's District, March Quarter, 1919, vol. 2c, p. 131); probate granted at London on 16/6/1920 to George Reeves, A.R.C.S.. – effects £1,746.11s.8d.

Reeves, William; RIC 34041; LDS 2097/269; born 1848, Co. Antrim; married on 6/2/1874 (Castleblayney Registrar's District, vol. 1, p. 463); 3rd SI 16/4/1868; musketry instructor at the Phoenix Park Depot from 19/12/1882 to 1/4/1887; CI 1/2/1893; King Edward VII Visit to Ireland Medal, 1903; County Inspector attached to Crime Department from 1/2/1893 to 3/4/1895; AIG 22/10/1906; Commandant of the Phoenix Park Depot from 22/10/1906 to 1/4/1908; pensioned 23/10/1909; his only son, Charles William, aged six years died of meningitis on 14/4/1889 at Armagh; (photo in the *Constabulary Gazette*, vol. XXV, no. 14, 19/6/1909, p. 212).

Regan, John Morton; RIC 64530; LDS 2098/240; born 31/1/1889, 95, North Queen Street, Belfast, Co. Antrim; son of Thomas Joseph Regan, DI, RIC and Euphemia Elizabeth Conlin; captain, 6th Battalion Royal Irish Rifles from 21/10/1915 to 24/5/1919; 3rd DI 13/3/1909; TCI

1/10/1920; pensioned 31/5/1922; transferred to the Royal Ulster Constabulary on 1/6/1922; county inspector, RUC, serving in Co. Tyrone and Co. Down; pensioned 11/11/1944 at which time he was appointed to the Control Commission, firstly in Germany and from 1945 in Greece where he was assistant inspector general. He resigned on 10/8/1948 and died on 26/8/1971; (WO 339/42952); (photo in the *Constabulary Gazette*, vol. XIII, no. 9, 23/5/1903 & vol. XXXIII, no. 24, 6/9/1913, p. 375).

Regan, Thomas Joseph; RIC 44360; LDS 2098/216; born 31/7/1858, Co. Dublin; father of John Martin Regan, DI, RIC; married on 9/6/1886 (Belfast Registrar's District, June Quarter, 1886, vol. 1, p. 472), wife a native of Belfast; 3rd DI 19/7/1906; pensioned 30/6/1919.

Reid, James; RIC 42084; LDS 2098/203; born 2/7/1857, Co. Fermanagh; wife a native of Co. Down; 3rd DI 4/1/1905; pensioned 31/5/1919; (photo in the *Constabulary Gazette*, vol. XXV, no. 18, 17/7/1909, p. 273).

Reid, Robert; RIC 30165; LDS 2097/326, born 1844, Co. Tipperary; 3rd DI 1/11/1882; pensioned 31/3/1905; died 15/10/1910 at Beech Hill, Downshire Park, Cregagh, Belfast, Co. Antrim; will proved on 14/12/1910 at Belfast by the oath of Ellen Stewart Reid, the widow – effects £209.17s.9d.

Reilly, John; RIC 27477; LDS 2098/024; born 1842, Co. Cavan; 3rd DI 1/5/1887; pensioned 25/6/1894; died 17/12/1916 at Auburn, Ravenhill Park, Belfast; will proved on 16/2/1917 at Belfast by the oath of Catherine Reilly, the widow and Alfred McConnell, solicitor – effects £620.8s.3d.

Reilly, Thomas; RIC 58222; LDS 2098/089B; born 28/2/1876, Co. Cavan; married on 3/2/1910, wife a native of Co. Cavan; 3rd DI 7/9/1919; pensioned 20/7/1922.

Reilly, William; RIC 61169; LDS 2098/177B; born 10/7/1881, Castlebar, Co. Mayo; (Castlebar Registrar's District, September Quarter, 1881, vol. 4, p. 116); awarded the Constabulary Medal on 8/12/1919; married on 7/1/1917, wife a native of Co. Kilkenny; 3rd DI 16/10/1920; pensioned 3/5/1922.

Rennison, Thomas; LDS 2097/170; born 1807, Kildimo, Co. Limerick; enlisted as a sub constable on 10/2/1832; 3rd SI 1/6/1848; accidentally killed on 4/3/1850 by being thrown form a car in Co. Limerick.

Rice, Arthur Cue; RIC 40921; LDS 2098/164; born 1879, Co. Longford; 3rd DI 1/11/1899.

Rice, William Henry; RIC 37115; LDS 2098/021; born 27/6/1852, Co. Longford; 3rd DI 1/8/1886; King Edward VII Visit to Ireland Medal, 1903; resident magistrate 3rd class 23/11/1905, 2nd class 14/4/1910; pensioned 1/6/1919; (p. 131, RM Records of Service Book, National Archives, Dublin); (photo in the *Constabulary Gazette*, vol. 1, no. 23, 4/9/1897 & vol. XVIII, no. 23, 24/2/1906).

Rich, John Sampson; LDS 2097/111; born 1789, Middlesex, London, England; lieutenant and captain half-pay, Royal Artillery from March 1808 to November 1829; 3rd SI 1/2/1837; received a compound fracture of the right ankle whilst on a tour of inspection in Co. Kerry on 23/12/1837; pensioned 5/12/1858; died 23/9/1880 at Limerick, Co. Limerick; (Limerick Registrar's District, 1880, December Quarter, vol. 5, p. 336).

Richards, William Beresford; LDS 2097/150; born 1820, Co. Wexford; he was one of the first four RIC officers to undergo training on 31/8/1861 at the School of Musketry, Fleetwood, North Lancs., England (*Cork Examiner* 26/8/1861); 3rd SI 9/11/1845; CI 16/6/1869; received a favourable record on 30/6/1871 for efficient and successful exertions for the capture of W. Slattery, charged with the murder of his wife; pensioned 1/4/1875; died 2/12/1886 at 103 Lower Baggot Street, Dublin; administration granted on 20/12/1887 at the Principal Registry to Solomon Richards, of Solsborough, Enniscorthy, Co. Wexford, lieutenant-general, the brother – effects £84.7s.0d.

Richardson, Joseph Barker; LDS 2097/101; born 1809, Middlesex, London, England; 3rd SI 1/10/1836; paymaster 1/10/1836 for King's County, Co. Kildare and Co. Dublin; residing at 3

Heytesbury Terrace, Wellington Road, Dublin in 1850; pensioned 31/5/1851 on the abolition of the office of paymaster; died 18/4/1875 at Lisburn, Co. Antrim; (Lisburn Registrar's District, 1875, vol. 1, p. 662).

Richardson, John Edward Herbert; RIC 61138; LDS 2098/194; born 1879, Co. Dublin; married on 12/2/1918 (Kilkenny Registrar's District, March Quarter, 1918, vol. 3, p. 345), Muriel Blunden, a native of Co. Kilkenny; 3rd DI 10/1/1904; King Edward VII Visit to Ireland Medal, 1903 as a cadet; TCI 1/10/1920; pensioned 16/5/1922.

Richmond, Archibald Hanward Robert; RIC 61140; LDS 2098/196; born 1879, London, England; schoolmaster for 3 years; New College, Oxford; major, 6th Battalion Royal Irish Rifles from 19/1/1916 to 27/3/1918; married on 2/8/1905, Miss E.M.N. Carna, a native of England; 3rd DI 10/10/1903; King Edward VII Visit to Ireland Medal, 1903 as a cadet; his son, Edward Archibald Gordon Richmond, aged two days, died at Abbeylands, Mountbellew, Co. Galway on 30/6/1906; he committed suicide by shooting himself with his revolver in his room at the Royal Hotel in New Ross, Co. Wexford on 18/1/1921.

Ridge, John Hardinge; LDS 2097/110; born 1819, Freshford, Co. Kilkenny; wife a native of Co. Tyrone; 3rd SI 14/1/1837; pensioned 1/4/1856; died 6/4/1872 at Ballymote House, Glenealy, Co. Wicklow; administration granted on 3/12/1872 at the Principal Registry to Anne Ridge, Church Street, Wicklow, Co. Wicklow – effects under £6,000.

Rigg, William Trevor; RIC 59037; LDS 2098/164; born 1874, Sevenoaks, Kent, England; (Sevenoaks Registrar's District, 1874, December Quarter, vol. 2a, p. 536); residing at 40, Stratford Road, Kensington, London in 1881 (Census) with his mother, Maria Sylvia Rigg (b.1843), Peterborough, Northampton; pupil in surveying office for 6 months in London; BA University College, Oxford; married on 21/8/1906, Lillian Knight Roche, a native of Co. Dublin; 3rd DI 1/11/1899; CI 1/8/1920; major, 6th Battalion Royal Irish Rifles from 20/1/1916 to 27/3/1919; wounded; awarded the Croix de Guerre with palms on 29/3/1919 for the Somme; awarded the Constabulary Medal on 30/11/1920; divisional commissioner 15/11/1920 in Dublin (Depot), Louth, Meath and Wicklow; pensioned 8/5/1922.

Ring,———; CarNB; baronial chief constable; died 5/7/1829; C.C. barony of Kinalea and Kerricurrihy, Co. Cork.

Riordan, Patrick; RIC 57642; LDS 2098/070B; born 26/11/1864, Co. Limerick; (Limerick Registrar's District, 1864, vol. 5, p. 464); married on 22/4/1903 (Limerick Registrar's District, June Quarter, 1903, vol. 5, p. 233), wife a native of Co. Limerick; 3rd DI 17/6/1916; allocated to the Crime Special Department at headquarters from 17/6/1916 to 1/9/1916; pensioned 31/8/1922; assisted in the Provisional Government in the formation of the Civic Guards (later styled the Garda Síochána) in February 1922 by serving on sub committee on training.

Roberts, Albert Augustine; RIC 52413; LDS 2098/031; born 1862, Co. Cork; tutor at Portarlington School for one year, Ballinamona Park, Waterford for one year and three months and at the Queen's Service Academy, 3, Ely Place, Dublin for one year; married firstly on 7/7/1898 (Rathdown Registrar's District, September Quarter, 1898, vol. 2, p. 791), wife a native of Dublin; married secondly on 10/12/1899, wife a native of Dublin; 3rd DI 1/6/1887; Queen Victoria's Visit to Ireland Medal, 1900; King Edward VII Visit to Ireland Medal, 1903; awarded the King's Police Medal 1909; CI 13/11/1909; AIG 1/4/1920; wounded 22/6/1920, Amien Street, Dublin; pensioned 4/10/1920.

Roberts, Charles Leslie; RIC 70845; LDS 2098/135B; born 9/5/1891, Norton, Oxon., England; (Norton Registrar's District, 1891, June Quarter, vol. 5b, p. 158); articles clerk for five years; major, Machine Gun Corps; awarded the Military Cross while serving during the Great War; specially appointed without examination; 3rd DI 15/6/1920; pensioned 7/6/1922; (Wedding photograph: *Irish Life Magazine*, 24/9/1920).

Roberts, John; CarNB; awarded one medal and two clasps for Vittoria and the Pyrenees; married, 1814; ensign, 71st Regiment of Foot (Fraser's Highlanders Regiment), 1808; lieutenant,

220   221

220 William Reilly, Trim, Co. Meath, 1922.   221 William Henry Rice.   222 Patrick Riordan.
223 Charles Leslie Roberts, wedding photo.

222   223

1809; captain unattached; stipendiary magistrate 25/5/1831 at Lahinch House, Ennistymon, Co. Clare with a detachment at Morris's Mills, Kilfenora, Co. Clare; his wife, Anne died at Castlecomer, Co. Kilkenny on 1/2/1845; transferred to Pettigo and Carndonagh, Co. Donegal in May 1832; resident magistrate 1/10/1836; retired as a RM on 16/6/1853; died 27/1/1857; (WO 25/ 772 fol. 248).

Roberts, John Cramer; CarNB; b.1796, Sallymount, Co. Kildare; son of Rev. John Cramer, of Sallymount, Co. Kildare, DL, who assumed by Royal licence the additional surname and the arms of Roberts on 9/10/1801, having married on 2/1/1794, Martha (b.29/9/1767), eldest daughter of Sir Thomas Roberts, Bt., of Glassenbury, Kent; ensign 5th Regiment of Foot (Northumberland Regiment), 18/1/1816; lieutenant, 15/6/1816; lieutenant half pay, 27/7/1816; lieutenant full pay 7/12/1816; lieutenant half pay 25/2/1817; lieutenant half pay 18th Regiment of Foot (Royal Irish Regiment), 16/7/1820; captain unattached (by purchase) 14/7/1821; lieutenant-colonel, 65th Regiment of Foot (2nd Yorkshire North Riding Regiment); ADC to the Governor of Malta; married at Malta, 12/11/1828, Marian, daughter of David Ross (by Marian, his wife, daughter of Col. Gall); his third son, Herbert William Cramer Roberts, aged 13 years died on 14/5/1851 of gastric fever at the Phoenix Park Training Depot, Dublin (*Cork Examiner* 14/5/1851) & (the *Dublin Evening Post*, Tuesday, 13/5/1851); AIG 11/6/1836; Commandant of the Phoenix Park Depot, 1842; DIG 4/12/1857; died 3/3/1864 in his 67th year, suddenly at Saint Leonards-on-Sea, formerly of No. 38, Fitzwilliam Place, Dublin (*Cork Examiner* 8/3/1864); will with two codicils proven at the Principal Registry on 5/5/1864 by the oaths of John David Cramer Roberts, of Highfield, Trant, Kent and William Cramer Roberts, of Thornton, Dunlavin, Newbridge, Esquires and two of the executors – effects under £4,000. (WO 25/772 fol. 317).

Robertson, Thomas Jeffrey Norris; RIC 29526; LDS 2097/248; born 1844, Co. Dublin; clerk in the Census Office Dublin from July 1861 to September 1862; 3rd SI 1/9/1864; pensioned 10/5/1886 at Bailieborough, Co. Monaghan; died 17/6/1887 in Dublin.

Robertson-Glasgow, Colin Campbell; RIC 59401; LDS 2098/158; born 1874, Kilwinning, Ayrshire, Scotland; son of Mr R. Bruce Robertson-Glasgow; educated at Lincoln College, Oxford; 3rd DI 1/9/1899; King Edward VII Visit to Ireland Medal, 1903; resigned 30/4/1911; Chief Constable of Ayrshire County Police on 1 May 1911 to March 1919.

Robinson, Henry Seymour; RIC 72004; LDS 2098/158B; born 12/10/1893, Co. Sligo; (Sligo Registrar's District, March Quarter, 1894, vol. 2, p. 283); lieutenant, 9th Lancers; 3rd DI 10/1/1920; pensioned 31/5/1922; transferred to the Royal Ulster Constabulary on 1/6/1922.

Robinson, Philip Andrew de La Pere; RIC 26021; LDS 2097/236; born 1840, Co. Galway; 3rd DI 23/8/1860; died 3/6/1869 at Portarlington, Co. Laois, late of Co. Tyrone; will proved at the Principal Registry on 3/11/1869 by the oath of Jessie F. Robinson, of Ballynavin, Borrisokane, Co. Tipperary, spinster, one of the executrixes – effects under £600.

Robison, Robert; LDS 2097/102; born 1792, King's County; ensign (by purchase), 26th Regiment of Foot (The Scotch Rifles Regiment), 24/4/1809; lieutenant, 3/10/1811; captain (unattached), 27/3/1827 to 30/4/1830; residing at Newcastle-upon-Tyne, 1827–8; 3rd SI 1/10/1836; paymaster 1/10/1836 for Counties Armagh, Louth and Monaghan; died 2/12/1846. (WO 25/772 fol. 255).

Roche, Richard; LDS 2097/079; born 1799, Co. Kilkenny; enlisted as a sub constable, 1/2/1823; wife a native of Co. Kilkenny; residing at Beechy Park, Hackettstown, Co. Carlow in 1828; his son, Matthew, died on 28/11/868 in Washington D.C., U.S.A. (*Cork Examiner* 15/1/1869); 3rd SI 1/1/1823; reduced from 1st class sub inspector to 2nd class sub inspector in 1850; pensioned 1/8/1859; died 1871 in the United States.

Roche, W.R.; CarNB; born 1794; resident magistrate 1/12/1837; pensioned 12/8/1841; died 1849.

Rock, Thomas; RIC 24611; LDS 2097/225; born 1838, Co. Kildare; worked at civil engineering from 1854 to 1857; 3rd SI 20/3/1859; died 9/6/1863, Dunfanaghy, Co. Donegal; letters of administration granted at Londonderry on 22/12/1863 to Mary Rock of Dunfanaghy, Co. Donegal, widow, the mother and only next of kin of the deceased.

Rodden, John Charles; LDS 2097/074; born 1790, King's County; PPF; private and sergeant in the Army from 7/8/1811 to 19/12/1822; enlisted as a constable, 1/5/1823; 3rd SI 15/3/1832; pensioned 1849; residing at The North Strand, Dublin in 1850; died 2/3/1863 at Newcomen Place, Dublin, aged 72 years (*Cork Examiner* 6/3/1863); will proved a the Principal Registry on 9/4/1863 by the oath of Elizabeth Rodden, of Newcomen Place, Dublin, widow of the deceased and sole executrix.

Roddy, Michael; RIC 55571; LDS 2098/145B; born 1871, Co. Mayo; married on 18/1/1905 (Waterford Registrar's District, March Quarter, 1905, vol. 5, p. 571), wife a native of Co. Waterford; 3rd DI 20/8/1920; pensioned 24/5/1922.

Rodger, Samuel Bevan; RIC 27988; LDS 2097/242; born 1840, Co. Limerick; 3rd SI 16/9/1862; CI 16/3/1887; pensioned 15/5/1902; died 17/6/1902 at Oldenburgh, Queenstown, Co. Cork, late of The Barracks, Tullamore, King's County; will proved on 21/7/1902 at the Principal Registry by the oath of Thomas C. Rodger – effects £2,688.9s.1d., Resworn £3,487.11s.11d.

Rodgers, John Sutton; CarNB; born 1792; died 28/5/1839; buried in the Church of Ireland Cemetery, Carndonagh, Co. Donegal; his headstone has the following inscription: 'Here lies the body of John Sutton Rodgers, Esq., late Sub Inspector of Constabulary Police who died on the 28th of May 1839, aged 47 years. This monument was erected in his memory by Louis Anderson, Esq., County Inspector and the Sub Inspectors, Head and other Constables of the County Donegal Establishment, 1843.'

Rodwell, George D'Urban; RIC 58407; LDS/ 2098/156; born 1878, Co. Cork; son of Thomas Rodwell, SI, RIC; 3rd DI 4/5/1899; musketry instructor at Richmond Barracks Sub Depot from 10/10/1907 to 15/04/1908; musketry instructor at the Phoenix Park Depot from 13/3/1909 to 13/3/1912; King George V Visit to Ireland Medal, 1911; seconded for service as Divisional Staff Officer for Musketry at Aldershot with the rank of Brigade Major from 23/11/1914 and Assistant Provost Marshal in France to 7/2/1919; awarded the Croix de Guerre; commandant and musketry instructor at the North Dublin Union on 18/3/1920; CI 1/8/1920; pensioned 15/5/1922; died 5/6/1958; (photo in the *Constabulary Gazette*, vol. XXXIII, no. 17, 5/7/1913, p. 268).

Rodwell, Thomas; LDS 2097/214; born 1831, Norfolk, England; father of George D'Urban Rodwell, CI, RIC; joined the Irish Revenue Police as a lieutenant on 24/11/1851; wife a native of Co. Derry; 3rd SI 1/12/1857; pensioned 24/11/1891; died 5/6/1913 at 8, Kenilworth Road, Rathgar, Dublin; will proved on 1/7/1913 at the Principal Registry to Margaret M. Rodwell and George D'Urban Rodwell, DI, RIC – effects £1,376.10s.1d.; buried in Mount Jerome Cemetery, Harold's Cross, Dublin with his wife, Marion who died on 6/5/1913, her sister Sara Douglas Givin, who died on 4/12/1923, aged 89 years.

Roe, James; LDS 2097/165; born 1826, Queen's County; 3rd SI 29/4/1848; pensioned 1/12/1886; died 23/2/1888; his daughter Elizabeth Florence (Lily) Drought, widow of A.E. Drought of Knockfin House, Rathdowney, Co. Laois on 11/9/1899 married at Donaghmore, Queen's County, William Augustus Drought, manager, Munster and Leinster Bank, Drumcollogher, Co. Limerick.

Roe, Peter Thomas; RIC 43500; LDS 2098/139; born 1856, Co. Dublin; the son of Thomas Roe and Louise Ogle; wife, Frances Phillips was a native of Queen's County and they had three children, George, Frank and William; 3rd DI 1/5/1898; King Edward VII Visit to Ireland Medal, 1903; awarded a certificate from the Irish Police and Constabulary Recognition Fund;

pensioned 10/6/1918; his son George Charles Frederick Roe attended the King's Hospital School, Oxmanstown, Dublin from 1906 to 1912.

Rogers, Francis William Lyttleton; RIC 38049; LDS 2097/287; born 1853, Co. Kilkenny; second son of Henry Lyttleton Rogers, RM; married on 11/4/1894 (Dublin South Registrar's District, June Quarter, 1894, vol. 2, p. 533), Hessle Mary Skerritt; 3rd SI 23/9/1871; pensioned 23/12/1910; died 24/2/1916 at 11, Merrion Square, Dublin, husband of Hessle Mary Rogers; will proved on 8/6/1910 at the Principal Registry by the oath of Charles E. Murphy, solicitor – effects £8, 498.16s.1d.

Rogers, Henry William Beamish; LDS 2097/153; born 1818, Co. Cork; son of Major (later Major-General) Edward Rogers, 3rd East Kent Regiment (The Buffs) and Barrackmaster Ordnance Department and Sarah Beamish, of Mount Beamish (m.1805) eldest daughter of Rev. Samuel Beamish (1753–1834), of Mount Beamish, Co. Cork and Mary Hamilton (m.1791); nephew of Col. Henry Rogers, Royal Artillery, Chief Storekeeper and Barrackmaster General for Ireland; 3rd SI 15/4/1846; he was offered the alternative of resigning which he did not accept and his name was struck off the strength of the Force on 1/4/1848.

Rogers, Henry Annesley Coxwell; RIC 43065; LDS 2097/295; born 6/2/1855, Dowdeswell, Glos., England; (Cheltenham Registrar's District, 1855, March Quarter, vol. 6, p. 361); the sixth son of Rev. William Rogers Coxwell-Rogers (1809–1896), MA, Rector of Dowdeswell, 1854–1894 and Charlotte Skinner, daughter of Frank Nicholls, barrister-at-law, of Trerereife, Cornwall who were married on 20/5/1841; his father assumed by Royal Licence on 26/10/1854 the additional name and arms of Rogers; married in 1895, Mary Georgina (d.28/7/1948), 2nd daughter of Edmund William Waller, of Ardtona, Dundrum, Co. Dublin and Elsinore, Bray, Co. Wicklow; 3rd SI 1/1/1878; musketry instructor at the Phoenix Park Depot from 3/4/1895 to 28/12/1896; Adjutant, Phoenix Park Depot from 28/12/1896 to 1/7/1899; CI 1/7/1899; King Edward VII Visit to Ireland Medal, 1903; AIG 26/10/1909; Commandant of the Phoenix Park Depot from 26/10/1909 until his death as a result of a riding accident on 15/4/1911 at the RIC Depot, Phoenix Park, Dublin; (Dublin South Registrar's District, 1911, June Quarter, vol. 2, p. 492); will proved on 24/8/1911 at the Principal Registry by the oath of Mary G. Coxwell Rogers, the widow – effects £783.14s.0d.

Rogers, John; LDS 2097/091; 3rd SI 1/12/1835; censured in September 1840.

Rogers, Joseph Henry Lyttleton; LDS 2097/119; born 1818, Co. Cork; 3rd SI 6/8/1838; resident magistrate 26/4/1860; died 18/10/1898.

Rolston, John; RIC 28328; LDS 2098/045; born 1845, Loughgilly, Co. Armagh; 3rd SI 1/5/1888; King Edward VII Visit to Ireland Medal, 1903; pensioned 16/5/1906; died 5/5/1912 at 44, Belgrave Square, Rathmines, Dublin; administration granted on 23/5/1912 to William Rolston – effects £780.2s.4d.

Roney, William; LDS 2097/092; born 1804, Co. Kildare; wife a native of Dublin City; his daughter, Maria Roney, died on 31/3/1864 (Longford Registrar's District, vol. 8, p. 171), aged 30 years, at Prospect, Co. Longford (*Cork Examiner* 6/4/1864); enlisted as a sub constable, 24/12/1824; 3rd SI 25/12/1835; received a grant from the Reward Fund on 31/3/1856 for zeal, tact and success in obtaining circumstantial evidence resulting in the conviction of the perpetrator of a barbarous murder; pensioned 15/8/1870; died 27/10/1886 at Sligo, Co. Sligo (Sligo Registrar's District, 1866, December Quarter, vol. 2, p. 197).

Rooke, William Duffield; RIC 24292; LDS 2097/224; born 1836, Co. Dublin; ensign in the Wicklow Rifles for eight months to 1/12/1858; married on 17/6/1864 at St Barnabas Church, South Kensington, Lydia, eldest daughter of James Windsor, Esq., retired Ordnance Storekeeper (*Cork Examiner* 21/6/1864); 3rd SI 15/1/1859; Private Secretary to the Inspector General from 8/5/1865 to 22/10/1868; died 22/10/1868 at Belgrave Terrace, Monkstown, Co. Dublin, formerly of Lower Fitzwilliam Street, Dublin; will proved at the Principal Registry on 23/11/1868 by the oath of Edward John Windsor, of Strathmore Terrace, Landsdowne Road,

Dublin, one of the executors – amended as to the residence of the deceased, by Registrar's Order of 16/1/1869 – effects under £600.

Ross-Lewin, Henry; LDS 2097/058; born 1778, Ross Hill, Kildysart, Co. Clare; son of George Ross-Lewin, of Ross Hill, Co. Clare, cornet 14th Dragoons and Anne, daughter of Thomas Lewin, of Cloghans, Co. Mayo; ensign and lieutenant in the Irish Militia for 18 years; ensign, lieutenant and major in the army from September 1808 to December 1819; brother of Lieutenant (3/10/1811) Edward Ross-Lewin, 9th Regiment of Foot (Royal Norfolk Regiment), slightly wounded during the Retreat from Burgos on 25/10/1812 and was killed at the Storming of San Sebastian on 31/8/1813; elder brother also of Lieutenant (15/12/1808) Thomas Ross-Lewin, 32nd Regiment of Foot (Duke of Cornwall's Light Infantry) who was slightly wounded in the Pyrenees on 30/7/1813 and died in 1857; Captain (7/9/1804) Henry Ross-Lewin 32nd Regiment of Foot (Duke of Cornwall's Light Infantry); served under General Henry Edward Fox in the rehabilitation of United Irishmen for overseas service in the British Army. He was stationed in Dublin during the Robert Emmet Rising and his assessment is one of the most fair and striking. He was present at eleven general actions and sieges, including the battles of Quatre Bras and Waterloo and was wounded in the last charge at Salamanca on 22/7/1812; promoted brevet Major on 4/6/1814, he married Anne (d.31/12/1876), daughter of William Burnett, of Eyrescourt, by Christine Mary his wife, daughter of Edward Donelan, of Hillswood, Co. Galway; 3rd SI 1/1/1825; died 27/4/1843; author of *The Life of a Soldier: a narrative of twenty seven years' service in various parts of the world* (London, 1834), 3 vols and *With the 32nd In the Peninsular and Other Campaigns*, by Major Harry Ross-Lewin, of Ross Hill, Co. Clare. Edited by John Wardell, M.A., Reader in Modern History in the University of Dublin and Professor of Jurisprudence and Political Economy in the Queen's College, Galway. Dublin: Hodges Figgis & Co., Ltd., publisher to the University. London: Simkin, Marshall & Co. Ltd., 1914.

Ross, Frederick Halloran; RIC 15468; LDS 2097/190; born 1833, Co. Antrim; son of James Ross, CI, RIC, RM (d.22/3/1882, aged 77 years) and Mary (d.22/11/1891, aged 88 years); 3rd SI 16/12/1851; CI 1/11/1856; pensioned 1/5/1894; died 9/12/1915 at No. 1, Brighton Terrace, Monkstown, Co. Dublin; will proved at the Principal Registry on 6/1/1916 by the oath of the Reverend Thomas Pearson, Clerk and Richard B. White, solicitor – effects £18,391.9s.10d., resworn £18,549.8s.9d. He left £300 to the Irish Auxiliary of the Society for Promoting Christianity among the Jews, £200 to the Representative Church Body of Ireland for the Sustentation Fund, £100 to the Hibernian Church Missionary Society, £100 to the Hibernian Bible Society, £50 to the Richmond Institution for the Blind, £50 to the Claremont Institution for the Deaf and Dumb, £50 to the Hospital for Incurables, Donnybrook; £200 to the Bishop of Down and Connor and Dromore for the Poor Parishes Fund, £50 to the Bird's Nest Mission, £100 to the Protestant Orphan Society and £100 to the Irish Distressed Ladies Fund; buried in Deansgrange Cemetery, Dublin (South Section, Row R, Vault No. 5) with his parents and his sister, Frances L. Ross who died on 27/11/1914, aged 68 years.

Ross, George C.; RIC 53973; LDS 2098/210; born 29/4/1870, Skibbereen, Co. Cork; (Skibbereen Registrar's District, 1870, vol. 10, p. 760); married on 1/3/1897, wife a native of Co. Limerick; 3rd DI 12/8/1905; chief police instructor at the Phoenix Park Depot from 14/4/1919 to 1/10/1920; CI 1/10/1920; pensioned 3/6/1922; died 14/12/1961 in Belfast.

Ross, James; RIC 43550; LDS 2098/119; born 1858, Co. Cavan; married on 26/2/1908 (Rathdown Registrar's District, March Quarter, 1908, vol. 2, p. 805), Caroline M. Read, a native of Co. Kerry; 3rd DI 2/10/1896; King Edward VII Visit to Ireland Medal, 1903; King George V Coronation Medal, 1911; pensioned 21/5/1918.

Ross, James; LDS 2097/056; born 1804, Co. Cork; father of Frederick Halloran Ross, DI, RIC; wife a native of Co. Antrim; 3rd SI 1/10/1824; CI 1/10/1824; was severely wounded by a blow of a stone when on duty at the Fair of Dromore, Co. Tyrone on 17/3/1828; resident magistrate 11/7/1853; died 23/3/1882 at 9, Clarinda Park East, Kingstown, Co. Dublin; administration

224 **224** George D'Urban Rodwell, Musketry instructor to the British Expeditionary Forces at Aldershot, 1916. **225** George C. Ross. **226** George C. Ross, address.

Address and Presentation to
George Ross Esq., D.I., R.I.C.,

On his leaving Belfast

Dear Mr Ross,

Your many friends in Belfast have learned with sorrow of your impending removal from their midst, after nine year's faithful service. The lot of a Constabulary Officer in a large community like ours is one that calls for the exercise of tact and firmness. You have displayed those qualities to a degree that has won for you the respect and esteem of all who have come in contact with you in your official position.

Far beyond the bounds of "C" District with which you have been principally identified, you have brought to bear on your duties an earnestness and sympathy that have won for you a reputation for fairness that is thoroughly well deserved. The relations between the Police and people in your district are of a most cordial nature, thanks largely to your untiring efforts in the public weal.

In private life your genial disposition and charm of manner have endeared you to a wide circle of citizens who deeply regret that the exigencie of the splendid force to which you have the honour to belong are about to entail your removal to Dublin. At the same time they rejoice that promotion has fallen to you, the authorities having realised your worth by calling you to fill a responsible position at the Depot in the Phoenix Park.

We trust that you will long be spared to adorn the ranks of the R.I.C., and that you will look back with pleasure and pride on that portion of your career which was spent in the City of Belfast, in the welfare of which you have taken such a deep interest.

The accompanying Gift, we hope will, ever remind you of your stay amongst us. It is but a small expression of our affection, but it is given with the heartiest good wishes for your future welfare.

Signed on behalf of the Subscribers

S.T.Mercier (High Sheriff), Chairman

F.Curley, J.P. Treasurer R.B. Andrews, Secretary

Committee

J.R.Hunter F.W.Ewart N.F.Whittaker

Wm. McComb John Condey C.J.Milligan, M.D.

226

granted on 27/5/1882 at the Principal registry to Mary Ross, of Crow Park, Trim, Co. Meath, widow and universal legatee for life – effects £452.2s.4d.; buried in Deansgrange Cemetery, Dublin on 25/3/1882 (South Section, Row R, Vault No. 5) with his wife Mary, daughter Frances L. and son Frederick Halloran Ross, DI, RIC.

Ross, James; RIC 3444; LDS 2097/261; born 1819, Co. Longford; as a second class head constable he was seconded to the Commissariat Department in the Crimea; musketry instructor at the Phoenix Park Depot from 1/10/1863 to 1/6/1864; 3rd SI 15/3/1867; received a favourable record on 30/6/1871 tracing the author of a threatening letter to a National Schoolmaster who was convicted and sentenced to eighteen months imprisonment with hard labour; pensioned 1/10/1882; died 12/2/1902 at 156, Belgrave Square, Rathmines, Dublin.

Ross, Thomas; LDS 2097/187; born 1824, Co. Down; daughter Josephine Maude, born on 16/2/1866 at Rossylongan House, Donegal, Co. Donegal (Donegal Registrar's District, vol. 7, p. 38) (*Cork Examiner* 23/2/1866); 3rd SI 6/5/1851; received a favourable record on 31/12/1868 for tracing the carcasses of stolen sheep to Dublin and capturing the offenders; received a favourable record on 30/6/1869 for the discovery of the writer of a threatening letter; pensioned 30/1/1891; died 22/8/1912 at 11, Morehampton Road, Dublin.

Roughan, Michael Joseph; RIC 43880; LDS 2097/297; born 1855, Co. Clare; 3rd SI 2/9/1868; resigned 31/8/1887.

Rowan, Hill Wilson; CarNB; born Beleisle, Co. Antrim; son of Robert Rowan (9/8/1754–12/9/1832), of Mulland, Garry and Belleisle, Co. Antrim and Eliza (d.1817), daughter of Hill Wilson, of Purdysburn, Co. Down, who were married on 6/4/1777; married, Eliza Villiers Jackson (died on 29/1/1862, aged 65 years, at Sutton, Howth, Co. Dublin, *Cork Examiner* 31/1/1862), sister of Mr Justice Jackson; stipendiary magistrate 8/4/1830 at Ballydangan House, Loughrea, Co. Galway; pensioned as a magistrate, 1844; died 1863; brother of Col. Sir Charles Rowan (1782–1850), KCB, Joint Commissioner of the London Metropolitan Police, 1829–1850, Assistant Adjutant-General, Light Division in the Peninsular War and Field Marshal Col. Sir William Rowan, GCB (b.1789), 52nd Regiment of Foot (The Oxfordshire Regiment), a distinguished officer, who served in Sicily, Portugal, France and Belgium (at Waterloo) and commanded the Forces in Canada, 1849 to 1855

Rowan, John; RIC 43982; LDS 2098/199; born 1858, Co. Mayo; married on 24/8/1890 (Naas Registrar's District, September Quarter, 1890, vol. 2, p. 716), wife a native of Co. Sligo; 3rd DI 5/8/1903; King Edward VII Visit to Ireland Medal, 1903; pensioned 15/6/1919.

Rowan, William Hamilton; LDS 2097/147; born 1823, Killyleagh Castle, Co. Down; third son of Sydney Hamilton Rowan, Esq. (b.1789) Co. Down who married the daughter of Henry Jackson, Carrickmacross, Co. Monaghan; married at Tralee Church on 27/2/1851 (Tralee Registrar's District, vol. 10, p. 435), Susan Moroney, eldest daughter of George Thomas Hare, Esq., late of Ballybrown, Co. Limerick; 3rd SI 2/11/1844; died on 18/8/1851 of consumption at Bridge Cottage, Carndonagh, Co. Donegal (*Cork Examiner* 27/8/1851).

Rowland, John Francis; LDS 2098/170B; born 11/11/1893, Castlebar, Co. Mayo; (Castlebar Registrar's District, December Quarter, 1893, vol. 4, p. 96); lieutenant, Kings Own Scottish Borderers; 3rd DI 10/1/1920; on 23/1/1921 he was awarded a 2nd class favourable record for conspicuous gallantry during an ambush at Moynalty, Co. Meath; pensioned 4/5/1922; (WO 339/47607).

Royse, Abraham Foord; LDS 2097/055; born 1794, Nantinan House, Nantinan, Co. Limerick; ensign in the Limerick County Militia from 29/4/1813 to 19/5/1813 (WO 13/3018–38); ensign, 87th Regiment of Foot (Royal Irish Fusiliers Regiment), 20/5/1813; lieutenant, 1815; lieutenant half pay, 1/4/1817; awarded one medal and three clasps for Nive, Orthes and Toulouse; wife a native of Co. Galway, Jeanette Victiore, entered the convent and in religion took the name Sister Jane Frances and she died aged 70 years, 'the widow of Abraham of F. Royse, Esq.,' on 15/12/1871 at Loretto Abbey, Rathfarnham, Co. Dublin (Dublin South

Registrar's District, vol. 17, p. 575) (*Cork Examiner*, 21/12/1871); 3rd SI 1/10/1824; CI 1/10/1836; died 9/9/1852 in Carlow; (Administration with will annexed proved in 1852 at the Prerogative Court, NA Reference: T/8784); (WO 25/772 fol. 302)

Royse, Edward Hoskins Fitzgibbons; RIC 17631; LDS 2097/200; born 1831, Nantinan House, Nantinan, Co. Limerick; clerk in the Provincial Bank of Ireland at Limerick for two and a half years; father of George Crosbie Royse, SI, RIC; 3rd SI 7/12/1853; pensioned 1/6/1878; died 7/5/1880 at Enniskillen, Co. Fermanagh (Enniskillen Registrar's District, 1880, June Quarter, vol. 2, p. 67), at Woodcote, Bournemouth, Hants., England; buried in Mount Jerome Cemetery, Dublin on 22/1/1902 (Grave No. A10–262–7174).

Royse, George Crosbie; RIC 49771; LDS 2097/320; born 1857, Co. Galway; son of Edward Hoskins Fitzgibbon Royse, SI, RIC; 3rd SI 13/9/1882; died 18/1/1902 at Woodcote East Cliffe, Bournemouth, late of 18, Prince Patrick Terrace, North Circular Road, Dublin by the oath of Lily Royse, the widow – effects £1,124.15s.8d.; his widow, Lily, daughter of William Alton, MD, FRCSI, Tralee, Co. Kerry, died at Wentworth Villa, Wicklow, Co. Wicklow on 16/9/1916.

Rudge, Augustus; LDS 2097/220; born 1828, Norfolk, England; joined the Irish Revenue Police as a lieutenant on 27/12/1854 and served in Dungloe, Co. Donegal; 3rd SI 1/4/1858; CI 20/7/1881; pensioned 16/5/1887; died 31/8/1901 at 1, Cassandra Villas, Bray, Co. Wicklow; buried in Enniskerry, Co. Wicklow on 3/9/1901; will proved on 23/10/1901 at the Principal Registry by the oath of Frances Rudge, widow and Wentworth Allen, Esq. – effects £5,282.12s.8d.

Russell, John; RIC 56361; LDS 2098/078B; born 5/1/1874, Ennistymon, Co. Clare; (Ennistymon Registrar's District, 1874, vol. 4, p. 301); married on 1/7/1902 (Rathdrum Registrar's District, September Quarter, 1902, vol. 2, p. 887), wife a native of Co. Wexford; 3rd DI 21/9/1917; pensioned 17/7/1922.

Ruthven, Frederick St Clair; RIC 31734; LDS 2097/257; born 1843, Co. Wicklow; wife from Burma; 3rd SI 1/7/1866; CI 22/10/1891; pensioned 1/7/1906; died 5/4/1919 at Charleville Cottage, Enniskerry, Co. Wicklow; will proved at the Principal Registry on 31/7/1919; (photo in the *Constabulary Gazette*, vol. 2, no. 36, 4/12/1897).

Rutland, George; LDS 2097/033; born 1793, Oxon., England; wife a native of Co. Waterford; 3rd SI 25/1/1823; CI 1/9/1839; residing at Jail Street, Ennis, Co. Clare in 1846 (Slater's Directory, 1846); died on 8/5/1852, at his residence, Millview Road, Ennis, Co. Clare (*Cork Examiner* 12/5/1852).

Ruttledge, George Bedell; RIC 53461; LDS 2098/048; born 1863, Co. Fermanagh; pupil in a land agent's office for two years; married on 24/4/1895 (Dublin South Registrar's District, June Quarter, 1895, vol. 2, p. 524), Winifred Herbert, a native of Co. Kerry; BA 1885, Trinity College Dublin; 3rd DI 1/4/1889; King Edward VII Visit to Ireland Medal, 1903; CI 24/5/1911; awarded in 1917 the King's Police Medal, 1909; awarded a certificate from the Irish Police and Constabulary Recognition Fund; pensioned 15/10/1920.

Ryan, Jeremiah F.; RIC 42452; LDS 2098/176; born 1858, Australia; joined from Co. Tipperary; married on 26/2/1892 (Cork Registrar's District, March Quarter, 1892, vol. 5, p. 87), wife a native of Co. Kerry; 3rd DI 16/2/1901; pensioned 30/6/1919.

Ryan, Joseph; RIC 52710; LDS 2098/206; born 7/12/1867, Co. Cavan; married on 23/4/1896 (Dungannon Registrar's District, June Quarter, 1896, vol. 1, p. 743); 3rd DI 29/5/1905; pensioned 31/8/1922.

Ryan, Thomas P.; RIC 72249; ADRIC CADET no. 85; LDS 2098/248B; born 17/1/1891; army; seconded for service with ADRIC; 3rd DI 2/7/1921; pensioned 7/7/1922.

227

227 John Rowan.

228

228 John Francis Rowland.

229 Frederick St Clair Ruthven.

230 William Henry Scott.

229

230

S

Sanson, Adam John Walker; RIC 71034; LDS 2098/112B; born 28/5/1897, Roxburgh, Scotland; lieutenant, Royal Field Artillery; 3rd DI 15/6/1921; pensioned 30/4/1922.

Sargent, Albert Ernest; RIC 72986; ADRIC CADET no. 450; LDS 2099/030; born 6/9/1890, Kent, England; lieutenant, Tank Corps; married Mary Giles of 105B Old Christchurch Road, Bournemouth; 3rd DI 25/6/1921; pensioned 27/4/1922.

Sargent, William; RIC 41488; LDS 2098/198; born 1857, Co. Kildare; eldest son of Joseph and Fannie Sargent, of Rathmore, Co. Kerry; married on 31/8/1886 (Galway Registrar's District, September Quarter, 1886, vol. 4, p. 97), wife a native of Co. Galway; 3rd DI 13/1/1905; died 10/11/1908 at Kanturk, Co. Cork; buried in Rathmore, Co. Kerry on 12/11/1908.

Saunderson, James Johnson; LDS 2097/037; born 1800, Co. Limerick; midshipman in the navy from January 1813 to December 1816; 3rd SI 28/1/1823; CI 9/2/1841; pensioned on 16/11/1858; died 4/4/1867 at No. 9, Fairview Avenue, Clontarf, Co. Dublin (Dublin North Registrar's District, 1867, vol. 7, p. 75); administration granted at the Principal Registry on 9/5/1867 to Rev. Francis Saunderson, of Kildallon, Ardlogher, Co. Cavan, the Cousin German and one of the next of kin of the deceased – effects under £6,000.

Saville, John Benjamin; RIC 44354; LDS 2097/300; born 1857, Co. Tipperary; 3rd SI 5/4/1879; died 21/4/1886 at Borrisokane, Co. Tipperary; administration granted on 27/11/1886 at the Principal Registry to Michael Gleeson, Nenagh, Co. Tipperary, the attorney of William Saville, brother – effects £911.19s.0d.

Saville, William; LDS 2097/159; born 1799, Redcross, Co. Wicklow; enlisted as a constable on 1/11/1823; 3rd SI 4/9/1847; pensioned 3/7/1869; died 13/2/1875 at 29 Gloucester Street, Dublin; will proved on 19/6/1875 at the Principal Registry by the oath of Samuel Hestor, of Tipperary, one of the surviving executors – effects under £2,000.

Scott, Andrew; RIC 61511; LDS 2098/221B; born 11/5/1881, Co. Derry; (Derry Registrar's District, June Quarter, 1881, vol. 2, p. 199); lieutenant, army; 3rd DI 12/1/1920; pensioned 31/5/1922; transferred to the Royal Ulster Constabulary on 1/6/1922.

Scott, George; RIC 537; LDS 2097/195; born 1810, Co. Fermanagh; father of William Henry Scott, SI, RIC; enlisted as a sub constable on 27/8/1828; married on 10/8/1832, wife a native of Co. Louth; 3rd SI 12/11/1852; pensioned 1/10/1870; died 25/12/1888 at 11, Hardwicke Place, Dublin; buried in Swinford, Co. Mayo on 28/12/1888; administration granted on 11/10/1889 at the Principal Registry to Jane Scott, Annesfield, Athlone, Co. Roscommon, universal legatee for life – effects £1,133.3s.3d.

Scott, Victor Henry; RIC 65127; LDS 2098/011B; born 16/6/1884, Cookstown, Co. Tyrone; (Cookstown Registrar's District, June Quarter, 1884, vol. 1, p. 488); lieutenant, Royal Inniskilling Fusiliers from 12/2/1904 to 1/4/1908; seconded for service as a captain and later promoted major in the 5th Battalion, Royal Inniskilling Fusiliers from 13/11/1914 to 10/3/1919; wounded; married on 18/6/1919, J.T. Neame, a native of Kent; 3rd DI 4/1/1910; Adjutant, Phoenix Park Depot from 25/9/1920 to 19/11/1920; TCI 14/2/1921; pensioned 31/3/1922; (WO 339/12802).

Scott, William Henry; RIC 27019; LDS 2097/240; born 1840, Co. Louth; son of George Scott, SI, RIC; 3rd SI 8/3/1862; CI 1/5/1888; pensioned 1/12/1901; his second daughter, Letitia Bunbury (Lillie) on 21/3/1899 at the Cathedral, Lisburn, Co. Antrim, married J.H.E.

Griffith, BA, BAI, TCD, son of Rev. J.H. Griffith, D.D., Rector of Ennis, Co. Clare; (photo in the *Constabulary Gazette*, vol. 1, no. 23, 4/9/1897).

Scott-Ross, Kenneth George; RIC 72257; ADRIC CADET no. 93; LDS 2098/208B; born 4/1/1887, Forfarshire, Scotland; divinity student; captain, King's Own Scottish Borderers; married on 3/12/1909; 3rd DI 12/1/1920; pensioned 16/5/1922.

Scully, Daniel; RIC 56717; LDS 2098/077B; born 20/7/1872, Milford, Co. Donegal; (Milford Registrar's District, 1872, vol. 12, p. 256); married on 23/3/1905, wife a native of Co. Kerry; 3rd DI 5/6/1917; pensioned 17/7/1922.

Scully, James; RIC 42996; LDS 2098/163; born, 1859, Co. Limerick; married on 20/6/1888 (Lisburn Registrar's District, June Quarter, 1888, vol. 1, p. 768), wife a native of Co. Kilkenny; 3rd DI 13/10/1899; died 21/6/1915 at Ardross, New Ross, Co. Wexford.

Scully, Michael; RIC 46212; LDS 2098/184; born 1859, Co. Limerick; married on 11/11/1896 (Dublin North Registrar's District, December Quarter, 1896, vol. 2, p. 526), wife a native of Co. Mayo; 3rd DI 12/2/1901; King Edward VII Visit to Ireland Medal, 1903; died 14/12/1917 at Inchville, Balbriggan, Co. Dublin; buried in Glasnevin Cemetery, Dublin on 16/12/1917; administration granted on 1/2/1918 at the Principal Registry on 1/2/1918.

Scully, Patrick J.; RIC 57698; LDS 2099/003; born 1878, Co. Carlow; (Carlow Registrar's District, 1878, March Quarter, vol. 3, p. 444); married on 7/9/1910, wife a native of Co. Cork; 3rd DI 4/1/1921; pensioned 3/4/1922.

Scully, Vincent William Thomas; LDS 2098/103B; born 1/9/1900, Co. Longford; private, Artists Rifles Officer Training Corps; 3rd DI 4/1/1920; pensioned 8/5/1922.

Seddall, Edward Thomas; RIC 45166; LDS 2097/306; born 1859, Malta; married on 5/11/1884 (Longford Registrar's District, December Quarter, 1884, vol. 3, p. 181), wife from Co. Westmeath; 3rd SI 1/5/1880; divisional sub inspector to the special resident magistrate from 14/9/1882 to 21/1/1885; resigned 24/5/1902 and took up residence in Liverpool and established a Private Enquiry Agency; (photo in the *Constabulary Gazette*, vol. 1, no. 16, 17/7/1897).

Seely, J.; LDS 2097/102; 3rd SI 1/10/1836; paymaster 1/10/1836; censured by the government on 19/7/1837; removed from the Force on 12/3/1839 in consequence of repeatedly absenting himself from his quarters; permitted to remain in the Force on the understanding that should any complaint be brought before the government his services would immediately be dispensed with; refused leave of absence on 8/5/1839; admonished on 1/10/1841 and dismissed on 30/11/1841.

Seton, George; LDS 2097/113; born 1787, Glasgow, Scotland; lieutenant 7th Royal Fusiliers, 31/5/1810; captain unattached, 15/5/1827 to 14/8/1836; residing at 4, Byford Street, Carlton Place, Glasgow, 1828; 3rd SI 1/5/1837; wife Anne; died 30/11/1845. (WO 25/773 fol. 145); (Will of George Seton of Potterhill, Pertshire – PRO, Kew, Catalogue Reference: PROB 11/1961 / Dept: Records of the Prerogative Court of Canterbury and related Probate Jurisdictions: Will Registers / Volume number: 6 Quire Numbers: 251–300 / Date: 18 April 1842 / Image Reference: 320/283).

Sewers, Thomas; LDS 2097/274; born 1820, Co. Monaghan; wife from Co. Leitrim; 3rd SI 17/6/1868; pensioned 1/3/1876; died 17/2/1885; his youngest daughter, Marion Louise married on 10/12/1888 at St George's Church, Arthur Stock, MD, Inchicore, Co. Dublin, second son of Martin Stock, automotive engineer, Broadstone, Dorset, England (*Cork Examiner* 13/12/1888).

Seymour, Charles Edward; RIC 32295; LDS 2097/260; born 1842, Co. Limerick; 3rd SI 1/1/1867; CI 23/12/1891; died 13/2/1899 at Portland, Downpatrick, Co. Down; buried in Downpatrick on 16/2/1899; administration granted on 10/4/1899 at Belfast to Louisa Matilda Seymour, of Portland, Downpatrick, Co. Down, widow, the universal legatee – effects £226.16s.6d.; (photo in the *Constabulary Gazette*, vol. V, no. 8, 10/4/1899).

Seymour, Joseph; LDS 2097/072; born 1806, Cork City, Co. Cork; PPF; enlisted as a sub constable, 21/10/1826; wife a native of Co. Kildare; 3rd SI 15/2/1832; CI 10/5/1852; pensioned 15/2/1866; died 20/12/1881at 13, Harrington Street, Dublin; buried in Mount Jerome Cemetery, Dublin on 23/12/1881; C.C. Blessington, Co. Wicklow; he was the father of Joseph Seymour, JP, born at Greenlanes, Verdon Avenue, Clontarf, Co. Dublin in 1844, who was educated at Trinity College Dublin; resided at Aghadoe House, Killeigh, Co. Cork and Ravens Court, Blackrock, Cork; lieutenant-colonel, 4th Battalion, Royal Irish Regiment (formerly the North Tipperary Light Infantry); senior partner in the firm of Eustace and Co., timber merchants; married firstly, in 1867, Helen Maria, daughter of Adam Newman Perry and granddaughter of Adam Perry, Rock Lodge, Co. Cork and Woodroofe, Co. Tipperary; married secondly in 1888, his second cousin, Annie Jane, daughter of Richard Gilbert, of Moygaddy, Co. Kildare and Ballinglen, Co. Wicklow. Lieut-Col. Seymour died on 16/2/1901; (portrait: Garda Museum & Archives, Dublin Castle, Dublin 2).

Shankey, John; RIC 59736; LDS 2098/136; born 1856, Co. Meath; married on 9/10/1883; wife a native of King's County; 3rd DI 14/12/1897; pensioned 31/10/1917.

Shannon, George Henry; RIC 44613; LDS 2097/302; born 1855, Dublin City, Co. Dublin; BA, BL; 3rd SI 8/8/1879; as a barrister-at-law he was employed by the RIC before the Riots Commission in Belfast in 1886; temporary resident magistrate 5/5/1888; permanent RM 3rd class 3/7/1889, 2nd class 9/8/1892, 1st class 26/12/1904; pensioned 7/7/1919; (p. 85, RM Records of Service Book, National Archives, Dublin).

Sharpe, John Robert; RIC 52407; LDS 2098/025; born 1866, Co. Meath; married on 4/6/1897, wife a native of Co. Kilkenny; 3rd DI 1/6/1887; CI 17/2/1910; pensioned 1/7/1920.

Sharpe, Robert; LDS 2097/171; born 1805, Co. Armagh; enlisted as a sub constable on 16/11/1825; 3rd SI 1/6/1848; pensioned 21/11/1857 in Co. Waterford; died 1874.

Shaw, Bernard George; RIC 24630; LDS 2097/228; born 1838, Belvelly, Co. Cork; only son of George Nathaniel Shaw, Monkstown Castle, Co. Cork; married on 1/7/1869, at St Anne's Church, Dublin (Dublin South Registrar's District, vol. 12, p. 547), Frances Maria, daughter of Rev. Alexander Dixon, of Ballymore, Co. Fermanagh and granddaughter of the late Roger Henty Keating, Esq. (*Cork Examiner* 5/7/1869); 3rd SI 2/6/1859; pensioned 21/6/1890; died 10/10/1920 at 1 Florence Terrace, Bray, Co. Wicklow; administration granted at the Principal Registry on 14/4/1920.

Shaw, George Foley; RIC 44767; LDS 2097/303; born 1856, Co. Dublin; eldest son of Dr George Foley Shaw, S.F.T.C.D.; 3rd SI 1/11/1879; pensioned 13/10/1899; died 2/1/1906 in London.

Shaw, John; CarNB; C.C. Binghamstown and Newport, Co. Mayo.

Shaw, Stanley; RIC 45165; LDS 2097/306; born 1858, Co. Dublin; LLB; 3rd SI 1/3/1880; resigned 16/5/1882.

Shaw-Kennedy, James (Sir), CB, KCB; born 13/10/1788, The Largs, Straiton Parish, Ayrshire, Scotland; the eldest son of Captain John Shaw, of Dalton, Kirkcudbrightshire, formerly of the 76th Regiment of Foot (Highlanders Regiment); educated at the Royal Military College and he joined the 43rd Regiment of Foot (Monmouthshire Light Infantry) at Hythe, Kent as an ensign in 18/4/1805. At that time the regiment was combined with the 52nd Regiment of Foot (Oxfordshire Regiment) and the 95th Regiment of Foot (Rifle Regiment) in a brigade under Major-General Sir John Moore. The brigade was trained exclusively as light infantry, and its methods were extremely popular with Shaw and the other young officers. Shaw became a lieutenant on 23/1/1806 and served throughout the Peninsula campaign as the aide-de-camp of General Robert Crawfurd, who commanded elements of Moore's original brigade in a unit referred to as the 'Light Division.' He first saw service in the Copenhagen Expedition, 1807 and under Sir David Baird took part in the Corunna Campaign of 1808–9. In the retreat Shaw contracted a fever from which he never fully recovered. The 43rd Regiment of Foot

231   232

231 Edward Thomas Seddall.   232 Joseph Seymour, oil painting portrait, Garda Museum, Dublin Castle.   233 John Robert Sharpe.

233

(Monmouthshire Regiment) was again engaged in the Douro and Talavera Campaigns and Shaw became adjutant of his now famous regiment at the battle of Talavera. After Crawfurd's death in the battle of Ciudad Rodrigo in 1812, Shaw was promoted captain on 16/7/1812 and helped to edit a manual of his tactics and training procedures entitled 'Standing Orders for the Light Division.' Although General Moore's and General Crawfurd's methods were not generally adopted by the British army during the Napoleonic Wars, Shaw's talents for reorganization attracted the attention of his superiors more than once. Once more in active service in 1815 as one of Charles Alten's staff officers, Captain Shaw by his reconnoitring skills and tactical judgement was of the greatest assistance to Alten and Wellington who promoted him brevet-major on 18/6/1815. Shaw, on 21/1/1819 was promoted to lieutenant-colonel again on Wellington's recommendation. During the occupation of France by the allied army, Shaw was commandant of Calais. In 1826 he was promoted adjutant-general for the military district of Belfast in Ireland, once again at Wellington's suggestion. After approximately a year in Ireland, Colonel Shaw was appointed assistant adjutant-general of England's Northern District and transferred to Manchester. During his nine years as military commander of Manchester, Shaw was called upon many occasions to suppress demonstrations by workingmen. His experience with light infantry was most valuable in developing tactics for dealing with civil disturbances. Shaw's work in Manchester eventually attracted the attention of the Home Office. In July 1829, the home secretary, Sir Robert Peel, offered Shaw one of the two commissionerships in the new 'London Metropolitan Police.' Peel wrote to Shaw: 'For one of these appointments I mean to select a military man and my intention is to take the officer whom I believe to be best qualified to discharge the confidential and very important duties which will devolve upon him ... As the experiment is a novel one and the undertaking arduous there will I think be a great opportunity for distinction and the office will become more important every day.' Shaw, however, desired to remain in the army, and after thanking Peel for his consideration, he respectfully declined the offer. Although Shaw remained in the army, he continued to develop his ideas on the use of troops as 'police' in support of civil authorities. His service in the light infantry had already taught him the value of discipline and mobility, and his correspondence indicates that his service in Manchester influenced the methodology that he would eventually employ with the Irish Constabulary. Shaw characterized his method an 'unceasing state of watching,' and described its function in a letter to Sir William Napier in November 1829: 'I cannot doubt therefore that the most humane course to pursue, and that will also best protect property, is to overcome the mob by their seeing that you hold in readiness such a force that can instantly support the civil power, and that civil authorities acting in understanding with the military, instantly proceed to meet and suppress every scene of riot that may take place, only showing the military when the civil force is evidently inadequate.' A year later, in another letter to Napier, Shaw wrote: 'I have spared no pains to prevent collision between the troops and the people: and this is chiefly to be effected by such good understanding with the magistrates as will prevent their continuing the imprudence of calling out the troops unnecessarily; a great deal may be done also by the way in which troops are stationed so that they may not be placed in actual contact with the people where irritation most exists but sufficiently near to reach such points and in force if absolutely necessary.' Shaw married in 1820 and took the name Shaw-Kennedy after inheriting the estate of Kirkmichael through his wife's family in 1834. His opportunity to test his theories lay not far off. In 1836, Shaw-Kennedy was asked to take command of the reformed Irish Constabulary. He accepted, and took up his appointment as its first inspector general on 1 June 1836. His tenure as inspector general lasted only until 15 March 1838, as he resigned his post after misunderstandings with the Irish executive over his authority in relation to the proper channels for the reports of stipendiary magistrates, and the fact that the government attempted to promote certain individuals without regard for his recommendations in the matter; author of *Standing Rules and Regulations of the Irish Constabulary* (1837); he was promoted colonel on 10/1/1837; major-general on 9/11/1846;

lieutenant-general on 20/6/1854 and he was made a full general on 19/8/1862; in August 1854 he was appointed Colonel of the 47th Regiment of Foot (Lancashire Regiment) and he had received the Waterloo Medal with three clasps; in 1838 he was made a Companion of the Bath and in 1861 he received a ribbon of a Knight Commander of the same distinguished Order; he died at 8 Royal Circus, Bath, Somerset, England on 30/5/1865; (Bath Registrar's District, June Quarter, 1865, vol. 5c, p. 182); (Annual Register, 1865, pp. 196–7); will proved at Bristol by the oath of Dame Mary Primrose Shaw-Kennedy, of 8, Royal Circus, Bath, aforesaid widow, the relict and sole executrix – effects under £7,000 in England.

Sheahan, Patrick; RIC 52398; LDS 2098/023B; born 15/10/1867, Kilrush, Co. Clare; (Kilrush Registrar's District, 1867, vol. 19, p. 375); married firstly on 11/1/1894; (Listowel Registrar's District, March Quarter, 1894, vol. 5, p. 307), wife a native of Co. Kerry; married secondly on 10/10/1915 (Limerick Registrar's District, December Quarter, 1915, vol. 5, p. 242); 3rd DI 19/3/1911; King Edward VII Visit to Ireland Medal, 1903 as a head constable; King George V Visit to Ireland Medal, 1911; pensioned 12/11/1920..

Sheals, H.F.; LDS 2097/176; born 1828, Co. Cavan; son of Peyton Sheals, SI, RIC; 3rd SI 7/10/1848; died 30/5/1857 in Co. Leitrim.

Sheals, Peyton; LDS 2097/051; born 1791, Ballymahon, Co. Longford; father of H.F. Sheals, SI, RIC; baronial chief constable from 26/12/1812 to 30/6/1824; recommended by Dowager Lady Rosse; his father died in 1814 leaving seven small children; wife a native of Renfrewshire, Scotland; his eldest daughter, Jane Maria Annette, of Fortview House, Co. Roscommon (niece to the late and cousin to the present, Sir Hew Crawford Pollok, of Pollok Castle, Renfrewshire, Scotland) married on 23/6/1869, at Grangegorman Church, John G. Persse, Esq., solicitor, of Castleblayney, Co. Monaghan, youngest son of the late Dominick Persse (1782–1867), Esq., 71st Regiment of Foot (Highland Regiment), of Spring Garden, Co. Galway (*Cork Examiner* 26/6/1869); 3rd SI 1/7/1824; C.C. Cootehill, Co. Cavan, 1831; pensioned 30/6/1858 in Co. Westmeath; died 25/10/1880 at Fortview House, Roscommon, Co. Roscommon; (Roscommon Registrar's District, 1880, December Quarter, vol. 3, p. 218).

Sheehan, John Barron; LDS 2097/211; born 25/12/1832, Co. Waterford; clerk in the Census Office for four years; Waterford Militia for one year and six months (WO 13/3288–309); married on 15/10/1882 (Dublin Registrar's District, December Quarter, 1882, vol. 2, p. 497); 3rd SI 15/9/1857; CI 1/1/1879; pensioned 26/12/1897; died 8/11/1910.

Sheehan, Timothy Powell; RIC 71651; LDS 2098/139B; born 19/8/1891, Co. Kildare; captain, Royal Irish Regiment; 3rd DI 8/7/1920; married on 4/9/1920 (Waterford Registrar's District, September Quarter, 1920, vol. 4, p. 389), wife a native of Co. Meath; pensioned 13/7/1922; died in Belfast, 4/9/1971.

Sheehy, Thomas; LDS 2098/004B; born 1/12/1872; Co. Kerry; married on 4/6/1901 (Newcastle Registrar's District, June Quarter, 1901, vol. 5, p. 296), wife a native of Co. Limerick; 3rd DI 11/11/1909; died 24/12/1918 at Rahans, Ballina, Co. Mayo; (Ballina Registrar's District, 1918, March Quarter, vol. 4, p. 1); will proved at Ballina on 15/3/1919.

Sheil, Henry Percy; RIC 50991; LDS 2097/330; born 11/3/1861, Co. Tyrone; married on 21/9/1886 (Larne Registrar's District, September Quarter, 1886, vol. 1, p. 661), wife a native of Co. Antrim; 3rd DI 4/9/1883; King Edward VII Visit to Ireland Medal, 1903; resident magistrate 3rd class 15/2/1908, 2nd class 1/1/1911; resigned 1/9/1911; (p. 136. RM Records of Service Book, National Archives, Dublin).

Sheil, John; LDS 2097/136; born 1813, Co. Derry; 3rd SI 3/6/1841; dismissed 12/8/1841.

Shepperd, Parker; CarNB; baronial chief constable; C.C. Tandragee, Co. Armagh.

Sheridan, Robert; RIC 45076; LDS 2098/235; born 1/10/1861, Co. Cavan; married on 8/8/1889, wife a native of Co. Fermanagh; 3rd DI 10/1/1908; pensioned 15/6/1920; died 31/3/1927.

234

235

234 Bernard George Shaw.

235 George Foley Shaw.

236 Hugh Shier.

237 William DeRinzy Shoveller.

236

237

Shier, Hugh; RIC 38728; LDS 2098/182; born, 1858, Adare, Co. Limerick; married on 22/12/1880, wife a native of London; 3rd DI 29/11/1901; Queen Victoria's Visit to Ireland Medal, 1900 as a head constable; King Edward VII Visit to Ireland Medal, 1903; pensioned 29/6/1914.

Shore, Patrick Bayard; RIC 52483; LDS 2098/045B; born 25/3/1868, Ennis, Co. Clare; (Ennis Registrar's District, 1868, vol. 4, p. 291); 3rd DI 27/2/1913; pensioned 31/1/1919.

Short, John; RIC 81515; LDS 2099/016.

Shoveller, William De Rinzy; RIC 35270; LDS 2097/277; born 1850, Townparks, Wexford, Co. Wexford; son of Major William King Shoveller (d.9/4/1887) RMLI and Georgina C. (DeRinzy) Shoveller (d.25/12/1891) who are buried in Deansgrange Cemetery, Dublin (South Section, Row L1, Grave No. 45); 3rd SI 20/3/1869; CI 1/9/1900; King Edward VII Visit to Ireland Medal, 1903; barrackmaster of the Phoenix Park Depot 1/9/1900; pensioned 17/2/1910; (photo in the *Constabulary Gazette*, vol. XIV, no. 17, 16/1/1904).

Sidley, William Henry Francis; RIC 64324; LDS 2098/233; born 19/11/1882, Granard, Co. Longford; (Granard Registrar's District, December Quarter, 1882, vol. 3, p. 3); son of Rev. Henry Francis DeBurgh Sidley (b.1856 King's County) and Catherine Mary (Co. Mayo); BA 1908, Trinity College Dublin; married on 30/3/1910 (Lurgan Registrar's District, march Quarter, 1910, vol. 1, p. 826), wife a native of Co. Armagh; 3rd DI 10/6/1908; TCI 10/11/1920; pensioned 14/7/1922; Commissioner of Police, Jamaica Constabulary; (photo: Garda Museum & Archives, Dublin Castle).

Silcock, James Charles Lionel; RIC 62657; LDS 2098/219; born 13/6/1882, Co. Down; assistant schoolmaster for five years; married on 14/4/1909 (Dublin South Registrar's District, June Quarter, 1909, vol. 2, p. 537), wife a native of India; 3rd DI 9/1/1907; Private Secretary to the Inspector General from 29/7/1920 to 18/12/1920; pensioned 31/5/1922; transferred to the Royal Ulster Constabulary on 1/6/1922; (photo in the *Constabulary Gazette*, vol. XXVII, no. 6, 23/4/1910, p. 84).

Simey, Alfred James Downes; RIC 59415; LDS 2098/175; born 9/5/1875, Sunderland, Durham, England; (Sunderland Registrar's District, 1875, June Quarter, vol. 10a, p. 840); analyst at Bass's Brewery for 3 years; married on 16/7/1901, Miss H.K. Stillinghurst, of Hampton, Chelmsford; captain, Royal Army Services Corps, 18/12/1915 (*London Gazette* dated 5/1/1916) and Assistant Provost Marshal in France, 16/10/1916; released from army service, 13/2/1919 and retained the rank of captain (*London Gazette* dated 24/2/1921); awarded the Croix de Guerre; 3rd DI 1/1/1901; Queen Victoria's Visit to Ireland Medal, 1900 as a head constable; King Edward VII Visit to Ireland Medal, 1903; pensioned 20/4/1922; (WO 339/50582).

Simpson, Robert; LDS 2097/175; born 1830, Co. Longford; son of Robert Simpson, CI, RIC; son born on 6/9/1855 at Liffey View, Blessington, Co. Wicklow (*Cork Examiner* 10/9/1855); daughter, Florinda Victoria, born on 15/8/1865 at Delvin, Co. Westmeath (Delvin Registrar's District, vol. 18, p. 193) (*Cork Examiner* 18/8/1865); 3rd SI 2/8/1848; dismissed 29/11/1868.

Simpson, Robert; LDS 2097/052; born 1782, Co. Derry; father of Robert Simpson, SI, RIC; married 11/8/1823; ensign and lieutenant, Londonderry Militia from February 1804 to October 1806 (WO 13/3039–58); ensign, 89th Regiment of Foot, 9/10/1806; lieutenant, 9/7/1808; lieutenant half pay, 1818; 3rd SI 1/8/1824; CI 1/12/1826; died 8/11/1849; (WO 25/774 fol. 8).

Singleton, Matthew; CarNB; born 1797, Castleblayney, Co. Monaghan; father of Richard Singleton, CI, RIC; 3rd SI 1822; CI and Paymaster for Co. Kerry 1/1/1828; chief magistrate 16/5/1831; PPF; resident magistrate 1/10/1836; residing at Landscape, Pallasgreen, Co. Tipperary in 1838 (Nenagh Guardian, 1838); died 27/1/1865 at Castleblayney, Co. Monaghan (Castleblayney Registrar's District, vol. 1, p. 340 & vol. 16, p. 285); will with one codicil proved at the Principal Registry on 21/2/1865 by the oath of Anne Singleton, of Castleblayney, widow and sole executrix – effects under £8,000; his eldest daughter Anne (b.1830)(d.15/3/1895), married firstly on 22/10/1846, at Sandys Street Presbyterian Church, Newry, Co. Down, Nathaniel Weir, solicitor (Newry Registrar's District, vol. 8, p. 703) and she married secondly on

4/3/1856, at St Peter's Church, Dublin (Dublin South Registrar's District, vol. 5, p. 298), Eldon Piers Butler (b.1831)(d.20/2/1903), fifth son of Espine Ward, Esq., of 64, Lower Charlemont Street, Dublin (*Cork Examiner* 7/3/1856). They are buried in Mount Jerome Cemetery, Dublin with their daughter Annie Singleton Ward (d.22/8/1914); C.C. Clonmel, Co. Tipperary; Tralee, Co. Kerry; Woodford, Co. Galway.

Singleton, Richard; RIC 21576; LDS 2097/123; born 1818, Co. Tipperary; eldest son of Matthew Singleton, CI, RIC, RM and father of Thomas French singleton, AIG, RIC; 3rd SI 1/1/1839; CI 18/7/1876; pensioned 21/4/1879; died 7/10/1880 at Dundalk, Co. Louth.

Singleton, Thomas French; LDS 2097/245; born 15/2/1845, Parish of Kilcolman, Co. Mayo and baptized on 18/2/1845; son of Richard Singleton, CI, RIC; married on 23/4/1873 (Larne Registrar's District, vol. 6, p. 703); 3rd SI 1/12/1863; member of the Royal Victorian Order, 1903; awarded the Queen's Jubilee Medal, 1897; CI 1/4/1887; Commissioner of Police and Town Inspector of Constabulary, Belfast from 3/10/1889 to 28/6/1896; AIG 28/6/1896; Commandant of the Phoenix Park Depot from 28/6/1896 to 1/4/1902; Queen Victoria's Visit to Ireland Medal, 1900; King Edward VII Visit to Ireland Medal, 1903; pensioned 15/2/1905; (photo in the *Constabulary Gazette*, vol. 2, no. 39, p. 1, 24/12/1897).

Slacke, Owen Randal; born 15/8/1837; resident magistrate, 1868–1882; divisional commissioner 1882 to 14/11/1897; captain; later Kt. (cr.1897) Sir. Born 15/8/1837; married firstly, 1863, Katherine Anne (died on 31/1/1872 at Carrick House, Carrick-on-Suir, Co. Waterford – *Cork Examiner* 2/2/1872), eldest daughter of Sir C. Lanyon, of The Abbey, Co. Antrim; daughter Helen Maria (Carrick-on-Suir Registrar's District, vol. 19, p. 637) born on 5/12/1869 at Carrick House, Carrick-on-Suir, Co. Tipperary (*Cork Examiner* 10/12/1869); married secondly, 1875, Fanny, daughter of P. Connellan, Coolmore, Co. Kilkenny; three sons and one daughter; Late Captain 10th Hussars; address: 31 Chesham Street, London S.W.; Clubs: Cavalry; Kildare Club; died 27/4/1910.

Slattery, John; RIC 25324; born 1841, Co. Kilkenny; married on 30/6/1884, wife a native of Co. Tipperary; 3rd DI 1/11/1889; police instructor and schoolmaster, Phoenix Park depot from 1/11/1889 to 1/2/1893; pensioned 1/2/1893.

Slattery, William; LDS 2097/118; born 1799, Co. Tipperary; 3rd SI 1/2/1838; received a grant from the Reward Fund on 31/3/1856 for zeal, tact and success in obtaining circumstantial evidence resulting in the conviction of the perpetrator of a barbarous murder; pensioned 12/12/1859; died 20/4/1861.

Sloane, A.C.; LDS 2097/112; 3rd SI 1/4/1837; dismissed 6/11/1838.

Smith, Henry; LDS 2097/164; born 1826, Clonooney House, Clones, Co. Monaghan; private, 3rd Light Dragoons for twenty eight days; he married on 30/8/1849 (Listowel Registrar's District, vol. 7, p. 276), Elizabeth Agnes (1/10/1828–29/8/1889), second daughter John Sandes (22/3/1791–31/5/1845), of Listowel, Co. Kerry and Agnes (1800–1858), daughter of John Sandes (his first cousin); 3rd SI 1/5/1848; received an approbation on 30/6/1852 for spirited exertions in saving life and property from fire; CI 1/11/1872; pensioned 1/5/1888; died 4/1/1909 at 12 Kevin's Park, Rathmines, Dublin; will proved on 6/2/1909 at the Principal Registry by the oath of Frances Smith, the widow and William Barrett, Gent. – effects £188.1s.8d.

Smith, Henry; CarNB; PPF; C.C. Tulla, Co. Clare; Moylough, Co. Galway.

Smith, Henry Wilson; RIC 33106; LDS 2097/263; born 1849, Co. Donegal; 3rd SI 1/8/1867; died 31/10/1876 at Buncrana, Co. Donegal; administration granted on 20/12/1876 at Derry to Rachel Henrietta Smith, of 10 Gardiner's Place, Dublin, widow of the deceased – effects under £450; (photo in the *Constabulary Gazette*, vol. VI, no. 13, 23/12/1899, p. 390).

Smith, Herbert Frederick; RIC 72333; ADRIC CADET no. 541; LDS 2098/203B; born 14/4/1887, Cambs., England; (Cambridge Registrar's District, 1887, June Quarter, vol. 3b, p. 499); lieutenant, King's African Rifles; 3rd DI 10/1/1920; resigned 30/12/1921; (WO 339/29593).

Smith, John Barnhill; RIC 6704; LDS 2097/283; born, 1826, Co. Tyrone; 3rd SI 5/1/1871; received a favourable record on 31/12/1871 securing a powerful lunatic and disarming him of a cleaver with which he attempted violence; married on 22/2/1872 at All Saints Church, Knightsbridge, London, Emily, third daughter of the late John Sutton, Esq., of New Clements Inn, London (*Cork Examiner* 29/2/1872); pensioned 16/4/1881; died 13/12/1903 at 2, Prince of Wales' Terrace, Ballsbridge, Dublin, and formerly on Lissavalley, Barnaderg, Co. Galway; administration granted on 19/4/1904 at the Principal Registry to Emily Smith, widow – effects £393.2s.3d.

Smith, Robert Allman; RIC 33944; LDS 2097/268; born 1844, Co. Dublin; son of Rev. G. Smith, DD, Rector of Omagh, Co. Tyrone; midshipman, Royal Navy and served in the Cape of Good Hope, Ceylon, Borneo, Hong Kong, Japan, Vancouver, Hawaii and the Falklands; married on 8/7/1874 (Coleraine Registrar's District, vol. 11, p. 493); 3rd SI 20/3/1868; CI 1/2/1894; pensioned 1/2/1908; died 4/5/1918 at Benedine Lodge, Nenagh, Co. Tipperary; will proved on 3/7/1918 at Limerick; in November 1906 his son, E.P. Allman Smith passed his final Littlego examinations in Trinity College Dublin, taking fourth place on the first class list of medical students; (photo in the *Constabulary Gazette*, vol. X, no. 25, 25/3/1902).

Smith, Samuel; LDS 2097/071; born 1795, Co. Wexford; PPF; enlisted as a sub constable on 17/3/1819; constable on 1/8/1823; 3rd SI 1/8/1831; received an injury to the leg while on duty at a Patron at Leenane, Co. Galway on 8/9/1836; pensioned 1/8/1848.

Smith, Thomas James (Sir); LDS 2097/321; born 1863, King's County; married on 9/2/1885 (Dublin South Registrar's District, March Quarter, 1885, vol. 2, p. 587), wife from Co. Wicklow; 3rd DI 16/10/1882; King Edward VII Visit to Ireland Medal, 1903; detective director at Belfast, 29/5/1905; CI 8/12/1905; King George V Coronation Medal, 1911; Commissioner of Police and Town Inspector of Constabulary, Belfast from 1/6/1909 to 11/3/1920; inspector general from 11/3/1920 to 15/5/1920; awarded in 1920 the King's Police Medal, 1909; CBE (Civil) 1919; KBE (Civil) 1920; died 15/9/1939 at Lissavalley, Les Vardes, St Peter Port, Guernsey; probate granted on 9/12/1939 at London to Dame Emma Louisa Smith, widow – effects resworn £1,538.7s.7d. in England; resworn £334.14s.2d.

Smith, Thomas; LDS 2097/073; born 1811, Co. Dublin; PPF; enlisted as a sub constable 27/8/1828; constable 1/11/1829; wife a native of Co. Limerick; daughter born on 17/1/1851 at Rathkeale, Co. Limerick (*Cork Examiner*, 23/1/1852); daughter born on 6/9/1856 at Ballymullen (*Cork Examiner* 15/9/1856); 3rd SI 18/2/1832; CI 11/9/1852; pensioned 1/1/1872; died 10/8/1893 in Dublin; buried in Mount Jerome, Dublin on 12/8/1893 (Grave No. B40–354–9068).

Smith, Thomas; LDS 2097/139; born 1805, Co. Meath; PPF; enlisted as a sub constable on 2/7/1823; wife a native of Co. Dublin; 3rd SI 13/6/1842; pensioned 1/8/1875; died 4/3/1893 in Ballina, Co. Mayo (Ballina Registrar's District, 1893, March Quarter, vol. 4, p. 2).

Smith, William; LDS 2097/067; born 1787; PPF; Dublin Police, 1812–20; 3rd SI 1/10/1820; C.C. Croom, Co. Limerick; arrested Fitzgibbon who was the principal in the murder of Major Going on 14/10/1821; arrested a man for the murder of Major Hare in 1821 who after a little judicious management became an approver and exposed the whole conspiracy; assaulted in a riot at Croom Fair on 3/5/1833; died 8/8/1838; wife Anne in receipt of a pension of £30p.a. from 9/8/1838.

Smith, William Alfred Scudemore; LDS 2098/205; born 19/3/1880, Gatertop, Leominster, Herefs., England; (West Ham Registrar's District, March Quarter, 1880, vol. 4a, p. 167); son of John Smith; BA (Hons.) Pembroke College, Cambridge; captain, Cambridge University Volunteer Rifles; married Alice second daughter of Major-General J. Graham, DL, late of the 1st Royal Dragoons, Mossknow, Dumfriesshire, Scotland on 15/10/1908 at Kirkpatrick-Fleming Church, Dumfriesshire; 3rd DI 8/1/1905; resigned 15/03/1910 on his appointment as Assistant Head Constable of Liverpool; on the outbreak of WW1, 188 Army and 19 Naval

238

239

238 William Henry Francis Sidley. 239 Thomas James Smith, Inspector General, RIC. 240 Col. William Alfred Smith, Assistant Head Constable, Liverpool Police. 241 Harry Smyth.

240

241

Reservists were recalled to the colours from the Liverpool City Police and a further 109 volunteered for active service, including Smith. In all close on 900 were to serve with 142 losing their lives; in 1915 be became second in command of a Kitchener Battalion of the Liverpool King's Regiment, subsequently becoming commanding officer of the 18th (Service) Battalion of the Manchester Regiment and he was killed on 9/7/1916 at the Glatz Redoubt near Montauban, Somme, France at the Divisions HQ where he was visiting with other senior officers with others by an unlucky shell; wife, Alice Smith (nee Graham) (b.24/1/1880, married at Kirkpatrick Parish Church on 15/10/1898); daughter, Felicity Mary Audley Smith (b.1/6/1912) at 8, Riversdale Road, Garston, Liverpool; will proved at the Principal Registry by the oath of his widow, Alice on 19/11/1916 – effects £134.0s.0d.; (WO 339/16380).

Smith, William Frederick Hammersley; RIC 31908; LDS 2097/258; born 16/5/1843, Dublin City; 3rd SI 7/9/1866; Private Secretary to the Inspector General from 12/8/1879 to his appointment as a temporary resident magistrate on 25/10/1880; permanent RM 3rd class 6/6/1881, 2nd class 9/10/1882, 1st class 4/6/1894; pensioned 16/5/1908; (p. 68, RM Records of Service Book, National Archives, Dublin).

Smith, William Robert; RIC 66986; LDS 2098/041B; born 8/9/1890, Mohill, Co. Leitrim; (Mohill Registrar's District, December Quarter, 1890, vol. 3, p. 167): assistant master; 3rd DI 18/2/1913; died of typhoid fever, 7/3/1916.

Smylie, Robert Samuel; CarNB; lieutenant; 3rd SI 1820; died 1/12/1827; C.C. Tralee, Co. Kerry; his son, Samuel Smylie, Esq., JP, died in New York on 12/3/1871, aged 52 years, late of Woodley Park and Rochelle, Co. Dublin (*Cork Examiner* 4/4/1871).

Smyth, Devaynes; RIC 29867; LDS 2097/251; born 1845, King's County; employed as a clerk with the Customs & Excise, Liverpool; 3rd SI 1/1/1865; resigned 7/8/1877.

Smyth, Frederick John; RIC 51162; LDS 2097/335; born 1860, Co. Mayo; married on 14/6/1899 (Dublin South Registrar's District, June Quarter, vol. 2, p. 586), Ermine Jane Wills, a native of Co. Westmeath; 3rd DI 12/7/1884; King George V Visit to Ireland Medal, 1911; pensioned 4/2/1920.

Smyth, Gerard Bryce Ferguson; born 7/9/1885, Dalhouise, Punjab, India; son of Mr George Smyth, of Milltown, who had a distinguished career in the Bengal Civil Service, and Helen Smyth; a grandson of Mr Thomas Ferguson, JP, Edenderry House, Banbridge, Co. Down; educated at Shrewsbury School, January 1899 to January 1901 and had private tuition from October 1901 to February 1903; entered the Royal Engineers from Woolwich on 29 July 1906 and was promoted to the rank of lieutenant on 3 February 1908. He went to France with the original Expeditionary Force in August 1914, and served with distinction on the western front throughout the war. He was wounded on no fewer than six occasions, was decorated by the King and the President of the French Republic for his brilliant services, and rose from the rank of lieutenant to that of Brigadier-General. He was awarded the Distinguished Service Order in December, 1914, the official announcement stating that the decoration was granted 'for consistent skill, daring, and hard work, in reconnaissance and defensive preparations night and day throughout the campaign, and specially throughout the battle of the Aisne, and in the trenches of Givenchy, although wounded on 20 October 1914, by a shell, entailing the loss of his left arm.' He was frequently mentioned in despatches by Field-Marshals Viscount French and Earl Haig, and was specially promoted to the rank of brevet major on the occasion of the King's birthday in 1916, in recognition of his distinguished service in the field; divisional commissioner, 14/4/1920; killed on 17/7/1920 at the Cork & County Club, Cork City; his brother, Major George Osbert Stirling Smyth, DSO, MC, Royal Field Artillery, aged 30 years was killed during a raid at the house of Professor Carolan, Drumcondra, Dublin on 12/10/1920. Osbert was on army service in Cairo, Egypt, when his brother was assassinated in Cork City. He came to Dublin Castle shortly after he buried his brother with eleven hand-picked officers. These men were known to Sinn Féin as 'The

Cairo Gang' or 'The Murder Gang' and all eleven were assassinated by Michael Collins' Squad on 11/11/1920.

Smyth, Harry; RIC 59040; LDS 2098/162; born 1874, Herts., England, youngest son of Hugh Smyth, Esq., Baldock, Herts., England; 3rd DI 2/10/1899; BA, Lincoln College, Oxford; married on 21/8/1900 (Dublin South Registrar's District, September Quarter, 1900, vol. 2, p. 545), at St Mary's Church, Donnybrook, Dublin, Georgine Eveleen (Evie), daughter of D. MacNair, Java and Mrs Caeron Macnair, Park Avenue, Sydney Parade, Dublin; daughter born at Shinrone, King's County on 31/5/1901; killed 28/4/1916, Ashbourne, Co. Meath; buried in Ardbracken Cemetery, Navan, Co. Meath; awarded the Constabulary Medal, posthumously on 27/7/1916; administration granted on 1/9/1916 at London to Georgina E. Smyth, the widow – effects in Ireland £223.10s.0d., resealed at Dublin; (WO 339/6322).

Smyth, Henry William; RIC 37898; LDS 2097/286; born, 1852, Co. Mayo; married on 16/9/1879, wife a native of Co. Carlow; 3rd SI 9/8/1871; died 30/4/1883; buried within the walls of the Augustinian Abbey, Dunmore, Co. Galway; his headstone has the following inscription: 'In memory of Henry William Smyth, Esq., Sub Inspector R.I. Constabulary who departed this life 30th April 1883 – beloved and regretted by the men of his command by whom this monument is erected as a mark of their esteem.'

Smyth, John Joseph; LDS 2098/209B; born 4/12/1895, Magherafelt, Co. Derry; (Magherafelt Registrar's District, December Quarter, 1895, vol. 1, p. 683); lieutenant, Black Watch; ADRIC; married on 2/9/1920, wife a native of Surrey; 3rd DI 12/1/1920; pensioned 20/4/1922; died 28/3/1932.

Smyth, Joseph; RIC 39221; LDS 2098/165; born 1854, Co. Kerry; married on 9/12/1884 (Cookstown Registrar's District, December Quarter, 1884, vol. 1, p. 627), wife a native of Co. Tyrone; 3rd DI 1/12/1899; King Edward VII Visit to Ireland Medal, 1903; pensioned 10/12/1913; died 15/1/1928 in Dublin; (Dublin South Registrar's District, 1928, March Quarter, vol. 2, p. 340); buried in St James Cemetery, Dublin.

Smyth, William; RIC 5827; LDS 2097/275; born 1826, Co. Kildare; wife a native of Co. Galway; 3rd SI 1/2/1869; died 25/2/1880 at Waterford, Co. Waterford; (Waterford Registrar's District, 1880, September Quarter, vol. 4, p. 533).

Somerville, Bellingham Arthur; RIC 38805; LDS 2097/290; born 1854, Co. Dublin; son of Tenison Alan Somerville and brother of Henry Bellingham Somerville, SI, RIC; married on 27/8/1879; 3rd SI 24/8/1872; pensioned 25/2/1891; died 20/1/1916 at Chermont, Rathnew, Co. Wicklow; will proved on 10/4/1916 at the Principal Registry by the oath of Thomas Meskall, accountant and Margaret H. Somerville, the widow – effects £3,158.19s.1d.

Somerville, Henry Bellingham; RIC 33011; LDS 2097/262; born 1849, Co. Dublin; son of Tenison Alan Somerville and brother of Bellingham Arthur Somerville; 3rd SI 1/7/1867; pensioned 31/5/1897; died 14/2/1915 at 74, Morehampton Road, Donnybrook, Dublin; will proved on 14/2/1915 at the Principal Registry by the oath of Mary Somerville, the widow – effects £5,167.1s.0d.

Somerville, James; RIC 16551; LDS 2097/196; born 1830, Co. Cork; assistant in the office of a mercantile establishment; 3rd SI 1/2/1853; pensioned 16/8/1887; died 8/2/1913 at Mardyke House, Skibbereen, Co. Cork; will proved on 15/3/1913 at the Principal Registry to the Rev. George B. Sweetman, Clerk – effects £864.2s.4d.

Somerville, Robert; LDS 2097/082; born 1798, Co. Fermanagh; enlisted as a sub constable, 1/3/1823; his wife Susan, a native of Co. Fermanagh, died 31/8/1834, aged 35 years and their daughter Jane died 28/8/1835, aged eight years and they are both buried in Ballincollig Military Cemetery, Ballincollig, Co. Cork; sub constable, 1/3/1823; constable 1/10/1824; 3rd SI 14/2/1833; CI 17/11/1858; pensioned 1/10/1867; died 22/2/1874 at Ballincollig, Co. Cork, late of Kinsale, Co. Cork; will proved on 19/3/1874 at Cork by the oath of David Somerville, of Ballincollig, Co. Cork – effects £100.

Sparling, Edward; LDS 2097/083; 3rd SI 1/4/1833; still serving in 1839 – record incomplete.
Sparrow, Robert; RIC 52877; LDS 2098/038; born 11/12/1862, Co. Tipperary; master in Carrig School, Kingstown and Rathmines School for five years; Medalist, BA Trinity College Dublin; married Adelaide (1874–1951), daughter of Thomas Walter and Elizabeth Lambert, Kilquane, Co. Galway; 3rd DI 16/3/1888; King Edward VII Visit to Ireland Medal, 1903; chief police instructor at the Phoenix Park Depot from 1/4/1905 to 18/3/1910; resident magistrate 3rd class 18/3/1910, 2nd class 28/1/1913; appointed for special duty at Dublin Castle from 25/11/1920 to 7/3/1921; pensioned 15/8/1921; died in 1923; buried in Mount Jerome Cemetery, Dublin with his wife and two sons, Robert Francis Garnett born at Newport, Co. Tipperary on 16/12/1901 and died in 1951 and William La Barth (1906–72); (p. 142, RM Records of Service Book, National Archives, Dublin).
Spears, Reginald Rowland; RIC 67607; LDS 2098/048B; born 11/6/1892, 48, Hollybrook, Drumcondra, Co. Dublin; (Dublin South Registrar's District, September Quarter, 1892, vol. 2, p. 535); second divisional clerk in the Department of Agriculture from January 1912 to November 1913; 2nd lieutenant, Army Service Corps, 9/10/1915 (*London Gazette* dated 23/10/1915); attached to 4th Battalion, Royal Irish Regiment, 26/2/1918; served in Salonica,1/2/1916–30/7/1916 and France, 1/6/1918–27/1/1919; relinquished his commission on completion of service and permitted to retain the rank of lieutenant, 28/1/1919 (*London Gazette* dated 28/7/1922); married on 1/12/1920 (Dublin South Registrar's District, December Quarter, 1920, vol. 2, p. 497), Edith May Robertson; 3rd DI 1/11/1914; pensioned 7/6/1922; (WO 339/44182); transferred to the Royal Ulster Constabulary on 8/6/1922.
Spellman, Owen; RIC 55460; LDS 2098/095B; born 19/4/1872, Co. Roscommon; married on 21/8/1917 (Kilkenny Registrar's District, September Quarter, 1917, vol. 3, p. 327), wife a native of Co. Kilkenny; 3rd DI 7/9/1919; pensioned 16/5/1922.
Spotiswood, Andrew; CarNB; born 1797; son of the rector of Bellaghy, Co. Derry diocese; 3rd SI 1825; on 30/1/1827 he applied for leave on the death of his mother; on 11/7/1831 he tenders his resignation as he had been appointed agent of the Magherafelt estate by the Marquis of Londonderry and Sir Robert Bateson, Bt.; C.C. Newtownards, Co. Down.
Sproule, John; RIC 7054; LDS 2097/283; born 1826, Co. Westmeath; wife from Co. Clare; 3rd SI 5/4/1871; received an approbation on 30/6/1872 for spirited and zealous conduct in extinguishing fire on the premises of a dealer in gunpowder; assisted by a tradesman, he removed a quantity of gunpowder from the burning house; pensioned 15/4/1875; died 21/5/1893 at Flower Hill, Navan, Co. Meath; will proved on 13/7/1893 at the Principal Registry by the oath of Arabella Sproule, the widow, one of the executors – effects £661.13s.9d.
St George, John Edward; RIC 52410; LDS 2098/027; born 20/2/1864, Kilrush House, Freshford, Co. Kilkenny; (Urlingford Registrar's District,1864, vol. 3, p. 723); married on 4/7/1899, wife a native of Co. Dublin; captain, 5th Battalion, Royal Irish Regiment; 3rd DI 11/6/1886; Queen Victoria's Visit to Ireland Medal, 1900; King Edward VII Visit to Ireland Medal, 1903; Private Secretary to the Inspector General from 6/5/1903 until his appointment as a resident magistrate 3rd class 26/9/1908, 2nd class 26/10/1911; pensioned 12/3/1921; died 1940; (p. 139, RM Records of Service Book, National Archives, Dublin).
St Leger, William Henry; LDS 2097/130; born 1817, Co. Waterford; son of Colonel, The Hon. Richard St Leger; junior clerk in the Constabulary Office from 25/6/1836 to 7/2/1840; wife a native of the Cape of Good Hope with family connections in Co. Limerick; 3rd SI 7/2/1840; CI 1/8/1867; pensioned 1/10/1882; died 3/5/1886 at Wentworth House, Wicklow; buried in Mount Jerome Cemetery, Dublin on 7/5/1886 (Grave No. C108–364).
Stack, Thaddeus J.G.; RIC 27853; LDS 2097/241; born 1840, Co. Limerick; temporary clerk in the Military Store Service, Pimlico for three years; married on 4/7/1864 at Ballygar Church, Co. Galway (Mountbellew Registrar's District, vol. 14, p. 193), Martha, daughter of William

Nowlan, of Ballygar, Co. Galway (*Cork Examiner* 8/7/1864); 3rd SI 1/7/1862; dismissed 5/11/1866, having been found guilty of certain charges before a Court of Inquiry.

Stafford, Arthur Willoughby; LDS 2097/144; born 1819, Co. Cavan; son of Major Stafford of the Londonderry Militia; 3rd SI 1/1/1845; CI 26/5/1869; pensioned 15/2/1880; died 28/12/1903 at Gardenmore, Larne, Co. Antrim; administration granted on 30/11/1904 (T.11593 / National Archives) at Belfast to Jane Hall and Elizabeth R. Nelson – effects £3,292.11s.0d.

Stanhope, William Henry; LDS 2097/102; born 1790; 3rd SI 1/10/1836; paymaster 1/10/1836; appointment not taken up by him; died on 21/6/1872 at his residence in Spring Gardens, London (*Cork Examiner* 28/6/1872).

Stapleton, Thomas; LDS 2099/012; born 1878, United States; married on 21/10/1903 (Dublin North Registrar's District, December Quarter, 1903, vol. 2, p. 555), wife a native of Co. Waterford; 3rd DI 6/12/1921; pensioned 30/4/1922.

Starkie, Robert Fitzwilliam; RIC 44399; LDS 2097/301; born 21/11/1855, William Street, Belmullet, Co. Mayo (*Cork Examiner* 28/11/855), third son of William Robert Starkie (b.1825), Resident Magistrate 25/11/1854–12/6/1897, JP, Cregane Manor, Roscarbery, Co. Cork and Frances Maria, youngest daughter of Michael Power of Waterford, who were married in Dublin on 29/10/1850 (Dublin North Registrar's District, vol. 5, p. 158) (*Cork Examiner* 30/10/1850); grandson of Walter Starkie, Esq., died at Newtown, near Roscarbery, Co. Cork on 23/9/1853, aged 65 years, late captain, 82nd Regiment of Foot (South Lancashire Regiment), veteran of the Peninsular Wars, for which he obtained the medal and seven clasps, and who had a miraculous escape in 1816 from the wreck of the *Boadicea* which sank with the *Lord Melville* while returning from the Battle of Waterloo in a storm with a loss of 267 lives off Garretstown, Co. Cork; his eldest brother, Robert Fitzwilliam Starkie, died on 16/5/1855, of water on the brain at Belmullet, Co. Mayo (*Cork Examiner* 25/5/1855); his second eldest brother, Walter J. Starkie was head of the Board of National Education; private 19th Hussars for six months and clerk in the National Bank of Ireland for two and a half years; 3rd SI 12/5/1879; Adjutant, Phoenix Park Depot from 10/3/1891 to 1/9/1893; Private Secretary to the Inspector General from 1/9/1893 to 18/6/1895; resident magistrate 3rd class 12/6/1895, 2nd class 1/8/1902, 1st class 28/1/1913; married on 11/9/1905, at St Mary Abbots, Kensington, London, Marion Awdry, daughter of William E. Robinson, Rochdale and Mrs Edward Harvey; Member of the Commissions of Inquiry at Dublin Castle, 1901, 1908 and 1914; Chairman of Munitions Tribunal for Southern Ireland; Chairman of Courts of Referees under the Employment Insurance Acts at Cork, Mallow and Fermoy; CB, 1916; pensioned 21/11/1920; (p. 104, RM Records of Service Book, National Archives, Dublin).

Steadman, David Addie; RIC 53459; LDS 2098/047; born 1865, Fifeshire, Scotland; tutor at Bates Academy, 29 Gardiner Place from 1885 to 1886 and at Farranfore, Co. Kerry in 1888; married on 3/11/1904, wife a native of London; barrister-at-law; 3rd DI 1/1/1889; Queen Victoria's Visit to Ireland Medal, 1900; King Edward VII Visit to Ireland Medal, 1903; CI 19/3/1911; pensioned 1/3/1921; (photo in the *Constabulary Gazette*, vol. VI, no. 25, 11/3/1899).

Stephens, Samuel Henry; LDS 2097/215; born 1834, Co. Galway; joined the Irish Revenue Police as a lieutenant on 25/1/1854 and served in Arva, Co. Cavan; 3rd SI 1/12/1857; pensioned 1/5/1894; died 7/1/1908 at Rathvinden Cottage, Leighlinbridge, Carlow; buried in Innislonagh Churchyard, Marlfield, Co. Tipperary; will proved on 28/2/1908 at the Principal Registry by the oath of Grace H. Stephens, widow – effects £1,629.8s.9d.

Stephens, William; RIC 17313; LDS 2097/310; born 1835, Co. Tyrone; 3rd SI 14/12/1880; pensioned 10/10/1891; died 15/4/1895 at Balbriggan, Co. Dublin, formerly of Oughterard, Co. Galway (Balrothery Registrar's District, 1895, June Quarter, vol. 2, p. 301); will proved at the

242

243

242 Reginald Rowland Spears.   243 James Verdier Stevenson, Chief Constable of Glasgow, 1902.   244 Kerry Leyne Supple.   245 Oswald Ross Swanzy.

245

244

Principal Registry by the oath of Elizabeth Stephens, of Dublin Street, Balbriggan, Co. Dublin, widow – effects £294.4s.10d.

Stevenson, Edward James P.; RIC 72024; LDS 2098/196B; born 7/7/1898, Belfast, Co. Antrim; (Belfast Registrar's District, 1898, September Quarter, vol. 1, p. 407); son of James Verdier Stevenson, DI, RIC; lieutenant, Black Watch; 3rd DI 10/1/1920; killed 2/6/1921, Westpoint / Leenane Road, Carrowkennedy, Co. Mayo.

Stevenson, James Verdier; LDS 2098/004; born 1858, Athlone, Co. Westmeath, son of William Stevenson and Jane Salisbury. Educated at Ranelagh School, Athlone. Seven years as a clerk in the Civil Service, 1877–84 (Postmaster General's Office, London and Commissioners of Woods and Forests, Dublin); married on 27/8/1899 (Newtownards Registrar's District, December Quarter, 1899, vol. 1, p. 1133), Helen Bingham, daughter of John Little, Ballina, Co. Mayo and widow of Robert A. Bingham (son of Major Denis Bingham, Bingham Castle, Co. Mayo) and they had three sons and three daughters; his son RIC DI Edward J. Stevenson, was murdered at Westpoint / Leenane Road, Carrowkennedy, Co. Mayo on 2/6/1921; 3rd DI 1/12/1885; resigned 2/4/1902 on his appointment as Chief Constable of Glasgow City Police; awarded the King's Police Medal, 1913; MVO, 1914; CBE, 1918. He retired on 1/4/1922 and died 15/11/1933 at Moyne, Blacksole, Herne Bay, Sussex, England; (Blean Registrar's District, December Quarter, 1933, vol. 2a, p. 1,231); probate granted at London on 7/3/1934 to Helen Halliday Stevenson, widow – effects £1,191.7s.1d.

Stewart, Thomas; LDS 2097/063; born 1783, Co. Donegal; lieutenant in the yeomanry from July 1803 to September 1814; 3rd SI 1/10/1825; pensioned 16/9/1845; died 1854.

Stewart, William T.; CarNB; Prince of Wales' Own Donegal Militia (WO 13/2751–71); PPF chief magistrate in Westmeath in 1821, residing at Garristown; replaced Richard Going in Limerick when he was murdered on 14/10/1821.

Stock, Edwin Henry Douglas; RIC 31909; LDS 2097/259; born 1846, Isle of Man; wife a native of Co. Limerick; 3rd SI 15/9/1866; resigned 1/2/1873.

Stoker, George Worthington; RIC 18700; LDS 2097/203; born 1836, Queen's County; married on 21/1/1864 (Scarriff Registrar's District, vol. 4, p. 473), at the Cathedral, Killaloe, Co. Clare, Elizabeth Vereker, daughter of the late Captain Jervis, 6th Dragoon Guards and widow of the late Richard Rose, Esq., JP, of Ahabeg, Caherconlish, Co. Limerick (*Cork Examiner* 25/1/1864); 3rd SI 21/8/1854; dismissed 27/7/1866.

Stoker, John; LDS 2097/075; born 1799, Queen's County; PPF; enlisted as a sub constable, 10/2/1823; constable, 1/11/1823; 3rd SI 1/6/1832; dismissed 20/7/1847.

Stoker, John; LDS 2097/085; born 1799, Queen's County; enlisted as a sub constable, 18/3/1822; wife a native of Co. Carlow; 3rd SI 16/4/1834; CI 1/3/1859; pensioned 1/3/1867.

Stokes Robert Baret (Sir); born 10/2/1833, Jersey, Channel Islands; second son of Robert Day Stokes, Dromoulton, Co. Kerry and Eliza, daughter of Robert Baret, of Horstead Hall, Norfolk; married Marjorie, daughter of John Simpson, Oakfield, Ontario, Canada; educated at the Royal Military College, Sandhurst; joined 54th West Norfolk Regiment, 1850; lieutenant, 1854; captain,1857; served in the Indian Mutiny, D.A.Q.M.G Allahabad Brigade, 1858–9; passed Staff College, 1859; major of Brigade B.N. America, 1862–7; temporary resident magistrate 31/12/1870; permanent RM 3rd class 16/1/1872, 2nd class 5/1/1881, 1st class 1/1/1888; divisional commissioner 16/1/1888–1/2/1898 in RIC Midland Division, 1888–93 and RIC South Eastern Division, 1893–98; CB (Civil), 1895; Kt. (Cr.1898); died 4/9/1899 at Heidelberg, Germany, late of Eversleigh, Middle Glanmire Road, Cork; administration of the estate (with the will) granted on 16/3/1900 at the Principal Registry to Margaret Augusta Stokes, the widow – effects £3,553.9s.5d.; (p. 71, RM Records of Service Book, National Archives, Dublin).

Stokes, Thomas; RIC 20090; LDS 2097/323; born 1837, Co. Tipperary; wife a native of Co. Limerick; 3rd DI 18/10/1882; died 18/7/1885.

Stovin, Frederick (Sir); CarNB; PPF; born 1783, Whitgift, near Howden, Yorkshire; provincial inspector general 1833–36; son of James Stovin, of Whitgift, near Howden, Yorkshire; ensign 52 Foot, 22/3/1800; captain, 62nd Regiment of Foot (Wiltshire Regiment), 24/6/1802; placed on half pay; captain 28th Regiment of Foot (North Gloucestershire Regiment), 9/7/1803; major 9/5/1816 to 2/9/1819; assistant adjutant general to the third division in Peninsula 1811 to end of the war; received the gold cross with two clasps; deputy adjutant general to the expeditionary force against coasts of the United States 1814; lieut. col. of 92nd Regiment of Foot (Highland Regiment) 2/9/1819, and of 90th Regiment of Foot (Perthshire Volunteers Regiment), 9/8/1821, placed on half pay 23/4/1829; private secretary to the lord lieutenant, 1831; groom-in-waiting to the Queen 1837–59, extra groom-in-waiting to the Queen 28/3/1860 to his death; colonel, 83rd Regiment of Foot, 1/9/1848 to his death; general 14/8/1859; KCB 2/1/1815; GCB 18/5/1860; KCMG 26/2/1820. In 1815 he married Anne Elizabeth, second daughter of Sir Sitwell Sitwell, Bt., Renishaw Hall, Derbyshire. She died at Brighton on 3/4/1856, aged 63; (Hesming Registrar's District, June Quarter, 1856, vol. 2b, p. 137); he died at St James Palace, London 16/8/1865; (St Martin's Registrar's District, September Quarter, 1865, vol. 1a, p. 253); will with a codicil proved at the Principal Registry by the oath of William Warburton, Esq., GCB, a General in the Army, of the Foreign Office in the County of Middlesex, the great-nephew, the sole executor – effects under £7,000.

Strain, James; LDS 2097/156; born 1818, Co. Mayo; enlisted as a sub constable on 1/9/1835; 3rd SI 21/2/1847; CI 10/11/1852; pensioned 1/1/1876; died 5/10/1891 at Richmond, Yorks., England, the residence of his son-in-law, Rev. Agmondisham Vesey.

Stritch, Matthew Michael; RIC 37549; LDS 2097/284; born 1847, Co. Roscommon; married on 8/6/1892, wife from Co. Dublin; 3rd SI 25/4/1871; pensioned 26/5/1894.

Stuart, George Beatty West; RIC 32212; LDS 2097/260; born 1845, King's County; son of John Simson Stuart, SI, RIC; married on 15/4/1871; 3rd SI 1/10/1867; King Edward VII Visit to Ireland Medal, 1903; pensioned 1/2/1907; died 7/1/1922; buried in Deansgrange Cemetery, Dublin (South West Section, Row Q, Grave No. 70) with his wife Maria Louisa Stuart (d.3/9/1930) and his son John Simson Stuart (d.6/6/1939).

Stuart, John Simson; LDS 2097/085; born 1807, Co. Antrim; father of George Beatty West, SI, RIC; wife a native of Co. Leitrim; 3rd SI 1/7/1834; CI 1/5/1859; pensioned 26/9/1868; died 13/12/1886 at 1, Sun Lodge, Blackrock, Cork; buried in the New Cemetery, Galway, Co. Galway; will proved on 14/1/1887 at Cork by the oath of Samuel Duguid Budd, Woodview, Ballintemple, Cork, bank accountant, sole executor – effects £95.10s.0d.

Studdert, John Fitzgerald; RIC 52412; LDS 2098/030; born 1866, Co. Carlow; married on 22/9/1890, wife a native of Co. Galway; 3rd DI 23/9/1887; King Edward VII Visit to Ireland Medal, 1903; pensioned 30/9/1920.

Studdert, John Fitzgerald; RIC 12831; LDS 2097/178; born 1828, Co. Clare; ensign in the army from 14/5/1846 to 1/9/1847; 3rd SI 21/4/1849; seconded to the Commissariat Department in the Crimea on 11/7/1854 where he was killed on 7/2/1855.

Studdert, Jon; LDS 2097/216; born 1831, Co. Limerick; Limerick County Militia for eight months (WO 13/3018–38); civil engineer for eight years; joined the Irish Revenue Police as a lieutenant on 3/4/1855 and served in Logduff, Co. Donegal; 3rd SI 1/12/1857; dismissed 25/8/1876.

Studdert, Stewart Blacker; LDS 2097/139; born 1815, Co. Dublin; 3rd SI 30/3/1842; died 7/2/1854 in Co. Antrim.

Sugrue, James; RIC 55281; LDS 2098/122B; born 2/2/1871, Co. Kerry; married on 23/7/1912 (Dublin North Registrar's District, September Quarter, 1912, vol. 2, p. 555), wife a native of Dublin City; 3rd DI 14/5/1920; awarded the Constabulary Medal on 19/9/1921 for gallant conduct during the battle of Maam, Co. Galway; pensioned 19/5/1922.

Sullivan, Robert Ievers; LDS 2097/331; born 1859, Co. Limerick; son of John Sullivan, MD and Letitia Ievers (b.1831) (m.1857); MA, LLB; married on 19/6/1890 (Gorey Registrar's District, June Quarter, 1890, vol. 2, p. 668), wife a native of Co. Wexford; 3rd DI 8/9/1883; King Edward VII Visit to Ireland Medal, 1903; CI 4/4/1908; King George V Coronation Medal, 1911; pensioned 15/6/1920.

Supple, Edward Kerry; RIC 15215; LDS 2097/188; born 1833, Ballyhorgan House, Ballyhennessy, Co. Kerry; son of Kerry Supple, Esq., Ballyhorgan House, Co. Kerry; father of Kerry Leyne Supple, DI, RIC; another son, Lieutenant Edward James Collis Supple, 6th Battalion, Duke of Wellington's Regiment, died aged 33 years from wounds he received in action on 22/7/1915; his youngest sister, Annie, married on 9/11/1862 at Ballyduff, Co. Kerry, Morty O'Sullivan, Esq., JP, of West Cove, Co. Kerry (*Cork Examiner* 11/10/1862); married on 7/7/1856, at Castletownberehaven, Co. Cork, Emily Trotter, eldest daughter of Lieutenant Thomas Hungerford, Royal Navy, Coast Guard Service (*Cork Examiner* 9/7/1856); son Henry Guy (Dundalk Registrar's District, vol. 7, p. 850) born on 10/4/1869 at Dundalk, Co. Louth (*Cork Examiner* 16/4/1869); 3rd SI 1/9/1851; pensioned 2/8/1893; died 7/3/1918 at Glenmore, Greystones, Co. Dublin: (Rathdown Registrar's District, 1918, March Quarter, vol. 2, p. 651); will proved at the Principal Registry on 8/5/1918.

Supple, Kerry Leyne; RIC 50989; LDS 2097/330; born 1863, Co. Louth; son of Edward Kerry Supple, SI, RIC; married on 6/6/1917 (Abbeyleix Registrar's District, June Quarter, 1917, vol. 3, p. 263), Mrs C. Bell who owned a farm in Queen's County; 3rd DI 16/7/1883; King Edward VII Visit to Ireland Medal, 1903; CI 1/2/1908; King George V Coronation Medal, 1911; (photo in the *Constabulary Gazette*, February 25, 1899 and a review of his book *The Irish Justice of the Peace for Justices, Members of the R.I.C., P. S. Clerks, etc.* published 1899; author of *The Magistrate's Guide*); pensioned 1/3/1921; died 14/8/1921 at Jesmond Terrace, Newcastle-Upon-Tyne, Northumberland, England, late of Naas, Co. Kildare and formerly of Farmleigh, Abbeyleix, Queen's County; (Newcastle-upon-Tyne Registrar's District, September Quarter, 1921, vol. 10b, p. 152); will proved at the Principal Registry on 7/11/1921 by the oath of Whiteside Dane, DL – effects £590.19s.11d. in England, sealed at London on 23/12/1921.

Sutherland, Oliver; LDS 2097/049; born 1802, Co. Galway; 3rd SI 26/1/1824; C.C. Bailieboro, Co. Monaghan, 1824, Hillsboro, Co. Down, 1828; Garva, 1830; pensioned 16/3/1842; died 26/11/1858.

Swanzy, Oswald Ross; RIC 61367; LDS 2098/204; born 15/8/1881, Castleblayney, Co. Monaghan; (Castleblayney Registrar's District, September Quarter, 1881, vol. 1, p. 429); son of James Swanzy, solicitor, Castle Square, Castleblayney, Co. Monaghan and Elizabeth G. Ross; 3rd DI 5/6/1905; District Inspector in Cork City North from 1/1/1916 to 15/5/1920; allegedly involved in a raid on the home of Tomas McCurtin, Lord Mayor of Cork in which McCurtin was killed. As a reprisal Swanzy was shot dead near Christchurch Cathedral at Market Street, Lisburn, Co. Antrim on 22/8/1920. He is buried in Mount Jerome Cemetery, Dublin (Grave No. C108–3156). After his death his mother and sister Irene moved to Dublin and in 1922 his mother died. Irene went on a world trip and settled in the Fiji Islands, marrying a Civil Engineer and Director of Public Works in Fiji, becoming Mrs Irene F.E. Wise, 197, Princes Road, Tamaranua, Suva, Fiji and was still residing there in the 1970s. His number one dress uniform was acquired by the PSNI Museum, Belfast from a collector in New Zealand.

Sweeney, James; RIC 62074; LDS 2098/120B; born 2/12/1883, Co. Donegal; 3rd DI 15/6/1920; pensioned 31/8/1922.

Sweeny, Patrick; LDS 2097/107; born 1806, Co. Mayo; 3rd SI 16/11/1836; on 9/5/1845 he was arrested at the suit of Commissioners of Revenue on a bond of recognizance in which he was a joined security for a Mr Rankin, Sub Inspector of Revenue Police; died 28/4/1876 at Ballinasloe, Co. Galway; administration granted on 11/7/1876 at the Principal Registry to Mary

Sweeny Robins (wife of Patrick Robins, Esq.,), of Moate, Co. Westmeath and Eleanor MacDermott, of Boyle, Co. Roscommon, the nieces of the deceased.

Sweet, William; LDS 2097/293; born, 1836, Kent, England; sergeant major, 1st Royal Dragoons for 18 years and 4 months; 3rd SI 1/5/1873; RIC Riding Master, 1/5/1873 until his death on 10/8/1875; buried in Arbour Hill Cemetery, Dublin; (photo in the *Constabulary Gazette*, vol. VI, no. 13, 23/12/1899, p. 390).

T

Taaffe, Patrick P.; LDS 2097/120; born 1812, Killukin, Co. Roscommon; 3rd SI 4/10/1838; paymaster 4/10/1838 for Counties Fermanagh and Longford; resigned 1/8/1847.

Tabuteau, Joseph; CarNB; born 1798, Tullamore, Clonyhurk, King's County; son of Joseph Brions Tabuteau, MD, surgeon in King's County Infirmary and Eleanor Batt; an older brother was a JP for King's County and a younger brother was Consul for the Netherlands in Dublin; 3rd SI 1/4/1826; chief magistrate 15/2/1832; resident magistrate 1/10/1836; pensioned as a RM on 14/8/1860 at Miltown Malbay, Co. Clare; died 2/9/1879; (Dublin South Registrar's District, 1879, September Quarter, vol. 2, p. 437).

Talbot, Gilbert James; RIC 31545; LDS 2097/256; born 1844, Dublin; 3rd SI 15/4/1866; CI 14/8/1893; married on 16/12/1870 at St Anne's Church, Dublin Emily Adelaide, youngest daughter of the late John Townley, Esq., Tulliven House, Co. Cavan (*Cork Examiner* 20/12/1870); daughter born in Lucan, Co. Dublin on 7/10/1874; pensioned 1/9/1906; died 6/11/1916 at 7, Knapton Terrace, Kingstown, Co. Dublin; will proved on 17/1/1917 at the Principal Registry by the oath of Emily A. Talbot – effects £8,815.1s.4d.; (photo in the *Constabulary Gazette*, vol. V, no. 6, 6/5/1899 & vol. V, no. 26, 23/9/1899).

Tandy, James; CarNB; PPF; major; chief magistrate 1/12/1819 in Dublin, Carlow, parts of Kildare, and Cork; resident magistrate 1/1/1824 for Co. Kildare, Wicklow and Carlow, based at Annsfield, Grangebeg, Kilcullen, Co. Kildare and Millbank, Naas, Co. Kildare; pensioned 15/11/1836.

Taylor, James; LDS 2097/025; born 1780, Co. Donegal; lieutenant, Prince of Wales' Own Donegal Militia (WO 13/2751–71); 3rd SI 1/4/1820; CI 1/4/1824; paymaster 1/10/1836; pensioned 31/5/1851; died 19/5/1865 at Rosslinn Bridge, Londonderry; will proved at the Principal Registry on 15/7/1865 by the oath of James Hayden of the City of Londonderry, solicitor; and one of the executors – effects under £4,000; C.C. Raphoe, Co. Donegal.

Taylor, Joseph Oliver; RIC 46774; LDS 2097/310; born 1859, Co. Dublin; BA, Trinity College Dublin, LLD 1890; married on 27/7/1887 (Dublin South Registrar's District, September Quarter, 1887, vol. 2, p. 495), wife a native of Co. Kildare; 3rd SI 29/4/1881; King Edward VII Visit to Ireland Medal, 1903; King George V Visit to Ireland Medal, 1911; pensioned 6/11/1917.

Taylor, William; RIC 17122; LDS 2097/198; born 1830, Co. Dublin; employed in the Belfast Bank, Dundalk, Co. Louth for two months; BA 1852, Trinity College Dublin; 3rd SI 12/8/1853; died 4/11/1870 at Hillsborough, Co. Down; administration granted on 19/12/1870 at the Principal Registry to Nathaniel Sneyd Taylor, Mullagh, Co. Cavan, next of kin – effects under £1,000.

Taylour, Herbert Featherstonehaugh; RIC 55991; LDS 2098/099; born 1868, Co. Dublin; (Dublin North Registrar's District, 1868, vol. 12, p. 519); married on 22/4/1900 (Dublin South Registrar's District, vol. 2, p. 511), Helen Allardice Webb, of Rathmines, Co. Dublin; lieutenant, 3rd Battalion Leinster Regiment from 1889 to 1891; 3rd DI 1/3/1894; King Edward VII Visit to Ireland Medal, 1903; CI 22/4/1920; pensioned 13/5/1922; his daughter, Fay Taylour (1908–83), born in Birr, Co. Offaly and educated at Alexandra College, Dublin was a pioneer speedway rider when the sport came to Britain in 1928 from Australia. She won the Australian Speedway Championship in 1929 (being the first 'British' person to do so). When the Auto Cycle Union banned the girls after one of them fell off her bike in a pre-meeting parade in Wembley and was injured, Fay turned to four wheels making international midget car racing her speciality until the mid 1950s.

Teeling, Charles George; LDS 2097/134; born 1805, Co. Monaghan; son of Charles Hamilton Teeling, of Belfast and Catherine Anne Teeling, who died on 24/9/1854 at the residence of her son-in-law, Thomas O'Hagan, Esq., QC, Gardiner's Place, Belfast (*Cork Examiner* 29/9/1854); served in the British Auxiliary Legion of Spain and in Egypt in the service of Mahomet Ali as his ADC; his sister, Kate, in Religion, Mother Mary, died on 23/12/1871 at the Convent of the Immaculate Conception, Lakelands, Sandymount, Co. Dublin (*Cork Examiner* 2/1/1872); wife a native of Co. Cork; his fourth son, Samuel, married on 8/8/1872 Mary, eldest daughter of the late Peter T. Foley, Esq., of Ballyaid House, Tralee, Co. Kerry, at the Catholic Church, Anna, Tralee, by the Very Rev. Dean Mawe, assisted by the Rev. J. McCarthy (*Cork Examiner* 14/8/1872); 3rd SI 26/2/1841; pensioned 14/4/1868; died 20/5/1875 at No. 1, Sherrard Street, Dublin.

Telford, George; CarNB; C.C. Kilconnell, Co. Galway.

Thacker, James Henry Joseph; LDS 2098/087B; born 5/8/1889, Temple Gardens, Montrose, Co. Dublin; (Dublin South Registrar's District, September Quarter, 1889, vol. 2, p. 557); educated at Strangeways and Dublin University; BA 1910, Trinity College Dublin; lieutenant, Army Service Corps, 16/10/1915 (*London Gazette* dated 5/11/1915); relinquished his commission on the grounds of ill health and retained the rank of lieutenant 14/9/1917 (*London Gazette* dated 8/10/1917); 3rd DI 12/11/1913; pensioned 31/8/1922; (WO 339/46219).

Thompson, Henry Walker; LDS 2097/050; born 1797, Co. Mayo; ensign and lieutenant in the North Mayo Militia from June 1811 to 15/9/1813 (WO 13/3101–20); ensign, 71st Regiment of Foot (Fraser's Highlanders), 16/9/1813; lieutenant, 1815; lieutenant half pay, 10/3/1816; lieutenant, 74th Regiment of Foot (Highlanders Regiment), 1/4/1816; lieutenant half pay, 24/3/1817; awarded one medal for Waterloo; applied to join on 14/10/1823 from 10, Jervis Street, Dublin; 3rd SI 1/5/1824; CI 1/4/1826; to the Commission of Peace on 1/5/1832; resided at Belvedere, Clontarf, Co. Dublin, 1836; AIG 9/6/1848; pensioned 1/3/1863; died 12/5/1877 at 2, Rostrevor Terrace, Dublin; will proved on 14/6/1877 at the Principal Registry to Elena Walker, of 2, Rostrevor Terrace, Dublin, spinster and executrix – effects under £1,500; (WO 25/776 fol. 79).

Thompson, Robert; CarNB; baronial chief constable; C.C. Dunkerron, Co. Kerry; Annadale, Co. Kerry; Borrisokane, Co. Tipperary.

Thompson, Robert Alexander; RIC 54175; LDS 2098/065; born 1865, Co. Dublin; son of William Thompson, accountant, Great Northern Railway; classical master, Drogheda, Co. Louth for nine months, Fermoy, Co. Cork for five months and Carrig School, Kingstown, Co. Dublin for two months; 3rd DI 21/6/1890; pensioned 11/10/1897; died 8/2/1917 at St Patrick's Hospital, Dublin.

Thompson, Thomas; LDS 2097/104; born 1813, Co. Kerry; 3rd SI 1/11/1836; rewarded with an ornamental sword on 1/11/1842; resigned on 1/2/1845 on his appointment as superintendent of police in Colombo, Ceylon, from the Sinhalese town he took charge of policing the whole island. He received his commission from Queen Victoria, his calibre being classed of such a high standard that his appointment took precedence over sergeant J.S. Colepepper of the London Metropolitan Police, who had taken charge of the capital, Kandy in 1844 and who naturally anticipated promotion to Colombo. Thompson became ill and rejoined the Irish Constabulary on 1/12/1847 and was replaced by another Sub Inspector William Macartney of the Irish Constabulary; CI 1/9/1865; pensioned 1/7/1871; died 19/5/1884.

Thornhill, Henry Badham; RIC 16221; LDS 2097/194; born 17/11/1831, Castlekevin, Mallow, Co. Cork; the eldest son of Edward Badham Thornhill (b.1808, Castlekevin, Mallow, Co. Cork and d.1881, Dublin) and Elizabeth (b.1810 and d.1893, Dublin); grandson of Henry Badham Thornhill and Catherine Odell who were married on 6/7/1802 at Castletownroche, Co. Cork; married Mary Hardman on 15/6/1858 at Kiltoghert, Carrick-on-Shannon, Co. Leitrim

(Carrick-on-Shannon Registrar's District, vol. 3, p. 242); 3rd SI 21/10/1852; seconded to the Commissariat Department in the Crimea on 1/9/1854 to 8/2/1855; died 18/2/1861 at Strabane, Co. Tyrone (*Cork Examiner* 1/3/1861); a gratuity of £39.9s.1d. was granted to his widow on 4/3/1861; administration granted at the Principal Registry on 21/3/1861 to Mary Badham Thornhill, of No. 61, Harcourt Street, Dublin, the widow of the deceased – effects under £200. (Mary Badham, born on 11/6/1839, was the daughter of Edward T. Hardman, M.D., of Newbliss, Co. Monaghan and Sarah Walker). Following the death of Dr E.T. Hardman, Sarah (d.1886), his widow, married Abraham Slater Waters (1816–89) on 20/9/1845.

Thornley, Thomas; LDS 2097/116; born 1797, Lancs., England; ensign, 43rd Regiment of Foot (Monmouthshire Regiment), 21/10/1813; lieutenant, 1815 to 2/4/1817; married firstly 2/2/1817, Matilda Blake, at Ballyhaunis, Co. Mayo and she died in Sligo in October 1835 (*Ballyshannon Herald*); their son Richard died in Sligo in 1834 and their eldest daughter, Charlotte Matilda Blake Thornley, married in 1844, Abraham Stoker (1799–12/10/1876), a Dublin Castle civil servant and they had a son (Abraham) 'Bram Stoker' (8/11/1847–20/4/1912), author of *Dracula*, who married Florence Anne Lemon Balcombe (17/7/1858–25/5/1937) on 4/12/1878, at St Ann's Church, Dublin; 3rd SI 19/9/1837; Thomas Thornley married secondly, Claudia Gamble of Londonderry; received a severe injury to his head, shoulder and other body parts at Cushendall, Co. Antrim on 12/12/1849 and he died on 30/4/1850; (WO 25/776 fol. 120).

Thynne, Henry (Sir); RIC 25257; LDS 2097/232; born 1838, Ennistymon, Co. Clare, son of Edward Thynne, Esq., of Ipswich, Queensland and Bridget Stuart (nee Fitzgerald); CB (Civil) 1890; knighted, 1898; BA, 1859, with treble first honours; LLB, 1873; Gold Medallist; LLD, MA, Queens University of Ireland, 1882; he was educated by the local Christian Brothers and by a private tutor and spent some time in Queens College Cork as well as Queens College Galway (QUI Calendar, 1882, p. 323). He was awarded three junior scholarships in QCG, 1855–6 to 1857–8 (science division of the Arts faculty) and two senior scholarships, Natural Philosophy in 1859–60 and Mathematics in 1860–1. He was awarded the BA in 1859 and gained first class honours in Mathematics, Mathematical Physics and Experimental Physics. He was awarded a first class honours in the LLB in 1873 and received a gold medal. He was awarded an honorary MA and LLD by the QUI in 1882. Both he and his brother Andrew Joseph (b.30/10/1847) (d.27/2/1927) were expert competitive rifle marksmen; his brother Andrew Joseph and parents emigrated to Queensland in 1864; Andrew Joseph after a short time as a civil servant became a very successful solicitor, establishing the law firm Thynne & Macartney (with Edward Macartney, son of RIC Sub Inspector, William Isaac Macartney), and was elected to the Legislative Council in 1882 to 1922 and served successfully as Minister for Justice, Minister without portfolio, Postmaster-General and Secretary for Agriculture. He was appointed to the first senate of the University of Queensland in April 1910, elected vice chancellor in 1916 and chancellor in 1925, a position he held until his death in 1927 and he was given a state funeral; 3rd SI 4/11/1859; resident magistrate 3rd class 18/11/1878, 2nd class 6/10/1882; served as a RM in Donegal from 18/11/1878 and Kilkenny from 1/8/1882; DIG 30/11/1886; died 10/12/1915 at The Plantation, Donnybrook, Dublin; will proved on 13/1/1916 at the Principal Registry by William Arthur O'Connell, Deputy Inspector General, RIC – effects £6,892.2s.8d.; (p. 72, RM Records of Service Book, National Archives, Dublin); (photo in the *Constabulary Gazette*, vol. VI, no. 13, 23/12/1899, p. 390).

Tiley, Howard Douglas D.C.; RIC 82946; ADRIC CADET no. 36; LDS 2099/051; born 1890, Middlesex, England; (Brentford Registrar's District, 1890, March Quarter, vol. 3a, p. 116); army service, 1915–19; ADRIC, October 1920 to September 1921; 3rd DI 20/9/1921; pensioned 15/3/1922; joined the Palestine Police on 16/3/1922.

Tilly, James Crofton; RIC 52879; LDS 2098/042; born 1869, Co. Dublin; son of Robert Murray Tilly, CI and Barrackmaster, RIC; 3rd DI 17/7/1888; died 11/1/1893 at 12, Belfast Terrace, North Circular Road, Dublin, late of New Ross, Co. Wexford; administration granted on

31/1/1893 at the Principal Registry to Robert Murray Tilly, 12 Belfast Terrace, North Circular Road, Dublin, the father – effects £600.16s.0d.; buried in Mount Jerome Cemetery, Dublin.

Tilly, Robert Murray; RIC 27173; LDS 2097/240; born 1842, Co. Dublin; employed in the Census Office, Dublin for two months; son of Benjamin Tilly (b.1813, Co. Dublin); BA Vern., 1834, Trinity College Dublin; father of James Crofton Tilly, DI, RIC; 3rd SI 9/3/1862; barrackmaster of the Phoenix Park Depot 7/3/1890; died 10/8/1893 at 1 Wentworth Villa, Wicklow, Co. Wicklow; will proved on 22/7/1893 at the Principal Registry by the oath of Reverend Gilbert Mahaffy, of St Paul's Parsonage, North Circular Road, Dublin, one of the executors – effects £685.14s.8d.; buried in Mount Jerome Cemetery, Dublin on 14/8/1893 with his wife Catherine Crofton Tilly, died 6/4/1924, aged 83 years, his sons Charles Henry Tilly, died 6/2/1892, aged 20 years, James Crofton Tilly, DI, RIC, died 11/1/1893, aged 24 years and his daughter Ina Eveleen Tilly, died 23/7/1962.

Toppin, Henry; RIC 54944; LDS 2098/075; born 15/6/1868, Philipstown House, Tipperary, Co. Tipperary; son of Rev. Canon Toppin of Tramore, Co. Waterford and grandson of Charles Samuel Tandy, of Sion Lodge, Waterford; educated at TCD and Germany; married on 14/4/1893 (Dublin South Registrar's District, June Quarter, 1893, vol. 2, p. 557), Amy Constance, daughter of John Greene, JP, of Gaulstown, Co. Meath; 3rd DI 27/5/1891; resident magistrate 4/2/1913; served in WWI until 19/10/1920 with the temporary rank of Lieutenant Colonel; (p. 156, RM Records of Service Book, National Archives, Dublin).

Tottenham, Lowry Cliffe Loftus; RIC 47733; LDS 2097/313; born 12/4/1858, Co. Dublin; second son of Henry Loftus Tottenhan, BA, Barrister-at-Law (16/1/1814–26/4/1896) and Joyce (d.27/9/1892), daughter of James Lowry and widow of Edward Leslie Colvill; father of Reginald Tottenham, DI, RIC; worked in the Bank of Ireland for four years and six months; married 18/9/1888, Isabella Ogle, only child of Ven. William Creek, D.D., Archdeacon of Kilmore and Rector of Kildallon, Co. Cavan; two of his sons, were killed in action in WWI: 2nd Lieutenant Arthur Henry Tottenham, 'C' Company, 2nd Battalion, Royal Inniskilling Fusiliers, aged 20 years, killed at the Somme, France on 27/6/1916 and 2nd Lieutenant Edward Lowry Loftus Tottenham, MC, 11th Battalion (attached 6th Battalion) The Loyal North Lancashire Regiment, aged 21 years, killed in Mesopotamia (Iraq) on 9/4/1916; 3rd SI 22/10/1881; pensioned 15/10/1904.

Tottenham, Reginald; RIC 72001; LDS 2098/163B; born 1/7/1893, Enniscorthy, Co. Wexford; (Enniscorthy Registrar's District, September Quarter, 1893, vol. 3, p. 349); third son of Lowry Cliffe Loftus Tottenham, DI, RIC; educated at St Bee's College and Trinity College Dublin; lieutenant, Tank Corps; R.U.W.W. Police; 3rd DI 10/1/1920; Private Secretary to the Inspector General from 7/7/1921 to 18/7/1922; pensioned 18/7/1922; (WO 374/69215); joined the Colonial Police Service; married in 1931, Nysalie Pearse; CBE (1949).

Towers, James; LDS 2097/169; born 1804, Dublin City, Co. Dublin; enlisted as a sub constable on 20/3/1820; wife a native of Co. Wicklow; 3rd SI 1/6/1848; died 11/1/1852 in Co. Kildare.

Townsend, Edward Synge; LDS 2097/060; born 1773, Co. Cork, son of Edward Synge Townsend (18/1/1741–2/1/1819), Rector of Clondrohid, Macroom, Co. Cork and Elizabeth (d.12/4/1831), 3rd daughter of Horatio Townshend, of Bridgemount; grandson of Rev. Horatio Townsend (1/9/1706–1772), Rector of Donoughmore, Co. Cork and Mary Hungerford, of Inchydoney, Co. Cork; widower with one son and three daughters on appointment; 3rd SI 1/1/1825; received injuries on two occasions whilst in the Force by falls from his horse; died 8/8/1843.

Townsend, Henry; LDS 2097/043; born 1801, Co. Cork; third son of Samuel Townsend (1768–1836), of Whitehall, Skibbereen, Co. Cork, DL, JP, High Sheriff, 1798 and Mercy (m.1794), youngest daughter of Walter Baldwin, of Curravordy, Co. Cork; married in 1838, Annabella, youngest daughter of Robert Westropp, Fort Anne, Co. Clare; served nearly two years in the West Carbery Armed Association prior to his appointment; 3rd SI 1/9/1823; CI 4/7/1832; pensioned 1/2/1866; died 7/11/1872 at Mount Alto, Queenstown, Co. Cork;

246

247

246 Henry Thynne, Assistant Inspector General, RIC. 247 Henry Toppin. 248 Lowry Cliffe Loftus Tottenham. 249 Brigadier General Sir Henry Hugh Tudor.

248

249

302   *The Royal Irish Constabulary Officers*

administration granted on 6/12/1872 at Cork to Annabella Townsend, Mount Alto, Queenstown, Co. Cork, widow of the deceased – effects under £14,000.

Townsend, Norman Lionel; RIC 33015; LDS 2097/263; born 6/9/1846, Inistioge, Co. Kilkenny; third son of Rev. Thomas Uniacke Townshend, Vicar of Inistioge, Co. Kilkenny and Elizabeth (m.1839) (d.1876), eldest daughter of Edward Carr, of Arnestown, Co. Wexford; married, Annabella, youngest daughter of Major-General Philip Barry, RE and Mary Ann Jackson, daughter of John Jackson; father of Thomas Philip Barry Townshend, DI RIC; his son Richard Stapleton Barry Townsend, lieutenant Royal Irish Fusiliers was killed at the Battle of the Somme on 1/7/1916, aged 32 years, who is commemorated in a memorial in St Patrick's Cathedral, Armagh; (WO 339/14291); another son, Harvey Arthur Barry Townsend, captain, 10th Battalion, Royal Irish Fusiliers, died 1959; wife from Co. Dublin; 3rd SI 10/7/1867; received a favourable record and a grant from the Reward Fund on 31/12/1870 for the capture of armed offenders, for whom they lay in ambush and who fired upon the police; temporary resident magistrate 1/10/1886; permanent RM 3rd class, 1/1/1888, 2nd class 27/2/1892, 1st class 1/8/1903; pensioned 6/9/1911; (p. 73, RM Records of Service Book, National Archives, Dublin).

Townsend, Thomas Philip Barry; RIC 58073; LDS 2098/133; born 12/2/1875, Co. Westmeath; son of Norman Lionel Townshend, RM, RIC and Annabella, youngest daughter of Major-General Philip Barry, Royal Engineers who built Sheerness Docks; 3rd DI 18/12/1897; pensioned 16/7/1921; (photo in the *Constabulary Gazette*, vol. 2, no. 39, p. 1, 24/12/1897 & vol. XVI, no. 12, 10/12/1904).

Tracy, William Samuel; LDS 2097/055; 3rd SI 10/8/1824; JP, 8/2/1833; resident magistrate 1/9/1838; retired as a RM on 4/11/1868.

Trant, Thomas; LDS 2097/089; born 1812, Co. Dublin; resident warder, Royal Gun Carriage Yard and Ordnance Stores, Dublin Castle from March 1824 to 1834; wife, Eliza Sophia (b.1812) was a native of Co. Dublin; 3rd SI 8/4/1835; received a grant for the Reward Fund on 31/5/1848 for indefatigable and successful exertions in the arrest of Larkin and Daniel for the murder of Mr Prim, pay clerk and sub constable John Yates, RIC 3848 on 15/3/1847; awarded the Constabulary Medal, 1/9/1848 and a reward of £50 for his successful defence of the Warhouse at Boulagh Common, Co. Tipperary against a considerable amount of rebels on 29/7/1848; author of *Reply to Fr Fitzgerald's Pamphlet entitled 'His Personal Recollections of the Insurrection at Ballingarry in July, 1848'* (Dublin, 1862); pensioned 18/1/1859 in Ennistymon, Co. Clare; died on 3/11/1867 as a result of chronic bronchitis at No. 119, Upper Rathmines, Co. Dublin (*Irish Times*, 4/11/1867); buried in Mount Jerome Cemetery, Dublin on 5/11/1867 (Registry No. 1071) (Section C, Sub Division 67, Grant No. 3171); will and one codicil proved at the Principal Registry by the oath of Eliza Sophia Trant, the widow and sole executrix – effects under £300; his widow, Eliza Sophia died on 9/3/1894, aged 82 years, at 9, Newgrove Avenue, Sandymount, Dublin (*Irish Times*, 10/9/1894) and is also buried in Mount Jerome Cemetery, Dublin.

Treacy, James; LDS 2099/004.

Trench, William Power; LDS 2097/030; captain; 3rd SI 1/5/1822; C.C. Castlecomer, 1833 (the *Morning Register*, Dublin, vol. ix, Thursday 26/9/1833); C.C. Wexford (the *Morning Register*, Dublin, vol. x, Monday 4/11/1833).

Trimble, Henry; LDS 2097/172; born 1805, Clonbroney, Co. Longford; enlisted as a sub constable on 8/5/1824; married on 9/5/1850, Helena, second daughter of John Buchanan (Manorhamilton Registrar's District, vol. 8, p. 50); wife a native of Co. Leitrim; 3rd SI 1/6/1848; pensioned 16/12/1852; died in 1855.

Triscott, Andrew Hamond Edmund; RIC 35093; LDS 2097/274; born 1848, Alverstole, Hants., England; (Alverstole Registrar's District, 1848, March Quarter, vol. 7, p. 26); married on 25/11/1879 (Dublin North Registrar's District, vol. 2, p. 500), wife from Co. Tipperary N.R.; 3rd SI 30/1/1869; pensioned 18/12/1908; died 1/4/1916 at 3, St Kevin's Park, Rathgar, Dublin, formerly of Mullingar, Enniskillen and Bray; will proved on 1/7/1916 at the Principal Registry by the oath of Kathleen Triscott, the widow – effects – £1,514.7s.1d.

Tronson, J.D.; LDS 2097/083; born 1810, Co. Meath; PPF; 3rd SI 23/2/1833; pensioned 1/12/1839; C.C. Pilltown, Co. Kilkenny.

Tronson, Joseph Charles; RIC 53576; LDS 2098/084B; born 15/6/1861, Co. Louth; married on 12/6/1907 (Dublin North Registrar's District, June Quarter, 1907, vol. 2, p. 544), wife a native of Co. Cavan; 3rd DI 31/12/1917; attached to Crime Department at headquarters from 7/11/1920; pensioned 31/8/1922.

Tuckey, Charles Henry; LDS 2097/042; born Co. Cork; 3rd SI 23/8/1823; resident magistrate 15/9/1837; daughter born on 14/10/1850 (*Cork Examiner* 18/10/1850); daughter born on 20/8/1854 in Carlow (*Cork Examiner* 1/9/1854); retired as a RM at Carlow, Co. Carlow on 12/9/1859; C.C. Bridgetstown, Wexford in 1828 and Kilkenny in 1831.

Tudor, Henry Hugh Major-General (Sir); born 1871, son of Rev. Harry Tudor, Sub-Dean of Exeter; entered the Royal Artillery, 1890; promoted Major in 1908, Lieutenant-Colonel, 1914, Brevet-Colonel, 1917 and major-general, 1919; Temporary Air Vice-Marshal, 1923–4; South African War, 1899–1902 (severely wounded, despatches, Queen's medal with four clasps, King's Medal with two clasps); European War, 1914–18, commanding 9th Division (wounded, despatches ten times); CMG, 1916; CB (Military), 1918; KCB (Civil), 1923; Order of Leopold of Belgium; French Croix de Guerre with Palm; Belgian Croix de Guerre; inspector general of the RIC from 15 May 1920 to 14 June 1922; inspector general of police and prisons, Palestine, 15/6/1922; retired 1925; and resided at 19, Churchill Square Apartments, St Johns, Newfoundland; married in 1903, Eva Gertrude Josephine (d.1958), daughter of Lea Priestly Edwards; one son RAF Group Captain Hugh Henry Lea Tudor, DFC, AFC (b.1910) and three daughters, Elizabeth Aurora (b.1910), Mary Margaret (b.1907) and Helen Eva (b.1913); died on 25/9/1965, Newfoundland.

Turnbull, Hugh Stephenson; LDS 2098/234; born 25/8/1882, Poong, India; son of Major-General Peter Stephenson Turnbull (1836–1921), MD, KHS, HM Indian Army, surgeon to the King, 1902 and Mary, second daughter of George Oliver Hawick; educated at Merchiston Castle School, Edinburgh, and Royal Military College, Sandhurst; lieutenant, Indian Army service 1901–8; 3rd DI 15/10/1908; resigned 31/5/1913 on his appointment as Chief Constable of Argyllshire County Police on 31/5/1913 to 31/7/1920; (recalled to army, 1915–18, Major, Argyll and Sutherland Highlanders, Lt. Col. 1916). Chief Constable of Westmoreland & Cumberland County Constabulary 1/8/1920 to August 1925; Commissioner of Police in the City of London, September 1925 to 1950; awarded KBE 1929, KPM 1936, KCVO 1937. He married 20 October 1909 Jean Grant; 2 sons and 1 daughter; died 9 January 1973, Grantown-on-Spey, Morayshire.

Turner, Sir Alfred; KCB (created 1902) (military CB) (civil CB); major-general; born 10/3/1833, London, eldest son of Richard E. Turner, BL, Bencher, Inner Temple and Frances, daughter of Charles Johnstone; married firstly, 1865, Blanche (d.1899), daughter of Charles Hopkinson of Wotton Court, Gloucester; married secondly, Juliette Elizabeth Marie, only daughter of Henry Whiting; two sons and one daughter; educated at Westminster School; Addiscombe; joined Royal Artillery, 1860; A.D.C. and military private secretary to Viceroy of Ireland, 1882–4; D.A.A.G. Nile Expedition, 1884–5 (despatches, medal and clasp, bronze star; assistant military secretary Commander-in-Chief in Ireland, 1885–6; private secretary, Viceroy of Ireland, 1886; Divisional Commissioner Cork, Kerry, Clare and Limerick, 1886–92; Assistant Adjutant-General, Royal Artillery, Army Headquarters, 1895–8; Inspectoral-General of Auxiliary Forces, 1900–4; President of Salon; Member of Japanese Society; Chairman of the Alliance, Franco-Brittanique; decorated for civil service in Ireland (civil CB); for military services and being mentioned in despatches (Mil. CB); publications: *The Retreat from Moscow and Passage of the Beresina*; *From Weissenburg to Sedan*; *Sixty Years of a Soldier's Life*, 1912; address: Carlyle House, Chelsea Embankment, London SW; died 20/11/1918.

Turner, Henry; RIC 36838; LDS 2097/280; born 3/8/1848, Co. Kilkenny; wife from Co. Dublin; 3rd SI 26/8/1870; received a favourable record on 30/6/1871, whereby a threatening letter was handed to him by the person to whom it was sent. The signature was 'Rory' but the writer had inadvertently commenced a signature with the letter 'G,' and apparently endeavoured

250

251

250 Hugh Stephenson Turnbull, Chief Constable of Argyle County Constabulary, 1913–20.
251 Ernest Phillips Tyacke.   252 John Tyson, Riding Master.   253 Andrew Walsh.

252

253

to obliterate it with his finger. SI Turner concluded that the writer's real name commenced with G and by this and other grounds of suspicion, traced the writer who was arrested; temporary resident magistrate 31/8/1881; permanent resident magistrate 3rd class 25/10/ 1882, 2nd class 19/3/1887, 1st class 22/5/1897; pensioned 1/1/1911.

Tweedy, Thomas; RIC 51002; LDS 2097/332; born 1861, Co. Dublin; 3rd DI 19/9/1883; CI 6/7/1908; King George V Coronation Medal, 1911; died 22/12/1918 of pleurisy following influenza at Fitzwilliam Nursing Home, Upper Pembroke Street, Dublin, late of Kilbrogan Hill, Bandon, Co. Cork; will proved on 21/1/1919 at the Principal Registry; (photo in *The Constabulary Gazette*, vol. XIII, no. 12, 13/6/1903 & vol. XV, no. 15, 2/7/1904).

Tyacke, Ernest Phillips; RIC 44153; LDS 2097/299; born 1856, Chichester, Sussex, England; (Chichester Registrar's District, 1856, June Quarter, vol. 2b, p. 308); married on 17/7/1900 (Rathdrum Registrar's District, September Quarter, 1900, vol. 2, p. 831), Helena Mary Laura Hudson, a native of Co. Wicklow on 17/7/1900; 3rd SI 7/1/1879; CI 1/12/1899; King George V Coronation Medal, 1911; pensioned 15/9/1917.

Tyacke, Henry Donati; RIC 45467; LDS 2097/309; born 1859, London, England; married on 2/12/1896 (Dublin South Registrar's District, December Quarter, 1896, vol. 2, p. 560), wife a native of King's County; 3rd SI 1/12/1880; CI 15/5/1902; King Edward VII Visit to Ireland Medal, 1903; AIG 1/7/1912; pensioned 1/4/1920; (photo in *The Constabulary Gazette*, vol. XXXIV, no. 5, 11/10/1913).

Tyndall, John Francis; RIC 55267; LDS 2098/068B; born 16/9/1872, Co. Waterford; (Waterford Registrar's District, 1872, vol. 19, p. 929); married on 6/6/1899 (Kilmacthomas Registrar's District, June Quarter, 1899, vol. 2, p. 32), wife, Mary Elizabeth Frances; his sons attended The King's Hospital School, Oxmanstown, Dublin — Charles John Tyndall (1912–18) and George Francis Tyndall (1914–18), respectively; 3rd DI 6/1/1916; awarded the medal and clasp of the Royal Humane Society; pensioned 9/6/1922.

Tyrrell, Frederick Rufane St Lawrence; RIC 55034; LDS 2098/080; born 28/9/1871, Tuam, Co. Galway (*Cork Examiner* 3/10/1871); son of William St Lawrence Tyrrell, SI, RIC; married on 17/11/1909, Miss Moutray Reed, a native of England; 3rd DI 24/11/1891; King Edward VII Visit to Ireland Medal, 1903; Temporary Adjutant, Phoenix Park Depot from 8/5/1903 to 1/4/1907 and Adjutant from 8/5/1907 to 16/10/1912; King George V Visit to Ireland Medal, 1911; CI 8/3/1916; pensioned 1/6/1922; transferred to the Royal Ulster Constabulary on 1/6/1922.

Tyrrell, William St Lawrence; LDS 2097/221; born 1833, Co. Down; father of Frederick Rufane St Lawrence Tyrrell, CI, RIC (*Cork Examiner* 3/10/1871); joined the Irish Revenue Police as a lieutenant on 29/12/1853 and served in Guidore, Co. Donegal; 3rd SI 25/3/1858; died 22/7/1885 at Kinsale, Co. Cork (Kinsale Registrar's District, 1885, September Quarter, vol. 5, p. 248); his wife, Cecilia Louisa, daughter of George David Dunkin, 7th Royal Fusiliers, of Wyfield Court, Oxford, died at Ison Mount, Forest Road, Southport on 8/5/1895

Tyson, John; LDS 2097/294; born 1840, Chester, Ches., England; ex-regimental sergeant major, 4th Dragoon Guards, in which he spent 18 years and 8 months; 3rd SI 24/8/1876; RIC Riding Master; awarded the Queen's Jubilee Medal, 1897; Queen Victoria's Visit to Ireland Medal, 1900; his son was accorded first place at the Irish Veterinary College in August 1901; pensioned 30/6/1903; died 10/7/1916 at 69, Hollybrook Road, Clontarf, Co. Dublin; will proved on 19/8/1916 at the Principal Registry by Harriet Tyson, spinster – effects £607.5s.8d.; buried in Glasnevin Cemetery, Dublin (Grave No. XB61 South); his son, John Millward Tyson, aged two years and four months died on 4/12/1883 at the Phoenix Park Depot, Dublin and was buried in Grangegorman Cemetery, Dublin on 5/12/1883; (photo in *The Constabulary Gazette*, vol. 1, no. 22, 28/8/1897 & vol. 2, no. 39, p. 1, 24/12/1897).

U

Urquhart, Beauchamp Colclough; CarNB; born 1796, Co. Carlow; the son of Lieutenant Colonel George Urquhart and Bridget, daughter of Beauchamp Colclough (d.26/11/1858 at Finglas, Co. Dublin), of Bohermore, Co. Carlow; married Ann Jane Fitzsimons (d.1862), Streamstown, Co. Westmeath; resigned 1830; died 1861; C.C. Kilkenny, Co. Kilkenny; Parsonstown, Co. Meath; Edenderry, King's County.

V

Valentine, Francis; LDS 2097/176; born 1803, Dublin; 3rd SI 24/8/1848; pensioned 10/8/1867; died 18/10/1877 at 34, Albert Road, Sandycove, Kingstown, Co. Dublin; will proved on 14/11/1877 at the Principal Registry by the oath of William Bloomfield, of 25, Eustace Street, Dublin, solicitor and Henry Kirwan, of 1, Regent Terrace, Albert Road, Sandycove, Co. Dublin, executors, effects under £7,000.

Vallancey, William Henry; LDS 2097/217; born 1836, Co. Clare; joined the Irish Revenue Police as a lieutenant on 6/6/1857; 3rd SI 1/12/1857; dismissed 25/5/1874.

Vanston, William; RIC 34770; LDS 2098/129; born 1851, Clonenagh, Queen's County; 3rd DI 1/1/1897; King Edward VII Visit to Ireland Medal, 1903; pensioned 18/7/1910.

Verling, Dominick W.; LDS 2097/117; born 1815, Castlelyons, Co. Cork; 3rd SI 12/10/1837; died 9/6/1854.

Verrall, Ernest; RIC 51003; LDS 2097/332; born 1859, Iford, Sussex, England; son of John Verrall, of Swansborough Grange, Sussex and Frances Verrall (b.1834) Ilford, West Thurrock, Essex; residing at Wallands Crescent, Lewes St John, Southover, Sussex in 1881 (Census); 3rd DI 22/9/1883; musketry instructor at the Phoenix Park Depot from 1/10/1904 until his death on 10/3/1907 at the RIC Depot, Phoenix Park, Dublin; will proved on 4/4/1907 at the Principal Registry by the oath of Florence F. Verrall and Marion F. Verrall, spinsters – effects £8,758.4s.4d. (photo in the *Constabulary Gazette*, vol. 2, no. 36, 4/12/1897, p. 1)

Vignoles, Samuel; CarNB; born Newtown, Co. Westmeath; captain; stipendiary magistrate 4/4/1831, Ennis, Co. Clare and in Cork West Riding 1833–4; presentation and address made to him at Bandon, Co. Cork on 12/4/1834 (Cork Evening Herald, 16/4/1834); residing at Mount Pleasant, Tullamore, King's County, 1835; removed 7/12/1839; died 1843.

Villar, Robert Peter; LDS 2098/026B; born 16/6/1887, Taunton, Somerset, England; (Taunton Registrar's District, 1887, September Quarter, vol. 5c, p. 333); son of William James and Annie Elizabeth Villar, Tauntfield House, Taunton; teacher in a preparatory school, Silcock, Cumberland for one year and employed as a solicitor's articles clerk in Stogumber, Somerset for one year; 3rd DI 15/11/1911; King George V Visit to Ireland Medal, 1911; captain and major, 15th (2nd Reserve) Battalion (Lancashire Hussars), The King's (Liverpool Regiment), 18th (Lancashire Hussars) Battalion from 18/4/1916; killed 22/3/1918, Somme, France; buried in Pozieres Memorial Cemetery, Somme.

Vokes, Thomas Phillip; CarNB; PPF; Justice of the Peace, 10/5/1813; chief magistrate 19/11/1821; married in 1806, Susanna, daughter of Richard Brew, Tullycrine, Co. Clare (d.15/3/1827); resident magistrate 1/10/1836; pensioned in 1847; died 1852, Spa, Belgium; on 14/1/1849, his granddaughter, Georgina Ann Sarah, aged 12 years died at Arlington Street, Mornington Crescent, London. She was the eldest daughter of Captain Burslem, 48th Regiment of Foot (Northamptonshire Regiment) and granddaughter of Colonel Burslem, KH, of Harwood Lodge, Berkshire; his youngest daughter, Anne Charlotte, married on 12/6/1852 at St Mary's, Bryanston Square, Count Alfred Edward, son of Lieutenant-General Count de Bylandt, KCH (*Cork Examiner* 18/6/1852).

W

Wade, Frederick Sidney; RIC 51110; LDS 2097/335; born, 1863, Surrey, England; married on 1/9/1885 (Dublin North Registrar's District, September Quarter, 1885, vol. 2, p. 385), wife from Co. Dublin; 3rd DI 29/2/1884; King Edward VII Visit to Ireland Medal, 1903; pensioned 13/4/1907; died 2/8/1910.

Wade, George; LDS 2097/052; born 1791, Co. Meath; lieutenant in the Co. Wexford Militia from 1813 to 1824 (WO 13/3330–50); wife a native of Co. Dublin; his daughter, Susan Annabella, married on 29/4/1852, at Omagh, Co. Tyrone (Omagh Registrar's District, vol. 9, p. 395), George Molony, Esq., son of Walter Molony, RM (*Cork Examiner* 7/5/1852); 3rd SI 1/8/1824; CI 1/7/1826; pensioned 1/5/1851; died 1/6/1852.

Wade, George; LDS 2097/140; born 1811, Co. Tipperary; wife a native of Co. Dublin; 3rd SI 15/4/1843; died 15/10/1859.

Waldron, Francis; LDS 2097/166; born 1814, Athleague, Co. Roscommon; Justice of the Peace for Counties Roscommon and Leitrim; 3rd SI 15/5/1848; paymaster 15/5/1848 for counties Longford and Cavan; pensioned 31/5/1851 on the abolition of the paymasters.

Walker, Andrew; RIC 13123; LDS 2097/180; born 1825, Co. Sligo; 3rd SI 23/6/1849; discharged on 6/12/1858 on a gratuity of £64.5s.3d.

Walker, James; LDS 2097/088; born 1798, Co. Meath; enlisted as a sub constable, 15/1/1823; wife a native of Co. Louth; 3rd SI 24/2/1835; pensioned 1/5/1856 from Cork City; died 29/7/1872 at Longford Place, Monkstown, Co. Dublin; will proved on 14/9/1872 at Wakefield, Yorks., England and resealed at the Principal Registry on 28/10/1872 – effects £2,044.4s.1d.

Wall, Michael; RIC 29711; LDS 2098/040; born 1846, Co. Kilkenny; 3rd DI 10/2/1888; pensioned 1/12/1906; died 12/3/1916 at Midleton, Co. Cork; (Midleton Registrar's District, 1916, March Quarter, vol. 4, p. 442).

Wall, Patrick; RIC 56368; LDS 2098/181B; born 5/3/1872, Loughrea, Co. Galway; (Loughrea Registrar's District, 1872, vol. 4, p. 479); married on 28/9/1915, wife a native of Co. Tipperary S.R.; 3rd DI 16/12/1920; pensioned 8/5/1922.

Wallace, Frederick Campbell; RIC 53462; LDS 2098/049; born 1865, Newtownards, Co. Down; son of Samuel Beatty Wallace, DI, RIC and brother of Jeremiah Thomas Wallace, DI, RIC; married on 12/9/1894 (Newry Registrar's District, December Quarter, 1894, vol. 1, p. 975), Ethel M.A. Ternan, a native of England; 3rd DI 1/6/1889; CI 15/11/1911; died 29/10/1914 at Saul Street, Downpatrick, Co. Down, formerly of The Diamond, Raphoe, Co. Donegal; will proved on 30/11/1914 at Belfast by the oath of Ethel J.A. Wallace, the widow – effects £828.18s.10d.; his son was born in Belmullet, Co. Mayo on 12/3/1900; (photo in the *Constabulary Gazette*, vol. IX, no. 12, 15/6/1901).

Wallace, Jeremiah Thomas; RIC 52178; LDS 2098/062B; born 12/12/1868, Newtownards, Co. Down; (Newtownards Registrar's District, 1868, vol. 16, p. 786); son of Samuel Beatty Wallace, DI, RIC and brother of Frederick Campbell Wallace, DI, RIC; married on 27/6/1906 (Dublin South Registrar's District, June Quarter, 1906, vol. 2, p. 580), wife a native of Co. Cavan; 3rd DI 15/02/1915; pensioned 1/2/1921.

Wallace, Samuel Beatty; RIC 28157; LDS 2097/242; born 1843, King's County; father of Frederick Campbell Wallace, DI, RIC and Jeremiah Thomas Wallace, DI, RIC; worked in the Census Office, Dublin for one year and one month; married on 21/7/1864 (Dublin South

Registrar's District, vol. 17, p. 633), at St Peter's Church, Dublin, Margaret (d.19/3/1919), daughter of the late Robert Fair, Esq., of Cloone Castle, Co. Galway and Lisavalley Lodge, Co. Mayo (*Cork Examiner* 23/7/1864); 3rd SI 2/11/1862; died 20/11/1867 at Schull, Co. Cork (Schull Registrar's District, vol. 20, p. 404); administration granted on 18/2/1868 in the Principal Registry to Margaret Wallace, of Fermoy, Co. Cork, the widow of said deceased – effects under £297.

Walsh, Andrew; RIC 40442; LDS 2098/190; born 8/6/1854, Co. Mayo; married firstly on 23/4/1892 (Rathdown Registrar's District, June Quarter, 1892, vol. 2, p. 751); wife a native of Co. Mayo; married secondly on 13/9/1911 (Clonakilty Registrar's District, December Quarter, 1911, vol. 5, p. 29), wife a native of Co. Wicklow; 3rd DI 7/1/1902; King Edward VII Visit to Ireland Medal, 1903; pensioned 7/7/1914.

Walsh, Charles Arthur (Sir); RIC 55388; LDS 2098/090; born 1869, Clogheen, Co. Tipperary, son of Richard Walsh, LRCP, of Clogheen; BA, Royal University of Ireland; married on 10/5/1898 (Armagh Registrar's District, June Quarter, 1898, vol. 1, p. 96), Isabel, daughter of Robert Malcolmson, Bennykerry Lodge, solicitor, of Carlow. Her sister Elizabeth, married John Charles Milling (1873–1919), CI, RIC; 3rd DI 1/9/1892; King George V Visit to Ireland Medal, 1911; CI 21/9/1917; DIG 13/3/1920; pensioned 31/8/1922; KBE (Civil), 1922; died 1949.

Walsh, Henry John; RIC 31298; LDS 2097/327; born 1845, Co. Limerick; 3rd DI 1/11/1882; pensioned 1/2/1906.

Walsh, Hill J.M.; LDS 2097/041; born 1804, Co. Wicklow; 3rd SI 30/6/1823; CI 8/1/1854; died 30/9/1860 at Leinster Square, Dublin; buried in Mount Jerome Cemetery, Dublin (Registry No. 749).

Walsh, James Joseph; RIC 82929; LDS 2099/036; born 28/9/1895, Louistown, Co. Wexford; captain, Royal Dublin Fusiliers; 3rd DI 20/9/1921; married Heartsease Dora Oldbury-Byrne (b.India) on 4/6/1921. His wife's address was given as c/o Henry S. King, 9 Pall Mall, London. His car was hijacked in February 1922 near Collooney, Co. Sligo where he had been stationed since 1/10/1921 and his wife was injured in the incident. He was discharged from the Force on having been allowed to tender his resignation by the Chief of Police and the Under Secretary to the Lord Lieutenant, Sir Alfred C. Cope. He was called to the Bar in November 1922. He was taken ill while involved in a court case and died in Tipperary Town in 1938.

Walsh, Patrick; LDS 2097/164; born 1810, Co. Limerick; enlisted as a sub constable on 23/10/1832; married in May, 1840; wife, Mary, was a native of Tipperary N.R.; 3rd SI 3/3/1848; died 24/11/1851 in Queen's County.

Walsh, Patrick; RIC 54567; LDS 2098/028B; born 18/6/1871, Co. Monaghan; 3rd DI 24/6/1911; married on 15/2/1906 (Killarney Registrar's District, March Quarter, 1906, vol. 5, p. 243), wife a native of Co. Kerry; on 7/2/1922 when stationed at Letterkenny, Co. Donegal he received a letter from Michael Collins inviting him to join the committee set up by the Provisional Government to organize a new police force to replace the RIC. He travelled to Dublin the following day and was present at the Gresham Hotel on 9/2/1922 at the first meeting of the organizing committee; pensioned 5/4/1922; appointed deputy commissioner in the Garda Síochána on 6/4/1922; in May 1922 when a faction of the Garda Síochána mutinied in Kildare and Commissioner Michael Staines tendered his resignation, Patrick Walsh also resigned in loyalty to the Commissioner, but continued to serve the Provisional Government as a civilian advisor. On the recommendation of Commissioner Eoin O'Duffy, he was appointed assistant commissioner, his former office having been filled by deputy commissioner Eamon Coogan; retired from the Garda Síochána, 1936; died 1957; (photo: *The Garda Síochána: Policing Independent Ireland, 1922–1982*, by Gregory Allen, Gill & MacMillan Ltd, Dublin 1999).

Walsh, Thomas; RIC 45370; LDS 2098/021B; born 4/5/1865, Co. Mayo; married on 14/10/1891 (Dublin North Registrar's District, December Quarter, 1891, vol. 2, p. 474), wife a native of Co. Mayo; 3rd DI 10/1/1910; pensioned 8/5/1922; died 14/5/1924.

254   255

254 Charles Arthur Walsh, Deputy Inspector General, RIC. 255 Patrick Walsh. 256 Patrick
Walsh, Deputy Commissioner Garda Síochána. 257 Thomas J. Walsh.

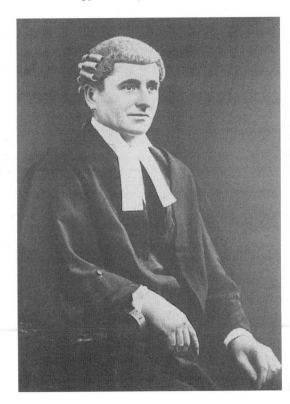

256   257

Walsh, William; RIC 19016; LDS 2097/207; born 1834, Co. Tipperary; 3rd SI 1/11/1855; died 23/11/1866, Dungarvan, Co. Waterford (Dungarvan Registrar's District, 1867, vol. 4, p. 551).

Walshe, Denis; RIC 2097/125; born 1805, Co. Waterford; 3rd SI 4/3/1839; died 6/12/1853 in Westport, Co. Mayo 'after a long and painful illness' (*Cork Examiner* 16/12/1853).

Walshe, Henry Jordan; RIC 74789; LDS 2098/207B; born 16/6/1890, Westport, Co. Mayo; (Westport Registrar's District, December Quarter, 1890, vol. 4, p. 414); lieutenant, army; married on 26/9/1918 (Gorey Registrar's District, September Quarter, 1918, vol. 2, p. 709); 3rd DI 12/1/1920; pensioned 31/5/1922; transferred to the Royal Ulster Constabulary on 1/6/1922.

Walwood, Robert; RIC 55885; LDS 2098/182B; born 16/7/1872, Mohill, Co. Leitrim; (Mohill Registrar's District, 1872, vol. 13, p. 254); 3rd DI 16/10/1920; pensioned 12/5/1922.

Wansborough, Alfred Joseph; RIC 47334; LDS 2097/313; born 1857, Somerset, England; 3rd DI 8/9/1881; Queen Victoria's Visit to Ireland Medal, 1900; pensioned 15/12/1920.

Warburton, Bartholomew; born in Garryhinch, King's County, the son of Richard Warburton, Garryhinch and brother of Major George Warburton (1777–1846); CarNB; his sister, Mary (the fourth daughter of Richard Warburton and niece of the Dowager Lady Carden, of Mountbutler, King's County) married on 10/7/1855 (Roscrea Registrar's District, vol. 10, p. 9), James S. Birch, of Birchgrove, Co. Tipperary, at Corbally, Queen's County (*Cork Examiner* 13/7/1855); stipendiary magistrate 1/4/1825 and residing at Somerset, Laurencetown, Co. Galway; residing at Crinkill Lodge, Parsonstown, King's County in 1825–6; resident magistrate 1/10/1836; retired as a RM on 29/8/1859 and residing at 31, Holles Street, Dublin; died 16/12/1860 at Kilbeggan, Co. Westmeath; letters of administration granted at the Principal Registry to Anna Lucinda Warburton, Kilbeggan, Co. Westmeath on 21/2/1861, widow, the universal legatee in trust for life – effects under £200.

Warburton, Edward Bayly; LDS 2097/143; born, 1823, Dublin City, Co. Dublin; 3rd SI 8/4/1844; resident magistrate 3rd class 30/12/1859, 2nd class 17/2/1864, 1st class 21/1/1877; died 2/12/1888 at Bantry, Co. Cork; (Bantry Registrar's District, 1888, December Quarter, vol. 5, p. 16); administration granted at the Principal Registry on 12/7/1889 to Emily Warburton, Bantry, Co. Cork, the widow – effects £1,385.6s.8d.; (p. 76, RM Records of Service Book, National Archives, Dublin).

Warburton, George; CarNB; born 1777, Garryhinch, King's County, the son of Bartholomew Boyd Warburton, Birrview, Garryhinch, King's County (d.22/2/1823 in Dublin) (the *Constitution* or *Cork Morning Post*, Monday 24/2/1823) and Elizabeth Batt (her nephew was William Holmes Batt, chief constable, PPF); appointed 1/10/1802; PPF Chief Magistrate for Co. Clare and based in Kilrush, 1816–1823; yeomanry major; provincial inspector general for Connaught 1823–36, residing at Castlegar and Oatfield House, Aughrim, Co. Galway; DIG 1/6/1836; inspector general 15/3/1838; pensioned 1/7/1838; died 24/3/1846; (will of George Warburton – PRO, Kew, Catalogue Reference: PROB 11/2030 / Dept: Records of the Prerogative Court of Canterbury and related Probate Jurisdictions: Will Registers / Volume number: 2 Quire Numbers: 51–100 / Date: 21 January 1846 / Image Reference: 200/178). The only river police organized at that time was initiated by Warburton in November, 1821, when he arranged for six boats as a patrol in the Shannon estuary to prevent the importation of arms from adjoining counties. To take charge of the party he swore in Lieutenant John Read Bindon, R.N., as Chief Constable at Kildysart on 21/10/1821. Government did not think the Waterguard Police good value for money, and by May 1823 Warburton had disposed of four of his boats, retaining two as a communication with Co. Limerick, and transferring Bindon to ordinary duty at O'Brien's Bridge. As Provincial Inspector General for Connaught in 1825, George Warburton was based at Oatfield House, Ballinasloe, Co. Galway and later at Castlegar, near Ahascragh, Co. Galway. George Warburton married on 6/7/1800 Anne Maria, daughter of Thomas Acton (1780–1817); (Marriage Licence granted in 1806 at the Dublin & Glendalough Diocese, NA

Reference: M/2464), of Westaston Demesne, Dunganstown, Co. Wicklow and Sidney Davis (daughter of Joshua Davis, BL, Dublin). They had four sons, all of whom left Ireland; Bartholomew Eliot George (1810–52), a peripatetic writer on historical and literary subjects; Thomas Acton (1813–94), Captain George Drought (1816–57), a Wicklow JP named after his father's brother-in-law, Captain George Drought, who saw long service as a police magistrate in the City of Limerick (1821–1836); and two daughters, Sidney (1807–1858) and Anna Matilda (1814–53). His wife was buried in Iffley churchyard, near Oxford on 12 December 1870. His daughter, Sidney died at Clifton, near Oxford and was buried in Iffley churchyard on 23 June 1858. Another daughter, Anna Matilda died in St Mary of Magdalen Parish, Oxford and was buried in Iffley churchyard on 12 August 1853. The eldest son was Bartholomew Eliot George Warburton born in 1810, near Tullamore, King's County; educated at Queen's College, Cambridge; migrated to Trinity College Dublin 23/2/1830; BA 1834; MA 1837; barrister King's Inns 1837; traveled in Syria, Palestine and Egypt 1843; author of *The Crescent and the Cross, or romance and realities of eastern travel*, 2 vols, 1844, *Zoe: an episode of the Greek War*, 1847; *Memoirs of Prince Rupert and the cavaliers, with the private correspondence*, 3 vols 1849, *French translations*, 1851; *Reginald Hastings: a tale of the troubles*, 1850; *Darien, or the merchant prince: an historical romance*, 3 vols 1851; deputed by the Atlantic and Pacific junction company to arrange a friendly understanding with the Indian tribes on the isthmus of Darien 1851; he was drowned on 4/1/1852 on the steamer *Amazon* which departed Southampton and was burnt off Land's End. There was a memorial window erected to him in the Parish Church of St Mary the Virgin, Iffley, near Oxford. His son George Drought Warburton was born in Co. Wicklow in 1816; educated at the Royal Military College, Woolwich; 2nd Lieutenant Royal Artillery 21/6/1833, captain 1/11/1848; retired on full pay 29/11/1853; brevet major 28/11/1854; sent to assist the Spanish Legion in Spain 1837, and was severely wounded in action; served in Canada 1844–6; stationed in Landguard Fort, near Norwich; MP for Norwich 28/3/1857 to his death; author of *Hochelega, or, England in the new world*, 2 vols 1846, anon., 6 ed., 1855; *The Conquest of Canada; By the author of Hochelega*, 2 vols 1849, 4 ed. with author's name; *Memoir of Charles Mordaunt, Earl of Peterborough and Monmouth, by the author of Hochelega*, 2 vols 1853. He shot himself through the head at Henley House, Frant, near Turnbridge Wells, Sussex on 23/10/1857. He is buried at Iffley Churchyard, near Oxford. His son Thomas Acton Warburton, born 1813; educated at Trinity College, Dublin; BA 1835; LLB and LLD 1852; barrister IT 8/5/1840; ordained deacon 1851 and priest 1852; Curate of Horspath, Oxfordshire, 1851–3; Vicar of Iffley, near Oxford, 1853–76; Rural Dean of Cuddesdon, 1871–6; Vicar of St John the Evangelist, East Dulwich from 1876 to 1888. He was the author of *Rollo and his Race, or footsteps of the Normans*, 2 vols 1848, 2nd ed. 1848. He died at Hastings Lodge, Dulwich Wood Park, on 22/8/1894 and is buried at Iffley churchyard. His son George Hartop Eliot Warburton and his wife Isabel Warburton were residing at 94, Alexandra Street, Palmerston North, Wellington, New Zealand, when their son sapper Piers Acton Eliot Warburton of the New Zealand Engineers, aged 30 years died 30 April 1915 of wounds received in action at the Anzac Bay Landing.

Warburton, Henry Benjamin; LDS 2097/105; born 1806, Garryhinch, King's County; secretary to the Naval Commander-in-Chief in the East Indies for four years; served with Rear-Admiral Sir Edward Owen, KCB in the East Indies; had charge of an office at Dublin Castle for one year; 3rd SI 1/11/1836; died 18/4/1850.

Warburton, John; RIC 33795; LDS 2097/267; born 1848, Cambs., England; son of John Warburton, Esq., of Cahirville House, Co. Tipperary; married on 18/5/1872, Emma Louisa, youngest daughter of John Finlay, Esq., JP, of Brackley House, Co. Cavan; (*Cork Examiner* 26/4/1872) (Bawnboy Registrar's District, vol. 8, p. 41), wife from Co. Cavan; 3rd SI 1/2/1868; CI 1/2/1893; pensioned 17/1/1908.

Warburton, Peter; CarNB; PPF; chief magistrate at Ballyhaise, Co. Cavan in December 1826 when he and a party of police with Chief Constable Robert Ormsby were attacked.

Warburton, Richard; CarNB; born 1778, Garryhinch, Portarlington; brother of Major George Warburton (1777–1846); 3rd SI 30/10/1822; married Anne, daughter of Thomas Kemmis, Dublin; had ten sons and four daughters; third son George, b.1805; 4th son, William, Dean of Elphin, b.1806, married Emma Margaret, daughter of Major-General Richard Stovin; on 19/7/1824 he wrote to Goulburn asking that the county cess collection be postponed until the harvest was saved and mentions that the local police stopped local people dancing in the neighbourhood of his demesne, but he is all in favour of the dancing.

Ward, Henry Frederick; LDS 2097/213; born 1827, England; joined the Irish Revenue Police as a lieutenant on 21/6/1850 and served in Oughterard, Co. Galway; 3rd SI 1/12/1857; pensioned 21/6/1890; died 10/12/1910 at The George Hotel, Stranraer, New Brunswick, late of Esdale Terrace, Coleraine, Co. Derry; administration granted on 10/4/1911 to William H. Ward, bank official – effects £205.19s.9d.

Ware, Henry; LDS 2097/222; born 1827, Enniskeane, Co. Cork; son of William Ware; scholar TCD on 13/10/1843, BA 1848, Trinity College Dublin; joined the Irish Revenue Police as a lieutenant on 11/11/1853 and served in Rosnakil, Co. Donegal; daughter born on 2/8/1863 at Ballyjamesduff, Co. Cavan (*Cork Examiner* 4/8/1863) and a son born on 23/9/1864 at Ballyjamesduff (*Cork Examiner* 26/9/1864); daughter Catherine Rebecca (Oldcastle Registrar's District, vol. 13, p. 326) born on 18/8/1869 at Ballyjamesduff (*Cork Examiner* 19/8/1869); his son, Henry Thornhill Ware, aged ten months, died on 20/7/1865 (Cork Registrar's District, vol. 15, p. 46), at 12 Patrick's Hill, Cork (*Cork Examiner* 14/8/1865); sons, Charles Henry Totten born on 30/3/1871 (*Cork Examiner* 1/4/1871) and Nathaniel Webb on 29/4/1872 at Ballyjamesduff, Co. Cavan (*Cork Examiner* 8/5/1872); 3rd SI 15/6/1858; received a favourable record on 30/6/1871, whereby a threatening letter was put in his hands and he formed an opinion as to the writer, searched the house where he was staying, found a number of manuscripts there, discovering one in the identical handwriting and cleverly obtained from the suspected person an acknowledgement that the manuscript was written by him – he was arrested, tried and convicted; pensioned 1/4/1879; died 6/6/1880.

Warren, John Henry; RIC 37548; LDS 2097/285; born 1849, Co. Dublin; spent two years at sea in the Merchant navy and two years in the Loan Fund Office, Dublin Castle; 3rd SI 27/4/1871; resigned 21/10/1874.

Waters, Abraham Slater; RIC 2069; LDS 2097/154; born 1/3/1816, Dublin City; son of William Waters, SI, RIC and Samuel Abraham Walker Waters; enlisted as a sub constable on 1/5/1835; 3rd SI 3/10/1846; CI 15/12/1869; married in St Catherine's Parish, Dublin on 20/9/1845; pensioned 1/3/1876; died 3/4/1889 at the residence of his son-in-law, Dr Olpherts, Downpatrick, Co. Down; buried in Deansgrange Cemetery (South Section, Row X, grave No. 5) with his wife Sarah Walker (d.30/5/1886 at Downpatrick, Co. Down), widow of Edward Townley Hardman, his son Abraham Samuel Walker Waters and his wife Helen; administration granted on 13/5/1889 at the Principal Registry to Samuel Abraham Walker Waters, 65, Park Avenue, Sandymount, Co. Dublin, the son – effects £210.2s.11d.

Waters, John; RIC 35576; LDS 2098/105; born 1850, Co. Sligo; 3rd SI 25/6/1894; King Edward VII Visit to Ireland Medal, 1903; pensioned 3/2/1910; died 23/11/1920 at Carrickacroghery, Dromahair, Co. Leitrim; (Manorhamilton Registrar's District, 1920, December Quarter, vol. 72, p. 137); administration granted at the Principal Registry on 23/11/1920.

Waters, Samuel Abraham Walker; RIC 31735; LDS 2097/257; born, 20/10/1846, Prussia Street, Dublin, Co. Dublin; son of Abraham Slater Waters (1816–1889), CI, RIC and grandson of William Waters (b.1790), SI, RIC; married Margaret Helen (d.7/6/1926), youngest daughter of the late James MacNab, of Mona Lodge, O'Brien's Bridge, Co. Limerick, on 4/1/1872 at Castleconnell, Co. Limerick, by Rev. J.H. Revington, S.A. (*Cork Examiner* 9/1/1872); 3rd SI 1/7/1866; Detective Director from 20/4/1883 to 1/4/1889; CI 1/4/1889; County Inspector

258

259

258 Alfred Joseph Wansborough.   259 John Warburton.   260 Abraham Samuel Waters.

260

261

262

261 Samuel Abraham Walker Waters.

262 Samuel Abraham Walker Waters, Assistant Inspector General, RIC.

attached to Crime Department, 1/4/1889 to 31/1/1891; Queen Victoria's Visit to Ireland Medal, 1900; AIG 27/4/1901; King Edward VII Visit to Ireland Medal, 1903; pensioned 22/10/1906; died 4/3/1936 at Woodview, Stillorgan, Co. Dublin; will proved at Dublin by the oaths of James A.H. Waters, civil servant and George Christie, bank official; his daughter, Helen Gunning Walker Waters, in 1897 married Sir Walter Edgeworth-Johnstone (1863–1936), Lieutenant-Colonel, Royal Irish Regiment; RM, 1904–15, Chief Commissioner, DMP, 1915–23; S.A.W. Waters was buried in Deansgrange Cemetery (South Section, Row X, grave No. 5) with his wife Helen (d.30/5/1886), his father Abraham Samuel Waters (d.3/4/1889) and his mother, Sarah (d.30/5/1886); (*A Policeman's Ireland – Recollections of Samuel Waters, RIC*, edited by Stephen Ball, Cork University Press, Cork, 1999); (photo in the *Constabulary Gazette*, vol. 1, no. 13, 26/6/1897); (photo: Garda Museum & Archives, Dublin Castle).

Waters, William; LDS 2097/024; born 1789, Co. Wicklow; served as a Peace Officer in the Castle Division of the Dublin Police from 19/3/1810 to 12/2/1820; father of Abraham Samuel Waters (1816–89), CI, RIC and grandfather of Samuel Abraham Walker Waters (1846–1936), AIG, RIC; married on 30/8/1809 Ann McDowell (d.2/3/1873, aged 85 years), Dublin; buried in Mount Jerome Cemetery, Dublin; transferred to the Peace Preservation Force, 12/2/1820; 3rd SI 9/8/1824; received a severe injury of the right knee from a fall when on patrol at night in December 1820; discharged 1/10/1840; government refused to restore Mr Waters but offered to find a passage to the Colonies for his family.

Watkins, John S.; LDS 2097/158; born 1829, Cork City, Co. Cork; 3rd SI 10/5/1847; seconded to the Commissariat Department in the Crimea from 3/8/1854 to 15/1/1855; musketry instructor at the Phoenix Park Depot from 16/1/1864 to 1/2/1869; Adjutant, Phoenix Park Depot from 1/2/1869 to 15/8/1870; CI 15/8/1870; pensioned after 1876.

Watkins, Westropp Peard; LDS 2097/040; born 1797; son of Westropp Watkins and Dorcas, daughter of Richard Peard, Esq., of Carrigeen and Elizabeth Vowel; lieutenant 102nd Regiment of Foot (Royal Dublin Fusiliers) and 80th Regiment of Foot (South Staffordshire Regiment); married 6/7/1822, Knockmourne, Co. Cork; wife a native of Co. Cork; 3rd SI 13/5/1823; residing at Church Street, Ennis, Co. Clare in 1824 (Pigot's Directory, 1824); reported to be of unsound mind on 5/1/1839; pensioned 16/4/1839; died 2/6/1846; (WO 25/777 fol. 134).

Webb, Charles William Vincent; RIC 78626; LDS 2098/246B; born 24/3/1887, Preston, Lancs., England; (Preston Registrar's District, 1887, June Quarter, vol. 8e, p. 680); army; seconded for service with ADRIC; 3rd DI 2/7/1920; pensioned 30/4/1922.

Webb, John Gregory; RIC 17385; LDS 2097/199; born 1830, Killucan, Co. Westmeath; employed as an engineer under Sir John McNeill for two years; son, George Cuppage born on 15/11/1864 at Athy, Co. Kildare (Athy Registrar's District, vol. 18, p. 405) (*Cork Examiner* 17/11/1864); 3rd SI 27/8/1853; received an approbation on 31/3/1856 for cool and forbearing conduct when being on patrol in the streets of Castlebar, Co. Mayo, an attack was made on the police by a large number of riotous soldiers – eliciting the approbation of the judge before whom the case was tried; received an approbation on 31/12/1868 for meritorious exertions in extinguishing a fire with a party; received a favourable record on 30/6/1869 for indefatigable (though unsuccessful) efforts to make a murderer amenable; pensioned 1/12/1882; died 2/1/1913.

Webb, William; CarNB; PPF; chief magistrate in Co. Donegal (baronies of Ennishowen and Raphoe) in 1822.

Webster, John; RIC 34903; LDS 2098/094; born 1850, Clones, Co. Monaghan; 3rd DI 12/11/1892; King Edward VII Visit to Ireland Medal, 1903; pensioned 4/8/1911; in September 1905 his son, Mr G.P. Webster secured third place in the United Kingdom for a cadetship in the Indian Police Service; another son took first place in the United Kingdom as a naval clerk in the Royal Navy.

Webster, Robert; CarNB; C.C. Innishowen, Co. Donegal; Galway, Co. Galway.

Weldon, Patrick Campbell; CarNB; PPF; 3rd SI 1821; on 14/5/1821 the turn-key of Ennis Gaol contrived to leave, taking with him two convicts in disguise, under sentence of transportation. Weldon gave immediate pursuit and captured the turn-key and one of the convicts. The other convict was captured by another policeman while attempting to cross the Shannon; in 1826 allegations were made and withdrawn by a Bridget McMahon, of Carrick-on-Shannon, formerly of Ennis that she had two children by Weldon and followed him to Carrick-on-Shannon when he was transferred from Ennis. Major Warburton said the complainant was 'a wretched Christian unworthy of any attention'; (Will proved in the Prerogative Court in 1836, granted to F. Weldon, Ballinasloe, Co. Galway, NA Reference: IWR/1836/F/438); C.C. Ennis, Co. Clare; Carrick-on-Shannon, Co. Leitrim; Ahascragh and Ballinrobe, Co. Galway.

West, Edward; RIC 54676; LDS 2098/150B; born 1872, Co. Kerry; married on 16/9/1902 (Tralee Registrar's District, September Quarter, 1902, vol. 5, p. 307), wife a native of Co. Kerry; 3rd DI 20/9/1920; pensioned 26/4/1922.

Westropp, Robert; LDS 2097/109; born 1810, Fort Anne, Co. Clare; son of Robert Westropp, Esq., of Fort Anne, Co. Clare; 3rd SI 25/11/1836; married 27/1/1836 Anne (died 14/10/1879), daughter of William Colclough, Clonmel, Co. Tipperary; Anne remarried on 28/2/1854 (Rathdown Registrar's District, vol. 9, p. 543), James Scott, Esq., youngest son of the late William Scott, of Scottsborough, Co. Fermanagh (*Cork Examiner* 8/3/1854); died 22/8/1849 at Longford, Co. Longford (*Cork Examiner* 31/8/1849).

Whelan, Thomas; RIC 24081; LDS 2097/223; born 1838, Co. Wicklow; son of John Whelan, Rath, Co. Wicklow; clerk in the Great Northern Railway of Peterborough and Doncaster from February 1855 to September 1858; 3rd SI 13/10/1858; CI 14/9/1882; AIG 10/9/1891; Commissioner of Police for Belfast, 1/2/1898; Queen Victoria's Visit to Ireland Medal, 1900; pensioned 1/4/1902; died 26/11/1911 at Saval Villa, Barnhill Road, Dalkey, Co. Dublin;

administration granted on 21/12/1911 at the Principal Registry to Harry R. Whelan, solicitor – effects £7,603.1s.5d.

Wherry, Alexander; LDS 2097/186; born 1807, Co. Fermanagh; enlisted as a sub constable on 1/9/1827; 3rd SI 1/6/1848; died 1/7/1849 in Co. Wexford; his children, one boy and four girls received a gratuity of £38.5s.4d. from the Reward Fund on 8/10/1849.

White, Frederick Augustus; RIC 29662; LDS 2097/250; born 1845, Carlow, Co. Carlow; youngest son of Matthew Lawrence White of Carlow, Co. Carlow; daughter born on 25/2/1869 at Foxford, Co. Mayo (*Cork Examiner* 23/1869); 3rd SI 1/9/1864; CI 3/10/1889; died 7/11/1893 at Ennis, Co. Clare; administration granted on 6/2/1894 at the Principal Registry to Annie Winston 4 of 39, Synge Street, Dublin, the widow – effects £176.17s.5d.; buried in Ennis, Co. Clare on 9/11/1893.

White, George; LDS 2097/075; born 1792, Co. Dublin; PPF; enlisted as a sub constable, 7/4/1820; wife a native of Co. Wexford; 3rd SI 13/4/1832; received a ball wound by accident while on duty at Ballinasloe in June, 1831; received seven wounds from stones thrown by a party at the Fair of Innistiogue on 12/10/1835; C.C. Rossbercon, New Ross, Co. Wexford, 1835; pensioned 10/1/1852; died 24/10/1874 at Shrubs, Co. Dublin; will proved on 26/11/1874 at the Principal Registry by the oath of Mary Catherine White, of Shrubs, Co. Dublin – effects under £12,000.

White, Matthew O'Byrne; RIC 56628, LDS 2098/116; born 30/7/1870, Tubbercurry, Co. Sligo; (Tubbercurry Registrar's District, 1870, vol. 14, p. 555); temporary clerk in the Land Commission for two years and in the Census Office for one year; married on 2/2/1905 (Gort Registrar's District, March Quarter, 1905, vol. 4, p. 207), May (d.1/10/1971), eldest daughter of Francis Fitz Adelm Persse (b.26/4/1854) of Gort, Co. Galway, JP and Mary (d.27/11/1909), daughter of William Monahan, of Templemartin, Co. Galway who were married on 20/7/1880; 3rd DI 18/6/1895; pensioned 30/9/1917; died 31/3/1943; buried with his wife May in Grangegorman Military Cemetery, Blackhorse Avenue, Dublin; (photo in the *Constabulary Gazette*, vol. XIV, no. 16, 9/1/1904).

White, William Eugene; RIC 71611; LDS 2098/126B; born 13/8/1893, Strokestown, Co. Roscommon; (Strokestown Registrar's District, September Quarter, 1893, vol. 3, p. 349); lieutenant, Royal Field Artillery; married on 13/8/1920 (Dublin South Registrar's District, December Quarter, 1920, vol. 2, p. 669), Belinda Mary Angela Ryan; 3rd DI 8/7/1920; pensioned 6/4/1922.

Whitehead, J.D.; LDS 2097/133; born 1817, Co. Dublin; clerk in the office of the Commission for inquiring into the State of the Poor in Ireland from 23/12/1834 to 7/5/1836; junior clerk in the Constabulary Office from 23/7/1836 to 24/11/1840; resigned 22/5/1854.

Whittaker, John; LDS 2097/044; born 1800, Co. Fermanagh; 3rd SI 8/10/1823.

Whyte, Francis Ignatius; LDS 2098/015B; born 7/3/1886, Cullenstown, Duncormick, Co. Wexford; (Wexford Registrar's District, March Quarter, 1886, vol. 4, p. 804); tutor for eight months at Skerry's Academy, Dublin; married on 20/11/1915 (Dublin South Registrar's District, December Quarter, 1915, vol. 2, p. 553), Charlotte La Touche Vaugh, daughter of Wilton Vaugh (27/11/1847–16/10/1925), Sub Sheriff of Co. Leitrim and Susan Taylor, of 4, Clarinda Park, Kingstown, Co. Dublin, who were married on 30/5/1884, a native of Co. Leitrim and they had three daughters Camille, Una and Marguerite; 3rd DI 9/10/1910; TCI 8/11/1920; pensioned 15/4/1922; died in 1964; buried in Dromahair Catholic Cemetery, Co. Leitrim; (photo in the *Constabulary Gazette*, vol. XXXIII, no. 9, 10/5/1913).

Wickham, Charles George; born 1/9/1879, Tadcaster, Yorks., England; (Tadcaster Registrar's District, 1879, December Quarter, vol. 9c, p. 768); youngest son of Mr William Wickham Wickham (b.1836) Lightcliffe, Halifax, Yorkshire, of Boston Spa, Yorkshire and Katharine Henta Wickham (b.1843) Newton Kyme, Yorkshire; residing at Newton Kyme Hall, Newton Kyme, Cum Towlston, Yorkshire in 1881 (Census); began his military career with the Norfolk Regiment in 1899, and served in the Mounted Infantry in the South African Campaign, 1899–1902. He was wounded during the operations against the Boers, and in recognition of his services he was awarded the DSO, was mentioned in despatches and held the Queen's and King's Medals with seven clasps; 3rd DI 3/4/1905; divisional commissioner 21/10/1920 at Belfast; pensioned 31/5/1922; transferred to the Royal Ulster Constabulary on 1/6/1922; KCMG, KBE, DSO; Inspector General of the Royal Ulster Constabulary from 1 June 1922 to July 1945; died 1971 Comber, Co. Down.

Wickham, James Carr; LDS 2097/135; born 1814, Co. Limerick; wife a native of Co. Donegal; 3rd SI 6/5/1841; pensioned 28/9/1868; died 4/6/1886 at Killarney, Co. Kerry; (Killarney Registrar's District, 1886, June Quarter, vol. 5, p. 242).

Wigan, Yeoman Ramsay Douglas; RIC 73008; ADRIC CADET no. 454; LDS 2099/038; born 1891, Portsea, Kent, England; (Portsea Registrar's District, 1891, June Quarter, vol. 2, p. 514); married on 29/1/1918, wife from 36, Endsleigh Gardens, Ilford, Essex; captain, Royal Berkshire Regiment; 3rd DI 20/9/1921; pensioned 31/3/1922.

Wilbond, James; RIC 55389; LDS 2098/089; born 1869, Devon, England; BA RUI; 3rd DI 1/2/1893; CI 11/10/1918; divisional commissioner 16/3/1920 at Athlone; pensioned 22/4/1922.

Wilder, William; LDS 2097/078; born Abbeyshrule, Co. Longford; PPF; 3rd SI 1/12/1832; C.C. Mullinavat and Mount Argula, Innistiogue, Co. Kilkenny, 1835.

Wilkins, Charles Henry; RIC 72157; ADRIC CADET no. 30; LDS 2098/205B; born 3/9/1893, Pancras, London, England; (Pancras Registrar's District, 1893, December Quarter, vol. 1b, p. 43); lieutenant, Royal Air Force; married on 19/2/1921, wife a native of Essex; 3rd DI 12/1/1920; received a first class favourable record for good duty during an ambush at Crossard, Co. Mayo on 1/4/1921; pensioned 21/6/1922; (WO 374/74422).

Wilkinson, Arthur; CarNB; PPF; residing in Charlemont House, Dublin, he spent thirty years in the army; he had been a lieutenant-colonel when his regiment was ordered to India and couldn't pay his way with a wife and six daughters, four of who were infants, therefore he accepted the situation as secretary to the Co. Cork PPF under Major Samson Carter who was his brother-in-law; (will of Arthur Wilkinson, Fort Lewis, Doneraile, Co. Cork, proved in the Prerogative Court in 1830, grant to Anne Wilkinson, NA Reference: IWR/1830/F/152 & T/10371); C.C. Doneraile, Co. Cork.

Willcocks, John; CarNB; born 1795, Palmerston, Co. Dublin; second son of Major Sir Richard Willcocks (1768–1834); 3rd SI 1/10/1821; stipendiary magistrate 15/2/1832; resident magistrate 1/10/1836; retired as a RM on 1/6/1860 and residing at Tullamore, King's County; died 4/11/1872 at St Laurence, Chapelizod, Co. Dublin; will proved on 3/1/1873 at the Principal Registry by the oath of John Willcocks, Junior, Esq., the sole executor – effects under £100; buried in St Laurence Church of Ireland Cemetery, Chapelizod, Dublin with Mary Anne, who died 4/3/1863, aged 59 years, daughter of Dr Ambrose Going, Ballyphilip, superintending magistrate of Co. Limerick; his son John Willcocks, JP, late Captain 3rd Middlesex Militia, died 31/5/1882, aged 50 years and his widow Annie Adela Waller Willcocks, née Biddulph, whom he married in 1867, afterwards wife of John Ouseley Murphy (father of Charles Ouseley Murphy, DI, RIC) and, died 21/4/1926 aged 79 years; his parents Sir Richard and Lady Lucy and brothers, Robert Henry and Rev. William are buried in the adjacent vault; C.C. Cashel, Co. Tipperary.

Willcocks, Richard (Sir); CarNB; born 1768, Palmerston, Dublin; PPF; captain, Palmerston yeomanry which he raised in 1803; appointed special government magistrate by the Duke of Wellington in Co. Limerick, 1808, Co. Waterford, 1810, Co. Tipperary, 1811, Co. Kilkenny, Garristown, Co. Meath and Co. Westmeath; major; appointed the first chief magistrate 6/9/1814 by Robert Peel in the barony of Middlethird, Co. Tipperary and based at Cashel; the success of Peel's Peace Preservation Force was due primarily to the extensive work of Richard Willcocks

263

264

263 Francis Ignatius Whyte. 264 Charles George Wickham, Inspector General Royal Ulster Constabulary, 1922–45. 265 Charles Henry Wilkins.

265

(*Mr Secretary Peel – The life of Sir Robert Peel to 1830* by Norman Gash, Harvard University Press, Cambridge, Massachusetts, 1961, pp. 182/3, 200/1); Willcocks sent a letter of thanks to Robert Peel for granting him leave to visit his family from Cashel to Palmerston at Christmas 1817; Rathkeale, Co. Limerick,1820; provincial inspector general from 6/11/1822. He tendered his resignation on 14/10/1827, 'owing to my late very severe illness and the general debilitated state of my health.' His reply pays high tribute and adds that the Lord Lieutenant 'feels it to be a duty to provide adequately for the retirement of a respectable and deserving public servant,' all meticulously set down in Wellesley's own hand; knighted 1827; a summary in 1827 of the service and the esteem in which Sir Richard Willcocks was held appears in the papers of Sir Edward John Littleton (1791–1863), 1st Baron Hatherton, Chief Secretary to the Lord Lieutenant of Ireland, 1833–4 (Staffordshire Record Office D260/M/01/1086): '1827, Sir Richard Willcocks – In 1803, he obtained and communicated to the Government the first information of Emmet's designs, and thereby prevented the insurgents from gaining possession of Dublin. On that occasion he narrowly escaped assassination; eight persons having been stationed in different places for the purpose of attacking him. Immediately afterwards he organized a Yeomanry Corps in the County of Dublin, with the assistance of which he maintained the tranquillity of his own neighbourhood. He apprehended and committed to prison 35 persons concerned in Emmet's insurrection. He was subsequently employed from 1807, to 1827, in active service in different parts of Ireland. He was sent as a Stipendiary Magistrate, from time to time, into the Counties of Kerry, Limerick, Tipperary, Cork, Waterford, Kilkenny, Meath, and Westmeath; by his own exertions unaided by police, he successively tranquillized those counties. This was affected chiefly by obtaining private information, apprehending the principal offenders, bringing them to trial, securing witnesses, and preventing them from being tampered with. He was afterwards appointed Chief Magistrate under the Peace Preservation Act, and ultimately Inspector General of Munster, under the Constabulary Act. It is universally allowed that there never was a more efficient Magistrate. The honour of Knighthood was conferred on him on retiring. 'His allowances were the same as those of Major Mills'; his eldest daughter, Sarah, married William Clarke, son of Edward Clarke, Palmerston in January 1812 at Palmerston; he died 7/4/1834 at Palmerston, Co. Dublin; C.C. Cashel, Co. Tipperary; buried in St Laurence Church of Ireland Cemetery, Chapelizod, Dublin with his wife Lady Lucy Willcocks, died 27/3/1840, aged 73 years; his eldest son, Robert Henry Willcocks, formerly Lieutenant Colonel 81st Regiment of Foot (Loyal Lincoln Volunteers Regiment), who died 14/4/1859, aged 65 years; his third and youngest son Rev. William Willcocks, rector of the Parish of Palmerston for 36 years, who died on 28/2/1871, aged 70 years, BA Vern., 1822, MA, 1832, having rebuilt St Laurence Church, Chapelizod in 1839; his grandson, John Willcocks of Palmerston, only son of Captain John and Annie Willcocks, nee Biddulph, born 14/4/1872, died 7/3/1918 and also Florence, wife (married in 1897) of Captain Benjamin Ivan Tilly (d.1953) and youngest daughter of Captain John Willcocks, JP, born 29/1/1877, died 29/10/1925. Sir Richard's epitaph reads: 'Praises on Tombs are trifles vainly spent; a man's good name is his own monument.' His death notice in the *Cork Evening Herald* of 9/4/1834 reads: 'Sir Richard Willcocks, one of the oldest and most respected members of the county of Dublin magistracy died at his late Dublin residence, Palmerston, yesterday. He was many years inspector general of constabulary and upon his retirement in 1827 he received the honour of Knighthood at the hands of the Marquess Wellesley as a well earned mark of approval for the zealous and efficient discharge of his onerous public duties. He was in private life a most inestimable character, and in public, everything that activity, sound discrimination and honesty of purpose could make a man.'

Williams, Frank Bertram; RIC 72242; ADRIC CADET no. 78; LDS 2098/225B; born 5/9/1890, Birmingham, Warks., England; (Birmingham Registrar's District, September Quarter, 1890, vol. 6d, p. 171); army; 3rd DI 12/1/1920; pensioned 15/4/1922.

Williams, George; RIC 58791; LDS 2098/152B; born 1879, Co. Sligo; (Sligo Registrar's

District, March Quarter, 1879, vol. 2, p. 337); 3rd DI 20/9/1920; pensioned 31/5/1922; transferred to the Royal Ulster Constabulary on 1/6/1922.

Williams, Henry; RIC 485; LDS 2097/179; born 1805, Co. Kerry; enlisted as a sub constable on 6/11/1827; wife a native of Co. Tipperary; his eldest daughter, Marianne married on 4/9/1854 at Riverstown, Co. Cork, George B. O'Callaghan, Inspector of National Schools; 3rd SI 15/6/1849; pensioned 9/11/1869; died 26/6/1891 at Shannon View Cottage, Portumna, Co. Galway; will proved on 30/7/1891 at the Principal Registry by the oath of Jane Ada Williams, of 6, D'Olier Street, Dublin, widow, the sole executrix – effects £113.16s.10d.

Williams, James; CarNB; father of John De Lacy Williams, SI, RIC: C.C. Abbeyshrule, Granard, Co. Longford, 1826 and Archerstown Castkletowndelvin, Co. Westmeath, 1835.

Williams, John De Lacy; RIC 15583; LDS 2097/190; born 1828, Granard, Co. Longford; son of James Williams, II, RIC; 3rd SI 11/2/1852; discharged on a gratuity of £24.16s.8d. on 17/7/1855 in Co. Down.

Williams, Thomas; CarNB; PPF; in January 1831 he was in poor health through activities in winter arresting a gang; he was given £25 for services rendered and he went to live in Loughrea with his family as the mountain air in Woodford was not agreeable to his pulmonary complaint; died in March 1831 leaving his widow, Anne and four children; C.C. barony of Leitrim, Woodford, Co. Galway, 1825.

Williams, William; LDS 2097/077; born 1804, Co. Kilkenny; wife a native of Dublin City; daughters born on 29/4/1855 and 5/2/1857 at Ballymena, Co. Antrim (*Cork Examiner* 4/5/1855 and *Cork Examiner* 11/2/1857) and a son born on 29/8/1861 at Belfast (*Cork Examiner* 30/8/1861); 3rd SI 9/11/1832; CI 5/2/1853; pensioned 4/3/1870; died 1/10/1880 at 88, Fitzroy Avenue, Belfast, late of 14 Cromwell Terrace and The Plains, Belfast; will proved on 24/11/1880 at Belfast by the oath of Edward Collingwood Bell, of Corbally Cottage, near Limerick (Gent.) and Benjamin Henry Spedding, of Belfast, MD, the executors – effects under £6,000.

Williamson, Robert Cecil; RIC 68424; 2098/059B; born 16/8/1891, Co. Dublin; (Dublin South Registrar's District, September Quarter, 1891, vol. 2, p. 562); son of William George Williamson, CI, RIC; BA 1913, LLB 1914, Trinity College Dublin, Barrister-at-Law; married on 21/2/1917 (Dublin South Registrar's District, March Quarter, 1917, vol. 2, p. 585), Miss Crowe; 3rd DI 27/2/1915; pensioned 31/8/1922.

Williamson, William George; RIC 34567; LDS 2097/271; born 1847, Co. Derry; father of Robert Cecil Williamson, DI, RIC; 3rd SI 21/8/1868; Adjutant, Phoenix Park Depot from 10/3/1885 to 10/3/1891; CI 1/5/1894; pensioned 6/7/1908.

Wills, Henry; RIC 19694; LDS 2097/316; born 1836, Co. Kildare; 3rd SI 16/1/1882; pensioned 1/6/1896; died 20/3/1905.

Wills, Henry; RIC 19694; LDS 2097/296; born 1836, Co. Kildare; married on 3/6/1868; wife a native of Queens County; 3rd S.I. 16/1/1882; pensioned on 1/8/1896; died at the residence of his son-in-law at Clarehayes, Churchtaunton, Honiton, Devon on 30/6/1922, husband of Lizzie P. Wills (*Irish Times*, 7/7/1922).

Wills, John; CarNB; born 1788; PPF; of Esker Lodge, Lucan, Co. Dublin; a veteran of the Dublin Police, 1797–1812; was one of three of the first government (others being Richard Willcocks and Edward Wilson) appointed magistrates on the recommendation of Lord Cathcart by the Earl of Hardwicke in 1802 sent out without police; special magistrate 1808; in 1813 he was ordered to take charge of the disturbed areas of Cos. Roscommon, Galway, Leitrim, Cavan, Wexford and Westmeath; as a chief magistrate 14/12/1815 he took charge of the barony of Clanwilliam, Co. Tipperary; in February 1817 took charge of the proclaimed barony of Castleraghan, Co. Cavan; removed with the Revenue Police in April 1817 to the proclaimed baronies of Offaly, Kilcullen, Connell, Carberry, Clane and Naas in Co. Kildare and Philipstown in King's County; in November 1818 sent to Donegal to organize the Revenue Police; recalled in

February 1819 to take charge of the proclaimed parishes of Killyon, Killyconnigan and Clonard in the baronies of Clune and Moypenrath, Co. Meath; on 14/11/1819 he was sent to Co. Roscommon, residing in Rockley Park, Roscommon and remained there until the County Constabulary came into operation on 24/4/1824 when he retired to Esker Lodge, Lucan, Co. Dublin on a pension of £500 per annum; (Probate granted in respect of Major John Wills, Willsbrook, Co. Dublin in the Prerogative Court on 27/6/1853, NA Reference: T/13994 & Char1/15/p50).

Wilson, Edward; CarNB; served in the Dublin Police from 1788 to 1808 as Chief Peace Officer, Workhouse Division; arrests made by him mentioned in the *Freeman's Journal* of 25/10/1793, 6/6/1801, 9/8/1803, 2/8/1804, 25/9/1804, 4/10/1804 and 6/4/1805 and made several arrests of the leaders in Robert Emmet's Rising in 1803; appointed a special government magistrate, 1808, by the Duke of Wellington; from 1811 he served as a special magistrate for Dublin Castle in Roscommon, Westmeath, Waterford and Queen's County; PPF, barony of Kilnamanagh, Co. Tipperary; major; chief magistrate 3/5/1815; pensioned 1828; his eldest son, Edward Wilson Esq., Cahirconlish House, Co. Limerick, married Isabella, daughter of the late Captain Thomas Goodrich Peacock (d.1817), 55th Regiment of Foot (Westmoreland Regiment), of Fort Etna, Co. Limerick at Kilkeedy Church on 29/8/1820; his wife died at Brasfort, Co. Tipperary in the 52nd year of her age on 7/2/1822; C.C. barony of Kilnamanagh, Co. Tipperary, 1820.

Wilson, Timothy Bunting; RIC 24637; LDS 2097/229; born 1838, Co. Limerick; married by his brother, Rev. Richard Wilson, M.A., Vicar of Kilselly, Co. Clare on 23/4/1859 at St Ann's, Shandon, Cork, Mary Hampton, only daughter of Richard Pennefeather Lloyd, Esq., of Muckton House, Co. Galway; 3rd SI 3/6/1859; pensioned 1/7/1899; one son was born at Airmount, New Ross, Co. Wexford on 19/1/1880; died 26/12/1910 at Adelaide House, Clonmel, Co. Tipperary; will proved on 19/6/1911 at the Principal Registry by the oath of William A. Riall, DL, David J. Higgins, solicitor and Caroline O'D. G. Wilson, the widow – effects £31,798.2s.11d.

Wilson, William Harding; RIC 50239; LDS 2098/019B; born 1864, Ballycumber, King's County; (Parsonstown Registrar's District, 1864, vol. 13, p. 648); married on 1/8/1893 (Dublin North Registrar's District, September Quarter, 1893, vol. 2, p. 385), wife, Frances Clarke, a native of Ballymote, Co. Sligo and sister of sergeant Edward William Clarke, RIC 44161 and sergeant Eccles Clarke, RIC 53544; 3rd DI 9/10/1910; killed 16/8/1920, George's Street, Templemore, Co. Tipperary; late of Manor Cottage, Templemore; buried in St Mary's Church of Ireland Cemetery, Templemore; his epitaph reads: 'His life to his country, his soul to God'; administration granted at Limerick on 8/10/1920.

Wilton, Henry; RIC 29661; LDS 2097/249; born 1844, Crosserlough, Co. Cavan; clerk in the Irish Railway clearing house from November 1861 to May 1862; 3rd SI 1/9/1864; died 30/11/1886 at The Yews, Antrim, Co. Antrim; (Antrim Registrar's District, 1886, December Quarter, vol. 1, p. 2).

Winder, Edward Henry; RIC 45148; LDS 2097/305; born 1857, Co. Dublin; married on 13/1/1881 (Dublin North Registrar's District, March Quarter, 1881, vol. 2, p. 641), wife a native of Co. Dublin; brother of Frank Winder, MD and Percy Winder; his mother, Mary Anne Winder, died in November 1912, aged 83 years at Tourville, Rathfarnham, Co. Dublin; buried in Stillorgan, Co. Dublin; 3rd DI 1/3/1880; pensioned 7/1/1920.

Winslow, Daniel T.; LDS 2097/062; born 1781, Dresternan, Cloghan, Co. Fermanagh; father of William Frederick Winslow, SI, RIC; ensign and lieutenant in the Fermanagh Militia from 1796 to 1804 (WO 13/2861–81); widower on appointment; 3rd SI 20/9/1825; died 23/5/1840.

Winslow, William Frederick; LDS 2097/132; born 1813, Cloghan, Co. Fermanagh; son of Daniel T. Winslow, SI, RIC; wife a native of Co. Kilkenny; 3rd SI 18/9/1840; died 7/3/1862 at Trim, Co. Meath; administration granted at the Principal Registry on 14/2/1863 to Anne Winslow, of the Parade in the City of Kilkenny, the widow of the deceased – effects under £600.

Wise, Arthur; CarNB; PPF; PPF Clerk 25/3/1817.

Wood, Henry Archdall; 2097/222; born 1829, Co. Cork; joined the Irish Revenue Police as a lieutenant on 31/1/1852 and served in Boyle, Co. Roscommon; temporary clerk in the Commissariat for two years; 3rd SI 11/6/1858; received an approbation on 31/12/1870 for strenuous exertions at a burning mill, saving the dwelling house, gasometer, engine, stables and horses, at great risk; died 11/12/1874 at Donaghmore, Co. Antrim; (Donaghmore Registrar's District, 1874, vol. 18, p. 348).

Wood, John Stewart (Sir); born 1813, Southampton, Hants., England, the son of Major John Thomas Wood, Middlesex, England and Hannah Elizabeth, daughter of Major-General John Stewart, Royal Artillery; educated at the Royal Military College, Sandhurst; ensign, 48th Regiment of Foot (Northamptonshire Regiment) 3/5/1831; lieutenant, 13th Regiment of Foot (Prince Albert's Somersetshire Light Infantry) 22/8/1835; major, 13/2/1855 to 25/1/1866 when placed on half pay; assistant adjutant general at Aldershot, 1856–60; served in the Coorg campaign in India 1834, Afghanistan and Koohistan campaigns 1838–42, and in the Crimean War; medal for Ghuznie; medal for Jellalabad; medal for Cabul; medal and three clasps for the Crimea; the Turkish Medal; Knight of the Legion of Honour; Fourth Class of the Turkish Order of the Medidjeh; married 1844, Isabella Frances, 3rd daughter of George Baker, esq., of Beverly, St Stephens, Kent; DIG 7/8/1860; inspector general 8/5/1865 to 19/9/1876; KCB, 1870; author of *Standing Rules and Regulations of the RIC* (Dublin, 1872); died 9/9/1880 at Hobarton House, Dover Street, Ryde, Isle of Wight, late of 34, Brunswick Place, Brighton; (*Times*, 14/9/1880, p. 8); (Isle of Wight, Registrar's District, September Quarter, 1880, vol. 2b, p. 394); will proved at the Principal Registry on 23/10/1880 by the oath of Dame Isabella Frances Wood, of 34 Brunswick Place, Brighton, the relict, the sole executrix – effects Personal estate under £25,000.

Wood, Thomas Dawson; CarNB; C.C. Tullow, Co. Carlow; Kilcock, Kildare.

Woodburn, Henry; CarNB; PPF; 3rd SI 1830 from PPF; chief clerk to Major Thomas Philip Vokes, Limerick, 15/8/1820 and C.C., 31/1/1826; C.C. Ballingarry, Co. Limerick in 1829.

Woodhouse, Archibald; LDS 2097/087; born 1809, Drumcree, Co. Armagh; 3rd SI 1/12/1834; died 23/2/1842.

Woods, Benjamin; PPF; born in King's County in 1787, the fifth of six children born to Ann Wilkinson and her husband, Jonathan Woods, a shopkeeper. He married in Dublin, having obtained a marriage licence on 23 November 1812. His wife, like his mother, was called Ann Wilkinson. They had four children. Benjamin Woods was to be the important police officer in northern New Zealand between 1840 and 1853. During the Napoleonic wars Woods probably served in the army, and in 1815 joined the newly formed Irish Peace Preservation Force. He worked his way up to the position of district head constable in the Irish Constabulary before moving on to clerical work. In 1839 Woods and his family sailed on the *China* to Sydney, Australia. He was still seeking employment when in early 1840 the recently appointed chief police magistrate for New Zealand, Wiloughby Shortland, offered him the position of chief constable. Woods accepted, and located two non-commissioned officers to assist him before travelling with his family to New Zealand on the *Westminster*. Also aboard the vessel, which left Sydney on 4 March 1840, were Lieutenant Henry Dalton Smart, a corporal, four privates, and ten troop horses to serve as mounts for this force and for the five New South Wales troopers who had accompanied Lieutenant Governor William Hobson to New Zealand earlier in the year. For a period after their arrival at the Bay of Islands the Woods family were forced to live in a tent. Working conditions were difficult and lawlessness was rife. Undaunted by these problems, Woods began appointing constables in Kororareka (Russell). Although he was responsible to the police magistrate at the Bay of Islands, Woods was the effective head of police in the region and by late 1840 had established a police barracks at Kororareka. In December he was chosen by Hobson to become the first chief constable at Auckland, which was to be the new capital. However, the new police magistrate at the Bay of Islands, Thomas Beckham, had this appointment rescinded, so Woods remained in the north. In 1844 Woods provoked an incident which threatened to disturb the peace between Maori and Pakeha. Whilst forcibly entering Joseph Bryars's dwelling near Kawakawa on 22 September at 3 a.m. with an arrest warrant, he accidentally injured with his sword Kohu, a woman of rank from Kawiti's hapu. Her brother, Hori Kingi tahua, demanded compensation. When Tahua appeared at Kororareka with a large armed party the magistrate, Beckham, gave him (with a bad grace) a horse worth £10. Governor Robert Fitzroy commented, 'I wish the constables had gone unarmed and waited at the man's house till daylight'. Woods was castigated for his provocative conduct. However, this was but one of a series of such incidents which preceded the outbreak of war in 1845, signifying a general deterioration in race relations. After the sacking of Kororareka in 1845 Woods was, for almost a year, responsible for policing the suburbs of Auckland. He worked at this task in conjunction with Auckland's chief constable, James, who controlled the centre of the town. From 1 April 1846 Woods became chief constable of Kororareka (by now known as Russell). In February 1847 he was enrolled, on Governor George Grey's instructions, as a sergeant major in the new Auckland Armed Police Force, which had been established by the Constabulary Force Ordinance in 1846. Inspector T.R. Atkyns, Wood's new superior officer in Auckland, sent him a detachment of four armed constables. From 1848 until 1853 the Auckland Armed Police Force was one of the two main detachments of the Armed Police Force of New Ulster. Armed police were stationed at Auckland, Howick, Onehunga, the Bay of Islands and Mangonui. The services carried out by these men included the carriage of mail, an effective way of gathering intelligence and providing security for those on the delivery routes. In 1853, at the beginning of provincial government, Woods retired from the police force. He returned to Auckland to become bailiff at the Resident Magistrate's Court, retiring from that position in 1859. He died at Auckland on 6 November 1867 and was buried in the Grafton Cemetery. In 1986, during the New Zealand Police centennial celebrations, police and some of his descendants unveiled a monument to him there.

Woods, William; RIC 41140; LDS 2098/153; born 1855, Co. Armagh; married on 18/10/1882, wife a native of Co. Roscommon; 3rd DI 3/3/1899; King Edward VII Visit to Ireland Medal, 1903; pensioned 30/11/1917.

Woods, William Alexander; RIC 61492; LDS 2098/207; born 9/6/1885, Yorks., England; married on 1/12/1914, Mrs F.D. Jameson, a native of England; 3rd DI 12/6/1905; captain, 6th (service) Battalion, Royal Irish Fusiliers, 21/10/1914 and Assistant Provost Marshal (grade as staff captain) Dublin District, 7/2/1916; relinquished his appointment and granted the rank of captain, 2/5/1918; wounded at Gallipoli, 1916; resident magistrate 3rd class 23/7/1920; (p. 185, RM Records of Service Book, National Archives, Dublin); died at 7, West Parade, Anlaby Road, Hull on 5/8/1928; (WO 339/13579).

Workman, John Edward; RIC 82583; ADRIC CADET no. 1750; born 23/6/1897, Dursley, Glos., England; (Dursley Registrar's District, 1897, September Quarter, vol. 6a, p. 246); private, Gloucestershire Regiment, 1915; 2nd Lieutenant, King's Regiment (Liverpool); Royal Flying Corps; Royal Air Force, 1/4/1918; ADRIC, Temporary Cadet 23/2/1921; Platoon Commander, Royal Ulster Special Constabulary, 1921; Assistant Commissioner of Police, Gold Coast, January 1925; Commissioner of Police Gold Coast, 1933; Commissioner of Police and Commandant Defence Force, Fiji, 1937; Commissioner of Police Northern Rhodesia, 12/4/1947; retired August 1951; died 13/9/1975.

Worsley, Robert Lewkenor; RIC 79136; ADRIC CADET no. 770; LDS 2099/043; born 1894, Brackley, Northampton, England; (Brackley Registrar's District, 1894, March Quarter, vol. 3b, p. 4); lieutenant, army 1914–19; ADRIC, 18/10/1920–25/8/1921; 3rd DI 20/9/1921; pensioned 19/3/1922; joined the Palestine Police on 20/3/1922; (WO 374/78913).

Worsnop, Francis Edgar; RIC 72228; ADRIC CADET no. 64; LDS 2098/227B; born 23/5/1890, Natal, India; lieutenant, Royal Navy; 3rd DI 12/1/1920; dismissed 29/8/1921.

266

267

266 Family vault (in foreground) of Major Sir Richard Willcocks, Chief Magistrate, Peace Preservation Force, 1814–22 and Inspector General for Munster, 1822–27, St Laurence Church of Ireland Cemetery, Chapelizod, Dublin. 267 William Harding Wilson, grave in Templemore, Co. Tipperary. 268 John Workman, Commissioner of Police Northern Rhodesia, 1947. 269 George Hill Wray.

268

269

Wray, George Hill; LDS 2097/219; born 1834, King's County; joined the Irish Revenue Police as a lieutenant in 1854; 3rd SI 18/5/1858; CI 1/3/1879; pensioned 18/3/1886; died 19/7/1886, at Ballynahinch, Co. Down.

Wray, Henry William; LDS 2097/066; born 1804, Convoy, Co. Donegal; wife a native of Co. Cavan; his daughter, Mary Mabel Wray, aged 15 years died on 18/3/1855 at Queenstown, Co. Cork (*Cork Examiner* 23/3/1855); 3rd SI 1/1/1827; CI 1/5/1851; died 28/3/1866 at Julia Mount, Wexford, Co. Wexford; administration with will annexed granted at the Principal Registry on 7/5/1866 to Elizabeth Jane Wray, of Sidmonton Road, Bray, Co. Wicklow, widow and residuary legatee – effects under £800.

Wray, Hugh Boyd; LDS 2097/026; born 1794, King's County; ensign, 40th Regiment of Foot, 1/1/1811; lieutenant, 10/9/1812; lieutenant half pay, 1817; veteran of the Battle of Vittoria, Pyrenees and Waterloo; 3rd SI 10/5/1821; tried and acquitted of murder at Kilkenny Assizes, August, 1822, after which he was transferred to Queen's County; married 10/5/1823, Rathdowney, Queen's County; son Jackson Wray, born 22/3/1824; CI 1/2/1824; JP, 1/1/1832; resident magistrate 17/2/1848; retired as a RM in 1848; died 23/2/1873 at 4, Clifton Place, Monkstown, Co. Dublin; buried in Deansgrange Cemetery, Dublin (South Section, Row M, Grave No. 19) with his son Jackson Wray; will proved on 21/4/1873 at the Principal Registry by the oath of Nicholas Biddulph, Congor House, Borrisokane, Co. Tipperary and Charles Sibthorpe, 36, Upper Leeson Street, Dublin, the executors – effects under £2,000; (WO 25/767 fol. 99); C.C. Borris-in-Ossory.

Wray, John; CarNB; born Co. Donegal; on 11/5/1825 he applied for a month's leave to arrange family affairs in Co. Donegal but was refused; C.C. Swanlinbar, Co. Cavan.

Wray, William; LDS 2097/175; born 1802, Co. Meath; enlisted as a sub constable on 28/10/1823; his son, John Thomas, aged 15 years died on 16/6/1853 at Rathfriland, Co. Down (*Cork Examiner* 24/6/1853); 3rd SI 11/8/1843; died 5/6/1862 in Co. Down.

Wright, Bernard; LDS 2099/054; born 19/10/1899, Co. Cavan; enlisted in Royal Artillery, lieutenant, Royal Artillery, 17/9/1917–5/11/1919; 3rd DI 8/1/1921; pensioned 22/7/1922.

Wright, George; LDS 2097/109; born 1794, Waterford City; high constable, Waterford City Corporation from 1/7/1813 to 12/1/1837; 3rd SI 13/1/1837; died 29/3/1852 in Co. Galway.

Wright, James Browne; RIC 52506; LDS 2098/033; born 1861, son of Samuel Wright, JP, land agent, Newbliss, Co. Monaghan; married on 28/9/1897 (Belfast Registrar's District, September Quarter, 1897, vol. 1, p. 307), Zara, daughter of Trevor Corry, of Bellmont, Newry, Co. Down; educated at Trinity College, Dublin, BA (Hons.) and LLB 1881, Trinity College Dublin; Honorary LLD in 1906, TCD; 3rd DI 1/1/1888; resigned 2/2/1899 on his appointment as Chief Constable of Newcastle-upon-Tyne City Police to July 1925; Mobilizing Officer of Fire Brigades, N.E. Area, 1917–25; Member of the Commission on Irish Police Pay, 1919; Member of the Police Council, 1920–2; King's Police Medal and King's Coronation Medal; died 20/6/1926 at 1, Park Terrace, Newcastle-upon-Tyne, late of 3, Camp Terrace, North Shields; (Newcastle-upon-Tyne Registrar's District, June Quarter, 1926, vol. 1b, p. 175); probate granted to Zara Wright, widow, Frederick Edwin Foster, solicitor and the Rev. John Hamill McConachie, clerk – effects, £5,229.5s.10d.; (photo in the *Constabulary Gazette*, vol. IV, no. 17, 21/1/1899).

Wright, John; LDS 2097/056; born 1784, Tedavnet, Co. Monaghan; son-in-law of Chief Constable William Hunt (d.1830); baronial chief constable from March 1819 to March 1820; surgeon 88th Regiment of Foot (Connaught Rangers); widower with one son and three daughters on appointment; 3rd SI 1/10/1824; died 22/1/1842.

Wright, John; LDS 2097/025; born 1783; PPF; PPF Clerk 29/7/1817; 3rd SI 1/10/1817; pensioned 1/3/1839; died in 1853. (Will probated on 2/7/1853 in the Down & Connor Diocese, NA Reference: Down & Connor Will & Grant Book/6994); C.C. Carthage, Moville, Co. Donegal, 1824 and barony of Banagh, Mountcharles, Co. Donegal.

270   271

270 James Brown Wright, 1897. 271 Sketch of James Brown Wright, Chief Constable, Newcastle-on-Tyne, 1899. 272 Edward Melville Phillips Wynne, Private Secretary to the Inspector General, 1900. 273 Owen Wynne.

273

272

Wright, Meade N.; LDS 2097/054; born 1796, Co. Kilkenny; private and non-commissioned officer in the army from 1/6/1813 to 20/12/1820; enlisted as a constable, 1/7/1822; 3rd SI 10/8/1824; C.C. Antrim, Co. Antrim; pensioned 1/10/1848; died in 1853.

Wright, Neptune Blood; LDS 2097/085; born 1817, Co. Monaghan; 3rd SI 24/7/1834; dismissed 14/4/1840.

Wright, Robert W.; LDS 2097/031; born 1782, Co. Kilkenny; 3rd SI 13/12/1822; died 20/4/1844.

Wynne, Edward Melville Philips; RIC 50740; LDS 2097/326; born 24/3/1859, Shoeburyness, Essex, England; (Rochford Registrar's District, 1859, June Quarter, vol. 4a, p. 188); spent three years in Stafford Militia; educated at Eton and Oxford, passed the responsor's and moderators examinations; 3rd DI 15/12/1882; Queen Victoria's Visit to Ireland Medal, 1900; Private Secretary to the Inspector General from 29/9/1898 until his appointment as a resident magistrate 3rd class 1/5/1903, 2nd class 8/2/1909, 1st class 27/3/1920; pensioned 1/1/1921; (p. 125, RM Records of Service Book, National Archives, Dublin).

Wynne, John; LDS 2097/033; born 1773, Cairy, Co. Sligo; major in the army from 8/7/1794 to 30/3/1817; 3rd SI 23/1/1823; C.C. Skull, Co. Cork; pensioned 1/1/1840; died 1846.

Wynne, Owen; RIC 46828; LDS 2097/311; born 1857, Middlesex, England; youngest son of James Wynne, BL; 3rd SI 10/5/1881; died 23/10/1898 in England; buried in Mount Jerome Cemetery, Dublin on 26/10/1898; (Grave No. C112–5021).

Wynne, Samuel Richard; RIC 57234; LDS 2098/228B; born 30/10/1876, Tralee, Co. Kerry; (Tralee Registrar's District, 1876, vol. 20, p. 623); 3rd DI 1/1/1921; pensioned 4/6/1922.

Wyse, Thomas; LDS 2097/157; born 1823, Rathculliheen, Co. Wexford; third son of Francis Wyse and Mary Catherine Scally, who died on 7/1/1865 (Midleton Registrar's District, vol. 4, p. 634), aged 68 years at Lakeview, Midleton, Co. Cork (*Cork Examiner* 10/1/1865); 3rd SI 20/4/1847; CI 20/9/1870; married on 23/4/1857, at the Cathedral, Marlborough Street, Dublin, his second cousin, Frances 'Fanny' Maria Wyse (d.6/1/1870, aged 38 years, at Youghal, Co. Cork (Youghal Registrar's District, vol. 4, p. 791), following the birth of an infant son, John Edward Wyse (Youghal Registrar's District, vol. 4, p. 1096) on 1/1/1870 and who died (Youghal Registrar's District, vol. 4, p. 792) on 10/1/1870 – *Cork Examiner* 13/1/1870), daughter of Francis Wyse, of Rathculliheen, Co. Waterford; his paternal first cousins were George Wyse, born 1793 who died at Bray, Co. Wicklow on 4/11/1867 (Rathdown Registrar's District, vol. 17, p. 663) (*Cork Examiner* 6/11/1867), of 22, Upper Leeson Street, Dublin, barrister-at-law and Senior Dublin Police Magistrate, former officer with the 6th Regiment of Foot (1st Warwickshire Regiment) and Sir Thomas Wyse (9/12/1791–16/4/1862), KCB, British Ambassador to Athens, who married on 4/3/1821, Letitia Christine Bonaparte (11/12/1804–15/3/1871), daughter of Lucien Bonaparte (21/5/1775–29/6/1840), Prince of Canino, by his second wife whom he married in 1802, Alexandrine de Bluchampe (11/12/1804–15/3/1871) and brother of Napoleon I Bonaparte (15/8/1769–5/5/1821), Emperor of the French; Thomas and Frances Wyse had seven children; daughter born on 24/1/1862 at Riverstown House, Newtownbarry, Co. Wexford (*Cork Examiner* 28/1/1862); Thomas Wyse drowned in a lake at Loughrea, Co. Galway, 7/4/1878; administration granted on 24/5/1878 at Tuam to his sister, Mary Hore, widow of Richard Hore, the curatrix of the minor children of said deceased – effects under £300.

Y

Yates, Henry Edmund Wingfield; RIC 48491; LDS 2097/318; born 1858, Colney, Herts., England; father of Lionel Westropp Peel Yates, CI, RIC; residing at The Vicarage House, St Albans, St Peter, Hertfordshire in 1881 (Census); married on 14/3/1886 (Tullamore Registrar's District, March Quarter, 1886, vol. 3, p. 559); 3rd SI 17/3/1882; King Edward VII Visit to Ireland Medal, 1903; CI 10/10/1903; King George V Coronation Medal, 1911; awarded in 1919, the King's Police Medal, 1909; pensioned 15/6/1920; (photo in the *Constabulary Gazette*, vol. XII, no. 19, 31/1/1903).

Yates, Lionel Westropp Peel; RIC 64529; LDS 2098/241; born 29/5/1888, Kanturk, Co. Cork; (Kanturk Registrar's District, June Quarter, 1888, vol. 5, p. 239); son of Henry Edmund Wingfield Yates, CI, RIC; educated at Cranleigh School and Trinity College Dublin; lieutenant, 6th (Service) Battalion Royal Inniskilling Fusiliers, 30/10/1914; prisoner of war, 21/3/1918 in the village of Ronssoy; repatriated, 9/12/1918; major, 20/1/1919; released from military duties, 20/3/1919 and permitted to retain the rank of major; 3rd SI 6/2/1909; TCI 19/11/1920; pensioned 13/7/1922; co-author with Honor Goodhard of *The Eclipse of James Trent DI* (London, 1924); Chief Constable of Dorset County Constabulary from 19 April 1924 to 28 February 1955; (WO 339/11956).

Yeates, William Henry; RIC 45468; LDS 2097/309; born 1859, Co. Dublin; teacher; 3rd SI 1/12/1880; King Edward VII Visit to Ireland Medal, 1903; pensioned 30/6/1919.

Yeldham, Charles Cecil; RIC 54174; LDS 2098/063; born 1863, Ipswich, Suffolk, England; (Ipswich Registrar's District, 1863, December Quarter, vol. 4a, p. 555); he worked with the Electric Sun Lamp Company for one and a half years and spent two months in a metal broker's office (Morris and Kenewick, London); 3rd DI 21/5/1890; Queen Victoria's Visit to Ireland Medal, 1900; King Edward VII Visit to Ireland Medal, 1903; CI 11/9/1912; pensioned 5/7/1920; Co-founder of the Irish Automobile Club on 22 January 1901, at the Metropole Hotel, Sackville Street (O'Connell Street), Dublin; his wife, Kate Frances died at Rock Cottage, Sixmilebridge, Co. Clare on 11/4/1897; (photo in the *Constabulary Gazette*, vol. IV, no. 19, 4/2/1899).

Young, Francis Smyth; LDS 2097/047; born 1790, Co. Cavan; ensign and lieutenant in the army from 31/7/1809; 3rd SI 1/11/1823; received an injury to his right shoulder when thrown from a jig when on duty on 27/8/1834; pensioned 31/8/1847; died on 27/5/1852 at Bagenalstown, Co. Carlow (*Cork Examiner* 4/6/1852).

Young, George Edward Saville; LDS 2098/225; born 20/1/1884, Thame, Oxon., England; (Thame Registrar's District, 1884, March Quarter, vol. 1d, p. 857); son of Rev. Henry Saville Young and Rebecca Isabel Young, of Mallard's Court, Stokenchurch, High Wycombe; married Alison Jane Young, of Chelsworth Cottage, Warley, Essex; 3rd DI 4/7/1908; major, 2nd Battalion Irish Guards on 12/10/1914 and later major, 1st Battalion Irish Guards; killed 31/3/1917, Somme, France; buried in Grove Town Cemetery, Meaulte, Somme (Grave III.A.2).

Young, J.J.; LDS 2097/151; born 1815, Dublin; wife a native of Co. Dublin; 3rd SI 10/12/1845; died 1/1/1856 in Co. Wexford.

Young, Joseph; RIC 52507; LDS 2098/113B; born 9/8/1867, Borrisokane, Co. Tipperary; (Borrisokane Registrar's District, 1867, vol. 13, p. 428); 3rd DI 14/5/1920; pensioned 31/8/1922.

Young, William; LDS 2097/259; born 1823, Co. Tyrone; wife from Co. Dublin; 3rd DI 1/9/1866; pensioned 1/10/1882.

Appendices

APPENDIX 1: STATISTICAL TABLES CONCERNING OFFICERS WHO
SERVED IN THE PEACE PRESERVATION FORCE, THE COUNTY
CONSTABULARY, THE IRISH CONSTABULARY AND THE ROYAL IRISH
CONSTABULARY BETWEEN 1814 AND 1922

The tables cover all those 1,700 officers who served in the Peace Preservation Force, the County Constabulary (1822–1836), the Irish Constabulary (1836–1867), and the Royal Irish Constabulary (1867–1922) whose names have been found as officers in the records of the former State Paper Office, Dublin Castle, the Chief Secretary's Office Registered Papers in the National Archives, Dublin and those whose names appear on the officers register of service in the Home Office Series in the Public Record Office, Kew, Richmond Surrey, arranged alphabetically by personal name.

The officers found in the State Papers in the old State Paper Office, Dublin Castle and identified by Patrick Carroll were 169 officers of the Peace Preservation Force and County Constabulary, who had left the constabulary prior to the formation of the Irish Constabulary in 1836. The officers found and identified in the Home Office Series, at the Public Record Office, Kew, Richmond, Surrey amounted to 937 officers and in HO.184/45 Vol. 1 (31/1/1817–14/3/1884); 491 officers in HO/184/46 Vol. 2 (14/3/1884–22/12/1908) & HO/184/46 Vol. 3 (19/3/1909–1/4/1921) and 56 officers in HO/184/48 Vol. 4 (1/4/1921–17/9/1921). The remaining 47 officers were appointed direct by government.

Of the 1,700 officers found, 1245 were identified as being Irish-born, 225 were non-Irish and the country of birth of the remaining 230 is unknown.

Table A illustrates the numbers per native county of Irish-born officers of the RIC.

Table B illustrates the numbers per native country of foreign-born officers of the RIC.

Table C illustrates the numbers of officers of the RIC who were killed on duty between 1816 and 1922.

Table D illustrates the numbers of officers of the RIC who volunteered for service in the British Army, were killed or wounded and or rejoined the RIC during World War One.

Table E illustrates the numbers of officers of the RIC who were awarded the Constabulary Medal for gallantry between 1842 and 1922.

Table F illustrates the numbers of officers who were awarded the King's Police Medal between 1909 and 1922 for distinguished service.

Table G illustrates the numbers of officers by ranks who were awarded the Queen Victoria Visit to Ireland Medal, 1900.

Table H illustrates the numbers of officers by ranks who were awarded the King Edward VII Visit to Ireland Medal, 1903.

Table I illustrates the numbers of officers by ranks who were awarded the King George V Visit to Ireland Medal, 1911.

Table J illustrates the numbers of officers by ranks who were awarded the King George V Coronation Medal, 1911.

Table K illustrates the number of Officers of the Royal Irish Constabulary who were killed or wounded during the Irish War of Independence

Table A: Native county of Irish-born officers of the (Royal) Irish Constabulary, 1816–1922

County	Number	County	Number
Antrim	41	Londonderry	24
Armagh	25	Longford	24
Carlow	14	Louth	22
Cavan	37	Mayo	43
Clare	52	Meath	20
Cork	98	Monaghan	35
Donegal	19	Queen's (Laois)	28
Down	23	Roscommon	46
Dublin	124	Sligo	45
Fermanagh	31	Tipperary	63
Galway	68	Tyrone	28
Kerry	49	Waterford	22
Kildare	21	Westmeath	28
Kilkenny	36	Wexford	23
King's (Offaly)	42	Wicklow	27
Leitrim	25		
Limerick	62	Total	1245

Table B: Native country of foreign-born officers of the (Royal) Irish Constabulary, 1816–1922

Country	Number	Country	Number
Africa	1	India	9
Australia	1	Isle of Man	1
Austria	1	Malta	2
Belgium	1	Prussia	1
Bermuda	1	Scotland	21
British Guiana	1	Singapore	1
Canada	6	Spain	1
China	1	United States	2
England	164	Wales	6
France	4	Total	225

Table C: Officers of the (Royal) Irish Constabulary who were killed on duty between 1816 and 1922

Year	Number	Year	Number
1821	1	1908	1
1827	1	1913	1
1831	1	1915	1
1845	1	1916	5
1850	2	1917	1
1853	1	1918	1
1854	2	1919	2
1855	2	1920	10
1878	1	1921	13
1880	1	1922	1
1889	1	Total	50

Table D: Officers of the Royal Irish Constabulary who volunteered for service in the British Army, were killed or wounded and or rejoined the RIC during World War One

Year	Enlisted	Killed	Wounded	Rejoined	Not Rejoin
1914	–	–	–	–	–
1915	–	I	I	–	–
1916	–	3	3	–	I
1917	–	I	3	I	I
1918	–	I	2	5	I
1919	–	–	–	19	–
1920	–	–	–	I	–
Total	35	6	9	26	3

1 CI + 33 DIs enlisted and William Alfred Smith ex-DI

3 wounded in the 1916 Rising,
3 wounded in 1919
2 wounded in 1920
1 wounded in 1922

Table E: Officers of the Royal Irish Constabulary who were awarded the Constabulary Medal between 1842 and 1922

Year	Numbers of Medals
1848	2
1867	3
1916	I
1917	I
1920	I
1921	2
1922	I
Total	11

Table F: Officers of the Royal Irish Constabulary who were awarded the King's Police Medal between 1909 and 1922

Year	Numbers of Medals	Year	Number of Medals
1909	I	1917	2
1910	I	1918	–
1911	–	1919	3
1912	I	1920	I
1913	I	1921	4
1914	I	1922	3
1915	–		
1916	–	Total	18

Table G: Total number of officers of the RIC who were awarded the Queen Victoria Visit to Ireland Medal, 1900

Rank	Number of Medals
DIG	1
AIG	1
Surgeon	1
Veterinary Surgeon	1
CI	3
DI	19
Cadet	5
Total	31

Table H: Total number of officers of the RIC who were awarded the King Edward VII Visit to Ireland Medal, 1903

Rank	Number of Medals
IG	1
DIG	1
AIG	3
Surgeon	1
Veterinary Surgeon	1
CI	15
DI	115
Cadet	4
Total	141

Table I: Total number of officers of the RIC who were awarded the King George V Visit to Ireland Medal, 1911

Rank	Number of Medals
AIG	1
Surgeon	1
Veterinary Surgeon	1
CI	5
DI	22
Cadet	–
Total	30

Table J: Total number of officers of the RIC who were awarded the King George V Coronation Medal, 1911

Rank	Number of Medals
IG	1
AIG	–
Surgeon	–
Veterinary Surgeon	–

CI	23
DI	8
Cadet	–
Total	32

Table K: Officers of the Royal Irish Constabulary who were killed or wounded during the Irish War of Independence

Year	Killed	Wounded
1919	2	–
1920	10	3
1921	13	2
1922	1	1
Total	26	6

Names of wounded officers

1920 = Albert Augustine Roberts; Philip Valentine McDonagh; Michael Fallon.
1921 = William Herbert King; Frederick George Lancaster.
1922 = Hubert Leslie Baynham

APPENDIX 2   RIC OFFICERS ROLL OF HONOUR

MAJOR RICHARD GOING
Chief Police Magistrate
Peace Preservation Force
Born 1769, Co. Tipperary
Killed 14 October 1821.
Curraheen Cross, Co. Tipperary.

JAMES WOLFE McNEALE
Chief Constable
Irish Constabulary
Born, Carlingford, Co. Louth.
Severely wounded 24 June 1826
Monaghan, Co. Monaghan
Died of wounds January 1827.

JAMES GIBBONS
Chief Constable
Irish Constabulary
Killed 14 December 1831.
Carrickshock, Co. Kilkenny.

CAPTAIN JOHN MacLEOD RM
Resident Magistrate
Ex-County Inspector, Irish Constabulary
Born 1791
Killed 29 January 1845.
Garradice, Ballinamore, Co. Leitrim

THOMAS RENNISON
Sub Inspector
Irish Constabulary
Born 1807, Kildimo, Co. Limerick
Died 4 March 1850

THOMAS THORNLEY
Lieutenant Sub Inspector
Irish Constabulary
Born 1797, Lancashire, England
Severely wounded 12 December 1849
Cushendall, Co. Antrim
Died of wounds 30 April 1850

GEORGE DU BOURDIEU
2nd Class Sub Inspector
Irish Constabulary
Born 1826, Portsmouth, England
Killed 3 August 1854
Crimea

THOMAS C. ANDERSON
2nd Class Sub Inspector
Irish Constabulary
Born 1823, Co. Kildare
Killed 11 August 1854
Crimea

JOHN FITZGERALD STUDDERT
3rd Class Sub Inspector 12831
Irish Constabulary
Born 1828, Co. Clare
Killed 7 February 1855
Crimea

WILLIAM PETER COPPINGER
2nd Class Sub Inspector
Irish Constabulary
Born 1826, Co. Wexford
Killed 11 August 1855
Crimea

THOMAS WYSE
County Inspector
Royal Irish Constabulary
Born 1823, Rathculliheen, Co. Wexford
Drowned 7 April 1878
Loughrea, Co. Galway

SAMUEL BOYCE
Sub Inspector
Royal Irish Constabulary
Born 1839, Brooke-Hill, Coleraine, Co. Derry
Killed 23 June 1880
Waringstown, Co. Down

WILLIAM LIMERICK MARTIN
District Inspector
Royal Irish Constabulary
Born 1845, Co. Clare
Killed 3 February 1889
Derrybeg, Gweedore, Co. Donegal.

FRANK MICHAEL FEELY
District Inspector
Royal Irish Constabulary
Born 1865, Co. Cork
Injured 30 December 1907
Died 11 January 1908
Stapleton Place, Dundalk, Co. Louth

OSWALD ALEXANDER CAMERON
District Inspector
Royal Irish Constabulary
Born 17 November 1890, Middlesex, England
Killed 17 February 1913
Sligo, Co. Sligo

CAPTAIN EDWARD GRAHAM MYLNE
1st Battalion, Irish Guards
District Inspector 61505
Royal Irish Constabulary
Born 19 January 1883, Bombay, India
Killed 12 June 1915
Rouen, France.

CAPTAIN OSBOURNE GEORGE DE COURCY BALDWIN
'C' Coy, 8th Battalion, Royal Munster Fusiliers
District Inspector 65959
Royal Irish Constabulary
Born 4 April 1885, Yorkshire, England
Killed 26 January 1916
Pas de Calais, France.

CAPTAIN VALENTINE CHARLES JOSEPH BLAKE
1st Battalion, Irish Guards
District Inspector 63671
Royal Irish Constabulary
Born 17 December 1885, Co. Mayo
Killed 28 January 1916
Pas de Calais, France.

HARRY SMYTH
District Inspector 59040
Royal Irish Constabulary
Born 1874, Hertfordshire, England
Killed 28 April 1916
Ashbourne, Co. Meath.

ALEXANDER GRAY
County Inspector
Royal Irish Constabulary
Born 1858, Co. Tyrone
Wounded 28 April 1916
Ashbourne, Co. Meath.
Died of wounds 10 May 1916

LIEUTENANT-COLONEL WILLIAM SCUDEMORE ALFRED SMITH
Ex-District Inspector
Royal Irish Constabulary
Born 19 March 1880, Gatertop, Herefordshire, England
Killed 9 July 1916
Somme, France.

CAPTAIN GEORGE EDWARD SAVILLE YOUNG
1st Battalion, Irish Guards
District Inspector
Royal Irish Constabulary
Born 20 January 1884, Oxfordshire, England
Killed 31 March 1917
Somme, France.

CAPTAIN ROBERT PETER VILLAR
18th (Lancashire Hussars) Battalion, The King's (Liverpool Regiment)
District Inspector
Royal Irish Constabulary
Born 16 June 1887, Somerset, England.
Killed 22 March 1918
Somme, France.

JOHN CHARLES MILLING RM
Resident Magistrate
Ex-District Inspector 56627
Royal Irish Constabulary
Born 27 March 1873, Co. Westmeath
Wounded 29 March 1919
Westport, Co. Mayo.
Died of wounds 30 March 1919

MICHAEL HUNT
District Inspector 55727
Royal Irish Constabulary
Born 3 September 1873, Co. Sligo
Killed 23 June 1919
Thurles, Co. Tipperary.

WILLIAM CHARLES FORBES REDMOND
Second Assistant Commissioner, Dublin Metropolitan Police
Ex-District Inspector 57951
Royal Irish Constabulary
Born 1873, Co. Armagh
Killed 21 January 1920
Harcourt Street, Dublin.

ALAN BELL RM
Resident Magistrate
Ex-District Inspector 44799
Royal Irish Constabulary
Born 8 August 1857, Banagher, Co. Offaly
Killed 26 March 1920
Merrion, Dublin.

PERCIVAL SAMUEL LEA-WILSON
District Inspector 65448
Royal Irish Constabulary
Born 22 April 1887, Kent, England
Killed 15 June 1920
Gorey, Co. Wexford.

BREVET LIEUTENANT-COLONEL GERARD BRYCE FERGUSON SMYTH DSO
Divisional Commissioner for Munster
Royal Irish Constabulary
Born 7 September 1885, Dalhouise, India
Killed 17 July 1920
Cork & County Club, Cork City.

WILLIAM HARDING WILSON
District Inspector 50239
Royal Irish Constabulary
Born 1864, Co. Offaly
Killed 16 August 1920
Main Street, Templemore, Co. Tipperary.

OSWALD ROSS SWANZY
District Inspector 61367
Royal Irish Constabulary
Born 15 July 1881, Co. Monaghan
Killed 22 August 1920
Christchurch Cathedral, Lisburn, Co. Antrim.

JAMES JOSEPH MARY BRADY
District Inspector 70381
Royal Irish Constabulary
Born 9 October 1898, Co. Dublin
Killed 30 September 1920
Chafpool, Co. Sligo.

PHILIP ST JOHN HOWLETT KELLEHER
District Inspector
Royal Irish Constabulary
Born 1 July 1897, Macroom, Co. Cork
Killed 31 October 1920
Granard, Co. Longford.

FRANCIS WILLIAM CRAKE
District Inspector 72473
Royal Irish Constabulary
Born 19 April 1893, Northumberland, England
Killed 28 November 1920
Kilmichael, Co. Cork.

PHILIP JOHN O'SULLIVAN
District Inspector 72019
Royal Irish Constabulary
Born 6 August 1897, Kinsale, Co. Cork
Killed 17 December 1920
Henry Street, Dublin.

THOMAS JAMES MCGRATH
MM District Inspector 65788
Royal Irish Constabulary
Born 30 August 1890, Co. Limerick
Killed 7 January 1921
Ballinalee, Co. Longford.

TOBIAS O'SULLIVAN
District Inspector 59193
Royal Irish Constabulary
Born 1877, Co. Galway
Killed 20 January 1921
Listowel, Co. Kerry.

WILLIAM CLARKE
District Inspector 72020
Royal Irish Constabulary
Born 2 August 1892, Co. Armagh
Killed 20 January 1921
Glenwood, Co. Clare.

PHILIP ARMSTRONG HOLMES
Divisional Commissioner 58074
Royal Irish Constabulary
Born 1876, Co. Cork
Wounded on 28 January 1921
Toureengarriv, Co. Cork.
Died of wounds 29 January 1921

FRANCIS WORTHINGTON CRAVEN DSO DSC DSM
District Inspector 80043
Royal Irish Constabulary
Born 29 February 1898, Barrow-in-Furness, Cumbria, England
Killed 2 February 1921
Ballinalee, Co. Longford.

MAJOR JAMES SEAFIELD-GRANT MC
Commandant 79885, ADRIC 1179
Auxiliary Division, Royal Irish Constabulary
Born 1891, Adeburgh, Suffolk, England
Killed 25 February 1921
Coolavorig, Ballyvourney, Co. Cork.

MAJOR JOHN ALISTER MACKINNON MC DCM MM
ADRIC Cadet 917
Auxiliary Division, Royal Irish Constabulary
Born 1889
Tralee, Co. Kerry
Killed 15 April 1921

MICHAEL JOSEPH CAHILL
District Inspector 72022
Royal Irish Constabulary
Born 16 August 1895, Co. Tipperary
Killed 23 April 1921
Swords, Co. Dublin.

GILBERT NORMAN POTTER
District Inspector 59414
Royal Irish Constabulary
Born 10 July 1878, Dromahair, Co. Leitrim
Killed 27 April 1921
Clogheen, Co. Tipperary.

HARRY BIGGS
District Inspector 76116
Royal Irish Constabulary
Born 20 June 1894, Hampshire, England
Killed 14 May 1921
Coolboreen, Co. Tipperary.

CECIL ARTHUR MAURICE BLAKE
District Inspector 76106
Royal Irish Constabulary
Born 20 February 1885, Hampshire, England
Killed 15 May 1921
Ballyturin House, Gort, Co. Galway.

MICHAEL FRANCIS MCCAUGHEY
District Inspector 67290
Royal Irish Constabulary
Born 19 December 1892, Co. Down
Killed 1 June 1921
Castlemaine, Co. Kerry.

EDWARD JAMES P. STEVENSON
District Inspector 72024
Royal Irish Constabulary
Born 7 July 1898, Belfast, Co. Antrim
Killed 2 June 1921
Carrowkennedy, Co. Mayo

CYRIL ROBERT MASON
District Inspector 77809
Royal Irish Constabulary
Born 25 October 1895, Cheshire, England
Killed 16 June 1921
Wexford, Co. Wexford.

MICHAEL KEANY
District Inspector 53643
Royal Irish Constabulary
Born 24 September 1867, Curracloona, Manor Hamilton, Co. Leitrim
Killed 11 February 1922
Clonakilty, Co. Cork.

APPENDIX 3: INSPECTORS–GENERAL OF THE
*ROYAL IRISH CONSTABULARY, 1836–1922

Lieutenant-General James Shaw Kennedy	1 June 1836
Major George Warburton	15 Mar. 1838
General Sir Duncan McGregor	1 July 1838
Sir Henry John Brownrigg	19 Oct. 1838
Colonel Sir John Stewart Wood	8 May 1865
Lieutenant-Colonel George Edward Hillier	19 Sept. 1876
Colonel Robert Bruce	12 May 1882
Sir Andrew Reed	21 Sept. 1885
Colonel Sir Neville Francis F. Chamberlain	1 Sept. 1900
Brigadier-General Sir Joseph A. Byrne	1 Aug. 1916
Sir Thomas James Smith	11 Mar. 1920
Major-General Sir Henry Hugh Tudor	15 May 1920

*Irish Constabulary consolidated under 6th William IV, cap.13 and renamed the Royal Irish Constabulary in September 1867. 1 Inspector General, 1 Deputy Inspector General and 2 Assistant Inspector Generals under 22nd & 23rd, Victoria, cap.22.

APPENDIX 4: DEPUTY INSPECTORS–GENERAL OF THE
*ROYAL IRISH CONSTABULARY, 1836–1922

Major George Warburton	1 June 1836	15 Mar. 1838	(IG)
Colonel William Miller	1 June 1836	9 June 1848	(Pens.)
Major Edward Jonathan Priestley	11 June 1836	4 Dec. 1857	(Pens.)
Colonel Stephen Holmes, K.H.	15 Mar. 1838	1 July 1838	(Pens.)
Major John Gallwey	1 July 1839	3 Mar. 1845	(Died)
Lieutenant Henry John Brownrigg	9 June 1848	19 Oct. 1858	(IG)
Lieutenant-Colonel John Cramer Roberts	4 Dec. 1857	13 Mar. 1864	(Died)
Lieutenant-Colonel George Ashley Maude	19 Oct. 1858	7 Aug. 1860	(Pens.)
Major John Stewart Wood	7 Aug. 1860	8 May 1865	(IG)
Major Thomas Esmonde VC	8 May 1865	30 July 1867	(Gratuity)
Lieutenant-Colonel George Edward Hillier	30 July 1867	19 Sept. 1876	(IG)

Rowland Francis Nichol Fanning	16 Nov. 1876	11 Nov. 1886	(Pens.)
Colonel Robert Bruce	1 Jan. 1877	12 May 1882	(IG)
Henry Thynne	30 Nov. 1886	10 Dec. 1915	(Died)
Heffernan Fritz James Jos. John Considine	18 Apr. 1900	8 Nov. 1911	(Pens.)
William Arthur O'Connell	9 Nov. 1911	15 Dec.1916	(Pens.)
William Moorehouse Davies	15 Dec. 1916	13 Mar. 1920	(Pens.)
Charles Arthur Walsh	13 Mar. 1920	31 Aug. 1922	(Pens.)

APPENDIX 5: ASSISTANT INSPECTORS–GENERAL OF THE *ROYAL IRISH CONSTABULARY, 1836–1922

Edward Jonathan Priestley (DIG 9 Jan. 1845)	11 June 1836	11 June 1842	(RM11 June 1842)
John Cramer Roberts	11 June 1836	4 Dec. 1857	(DIG)
Henry John Brownrigg	1 Sept. 1838	9 June 1848	(DIG)
Henry Walker Thompson	9 June 1848	1 Mar. 1863	(Pens.)
Francis Percy	1 Jan. 1857	1 Jan. 1860	(Pens.)
Thomas Esmonde VC	24 Nov. 1859	8 May 1865	(DIG)
George Edward Hillier	1 Jan. 1860	30 July 1867	(DIG)
Shuldham Pooley Crawford	1 Jan. 1863	26 Nov. 1873	(Pens.)
John Duncan	30 July 1867	1 Oct. 1882	(Pens.)
John Manby Colegrave	11 Feb. 1869	17 Jan. 1880	(RM)
William Rickard Burke	8 Apr. 1872	16 Nov. 1876	(Pens.)
Rowland Francis Nichol Fanning	16 Nov. 1876	14 Sept. 1882	(DIG)
Wellington Colomb	16 Oct. 1877	10 Sept. 1891	(Pens.)
Andrew Reed	14 Sept. 1882	21 Sept. 1885	(IG)
George Edward Newland	1 Sept. 1882	1 Oct. 1888	(Pens.)
Francis Nesbitt Cullen	20 Sept. 1885	2 Oct. 1889	(Died)
Edwin Grundy Pennington	1 Oct. 1888	27 June 1896	(Died)
Charles Ewen Allen Cameron	3 Oct. 1889	27 Apr.1901	(Pens.)
Thomas Whelan	10 Sept. 1891	1 Apr. 1902	(Pens.)
Thomas French Singleton	28 June 1896	15 Feb. 1905	(Pens.)
Samuel Abraham Walker Waters	27 Apr. 1901	22 Oct. 1906	(Pens.)
Alexander Gambell	1 Apr. 1902	16 Feb. 1905	(Pens.)
Sackville Berkley Hamilton	16 Feb. 1905	1 Apr. 1908	(Pens.)
William Reeves	22 Oct. 1906	23 Oct. 1909	(Pens.)
Frederick James Ball	1 Apr. 1908	26 Oct. 1909	(Pens.)
Henry Annesley Coxwell Rogers	26 Oct. 1909	15 Apr. 1911	(Died)
William Moorehouse Davies	17 Feb. 1910	15 Dec. 1916	(Pens.)
William Arthur O'Connell	19 Apr. 1911	9 Nov. 1911	(DIG)
Edward Humble Pearson	9 Nov. 1911	8 June 1920	(Pens.)
Henry Donati Tyacke	1 July 1912	1 Apr. 1920	(Pens.)
Robert Glover Cook Flower	30 Dec. 1916	15 Apr. 1920	(Pens.)
Albert Augustus Roberts	1 Apr. 1920	4 Oct. 1920	(Pens.)
Edward Myles Clayton	15 Apr. 1920	31 Aug. 1922	(Pens.)
Ivon Henry Price	1 Oct. 1920	8 June.1922	(Pens.).

APPENDIX 6: COMMISSIONERS OF POLICE AND TOWN INSPECTORS OF CONSTABULARY, BELFAST (1865–1922)

Belfast Police were disbanded under 28 & 29 Victoria, cap.70 & Londonderry Police disbanded under 33 & 34 Victoria, cap.83.

James Luttrel Bailey	1 Sept. 1865	1 Oct. 1882	(Pens.)
Francis Nesbitt Cullen	1 Oct. 1882	20 Sept. 1885	(AIG)
Thomas Peter Carr	25 Sept. 1885	15 Mar. 1887	(Pens.)
Charles Ewen Allen Cameron	15 Mar. 1887	3 Oct. 1889	(AIG)
Thomas French Singleton	3 Oct. 1889	28 June 1896	(AIG)
Thomas Moriarty	28 Sept. 1896	1 Dec. 1901	(Pens.)
Charles Western Leatham	1 Dec. 1901	1 Apr. 1906	(Pens.)
Hugh O'Halloran Hill	1 Apr. 1906	1 June 1909	(Pens.)
Thomas James Smith	1 June 1909	11 Mar. 1920	(IG)
John Fitzhugh Gelston	11 Mar. 1920	31 May 1922	(RUC)

Held the rank of RIC County Inspector.

APPENDIX 7: *COMMANDANTS OF THE RIC TRAINING DEPOT, PHOENIX PARK, DUBLIN, 1842–1922

*Capt., John Cramer Roberts	1 Nov. 1842	1 Jan. 1860	(DIG)
Lt. Col. George E. Hillier	1 Jan. 1860	1 Aug. 1867	(DIG)
John Duncan	1 Aug. 1867	1 Oct. 1882	(Pens.)
George Edward Newland	1 Oct. 1882	1 Oct. 1888	(Pens.)
Edwin Grundy Pennington	1 Oct. 1888	27 June 1896	(Died)
Thomas French Singleton	28 June 1896	1 Apr. 1902	(Pens. 1905)
Alexander Gambell	1 Apr. 1902	16 Feb. 1905	(Pens. 1910)
Sackville Berkley Hamilton	16 Feb. 1905	22 Oct. 1906	(Pens. 1908)
William Reeves	22 Oct. 1906	1 Apr. 1908	(Pens. 1909)
Frederick James Ball	1 Apr. 1908	26 Oct. 1909	(Pens. 1909)
Henry Annesley Coxwell Rogers	26 Oct. 1909	15 Apr. 1911	(Died)
William Arthur O'Connell	19 Apr. 1911	9 Nov. 1911	(DIG)
Edward Humble Pearson	9 Nov. 1911	24 Apr. 1920	(Pens.)
George Bennett Heard	24 Apr. 1920	17 May 1922	(CI)

*Held the rank of County Inspector from 1842 and Assistant Inspector General from 4 Dec. 1857

APPENDIX 8: *ADJUTANTS OF THE RIC TRAINING DEPOT, PHOENIX PARK, DUBLIN, 1842–1922

Thomas Fleming	1 June 1848	1 May 1854	(Temp. Appt.)
Richard Robert Fulton	1 May 1854	30 June 1855	(Pens 1 July 1886)
Thomas Marcus Brownrigg	30 June 1855	30 June 1862	(RM)
Neptune Blood Gallwey	1 July 1862	24 Jan. 1869	(CI)
John S. Watkins	1 Feb. 1869	15 Aug. 1870	(CI)
Arthur Curling	15 Aug. 1870	15 May 1872	(CI)

Wellington Colomb	15 May 1872	15 Oct. 1875	(CI)
Patrick James Bracken	15 Oct. 1875	10 Mar. 1885	(Pens.)
William George Williamson	10 Mar. 1885	10 Mar. 1891	(CI)
Robert Fitzwilliam Starkie	10 Mar. 1891	1 Sept. 1893	(P/Sec.) (RM 18 June 1893)
Richard Middleton Hill	1 Sept. 1893	28 Dec. 1896	(Chief Constable Cornwall)
Henry Annesley Coxwell Rogers	28 Dec. 1896	1 July 1899	(CI)
William Arthur O'Connell	1 July 1899	9 May 1901	(CI)
John Peter Byrne	9 May 1901	1 May 1903	(RM)
John M. Poer O'Shee	8 May 1903	1 Apr. 1907	(Adjt. Richmond Bks.) (Comdt Gormanston)
F.R. St Lawrence Tyrrell	17 Sept. 1907	10 Apr. 1907	(Temp.)
F.R. St Lawrence Tyrrell	8 May 1907	16 Oct. 1912	(CI)
Cyril Francis Fleming	16 Oct. 1912	16 May 1915	(WW1)
George Archiebald Morant	9 Dec. 1915	1 Nov. 1916	(Chief Police Instr.) (P/Sec.)
Robert Alfred Madden.	1 Nov. 1916	1 Aug. 1918	(CI)
Francis C. Burke	1 Aug. 1919	27 Apr. 1919	(RM)
Cyril Francis Fleming	27 Apr. 1919	15 June 1920	(CI)
Charles Frederick Fellowes Davies	15 June 1920	25 Sept. 1920	(Comdt. Gormanston) (RUC)
Victor Henry Scott	25 Sept. 1920	16 Nov. 1920	(TCI)
John Kearney Gorman	16 Nov. 1920	14 May 1922	(RUC)

APPENDIX 9: BARRACKMASTERS & STOREKEEPERS OF THE RIC TRAINING DEPOT, PHOENIX PARK, DUBLIN, 1842–1922

John Mason Pooley	1 Aug. 1841	8 Nov. 1850	(Resigned).
Depot Paymaster & Barrackmaster			
Henry Crawford, Constable 2907	1 July 1842	1 June 1850	
Assistant Store-keeper			
*John George Browne	1 May 1854	7 June 1865	(Died) nephew of DMP Commr. Browne.
*Depot Paymaster, Barrackmaster & Storekeeper			
James Moore Frith	8 June 1865	18 June 1880	(Pens.)
Michael Stephen Egan	23 June 1880	6 Mar. 1890	(Died)
Robert Murray Tilly	7 Mar. 1890	10 Aug. 1893	(Died)
Michael Hurley	11 Aug. 1893	1 Sept. 1900	(Pens.)
William de Rinzy Shoveller	1 Sept. 1900	7 Feb. 1910	(Pens.)
O'Neill Ferguson Kelly	7 Feb. 1910	1 Oct. 1919	(Pens.)
Alfred Valentine McClelland	1 Oct. 1919	31 Aug. 1922	(Pens.)
(Relative rank of County Inspector)			

APPENDIX 10: PRIVATE SECRETARIES TO THE INSPECTORS-GENERAL OF THE ROYAL IRISH CONSTABULARY, 1860–1922

Rodolphus Harvey	1 Jan. 1860	1 Jan. 1864	(RM 16 June 1872)
William Duffield Rooke	8 May 1865	22 Oct.1868	(Died)
Andrew Reed	1 Nov. 1868	21 July 1879	(IG)
William Frederick Hammersley Smith	12 Aug. 1879	11 Nov. 1880	(RM)
Andrew Monds Harper	3 Aug. 1882	24 Nov. 1885	(RM)
Michael Hurley	24 Nov. 1885	11 Aug. 1893	(Pens.)
Robert Fitzwilliam Starkie	1 Sept. 1893	18 June 1895	(RM)
Charles Paston Crane	18 June 1895	9 Sept. 1897	(RM)
William Vesey Harrel	9 Sept. 1897	29 Sept. 1898	(Inspector of Prisons)
Edward M.P. Wynne	29 Sept. 1898	6 May 1903	(RM)
John Edward St George	6 May 1903	5 Oct. 1908	(RM)
William Crawford Gore Moriarty	5 Oct. 1908	27 Jan. 1911	(RM)
George Hugh Mercer	27 Jan. 1911	28 Mar. 1918	(RM)
William Alexander Woods	28 Mar. 1918	29 July 1920	(RM)
John Charles Lionel Silcock	29 Mar. 1920	18 Dec. 1920	(RUC 1 June.1922)
George Archiebald Morant	18 Dec. 1920	8 Mar. 1921	
Reginald Tottenham	7 July 1921	18 July 1922	(Disbanded)

APPENDIX 11: SURGEONS APPOINTED TO THE ROYAL IRISH CONSTABULARY, 1839–1922

James Kerin	7 Nov. 1839	16 Mar. 1848	(died 1848).
George Melville Hatchell	16 Mar.1848	1 July 1857	
Eugene Le Clerc	1 July 1857	19 Apr. 1880	
Samuel Thomas Gordon	19 Apr. 1880	1 Aug. 1914	
Pryce Peacock	1 Aug. 1914	12 July 1922	
(Relative rank of County Inspector)			

APPENDIX 12: VETERINARY SURGEONS APPOINTED TO THE ROYAL IRISH CONSTABULARY, 1842–1916

Edward Dycer	18 Nov. 1842	23 May 1855
James John Farrell	23 May 1855	1 May 1870
John William Gloag	1 May 1870	1 Oct. 1886
DI James Vincent Daly	1 Oct. 1886	1 Dec. 1916
(Relative rank of County Inspector)		

APPENDIX 13: DETECTIVE DIRECTORS OF THE
ROYAL IRISH CONSTABULARY, 1869–1920

NB: When the divisional system was re-organized in October 1883 by E.G. Jenkinson, the Crime Department was divided into 'Ordinary' and 'Special' branches. The Crime Ordinary Branch handled all reports relating to outrages, the ordinary investigation of crime, the preservation of peace, illegal assemblies and personal protection. The Crime Special Department collected and transmitted all secret information and in very special cases assisted the local Constabulary in inquiries into cases of serious outrage. Before this there were no full-time detectives outside of Belfast and 'disposable men'.

Rodolphus Harvey	14 Dec 1869	18 June 1872	
James Ellis French	18 June 1872	Arrested 15 July 1884 for his involvement with a homosexual group of Dublin Castle officials. Tried on plea of insanity on 19 Aug. 1884 & 30 Oct. 1884. Tried for Conspiracy on 31 Oct. 1884, 3 Nov. 1884 & 19 Dec. 1884. Found guilty on 20 Dec. 1884 and sentenced to two years imprisonment with hard labour from the date of his arrest.	
Samuel Abraham Walker Waters	20 Apr. 1883 & 1 Apr.1889 (Detective Director)		
Henry James Bourchier	14 Sept. 1892	1 Apr. 1893	(Crime Special) (CI)
James Samuel Gibbons	1 Mar. 1890	1 Apr. 1893	(Crime Special) (CI)
William Reeves	1 Apr. 1893	3 Apr. 1895	(Crime Special) (CI)
John Concannon	3 Apr. 1895	16 Jan. 1902	(DI Crime Dept @ HQ)
John Mathew Galwey Foley	1 May 1901	1 Nov. 1902	(Crime Special) (CI)
William Arthur O'Connell	1 Nov.1902	22 May 1907	(Crime Special) (CI)
Edward Humble Pearson	14 Aug. 1907	5 Nov. 1911	(Crime Special) (CI) (Temp)
Edward Humble Pearson	16 Nov. 1907	9 Nov. 1911	(Crime Special) (CI)
Joseph Edward Leo Holmes	9 Nov. 1911	18 July 1920	(Crime Special) (CI)
Patrick Riordan	17 June 1916	1 Sept. 1916	(DI Crime Dept @ HQ)
Thomas Neylon	1 Oct. 1919	15 June 1920	(DI Crime Dept @ HQ)
Joseph Charles Tronson	7 Nov. 1920	31 Aug. 1922	(DI Crime Dept @ HQ)
Andrew Martin Mooney	15 July 1920	1 Oct. 1920	(DI Crime Dept @ HQ)
Ivon Henry Price	16 Apr. 1903	1 Oct.1908	(Crime Special) (DI)
Hume Riversdale Jones	1 Oct. 1908	1 Oct. 1914	(Crime Special) (DI)
Cecil Charles Hudson Moriarty	1 Feb.1914	7 July 1918	(Crime Special) (DI)
Charles Cheesman	17 Aug. 1917	3 Dec. 1917	(Crime Special) (DI)
Charles Cheesman	3 Dec. 1917	18 June 1918	(Crime Special) (DI)
Joseph J T Carroll	24 Sept. 1918	1 May 1920	(Crime Special) (DI)

APPENDIX 14: POLICE INSTRUCTORS AT THE RIC TRAINING DEPOT, PHOENIX PARK, 1846–1922

DEPOT SCHOOLMASTER

John Nixon RIC 8883	Constable – October 1846	
John Corbett RIC 8919	Constable, with precedence of a 2nd Head Constable – 1854.	

POLICE INSTRUCTOR & SCHOOLMASTER

John Egan RIC 04438	1st Head Constable	1 Nov. 1869
Vacant		
John Bodley RIC 10049	1st Head Constable	12 Dec. 1877
John Bodley	DI	1 Jan. 1884
John Slattery RIC 25324	DI	1 Nov. 1889

CHIEF POLICE INSTRUCTORS

Connor Berne	1 Feb. 1893	1 Feb. 1902
William Charles Patrick Hetreed	1 Jan. 1902	1 Apr. 1905
Robert Sparrow	1 Apr. 1905	18 Mar. 1910 (RM) [Ex-Teacher]
Charles Henry O'Hara	28 Mar. 1910	29 Mar. 1915 [Ex-Teacher]
George Archiebald Morant	29 Mar. 1915	31 Oct. 1915
George Archiebald Morant	1 Nov. 1916	14 Apr. 1919
George Ross	14 Apr. 1919	1 Oct. 1920
Andrew Martin Mooney	1 Oct. 1920	11 Feb. 1921
Robert Long	25 Mar. 1921	31 July 1922

APPENDIX 15: RIDING MASTERS OF THE ROYAL IRISH CONSTABULARY, 1843–1917

Richard Pilkington, RIC 5509, 1st Head Constable attached to the Reserve Force in charge of Cavalry and Drill on 21 July 1843 – special appointment from the 5th Dragoon Guards. Resigned on 24 January 1867 on his appointment as Deputy Marshal of the Four Courts Marshalsea, Dublin. Sub Inspector George Roche Cronin was in charge of the Mounted Troop for 10 years until his appointment as a Resident Magistrate on 1 March 1866.

John Mulcahy, appointed on 15 March 1866.
He was born in Co. Tipperary S.R. in 1828. He joined the RIC in January 1858 as a sub constable, reg. no. 22742, having served with the 13th Light Dragoons in the Charge of the Light Brigade, in the Crimea. He was awarded the Crimean Medal and four Clasps for Alma, Balaklava, Inkerman, Sebastopol and the Turkish Medal. Also awarded the Distinguished Conduct Medal. His wife was from Co. Tipperary. He was promoted 2nd Class Head Constable on 1 January 1858, 1st Class Head Constable on 1 August 1858, appointed a 3rd Class SI on 15 June 1866 and Riding Master at the Reserve in the Phoenix Park Depot. He had one unfavourable record for being drunk on 18 October 1870. He died on 10 June 1872, aged 44 years and he is buried in Glasnevin Cemetery, Dublin. (Grave No. XE 134 Garden).

James Douglas, appointed on 1 July 1872.
He was born in Lancs., England in 1838, ex-Sergeant Major in the 18th Hussars from 17 April 1858 to 30 June 1872. He died on 11 March 1873 aged 35 years.

William Sweet, appointed on 1 May 1873.
He was born in Kent, England in 1836, ex-Regimental Sergeant Major in the 1st Royal Dragoons, in which he spent 18 years and 4 months. He died on 10 August 1875, aged 39 years. Buried in Arbour Hill Military Cemetery, Dublin

Alfred Fry, appointed on 1 October 1875.
He was born in Yorks., England in 1841, ex-Troop Sergeant Major in the 5th Dragoon Guards, in which he spent 17 years and 6 months. His wife was from Co. Roscommon. He died on 28 July 1876, aged 35 years.

John Tyson, appointed on 24 August 1876.
He was born in Chester, Cheshire, England in 1840, ex-Regimental Sergeant Major in the 4th Dragoon Guards in which he spent 18 years and 8 months). He was granted the Queen's Jubilee Medal for taking part in Queen Victoria's Diamond Jubilee Procession in London on 29 June 1897. (Plate 23 – *Arresting Memories*). He retired on 15 June 1903 and died on 10 July 1916. Buried in Glasnevin Cemetery, Dublin (Grave XB61 South).

Richard Edwin Odlum appointed on 1 September 1903.
He was born in Dublin in 1854 and he was married in October 1886 (wife from Co. Dublin). He was an ex-Major & Riding Master with the 7th Hussars & 14th Hussars for 22 years. He retired on 7 December 1917.

APPENDIX 16: PAYMASTERS OF THE IRISH CONSTABULARY, 1836–1851

Appointed under 6 & 7 William IV, cap. 36 and discontinued under 14 & 15 Victoria, cap.85.

Edward Eustace Hill	1 Oct. 1836	20 Dec. 1838	(RM.)
John Bews	1 Oct. 1836	1 Aug. 1841	(Dismissed)
B H Stanhope	1 Oct. 1836	1 Oct. 1836	
John Blake	1 Oct. 1836	13 Mar. 1845	(Dismissed)
M. O'Meara	1 Oct. 1836	7 Nov. 1839	
J Seely	1 Oct. 1836	30 Nov. 1841	(Dismissed)
Robert Robison	1 Oct. 1836	2 Dec. 1846	
David Brudenell Franks	1 Oct. 1836	11 Apr. 1849	(RM)
David William Bissett	1 Oct. 1836	31 May 1851	(Pens.)
William Galbraith	1 Oct. 1836	31 May 1851	(Pens.)
David B Graham	1 Oct. 1836	31 May 1851	(d.1861)
Aaron Moffatt	1 Oct. 1836	31 May 1851	(d.1861)
Mathew Thomas O'Halloran	1 Oct. 1836	31 May 1851	(d.1862)
Joseph Barker Richardson	1 Oct. 1836	31 May 1851	(d.1875)
James Taylor	1 Oct. 1836	31 May 1851	
Robert Joseph O'Brien	1 Oct. 1836	31 Aug.1851	
William Brett	1 Oct. 1836	31 May 1851	(Pens.)
Patrick Browne	1 Oct. 1836	10 June 1869	(Pens.)
William Walter Congreve	24 Oct. 1836	1 Jan. 1852	(Pens.)
Patrick P Taaffe	4 Oct. 1838	1 Aug. 1847	(Res.)
Benjamin Hayes Holmes	1 Dec. 1839	16 Aug. 1842	(RM)

16 Aug. 1842	22 Jan. 1844	(RM)	
James Coleman	1 May 1841	31 May 1851	
John Mason Pooley	1 Aug. 1841	8 Nov. 1850	(Res.)
Peter Coleman	1 Aug. 1841	31 May 1851	(d.1895)
John O'Brien	22 Jan. 1844	31 Oct. 1846	(RM)
Gerald Fitzgibbon	13 Mar. 1845	31 May 1851	
Bryan O'Loghlen	8 Oct. 1846	18 Jan. 1859	
George Devonport Comyns	8 Oct. 1846	9 Aug. 1852	(Pens)
James O'Callaghan	22 Oct. 1846	4 Apr. 1849	(Dismissed)
James Gallaher	1 Sept.1847	31 May 1851	
Francis Waldron	15 May 1848	31 May 1851	
Burowes Kelly	1 May 1849	31 May 1851	

APPENDIX 17: OFFICERS IN CHARGE OF THE ROYAL IRISH CONSTABULARY SUB DEPOTS, 1907–1922

RICHMOND BARRACKS SUB DEPOT

John Marcus Poer O'Shee		
– Assistant Commandant		
& Adjutant	17 Sept. 1907	10 Apr. 1908
George D'Urban Rodwell		
– Musketry Instructor	10 Oct. 1907	15 Apr. 1908
Richard Francis Raleigh Cruise	17 Sept. 1907	10 Apr. 1908
Master	1 July 1908	15 Oct. 1908
John Bowyer Bird	1 July 1908	10 Nov. 1908

NORTH DUBLIN UNION SUB DEPOT

George D'Urban Rodwell		
– Commandant & Musketry		
Instructor	18 Mar. 1920	14 Aug. 1920
Michael J A Egan – Adjutant	18 Mar. 1920	31 Aug. 1920
Robert Long – Company Officer	18 Mar. 1920	25 Mar. 1921

BEGGARS BUSH AUXILIARY DIVISION RIC DEPOT

William Farrell Martinson		
– Commandant	7 Feb. 1921	16 Mar. 1922
(To Palestine)		

RIC CAMP GORMANSTOWN, CO. DUBLIN

John Marcus Poer O'Shee	Commandant	11 Sept. 1920	22 Nov. 1920
Charles Frederick Fellowes Davies	Commandant	22 Nov. 1920	1 Mar. 1922
Thomas Dawson Morrison	Adjutant (Temp)	14 Sept. 1920	22 Nov. 1920
	Adjutant	22 Nov. 1920	15 Mar. 1922
Michael Joseph McConnell	Convoy Officer	8 Dec. 1920	25 Mar. 1922

RIC CAMP NEWTOWNARDS, CO. DOWN

William John McBride	Police Instructor	8 Nov. 1920	31 May 1922
	(Temp)		

APPENDIX 18: ALLOCATION OF RIC OFFICERS TO CONSTABULARY DIVISIONS & DISTRICTS

Districts	DI	CI	AIG	DIG	IG
County of Antrim					
Lisburn	1	1			
Antrim	1				
Ballymena	1				
Ballymoney	1				
Loughguile	1				
City of Belfast					
Commissioner's Office	1				
Detective Department	1				
Police Office					
Musgrave Street	1				
Springfield Road	1				
Brown Square	1				
Glenravel Street	1				
Mountpottinger	1				
County of Armagh					
Armagh	1	1			
Lurgan	1				
Newtownhamilton	1				
Portadown	1				
County of Carlow					
Carlow	1	1			
Bagenalstown	1				
County of Cavan					
Cavan	1	1			
Bailieboro'	1				
Ballyjamesduff	1				
Swanlinbar	1				
County of Clare					
Ennis	1	1			
Ballyvaughan	1				
Corofin	1				
Ennistymon	1				
Killaloe	1				
Kilrush	1				
Sixmilebridge	1				
Tulla	1				
City of Cork					
South District					
Union Quay	1	1			
North District					

Districts	DI	CI	AIG	DIG	IG
King Street	I				
County of Cork E.R.					
Ballincollig	I				
Charleville	I				
Fermoy	I				
Kanturk	I				
Kinsale	I				
Mallow	I				
Midleton	I				
Mitchelstown	I				
Newmarket	I				
Queenstown	I				
Youghal	I				
County of Cork W.R.					
Bandon	I	I			
Bantry	I				
Castletownbere	I				
Clonakilty	I				
Dunmanway	I				
Macroom	I				
Skibbereen	I				
County of Donegal					
Letterkenny	I	I			
Ardara	I				
Ballyshannon	I				
Buncrana	I				
Dunfanaghy	I				
Dungloe	I				
Moville	I				
Raphoe	I				
Rathmullen	I				
County of Down					
Downpatrick	I	I			
Banbridge	I				
Newry	I				
Newtownards	I				
County of Dublin					
Balbriggan	I	I			
Dundrum	I				
Howth	I				
Lucan	I				
County of Fermanagh					
Enniskillen	I	I			
Belcoo	I				
Kesh	I				

Districts	DI	CI	AIG	DIG	IG
Lisnaskea	I				
County of Galway E.R.					
Ballinasloe	I	I			
Athenry	I				
Loughrea	I				
Mountbellew	I				
Portumna	I				
Woodford	I				
County of Galway W.R.					
Galway	I	I			
Clifden	I				
Dunmore, Tuam	I				
Gort	I				
Oughterard	I				
Roundstone	I				
Tuam	I				
County of Kerry					
Tralee	I	I			
Cahirciveen	I				
Castleisland	I				
Dingle	I				
Kenmare	I				
Killarney	I				
Killorglin	I				
Listowel	I				
County of Kildare					
Naas	I	I			
Athy	I				
Kildare	I				
County of Kilkenny					
Kilkenny – Parliament Street	I	I			
Callan	I				
Castlecomer	I				
Johnstown	I				
Piltown	I				
Thomastown	I				
King's County – Offaly					
Tullamore	I	I			
Banagher	I				
Birr	I				
Edenderry	I				
Shinrone	I				
County of Leitrim					
Carrick-on-Shannon	I	I			

Districts	DI	CI	AIG	DIG	IG
Ballinamore	I				
Manorhamilton	I				
Mohill	I				
City of Limerick					
Limerick – William Street	I	I			
County of Limerick					
Abbeyfeale	I				
Adare	I				
Bruff	I				
Kilfinane	I				
Newcastle West	I				
Newpallas	I				
Rathkeale	I				
City of Londonderry					
Londonderry – Victoria Stn.	I	I			
County of Londonderry					
Coleraine	I				
Limavady	I				
Magherafelt	I				
County of Longford					
Longford	I	I			
Ballymahon	I				
Granard	I				
County of Louth					
Dundalk – Anne Street	I	I			
Drogheda – West Gate	I				
County of Mayo					
Castlebar	I	I			
Ballina	I				
Ballinrobe	I				
Claremorris	I				
Newport	I				
Swinford	I				
Westport	I				
County of Meath					
Navan	I	I			
Dunshaughlin	I				
Kells	I				
Slane	I				
Trim	I				
County of Monaghan					
Monaghan	I	I			
Carrickmacross	I				

Districts	DI	CI	AIG	DIG	IG
Clones	I				
Queen's County – Laois					
Maryborough (Portlaoise)	I	I			
Abbeyleix	I				
Mountrath	I				
County of Roscommon					
Roscommon	I	I			
Ballaghadereen	I				
Boyle	I				
Castlerea	I				
Strokestown	I				
County of Sligo					
Sligo	I	I			
Ballymote	I				
Collooney	I				
Easkey	I				
Tubbercurry	I				
County of Tipperary N.R.					
Nenagh	I	I			
Borrisokane	I				
Newport	I				
Roscrea	I				
Templemore	I				
Thurles	I				
County of Tipperary S.R.					
Clonmel	I	I			
Cahir	I				
Cappawhite	I				
Carrick on Suir	I				
Cashel	I				
Killenaule	I				
Tipperary	I				
County of Tyrone					
Omagh	I	I			
Aughnacloy	I				
Cookstown	I				
Dungannon	I				
Newtownstewart	I				
Strabane	I				
City of Waterford					
Waterford – Lady Lane	I	I			
County of Waterford					
Cappoquin	I				
Dungarvan	I				

Districts	DI	CI	AIG	DIG	IG
Portlaw	I				
County of Westmeath					
Mullingar	I	I			
Athlone	I				
Castlepollard	I				
Delvin	I				
Moate	I				
County of Wexford					
Wexford – Main Street, South	I	I			
Enniscorthy	I				
Gorey	I				
New Ross	I				
Taghmon	I				
County of Wicklow					
Wicklow	I	I			
Arklow	I				
Bray	I				
Dunlavin	I				
Reserve & Depot					
Inspector General	I				
Deputy Inspector General	I				
Assistant Inspector General	I				
Commandant of the Depot	I				
Barrackmaster & Storekeeper	I				
Surgeon – CI (1)	I				
Veterinary Surgeon – C.I (1)	I				
Crime Special / Dublin Castle	I				
Instructor of Musketry	I				
Police Instructor	I				
No. 1 Company (Munster)	I				
No. 2 Company (Ulster)	I				
No. 3 Company (Leinster)	I				
No. 4 Company (Connaught)	I				
No. 5 Company & Riding Master	I				
Richmond Barracks sub Depot					
(17 Sept. 1907–10 Nov. 1908)					
Assistant Commandant & Adjutant	I				
Musketry Instructor	I				
North Dublin Union Sub Depot					
(18 Mar. 1920–25 Mar. 1921)					
Commandant & Musketry Instructor	I				
Adjutant	I				
Company Officer	I				

Districts	DI	CI	AIG	DIG	IG
Beggars Bush A.D.R.I.C. Depot					
(7 Feb. 1921–16.Mar. 1922)					
Commandant	1				
RIC Camp Gormanstown					
(11 Sept. 1920–25 Mar. 1922)					
Officer Commanding	1				
Adjutant	1				
No. 6 Company	1				
No. 7 Company	1				
No. 8 Company	1				
RIC Camp Newtownards,					
Co. Down (8 Nov. 1920–31 May 1922)					
Police Instructor	1				
TOTAL	209	41	2	1	1

APPENDIX 19: RIC EQUIVALENT ARMY RANKS AND TITLES

RIC	*Army*
Inspector General	General
Deputy Inspector General	Lieutenant-General
Assistant Inspector General	Major-General
Commandant of the Depot (AIG)	Major-General / Commandant
County Inspector	Colonel
Surgeon to the Force (CI)	Surgeon / Major
Adjutant of the Depot (1st Class DI)	Adjutant
Musketry Instructor (1st Class DI)	Captain / Musketry Instructor
1st Class District Inspector	Major
2nd Class District Inspector	Captain
3rd Class District Inspector	Lieutenant
Depot Schoolmaster (DI)	Inspector of Schools
Cadet at training in Depot for DI	Ensign
Head Constable Major at Depot	Depot Sergeant Major
Head Constable (Reserve)	Sergeant-Major
Head Constable Storekeeper at Depot	Barrack Quartermaster Sergeant
Drill Instructors at Depot	Drill Sergeants
Canteen Sergeant at Depot	Canteen Sergeant
Librarian Sergeant	Librarian Sergeant
Sergeant	Sergeant
Acting Sergeant	Corporal
Constable	Private

Mounted troop	Cavalry
Riding Master (D.I)	Captain (Superintending, etc.,)
Veterinary Surgeon to the Force	Army Veterinary Staff Surgeon
Head Constable Mounted Troop	Sergeant Major
Rough Riding Sergeant	Rough Riding Sergeant
Rough Riding Acting Sergeant	Rough Riding Corporal
Sergeant Mounted Troop	Lance Sergeant
Acting Sergeant Mounted Troop	Lance Corporal
Constable Mounted Troop	Private

	Band
Bandmaster	Regimental Bandmaster
Band Sergeant	Band Sergeant
Band Acting Sergeant	Band Corporal
Band Constable	Band Private

Illustrations

Mam

Cerddi gan Famau,
Cerddi am Famau

Cyhoeddiadau
Barddas

Cyhoeddiadau
Barddas

℗ Mari George / Cyhoeddiadau Barddas ©
℗ Y cerddi Y beirdd ©

Argraffiad cyntaf: 2019

ISBN 978-1-911584-21-6

Cyhoeddwyd gan Gyhoeddiadau Barddas.

Mae'r cyhoeddwr yn cydnabod
cefnogaeth ariannol Cyngor Llyfrau Cymru.

Argraffwyd gan Y Lolfa, Tal-y-bont.

Dyluniwyd gan Tanwen Haf.
Darlun clawr gan Valériane Leblond.

Mam

Cerddi gan Famau,
Cerddi am Famau

Golygwyd gan **Mari George**

Cyflwynir y gyfrol hon i
Hefina, Kitty a Lois.

Cynnwys

Rhagair

Roeddwn wrth fy modd yn mynd i'r afael â'r dasg o gasglu cerddi ynghyd ar gyfer y gyfrol hon. Alaw Mai Edwards feddyliodd am y syniad ac mae'n syndod nad oes cyfrol debyg yn bodoli eisoes. Roeddwn am i'r gyfrol fod yn gasgliad o gerddi sy'n dathlu'r fam yn gyffredinol, boed yn gerddi gan famau neu'n gerddi'n talu teyrnged i famau, rhai ohonynt yn adnabyddus a rhai wedi eu cyfansoddi'n arbennig ar gyfer y gyfrol hon. Ymhlith y cerddi, mae atgofion penodol am famau fel yn achos cerdd hyfryd Huw Meirion Edwards am ei blentyndod a'i fam, a oedd yn digwydd bod yn athrawes Gymraeg arna i ac yn ddylanwad enfawr. Felly hefyd teyrnged Myrddin ap Dafydd i'w fam a'i fam-gu, marwnadau i famau fel englyn W. Rhys Nicholas a cherddi ingol yn disgrifio dirywiad neu farwolaeth mam, yn benodol y detholiad o awdl fuddugol Elwyn Edwards yn Eisteddfod Genedlaethol Casnewydd 1988. Yn ogystal, ceir cerddi sy'n sôn yn uniongyrchol am y profiad o fod yn fam ac y mae nifer o'r rheini'n defnyddio hiwmor fel yng ngwaith Casia Wiliam a Gwennan Evans. Yn britho'r casgliad mae hefyd gerddi a hwiangerddi traddodiadol a fydd, gobeithio, yn codi gwên hiraethus am y cof o eistedd ar lin mam yn canu. Gobeithio y gwnewch fwynhau pori drwy'r gyfrol hardd hon ac y bydd yn anrheg ddelfrydol i unrhyw fam ar Sul y Mamau.

Mari George

Enaid bach yn
llond y byd

Mam

Nid oes angen geiriau heddiw
I gyfleu 'nheimladau i,
Dim ond gair o ddiolchgarwch
Am dy fod yn fam i mi.

Menna Medi

12

Y Sylweddoliad

Mae'r cyfarfod yn hir.
Pawb yn gwisgo'i Saesneg gorau,
yn gwneud nodiadau'n lle gwrando.

Rydw innau'n trio ffitio mewn,
ond yn hel meddyliau am dudalennau gwag.

Daw rhywun â syniad newydd sydd
fel ebol blwydd, yn goesau i gyd ar hyd y bwrdd,
a dwinna'n deffro tu ôl i fy llygaid

ac yn cyfri'r wythnosau ac yn gwybod,
yn yr union ennyd yna,
amdanat ti.

Digon pethma oedd y cofnodion,
a dim ond fi sy'n gwybod dy fo' ti
yn swatio rhwng eu llinellau.

Casia Wiliam

Wrth Enwi ein Mab

Adda, Artro, Anarawd, Aldwyn,
oedd dechrau ei restr 'Hoff enwau i hogyn'.
Tybed a fyddai y Bs yn fwy addas?
Baeddan, Barach, Bedyn, Bedwas.

O, Gruff! Mae 'na beryg caiff Cador neu Clydno
neu Camber neu Carn neu Cynfelyn ei fwlio.
Mae Deicws a Dyfnwal yn enwau go soled,
ond yn yr un modd, Tomos, Dafydd ac Aled.

Mae Ednowain, Edernog, Eudwaf ac Edernol
a Glander a Glewas, i mi'n *rhy* ddiddorol.
O ba gracer y cest ti Hoen, Hwmffre a Hebog,
Idloe a Lawnslod, Melwas a Morfaelog?

A 'dyw Nwython nac Onfael nac Orchwy nac Oleuli
ddim yn cael dod yn agos i'r tystysgrif geni!
A allwch ddychmygu fi'n galw yn dyner,
'Penwyn,' neu 'Peryf, der' lawr i gael swper!'?

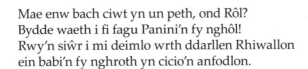

Mae enw bach ciwt yn un peth, ond Rôl?
Bydde waeth i fi fagu Panini'n fy nghôl!
Rwy'n siŵr i mi deimlo wrth ddarllen Rhiwallon
ein babi'n fy nghroth yn cicio'n anfodlon.

Rwy'n deall fod enwau sy'n gorffen 'da 'march'
mewn ambell gyd-destun yn ennyn cryn barch,
ond Rhyngfarch a Rhwyfarch? Ar ba blaned ti'n byw?
Be sy'n bod ar gael Ceri, neu Hari neu Huw?

Sadwrn? Na. Samlet? Na. Seithenyn? Mawredd dad!
Meddwyn anghofus da-i-ddim foddodd wlad
oedd hwnnw. Rêl *loser*. A go brin byddai Tewdur
yn gwneud dim i hygrededd na *street-cred* y cr'adur.

Tyfyriog a Teler a Tudfwlch yn enwedig
sy'n enwau ymhonnus i gyntaf-anedig.
Mae'r rhestr yn cloi gydag Ungoed ac Wyrydd
(sy'n addas i fachgen neu ferch fel ei gilydd).

Es 'nôl reit i gychwyn y rhestr ryfedda
ac wfft i wreiddioldeb – fe'i galwn yn Adda.

Gwennan Evans

15

Bochio

'Sgwyda,' fyddai Taid yn arfer ddweud,
'i'r jeli fynd i'r corneli'.
Ond erbyn hyn does dim cornel wag,
dim ond onglau crwm.

Dwi megis hanner cwafer,
fy mol yn gân i gyd.

Ganol nos mae'r symffoni yn ffromi
nes 'mod i'n eistedd yn arweinydd cefnsyth
a'r asid yn pydru fy nannedd.

Taswn i 'mond yn gwybod, Taid,
mai hyn fyddai fy hanes i,
wedi'r holl sgwrio
mi fyddwn i wedi mynd am ail bowlennaid,
a llyncu'r llysnafedd coch
bob tamaid.

Casia Wiliam

Cyfarchiad Tad i Fam ar Awr Geni

Bu hir y disgwyl, f'anwylyd, – yn drwm
　　Ar dy droed, ond gwynfyd
　　Yw cael, o'r oriau celyd
　Wyrth o beth sy'n werth y byd.

J. Eirian Davies

17

Anadl

Bu'r gwacter
yn dy ddisgwyl.

Gweld
siâp dy wyneb
ym mhob siarad.

A daeth
dy sgrech gyntaf …
mor gyfarwydd
â ddoe
a ninnau
yn dy nabod.

Ac fe gipiaist ti rywbeth …
… rhywbeth
na wyddem ei fod gennym
o'r blaen.

Mari George

18

Caio

(a anwyd ar yr 22ain o Ragfyr, 2016 – blwyddyn Brexit a blwyddyn Trump)

Mewn eiliad llithrodd y llynedd i'w lle yn y llyfrau hanes
– ei helynt a'i cholledion yn ei chôl –
a phawb yn falch o weld ei chefn hi.

Ond i ni, cyn bod y stori ar ben,
dest ti, Caio, yn bennod newydd berffaith.

Llenwaist dy dudalen wen â sgrech
a ddeffrodd ddesibelau diarth yng nghlust ein calonnau.

Yn un sbloets o inc coch a gwyn y gwaed a'r theatr,
lliwiaist ein byd â gwawr na wyddem amdani cynt.

Daeth dy fysedd traed hirion yn frawddegau cyfarwydd,
yn plethu'r tri ohonom yn gwlwm o blot.

Ti yw awdur ein bywydau ni nawr:
a gyda'th eni a'th enw rhoddaist
enwau a geiriau o'r newydd i ninnau hefyd.

Mewn eiliad llithrodd y llynedd i'w lle yn y llyfrau hanes
ond cyn yr atalnod olaf dest ti â dy lygaid gleision a dy gariad i'n côl,
ac roedd pawb, o, mor falch o dy weld.

Casia Wiliam

Bore Oes

Mae'r dydd ar fin y diwedd,
dydd sy'n nos,
mae'r wawr rhwng pell ac agos,
lleuad dlos;
mae'r awr yn fân ei chyllyll,
llym eu llafn,
mae'r eneth ifanc heno'n
dod yn fam.

Mae greddfau'r gwthio, gwthio'n
rhwygo'n rhydd,
rhwng ofn a gwefr yn nofio
at y dydd;
mae'r diwedd heddiw'n ddechrau,
mae mor hen,
mae'r clwyf yn ceulo'r golau,
geni'r wên.

Rwy'n chwalu'r gragen fregus,
blasu'r môr,
yn ddiofyn a diddewis,
agor dôr;
gadael geneth ifanc,
merch ddi-nam.

I sgrech y byd daeth bachgen –
a daeth Mam;
i grud y byd
un bachgen bach
ei fam.

Mererid Hopwood

... a dangosaf
iti'r glendid
sydd yn llygaid
glas dy fam

Mam

Mam bach annwyl,
Mam bach fi,
fi bia Mam
a Mam bia fi.

Anhysbys

Amser Stori

Rho, Mam, y stori i mi – ac fe gaf
　Ei gweld yn dy gwmni;
　Mae'n drysor i'm diddori
　Mewn geiriau a lluniau'n lli.

John Emyr

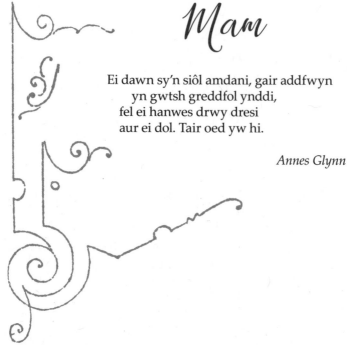

Mam

Ei dawn sy'n siôl amdani, gair addfwyn
yn gwtsh greddfol ynddi,
fel ei hanwes drwy dresi
aur ei dol. Tair oed yw hi.

Annes Glynn

Mynd Drot Drot

Mynd drot drot ar y gaseg wen,
 mynd drot drot i'r dre,
Mami'n dod 'nôl dros fryn a dôl
 a rhywbeth neis neis i de.

Teisen i Sil, banana i Bil
 a thamaid i'r gath a'r ci,
afal mawr iach i Ben y gwas bach
 a rhywbeth neis neis i fi.

Anhysbys

Dadeni

(detholiad)

Dere'r un bach, mae'r machlud
yn bwrw'i aur, ac mae'n bryd
cloi corlan dy deganau
a hi'r nos oer yn nesáu.
Dere i wrando'r stori
am y wawr, a gad i mi
mewn nyth twt, am unwaith 'to,
dy ddal. Estyn dy ddwylo
bach gwyn yn dynn amdanaf
cyn llithro heno i'th haf.
Dere, fe ddaw'r bore bach
â'i Frenin a'i gyfrinach.
Cwsg, cwsg, fy nhywysog gwyn,
darfod mae'r dydd diderfyn.

Mererid Hopwood

Suo Gân

Huna blentyn ar fy mynwes,
Clyd a chynnes ydyw hon;
Breichiau mam sy'n dynn amdanat,
Cariad mam sy' dan fy mron;
Ni chaiff dim amharu'th gyntun,
Ni wna undyn â thi gam;
Huna'n dawel, annwyl blentyn,
Huna'n fwyn ar fron dy fam.

Huna'n dawel, heno, huna,
Huna'n fwyn, y tlws ei lun;
Pam yr wyt yn awr yn gwenu,
Gwenu'n dirion yn dy hun?
Ai angylion fry sy'n gwenu,
Arnat ti yn gwenu'n llon,
Tithau'n gwenu'n ôl dan huno,
Huno'n dawel ar fy mron?

Paid ag ofni, dim ond deilen
Gura, gura ar y ddôr;
Paid ag ofni, ton fach unig
Sua, sua ar lan y môr;
Huna blentyn, nid oes yma
Ddim i roddi iti fraw;
Gwena'n dawel yn fy mynwes
Ar yr engyl gwynion draw.

Anhysbys

27

Nos Da, Mam

Fy mrawd a mi yn ein gwlâu bach clyd
A'r gwynt a'r glaw yn chwipio'r byd,
A llygid Mam a'i gwên dawel hi
A Huwcyn Cwsg sy'n gwylio ni.
Nos da, Mam, nos da, Mam,
Mi wela i chdi yn fy mreuddwyd i,
Nos da, Mam.

Mae'r bochdew bach yn ei nyth blawd llif
Yn edrach ymlaen at gael mwythau gen i,
Mae'r beiciau yn y cwt, Twm y ci yn y tŷ,
'Toes 'na unman gwell na'n tŷ ni ar nos Sul.
Nos da, Mam, nos da, Mam,
Mi wela i chdi yn fy mreuddwyd i,
Nos da, Mam.

Dwi'n clywad Dad yn rhoi coed ar y tân
A dwi'n swatio'n dynn wedi blino'n lân.
Nos da, Mam, nos da, Mam,
Mi wela i chdi yn fy mreuddwyd i,
Nos da, Mam.

Steve Eaves

Ni chrëwyd mwy
na chariad mam

Hel Caffis

Gwymon y Fenai a cherrig mân
a heli'r Foryd, gwylan a'i chân,
a Phont yr Aber, ewyn a broc
a'r glaw yn crio ar Stryd Dan Cloc,
a bygi, bagiau a mab a mam
yn cyrchu coffi a brechdan ham.
Wrth Siop y Pentan, powlio yn slei
mae mwg y trothwy o Caffi Cei
a'i seti mwstard, a'i nicotîn
a'i stêm paneidiau, a'i sawl hen gwîn.
Dan ffenest Nelson's, Rochelle's sy'n flas
o bolish derw a charped glas,
teisennau mewn gwydr a thanau nwy
ar bedair olwyn; *gateaux* ar lwy.

Mae to'r Majestic 'dal uwch y dre,
egsôsts y Crosvilles yn rhu trwy'r lle
a fry yn Gronant, ar dop Penrallt
mae 'na fîns ar dost a phyrms mewn gwallt.
Weithiau'r Bell Tower, a'r goets yn strach
dros risiau llechi, a bisgits bach
neu'r Neuadd Farchnad a chornel dynn
a lliain sgwariau bach coch a gwyn.
Rywbryd y cyfan 'lithrodd dros go'
yn llanw'r Foryd a thrai'r Lee-Ho
fel broc a gwymon. A mab a mam
yn cyrchu'r domen â'u sgerbwd pram.

Rhys Iorwerth

Cawod Eira

(wrth ddychwelyd i'r gwaith ar ôl fy nghyfnod mamolaeth)

Disgynnodd cawod eira dros ein byd
a ninnau'n stond, yn llawn rhyfeddod syn.
Mae'r cyfan bron â dadmer nawr i gyd.

Y cyngor oedd i aros adre'n glyd
a gafael ymhob eiliad fach yn dynn.
Disgynnodd cawod eira dros ein byd.

Â'm camera, ceisiais gadw cof o'r hud
mewn lluniau sydd fel cardiau post o wyn.
Mae'r cyfan bron â dadmer nawr i gyd.

Caf wên neu sgwrs yn amlach ar y stryd
a phawb yn oedi'n hwy y dyddie hyn.
Disgynnodd cawod eira dros ein byd.

Mae'r rhew yn toddi'n gynt a chynt o hyd
a'r dŵr yn llifo nawr i'r lle y myn.
Mae'r cyfan bron â dadmer nawr i gyd.

Mae'n amser cadw'r pram a'r mat a'r crud.
Oes peth i'w weld ar ôl ar gopa'r bryn?
Disgynnodd cawod eira dros ein byd.
Mae'r cyfan bron â dadmer nawr i gyd.

Gwennan Evans

Ffynnon

Milgwaith a mwy.
Y sgidadlu dyddiol, defodol,
i'r clos am hanner awr 'di tri.

Gwylio ffrwd diwetydd
yn byrlymu drwy'r iet,
yn troi'n gant o ffynhonnau bychain
o arian byw.

Clywed grwndi'r bwcedi metel
yn fintai sgleiniog ar hyd y palmentydd
yn aros i gasglu'r cyfoeth gloyw.

Ar raff o lôn hir
sy'n ein halio yn ôl at aelwyd,
rhwng crychiad ael a gwefus gellweirus,
ac o gylch llygaid disglair a bysedd buan,
clywn hanesion yn tasgu,
brawddegau'n hollti,
syniadau'n plethu
blith draphlith.
Yn ddelta o ddiwrnod
mewn bywyd plentyn.

Ac er y sarnu a'r tollti
ar y siwrnai 'nôl,
daw diferion drachefn i oreuro'r hwyr
ac arllwys drwy gysgodion min nos,
i lenwi corneli stafelloedd tawel.
Yn haenen arall o'n hanes ni,
yn stori i'r muriau anadlu.

Elinor Gwynn

Braint

Fe redan nhw drwy fy egni
gyda'u dyrnau brwnt
a syllaf ar ein staen jam
o gartre.

Yn sŵn briwsion
a nodau poenus piano
camaf ar ddarn o Lego
a dyna hi.
Af drwy'r drws yn drwm
a'i chwalu ar gau,
at y lôn
y breuddwydiaf amdani.

Cerdded drwy'i llonyddwch
a diolch am dawelwch.
Ond daw cecru adar yr hwyr
a chic rhyw bêl o bell
i'm baglu.

A throf yn ôl
yn yr haul marw,
troi am y drws
a'r sŵn
sy'n chwilio amdana' i.

Mari George

36

'Cer di'

Ym murmur ac ym mharabl
dieiriau dy stori,
rhyngom bwriwyd yr angor sy'n ddeall
ac ni all neb na dim dan haul
ei chodi hi yn llwyr o'm llaw,
ac ni ddaw dydd traul i'w haearn tryloyw,
na rhwd i'w rhaff;

ond mi wn,
gwn yn saff,
fel pob tad a mam,
y daw awr ei dirwyn,
am mai cariad yw dweud – 'cer di';

a rywfodd, bryd hynny,
pan fyddaf i'n gryfach,
a thithau'n ysu am daith,
wele fi'n gadael fynd
heb adael fynd ychwaith.

Mererid Hopwood

37

Stydi

(i Owain ar ddechrau ei gwrs DPhil ym maes Patristeg ym Mhrifysgol Rhydychen; ac mewn ymateb i Sant Sierôm yn ei stydi fel y darlunnir ef gan Antonello da Messina yn yr Oriel Genedlaethol, Llundain)

Rhwng ffurfioldeb y colofnau dysg
a mawredd coridorau cred,
cael hyd i'r gofod hwn o gartre'n
sioc o annibendod.

Bu'n rhaid ymgadw
rhag twtio dy dywel di-hid ar ei fachyn
a chorlannu'r sliperi strae;
rhag plygu jîns, gwneud peli twt o sanau;
rhag achub dalen wib
ar daith i'r llawr
a chau cloriau rhag i haul
hwyr ein pnawn
frychu meddwl golau Origen ac Awstin:
llaw'r fam ar y Tadau.

Awn at y ffenest. Gwelaf
yn y gwydr,
rhwng ffrwst colomennod,
glugiar gwirionedd
a thragwyddoldeb paun,
a dacw ddau'n rhwyfo'n hamddenol
dros darmac – gwyliwch y beiciau, bois! –
tua chroes anochel y Merthyron
ar waelod Broad Street;
boddir cân bell amaethwr
gan ruo bws o flaen Blackwell's
a grwndi'r ceir
a'm cludodd yma'n ôl
i dy stydi ac i'n sgwrs,
i swynion hela dy lew di dy hunan
(mor anniogel dda,
mor frawychus felys
mewn stori, myth a hanes):
yr Aslan sy'n dal i browlan yma byth
gan geisio'i brae
rhwng colofnau dysg
ac ar hyd coridorau cred.

Cei di geisio dofi
gwylltni'r gofod meddwl hwn –
bodlonaf innau
ar gymoni'i gysgod.

Christine James

Esgidiau

Mae holl esgidiau'r plant 'ma wrth y drws,
Neu felly mae'n ymddangos imi nawr.
Fe ddryllir delwedd berffaith o dŷ tlws
Gan barau driphlith draphlith dros y llawr.
Mae ganddynt bâr i bob gweithgaredd, bron,
Sy'n llenwi eu plentyndod prysur, drud,
A rhaid yw prynu 'sgidiau newydd sbon,
A minnau'n gwisgo'r un hen bâr o hyd.
Ond gwn, wrth gwyno, fel y gŵyr pob mam
Sy'n didol a thacluso'r parau strae,
Na fydd hi eto'n hir cyn daw y cam
Pan fydd rhaid codi llaw ac ymbellhau.
Bryd hynny, er bydd gen i gyntedd tlws,
Bydd hiraeth am esgidiau wrth y drws.

Elin Meek

40

Roedd gan fy
mam ei border bach

Mam

Ei gwên yw'r awel gynnes – a gwyn fyd
    ei gwên fach, ddirodres;
  yn ei grudd mae cochni gwres
  y wên sy'n hŷn na hanes.

Gwnewch i'r angylion farddoni – a'i roi
    ar awen da Vinci,
  urddwch y wawr â'r cerddi –
  a dyna Mam, fy mam i!

Môr o heddwch im roddodd – yn nhonnau
    ei henaid fe'm carodd,
  môr o rin – a mwy a rodd,
  yn ei llanw fe'm lluniodd.

O'i derwen un fesen wyf fi – wreiddiodd
   ym mhridd y ffrwythloni,
heddiw rhof ddiolch iddi –
mwy na mam fu Mam i mi.

Nid ei chur ond ei chariad – nid ei gwg
   ond ei gwên a'r teimlad,
pa rodd fel gwir ymroddiad?
Pa rym fel mynnu parhad?

Hi yw 'ngwên er fy ngeni – hi yw'r tân
   a'r tes nad yw'n oeri!
Ond er nerth y coelcerthi
trodd y fflam o Mam i mi.

Robin Llwyd ab Owain

Nerth

Ger adwy'r tŷ, fe'i gwyliaf
ar ei gliniau'n gwaredu chwyn
ac yn codi briallu o'u crud i'w gwely,
eu lapio'n dyner dan gwrlid y border
a dyfrio ei swsus nos da drostynt.

Cymer ei gwynt ati wrth i weddi
ddenig o dwll dan grisiau ei chalon
a loetran ar ei gwefus.

Mae'n fy ngweld ac yn goglais gwên,
er gwybod fod y pridd yn llithro
fel ei phlant drwy'i dwylo.

Marged Tudur

44

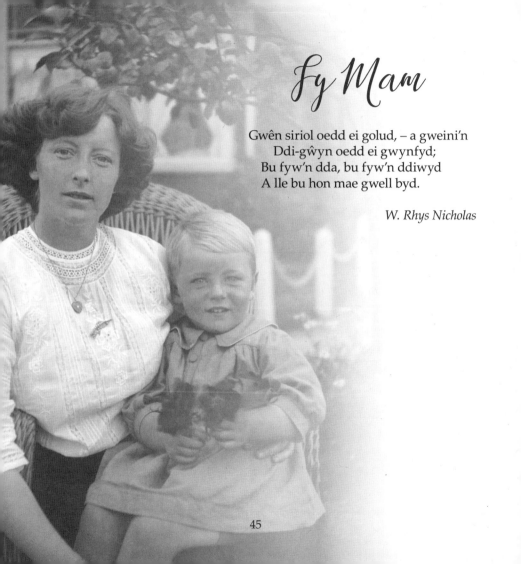

Fy Mam

Gwên siriol oedd ei golud, – a gweini'n
Ddi-gŵyn oedd ei gwynfyd;
Bu fyw'n dda, bu fyw'n ddiwyd
A lle bu hon mae gwell byd.

W. Rhys Nicholas

45

Poncie dan Eira

(i Mam)

Fel nodau'r ddawns wrth weindio'r
Hen degan fu dan glo,
Mae Poncie dy fagwraeth
Yn troelli yn fy ngho',
A Chapel Street yn swatio'n dynn
A llwch y glo dan orchudd gwyn.

Nid bwrw eira – 'odi'
A wnâi'n dy strydoedd di,
A threiglodd dy leferydd
I'n genau bychain ni:
Ni flasem finag Môn na phêr,
Roedd 'sur' a 'rhwnin' yn ein mêr!

Os trodd yr ôd yn eira,
Os toddodd trwch dy iaith,
Os llaesodd y degawdau
Dy linyn bogel maith,
Fe welwn ninnau'r eneth dlos
Sy'n dawnsio o hyd drwy fyd gwyn Rhos.

Huw Meirion Edwards

46

Cwrlid

(*Mam*)

Unwaith
fe'th wyliais
yn gwau edafedd
yn chwedlau lliwgar,
a'th bwythau cain
yn plethu'n eiriau
o ofal.

Heno,
a'r lliwiau'n bŵl
datod a wna'r pwythau cain,
ond ymhleth
yn yr hen rubanau,
mae geiriau'r chwedl
yno o hyd i'm cynnal.

Haf Llewelyn

Mam

Yn sŵn clician ei gweill diwyd
Lluniodd ddarluniau cain,
Llawn cysur.
Y pwythau gwastad yn dynn
A'r lliwiau'n cyfareddu.

Arafodd y gweill
A llaciodd y pwythau,
Cyn datod
O un i un.
Pylodd y lliwiau
Gan adael dim ond arlliw
O'r tanbeidrwydd a fu.

Ond heddiw,
A'r gweill mor dawel,
Mae'r darluniau eto
Yn llachar yn y cof.

Beryl Griffiths

... a heno â'r nos ynof
difesur yw cysur cof

Ar y Ffordd i Draeth Poppit

Odyn ni wedi bod 'ma o'r bla'n . . . ?

Mae'r haf yn dirwyn,
yn llif o atgofion at geg yr Aber.
Sgerbydau melyn troed-y-ceiliog yn codi'n bendrwm
o ganol y gwyrddni llychlyd,
a choesynnau'r brigwellt garw yn crafu'n welw
ar draws cynfas perffaith awyr Awst.

Mwyar cynta'r tymor yn fwclis blêr ar hyd gwar o glawdd;
Du fel jet, yn powlio'u galar dros olion diwedd tymor.
Sŵn crafllyd ceiliogod rhedyn, fel rîl bysgota,
yn towlu draw o'r tyfiant crin
ac o ddyddiau pell ein plentyndod;
Yn glanio o gylch ein traed
i ganol tawelwch blinder.

.
.

Wel, fues i erio'd 'ma o'r bla'n …

Dan bwysau'r haf eleni
roedd y gorwel, am y gwelwn,
yn estyn yn faith i gorneli'r cof
yn un hen lôn hir o hiraeth.

Haf diamser oedd hwn.
Haf o grwydro, yn ein hunfan,
ar hyd oes o flynyddoedd.
Ein bysedd yn troedio'n brysur
drwy lythyron cain a dyddiaduron cledr-llaw;
Datgymalu'r pentyrrau o gofnodion llaith,
oedd yn argaeau hyd loriau'r garej,
a'u datod o afael rhydlyd hen glipiau clustiau cŵn
cyn eu chwalu a'u didoli –
a gweld holl enwau ddoe yn tasgu 'nôl atom
o ganol y tudalennau.
Tawch oglau inc a llwydni'n treiddio'n dillad
a graen y teip, a'r papur rhad, yn rhwbio'n arw ar ein croen.
Gwibio drwy archif felen, fregus
o bytiau newyddion y gorffennol,
a rhythu ar orielau angof o wynebau
yn gwelwi a llacio'u gafael rhwng cloriau lliwgar.

A chwmni gwenoliaid duon gyda'r hwyr,
yn sgrechian, hefyd,
wrth sgrialu'n wyllt drwy goch y machlud.

·
·
·

Gallwn i aros 'ma am byth . . .

. . . Meddai'n dawel,
wrth rythu'n bell dros ddrych o aber ar ddiwedd p'nawn.
Ei bysedd yn crwydro'n ysgafn dros y brychni haul
a ledodd, gyda'r blynyddoedd, yn fap o fân gyfandiroedd
ar hyd croen ei dwylo.

Mae eiliadau tyner Awst yn lledu'n ddistaw fel llanw.
Y golau isel yn llifo i gefn fy llygade' a'u golchi fel dŵr afon,
ac awel fechan amser-mynd-adre yn hwylio meddyliau llonydd
i ganol cefnfor o las gwag.

. . . Finne' hefyd.

Elinor Gwynn

Glannau

(detholiad)

Llong hwyliau oedd hi
o weithdy troad y ganrif
cyn dyfod ager
i esmwytho ysgwydd a meddalu llaw.

Bellach
ar drugaredd y gwyntoedd
a'r cerrynt croes;
weithiau'n crafangu glan,
y graig yn rhoi
a'r tywod yn llithro,
broc môr.

Ymrwyfo, rhwyfo i rywle,
codi o'i chadair,
cynhyrfu, simsanu, syrthio:
dau fyd, dwy lan,
a rhyngom y môr,
weithiau'n ferw, weithiau'n falm
a glanio didario ar dro.

John Roderick Rees

Storm

(*detholiad*)

Yr oedd drwy ei rhuo hi – a'r mawrwynt
    storm arall yn cethri;
    ei haflwydd yn llef drwyddi,
    a'i rhu'n uwch i'n llorio ni.

Yn friw daeth i'n difrodi, – lledu'n wyllt
    yn ei holl gymhelri;
    taenu ei hing drwy'n tŷ ni,
    a lledodd i'n trallodi.

Fy mam glaf ym magl hen – y storom,
    mor ddi-stŵr â heulwen
    a dyrr drwy hèth ar darren,
    masg ei gwae'n gymysg â'i gwên.

Fy unfam yn gyfanfyd, – ynddi'r oedd
    rhuddin fy mychanfyd;
    yn fam awen fy mywyd,
    ei llaw fach oedd fy holl fyd.

Ddoe'n llewyrch a'n dyddiau'n llawen, – dyddiau
  pan nad oedd ond heulwen
  ifanc yn toi'r ffurfafen
  yn dân aur ar hyd y nen.

Ddifyrred myned ym Mai – ar adain
  yn ddireidus ddifai;
  yn y llethr ei cham yn llai,
  a'r direidi a redai.

Hon fy mhechod, fy meichiau, – fy nghyni,
  ond fy nghannwyll olau;
  hon y gyfraith lem weithiau,
  ond taeraf ffrind drwy ei ffrae.

Elwyn Edwards

Mam

Gwelais fy mam yn gwelwi
yn ddim, nes diflannodd hi.
Hirfaith yw un yn darfod,
ond byr yw peidio â bod.
Yn ei synau disynnwyr
araf iawn yw oriau'r hwyr.
Un ydwyf ag eiliadau
y nos a Mam yn gwanhau.
Ei hanadl yw f'anadl i,
un nos da cyn distewi.

Ond ddydd ar ôl dydd rwy'n dal
y gannwyll, dal i gynnal
oedfaon cyson y co'.
Un ennyd i benlinio
fy hunan mewn cynghanedd
bur, nes daw o glymau'r bedd,
heb boen, fy hen gwmpeini
o'i chur i fy nghyfarch i.

Gwion Lynch

56

Cân di bennill
fwyn i'th nain,
fe gân dy
nain i tithau

O Ffwrnais Awen

(i Ania Lili, wedi gweld casgliad Prifysgol Harvard o blanhigion gwydr)

Carwn ddangos iti'r breuder hwn:
harddwch creu o ffwrnais
awen dyn â dwylo'i grefft;
dawn efelychu roddodd fod
i batrwm pob un petal prin,
tryloywder lliw, gosodiad dail,
cyn clymu gwreiddiau blêr
y cannoedd rhywogaethau.

Carwn ddangos iti'r harddwch hwn:
trefn tymhorau'n saff am dro
mewn gardd o gasys gwydr,
blagur, blodau, ffrwythau, had,
yn ffrwydrad byw ail Eden
dan gysgod y gorchymyn
a gawsom oll i'w gwarchod
(er ein gwaethaf) hyd y diwedd.

A charwn ddangos iti hefyd 'rhain,
a dysgu iti hwiangerddi'u henwau:
Lili'r Wyddfa, Heboglys Eryri –
a Radur, Cerddinen Darren Fach
a'r Gerddinen Gymreig ... dysgu iti
gân eu tanio, Ania Lili, ac alaw
eu twf yn ein tir – rhag i'w gwydr
hwythau chwalu'n ulw yn y man.

Christine James

Rhwng y Ddwylan

Mae'n llond ei llygaid: rhyfeddodau'r dydd,
yn sgleinio rhwng ei blew amrannau hir,
glan môr, y trip i'r parc a'r chwarae rhydd
yn fêl ar dafod, ac mae'r lôn yn glir
wrth inni yrru adref. Cydia'n dynn
yn hud y diwrnod, mwytho'i pharsel llawn
profiadau, i'w ddadlapio gyda hyn.
Mae grŵn y car fel gwenyn bodlon iawn ...

Nes daw, ar Bont rhwng antur a dau glawr,
ei llais o'r cefn: 'Mae'n ysgol fory, Nain!'
'Dy ddiwrnod cynta! 'Dwyt ti'n hogan fawr!'
(Er gwres fy ngwên, synhwyraf awel fain.)
A 'nghalon chwithig, yno uwch y lli'n
dyheu am warchod haul ei syndod hi.

Annes Glynn

Twll yn yr Ardd

Rhyw bwten oedd hi, meddai Mam, man gwan
am swnian ar ei stôl pan oedd Mam-gu'n
tylino'r toes a chrasu'r bara can –
nes cael ei ffordd, cael powlen bridd y tŷ
o'i blaen, cael cyfle yn y gegin fach
i fod yn groten fawr. Hen siom, er hyn,
oedd stori'r toesiad cyntaf: fflat fel sach,
yn wastraff drud yng ngwae'r tridegau tyn.
'Anghofio'r burum wnest ti,' meddai'r fam.
'Dim gair. Fe awn â rhaw i lawr i ben
draw'r ardd, gwneud twll, a heb 'run geg fach gam,
o'r golwg yr aiff hwn. Am byth. Amen.'
Claddodd Mam-gu'r gymysgedd; mynd yn ôl
ac estyn powlen arall at ei stôl.

Myrddin ap Dafydd

Carthen Nain

(o weld paentiad melyn llorweddol
(acrylig a chnu) gan Paul Emmanuel)

Ym more hèth, mae'i brethyn
yn daer am freuddwydion dyn,
a glawio'i harogleuon
yn ddi-wad wna ddoeau hon;

yn anwesiad pwythiadau
mae solas o gynfas gwau'n
troi ffibrau'r oesau o ran
yn wefrau; yma'n hofran
fel opiwm, a'i batrwm byw
yn hel adre'n ddiledryw
i wâl oer a hiraeth les
y gwely, nes creu Gwales.

Llion Pryderi Roberts

Cledd â min yw claddu mam

Botwm Abi

(*ar fore angladd ei mam*)

Yr oedd un botwm yn rhydd
o wead dy ffrog newydd,
ac i'r stafell dest, felly,
blodyn, a gofyn, 'Mam-gu,
a wnei di ei winio'n dynn
a'i wneud-e' yn iawn wedyn?
A'i wneud-e' gyda'r edau
wen o hyd nad yw'n gwanhau?
Ei ail-greu fel ag yr oedd
a'i bwytho hyd fyth bythoedd?'

Felly Mam-gu â'i llaw gain
a g'wirodd y ffrog gywrain
heb liw dail na blodau haf
arni hi, dy ffrog aeaf.
Lle bu'r datod roedd nodwydd,
lle bu'n frau yr edau rydd,
yn y bwlch roedd botwm bach
wedi'i winio yn dynnach.

Er cystal gofal Mam-gu,
er ei cheinwaith, serch hynny,
erbyn y noson honno,
yr oedd, ta waeth, yn rhydd 'to.

Ond tra bo bwlch, neu tra bo
edau'r boreau'n breuo,
down ni, â'n hedau newydd,
i ymroi i'r botwm rhydd,
i wneud, wrth ei winio'n ôl,
wahaniaeth annigonol
i ti, Abi; gwneud rhywbeth,
ni waeth ei bwys, ni waeth beth.

Ceri Wyn Jones

Mam

Aethom yn ôl trwy gyfrolau'i hanes,
gan dynnu penodau'r
edwino. O! Mor denau,
wedyn, destun ein tristáu.

Tony Bianchi

Plentyn yn Angladd ei Fam

Yr oedd yno wrtho'i hun er bod tad,
Er bod torf i'w ganlyn.
Ddoe i'r fynwent aeth plentyn,
Ohoni ddoe daeth hen ddyn.

Gerallt Lloyd Owen

Mam

O'i gorthrymder i'r gweryd – yr aeth Mam;
  Hiraeth, mwy, fydd bywyd;
  Hyn rwy'n siŵr, er na sieryd
Mi gofiaf am Mam o hyd.

Gwilym Herber

Ar Garreg Fedd fy Mam

Er cau'r arch ni chaeir craith ein hiraeth,
        na lliniaru'n hartaith;
    ni chudd y priddyn ychwaith
    haelioni'r galon lanwaith.

Alan Llwyd

Cydnabyddiaethau

Alan Llwyd, *Cerddi Alan Llwyd: Yr Ail Gasgliad Cyflawn 1990–2015* (Cyhoeddiadau Barddas, 2015), 84.

Bethan Mair (gol.), *Hoff Gerddi Cymru* (Gwasg Gomer, 2002), 117–25.

Dafydd Islwyn (gol.), *100 o Englynion Barddas* (Cyhoeddiadau Barddas, 2009), 71.

Elwyn Edwards, *Aelwyd Gwlad* (Cyhoeddiadau Barddas, 1997), 72–8.

Gerallt Lloyd Owen, *Cilmeri a cherddi eraill* (Gwasg Gwynedd, 1991), 75.

Haf Llewelyn, *Llwybrau* (Cyhoeddiadau Barddas, 2009), 22.

Iwan Llwyd a Myrddin ap Dafydd (goln.), *Cywyddau Cyhoeddus* (Gwasg Carreg Gwalch, 1994), 34.

J. Eirian Davies, *Cyfrol o Gerddi* (Gwasg Gee, 1985), 62.

John Emyr a Luned Aaron, *Ennyd* (Gwasg Carreg Gwalch, 2017), 16.

Llion Pryderi Roberts, *Tipiadau* (Cyhoeddiadau Barddas, 2018), 36.

Mari George, *Siarad Siafins* (Gwasg Carreg Gwalch, 2014), 98.

Mererid Hopwood, *Nes Draw* (Gwasg Gomer, 2015), 42–3, 111–18.

Osian Rhys Jones a Llŷr Gwyn Lewis (goln.), *Bragdy'r Beirdd* (Cyhoeddiadau Barddas, 2018), 66–7, 86–7.

Tony Bianchi, *Rhwng Pladur a Blaguryn* (Cyhoeddiadau Barddas, 2018), 24.

Mae'r gyfrol hefyd yn cynnwys ambell gerdd gan Fardd y Mis, BBC Radio Cymru, rhai o gerddi *Talwrn y Beirdd* a cherddi o Gyfansoddiadau a Beirniadaethau Eisteddfod Genedlaethol Cymru: 1985, 1988, 2017 a 2018.

Diolch i Lenyddiaeth Cymru am yr ysgoloriaethau i rai o gyfranwyr y gyfrol hon.

Daw'r lluniau o gasgliadau personol y golygydd a'r cyhoeddwr ac eithrio t. 25: Chris Hellier/Alamy Stock Photo; t. 32: GP Library Limited/Alamy Stock Photo; t. 45: Steven Bramall/Alamy Stock Photo; t. 53: ClassicStock/Alamy Stock Photo; t. 55: Tony Henshaw/Alamy Stock Photo.